The American 1890s

THE
AMERICAN
1890s

A CULTURAL READER

★

Susan Harris Smith & Melanie Dawson,

Editors

Duke University Press Durham and London 2000

© 2000 Duke University Press   All rights reserved
Printed in the United States of America on acid-free paper ∞
Typeset in Trump Mediaeval by Tseng Information Systems, Inc.
Library of Congress Cataloging-in-Publication Data appear
on the last printed page of this book.

CONTENTS

LIST OF FIGURES

ACKNOWLEDGMENTS

W E WOULD LIKE to thank the Department of English of the University of Pittsburgh for two support grants and staff support, the Hillman library staff for special permissions, Steve Carr for encouraging us to design the original course on which this collection is based, Jean Ferguson Carr, Nancy Glazener, and Mary Briscoe for their helpful insights, Ken Wissoker and Katie Courtland at Duke University Press for their initial enthusiasm and continued support of the project, Phil Smith for his invaluable technical help, and the anonymous Duke Press readers who have been instrumental in shaping the final manuscript. And, of course, Phil and John. Finally, in working together on this project, our mutual respect for each other has deepened.

A TIMELINE OF AMERICA
AT CENTURY'S END: THE 1890S

1890

Wyoming and Idaho admitted as states

11 million acres of Sioux territory, ceded to U.S. government in 1889, opened for general settlement

Congress creates Sequoia and Yosemite National Parks

Sioux ghost dance and Battle of Wounded Knee; deaths of Sitting Bull and Big Foot

Sherman Anti-Trust Act

Jacob Riis, *How the Other Half Lives*

William James, *The Principles of Psychology*

William Dean Howells, *A Hazard of New Fortunes*

Emily Dickinson, *Poems* (first collected works published posthumously)

1891

People's (Populist) Party formed in Cincinnati

900,000 acres of Indian lands in Oklahoma opened for general settlement

Thomas Edison patents wireless telegraph and motion picture camera (Kinetograph)

International Copyright Act

Hamlin Garland, *Main-Travelled Roads*

Mary Wilkins Freeman, *A New England Nun and Other Stories*

1892

The Homestead, Pa., steel strike; Andrew Carnegie hires Pinkerton thugs

Chinese Exclusion Act renewed (immigration is prohibited for another ten years; the act stayed in effect until WWII)

Ellis Island opens as an immigration point of entry
Anna Julia Cooper, *A Voice from the South*
Walt Whitman, *Leaves of Grass* (final edition)

1893

World's Columbian Exposition in Chicago
Financial panic in May, crash in June
Mormon Temple dedicated in Salt Lake City
Anti-Saloon League organized
Thomas Edison exhibits the Kinetoscope in public
Frederick Jackson Turner announces the closing of the frontier in "The
    Significance of the Frontier in American History"
S. S. McClure begins publication of *McClure's Magazine*
Stephen Crane, *Maggie: A Girl of the Streets*

1894

"Coxey's Army" marches on Washington, D.C.
Pullman strike
American Railway Union strike
First Sunday comics
Bureau of Immigration created
Labor Day established as national holiday
Flagstaff observatory erected in Arizona
John Muir, *The Mountains of California*
Samuel Langhorn Clemens (Mark Twain), *The Tragedy of Pudd'nhead
    Wilson*

1895

Cuban rebellion against Spain
First professional football game played in Latrobe, Pa.
Income tax law declared unconstitutional
Yerkes observatory founded in Chicago
New York Public Library consolidated
Stephen Crane, *The Red Badge of Courage*

1896

William McKinley elected twenty-fifth president
Utah admitted as a state
First Ford automobile
First U.S. moving pictures shown in New York City in April
Supreme court upholds Louisiana's Jim Crow Law ("separate but equal") in
    Plessy v. Fergusson

Sarah Orne Jewett, *The Country of the Pointed Firs*
Harold Frederic, *The Damnation of Theron Ware*
Abraham Cahan, *Yekl: A Tale of the New York Ghetto*

1897

Klondike gold rush begins
Richard Harding Davis, *Soldiers of Fortune*

1898

U.S. battleship *Maine* explodes in Havana harbor in February
United States declares war on Spain in April
Col. Roosevelt's "Rough Riders" capture San Juan Hill in Cuba
Commodore Dewey wins at Manila Bay, the Philippines
Puerto Rico and Guam ceded to the United States
Roosevelt elected governor of New York
Charlotte Perkins Gilman, *Women and Economics*
Henry James, *The Turn of the Screw* (*Collier's Weekly* January–April)

1899

United Mine Workers organize
Thorstein Veblen, *The Theory of the Leisure Class*
Kate Chopin, *The Awakening*
Charles Chesnutt, *The Conjure Woman*
John Dewey, *The School and Society*
Frank Norris, *McTeague*

1900

Wright brothers fly a full-scale glider in September
William McKinley reelected, with Roosevelt as vice-president
Theodore Dreiser, *Sister Carrie*
Frank Baum, *The Wonderful Wizard of Oz*
Andrew Carnegie, *The Gospel of Wealth*
Pauline Hopkins, *Contending Forces*

1901

McKinley assassinated; Roosevelt becomes president
Formation of U.S. Steel, America's first billion-dollar company
John Muir, *Our National Parks*
Booker T. Washington, *Up from Slavery*
Charles W. Chesnutt, *The House Behind the Cedars*
Frank Norris, *The Octopus*

The American 1890s

INTRODUCTION

T HIS ANTHOLOGY INVITES you into
American culture from 1890 through 1900, the period known as the fin de
siècle. This decade was characterized by a widespread and radical alteration
in the ways that American life was perceived—an alteration precipitated
not by any one event but by a cultural shift brought about during a profound struggle to reinvent American society in light of an emergent, progressive, and reformist modernism. At the same time, Americans in the 1890s
were aware of the need to confront the changes wrought by a tumultuous
and receding nineteenth century, a period sometimes cloaked in conservative nostalgia. At issue were debates about cultural achievement and formal
education, anxieties arising from labor disputes and poor working conditions, fears surrounding immigration, controversies over full political and
social opportunities for minorities and women, and tensions arising from increased urbanization and expanding technologies. The authors whose writings appear in this cultural reader participated in shaping the century's end
by addressing these proliferating issues from sometimes sharply differing
points of view.

Invitation to the Decade

One way to understand the decade of the 1890s is to note significant events
and crises that widely affected the nation and completed its transformation from a former colony to an imperial power. As a result of the Panic of
1893, the United States experienced an economic depression that lasted until
1897. Capitalist industry was altered by the passage of the Sherman Anti-
Trust Act of 1890, which essentially forbade "every contract, combination,
... or conspiracy in restraint of trade or commerce." American corporations
had to deal not only with new regulations, but also with increasingly discon-

tented laborers, with tensions between managers and workers and between skilled and unskilled laborers; these tensions erupted in violent public disputes such as the Homestead and Pullman strikes over the right to unionize or the march on the nation's capital of "Coxey's Army" to demand jobs. Ethnic and racial turmoil also troubled a nation clinging to a conservative creed of Anglo-Saxon superiority. Federal troops clashed with Sioux Ghost Dancers in the Massacre at Wounded Knee in South Dakota in 1890. For African Americans, the U.S. Supreme Court's ruling in *Plessy v. Ferguson* (1896) continued the racially divisive practices of the post-Reconstruction years when it affirmed the constitutionality of "separate but equal" conditions for blacks and whites. Meanwhile, rapid technological advances allowed Americans to celebrate national accomplishments at the 1893 World's Columbian Exposition in Chicago and at the completion of the Great Northern Railroad. A few years later, the Spanish-American War over Cuba, the annexation of Hawaii, and the possession of the Philippines, Guam, and Puerto Rico marked America's military entry into global politics. In light of its growing international role, America's internal conflicts were especially problematic since the nation was attempting to assert a unified identity as a modern imperial power.

The essays and fiction in this collection address critical political and social debates at the century's end. They examine and debate the consequences of the decade's developments, conscious of a constantly shifting culture at a time of internal turmoil, political expansion, growing national consciousness, and engagement with modern ideas and new technologies. The articles and essays, therefore, are in contentious conversation with each other, either explicitly or implicitly. Furthermore, this collection demonstrates the vast differences among positions: nostalgic, protective, imperialist, progressive, egalitarian, and democratic. By including many voices, we have tried to capture a sense of the vigor and conviction with which arguments were generated and maintained in fin-de-siècle print culture. For instance, after reading a popular author of the decade such as Robert Grant reviling immigrants and condemning their preservation of "unAmerican" heritages, it is possible to understand better Abraham Cahan's harsh, realistic piece on the poverty and despair of the immigrant experience, which can be read as a response to the unsympathetic and xenophobic positions articulated by Grant and similarly minded authors.

In a period of increasing secularization and urbanization as well as intense social and economic reorganization, Americans were caught between the attractions of what seemed to be a stable and homogeneous past and the exciting promises of new technologies. The future also was made potentially threatening by women's emancipation, labor unrest, racial integration, and immigration. The nomenclature of the 1890s marked much as "new" (the

New Woman, the New Negro), a newness that posed both exciting possibilities and threatened stability. Period authors display a pronounced awareness of the imminence of the century's end, when Americans were facing cultural, demographic, geographical, and technological changes. Even something as seemingly innocuous as the "safety" bicycle, which precipitated a decade-long "craze," generated heated discussions about safety, health, decorum, dress reform, and genetic engineering.

Addressing a perceived shift in values meant that some authors in the 1890s took pointed, nationalist stances as they asserted a distinct "American" identity in the face of evidence that the country was changing. They responded to and helped produce a rise in patriotic nativism as they tried to establish claims to a consolidated national cultural identity, one that attempted to deny or distance those who threatened the narrow myth of Puritan "origin." The nativist impulse also spoke to the tension between a fading Europhilia and increasingly emergent "Americanness," which, in turn, was inextricably bound up with growing nationalism and imperial expansion. Through such public forums as national periodicals, writers addressed the contested issues of race, gender, ethnicity, class struggles, and international conflicts, which to some seemed to threaten the stability of the national narrative and to others to rightly question the underlying premises of that dominant narrative. At century's end, Americans experienced a heightened consciousness of both a national and an international identity. The increasing number and diversity of immigrants who were rapidly altering the country's demographics put Americans in frequent and contentious dialogue with the globe. Such tensions were particularly important to some of the authors in this collection, many of whom were immigrants or their recent descendants, and conscious of the stakes in claiming their place in a distinctly American culture.

The impulse to secure a national identity was in part a response to the national divisiveness and bloody fratricide of the Civil War as well as the ensuing failure of Reconstruction. In fact, the Civil War remained an uncomfortable presence from a not-so-distant past. The desires for civil unity, for a common destiny, and for a national identity often were manifested in a nostalgia for a rural, provincial, agrarian, and western frontier past. A perceived loss of mythologized, vanishing American types and institutions (among them the "wild" Indian, the cowboy, the originary Puritan, and the American West) fed the rising imperialist urge that culminated in the Spanish-American War of 1898. David Traxel in *1898: The Birth of the American Century* argues that this war was the inevitable consequence of the rising competition for international markets, of industrial expansion, and of racial and ethnic strife.

In the nineteenth century the ubiquitous term "Anglo-Saxon" figures as a marker of class distinction and the accompanying ideals of racial and ethnic "purity." Therefore, another way to understand the debates of the decade and the idea of origin is to point to the ways in which writers deployed the language of evolutionary theory and participated in ideas of progress that transcended national boundaries. An ongoing debate between Christianity and Darwinian thought as first expressed in *On the Origin of Species* (1859) continued to reverberate in America in the 1890s. Though Protestant Christianity was the country's dominant religion during the decade, Darwinian thought—especially its ideas about survival of the fittest, evolution, and environmental influences—had been assimilated (albeit uneasily) into public discourse and rhetoric. Evolutionary theory as explained by Herbert Spencer, the English philosopher and social theorist, in *First Principles* (1862), assured social progress. In fact, American writers had begun to respond to Darwinian thought as early as the 1870s, and by 1890 the vocabulary of this scientific, secular formulation of origin—evolution, instinct, descent, struggle for existence, survival, selection, extinction, degenerate, savage, and civilized—constituted the recognizable terms of evolutionary theory that permeate the essays and stories in this collection. One of the most pervasive debates focused on the influence of environment versus heredity, an issue of great concern, particularly to those who feared the dilution of Anglo-Saxon blood and a consequent "race suicide."

The 1890s long has been recognized as a period of sweeping change in American politics, society, and culture. For instance, Henry Steele Commager argued that the decade formed a "watershed of American history." Indeed, the most recent scholars of the period focus on the cultural reorientation that marks it; for instance, John Higham in *Writing American History* refers to a "reorientation" of American culture in the 1890s, and Richard Brodhead in *Cultures of Letters* to a "hierarchical reorganization of the literary sphere." Similarly marking the fin de siècle as a significant moment in the formation of modern cultural hierarchies, Lawrence Levine in *Highbrow/Lowbrow: The Emergence of Cultural Hierarchy in America* argues that "because the primary categories of culture have been the products of ideologies which were always subject to modifications and transformations, the perimeters of our cultural divisions have been permeable and shifting rather than fixed and immutable" (8). Because such studies have enriched and complicated an understanding of this formative American decade, one marked by cultural flux and dynamism, it is now impossible to describe Victorian America as simply "gilded" or the 1890s as merely "gay." The selections in this reader particularly stress the growing economic, gendered, racial, national, ethnic, and class-based complexities that fin-de-siècle Americans faced.

Such cultural changes affected all levels of society. An elitist culture, modeled after the European gentry, gradually was challenged by the desire for indigenous, nativist expression as well as by a more visibly advertisement-driven, mass-produced consumer culture, characterized by Thorstein Veblen as the culture of the "leisure class." As the influx of immigrants altered the cultural landscape, the processes of assimilation, acculturation, and preservation also vied for dominance. Both the rise of new technologies capable of producing still and moving images in photographs, X-rays, and moving pictures and the instantiation of a heightened aesthetics of realism produced anxiety about differentiating the "real thing" from an artful imitation. In the 1890s, women in particular were experiencing new freedoms: riding bicycles, attending colleges and universities, dressing for greater comfort and ease of physical movement, and entering the white-collar labor market. African Americans, blighted by the failure of Reconstruction, also were voicing their right and desire to become full participants in every arena of American life. And, as women and African Americans were gaining strength and recognition, the indigenous Amerind peoples, who had been battling for their freedom and sovereignty for decades, lost those same battles. In contrast to such developments, the fin de siècle was also the age of middle-class professionalization, which resulted in a self-conscious, progressive class composed of college-educated lawyers, teachers, doctors, and engineers, men with high material expectations and cultural aspirations who would be the leaders of the "Progressive Era."

It is important to note that although many Americans clung to the image of American life as dominated by white, male, Protestant professionals, others embraced change, calling into question assumptions about a hegemonic society, particularly in regard to people at or outside the margins of comfortable, affluent professional life. Certainly a growing middle class wanted to perpetuate, enhance, and solidify its racial and cultural dominance and create a secure sense of status and national homogeneity, but that goal was disrupted from within the middle class itself as well as from without by competing voices in an increasingly powerful, pluralistic nation. The resistant voices—from mild questioning to strident dissenting—challenged the exclusivity of political and cultural rights, sought to improve material conditions, and claimed a place for themselves as active producers and consumers of culture.

Hierarchies of Class and Cultural Positions

Debates over methods of acculturation are at the center of this cultural reader because the possibilities of upward striving inform the ideas that appear in subsequent sections that address issues of "types," social strife, labor, mental and physical training, the promises of formal education, and a future clearly marked by cultural change, all of which are engaged with ideas of personal or national "improvement." Our text begins with a section on the drive to acquire culture, a defining impulse of fin-de-siècle life. As ideas about culture provide an ideological basis for the selections in this first section, so too the language of "types" in the second section appears as a defining concept. While the opening selections set up expectations about acculturation, later sections problematize and test the boundaries of cultural promises—the value of physical conditioning and formal study, for example—frequently expressing anxiety about the dangers, limits, and false promises of future progress in an age of transition. Many essays and stories demonstrate a range of ideas about inhabiting a cultured, middle-class position, ranging from the perspective of individuals comfortably situated to those hoping to achieve that comfort and, with it, professional work, leisure time, and access to methods of self-improvement. Other selections aggressively question middle-class assumptions and point to the difficulty and questionable desirability of assuming those values.

Periodicals from which texts in this collection are drawn participated in this important cultural work at a time when a growing middle class questioned and debated the received ideas of cultural, national, and professional identity at a time of expanding national boundaries. While we want to emphasize the richness and diversity of the texts that spoke to one another from within a dynamic periodical culture and that sought to represent a multiplicity of social, ethnic, racial, and ideological positions, it is also important to recall that these publications were oriented to fairly affluent, culturally informed, bourgeois readers. It was a reading culture, in short, that held the voices of white, professional, well-educated, and nationalistic authors in particular esteem. Thus, a definite class-based uniformity is evident in the pieces collected here, and although not all of these selections speak from a middle-class position, they do speak to readers who inhabited or aspired to that status.

Delineations of class appealed to fin-de-siècle readers because of the mythologized argument that class positions were negotiable. The Horatio Alger "self-help" formula, fixed in the popular imagination since the late 1860s, posited that an individual could achieve a higher class status and economic advancement through determination and self-reliance alone. The dynamism associated with class was attractive to a wide range of readers, as images of a comfortable middle-class position offered models for advancement as well as confirmations of their own social status. The reality, of course, was that all hierarchical positions—class as well as culture—were intractable elements of material relations; the mill owner, for example, had greater access to class and culture than the mill hand.

What did it mean to be a middle-class American at the fin de siècle? That question circulates throughout this cultural reader, as it was one of the major concerns about identity facing late-nineteenth-century Americans. As Martin J. Burke has argued in *The Conundrum of Class: Public Discourse on the Social Order in America*, the terminology of class was a contested semantic problem throughout the 1880s. He cites the 1883 U.S. Senate investigation of the "Relations between Labor and Capital," noting the diversity of terms used to denote the complexities of class: the "working class," the "laboring class," the "non-laboring class," the "educated class," the "middle class," the "upper class," the "lower class," as well as terms such as "producers," "non-producers," the "privileged classes," and the "permanent classes" (160). Burke demonstrates that in 1883 there was not "a single 'language' or lexicon of class in American discourse. There was instead a variety of terms—some of them durable, others transitory—that Americans used, and a number of interpretive frameworks in which they used them" (160–61).

During the fin de siècle, "class," though primarily an economic marker, was but one dimension in the attempt to name, type, and locate oneself in a stratified society. For this reason, we focus attention on the central concerns of the upwardly striving and increasingly leisured bourgeoisie. But class position was problematic because of continual shifts in value; one needed to demonstrate mastery of cultural skills in order to claim a position, and although class was a significant marker of identity, there was no unified or comprehensive notion of what class could denote, or even what terms to use to define it. Therefore, class emerges as a central factor in American life, one linked to a host of other concerns. And while class is only one dimension of the contested identities addressed in this volume, notions of class or status intersect powerfully with identities based on race, ethnicity, regionalism, gender, and cultural status.

As the *Plessy v. Ferguson* ruling indicates, appearances had little to do with strict racial distinctions, nor could visible signs always reveal the complexities of ethnic or regional heritages that shaped identity. But though class affiliation largely dependent on capital seemed more negotiable, the acquisition of capital could not guarantee social access, nor could it provide assured familiarity with art, music, literature, or politics. As elusive as such markers of class were, however, stratifications based on culture were both more complex and, at times, more exact, hence their appeal to authors who "type" characters and detail their likenesses to familiar attitudes and practices. Learning to become a middle-class, cultured American was, in large measure, a matter of encountering examples of social "types" or categories of identity. As part of an impulse toward "self-culture," or a drive to improve, educate, and "strive" (in the language of Thomas Schlereth in *Victorian America*), increasing numbers of Americans sought guidance in articulating material, artistic, and intellectual markers of status. Periodicals offered readers access to wide-ranging instruction and edification, which were particularly important to rural and homebound readers.

"Culture" suggested a complex intersection of education, talent, and social behavior that could be attained by effort. Nonetheless, it is important to keep in mind that culture was contingent upon economic factors; access to goods and services was mediated by money and, as a consequence, striving to improve oneself was not necessarily a guarantee of success. Thus, it was possible to confuse an idealized internalization of culture with culture as merely a purchasable commodity. In the eyes of those who believed in acculturation, all forms of culture could improve the individual, but, as authors such as Thorstein Veblen and Edith Wharton point out, not all cultural forms or products were equally valuable. The rhetoric of culture nonetheless offered fin-de-siècle Americans a powerful enticement to enhance their lives by means of models and arguments for self-improvement. Indeed, the entire periodical culture offered readers the alluring promise of eluding class-based hierarchies. However, arguments about acculturation often overlooked economic issues of access in their zeal to promote striving.

Calls to cultural enrichment, while pointing to the desideratum of an accultured identity, also helped to create hierarchies by marking distinctions around social types and cultural practices. In addition, these ideas reflected and shaped the ways that the nation thought about itself by allowing readers to engage in a dialogue with broad ideals of acculturation voiced through the periodical market as well as other texts of advice. Thus, while notions of class and culture are significant features of fin-de-siècle writers and readers, these markers must be understood as related to terminologies in which identities were labeled or "typed," to use the language of the period. The language of "types," then, combines ideas of class with ideas about patriotism, upward mobility, and cultural skills. Concerns about "types" position the middle class as tension-ridden, anxious, and given to concerted and studied efforts to improve, develop, consolidate, exclude, and expand. Given the myriad possibilities associated with these terms, "type" and "class," the scope of this collection suggests the contested boundaries, the contradictory relations, and the unstable construction of an emergent middle-class lifestyle during the 1890s.

In a time of radical demographic change, the language of "types" could be deployed to create the illusion of stable hierarchies. In other words, the ideological dimension of such language conjured what was for some readers a reassuringly fixed state, or, as historian Henry Seidel Canby claimed, this was the last time in living memory "when everyone knew exactly what it meant to be an American." Some authors called this imaginary fixity into question by proposing new and alternative types that attempted to disrupt and reorganize vertical hierarchies. For example, Zitkala-Šă complicates the dominant image of the "wild" Indian with her portrait of an educated, self-aware modern Indian caught between two national identities. Susan B. Anthony, similarly, contrasts an older type of unobtrusive, subservient woman with a new type of publicly active woman. While some texts defend the dominant cultural hegemony of the United States, many others attempt to challenge its political and social axes, particularly works by Pauline Hopkins, Charles Chesnutt, Abraham Cahan, Paul Laurence Dunbar, Frederick Douglass, Simon Pokagon, and Booker T. Washington.

Thus, while many selections in this collection speak from and depict the lives of comfortable, relatively affluent Americans, other voices attempt to portray as well as speak from other positions, pointing to gaps and fissures in status. Many authors address the plight of the disenfranchised, some from the perspective of such well-known social reformers as Frederick Douglass and B. O. Flower. Other selections emphasize more measured and seemingly deferential voices; Simon Pokagon and Booker T. Washington, for example, reveal the need to negotiate the concerns, fears, and prejudices of a dominant white and largely unsympathetic audience. Still others, such as Robert Grant and Josiah Flynt, speak from the isolationist and combative stance of "true Americans," standing against immigration, against urbanization, against racial integration, and against women's rights and responsibilities as full citizens. From the personal to the political, from the informative to the aggressive, from the romantic to the realistic, these writers address their audience through an array of approaches, some of which were undoubtedly more comfortable than others for their readers. The selections here were tempered in many ways in order to engage rather than disturb; nonetheless, some of these selections did launch powerful critiques and addressed significant problems.

The section and author introductions in this volume often remind readers of the difficulty of resisting a dominant culture when resistance endangered the livelihoods and social relations of dissenters. Especially when readers today approach issues of ethnic and racial strife, there is a temptation to position dissenting individuals as spokespersons for an entire race or ethnic position, in part because history has made these figures prominent. It is important to recall that dissenters often spoke from personal experience in their attempt to reach a mainstream audience, not as leaders of a mobilized and widespread resistance, which would have been much more threatening to those readers. The rarity and difficulty of speaking against a dominant society should not be forgotten, especially in light of the way in which authors were careful to couch their criticism within the boundaries of acceptable rhetorical postures or narrative tropes when addressing readers who were likely to be resistant, if not hostile.

The Range and Scope of the Periodical Market

Although the period covered by this cultural reader is relatively concentrated, the materials range across the current disciplinary rubrics of history, sociology, economics, and literature. It is important to recall, however, that the original periodical readers for these selections encountered them as part of a unified market economy through the "general interest" periodical. Magazine readers of the fin de siècle, like readers in earlier decades, were accustomed to acquiring culture from publications that covered a wide range of subjects as announced in the subtitles. For instance, the *Atlantic Monthly* claimed "Literature, Science, Art, and Politics," and the *Colored American Magazine* "The Higher Culture of Religion, Literature, Science, Music and Art of the Negro." As the selections here attest, the well-informed reader of a hundred years ago experienced culture as broad, interdisciplinary, and dialogic; that is, the works of "political" or "scientific" writers existed in dialogue with "literary" or "historical" writings.

Selections in this collection range from those originally published in what were known as the "quality" monthlies (*Scribner's, Harper's, Century,* and the *Atlantic Monthly*) to the more political periodicals (the *North American Review* and *Forum*) and to a reformist magazine (the *Arena*). Additionally, this collection draws from newer general-information periodicals such as *Cosmopolitan* and *McClure's,* which were cheap, drew a larger audience, and accepted more advertising. We include selections from some specialty publications, among them the *Chautauquan* (whose readers considered themselves part of the "literary and scientific circle" that promoted specific courses of self-guided reading for personal improvement), *Outing* (a new and sport-oriented publication for outdoor men and women), and *Colored American Magazine* (which promoted and registered a love of higher culture in African American readers). While such periodicals sought to inculcate among readers a desire for culture because of a sincere belief in the political and social power afforded those who demonstrated cultural expertise, they were directed toward variously stratified, although often overlapping, groups of readers who identified themselves in relation to the middle class.

Of course, the concerns and debates of the 1890s can be found in a variety of literary or historical documents such as government legislation, newspapers, club or union documents, story papers, private letters, diaries, and memoranda. However, we have built this cultural reader from periodical materials in order to present a coherent sense of textual circulation and active debate in one prominent public forum. As Frank Luther Mott contended in his five-volume *A History of American Magazines,* the 1890s were the "golden age" of periodicals because magazines played a central role in informing and entertaining a broad array of American readers. During this decade, more than in earlier years, periodicals circulated widely through the culture because of technological improvements in printing and distribution of texts (especially in rural areas), rising literacy rates, increased competition, and lowered magazine prices (particularly after the financial panic of 1893). The force of the periodical at the fin de siècle can be demonstrated by its popularity. In *Selling Culture*, Richard Ohmann observes that "there were no modern, mass-circulation magazines in 1885, and by 1900 there were in the neighborhood of twenty—enough to make them a highly visible and much-noted cultural phenomenon" (29). Ohmann goes further, citing a rise in total periodical circulation, which increased from 4 million at the end of the Civil War to 18 million in 1890 and to 64 million in 1905, to claim that a national mass culture was first formed by magazines that "reestablished the American social order on a new basis" (vii).

Encompassing diverse aspects of fin-de-siècle life, magazines of the period were as important then as they are today, debating current events, expressing the desires, fears, and aspirations of middle-class American readers, and, through a combination of text and advertising, addressing readers as producers as well as consumers of culture. That periodicals were an essential component of a rapidly expanding consumer society is the argument in recent years of William Leach's *Land of Desire*, T. J. Jackson Lears's *Fables of Abundance* and *No Place of Grace*, Ellen Garvey's *The Adman in the Parlor*, Jennifer Scanlon's *Inarticulate Longings*, and Richard Ohmann's *Selling Culture*.

Periodicals, which became an attractive commodity as they formed their readers' interests in a diversity of concerns, perpetuated a continued interest in the burgeoning magazine industry itself. Furthermore, a broad circulation of periodicals meant that many more Americans had access to publications which promoted a middle-class ideology as well as images of how to purchase that life, particularly in the periodicals' advertisements. Susan Belasco Smith and Kenneth M. Price in *Periodical Literature in Nineteenth-Century America* contend that "the periodical—far more than the book—was a social text, involving complex relationships among writers, readers, editors, printers and distributors" (3). The very ubiquitousness of the periodical format made it a natural forum for the dissemination of general education and for the shaping of modern America.

Fiction and Nonfiction

The debates collected here take place in another way through the relation of fiction to nonfiction. The two modes complement and complicate one another, their productive tension illuminating literary trends, polemical arguments, and cultural issues of the 1890s. The fiction provides an imaginative interpretation of extant debates, allowing readers a sense of urgency, pathos, and even humor. During a period when realism was the dominant literary mode, authors claimed authenticity and authority through their commitment to representing a spectrum of social and political experiences, including reformist impulses. For example, some essays and short stories satirize economic and social differences (Josiah Flynt's "Club Life Among Outcasts" and Louise Betts Edwards's "Step-Brothers to Dives"); some address inequities through the voice of the disenfranchised (Zitkala-Šá's "School Days of an Indian Girl" and Abraham Cahan's "A Ghetto Wedding"); and others present anxieties about increased urbanization and technological advances in relation to the greater problems of cultural and social change (Frederick Jackson Turner's "The Problem of the West" and Robert Barr's "Within an Ace of the End of the World").

Like the essays, the fiction in this volume represents significant and recognized writers from the period (such as Stephen Crane and Elizabeth Stuart Phelps). As William Dean Howells pointed out at the time, a major trend in fin-de-siècle publishing was the short story. Short fiction, which often served as a writer's entrée to publication, introduced periodical readers to new authors and gave them the "credentials" that publishers increasingly demanded of aspiring novelists. A burgeoning interest in the short story contributed to the diversity of the periodical market; many writers in the 1890s put their energies into shorter fiction, among them Edith Wharton (who was not yet established) and Charles W. Chesnutt (whose lengthier fiction never met with the same success as his shorter works).

Fictional representations of the concerns characteristic of the 1890s, although often realistic, do a great deal more than illustrate existing arguments of the period; they pressure, redefine, and participate in ongoing conversations such as those devoted to charity, technology, and education. Like the essays, the fiction addresses the tensions of fin-de-siècle life, from the responsibilities of the privileged to the rights of the disenfranchised. Many stories attach their sympathy to the comfortable middle class, even as they explore the boundaries of class, custom, and community; other selections raise questions about a dominant cultural position (such as Pauline Hopkins's "Talma Gordon") or satirize trends (such as Paul Laurence Dunbar's "The Ingrate").

The authors whose work appears in this volume represent many career paths and hierarchical positions within the world of publishing. For example, Frederick Douglass and Susan B. Anthony were internationally prominent during the 1890s, but Theodore Roosevelt and Edith Wharton were not yet the famous figures they became. Roosevelt, although publicly prominent, was years from the presidency when he wrote "The College Graduate and Public Life," and Wharton was more than half a decade from composing her first major novel, *The House of Mirth*. By contrast, Robert Grant, Annie Payson Call, and Octave Thanet were prolific and widely recognized writers of the period. Although not widely popular in their own time, authors addressing issues of race and ethnicity, such as Charles Chesnutt, Pauline Hopkins, and Zitkala-Šá, had limited success during the fin de siècle; later, however, they seldom published. Thus, because their work has been recovered only in recent years, the history of their texts speaks powerfully to the hegemony of the period.

A Note from the Editors

An anthology, precisely because it is selective, cannot be comprehensive and, inevitably, there are noticeable exclusions. Although we include a few representative illustrations and advertisements in each thematic section, readers of this collection should know that many essays and stories were lavishly illustrated with line drawings or photographs and that periodicals were commercial ventures, often full of advertisements that usually have been removed from bound library volumes. With the exception of a few examples, the selections in this collection have not been reproduced with the images that would have accompanied or surrounded many of them in their original context—a context that highlights the close relations among text, image, and product.

Because the cultural debate was carried out more extensively in works of fiction and nonfiction, we have excluded drama and poetry. Some important writers associated with the 1890s are not represented here because some of their work was too lengthy, some is readily available in other anthologies, or they were not published in American periodicals during this decade. Also, we have made a few selective cuts in the selections themselves: a poem from Marguerite Merington's piece on the bicycle; extensive notes, a poem, and references to the illustrations of actresses from B. O. Flower's piece on dress reform; and the introduction and conclusion from Walter Wyckoff's essay on workers.

Computer scanning has allowed us to preserve the integrity of the original texts, many of which might be more familiar to modern readers in their expanded or revised forms as they later appeared in books. Because all original spellings and peculiarities of usage convey a flavor of 1890s writing and contribute to our understanding of the ways that texts circulated in the print culture of the period, we have retained them. However, readers should be aware that page layouts and typefaces have been modernized.

Finally, though we have divided this anthology into seven thematic sections, each focusing on a specific contested issue of the decade, we encourage readers to explore the connections to be made across the thematic divisions.

For instance, Thorstein Veblen's "The Economic Theory of Women's Dress" in section 1 can be productively read with Florence Kelley's "Women and Girls in Sweat-Shops" in section 3 and B. O. Flower's "Fashion's Slaves" in section 5. So, too, Andrew Carnegie's "Wealth" in section 1 can be read with Walter Wyckoff's "The Workers—The West" in section 3 and Louise Betts Edwards's "Step-Brothers to Dives" in section 4.

We hope that this cultural reader conveys something of the richness of the original periodicals of the American 1890s and that readers will continue to explore the texts of this vital and formative decade.

1 ★ BECOMING CULTURED AND CULTURE AS COMMODITY

Duing a decade filled with abundant advice on self-improvement, a major debate focused on the means by which an individual pursued his or her own cultural position. The articles grouped here range from definitions of culture to an examination of the processes by which cultural knowledge is claimed and demonstrated. Across the debates about kinds of culture, places and means for acquiring culture, levels of culture, and even the limits of culture, the overarching question was what counted as culture—what activities enhanced the status of those who participated in them. During a time when secondary education was not standardized and when the modern system of colleges and universities was still being established, many instructional and cultural functions were filled by university extensions, winter lyceum lectures and summer assemblies, expositions and fairs, and periodicals that circulated wide-ranging definitions of culture.

The *Chautauquan*, which promoted itself as "A Monthly Magazine Devoted to the Promotion of True Culture," also promised to initiate its readers into the processes of acculturation by directing them to lists of "required" reading. Periodicals such as *Harper's*, with longer and more prestigious histories, presented essays and literature by well-known or promising writers, but, assuming a certain level of cultural finesse on their readers' part, they rarely included lists or guidelines.

F. W. Gunsaulus's "The Ideal of Culture," from the *Chautauquan*, lays out a set of definitions about the pursuit of culture by questioning a type of education that he describes as merely intellectual and historical. Terming his audience "an army of idealists" and a "new band of the representatives of great forces in the past," he compares students of culture to Columbus on the brink of a new world, interjecting a need for the "Christian scholar" to find spiritual uplift in the humanities and to locate an ideal of culture that accords with Christian theology. In treating culture as a vehicle of ideology, in refusing to treat it as neutral and universal, Gunsaulus articulates one of the assumptions found throughout these essays—namely, that culture consists of arguments and contestations, not the "disinterested" study of art or philosophy.

Whereas Gunsaulus treats culture as an index of an individual's educational preparedness to function in a dynamic world, Andrew Carnegie, one of the richest American entrepreneurs at century's end, rationalizes personal wealth as the means to dispense culture to the masses. Thus, Carnegie naturalizes economic discrepancy and a system of inequality by suggesting that it is the philanthropic individual who creates public access to high culture through such institutions as the Carnegie public libraries and concert halls. In setting up a democratic ideal of culture, Carnegie positions the pursuit of culture as a vehicle for a larger set of ideas about public responsibility.

In contrast to such markedly idealistic, if self-serving, statements, selections from the *Critic* and the essay by George Clarke equate the relative sophistication of readers with particular class positions. Suggesting that there is an equation between a genre and the benefits to be gained from reading it, the *Critic*'s selections on the reading habit show an interest in cultivating readers across a broad range of social positions. Depicting the lady as well as the servant, the well-informed individual and the cultural initiate, these articles trace the habits and preferences of various classes of readers, noting the correlation between class and cultural preference. In the home of the "lady," for example, there is a "common fund of intellectual enjoyment" to which the entire family contributes, resulting in an educated family devoid of pretension. In the other contributions, which trace a young lady trying to anticipate the interests of her affianced readers in Chicago, and the servant readers in one home, there is a common sense that reading preferences "type" the reader. For example, one writer observes that while servants are drawn to "all the best novels," their criticisms are good but also "childlike" in their directness. George Clarke speaks to a larger concern, namely, the reading of novels, echoing earlier anxieties about the immoral and sensational appeal of an "addictive" and lesser literary form.

While such selections describe the formation of taste, it is the superficial performance of culture that Edith Wharton's short story "The Pelican" satirizes. Here, Wharton is openly critical of a demonstration of cultural knowledge when that knowledge is expounded by an individual devoid of both authenticity and reliability. The story's central character has no ability to digest information or to recall her reading accurately; like a pelican, she merely regurgitates the ideas of others. By demonstrating the increasing commodification of culture, Wharton dramatizes the moment when self-improvement degenerates into a display of compulsive consumerism, or an undiscriminating impulse to collect—an impulse also denounced by the economist Thorstein Veblen. One of the pervasive anxieties of the late nineteenth century was that "the real thing" was being replaced by "inauthentic" imitations. "Conspicuous consumption," the term coined by Veblen in *The Theory of the Leisure Class* (1899), describes the trend that Wharton indicted. Veblen argues that the purchase of culture ultimately becomes more important than discernment in a society characterized by excess capital and that, as a consequence, Americans were slipping down the evolutionary scale. In "The Economic Theory of Women's Dress," Veblen links fashion to waste and leisure, pointing to what he terms an "unproductive consumption" of valuable goods, which are now valued for their mere appearance and associations rather than for their actual worth as garments. This essay was part of Veblen's larger argument about a changing value system that distorts real or intrinsic worth and locates cultural power in visible commodities.

★

FRANK WAKELEY GUNSAULUS, D.D. *The Ideal of Culture*
Chautauquan 16 (October 1892): 59–64.

[A serious and didactic periodical, the *Chautauquan* was the foremost organ of the many adult education projects so important in this period. By the end of the century, 50,000 people had graduated from the *Chautauquan's* four-year course, and more than a quarter million people had taken classes. This essay calls attention to the emphasis placed on self-culture and character-building as essential to the Chautauquan project of producing an avowedly Christian and homogeneous American life.]

Mr. PRESIDENT, and Fellow Members of the Class of '92: I thank you for this most hearty greeting, which, I am sure, has less reference to myself than to the fact that to-day, with all joy and hope, this new section of the army of idealists, this new band of the representatives of great forces in the past, and of forces whose victories are still to come, go out into the world to do their work in God's name, and to carry before them the banner of the Chautauqua institute of culture. We have passed the arches; we have walked through the gate of gold; and we have learned, if anything at all has come to us, from these recent events that all culture results in the discovery of the fact that many lands lie still before us, and that really, every man and woman of scholarship is a veritable Columbus, standing upon the edge of some old east, and looking forward out into some larger west.

Mr. Emerson has told us that the great worth of a college course is to show to us its little avail; and in this suggestion he has intimated to all scholars what experience has taught to other minds long before, that the larger worlds still to conquer so greatly exceed the world which has already been conquered, that the little avail of what has done will grow distinct and clear, and the thought of it is only valuable as an inspiration for days to come. Surely, to-day, a class bearing the great name of "Columbians," a class which has written upon its heart "Seek and ye shall find," needs not to be told in an hour like this in our national, social, and literary history, that the immediate demand of the scholarship of the times is for that Columbian spirit which never rests, until, out of the seas, there do come to human sight vast continents of opportunity, new lands of privilege, great expanses upon which the higher forces of God and man shall work out the new products of the future. The discovery of America was the discovery of the future of mankind. Like all culture, it was brought about by a discovery of the past. The Renaissance was its birthplace; and that intellectual movement was a finding of the ancient world. Hope blossomed out of history. That is always the service of culture and it finds *Americas*.

It shall be my task for a brief while to invite your attention to the ideal of the culture which seems to me harmonious with this Chautauqua system of education to which we are all loyally devoted, and especially with this unique year. Never before, I think, in the history of humanity was there so deep a consciousness of the truth that no fact of life is safe, save as we use it for a starting point for the finding of new land, as a suggestion of pathways far out into the future, at the end of which there lie desirable goals. Nothing is more clearly recognized to-day in the policies of the intellectual world; nothing more certainly lifts itself out of sight in the seas of discussion, than this conviction that no truth which a man holds in his hand is safe to be held in any human hand; until we feel that all truth is lightning, and is safest as it passes from wire to wire, carrying the message of hope and love. By this idea are we protected from the perils which lie in every intellectual discovery, and saved from the larger distresses which come to man's mind by the faithless holding even of any noble idea. The atmosphere of our time is Columbian; the thought of our age has upon its forefront the words, "Seek and ye shall find." And a glorious fact about the things which men find is this, that every found thing is the suggestion of some larger unfound thing. Every range of mountains only serves to lift the mind higher that it may behold still loftier ranges, mingling with the clouds. Every star which is brought within man's ken is the bright suggestion in the sky of some farther constellation, some larger galaxy. The old scriptures open into new.

So, to-day, the culture of all time, wherever it is halting, wherever it is inefficient for practical service of the race, finds itself condemned by the Columbian spirit; and wherever culture, holding firmly to the duties of man, believes in the reality of the ideal, honestly trusts truth, has so firm faith in righteousness that it knows it will build its own bridges, bear its own weight, pay its own expenses, there culture marches on to victory, and every force of the present time is allied in its triumph. The culture to which you and I have been brought, my classmates, within the last four years of our reading, has certainly left our souls with some clear propositions that it is well to engraft into duty-loving work of our life, so that always, as we go out into the world here and there, we shall be carrying an idea of Christian culture. I think one of the first propositions is this: that man is the explanation of nature, its interpretation; and as he is the explanation and interpretation of nature, so he must always recognize himself to be its predestined king or its predestined slave. The revolutions of thought within the last fifty years have clothed man with an almost surpassing majesty. There were times when hesitant theologians stood and trembled and beheld nature becoming more and more beautiful, more and more nearly divine, as law after law swept up into those ever enlarging and ever more lofty ranges of activity, until at last the vision of man seemed destined to fade from human thought. But, to-day, even from our Darwins and Huxleys and Tyndalls—men who for so long were exiled from Christian pulpits—we are learning more surely the value and dignity of man. For, everywhere throughout nature, there is that distinct throb of aspiration toward man. Through all the ranges of life there seems to have been an effort for the creation of brain. Through all the brain there rises higher and higher aspiration toward the life of thought, and in all the transcendent world of thought there is a continuous leading on and tendency toward moral ideas. Man is crowned to-day by science, as almost never he was crowned by theology. He stands, prince in his world, listening to ten thousand voices of science telling him, with an eloquence almost equal to the eloquence of that old past: "This is your world, Adam, go out and subdue it." And the subjugation which man is giving to the world assures him that his own culture is going to be the larger and dearer. Everywhere throughout civilized life thought recognizes the greatness of humanity only as humanity is the crown and crowned thing in nature.

Ten thousand forces hitherto seemingly aimless have leaped into human service since you and I began to study nature through these books given to us in our Chautauqua course. New adaptations of power, new relationships of energies, fresh understandings of the value of the old powers—all these are part of that new vision of the greatness of nature and the grandeur of man which fills our minds to-day. Throughout the entire system of the universe with which we have dealt in these books we have found an ongoing movement, and words of which you and I were fearful four years ago have come to be necessary terms in our vocabulary. We feel that we are in a living universe. We know to-day, that, carrying forward into nature this new understanding of her processes and her hopes, we belong to that great evolution which at last smiled in the face of man, which at last gave us Shakespeare with his Hamlets, Pericles with his statesmanship, and Wagner with his music, which at last shall make man perfectly the son of God.

As we look through the history of chemic forces, powers in that world disclosed to us in our study of physics, energies which came to us as we looked far beyond the stars, we see that it is scientific truth, that "the whole creation groaneth and travaileth together in pain until now." And since that *"now"* has come; and humanity has stood in Jesus of Nazareth, in perfect mastery of the world, "the creation waiteth for the manifestation of the sons of God." No power that has come to us in the discoveries of nature but has indicated more and more the fact that man's destiny is sonship; that he is more than a manufactured product; infinitely more than even a created thing. He holds in his brain the very scepters of divine command; his crown is upon the forehead of his thought the instant he realizes in himself how surely there have been breathed into him divine destinies.

This is part of our message. We are to go forth in this great world of rocks and trees, of suns and stars, with the energies of earth mingling their power with the energies of heaven, to demonstrate continually the essential kingship of humanity. It is ours to take hold of every unknown force and bid it tell us its name. It is ours to touch every energy hitherto aimless and harness it to some divine ideal. The whole world of nature is an enigma without man; the life of nature is the darkest of problems without the supremacy of humanity. The power of humanity over nature is alone the explanation of its existence; and it is ours to tread the earth with some intimation of this regent power vouchsafed to us by Almighty God.

But we have been studying something else besides nature. We have found that just as the history of nature crowns itself in the history of humanity, just as to-day the forces of nature wait for their Bacons, Newtons, and Franklins in order that they may be eloquent or musical; so we find that the history of humanity holds within itself certain regent ideas without which man shall lose that kinship suggested in the life of nature. Hither we come, with this Christian culture as our birthright and gift, to tell our own hearts once again, to tell the world wherever we are to live and act, that the divine powers of the world are all ours; that the energies of omnipotence with all the powers and processes of history are vouchsafed to us—that the whole past belongs to him who holds worthy ideas as to ages past, sentiment as comprehensive as the centuries that have gone. That is the Christian scholar. He is the one human being who comes to the past with ideas large enough to throw about him a horizon everlasting. He is the one idealist who throws about the world of thought such a ring of hope and of sentiment as to make it all his. He is the one harvester of ten thousand years. He is the one gatherer of all victories. He is the one master of all triumphs.

The conviction which lies in the heart of every true Christian scholar is that every moment of the past is his ally and workman. Every chisel that touched the hard stone which through ages was gathered out of the quarries of time, every energy that smote that chisel sending out its curved line in beauty, until at last it became the representation of an idea, every power that lifted it at length and put it in triumph where it shines to-day—all these are ours, because in his brain and in his heart he has obtained the mastery of the ideas and sentiments for which these things stand. Every philosopher has ached in his brain for you and me; every Pythagoras at Alexandria has taught Plato for your son and mine. When Plato carried over into Athens a dream of a republic, he wrought for our republic. He was an inspiration upon history that our politics might be larger and truer. Every Socrates leaning with his walking stick against the marble porticos at Athens and stopping the young men of that city, teaching them how to ask and answer questions, makes your brain free and my heart fetterless. Every poet that spoke by the blue Ægean Sea with the richness of Sappho's love song, or with the thunder roll of Homer's majestic epic, or carved yonder for the heights of the Acropolis, that marvel of the Parthenon, spoke and sang and carved for you and me. Intellectual independence, spiritual ownership, the power that holds in this sublime mastery the forces of the future, is the gift of the past and makes every next moment altogether sublime.

Let us go forth men and women of the class of '92, with some intimation of the grandeur of the past out of which we come. Every orator in the past has thrilled his assemblies to make you and me eloquent. Every great soul which has touched the hand to canvas or carved on marble has allied himself with every great captain of any Marathon or Milvian Bridge, to make your life and my life worthy of the days in which we are to live. The past is ours, and, as George Eliot tells us "our finest hope is finest memory." So, therefore, my friends, must the whole world depend upon its cultured ones for its sight and hearing. The world of to-day with her facts almost so gigantic that they bewilder us with their dominance and prophesy a complete sovereignty over our souls, comes to the scholar, and that world begs at his feet for a perfect faith. It says to the scholar, "You know the past, you alone have threaded the ages; you have lived with Cromwell as you lived with Gustavus, from whom, when upon his knees, went up the cry—*Ein feste Burg ist unser Gott*; you were with Luther, as I have not been, when Luther nailed upon that cathedral door ninety-five propositions in the name of conscience; you helped to make with Calvin in the experiences of your intellectual life, the republics of Switzerland, you carved out in Germany with Charlemagne and with the great souls succeeding him, the possibilities of the empire; you taught the French spirit the idea of revolution; you gave eloquence to the lips of Mirabeau"; and our faltering age, heavy with facts, covered with the results which it has wrought out of the very depths of nature, comes to you and me, and, as we step out into the new life, it tells us, "O masters of the past, tell us where the ships of Almighty God land. You have walked upon the shore and have seen sails far out upon the billows of thought and sentiment. You know where the piers are to which these great ships come. You know whether or not, pacing this beach, men are waiting in vain for some message from the unknown. You, O masters of the past, help to make humanity master of the future."

And there is this great idea of the ministry of the Christian scholar that shall constantly give to the world that persuasion of the continuity of history, without which there is no real progress. We live often times as we believe, in these days, in a period of possible revolution. It is the scholar's function to teach humanity everywhere that revolution is the devil's word. It is ours continually to give to men to feel that the changes in politics, the overthrowing of crowns and scepters that do not in some living way connect themselves with the past, are productive of sorrow and distress in the future. It is ours to show men who have not studied history, whose relation to the past is not a living relationship, that all through the years there has been a steady growing tendency, a divine ideal working itself out; an immense impulse that has gone on from step to step with ever increasing victory, that to-day it means what it meant at the beginning, that it always will have but one message to humankind, and that its hope is the crowning of humanity in the name of our God and our Christ. Everywhere the world needs the inspiration which must come from the inspired scholar's heart. Evolution alone prevents revolution. *Evolution* is God's word in nature and history.

The disturbances in that great city so near to these shades of culture and of hope which pause for an instant this morning under the armed force of the State of New York [strike at Buffalo],—that is as valuable a fact to the modern Christian scholar as were the camps of Joshua, or the fall of Adam in Eden. Every page of history is absolutely sacred. There never was written a line of profane history. Coming out of that past, it is ours to instruct the belligerent hosts pause on the edge of revolution, that the tendency and force of all development, the power at the center of all history, the soul that breathes in all ages, is a power advancing on and on to the largest love of law and the truest use of liberty.

I hold that Christian thought, more than any other force in the world, is responsible for all the difficulties, and will be responsible for the solution of the problems that have come to us with regard to the labor problem. Fellow-Christians and fellow-scholars, do we not know that it is our Christianity which has sent the elements of the new truth into the brain of the laboring man and has so exalted him continually that at last, in holding power, new power, without the culture of Christian principles or without the chastening influence of noble sentiments, he stands with the torch in his hand forecasting a revolution not to be held by our force even in the name of God and law and liberty?

When Christianity came to the world, it met man in Rome in the presence of august institutions where the imperial sway of the Caesars was triumphant. It has taken him out of Rome. It has made another Rome everlastingly impossible. It has put St. Peter's in the place of Caesar's palace. It has made Rome the citadel of large and broad ideas, of hope, rather than of an oppressive, despotic government. It gave to man the Cross. It brought the prince and the pauper before that throne of goodness and told them both that they were equal before God. It has instructed power in all the ages; it has told power in every century that it has no right to exist, save as the minister of Jehovah. It has told this to the energy which makes money, as well as the energy which makes states. It has told the strength of brain and character which has made vast achievements in capital, as well as great achievements in poetry and in song, that it is the trustee of God Almighty's love and bounty. It has lifted the laboring man at last into the sublime region of self respect. He knows that something has made a Rome everywhere impossible. He stands upon the edge of industrial democracy by the power of Jesus Christ. He is in the new land of the industrial republic, by the might of the scarred hand alone. That has been the duty of Christian culture. The duty of Christian culture is the duty that Sam Adams performed in 1776, when that young man opened his lips to refute the idea that George the Third had the right to rule without any sense of responsibility. It must aid the evolution of the divine idea of the value of man above all else.

The duty of Christian culture everywhere is to tell capital that there is in nature and in man and through history a resistless current, that on the front of that current there are the words democracy and fraternity; that this current means in every rush of its wave broader privileges for the common man, larger opportunities for the being who, for ages before Christianity, was under the heel of want. It needs to tell capital, sitting behind its elegant lace curtains, that it is toying with the fiery forces of the times, and, as it sits upon velvet carpets, it needs to call up that page of history when at Versailles there sat the elegant wits of the court of the king who prayed with the unsuspected powers of the French revolution, and laughed, while France was growing more and more bloodthirsty and more and more sure of triumph. To prevent revolution, we must obey the divine ideal in the ages.

What is Christian culture to tell the laboring man? It is to tell the laboring man that the powers of history are all of them powers of law; that there is nothing so sacred in this Universe, in the name of liberty, as law; that God's government is the beginning and intimation of all government; that righteous obedience to law is the foundation of public liberty; that to destroy a dollar's worth of property upon any reason whatsoever, is to commit a crime.

That to bandage the eyes of ignorant men against the fact that there is and will be a righteous accumulation of wealth in the name of civilization, is to commit an outrage against truth.

But this labor problem is but one of the problems of our time. The laboring man of this moment wants your self-respect and your ideas. Fill his brain with noble ideas and impulses, and you will take the devil's lightning from beneath his skull. Give his heart just sentiments, such as those that were crucified on Calvary and rose at the grave of Joseph of Arimathaea, and you make civilization safe. But the poor man is not here. You, who represent the other class, must therefore pardon me, if I say more to you than I shall say to him. It is about the cheapest kind of oratory to come here and belabor and lecture the poor man. It will be one of the most earnest hours in which we may all live, if we recognize here that there are duties for us to perform. Everywhere in my short public career, I have had opportunities to speak to labor and I always urged obedience to law, self-respect, and that noble self-sacrifice and temperance that shall always inure to the common benefit. But let me tell the capital that sits here now, that what the poor man wants everywhere in this country, is not for it to build a hospital to cure his children, or for it even to build a library to inform his mind, or for it to build a mission to save his soul. He wants all these; these are all noble things; but he does not want any of them so badly as he wants a fair wage. He wants an honest distribution of the results of his labor, and then he can pay his own doctor's bill; he can put a little library over his own fireplace, and call it his own. And then, perhaps, he can save his own soul, too.

The ideals of Christian culture, however, are vastly more large and vastly more important than this, because in every direction they invite us into that large life which belongs to Christianity. No culture is Christian, in college or out of college, that does not recognize that the best discovery of moral or mental power within a soul is "a well of water springing up into everlasting life." Much of our culture has been upon the cistern plan. We have poured into our boys and girls rules, data of all sorts, dates, until at last the whole mass is unhealthy and untrue. I would have discovered in the dark depths of a boy's brain and heart living springs of thought, mastery of his own powers, sublime command of his own energies, a little living spring that holds the stars in its bosom in the night time, and is always fresh and pure, before I would say that his education has begun. That is genuine Christian culture. We must depend upon Christianity to make our culture all that this dream would suggest, and to make it all that it would suggest in politics and life everywhere. It must enthrone high above itself, above all ideas and sentiments, above all hopes and passions, the one great and noble leader, Jesus Christ the Lord. There, in His holiness, He must teach us law. There in His righteousness He must take the striker and make him obedient to law; that the law may be made right, if need be, by moral power. He must take the capitalist and teach him that all national life is fraternity, and all power is self sacrifice; and He must make you and me, in our labor in the world, missionaries of righteousness and truth.

Everywhere the Christ comes to our politics and social life and says, "I am the Truth. I am the Way. I am the Life." And civilization will stand until you and I help to teach it, stand like Karshish in Mr. Browning's poem, who, having found his way to Galilee, saw Lazarus, heard the story of his being raised from the dead, and writing a letter back to Abib, found his soul swaying back and forth between doubt and faith, until at last the spirit within the man broke forth in eloquence, and he said:

> "The very God! think, Abib; dost thou think?
> So, the All-Great were the All-Loving too—
> So through the thunder comes a human voice
> Saying, 'O heart I made, a heart beats here;
> Face my hands fashioned, see it in myself!
> Thou hast no power, nor mayst conceive of mine;
> But love I gave thee, with myself to love;
> And thou must love me, who hath died for thee!'
> The madman saith He said so; it is strange."

Let us make them sure of Christ and His power to save.

★

ANDREW CARNEGIE *Wealth*
North American Review 316 (June 1889): 653–664.

[Andrew Carnegie, one of America's wealthiest capitalists and most prominent philanthropists, here proclaims that "the gospel of wealth but echoes Christ's words." Applying Social Darwinism to "naturalize," justify, and perpetuate economic inequality, Carnegie insists that class distinctions based on wide economic differences show that civilization is progressing.]

THE PROBLEM of our age is the proper administration of wealth, that the ties of brotherhood may still bind together the rich and poor in harmonious relationship. The conditions of human life have not only been changed, but revolutionized, within the past few hundred years. In former days there was little difference between the dwelling, dress, food, and environment of the chief and those of his retainers. The Indians are to-day where civilized man then was. When visiting the Sioux, I was led to the wigwam of the chief. It was like the others in external appearance, and even within the difference was trifling between it and those of the poorest of his braves. The contrast between the palace of the millionaire and the cottage of the laborer with us today measures the change which has come with civilization.

This change, however, is not to be deplored, but welcomed as highly beneficial. It is well, nay, essential, for the progress of the race that the houses of some should be homes for all that is highest and best in literature and the arts, and for all the refinements of civilization, rather than that none should be so. Much better this great irregularity than universal squalor. Without wealth there can be no Maecenas. The "good old times" were not good old times. Neither master nor servant was as well situated then as to-day. A relapse to old conditions would be disastrous to both—not the least so to him who serves—and would sweep away civilization with it. But whether the change be for good or ill, it is upon us, beyond our power to alter, and, therefore, to be accepted and made the best of it. It is a waste of time to criticize the inevitable.

It is easy to see how the change has come. One illustration will serve for almost every phase of the cause. In the manufacture of products we have the whole story. It applies to all combinations of human industry, as stimulated and enlarged by the inventions of this scientific age. Formerly, articles were manufactured at the domestic hearth, or in small shops which formed part of the household. The master and his apprentices worked side by side, the latter living with the master, and therefore subject to the same conditions. When these apprentices rose to be masters, there was little or no change in their mode of life, and they, in turn, educated succeeding apprentices in the same routine. There was, substantially, social equality, and even political equality, for those engaged in industrial pursuits had then little or no voice in the State.

The inevitable result of such a mode of manufacture was crude articles at high prices. Today the world obtains commodities of excellent quality at prices which even the preceding generation would have deemed incredible. In the commercial world similar causes have produced similar results, and the race is benefited thereby. The poor enjoy what the rich could not before afford. What were the luxuries have become the necessaries of life. The laborer has now more comforts than the farmer had a few generations ago. The farmer has more luxuries than the landlord had, and is more richly clad and better housed. The landlord has books and pictures rarer and appointments more artistic than the King could then obtain.

The price we pay for this salutary change is, no doubt, great. We assemble thousands of operatives in the factory, and in the mine, of whom the employer can know little or nothing, and to whom he is little better than a myth. All intercourse between them is at an end. Rigid Castes are formed, and, as usual, mutual ignorance breeds mutual distrust. Each Caste is without sympathy with the other, and ready to credit anything disparaging in regard to it. Under the law of competition, the employer of thousands is forced into the strictest economies, among which the rates paid to labor figure prominently, and often there is friction between the employer and the employed, between capital and labor, between rich and poor. Human society loses homogeneity.

The price which society pays for the law of competition, like the price it pays for cheap comforts and luxuries, is also great; but the advantages of this law are also greater still than its cost—for it is to this law that we owe our wonderful material development, which brings improved conditions in its train. But, whether the law be benign or not, we must say of it, as we say of the change in the conditions of men to which we have referred: it is here; we cannot evade it; no substitutes for it have been found; and while the law may be sometimes hard for the individual, it is best for the race, because it insures the survival of the fittest in every department. We accept and welcome, therefore, as conditions to which we must accommodate ourselves, great inequality of environment; the concentration of business, industrial and commercial, in the hands of a few; and the law of competition between these, as being not only beneficial, but essential to the future progress of the race. Having accepted these, it follows that there must be great scope for the exercise of special ability in the merchant and in the manufacturer who has to conduct affairs upon a great scale. That this talent for organization and management is rare among men is proved by the fact that it invariably secures enormous rewards for its possessor, no matter where or under what laws or conditions. The experienced in affairs always rate the MAN whose services can be obtained as a partner as not only the first consideration, but such as render the question of his capitals scarcely worth considering: for able men soon create capital; in the hands of those without the special talent required, capital soon takes wings. Such men become interested in firms or corporations using millions; and, estimating only simple interest to be made upon the capital invested, it is inevitable that their income must exceed their expenditure and that they must, therefore, accumulate wealth. Nor is there any middle ground which such men can occupy, because the great manufacturing or commercial concern which does not earn at least interest upon its capital soon becomes bankrupt. It must either go forward or fall behind; to stand still is impossible. It is a condition essential to its successful operation that it should be thus far profitable, and even that, in addition to interest on capital, it should make profit. It is a law, as certain as any of the others named, that men possessed of this peculiar talent for affairs, under the free play of economic forces must, of necessity, soon be in receipt of more revenue than can be judiciously expended upon themselves; and this law is as beneficial for the race as the others.

Objections to the foundations upon which society is based are not in order, because the condition of the race is better with these than it has been with any other which has been tried. Of the effect of any new substitutes proposed we cannot be sure. The Socialist or Anarchist who seeks to overturn present conditions is to be regarded as attacking the foundation upon which civilization itself rests, for civilization took its start from the day when the capable, industrious workman said to his incompetent and lazy fellow, "If thou dost not sow, thou shalt not reap," and thus ended primitive Communism by separating the drones from the bees. One who studies this subject will soon be brought face to face with the conclusion that upon the sacredness of property civilization itself depends—the right of the laborer to his hundred dollars in the savings-bank, and equally the legal right of the millionaire to his millions. Every man must be allowed "to sit under his own vine and figtree, with none to make afraid," if human society is to advance, or even to remain so far advanced as it is. To those who propose to substitute Communism for this intense Individualism, the answer therefore is: The race has tried that. All progress from that barbarous day to the present time has resulted from its displacement. Not evil, but good, has come to the race from the accumulation of wealth by those who have had the ability and energy to produce it. But even if we admit for a moment that it might be better for the race to discard its present foundation, Individualism—that it is a nobler ideal that man should labor, not for himself alone, but in and for a brotherhood of his fellows, and share with them all in common, realizing Swedenborg's idea of Heaven, where as he says, the angels derive their happiness, not from laboring for self, but for each other,—even admit all this, and a sufficient answer is, This is not evolution, but revolution. It necessitates the changing of human nature itself—a work of eons, even if it were good to change it, which we cannot know. It is not practicable in our day or in our age. Even if desirable theoretically, it belongs to another and long-succeeding sociological stratum. Our duty is with what is practicable now— with the next step possible in our day and generation. It is criminal to waste our energies in endeavoring to uproot, when all we can profitably accomplish is to bend the universal tree of humanity a little in the direction most favorable to the production of good fruit under existing circumstances. We might as well urge the destruction of the highest existing type of man because he failed to reach our ideal as to favor the destruction of Individualism, Private Property, the Law of Accumulation of Wealth, and the Law of Competition; for these are the highest result of human experience, the soil in which society, so far, has produced the best fruit. Unequally or unjustly, perhaps, as these laws sometimes operate, and imperfect as they appear to the Idealist, they are, nevertheless, like the highest type of man, the best and most valuable of all that humanity has yet accomplished.

We start, then, with a condition of affairs under which the best interests of the race are promoted, but which inevitably gives wealth to the few. Thus far, accepting conditions as they exist, the situation can be surveyed and pronounced good. The question then arises—and if the foregoing be correct, it is the only question with which we have to deal—What is the proper mode of administering wealth after the laws upon which civilization is founded have thrown it into the hands of the few? And it is of this great question that I believe I offer the true solution. It will be understood that *fortunes* are here spoken of, not moderate sums saved by many years of effort, the returns from which are required for the comfortable maintenance and education of families. This is not *wealth*, but only *competence*, which it should be the aim of all to acquire.

There are but three modes in which surplus wealth can be disposed of. It can be left to the families of the decedents; or it can be bequeathed for public purposes; or, finally, it can be administered during their lives by its possessors. Under the first and second modes most of the wealth of the world that has reached the few has hitherto been applied. Let us in turn consider each of these modes. The first is the most injudicious. In monarchical countries, the estates and the greatest portion of the wealth are left to the first son, that the vanity of the parent may be gratified by the thought that his name and title are to descend to succeeding generations unimpaired. The condition of this class in Europe to-day teaches the futility of such hopes or ambitions. The successors have become impoverished through their follies or from the fall in the value of land. Even in Great Britain the strict law of entail has been found inadequate to maintain the status of an hereditary class. Its soil is rapidly passing into the hands of the stranger. Under republican institutions the division of property among the children is much fairer, but the question which forces itself upon thoughtful men in all lands is: Why should men leave great fortunes to their children? If this is done from affection, is it not misguided affection? Observation teaches that, generally speaking, it is not well for the children that they should be so burdened. Neither is it well for the state. Beyond providing for the wife and daughters moderate sources of income, and very moderate allowances indeed, if any, for the sons, men may well hesitate, for it is no longer questionable that great sums bequeathed oftener work more for the injury than for the good of the recipients. Wise men will soon conclude that, for the best interests of the members of their families and of the state, such bequests are an improper use of their means.

It is not suggested that men who have failed to educate their sons to earn a livelihood shall cast them adrift in poverty. If any man has seen fit to rear his sons with a view to their living idle lives, or, what is highly commendable, has instilled in them the sentiment that they are in a position to labor for public ends without reference to pecuniary considerations, then, of course,

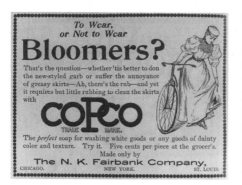

FIGURE I This soap advertisement borrows from *Hamlet*'s famous soliloquy, merging it with arguments about a modern woman's exercise wardrobe and with the new safety bicycle. Yoking high culture to commercial competition, the advertisement also positions the traditionally garbed bicycler against the more extreme woman who would wear bloomers. (*Cosmopolitan*, 1895)

the duty of the parent is to see that such are provided for *in moderation.* There are instances of millionaires' sons unspoiled by wealth, who, being rich, still perform great services in the community. Such are the very salt of the earth, as valuable as, unfortunately, they are rare; still it is not the exception, but the rule, that men must regard, and, looking at the usual result of enormous sums conferred upon legatees, the thoughtful man must shortly say, "I would as soon leave to my son a curse as the almighty dollar," and admit to himself that it is not the welfare of the children, but family pride, which inspires these enormous legacies.

As to the second mode, that of leaving wealth at death for public uses, it may be said that this is only a means for the disposal of wealth, provided a man is content to wait until he is dead before it becomes of much good in the world. Knowledge of the results of legacies bequeathed is not calculated to inspire the brightest hopes of much posthumous good being accomplished. The cases are not few in which the real object sought by the testator is not attained, nor are they few in which his real wishes are thwarted. In many cases the bequests are so used as to become only monuments of his folly. It is well to remember that it requires the exercise of not less ability than that which acquired the wealth to use it so as to be really beneficial to the community. Besides this, it may fairly be said that no man is to be extolled for doing what he cannot help doing, nor is he to be thanked by the community to which he only leaves wealth at death. Men who leave vast sums in this way may fairly be thought men who would not have left it at all, had they been able to take it with them. The memories of such cannot be held in grateful remembrance, for there is no grace in their gifts. It is not to be wondered at that such bequests seem so generally to lack the blessing.

The growing disposition to tax more and more heavily large estates left at death is a cheering indication of the growth of a salutary change in public opinion. The State of Pennsylvania now takes—subject to some exceptions—one-tenth of the property left by its citizens. The budget presented in the

British Parliament the other day proposes to increase the death-duties; and, most significant of all, the new tax is to be a graduated one. Of all forms of taxation, this seems the wisest. Men who continue hoarding great sums all their lives, the proper use of which for public ends would work good to the community, should be made to feel that the community, in the form of the state, cannot thus be deprived of its proper share. By taxing estates heavily at death the state marks its condemnation of the selfish millionaire's unworthy life.

It is desirable that nations should go much further in this direction. Indeed, it is difficult to set bounds to the share of a rich man's estate which should go at his death to the public through the agency of the state, and by all means such taxes should be graduated, beginning at nothing upon moderate sums to dependents, and increasing rapidly as the amounts swell, until of the millionaire's hoard, as of Shylock's, at least

> " —The other half
> Comes to the privy coffer of the state."

This policy would work powerfully to induce the rich man to attend to the administration of wealth during his life, which is the end that society should always have in view, as being that by far most fruitful for the people. Nor need it be feared that this policy would sap the root of enterprise and render men less anxious to accumulate, for to the class whose ambition it is to leave great fortunes and be talked about after their death, it will attract even more attention, and, indeed, be a somewhat nobler ambition to have enormous sums paid over to the state from their fortunes.

There remains, then, only one mode of using great fortunes; but in this we have the true antidote for the temporary unequal distribution of wealth, the reconciliation of the rich and the poor—a reign of harmony—another ideal, differing, indeed, from that of the Communist in requiring only the further evolution of existing conditions, not the total overthrow of our civilization. It is founded upon the present most intense individualism, and the race is prepared to put it in practice by degrees whenever it pleases. Under its sway we shall have an ideal state, in which the surplus wealth of the few will become, in the best sense, the property of the many, because administered for the common good, and this wealth, passing through the hands of the few, can be made a much more potent force for the elevation of our race than if it had been distributed in small sums to the people themselves. Even the poorest can be made to see this, and to agree that great sums gathered by some of their fellow-citizens and spent for public purposes, from which the masses reap the principal benefit, are more valuable to them than if scattered among them through the course of many years in trifling amounts.

If we consider what results flow from the Cooper Institute, for instance, to the best portion of the race in New York not possessed of means, and compare these with those which would have arisen for the good of the masses from an equal sum distributed by Mr. Cooper in his lifetime in the form of wages, which is the highest form of distribution, being for work done and not for charity, we can form some estimate of the possibilities for the improvement of the race which lie embedded in the present law of the accumulation of wealth. Much of this sum, if distributed in small quantities among the people, would have been wasted in the indulgence of appetite, some of it in excess, and it may be doubted whether even the part put to the best use, that of adding to the comforts of the home, would have yielded results for the race, as a race, at all comparable to those which are flowing and are to flow from the Cooper Institute from generation to generation. Let the advocate of violent or radical change ponder well this thought.

We might even go so far as to take another instance, that of Mr. Tilden's bequest of five millions of dollars for a free library in the city of New York, but in referring to this one cannot help saying involuntarily, How much better if Mr. Tilden had devoted the last years of his own life to the proper administration of this immense sum; in which case neither legal contest nor any other cause of delay could have interfered with his aims. But let us assume that Mr. Tilden's millions finally become the means of giving to this city a noble public library, where the treasures of the world contained in books will be open to all forever, without money and without price. Considering the good of that part of the race which congregates in and around Manhattan Island, would its permanent benefit have been better promoted had these millions been allowed to circulate in small sums through the hands of the masses? Even the most strenuous advocate of Communism must entertain a doubt upon this subject. Most of those who think will probably entertain no doubt whatever.

Poor and restricted are our opportunities in this life; narrow our horizon; our best work most imperfect; but rich men should be thankful for one inestimable boon. They have it in their power during their lives to busy themselves in organizing benefactions from which the masses of their fellows will derive lasting advantage, and thus dignify their own lives. The highest life is probably to be reached, not by such imitation of the life of Christ as Count Tolstoi gives us, but, while animated by Christ's spirit, by recognizing the changed conditions of this age, and adopting modes of expressing this spirit suitable to the changed conditions under which we live; still laboring for the good of our fellows, which was the essence of his life and teaching, but laboring in a different manner.

This, then, is held to be the duty of the man of Wealth: to set an example of modest, unostentatious living, shunning display or extravagance; to provide moderately for the legitimate wants of those dependent upon him; and, after doing so, to consider all surplus revenues which come to him simply as trust funds, which he is called upon to administer, and strictly bound as a matter of duty to administer in the manner which, in his judgment, is best calculated to produce the most beneficial results for the community—the man of wealth thus becoming the mere trustee and agent for his poorer brethren, bringing to their service his superior wisdom, experience, and ability to administer, doing for them better than they would or could do for themselves.

We are met here with the difficulty of determining what are moderate sums to leave to members of the family; what is modest, unostentatious living; what is the test of extravagance. There must be different standards for different conditions. The answer is that it is as impossible to name exact amounts or actions as it is to define good manners, good taste, or the rules of propriety; but, nevertheless, these are verities, well known although undefinable. Public sentiment is quick to know and to feel what offends these. So is the case of wealth. The rule in regard to good taste in the dress of men or women applies here. Whatever makes one conspicuous offends the canon. If any family be chiefly known for display, for extravagance in home, table, equipage, for enormous sums ostentatiously spent in any form upon itself,— if these be its chief distinctions, we have no difficulty in estimating its nature or culture. So likewise in regard to the use or abuse of its surplus wealth, or to generous, free-handed coöperation in good public use, or to unabated efforts to accumulate and hoard to the last, whether they administer or bequeath. The verdict rests with the best and most enlightened public sentiment. The community will surely judge, and its judgments will not often be wrong.

The best uses to which surplus wealth can be put have already been indicated. Those who would administer wisely must, indeed, be wise; for one of the serious obstacles to the improvement of our race is indiscriminate charity. It were better for mankind that the millions of the rich were thrown into the sea than so spent as to encourage the slothful, the drunken, the unworthy. Of every thousand dollars spent in so-called charity to-day, it is probable that $950 is unwisely spent—so spent, indeed, as to produce the very evils which it hopes to mitigate or cure. A well-known writer of philosophic books admitted the other day that he had given a quarter of a dollar to a man who approached him as he was coming to visit the house of his friend. He knew nothing of the habits of this beggar; knew not the use that would be made of this money; although he had every reason to suspect that it would be spent improperly. This man professed to be a disciple of Herbert Spencer; yet the quarter-dollar given that night will probably work more injury than all the money will do good which its thoughtless donor will ever be able to give in true charity will do. He only gratified his own feelings, saved himself from annoyance—and this was probably one of the most selfish and very worst actions of his life, for in all respects he is most worthy.

In bestowing charity, the main consideration should be to help those who will help themselves; to provide part of the means by which those who desire to improve may do so; to give those who desire to rise the aids by which they may rise; to assist, but rarely or never to do all. Neither the individual nor the race is improved by alms-giving. Those worthy of assistance, except in rare cases, seldom require assistance. The really valuable men of the race never do, except in cases of accident or sudden change. Everyone has, of course, cases of individuals brought to his own knowledge where temporary assistance can do genuine good, and these he will not overlook. But the amount which can be wisely given by the individual for individuals is necessarily limited by his lack of knowledge of the circumstances connected with each. He is the only true reformer who is as careful and anxious not to aid the unworthy as he is to aid the worthy, and, perhaps, even more so, for in alms-giving more injury is probably done by rewarding vice than by relieving virtue.

The rich man is thus almost restricted to following the examples of Peter Cooper, Enoch Pratt of Baltimore, Mr. Pratt of Brooklyn, Senator Stanford, and others, who know that the best means of benefiting the community is to place within its reach the ladders upon which the aspiring can rise—free libraries, parks, and means of recreation, by which men are helped in body and mind; works of art, certain to give pleasure and improve the public taste; and public institutions of various kinds, which will improve the general condition of the people; in this manner returning their surplus wealth to the mass of their fellows in the forms best calculated to do them lasting good.

Thus is the problem of Rich and Poor to be solved. The laws of accumulation will be left free, the laws of distribution free. Individualism will continue, but the millionaire will be but a trustee for the poor, intrusted for a season with a great part of the increased wealth of the community, but administering it for the community far better than it could or would have done for itself. The best minds will thus have reached a stage in the development of the race in which it is clearly seen that there is no mode of disposing of surplus wealth creditable to thoughtful and earnest men into whose hands it flows, save by using it year by year for the general good. This day already dawns. Men may die without incurring the pity of their fellows, still sharers in great business enterprises from which their capital cannot be or has not been withdrawn, and which is left chiefly at death for public uses; yet the day is not far distant when the man who dies leaving behind him millions of available wealth, which was free to him to administer during life, will pass away "unwept, unhonored, and unsung," no matter to what uses he leaves the dross which he cannot take with him. Of such as these the public verdict will then be: "The man who dies thus rich dies disgraced."

Such, in my opinion is the true Gospel concerning Wealth, obedience to which is destined some day to solve the problem of the Rich and the Poor, and to bring "Peace on earth, among men good will."

★

Brief Observations on the Habit of Reading
from the *Critic* (1892–1897)

[Begun in 1881, the *Critic* reprinted reviews of fiction, poetry, drama, and the fine arts from contemporary periodicals; it also responded to popular interests ranging from Rudyard Kipling to the bicycle to the *Trilby* craze. In these selections, the "habit of reading," the most overtly cultivated habit of the periodical market at large—its "daily bread," as labeled here—is presented as a source of cultivation to a wide spectrum of readers with diverse literary and nonliterary tastes. These selections allude to (without necessarily valorizing) the preferences of readers from various classes, educations, and backgrounds. To this diverse audience, reading thus appears as an object of concentrated study, a focal point of familial and marital responsibility, and as a means of exerting the moral discipline of leisure employment.]

★

The Reading Habit
[*Harper's Bazaar*], *Critic* 21 (July 30, 1892): 60

OF ALL THE HABITS that can be cultivated, none is more productive of pleasure and improvement than that of reading, provided the books be well chosen.

Reading is a recreation—the rest and refreshment that make one feel like a new being—but it is much more. It is not only the wine of mental life, it is its daily bread. The study of text books will by no means take the place of general and varied reading. One may be master of several languages and yet not be well read. One may have many accomplishments, and even be proficient in one or more branches of science, and yet be unintelligent on general subjects for lack of a habit of judicious reading.

The quantity of reading that may be done in a year by the employment of even small portions of time is surprising to those who have not observed the matter. It is a delight to think of the amount of information and keen intellectual pleasure obtained by those who follow the 'required readings' of the Chautauquan courses after spending less than an hour a day upon them, and equal advantages may follow more desultory reading if it be well chosen.

A lady whom we know is the head of a large family, entertaining much company, and doing a great deal of benevolent work. All these things leave her but little time, yet at the end of a year she will be found to have read more, and to have better assimilated what she has read, than the majority of men or women of leisure. In her the reading habit is very strong, and leads her to improve every chance moment. Her memory is good and her mental faculties clear, so that she can keep many separate threads of thought in mind without dropping or tangling any. Hence she finds it profitable to have several books on hand at once. For her own 'den,' where she is most likely to be found when she has more than a few moments at her disposal, she has always 'solid' work of some sort—history, biography, travel, or popularized science. In the sewing-room, where she may have to wait short intervals between 'fittings,' are kept volumes of selections. On her dressing-table is always another book. In her parlor a small-volumed Shakespeare is ever at hand. In the dining-room are newspapers and magazines. In a drawer in the hall table, ready to be taken when she is going out, are novels or books of short stories, to be read in carriage or horse-cars. Thus she is never obliged to wait idly through even those moments of waiting which are inevitable in every large family.

A very great advantage of this lady's habit is that her whole family receive the benefit of her ever-overflowing mind. Her children bring their studies, her husband his interests, and she her reading to the common fund of intellectual enjoyment. Their table hours are charming. The husband's business is one involving unusual cares and responsibilities, and he is often too tired to read, but, by his wife's flow of lively chat upon ever-fresh topics, his mind is, as he expresses it, so 'irrigated' that it becomes rich and fruitful, instead of the arid waste which a mind exhausted by business and unrefreshed from without must be. Her children derive from their mother's varied stores countless bits of information which enable them to better understand their lessons, and are constantly stimulated to greater efforts.

This useful and interesting woman makes no pretensions to learning, and with the exception of writing and speaking the English language with unusual purity and fluency, has no accomplishments; but she is singularly well informed.

★

Courses of Reading
[*Publishers' Circular*, London], *Critic* 21 (October 1, 1892): 184

A CORRESPONDENT has been applying to our contemporary the New York *Literary News* for advice regarding a course of reading. The counsel is sought by a friend, probably an elderly gentleman of benevolent instincts, on behalf of a young lady, and he is careful to state that 'the object is improvement as well as entertainment.' He confesses, with a candor rare in correspondents seeking advice, that the young lady has 'no marked literary tastes, but she is going to marry a man who is an amateur in English literature;' and she is anxious to qualify herself for the companionship of this distinguished patron of letters. She desires, in the words of her friend, to keep within 'hailing distance' of him—a laudable ambition in which we sincerely hope she will be successful, for if he should get out of her sight, intellectually speaking, there might be unpleasantness. When we learn that 'she is quiet, womanly, and capable of conscientious application,' we are encouraged to predict untold felicities for at least one cultured household in the United States. The editor, however, does not do much to help her. Knowing probably the facility with which good counsel is forgotten, he replies cautiously, the politic man, dodging as Mark Twain dodged in his famous letter to the Board of Aldermen of the city of San Francisco on the water lot question. He vaguely suggests that those who want books might do worse than consult a bookseller, and says some safe words about standard authors; but he positively declines to commit himself. Possibly he has experienced the penalties of taking too ardent an interest in those who desire to be directed in the paths of knowledge.

It is a practice with some people to write to busy men and women about books and courses of reading. Sometimes the object is to get the autograph of a celebrity; sometimes the letters are written purely as a pastime; too seldom, we fear, is there a genuine desire to obtain useful information. But supposing that all such letters are genuine, that is to say that they mean what they say, how is one to advise with any chance of doing good? Coleridge divides readers into four kinds: (1) Sponges, who absorb all they read and return it nearly in the same state, only little dirtied. (2) Sandglasses, who retain nothing and are content to get through a book for the sake of getting through time. (3) Strainbags, who retain merely the dregs of what they read. (4) Mogul diamonds, equally rare and valuable, who profit by what they read and enable others to profit by it also. If applicants for advice would state to which of these four great orders they belong, the person applied to might answer with some degree of certainty, some possibility of benefitting his correspondent. A physician examines a patient before prescribing, but a man of letters is supposed to be able to give proper prescriptions in total ignorance of the constitutions, habits, and circumstances of those who consult him, as if he were possessed of some magical power of divination, or as if all sorts of books were suited to all sorts of people. The young lady in question, for example, would like her course to comprise 'history, travel, fiction—in prose and poetry,' moreover she would prefer it to be 'in some sort progressive.' It is unfair to put conundrums under the guise of serious questions.

How, for instance, is one to make out prescriptions in history? There are certain historical works which all are agreed are good. But how is a man to know which to recommend on the indefinite applications that are generally made for guidance in reading? He might prescribe Gibbon when he ought to prescribe Macaulay, or Macaulay when Carlyle would produce better effects. He might have a leaning towards the classics and give Herodotus where it was Green or Bancroft that was really needed. There is no end to the mistakes he might commit. In words of travel, too the possibilities of blundering are infinite; but it is in fiction—prose and poetry—that the chief perils would lie. It is true that fiction is supposed to be light reading, and that there, at least, one cannot go wrong. But that is a superficial view of the matter. The reader with a natural appetite for (say) Eugene Sue, would scarcely be satisfied with Charles Lamb, even in the celebrated dissertation on roast pig. Similarly one with a taste for the religious novel would be very apt to feel some disappointment with 'Don Quixote.' We suppose it would always be safe to prescribe Scott; but it is not every one with whom Byron agrees, and there are those who speak slightingly of Dickens. To give Tennyson or Keats instead of Walt Whitman would be a fatal error, and it would never do to give Browning when the natural inclination is for Longfellow. To some constitutions Fielding would be a tonic, but for others he would be too strong; nor would the Rev. Laurence Sterne suit every one with a bent for theology. He would be bold who would recommend Shakespeare, and Milton is not to be thought of. The task of prescribing is indeed hopeless; and the only consolation is that those who really do care for books will, as Mr. Andrew Lang once pointed out, discover what is best for themselves.

★

What Chicago People Read

[*Daily Chronicle*, London, July 4], *Critic* 23 (September 23, 1893): 200

In CHICAGO the Grand Old Man would find little, if indeed any, scope for the pursuit of the interesting secondhand volume. On the other hand, he would find a larger number and a greater variety of new books under a single bookseller's roof than he could anywhere else. McClurg is the one bookseller of Chicago; his bookshop is like a great library; his name is synonymous with the sale of books over half the American continent.

Essentially, Chicago is a business city, with commercialism painted in red letters—a dreadfully business city, if you like. I had tried to learn whether Chicago people read much apart from the papers, and I had not succeeded in coming to any kind of conclusions. Better, I thought, go and hear what McClurg has to say on the matter. Gen. McClurg himself was in the country, but his partner Mr. F. B. Smith was good enough to take me in hand.

"Do Chicago people read much?" Mr. Smith repeated to himself when we had fairly opened the interview. "When you ask that question, you mean, I take it, do the well-to-do class and the middle class read much? Those classes are, I imagine, the great readers of books wherever you go. Allowing for the youth of Chicago, I certainly think we are very wide readers of books. Chicago people—those you would expect to read books—are a reading people. In Boston or New York more unusual, more rare books—many more—will be sold than here. But for the sale of books generally, I think we compare not at all unfavorably with the East. You would be surprised—as an Englishman especially you would be—to see some of the people who come to buy books. I mean, if you were to judge them by their coats, you would hardly set them down as book-buyers. Now, not long ago an unshaved young fellow in sombrero and top-boots walked in and began asking about books. I'm afraid I looked as if I was curious to discover just what kind of literature would suit my friend. Well, he saw this in my face. Says he, 'Perhaps you don't think I look much like a literary man.' Then he went on, 'I'm a Harvard graduate making a pretty good living as a cowboy out on the prairie. I wanted badly some new books, and I've come to get them.' With that he ordered quite a larger number of standard works in science and philosophy. He knew exactly what he wanted, and he pulled out a great bunch of notes and paid for his purchases. When Matthew Arnold—I'm going to tell you a pretty little story—visited Chicago, he was entertained by the Chicago Literary Club. There was the little speech of welcome on such occasions, and I recollect that it was a particularly happy speech. 'Now what,' asked Matthew Arnold, 'might that gentleman be who has just spoken?' 'A wholesale grocer,' somebody told him. Yes, he was a wholesale grocer, but in addition to that a scholarly man, nay, an excellent student."

"If I may distinguish between American and English literature which is more the largely favored? Rather, do American or English writers sell best?"

"Your question is a very difficult one, and I really doubt if I could answer it. All I could say is that there are American authors as great favorites as English authors, and English authors as great favorites as American ones. In Chicago, as I suppose in every great city in the world, fiction is most largely read. After fiction I should put history, then biography, travel, science, philosophy, and so on. To that, I might add that the bulk of our reading is in the works of modern writers. You would expect it to be so. Don't suppose, though, that the classics are not well sold, because indeed they are. Now I cannot say that poetry is much read in Chicago; it is not. Sometimes I wonder if poetry, except an occasional volume, is much read anywhere. Nevertheless, Longfellow, Tennyson, Browning, and the other great dead American and English poets are frequently asked for—Shakespeare particularly."

"And the old writers of Anglo-Saxon prose what about them?"

"Why, Dickens and Scott, taking merely those two great novelists, sell largely and continuously. How could it be otherwise? But I need not try, if I could, to go into any kind of details touching the sale of the masters of the English tongue—the masters born on one side of the Atlantic or the other. I could say nothing beyond what I have said—that they sell steadily, as they always must sell. Just to revert to poetry for a minute, there are two points which I might note—three points perhaps. First, have you recently had in England any sort of marked revival in Shelley? We have had a distinct revival here. Why I don't know, only so it is. Secondly, I'm afraid Wordsworth has almost gone out; and, thirdly, so has Byron. These points are by way of comment on my general statement concerning the sale of all the Anglo-Saxon classics. Oliver Wendell Holmes and W. D. Howells both sell largely. Mark Twain, I need hardly say, is most popular—has a great sale. Bret Harte, perhaps, is not quite so popular as he was at one time. It may be because he has written a great deal, and because other authors have grown up who write in the same vein, more or less. Henry James has never had the demand which some people consider he deserves. Mrs. Hudgson Burnett, Thomas Nelson Page, Mary E. Wilkins, and Gen. Lew Wallace are much sought after. 'Ben Hur,' by Gen. Lew Wallace, has been wonderfully successful in this part of America."

"So far as I can make out, the American writers most popular in England— we have not nearly covered them all—are the favorites in America—much more the favorites?"

"Probably it would be so; just as your favorites on the other side are also the favorites here. Yet, in one case, anyhow, there is an exception to your favorites being ours, and that is the case of Rudyard Kipling. At one time Rudyard Kipling had an immense name with American readers. He promised to become vastly popular, until one fine day he came round some of our American cities, and on a twenty-four hours' acquaintance, abused them up-hill and down-dale. You may remember what he said about Chicago—Chicago, in which he had only spent, comparatively speaking, a few hours—Chicago, of whose best people he had actually seen nothing."

"Then Kiplings's criticisms of American cities have hurt his circulation with American book-buyers—that's what it comes to?"

"Precisely: hurt his circulation to an enormous extent. 'Oh that Kipling,' folk say, using a little stronger language; 'we don't want anything to do with his books.' I don't discuss Kipling's criticisms upon America; I simply state one result of them. Kipling would have run a hard race with Robert Louis Stevenson for popularity if he had only held his tongue. American people like Stevenson; not merely like his books, but, for some reason, like him personally. They are attracted to the man as a man, and, after all, it is something for a writer of books to be popular personally."

40   BECOMING CULTURED

FIGURE 2 This advertisement for *Scribner's Monthly Magazine* appeared in its emergent competitor, *McClure's,* and heralds upcoming features. As an author concerned with everyday life and voicing a nationalist, protectionist view of life during the 1890s, Robert Grant is prominently featured in this appeal to *McClure's* readers, who are positioned as unsophisticated, "common sense" readers. (*McClure's,* 1895)

"Has Conan Doyle, might I ask, done anything to make the short story, as a short story, popular in America?"

"In America, as I have been told it is in England, readers prefer a continuous tale rather than a series of short stories. 'Sherlock Holmes's Adventures' have, in one instance, as some of Kipling's stories did before, broken down this preference. Conan Doyle is beginning to take a high position—a position already only a little behind James Matthew Barrie. Walter Besant would stand with Barrie, while Jerome K. Jerome has a good name for his 'Three Men in a Boat.' George Meredith holds as good a place as his English popularity warrants; Mrs. Humphry Ward's 'David Grieve' did very well; 'Ouida' and Miss Braddon are on the wane—they have written too much. Rider Haggard also is not the favorite he was, but Clark Russell is always being asked for. A sea-story—you know, well told—has a remarkable attraction for the man of Anglo-Saxon blood."

If every citizen of Chicago had not a well-stocked library it is not the fault of McClurg & Co.

★

A Note on Servants' Libraries
Critic n.s. 27 (March 13, 1897): 188

A CORRESPONDENT WRITES:

Will you allow me to take the liberty to ask you to reconsider what you say about the kitchen library, and to write a little more on the subject? You are always on the side of a broad humanitarianism, and your words have so much weight, that I should be glad and grateful to hear you lift up your voice on behalf of the faithful servants who are so mentally starved—by those who have a responsibility concerning them. Will you pardon me if I trouble you with a little personal experience? I should not do so except that I heard that one positive may disprove many negatives. For many years we have had a library for the servants in their sitting-room. It contains all the best novels— Thackeray, Dickens, Scott, Bulwer, George Eliot, Cooper, Dumas,—books of history and of natural history, books of travel, and various sets of books of general information, like "Chambers's Miscellanies." I assure you that they are constantly read and reread by the various men and women of the household. I do not mean that there are no dolts—alas, there are too many in Vanity Fair, among one's own circle. But the majority read, and read good books and give good criticisms—natural, spontaneous and simply direct—as a child's.

That I might have their standpoint, not my own, I have had (before writing this letter) a long talk with my maid, and the boy (who has been with us many years), about the other servants (I knew very well about these), and they assured me that the library is in constant use, and that even the grooms and the farm hands (for our home is in the country, New York is simply temporary) all come to read the books I have mentioned—especially the Miscellanies. Perhaps this will be a good illustration of the results of culture. I have been very ill for two or three years and have not given the library the same personal attention I used to, and as I was on the subject to-day, I asked, "Thomas, is there an encyclopedia in the library? I have forgotten." "No, madam, but I have bought a small one for myself." "And how about the books of poetry, I am afraid many of them have been lost"—for there is this practical objection: transient servants do carry them off if there is not supervision. "Yes, Madam, they have been, but they each have their own books of poetry—and they borrow them off of each other."

Perhaps you will say that it would be better to have some grammars in the library—and I grant it you,—but Thomas's answer proves my point. Thomas himself disclaims any interest in poetry—his specialty is history. But my cook, who was with me many years (leaving me last spring to be married), assured me that Shelley (much of whom she knew by heart) was the greatest delight she had—and when Dowden's Life of Shelley came out, we talked it over together.

★

GEORGE CLARKE, PH.D. *The Novel-Reading Habit*
Arena 19 (May 1898): 670–679

[George Clarke is concerned that escapist fiction is available to readers with little training or experience. Focusing on the social effects of reading, Clarke criticizes novels for allowing readers to avoid the realities of life and find refuge in fantasies (particularly those of class and privilege). The *Arena* both reviewed and published fiction, characteristically championing fiction with a strong social vision, particularly utopian novels. Here, Clarke suggests that only realistic fiction has redeeming social value.]

THE PREPONDERANCE of fiction in the literature of the closing decades of this century is the most salient feature in the literary history of our times which will strike the future historian. Fiction has been invading other provinces of literature to an extent which we should be glad to ascribe to an extraordinary abundance of imaginative and creative genius, if there were not a more probable explanation which is not quite so flattering. In order to understand and enjoy a novel there is no need of any previous special training or unusual mental capacity, so that the novel appeals to a wider circle of readers than any other kind of literature. As writers of every kind naturally desire to reach as large a public as possible, the consequence is that archaeologists, historians, philosophers, sociologists, scientists, theologians, and moralists have learned the art of diluting and sugaring with a love-story the substantial nourishment they offer us. Whether our enormous appetite for fiction is merely a temporary pathological condition or is destined to be permanent, it is certainly deserving of interest and attention.

The extraordinary fascination which fiction exercises is doubtless due to its power of lifting us up out of the region of the commonplace, and transporting us among scenes of enchanting interest. In proportion as our own lives are dull and monotonous the charm of fiction is more powerful. Happiness, Aristotle says, is essentially an activity, but many of us are by nature lethargic and disposed to shrink from the personal activity that would make our lives happy and interesting to ourselves. But the power which we have of sympathizing with others in their ambitions, joys, and sorrows—that gift of the imagination by which we are enabled to contemplate the careers of others with a personal interest by identifying ourselves for the moment with them—supplies us with a means of obtaining a sort of happiness by proxy, while our own attitude is entirely passive. It is by furnishing this kind happiness that the novel has won its immense popularity.

It must be admitted, too, that as a producer of enjoyment, fiction has some advantages over active existence. The sensations excited by fiction, though inferior in intensity and permanence, are superior in rapidity of succession to those of real life. A novel crowds for our enjoyment into the space of a few hours the most interesting sensations experienced during as many years by its principal characters, passing over in silence all that is commonplace and trivial. In the skilfully constructed novel every point capable of enhancing the effect is brought into relief, hidden details of character and incident, which in actual life would escape the eye of the ordinary observer, are illuminated by sidelights of humor or pathos, each act is plainly interpreted and its significance in the general course of events is explained, while the characters and plot are constructed expressly with a view to novelty and impressiveness. If the novelist is not gifted with the insight to detect the tragedy or comedy lurking beneath what seems merely commonplace, and with the skill to reveal it, he contrives to secure the interest of his reader by means of the marvelous and extravagant. But an incident or scene, even in real life, may be so described by a master of literary art that an ordinary person will derive more pleasure from hearing or reading the description than he would have felt as a spectator of the actual incident or scene itself. This does not imply an exaggeration or distortion of facts by the narrator, but that his vision is quick to perceive and interpret significant details which the common observer would pass over as trivial. Most of us have known persons so gifted with powers of narrative that their company in an adventure of any sort was valuable for the reason that the other participants never knew how thrilling the adventure really had been until they heard these specially gifted persons describe it afterwards. The spectators of any remarkable occurrence—a railway accident, a street riot, a court trial, or a horse-race—scan the newspaper account next day to find out how it all happened, knowing that the skilled eye of the journalistic craftsman has seen more than their own duller vision detected. And when a gifted narrator can do so much with plain facts, what is to be expected when he is at liberty, as in fiction, to lavish on the recital all the resources of his invention and imagination?

The novelist, moreover, chooses for his themes those which have the most absorbing and universal interest. Of all the objects of human desire, the most passionately sought are probably wealth and love. If we are to judge of the intensity of the passion of love by the rapture which a truly loving betrothed couple seem to enjoy, or by the delirious happiness of the average honeymoon, we shall have to admit that the most ecstatic pleasure of which normal human nature in its prime is capable results from the sentiment, emotion, passion, or whatever one may choose to call it, of love—love triumphant.

This is the theme, then, which is preeminently chosen by the novelist in order to excite the highest degree of sympathetic pleasure in his readers, and he relates over and over again, with altered scenes and incidents, the old story of the awakening, development, difficulties, and final triumph of love in two human hearts. The reader loses for the time being his own identity in that of the lovers, sharing in the anxious longing which precedes mutual acknowledgment, and in the rapture which follows it, in a degree depending on his own mental constitution and on the skill of the narrator.

In a similar manner the novelist uses for his purpose the passion for wealth, enlisting the reader's sympathy for the successful struggles of the hero against adverse fortune, or feasting his imagination with a picture of the luxuries enjoyed by the rich.

Here and there may be found a novel which does not depend for its interest on either of these themes, but to achieve a wide success such a novel must be written by a master hand.

As imagination is the faculty chiefly exercised both in the creation and in the enjoyment of fiction, it might be supposed that fondness for this kind of reading is an indication of a strong imagination and a superior type of mind. But this is far from being true. An unusual love for and addiction to literature of this class are perhaps evidence of a receptive and quick intelligence, of an ability to represent rapidly to the mind the idea presented in the printed word, and perhaps also of some appreciation of literary art, for no book that is interesting can be quite devoid of literary art. But an undiscriminating love of fiction, which accepts with avidity anything in the form of a story for the sake of dispelling ennui, is the mark of an indolent, unpractical, resourceless mental character.

Neither does unrestrained novel-reading tend to cultivate a strong imagination, for the render's imagination is never for a moment left to its own resources, but simply surrenders itself and follows blindly where the author chooses to lead. A mental faculty can be cultivated only by effort and exercise, and the effort required of the imagination in order to picture to itself scenes and situations of which the complete material is furnished to it is so slight as to be of insignificant value. The average novel, moreover, does not deal in those brilliant gleams of imagery which the best poetry flashes on our minds, and which remain imprinted there for our future delight and as an enduring treasure. The panorama unfolded by the story-teller makes only a transient impression, which pleases while it lasts, but which demands so little effort on our part that it is soon effaced by other impressions of a similar character. The constructive and creative imagination of the reader is allowed to lie torpid. Fiction has therefore especial attractions for persons who are deficient in mental energy and creative powers. It is true that many really great minds have found pleasure in reading novels, but it has always been the pleasure of relaxation, and not to be compared with the intense enjoyment which they have derived from the activity of their mental powers. The novelist performs for us moderns in some respects the same service as the rich man's jester rendered his master in former days. The jester's business was to produce at need the quips and conceits which amused his master's hours of ease and banished his ennui, the master meanwhile feeling that he had paid money to be amused, and was not called on to furnish any of the entertainment himself. The peculiar charm of novel-reading is that the reader's mind is simply receptive and no exertion is necessary for full enjoyment. When the novelist appeared the jester's business was doomed.

The effects of novel-reading have been well compared with those of indulgence in opium or intoxicating liquors. While we are under the influence of a novel (especially one of the "sensational" variety) our cares and anxieties are for the time forgotten, and our reasoning faculties are allowed to rest, while our imagination is delighted with a succession of fancies and visions. But this sort of indulgence is attended with danger, for frequent repetition of it will produce a habit and craving. The escape from tedium and anxiety is so pleasant that a person who has once experienced it is easily tempted to repeat the indulgence, and every new enjoyment of the pleasure adds to the temptation. Persons of an indolent disposition or who have an abundance of leisure time, and who have not acquired by education a healthy interest in subjects of serious study or a taste for what is best in literature, are the easiest victims. They find in a novel a means of passing through thrilling adventures, of falling in love and getting married, of enjoying sprightly conversation, and of associating, it may be, with princes and duchesses, without once quitting their easy-chair or being obliged, as in real society, to make some exertion for the entertainment of others. If the novel is tedious in parts, they are not restrained by motives of courtesy from "skipping," a liberty one cannot always take when bored by the conversation in a drawing-room. In this way the novel comes to be regarded as an unfailing resource for idle hours, all the habit of resorting to it may be formed as readily as the craving for narcotics or stimulants.

The formation of this habit, to the destruction of all relish for substantial and nourishing literature, is the chief of the pernicious consequences entailed by much reading of fiction. It is noticeable also that in the case of the novel-habit, as of the liquor-habit, it is not the pure and wholesome article of the finest brands that is most apt to produce the craving, but the impure and inferior stuff with which the market is flooded, and which a discriminating taste will reject. The effects of the novel-habit are not so conspicuous as those of tippling, and are doubtless less disastrous to mind and body, but it might fairly be urged that habitual debauches of novel-reading work sufficient havoc on the mental faculties to justify a crusade against the evil. If the production and consumption of fiction proceeds at its present rate we may perhaps one day see an Anti-fiction Society started, with pledges of total abstinence from novel-reading, and perhaps a new Dr. Keeley calling attention to a "cure" for the habit, which he will prove to be not so much a reprehensible vice as a hereditary disease for which its victims must not be held accountable.

Certainly the few workers in other fields of literature would have reason to hail such a "cure" with joy. Fiction has so nearly driven other kinds of literary production from the field that to the average reader the word "book" means only a novel, and "author" is synonymous with "novelist." In a recent number of one of our comic papers some verses appeared entitled "The A B C of Literature," each stanza being a squib on some popular living writer. That "literature" in its usual acceptation means hardly anything but "fiction," was shown by the fact that, with one exception, all the twenty-five authors mentioned are writers of fiction, and nearly all of them are known to the general public only as novelists. In popular estimation historians, essayists, and poets are almost ignored unless they have made their immortality sure by writing a novel.

The similarity of the novel-habit to dipsomania may be observed in the way in which it manifests itself. When the confirmed novel-reader has an idle hour the craving for his customary dissipation seizes him. Not being conscious of the viciousness of his habit, he offers less resistance than the toper, and proceeds at once to indulge it. If he has not at hand the means of doing so, he has only to proceed to the nearest public library, where his narcotic is dispensed gratis. The dipsomaniac has to pay dear for his indulgence, for public feeling is against him and legislation places difficulties in his way but the novel-fiend has everywhere the sympathy of a vast majority of tic voters, many of whom are victims like himsclf. Having secured his book he has hardly patience enough to wait until he reaches home, but will sometimes open it at once and read it in the public cars or as he walks along the street. Standing not long ago at the entrance to a public library in one of our cities, the present writer observed a young lady leave the building with the novel she had just borrowed there. Evidently she had been suffering from a bad attack of this craving, for she held the book open in her hand, reading with avidity; walked, still reading, to where her bicycle rested against the curb of the sidewalk; closed the book for a moment while she mounted her wheel; reopened it when she was safely launched, and placidly continued her reading as she pedalled her way along a moderately busy thoroughfare. There have been complaints from the publishing houses that the bicycle was damaging their business, but this incident would seem to show that the two interests are at least not necessarily hostile.

The principal fault of novels of the average sort is the negative one of being worthless, and they are dangerous only because they possess attractive qualities which give rise to a habit, to the exclusion of really profitable occupations. Almost any innocent occupation of one's time would be preferable to reading a poor novel. Even when idle one cannot exclude thought, and quiet contemplation is a mental exercise not without its value. If novels were more scarce much of the time now wasted on them would be given to books of a more profitable kind, a taste for good literature would be cultivated, and the best products of the best minds would not be, as they are now, a treasure unknown to the multitude. Among the millions who constitute the reading public how many individuals are there who ever think of opening a volume of poetry?

If our main object in the training of our children were to render them dependent for their intellectual entertainment on works of fiction, we could hardly pursue any method better calculated to produce that result than the plan at present followed. From the time that a child has learned to read words of one syllable he is supplied with stories written in a style and language adapted to his capacity. There is no difficulty in finding such books for him; hosts of writers and publishers are engaged in supplying the demand. There is a "Youth's Page" in the Sunday newspapers and family periodicals, and this department consists chiefly of stories. There are periodicals containing numerous tales, and published expressly for children. Every Christmas sees a new flood of tales and fables poured out for the enjoyment of young readers. Love of reading is considered a highly promising sign in a child, and is strongly encouraged by parents and teachers, who are generally satisfied with prohibiting books of an immoral or blood-thirsty kind, without extending their censorship to what is merely worthless and silly. Even the Sunday-schools contribute their share to the enervation of the young mind. The successful Sunday-school teacher is the one who can enliven his teaching with thrilling anecdotes, and the successful scholar receives as his reward a handsome volume containing, probably, the adventures of some boy-paragon, his struggle against allurements of cigarettes and naughty language, and his final triumph and apotheosis as a prosperous business man and pillar of Sunday-schools. One might almost suppose that the greater part of juvenile literature was deliberately designed to reduce the minds of the boys and girls who read it to fit a condition for the subsequent reception and enjoyment of the trash brought out for adults in the form of novels. It is tolerated on the ground that "any reading is better than no reading." But if the fiction placed within the reach of the young were immensely curtailed in quantity and only the best retained, their leisure reading might have as high an educational value as their school studies. And it is an error to suppose that reading trashy books will eventually lead to reading healthy literature.

While emphasizing here the harmful effects of the fiction that is morally unobjectionable, it is not intended to underrate the corrupt influence of immoral novels. But the novel that paints vice in attractive colors, that caters to ignoble or dissolute passions, or that gives currency to vicious principles of conduct, if it displays sufficient ability to make it deserving of notice, is at once branded by the critics as immoral and dangerous, its character is soon generally known, and anyone who reads it does so at his peril. It is true that the critics sometimes confound mere unconventionality or indecency with licentiousness, and stigmatize as immoral a book that is no more so than a treatise on anatomy. The most licentious books are not those of the realistic school.

There is, however, a fault which is very common in a certain class of fiction, and which generally escapes the critic's strictures, but which does considerable harm of its own—the fault namely, of ascribing a supreme importance to wealth and social station. The novel whose characters move only "in the best society," which casts a fascinating halo over the advantages of wealth, and conveys to the reader the idea that outside the pale of the "smart" people no human being deserves notice and life is not worth living, has a tendency to excite discontent with one's condition and to foster the propensity to cupidity that is only too strong in all of us. The discontent thus produced is not that "divine discontent" which has been so prolific for the amelioration and advancement of the race, and which is based on a perception of the possibilities open to ingenuity and industry; it is a purely personal and selfish feeling. The young man or woman of limited means who indulges much in light novels of the fashionable world cannot avoid contrasting his or her laborious life and restricted hours and means of pleasure with the gay existence of those who live for pleasure only, and the effect on the mind is likely to be a depreciation of the means of happiness within reach, and an envious feeling toward those whom the accident of birth or fortune has favored. When wealth is regarded as the supreme good, the character of the means by which it is secured must assume a secondary importance, and this large class of novels may fairly be charged with some share of responsibility for the scrambling after riches, the pliant conscience in speculative transactions, and the pretentious style of living on narrow means of which there is daily evidence.

It may with some justice be urged in favor of the society novel that even if it attaches false values to things and shows an indifference to some of the most serious phases of life, it at any rate acts as a vehicle for disseminating the ideas and sentiments which prevail in the upper strata of society, and which, as far as manners, taste, and even questions of personal honor are concerned represent a higher grade of culture than those in vogue in the social ranks to which the great mass of readers belong. It might even be maintained with truth that the average novel improves on those ideas and sentiments, representing their tone as higher than it really is. A novel of this class is not usually hampered by a determination to stick to the exact truth. Its hero is quite incapable of the most trifling deviation from the straight path of gentlemanly honor; the author would rather depict him as misled by passion into the gravest moral lapses than as playing the part of an eavesdropper for a moment (except unavoidably and with unutterable distress to himself) or as clearing himself from unjust reproach at the expense of the real culprit, if the latter happened to be a woman. To assist in diffusing a more delicate sense of honor, more chivalrous ideas regarding women and greater refinement in manners and language is undoubtedly a merit; and if to this merit be added that of affording a few hours' unprofitable entertainment we have made up the entire sum of the contribution made by the society novel to human well-being. The mental and moral interests of mankind would have little loss to record if all the books of this class that have been or are to be written should be suddenly swept out of actual or potential existence.

It may seem to be an injustice to dwell upon the mischievous effects of the inferior grades of fiction, and to say nothing of the wholesome and elevating influence of the best novels. It is quite true that human thinking and conduct have benefited from them to an extent that it would not be easy to overstate. They have raised the tone of morals and manners, championed many a depressed but righteous cause, contributed to the redressing of wrongs, and waged a successful warfare against cant, bigotry, and various sins of society. In proportion as they have been true in their descriptions of life, they have extended our knowledge and deepened our sympathies, and by minute analysis of character and motives they have helped us to understand ourselves. But the masterpieces of fiction need no herald of their praises: they may safely be left to work out their mission without aid and in spite of criticism. The misfortune is that the prestige which their eminent merits have won for fiction acts as a recommendation for books which have nothing in common with them but external form and the name of novel, and frequently differ from them *toto coelo* in character, aims, and influence.

★

EDITH WHARTON *The Pelican*
Scribner's 24 (November 1898): 620–629

[When this story appeared, Edith Wharton was beginning a lengthy and lucrative career that spanned the 1890s to the 1930s. Her insights into the complicated relations among social standing, perceived economic necessity, and cultural authority are evident in "The Pelican," which comments satirically on the consumption and performance of knowledge as well as the packaging of "intellectual" experience.]

SHE WAS VERY pretty when I first knew her, with the sweet straight nose and short upper lip of the cameo-brooch divinity, humanized by a dimple that flowered in her cheek whenever anything was said which possessed the outward attributes of humor without its intrinsic quality. For the dear lady was providentially deficient in humor: the least hint of the real thing clouded her lovely eye like the hovering shadow of an algebraic problem.

I do not think that nature had meant her to be "intellectual"; but what can a poor thing do, whose husband has died of drink when her baby is hardly six months old, and who finds that her coral necklace and her grandfather's edition of the British Dramatists are inadequate to the demands of the creditors?

Her mother, the celebrated Irene Astarte Pratt, had written a poem in blank verse on "The Fall of Man"; one of her aunts was dean of a girl's college; another had translated Euripides—with such a family, the poor child's fate was sealed in advance. The only way of paying her husband's debts and keeping the baby clothed was to be intellectual; and, after some hesitation as to the form that her mental activity was to take, it was unanimously decided that she was to give lectures.

They began by being drawing-room lectures. The first time I saw her she was standing by the piano, against a flippant background of Dresden china and photographs, telling a roomful of women preoccupied with their spring bonnets all that she thought she knew about Greek art. The ladies assembled to hear her had given me to understand that she was "doing it for the baby," and this fact, together with the shortness of her upper lip and the bewildering co-operation of her dimple, disposed me to listen leniently to her dissertation. Happily, at that time Greek art was still, if I may use the phrase, easily handled; it was as simple as walking down a museum-gallery lined with pleasant familiar Venuses and Apollos. All the later complications—the archaic and archaistic conundrums; the influences of Assyria and Asia Minor; the conflicting attributions and the wrangles of the erudite—still slumbered in the bosom of the future "scientific critic." Greek art in those days began with Phidias and ended with the Apollo Belvedere; and a child could travel from one to the other without danger of losing its way.

Mrs. Amyot had two fatal gifts: a capacious but inaccurate memory, and an extraordinary fluency of speech. There was nothing that she did not remember—wrongly; but her halting facts were swathed in so many layers of cotton-wool eloquence that their infirmities were imperceptible to her friendly critics. Besides, she had been taught Greek by the aunt who had translated Euripides; and the mere sound of the *aís* and *oís* which she now and then not unskilfully let slip (correcting herself, of course, with a start, and indulgently mistranslating the phrase), struck awe to the hearts of ladies whose only "accomplishment" was French—if you didn't speak too quickly.

I had then but a momentary glimpse of Mrs. Amyot, but a few months later I came upon her again in the New England university town where the celebrated Irene Astarte Pratt lived on the summit of a local Parnassus, with lesser muses and college professors respectfully grouped on the lower ledges of the sacred declivity. Mrs. Amyot, who, after her husband's death, had returned to the maternal roof (even during her father's lifetime the roof had been distinctively maternal), Mrs. Amyot, thanks to her upper lip, her dimple and her Greek, was already ensconced in a snug hollow of the Parnassian slope.

After the lecture was over it happened that I walked home with Mrs. Amyot. Judging from the incensed glances of two or three learned gentlemen who were hovering on the doorstep when we emerged, I inferred that Mrs. Amyot, at that period, did not often walk home alone; but I doubt whether any of my discomfited rivals, whatever his claims to favor, was ever treated to so ravishing a mixture of shyness and self-abandonment, of sham erudition and real teeth and hair, as it was my privilege to enjoy. Even at the incipience of her public career Mrs. Amyot had a tender eye for strangers, as possible links with successive centers of culture to which in due course the torch of Greek art might be handed on.

She began by telling me that she had never been so frightened in her life. She knew, of course, how dreadfully learned I was, and when, just as she was going to begin, her hostess had whispered to her that I was in the room, she had felt ready to sink through the floor. Then (with a flying dimple) she had remembered Emerson's line—wasn't it Emerson's?—that beauty is its own excuse for *seeing*, and that had made her feel a little more confident, since she was sure that no one *saw* beauty more vividly than she—as a child she used to sit for hours gazing at an Etruscan vase on the bookcase in the library while her sisters played with their dolls—and if *seeing* beauty was the only excuse one needed for talking about it, why, she was sure I would make allowances and not be *too* critical and sarcastic, especially if, as she thought probable, I had heard of her having lost her poor husband, and how she had to do it for the baby.

Being over-abundantly assured of my sympathy on these points, she went on to say that she had always wanted so much to consult me about her lectures. Of course, one subject wasn't enough (this view of the limitations of Greek art as a "subject" gave me a startling idea of the rate at which a successful lecturer might exhaust the universe); she must find others; she had not ventured on any as yet, but she had thought of Tennyson—didn't I *love* Tennyson? She *worshipped* him so that she was sure she could help others to understand him; or what did I think of a "course" on Raphael or Michelangelo—or on the heroines of Shakespeare? There were some fine steel-engravings of Raphael's Madonnas and of the Sistine ceiling in her mother's library, and she had seen Miss Cushman in several Shakespearian roles, so that on these subjects also she felt qualified to speak with authority.

When we reached her mother's door she begged me to come in and talk the matter over; she wanted me to see the baby—she felt as though I should understand her better if I saw the baby—and the dimple flashed through a tear.

The fear of encountering the author of "The Fall of Man," combined with the opportune recollection of a dinner engagement, made me evade this appeal with the promise of returning on the morrow. On the morrow, I left too early to redeem my promise; and for several years afterward I saw no more of Mrs. Amyot.

My calling at that time took me at irregular intervals from one to another of our larger cities, and as Mrs. Amyot was also peripatetic it was inevitable that sooner or later we should cross each other's path. It was therefore without surprise that, one snowy afternoon in Boston, I learned from the lady with whom I chanced to be lunching that, as soon as the meal was over, I was to be taken to hear Mrs. Amyot lecture.

"On Greek art?" I suggested.

"Oh, you've heard her then? No, this is one of the series called 'Homes and Haunts of the Poets.' Last week we had Wordsworth and the Lake Poets, today we are to have Goethe and Weimar. She is a wonderful creature—all the women of her family are geniuses. You know, of course, that her mother was Irene Astarte Pratt, who wrote a poem on 'The Fall of Man'; N. P. Willis called her the female Milton of America. One of Mrs. Amyot's aunts has translated Eurip—"

"And is she as pretty as ever?" I irrelevantly interposed.

My hostess stared. "She is excessively modest and retiring. She says it is actual suffering for her to speak in public. You know she only does it for the baby."

Punctually at the hour appointed, we took our seats in a lecture-hall full of strenuous females in ulsters. Mrs. Amyot was evidently a favorite with these austere sisters, for every corner was crowded, and as we entered a pale usher with an educated mispronunciation was setting forth to several dejected applicants the impossibility of supplying them with seats.

Our own were happily so near the front that when the curtains at the back of the platform parted, and Mrs. Amyot appeared, I was at once able to establish a rapid comparison between the lady placidly dimpling to the applause of her public and the shrinking drawing-room orator of my earlier recollections.

Mrs. Amyot was as pretty as ever, and there was the same curious discrepancy between the freshness of her aspect and the staleness of her theme, but something was gone of the blushing unsteadiness with which she had fired her first random shots at Greek art. It was not that the shots were less uncertain, but that she now had an air of assuming that, for her purpose, the bull's-eye was everywhere, so that there was no need to be flustered in taking aim. This assurance had so facilitated the flow of her circumlocutious diction that, as I listened, I had a curious sense that she was performing a trick analogous to that of the conjuror who pulls hundreds of yards of white paper out of his mouth. From a large assortment of stock adjectives she chose, with unerring deftness and rapidity, the one which taste and discrimination would most surely have rejected, fitting out her subject, as it were, with a whole wardrobe of slop-shot epithets irrelevant in cut and size. To the invaluable knack of not disturbing the association of ideas in her audience, she added the gift of what may be called a confidential manner—so that her fluent generalizations about Goethe and his place in literature (the lecture was, of course, manufactured out of Lewes's book) had the flavor of personal experience, of views sympathetically exchanged with her audience on the best way of knitting children's socks, or of putting up preserves for the winter. It was, I am sure, to this personal accent—the moral equivalent of her dimple—that Mrs. Amyot owed her prodigious, her irrational success. It was her art of transposing second-hand ideas into first-hand emotions that so endeared her to her feminine listeners.

To anyone not in search of "documents" Mrs. Amyot's success was hardly of a kind to make her more interesting, and my curiosity flagged with the growing conviction that the "suffering" entailed upon her by public speaking was at most a retrospective pang. I was sure that, as a matter of fact, she had reached the point of measuring and enjoying her effects, of deliberately manipulating her public; and there must indeed have been a certain exhilaration in attaining results so considerable by means involving so little conscious effort. Mrs. Amyot's art was simply an extension of coquetry: she flirted with her audience.

In this mood of enlightened skepticism I responded but languidly to my hostess's suggestion that I should go with her that evening to see Mrs. Amyot. The aunt who had translated Euripides was at home on Saturday evenings, and one met "thoughtful" people there, my hostess explained: it was one of the intellectual centres of Boston. My mood remained distinctly resentful of any connection between Mrs. Amyot and intellectuality, and I declined to go; but the next day I met Mrs. Amyot in the street.

She stopped me reproachfully. She had heard that I was in Boston; why had I not come last night? She had been told that I was at her lecture; and it had frightened her—yes, really, almost as much as years ago in Hillbridge. She never *could* get over that stupid shyness, and the whole business was as distasteful to her as ever; but what could she do? There was the baby— he was a big boy now, and boys were *so* expensive! But did I really think she had improved the least little bit? And why wouldn't I come home with her now, and see the boy, and tell her frankly what I had thought of the lecture? She had plenty of flattery—people were *so* kind, and every one knew that she did it for the baby but what she felt the need of was criticism, severe, discriminating criticism like mine—oh, she knew that I was dreadfully discriminating!

I went home with her and saw the boy. In the early heat of her Tennyson-worship Mrs. Amyot had christened him Lancelot and he looked it. Perhaps, however, it was his black velvet dress and the exasperating length of his yellow curls, together with the fact of his having been taught to recite Browning to visitors, that raised to fever heat the itching of my palms in his Infant-Samuel-like presence. I have since had reason to think that he would have preferred to be called Billy, and to hunt cats with the other boys in the block: his curls and his poetry were simply another outlet for Mrs. Amyot's irrepressible coquetry.

But if Lancelot was not genuine, his mother's love for him was. It justified everything—the lectures *were* for the baby, after all. I had not been ten minutes in the room before I was pledged to help Mrs. Amyot to carry out her triumphant fraud. If she wanted to lecture on Plato she should—Plato must take his chance like the rest of us! There was no use, of course, in being "discriminating." I preserved sufficient reason to avoid that pitfall, but I suggested "subjects" and made lists of books for her with a fatuity that became more obvious as time attenuated the remembrance of her smile; I even remember thinking that some men might have cut the knot by marrying her, but I handed over Plato as a hostage, and escaped by the afternoon train.

The next time I saw her was in New York, when she had become so fashionable that it was a part of the whole duty of women to be seen at her lectures. The lady who suggested that of course I ought to go and hear Mrs. Amyot, was not very clear about anything except that she was perfectly lovely, and had had a horrid husband, and was doing it to support her boy. The subject of the discourse (I think it proved to be on Ruskin) was clearly of minor importance, not only to my friend, but to the throng of well-dressed and absent-minded ladies who rustled in late, dropped their muffs and pocket-books, and undisguisedly lost themselves in the study of each other's apparel. They received Mrs. Amyot with warmth, but she evidently represented a social obligation like going to church, rather than any more personal interest; in fact, I suspect that every one of the ladies would have remained away, had it been ascertainable that none of the others were coming.

Whether Mrs. Amyot was disheartened by the lack of sympathy between herself and her hearers, or whether the sport of arousing it had become a task, she certainly imparted her platitudes with less convincing warmth than of old. Her voice had the same confidential inflections, but it was like a voice reproduced by a gramophone: the real woman seemed far away. She had grown stouter without losing her dewy freshness, and her smart gown might have been taken to indicate either the potentialities of a settled income, or a politic concession to the taste of her hearers. As I listened I reproached myself for ever having suspected her of self deception in declaring that she took no pleasure in her work. I was sure now that she did it only for Lancelot, and judging from the size of her audience and the price of the tickets I concluded that Lancelot must be receiving a liberal education.

I was living in New York that winter, and in the rotation of dinners I found myself one evening at Mrs. Amyot's side. The dimple came out at my greeting as punctually as a cuckoo in a Swiss clock and I detected the same automatic quality in the tone in which she made her usual pretty demand for advice. She was like a musical-box charged with popular airs. They succeeded one another with breathless rapidity, but there was a moment after each when the cylinders scraped and whizzed.

Mrs. Amyot, as I found when I called upon her, was living in a pleasant flat, with a sunny sitting-room full of flowers and a tea-table that had the air of expecting visitors. She owned that she had been ridiculously successful. It was delightful, of course, on Lancelot's account. Lancelot had been sent to the best school in the country, and if things went well and people didn't tire of his silly mother he was to go to Harvard afterward. During the next two or three years Mrs. Amyot kept her flat in New York, and radiated art and literature upon the suburbs. I saw her now and then, always stouter, better dressed, more successful and more automatic: she had become a lecturing-machine.

I went abroad for a year or two and when I came back she had disappeared. I asked several people about her, but life had closed over her. She had been last heard of as lecturing—still lecturing—but no one seemed to know when or where.

It was in Boston that I found her at last, forlornly swaying to the oscillations of an overhead strap in a crowded trolley-car. Her face had so changed that I lost myself in a startled reckoning of the time that had elapsed since our parting. She spoke to me shyly, as though aware of my hurried calculation, and conscious that in five years she ought not to have altered so much as to upset my notion of time. Then she seemed to set it down to her dress, for she nervously gathered her cloak over a gown that asked only to be concealed, and shrank into a vacant seat behind the line of prehensile bipeds blocking the aisle of the car.

It was perhaps because she so obviously avoided me that I felt for the first time that I might be of use to her; and when she left the car I made no excuse for following her.

She said nothing of needing advice and did not ask me to walk home with her, concealing, as we talked, her transparent preoccupations under the mask of a sudden interest in all that I had been doing since she had last seen me. Of what concerned her, I learned only that Lancelot was well and that for the present she was not lecturing—she was tired and her doctor had ordered her to rest. On the doorstep of a shabby house she paused and held out her hand. She had been so glad to see me and perhaps if I were in Boston again— the tired dimple, as it were, bowed me out and closed the door upon the conclusion of the phrase.

Two or three weeks later, at my club in New York, I found a letter from her. In it she owned that she was troubled, that of late she had been unsuccessful, and that, if I chanced to be coming back to Boston, and could spare her a little of that invaluable advice which—. A few days later the advice was at her disposal.

She told me frankly what had happened. Her public had grown tired of her. She had seen it coming on for some time, and was shrewd enough in detecting the causes. She had more rivals than formerly—younger women, she admitted, with a smile which could still afford to be generous—and then her audiences had grown more critical and consequently more exacting. Lecturing—as she understood it—used to be simple enough. You chose your topic—Raphael, Shakespeare, Gothic Architecture, or some such big familiar "subject"—and read up about it for a week or so at the Athenaeum or the Astor Library and then told your audience what you had read. Now, it appeared, that simple process was no longer adequate. People had tired of familiar "subjects"; it was the fashion to be interested in things that one hadn't always known about—natural selection, animal magnetism, sociology and comparative folk-lore; while, in literature, the demand had become equally difficult to meet, since Matthew Arnold had introduced the habit of studying the "influence" of one author on another. She had tried lecturing on influences, and had done very well as long as the public was satisfied with the tracing of such obvious influences as that of Turner on Ruskin, of Schiller on Goethe, of Shakespeare on the English drama; but such investigations had soon lost all charm for her too-sophisticated audiences, who now demanded either that the influence or the influenced should be absolutely unknown, or that there should be no perceptible connection between the two. The zest of the performance lay in the measure of ingenuity with which the lecturer established a relation between two people who had probably never heard of each other, much less read each other's works. A pretty Miss Williams with red hair had, for instance, been lecturing with great success on the influence of the Rosicrucians upon the poetry of Keats, while somebody else had given a "course" on the influence of St. Thomas Aquinas upon Professor Huxley.

Mrs. Amyot, warmed by my evident participation in her distress, went on to say that the growing demand for evolution was what most troubled her. Her grandfather had been a pillar of the Presbyterian ministry, and the idea of her lecturing on Darwin or Herbert Spencer was deeply shocking to her mother and aunts. In one sense the family had staked its literary as well as its spiritual hopes on the literal inspiration of Genesis: what became of "The Fall of Man" in the light of modern exegesis?

The upshot of it was that she had ceased to lecture because she could no longer sell tickets enough to pay for the hire of a lecture-hall; and as for the managers, they wouldn't look at her. She had tried her luck all through the Eastern States and as far South as Washington; but it was of no use, and unless she could get hold of some new subjects—or, better still, of some new audiences—she must simply go out of the business. That would mean the failure of all she had worked for, since Lancelot would have to leave Harvard. She paused, and wept some of the unbecoming tears that spring from real grief. Lancelot, it appeared, was to be a genius. He had passed his opening examinations brilliantly; he had "literary gifts"; he had written beautiful poetry, much of which his mother had copied out in reverentially slanting characters upon the pages of a velvet-bound volume which she drew from a locked drawer.

Lancelot's verse struck me as nothing more alarming than growing-pains; but it was not to learn this that she had summoned me. What she wanted was to be assured that he was worth working for, an assurance which I managed to convey by the simple strategy of remarking that the poems reminded me of Swinburne—and so they did, as well as of Browning, Tennyson, Rossetti, William Morris, and all the other poets who supply young authors with original inspirations.

This point being satisfactorily established, it remained to be decided by what means his mother was, in the French phrase, to pay herself the luxury of a poet. It was obvious that this indulgence could be bought only with counterfeit coin, and that the one way of helping Mrs. Amyot was to become a party to the circulation of such currency. My fetish of intellectual integrity went down like a ninepin before the appeal of a woman no longer young and distinctly foolish, but full of those dear contradictions and irrelevances that will always make flesh and blood prevail against a syllogism. When I took leave of Mrs. Amyot I had promised her a dozen letters to Western universities and had half pledged myself to sketch out for her a lecture on the reconciliation of science and religion.

In the West she achieved a success which for a year or more embittered my perusal of the morning papers. The fascination which lures the murderer back to the scene of his crime drew my eye to every paragraph celebrating Mrs. Amyot's last brilliant lecture on the influence of something upon somebody; and her own letters—she overwhelmed me with them—spared me no detail of the entertainment given in her honor by the Palimpsest Club of Omaha or of her reception at the University of Leadville. The college professors were especially kind: she assured me that she had never before met with such discriminating sympathy. I winced under the adjective, which cast a sudden light upon the vast machinery of fraud that I had set in motion. All over my native land, men of hitherto unblemished integrity were conniving with me in urging their friends to go and hear Mrs. Amyot lecture on the reconciliation of science and religion! My only hope was that, somewhere among the number of my accomplices, Mrs. Amyot might find one who would marry her in the defense of his literary convictions.

None, apparently, resorted to such heroic measures; for about two years later I was startled by the announcement that Mrs. Amyot was lecturing in Trenton, N.J., on modern theosophy in the light of the Vedas. The following week she was at Newark, discussing Schopenhauer in the light of recent psychology. The week after that I was on the deck of an ocean steamer, reconsidering my share in Mrs. Amyot's triumphs with the impartiality with which one views an episode that is being left behind at the rate of twenty knots an hour. After all, I had been helping a mother to educate her son.

The next decade of my life was spent in Europe, and when I came home the recollection of Mrs. Amyot had become as inoffensive as one of those pathetic ghosts who are said to strive in vain to make themselves visible to the living. I did not even notice the fact that I no longer heard her spoken of; she had dropped like a dead leaf from the bough of memory.

A year or two after my return I was condemned to one of the worst punishments that a worker can undergo—an enforced holiday. The doctors who pronounced the inhuman sentence decreed that it should be worked out in the South, and for a whole winter I carried my cough, my thermometer and my idleness from one fashionable orange-grove to another. In the vast and melancholy sea of my disoccupation I clutched like a drowning man at any human driftwood within reach. I took a critical and depreciatory interest in the coughs, the thermometers and the idleness of my fellow-sufferers; but to the healthy, the occupied, the transient I clung with undiscriminating enthusiasm.

In no other way can I explain, as I look back upon it, the importance which I attached to the leisurely confidences of a new arrival with a brown beard who, tilted back at my side on a hotel veranda hung with roses, imparted to me one afternoon the simple annals of his past. There was nothing in the tale to kindle the most inflammable imagination, and though the man had a pleasant frank face and a voice differing agreeably from the shrill inflections of our fellow-lodgers, it is probable that under different conditions his discursive history of successful business ventures in a Western city would have affected me somewhat in the manner of a lullaby.

Even at the time I was not sure that I liked his agreeable voice. It had a sonorous assertiveness out of keeping with the humdrum character of his recital, as though a breeze engaged in shaking out a table-cloth should have fancied itself inflating a banner. But this criticism may have been a mere mark of my own fastidious humor, for the man seemed a simple fellow, satisfied with his middling fortunes, and already (he was not much past thirty) deep-sunk in conjugal content.

He had just entered upon an anecdote connected with the cutting of his eldest boy's teeth, when a lady whom I knew, returning from her late drive, paused before us for a moment in the twilight, with the smile which is the feminine equivalent of beads to savages.

"Won't you take a ticket?" she said, sweetly.

Of course I would take a ticket—but for what? I ventured to inquire.

"Oh, that's *so* good of you—for the lecture this evening. You needn't go, you know; we are none of us going; most of us have been through it already at Aiken and at Saint Augustine and at Palm Beach. I've given away my tickets to some new people who've just come from the North, and some of us are going to send our maids, just to fill up the room."

"And may I ask to whom you are going to pay this delicate attention?"

"Oh, I thought you knew—to poor Mrs. Amyot. She's been lecturing all over the South this winter; she's simply *haunted* me ever since I left New

York—and we had six weeks of her at Bar Harbor last summer! One has to take tickets, you know, because she's a widow and does it for her son—to pay for his education. She's so plucky and nice about it, and talks about him in such a touching unaffected way, that everybody is sorry for her, and we all simply ruin ourselves in tickets. I do hope that boy's nearly educated!"

"Mrs. Amyot? Mrs. Amyot?" I repeated. "Is she *still* educating her son?"

"Oh, do you know about her? Has she been at it long? There's some comfort in that, for I suppose when the boy's provided for the poor thing will be able to take a rest—and give us one!"

She laughed and extended her hand.

"Here's your ticket. Did you say *tickets*—two? Oh, thanks. Of course you needn't go."

"But I mean to go. Mrs. Amyot is an old friend of mine."

"Do you really? That's awfully good of you. Perhaps I'll go too if I can persuade Charlie and the others to come. And I wonder"—in a well-directed aside—"if your friend—?"

I telegraphed her under cover of the dusk that my friend was of too recent standing to be drawn into her charitable toils, and she masked her mistake under a rattle of friendly adjurations not to be late, and to be sure to keep a seat for her, as she had quite made up her mind to go even if Charlie and the others wouldn't.

The flutter of her skirts subsided in the distance, and my neighbor, who had half turned away to light a cigar, made no effort to reopen the conversation. At length, fearing that he might have overheard the allusion to himself, I ventured to ask if he were going to the lecture that evening.

"Much obliged—I have a ticket," he said, abruptly.

This struck me as in such bad taste that I made no answer; and it was he who spoke next.

"Did I understand you to say that you were an old friend of Mrs. Amyot's?"

"I think I may claim to be, if it is the same Mrs. Amyot whom I had the pleasure of knowing many years ago. My Mrs. Amyot used to lecture too—"

"To pay for her son's education?"

"I believe so."

"Well—see you later."

He got up and walked into the house.

In the hotel drawing-room that evening there was but a meagre sprinkling of guests, among whom I discovered my brown-bearded friend sitting alone on a sofa, with his head against the wall. It was certainly not curiosity to see Mrs. Amyot which had impelled him to attend the performance, for it would have been impossible for him, without shifting his position, to command the improvised platform at the end of the room. When I looked at him he seemed lost in contemplation of the chandelier.

The lady from whom I had purchased my tickets fluttered in late, unattended by Charlie and the others, and assuring me that she should *scream* if we had the lecture on Ibsen—she had heard it three times already that winter. A glance at the programme reassured her: it informed us (in the lecturer's own slanting hand) that Mrs. Amyot was to lecture on the Cosmogony.

After a long pause, during which the small audience coughed and moved its chairs and showed signs of regretting that it had come, the door opened, and Mrs. Amyot stepped upon the platform. Ah, poor lady!

Someone said "Hush!" the coughing and chair-shifting subsided, and she began.

It was like looking at one's self early in the morning in a cracked mirror. I had no idea that I had grown so old. As for Lancelot, he must have a beard. A beard? The word struck me, and without knowing why I glanced across the room at my bearded friend on the sofa. Oddly enough he was looking at me, with a half-defiant, half-sullen expression; and as our glances crossed, and his fell, the conviction came to me that *he was Lancelot*.

I don't remember a word of the lecture; and yet there were enough of them to have filled a good-sized dictionary. The stream of Mrs. Amyot's eloquence had become a flood: one had the despairing sense that she had sprung a leak, and that until the plumber came there was nothing to be done about it.

The plumber came at length, in the shape of a clock striking ten; my companion, with a sigh of relief, drifted away in search of Charlie and the others; the audience scattered with the precipitation of people who had discharged a duty; and, without surprise, I found my brown-bearded acquaintance at my elbow.

We stood alone in the big bare-floored room, under the flaring chandelier.

"I think you told me this afternoon that you were an old friend of Mrs. Amyot's?" he began awkwardly.

I assented.

"Will you come in and see her?"

"Now? I shall be very glad to, if—"

"She's ready; she's expecting you," he interposed.

He offered no further explanation, and I followed him in silence. He led me down the long corridor, and pushed open the door of a sitting-room.

"Mother," he said, closing the door after we had entered, "here's the gentleman who says he used to know you."

Mrs. Amyot, who sat in an easy-chair stirring a cup of bouillon, looked up with a start. She had evidently not seen me in the audience, and her son's description had failed to convey my identity. I saw a frightened look in her eyes; then, like a frost flower on a window-pane, the dimple expanded on her wrinkled cheek, and she held out her hand to me.

"I'm so glad," she said, "so glad!"

She turned to her son, who stood watching us. "You must have told Lancelot all about me—you've known me so long!"

"I haven't had time to talk to your son—since I knew he was your son," I explained.

Her brow cleared. "Then you haven't had time to say anything very dreadful?" she said, with a laugh.

"It is he who has been saying dreadful things," I returned, trying to fall in with her tone.

I saw my mistake. "What things?" she faltered.

"Making me feel how old I am by telling me about his children."

"My grandchildren!" she exclaimed, with a blush.

"Well, if you choose to put it so."

She laughed again, vaguely, and was silent. I hesitated a moment, and then put out my hand.

"I see that you are tired. I shouldn't have ventured to come in at this hour if your son—"

The son stepped between us. "Yes, I asked him to come," he said to his mother, in his clear self-assertive voice. "*I* haven't told him anything yet; but you've got to now. That's what I brought him for."

His mother straightened herself, but I saw her eye waver.

"Lancelot—" she began.

"Mr. Amyot," I said, turning to the young man, "if your mother will allow me to come back to-morrow, I shall be very glad—"

He struck his hand hard against the table on which he was leaning.

"No, sir! It won't take long, but it's got to be said now."

He moved nearer to his mother, and I saw his lip twitch under his beard. After all, he was younger and less sure of himself than I had fancied.

"See here, mother," he went on, "there's something here that's got to be cleared up, and as you say this gentleman is an old friend of yours it had better be cleared up in his presence. Maybe he can help explain it—and if he can't, it's got to be explained to *him*."

Mrs. Amyot's lips moved, but she made no sound. She glanced at me helplessly and reseated herself. My early inclination to thrash Lancelot was beginning to reassert itself. I took up my hat and moved toward the door.

"Mrs. Amyot is certainly under no obligation to explain anything whatever to me," I said, curtly.

"Well! She's under an obligation to me, then—to explain something in your presence." He turned to her again. "Do you know what the people in this hotel are saying? Do you know what he thinks—what they all think? That you're doing this lecturing to support me—to pay for my education! They say you go round telling them so. That's what they buy the tickets for— they do it out of charity. Ask him if it isn't what they say—ask him if they weren't joking about it on the piazza before dinner. The others think I'm a little boy, but he's known you for years, and he must have known how old I was. *He* must have known it wasn't to pay for my education!"

He stood before her with his hands clenched, the veins beating in his temples. She had grown very pale, and her cheeks looked hollow. When she spoke her voice had an odd click in it.

"If—if these ladies and gentlemen have been coming to my lectures out of charity, I see nothing to be ashamed of in that—" she faltered.

"If they've been coming out of charity to me," he retorted, "don't you see you've been making me a party to a fraud? Isn't there any shame in that?" His forehead reddened. "Mother! Can't you see the shame of letting people think that I was a d—— beat, who sponged on you for my keep? Let alone making us both the laughing-stock of every place you go to!"

"I never did that, Lancelot!"

"Did what?"

"Made you a laughing-stock—"

He stepped close to her and caught her wrist.

"Will you look me in the face and swear you never told people that you were doing this lecturing business to support me?"

There was a long silence. He dropped her wrist, and she lifted a limp handkerchief to her frightened eyes. "I did do it—to support you—to educate you" she sobbed.

"We're not talking about what you did when I was a boy. Everybody who knows me knows I've been a grateful son. Have I ever taken a penny from you since I left college ten years ago?"

"I never said you had! How can you accuse your mother of such wickedness, Lancelot?"

"Have you never told anybody in this hotel—or anywhere else in the last ten years—that you were lecturing to support me? Answer me that!"

"How can you," she wept, "before a stranger?"

"Haven't you said such things about me to strangers?" he retorted.

"Lancelot!"

"Well—answer me, then. Say you haven't, mother!" His voice broke unexpectedly and he took her hand with a gentler touch. "I'll believe anything you tell me," he said, almost humbly.

She mistook his tone and raised her head with a rash clutch at dignity.

"I think you had better ask this gentleman to excuse you first."

"No, by God, I won't!" he shouted.

"This gentleman says he knows all about you and I mean him to know all about me too. I don't mean that he or anybody else under this roof shall go on thinking for another twenty-four hours that a cent of their money has ever gone into my pockets since I was old enough to shift for myself. And he shan't leave this room till you've made that clear to him."

He stepped back as he spoke and put his shoulders against the door.

"My dear young gentleman," I said, politely, "I shall leave this room exactly when I see fit to do so—and that is now. I have already told you that Mrs. Amyot owes me no explanation of her conduct."

"But I owe you an explanation of mine—you and every one who has bought a single one of her lecture tickets. Do you suppose a man who's been through what I went through while that woman was talking to you in the porch before dinner is going to hold his tongue, and not attempt to justify himself? No decent man is going to sit down under that sort of thing. It's enough to ruin his character. If you're my mother's friend, you owe it to me to hear what I've got to say."

He pulled out his handkerchief and wiped his forehead.

"Good God, mother!" he burst out suddenly, "what did you do it for? Haven't you had every thing you wanted ever since I was able to pay for it? Haven't I paid you back every cent you spent on me when I was in college? Have I ever gone back on you since I was big enough to work?" He turned to me with a laugh. "I thought she did it to amuse herself—and because there was such a demand for her lectures. *Such a demand!* That's what she always told me. When we asked her to come out and spend this winter with us in Minneapolis, she wrote back that she couldn't because she had engagements all through the South, and her manager wouldn't let her off. That's the reason why I came all the way on here to see her. We thought she was the most popular lecturer in the United States, my wife and I did! We were awfully proud of it too, I can tell you." He dropped into a chair, still laughing.

"How can you, Lancelot, how can you!" His mother, forgetful of my presence, was clinging to him with tentative caresses. "When you didn't need the money any longer I spent it all on the children—you know I did."

"Yes, on lace christening dresses and life-size rocking-horses with real manes! The kind of thing that children can't do without."

"Oh, Lancelot, Lancelot—I loved them so! How can you believe such falsehoods about me?"

"What falsehoods about you?"

"That I ever told anybody such dreadful things?"

He put her back gently, keeping his eyes on hers. "Did you never tell anybody in this house that you were lecturing to support your son?"

Her hands dropped from his shoulders, and she flashed round upon me in sudden anger.

"I know what I think of people who call themselves friends and who come between a mother and her son!"

"Oh, mother, mother!" he groaned.

I went up to him and laid my hand on his shoulder.

"My dear man," I said, "don't you see the uselessness of prolonging this?"

"Yes, I do," he answered, abruptly, and before I could forestall his move-ment he rose and walked out of the room.

There was a long silence, measured by the decreasing reverberations of his footsteps down the wooden floor of the corridor.

When they ceased I approached Mrs. Amyot, who had sunk into her chair. I held out my hand and she took it without a trace of resentment on her rav-aged face.

"I sent his wife a seal-skin jacket at Christmas!" she said, with the tears running down her cheeks.

★

DR. THORSTEIN VEBLEN *The Economic Theory of Women's Dress*

Popular Science Monthly 46 (December 1894): 198–205

[The creation of *Popular Science Monthly* in 1872 came in response to a growing interest in science among Americans, and the magazine soon be-came known for its scientific approaches to sociology, psychology, econom-ics, and politics as well as to natural science. Here, Thorstein Veblen, an economist, takes a cultural anthropologist's approach to the American con-sumer, pointing to the transvaluation of the work ethos, the "barbarian" be-havior of valuing leisure over work. He vilifies "conspicuous consumption" (by which individuals define their social status through material and un-necessary goods) over useful production. Veblen continues this argument in his most influential work, *The Theory of the Leisure Class* (1899).]

IN HUMAN APPAREL the element of dress is readily distinguishable from that of clothing. The two functions—of dress and of clothing the person— are to a great extent subserved by the same material goods, although the extent to which the same material serves both purposes will appear very much slighter on second thought than it does at first glance. A differentia-tion of materials has long been going on, by virtue of which many things that are worn for the one purpose no longer serve, and are no longer expected to serve, the other. The differentiation is by no means complete. Much of human apparel is worn both for physical comfort and for dress; still more of it is worn ostensibly for both purposes. But the differentiation is already very considerable and is visibly progressing.

But, however united in the same object, however the two pure purposes may be served by the same material goods, the purpose of physical comfort and that of a reputable appearance are not to be confounded by the mean-est understanding. The elements of clothing and of dress are distinct; not

FIGURE 3 This Charles Dana Gibson cartoon caricatures upwardly striving, professional people on a New York street, with the "Gibson girl" in the midst of posturing adults. Part of the Gibson girl's appeal was her aloofness from adult, consumer concerns, even as she was herself a symbol of vigor, beauty, and unquestionable affluence. (*Scribner's*, 1898)

only that, but they even verge on incompatibility; the purpose of either is frequently best subserved by special means which are adapted to perform only a single line of duty. It is often true, here as elsewhere, that the most efficient tool is the most highly specialized tool.

Of these two elements of apparel dress came first in order of development, and it continues to hold the primacy to this day. The element of clothing, the quality of affording comfort, was from the beginning, and to a great extent it continues to be, in some sort an afterthought.

The origin of dress is sought in the principle of adornment. This is a well-accepted fact of social evolution. But that principle furnished the point of departure for the evolution of dress rather than the norm of its development. It is true of dress, as of so much else of the apparatus of life, that its initial purpose has not remained its sole or dominant purpose throughout the course of its later growth. It may be stated broadly that adornment, in the naive aesthetic sense, is a factor of relatively slight importance in modern dress.

The line of progress during the initial stage of the evolution of apparel was from the simple concept of adornment of the person by supplementary accessions from without, to the complex concept of an adornment that should render the person pleasing, or of enviable presence, and at the same time serve to indicate the possession of other virtues than that of a well-favored person only. In this latter direction lies what was to evolve into dress. By the time dress emerged from the primitive efforts of the savage to beautify himself with gaudy additions to his person, it was already an economic factor of some importance. The change from a purely aesthetic character (ornament) to a mixture of the aesthetic and economic took place before the progress had been achieved from pigments and trinkets to what is commonly understood by apparel. Ornament is not properly an economic category, although the trinkets which serve the purpose of ornament may also do duty as an economic factor, and in so far be assimilated to dress. What constitutes dress an economic fact, properly falling within the scope of economic theory, is its function as an index of the wealth of its wearer—or, to be more precise, of its owner, for the wearer and owner are not necessarily the same person. It will hold with respect to more than one half the values currently recognized as "dress," especially that portion with which this paper is immediately concerned—woman's dress—that the wearer and the owner are different persons. But while they need not be united in the same person, they must be organic members of the same economic unit; and the dress is the index of the wealth of the economic unit which the wearer represents.

Under the patriarchal organization of society, where the social unit was the man (with his dependents), the dress of the women was an exponent of the wealth of the man whose chattels they were. In modern society, where the unit is the household, the woman's dress sets forth the wealth of the household to which she belongs. Still, even to-day, in spite of the nominal and somewhat celebrated demise of the patriarchal idea, there is that about the dress of women which suggests that the wearer is something in the nature of a chattel; indeed, the theory of woman's dress quite plainly involves the implication that the woman is a chattel. In this respect the dress of women differs from that of men. With this exception, which is not of first-rate importance, the essential principles of woman's dress are not different from those which govern the dress of men; but even apart from this added characteristic the element of dress is to be seen in a more unhampered development in the apparel of women. A discussion of the theory of dress in general will gain in brevity and conciseness by keeping in view the concrete facts of the highest manifestation of the principles with which it has to deal, and this highest manifestation of dress is unquestionably seen in the apparel of the women of the most advanced modern communities.

The basis of the award of social rank and popular respect is the success, or more precisely the efficiency, of the social unit, as evidenced by its visible success. When efficiency eventuates in possessions, in pecuniary strength, as it eminently does in the social system of our time, the basis of the award of social consideration becomes the visible pecuniary strength of the social unit. The immediate and obvious index of pecuniary strength is the visible ability to spend, to consume unproductively; and men early learned to put in evidence their ability to spend by displaying costly goods that afford no return to their owner, either in comfort or in gain. Almost as early did a differentiation set in, whereby it became the function of woman, in a peculiar degree, to exhibit the pecuniary strength of her social unit by means of a conspicuously unproductive consumption of valuable goods.

Reputability is in the last analysis, and especially in the long run, pretty fairly coincident with the pecuniary strength of the social unit in question. Woman, primarily, originally because she was herself a pecuniary possession, has become in a peculiar way the exponent of the pecuniary strength of her social group; and with the progress of specialization of functions in the social organism this duty tends to devolve more and more entirely upon the woman. The best, most advanced, most highly developed societies of our time have reached the point in their evolution where it has (ideally) become the great, peculiar, and almost the sole function of woman in the social system to put in evidence her economic unit's ability to pay. That is to say, woman's place (according to the ideal scheme of our social system) has come to be that of a means of conspicuously unproductive expenditure.

The admissible evidence of the woman's expensiveness has considerable range in respect of form and method, but in substance it is always the same. It may take the form of manners, breeding, and accomplishments that are, *prima facie*, impossible to acquire or maintain without such leisure as bespeaks a considerable and relatively long-continued possession of wealth. It may also express itself in a peculiar manner of life, on the same grounds and with much the same purpose. But the method in vogue always and everywhere, alone or in conjunction with other methods, is that of dress. "Dress," therefore, from the economic point of view, comes pretty near being synonymous with "display of wasteful expenditure."

The extra portion of butter, or other unguent, with which the wives of the magnates of the African interior anoint their persons, beyond what comfort requires, is a form of this kind of expenditure lying on the border between primitive personal embellishment and incipient dress. So also the brass-wire bracelets, anklets, etc., at times aggregating some thirty pounds in weight, worn by the same class of persons, as well as, to a less extent, by the male population of the same countries. So also the pelt of the arctic fur seal, which the women of civilized countries prefer to fabrics that are preferable to it in all respects but that of expense. So also the ostrich plumes and the many curious effigies of plants and animals that are dealt in by the milliners. The list is inexhaustible, for there is scarcely an article of apparel of male or female, civilized or uncivilized, that does not partake largely of this element, and very many may be said, in point of economic principle, to consist of virtually nothing else.

It is not that the wearers or the buyers of these wasteful goods desire the waste. They desire to make manifest their ability to pay. What is sought is not the *de facto* waste, but the appearance of waste. Hence there is a constant effort on the part of the consumers of these goods to obtain them at as good a bargain as may be; and hence a constant effort on the part of the producers of these goods to lower the cost of their production, and consequently to lower the price. But as fast as the price of the goods declines to such a figure that their consumption is no longer *prima facie* evidence of a considerable ability to pay, the particular goods in question fall out of favor, and consumption is diverted to something which more accurately manifests the wearer's ability to afford wasteful consumption.

This fact, that the object sought is not the waste but the display of waste, develops into a principle of pseudo-economy in the use of material; so that it has come to be recognized as a canon of good form that apparel should not show lavish expenditure simply. The material used must be chosen so as to give evidence of the wearer's (owner's) capacity for making it go as far in the way of display as may be; otherwise it would suggest incapacity on the part of the owner, and so partially defeat the main purpose of the display. But what is more to the point is that such a mere display of crude waste would also suggest that the means of this display had been acquired so recently as not to have permitted that long-continued test of time and effort required for mastering the most effective methods of display. It would argue recent acquisition of means; and we are still near enough to the tradition of pedigree and aristocracy of birth to make long-continued possession of means second in point of desirability only to the possession of large means. The greatness of the means possessed is manifested by the volume of display; the length of possession is, in some degree, evidenced by the manifestation of a thorough habituation to the methods of display. Evidence of a knowledge and habit of good form in dress (as in manners) is chiefly to be valued because it argues that much time has been spent in the acquisition of this accomplishment; and as the accomplishment is in no wise of direct economic value, it argues pecuniary ability to waste time and labor. Such accomplishment, therefore, when possessed in a high degree, is evidence of a life (or of more than one life) spent to no useful purpose; which, for purposes of respectability, goes as far as a very considerable unproductive consumption of goods. The offensiveness of crude taste and vulgar display in matters of dress is, in the last analysis, due to the fact that they argue the absence of ability to afford a reputable amount of waste of time and effort.

Effective use of the means at hand may, further, be taken to argue efficiency in the person making the display; and the display of efficiency, so long as it does not manifestly result in pecuniary gain or increased personal comfort, is a great social desideratum. Hence it happens that, surprising as it may seem at first glance, a principle of pseudo-economy in the use of materials has come to hold a well-secured though pretty narrowly circumscribed place in the theory of dress, as that theory expresses itself in the facts of life. This principle, acting in concert with certain other requirements of dress, produces some curious and otherwise inexplicable results, which will be spoken of in their place.

The first principle of dress, therefore, is conspicuous expensiveness. As a corollary under this principle, but of such magnificent scope and consequence as to claim rank as a second fundamental principle, there is the evidence of expenditure afforded by a constant supersession of one wasteful garment or trinket by a new one. This principle inculcates the desirability, amounting to a necessity wherever circumstances allow, of wearing nothing that is out of date. In the most advanced communities of our time, and so far as concerns the highest manifestations of dress—e.g., in ball dress and the apparel worn on similar ceremonial occasions, when the canons of dress rule unhampered by extraneous considerations—this principle expresses itself in the maxim that no outer garment may be worn more than once.

This requirement of novelty is the underlying principle of the whole of the difficult and interesting domain of fashion. Fashion does not demand continual flux and change simply because that way of doing is foolish; flux and change and novelty are demanded by the central principle of all dress-conspicuous waste.

This principle of novelty, acting in concert with the motive of pseudo-economy already spoken of, is answerable for that system of shams that figures so largely, openly and aboveboard, in the accepted code of dress. The motive of economy, or effective use of material, furnishes the point of departure, and this being given, the requirement of novelty acts to develop a complex and extensive system of pretenses, ever varying and transient in point of detail, but each imperative during its allotted time—facings, edgings, and the many (pseudo) deceptive contrivances that will occur to any one that is at all familiar with the technique of dress. This pretense of deception is often developed into a pathetic, child-like make-believe. The realities which it simulates, or rather symbolizes, could not be tolerated. They would be in some cases too crudely expensive, in others inexpensive and more nearly adapted to minister to personal comfort than to visible expense; and either alternative is obnoxious to the canons of good form.

But apart from the exhibition of pecuniary strength afforded by an aggressive wasteful expenditure, the same purpose may also be served by conspicuous abstention from useful effort. The woman is, by virtue of the specialization of social functions, the exponent of the economic unit's pecuniary strength, and it consequently also devolves on her to exhibit the unit's capacity to endure this passive form of pecuniary damage. She can do this by putting in evidence the fact (often a fiction) that she leads a useless life. Dress is her chief means of doing so. The ideal of dress, on this head, is to demonstrate to all observers, and to compel observation of the fact, that the wearer is manifestly incapable of doing anything that is of any use. The modern civilized woman's dress attempts this demonstration of habitual idleness, and succeeds measurably.

Herein lies the secret of the persistence, in modern dress, of the skirt and of all the cumbrous and otherwise meaningless drapery which the skirt typifies. The skirt persists because it is cumbrous. It hampers the movements of the wearer and disables her, in great measure, for any useful occupation. So it serves as an advertisement (often disingenuous) that the wearer is backed by sufficient means to be able to afford the idleness, or impaired efficiency, which the skirt implies. The like is true of the high heel, and in less degree of several other features of modern dress.

Herein is also to be sought the ground of the persistence (probably not the origin) of the one great mutilation practiced by civilized Occidental womankind—the constricted waist, as well as of the analogous practice of the abortive foot among their Chinese sisters. This modern mutilation of woman is perhaps not to be classed strictly under the category of dress; but it is scarcely possible to draw the line so as to exclude it from the theory, and it is so closely coincident with that category in point of principle that an outline of the theory would be incomplete without reference to it.

A corollary of some significance follows from this general principle. The fact that voluntarily accepted physical incapacity argues the possession of wealth practically establishes the futility of any attempted reform of woman's dress in the direction of convenience, comfort, or health. It is of the essence of dress that it should (appear to) hamper, incommode, and injure the wearer, for in so doing it proclaims the wearer's pecuniary ability to endure idleness and physical incapacity.

It may be noted, by the way, that this requirement, that women must appear to be idle in order to be respectable, is an unfortunate circumstance for women who are compelled to provide their own livelihood. They have to supply not only the means of living, but also the means of advertising the fiction that they live without any gainful occupation; and they have to do all this while encumbered with garments specially designed to hamper their movements and decrease their industrial efficiency.

The cardinal principles of the theory of woman's dress, then, are these three:

1. Expensiveness: Considered with respect to its effectiveness as clothing, apparel must be uneconomical. It must afford evidence of the ability of the

wearer's economic group to pay for things that are in themselves of no use to any one concerned—to pay without getting an equivalent in comfort or in gain. From this principle there is no exception.

2. Novelty: Woman's apparel must afford *prima facie* evidence of having been worn but for a relatively short time, as well as, with respect to many articles, evidence of inability to withstand any appreciable amount of wear. Exceptions from this rule are such things as are of sufficient permanence to become heirlooms, and of such surpassing expensiveness as normally to be possessed only by persons of superior (pecuniary) rank. The possession of an heirloom is to be commended because it argues the practice of waste through more than one generation.

3. Ineptitude: It must afford *prima facie* evidence of incapacitating the wearer for any gainful occupation; and it should also make it apparent that she is permanently unfit for any useful effort, even after the restraint of the apparel is removed. From this rule there is no exception.

Besides these three, the principle of adornment, in the aesthetic sense, plays some part in dress. It has a certain degree of economic importance, and applies with a good deal of generality; but it is by no means imperatively present, and when it is present its application is closely circumscribed by the three principles already laid down. Indeed, the office of the principle of adornment in dress is that of handmaid to the principle of novelty, rather than that of an independent or co-ordinate factor. There are, further, minor principles that may or may not be present, some of which are derivatives of the great central requisite of conspicuous waste; others are of alien origin, but all are none the less subject to the controlling presence of the three cardinal principles enumerated above. These three are essential and constitute the substantial norm of woman's dress, and no exigency can permanently set them aside so long as the chance of rivalry between persons in respect of wealth remains. Given the possibility of a difference in wealth, and the sway of this norm of dress is inevitable. Some spasm of sense, or sentiment, or what not, may from time to time create a temporary and local diversion in woman's apparel; but the great norm of "conspicuous waste" can not be set aside or appreciably qualified as long as this its economic ground remains.

To single out an example of the temporary effect of a given drift of sentiment, there has, within the past few years, come, and very nearly gone, a recrudescence of the element of physical comfort of the wearer, as one of the usual requirements of good form in dress. The meaning of this proposition, of course, is not what appears on its face; that seldom happens in matters of dress. It was the show of personal comfort that was lately imperative, and the show was often attained only at the sacrifice of the substance. This development, by the way, seems to have been due to a ramification of the sentimental athleticism (flesh-worship) that has been dominant of late; and now that the crest of this wave of sentiment has passed, this alien motive in dress is also receding.

The theory of which an outline has now been given is claimed to apply in full force only to modern woman's dress. It is obvious that if the principles arrived at are to be applied as all-deciding criteria, "woman's dress" will include the apparel of a large class of persons who, in the crude biological sense, are men. This feature does not act to invalidate the theory. A classification for the purpose of economic theory must be made on economic grounds alone, and can not permit considerations whose validity does not extend beyond the narrower domain of the natural sciences to mar its symmetry so far as to exclude this genial volunteer contingent from the ranks of womankind.

There is also a second, very analogous class of persons, whose apparel likewise, though to a less degree, conforms to the canons of woman's dress. This class is made up of the children of civilized society. The children, with some slight reservation of course, are, for the purpose of the theory, to be regarded as ancillary material serving to round out the great function of civilized womankind as the conspicuous consumers of goods. The child in the hands of civilized woman is an accessory organ of conspicuous consumption, much as any tool in the hands of a laborer is an accessory organ of productive efficiency.

R EFERENCES TO "TYPES" fre-
quently appear in periodicals of the 1890s, emphasizing continued and often
conflicting efforts to define identities and confirm prejudices about where
and how individuals fit into society. Types also figure prominently in advertisements and illustrations, especially as they appeared in periodicals,
which increasingly based their profits on advertising instead of subscriptions. Allowing for broad generalizations about large groups of people, the
language of types grants authors a means to categorize the mood of a nation
(as does William Dean Howells) or the characteristics of rural Americans
(Octave Thanet) or the problems of a growing and changing nation (Robert
Grant). Many of the authors here—among them Pauline Hopkins, Booker T.
Washington, Susan B. Anthony, and Theodore Roosevelt—work against conventional stereotypes, articulating complex relationships between individuals and group affiliations and resist reinscribing extant racial, gendered, and
ethnic expectations.

One topic of interest to the authors here is the "American type" and the circumstances that produce it. As the spokesperson for a generation of Americans, William Dean Howells, the era's most successful editor, essayist, and
novelist, composes a defense of modern America, defining the character of
a nation that was reconstituting its identity after the divisive Civil War.
Tracing the mood of "modern" America back to Reconstruction, Howells
upholds the primacy of American democracy and describes a fin-de-siècle
American modesty in regard to the arts, arguing that the vainglory of the
past is gone as American arts take their place in an international arena.
Howells locates one substantial challenge to American artistic development
in the love of wealth, but he also predicts that "the time is past" when men
abandoned their artistic ambitions for "the greater allurements of money-

making." In contrast to Howells's measured optimism, Octave Thanet produces admiring portraits of "the provincials," or rural Americans. A realist and local color writer, Thanet projected throughout her work a social Darwinist belief that social difficulties cure themselves as society rewards the fittest and the most virtuous. In "The Provincials," Thanet explores the "picturesque and the gentle side" of the national character, based on the rural American "at his best." Brought up in small cities, towns, and villages, her provincials live plainly and practically, applying solid and reliable values to all that they encounter, and her eccentric subjects imbibe their culture from the magazines, reading broadly and carrying the benefits of those publications with them.

While Thanet's exploration of what she terms an authentic "American type" hints at the presumed deficiencies and threats of foreigners, Robert Grant openly attacks immigrants, indicting them for the corruption and spoiling of American values. Grant supports his conservative views by evoking Ralph Waldo Emerson's *The Conduct of Life* (1860), a series of essays on behavior and values in American society by one of the country's most respected men of letters. In "The Conduct of Life," the last essay in a series entitled "The Art of Living" composed for *Scribner's* in 1895, Grant contrasts his American ideal of Abraham Lincoln, held up as natural, self-reliant, and energetic, with immigrants who are "ruffians," "malcontents," and "thugs." Warning against foreign merchants (i.e., Jews) taking over "American" businesses, and blaming European influences and shallow social pretensions, he charges the professional classes with the responsibility for leading America.

The fiction in this section, while invoking expectations of types, complicates an easy recognition of group affiliations. Pauline E. Hopkins, a novelist and the editor of *Colored American Magazine*, questions her readers' most basic assumptions about race and ability, behavior, and personal value. She often stated that her fiction was meant to encourage and incite social change among black Americans and, as a consequence, her black characters are often role models of virtue and self-control. "Talma Gordon," the story of a lovely African American woman, aggressively attacks legible types; raised as white, Talma's supposed faults are recognizable to her father as characteristics of her faint African American ancestry. In its portrayal of Talma and her champion, Dr. Thorton, the story continually works against an easy categorization of its characters and their motives as it portrays a deliberate reinterpretation of identity and a consequent effort to reconsider the bases of group affiliations.

Theodore Roosevelt, Booker T. Washington, and Susan B. Anthony also challenge expectations based on types and prevailing conceptions of specific groups. For Roosevelt, the young American male who graduated from college needed to be apprised of his duties to the state, to the populace, and to national defense. At a time when only 157,000 Americans were college graduates (as opposed to 16 million today), Roosevelt addressed an elite audience. Overriding the importance of intellectual work alone, he redefined young graduates primarily as American citizens and potential military patriots. Booker T. Washington's "The Awakening of the Negro" also rejects a stereotype; countering the characterization of the African American man as shiftless and dangerous, Washington points instead to a "new" Negro produced in industrial training schools, a man who works for his own profit and who will serve as a beacon to "our people in the Black Belt of the South." This man, furthermore, will redress a long-standing racial imbalance by commanding the respect of the white man. Though his article focuses on the new possibilities for black identity, Washington hints at the urgency of reforming the millions of desperate and poverty-stricken Southern blacks, suggesting the black man's violent response should these needs not be met. Just as Washington points to the past in order to measure the progress gained in the present, so Susan B. Anthony, suffragist leader, contrasts past inequities for women with new possibilities, such as full educational opportunities, economic rights, and individual freedoms.

★

WILLIAM DEAN HOWELLS *The Modern American Mood*
Harper's 95 (July 1897): 199–204

[William Dean Howells, nicknamed "the dean of American letters," during his long career was associated with *Harper's*, *Atlantic Monthly*, and *Cosmopolitan*. In his fiction, but most especially in his criticism, Howells promoted Realism, the dominant literary style of the late nineteenth century. Here, Howells types turn-of-the-century Americans as participating in the healing impulse thirty years after a devastating war.]

THE OBSERVANT AMERICAN whose memory runs back to the effulgent days following the close of the civil war must be aware of a signal change since then in the mood of his fellow-citizens concerning themselves and the republic. I do not think this is the effect merely of increasing years and of widened experience, but I think it is the result also of a self-scrutiny much more unsparing than we once used; and it appears to me that it is not a morbid or despondent mood, but simply serious, and altogether wholesome.

I. The grounds of confidence and of diffidence with us are the same that they have always been; our problem has grown larger, but it has not grown much more complex; and it is chiefly in its dimensions that it is so formidable to the imagination. We did mightier things in the green wood relatively than are now laid upon us to do in the dry; and I have no doubt that if we are tolerably faithful and honest we shall come out all right in the end, as every good American used to say we should.

I do not mean that it is easy to be faithful and honest, or at least so easy as to be heroic and magnanimous: a man or a nation can meet a brief demand upon the moral forces of far greater stress than the steady pull of ordinary duties and responsibilities. But I do mean that if we are coming generally to see that there is no hope for us but in fidelity and honesty, we are in a fair way to possess and to live those virtues. In former years, before the present thoughtful mood overcame us as a people, we had no doubt of the embodiment of those virtues in the national life; and if any one else doubted the fact, we laughed. We had some good reasons for our vainglory, or at least as good as any nation ever had. We had risen in arms above the greatest rebellion known to history, and had destroyed slavery in a conflict that perpetuated and democratized the Union. Better still, we had been morally equal to our victory, and had forgiven the vanquished; in us for the first time in the annals of the race Christianity had governed the action of a Christian people. There is no doubt but that in this magnificent moment we were the admiration and despair of the powers which had hated us and hoped for our ruin. No one who knew Europe during our civil war, or immediately after it, could doubt the existence of the feeling there that invited us to pose, and to pose, as we may say, arrogantly.

We certainly availed ourselves of the invitation. We took ourselves most seriously as the one accomplished fact in a world of experiments and failures. This was the tone in public and in private at home, and when we went abroad we at least did not change it; in fact, it might be fairly said that in those days we patronized Europe. We were altogether too great to be rancorous; but we went exulting and deriding and pitying through the Old World, which after all its ages had still not solved the riddle of the painful earth, while we had done it, and done it in much less than a century. Wherever two Americans met in France, or in Italy, or in Germany, or in England, and above all in England, this was the temper of their congratulations and this was the temper of our travel and criticism as it expressed itself in journalism and in literature.

All that was ours was good; if not apparently good, then really good. The absorption of the army into the people; the pardon and reconstruction of the South; the enormous expansion of values in the North, and the rise of the colossal fortunes which we innocently took for a token instead of a result of the general well-being; the rise even of the colossal corruptions, which were proofs that we could stand anything and still come out right in the end; all conduced to our self-satisfaction. What if our merchant marine was wiped from the seas? The volume of our commerce was never so vast; and our war-worn wooden ships carried among the steel-clad monsters of all the seas a flag that no power durst affront. At home, if we paid three prices for everything, very well: we had the money to pay the three prices. In those rapturous years our journalism began to constitute itself upon a scale larger than any in the world, and we saw the beginning of a truly national literature. The arts struck root so vigorously among us that we almost began to believe the arts were American.

II. It is easy to say how our vainglory began, but it is not so easy to say how it began to vanish, or why. But whatever Europe may think to the contrary, we are now really a modest people. The national attitude is self-critical, and if the standards by which we try ourselves are not those of Europe, but are largely derived from within ourselves, they are none the less severe and none the less just. They incline us, in the presence of other civilizations, to shame for our own defects rather than triumph in alien shortcomings. The American who now goes exulting and deriding and pitying through Europe, if there is such an American at all, is infinitely outnumbered by his compatriots who are quite silent in making comparisons which may be in our favor but which cannot flatter us when we consider our advantages. In moments of very intoxicated jingoism we may still threaten the coercion and even destruction of equal powers but this is not at any time the disposition of the American masses, and it is not commonly the temper of their servants in the political offices or their spokesmen in the newspaper offices. In letters we are but too meekly attentive to what they say of us over there, and in the arts our study of European methods and monuments has been so diligent that it would be hard to find anything distinctively American in many of our paintings, statues, and edifices. We even take seriously the comments of French travellers upon our life, and our richer people conform as strictly as they can to the social usages of the English aristocracy.

In fact, our present danger is not that we shall praise ourselves too much, but that we shall accuse ourselves too much and blame ourselves for effects from conditions that are the conditions of the whole world. But if this is better than to rest content with our conditions because they seem to be ours alone, if it is sometimes a good thing to recognize that we are socially and economically sick, it is also a good thing to know that we have in our own political system the power of recuperation against the universal disorder.

This power is the republic, the political institution of the government upon the basis of self-rule, and no one questions this in our present sober mood, any more than in our former transports. No one really doubts the adequacy of the republic to any imaginable emergency; or if there is here and there one whose heart misgives him, he has nothing to suggest in place of it. In a completer sense than we always realize, it is the republic or nothing for us. In the same completer sense there is no past for us; there is only a future. Something that is still untried may serve our turn, but nothing that has been tried and failed will serve our turn. If we think, what for us is almost unthinkable, the end of the republic, we think chaos. Our minds cannot conceive of the rise of the nation from such a downfall in any prosperous shape of oligarchy or monarchy; we can only grope in the unexplored regions beyond the republic for some yet more vital democracy, or equality, or fraternity, to save us from the ruin into which our own recreancy may have plunged us.

Love of the republic with us is something like loyalty in the subjects of a king, but it is loyalty to the ideal of humanity, not to some man, self-elected prince in the past, and perpetuated in his descendants through the abeyance of common-sense. It is not the effect of any such affirmation as loyalty is constantly making; it is the result of that wary and calculated assent by which alone republics can exist. We may not think the republic is the best thing that can ever be, but we feel that it is the best we can have for the present; and that anything better must be something more rather than something less of it.

III. We see that the republic measurably exists wherever any sort of popular check is put upon the will of the ruler; and we think it more becoming reasonable men to choose their prince than to let his ancestors choose him, we regard an election, grotesque and vulgar and imperfect though the process often is, as a civic event; and we regard a parturition, though surrounded by all the dignity of state, as a domestic event, not logically of political significance, and comparatively inadequate as an expression of the popular will in the choice of a prince. Our opinion and our usage in this matter are what mainly distinguish us from such monarchical republics as England, Italy, Sweden, Belgium, and Holland; and with all our diffidence we cannot help thinking that, as compared with ours, their way of choosing a ruler is of the quality of comic opera, though, in its order, we look upon the birth of a fellow-being as a most serious and respectable incident. Where the republic does not exist at all, as in China and Russia and Turkey, or as in Germany, where it exists so feebly and passively that any violent impulse of the prince may annul it, we find indefinitely greater cause for satisfaction with our own democratic republic. So far as the peoples of these countries acquiesce in their several despotisms, they appear to us immature; so far as the English, Italians, Swedes, Dutch, and Belgians limit their respective republics by the birth-choice of a prince, they seem to us not fully responsive to the different sorts of revolutions which called their republics, like our own, into being. Even the elective French republic, where the outlawed titles of nobility are still permitted social currency, strikes us as retarded in its fulfillment of the democratic destiny. But we make excuses for France, as we do for England, Italy, Belgium, Sweden, and Holland, though we cannot help seeing our own advantage in these respects over republics which are each in some things freer than our own.

We believe that the republic as we have it is, upon the whole, the best form of government in the world; but we no longer deny that other peoples have the republic because they have hereditary princes. We believe that the republic as we have it, and the yet more fully developed republic as we shall have it, is the destined form of government for all nations, but we are no longer eager to thrust our happiness upon them; and we do not expect them at once to prefer our happiness when it is quite within their reach. We perceive that in none of these free states called kingdoms is the divine right of kings recognized and if in the freest of them the form without the fact of recognition is still kept up; if the queen's ministers go down upon their knees to her in assuming the powers of government which she cannot really bestow, and can never exercise, and can scarcely influence, still we see that it is merely a form. It is a droll anomaly which we are rid of, and the spectacle of it in a monarchical republic might perhaps foster an inordinate pride in us if the democratic republic, as we have it, were not so essentially unflattering.

If we all take it for no more than it is, it insists in turn upon our finally taking ourselves severally for no more than we are. It bids us be men, but not imagine that we can be more than men by any device of heraldry or any trick of sovereign legerdemain. We cannot, any of us, kneel down John Smith, and rise Sir John, by effect of virtue in the executive, who would be extremely surprised and disgusted if we knelt to him at all, or even kissed his hand. The sense, the wisdom of this most important fact of an equal humanity has at last got into our blood and our breath; it pulsates and respires in us; but with such effect that the least of us is beginning to realize that others are as good as he, and not merely that he is as good as others. I know we try to deny this socially, though the forms of society mean equality for all who are in it; but we affirm it politically, and we act upon it politically. We are all well content with the fact, except some weaker brethren who cannot find recognition in our system for the superiority they ascribe to themselves, and are forced to lead a life of rather undignified and unpitied exile in other countries. By virtue of this reasoned humility with respect to each other, we forbear to vaunt ourselves with regard to peoples who are not necessarily characterized by their archaic, not to say barbaric, ceremonies.

IV. With us the danger has been not that we should attach a mystical value to birth, but that we should bow our reason to wealth, yet I think there is already less of this danger than there once was. Our ideal of great wealth has been rudely shaken, not only by its enemies, but by the example of its possessors, who have shown at least that humanity does not always better itself by accumulating the means of luxury. Without the duties and responsibilities of wealth in the countries where it is nearly always joined with rank, it

FIGURE 4   This Charles Dana Gibson cartoon "types" the men waiting in a bread line,
exaggerating physical differences and postures as signs of character as well as markers
of national and ethnic heritages. The illustration underscores a firm belief in "reading"
phenotype, a belief propelled by both photographic developments and literary realism.
(*Scribner's*, 1898)

is here often a spectacle that awakens in the beholder no emotions nobler
than envy and greed. After once indulging a riotous exultation that we had
more millionaires than any other nation in the world, it is safe to say that our
national pride no longer centres in them, or even in their money. Many of us
have our doubts whether a very rich American can be a very good American,
and we feel that the burden of proof rests heavily with such an American.

Wealth is without social ultimation among us, and is less harmful than
anywhere else. It may go on and become greater and greater wealth, but
it never can become birth; our plutocracy cannot turn aristocracy on this
soil. It may buy birth, but it must then go where birth counts. If it desires
rank, it must seek it in exile. The millionaire who marries his daughter to
a French or English noble banishes her; this can no longer be her home; his
grandchildren cannot inherit him here in the state they are born to abroad.
In fact, great wealth expatriates itself whether it goes or whether it stays.
If it stays, it stays in a wholly alien circumstance. It surrounds itself with
the service of foreign menials, in an ideal of life wholly foreign to the life

of America, which is the life of work. It eliminates itself from the fellow-citizenship which regards it askance, in tacit irony or open sarcasm. American wealth does not penetrate its European shell with the corruption that wealth sends out beneath and about it in other countries where it ultimates in rank and civic importance. Within its gates and portals it is shut up with the miasms which money must breed whenever it is not actively employed in the industries.

It is not merely the old-fashioned American who looks upon it with misgiving. It is the newest fashioned American, the best-educated, the most finely equipped, the young man choosing deliberately a high calling in which he cannot hope to make a fortune—it is he who regards the vast accumulations of money, once our admiration, with generous content in his higher aim. The time is past when it could be said that our best young men were tempted away from the arts and the humanities by the greater allurements of money-making.

V. On the threshold of a new century, the portal of the future, we see more clearly than ever that America is the home of work, of endeavor, of the busy effort in which man loses the heavy sense of self as he can in no pleasures and tastes the happiness of doing something, making something, creating something. Our problem is how to keep the chance of this free to all: how to find work for all; how to render drones impossible, either rich drones or poor drones, voluntary or involuntary. Perhaps the vastness of this problem is what has rendered us less selfsatisfied in the presence of others' difficulties, such difficulties as we surmounted when we left royalty and rank behind, and trusted our lives, our fortunes, and our sacred honor to the common good-will of common men. They are still confronted over there in the Old World with questions which we solved a century ago; but our problem is none the less serious for that. We do not feel the gay buoyancy of our nonage under the burden, but we are not discouraged, though we are so much more serious. We have been a little drunk with our prosperity; our luck had gone to our heads, perhaps; but we have not forgotten our duty, which is not the duty of people to prince, of class to class, but of man to man. We recognize fully that we are in each other's keeping as no people ever were before; and that if we are true to ourselves, equal to our opportunities, there is no good that we may not achieve for the common advantage.

I think that much of the self-criticism which has characterized us in these later, these wiser years is an effect of the unfathomable confidence we have in our destiny, which is one with our duty as well as our glory. We have it laid upon us to leave no question unasked which, if answered, may help us to know our duty. What has been our fault that we have any knotty problem, after a hundred years of absolute freedom and of almost unbroken prosperity? In what have we been false to ourselves? How have we failed to remember that there is no good but the good of all? What are the recoverable chances that we have thrown away? What is the secret of our stupidity, our heedlessness, our blindness?

We ask all this in terms of greater or less severity, but whatever we find the answer to be, not one of us dreams of looking for the remedy outside of democracy. No one proposes to revert to a former condition, of any sort whatever. It is not pretended, even in the wildest burlesque, that we could by any manner of means help ourselves, or save ourselves, through monarchy or aristocracy or autocracy. These things are logically so impossible for us that we are not even afraid of them. We intend the good of all; that is what we understand America to mean; and those forms have been found by quite sufficient experiment never to be for the good of any. Would a change (a wholly unimaginable change) to them put food in the mouths, clothes on the backs, knowledge in the heads of the common people? We ourselves are the common people, and we know what the common people need.

VI. It is in no overweening mood of optimism that we trust the republic to save itself. There are almost as few mere optimists as mere pessimists among us. Question those who seem to be the one or the other, and you find that at the bottom of their hearts they have the same doubts, the same hopes. The blandest optimist does not deny that there are a good many screws loose; the bleakest pessimist does not affirm that there is no means within our democracy of tightening them again, or that there is any means outside of democracy.

We trust the republic with itself; that is, we trust one another, and we trust one another the most implicitly when we affirm the most clamorously, one half of us, that the other half is plunging the whole of us in irreparable ruin. That is merely our way of calling all to the duty we owe to each. It is not a very dignified way, but the entire nation is in the joke, and it is not so mischievous as it might seem. By-and-by, probably, we shall change it. We should certainly change it in the presence of any vital danger; for one reason, because we should then be all of one mind, in devotion to the republic.

Nothing in our modern mood, I think, is more notable than the quiet of our patriotism. In this we are like people whose religion has become their life, it is no longer an enthusiasm, and it is certainly not a ceremonial. They do not seek for a sign; the light is in them. I cannot answer for the new generation which is soon to inherit America, but I believe we who are about bequeathing it to them desire nothing so little as a miracle. We have had many miracles in our time, and we have not found that they permanently profited, even as a foundation of faith. But the age of miracles is past with us, and we are glad it is past. They are never concerned with things of the mind, or things of the soul; it is as difficult to be good as to be wise; either of these states is the effect of long and slow endeavor; and neither is the effect of miracles. These gave us no righteous men and no great men, though they gave us many rich ones.

VII. With the popular American love of quantity there was always an underlying, or innerlying, love of quality; and I hope I do not too fondly believe that it is this which is coming to characterize us nationally. It is this essential fineness which has made us cherish most the delicate effects in poetry and fiction; in our painting it has sought the expression of the same subtle beauty through an earlier simplicity and a later virtuosity; in our sculpture it endeavors for a modern soul in antique perfection of form; in our necessarily eclectic architecture it chooses the elegance which it arrived too late, perhaps, to create.

Shall I go a little farther and say that this American world of thought and feeling shows the effect, beyond any other world, of the honor paid to woman? It is not for nothing that we have privileged women socially and morally beyond any other people; if we have made them free, they have used their freedom to make the whole national life the purest and best of any that has ever been. Our women are in rare degree the keepers of our consciences; they influence men here as women influence men nowhere else on earth, and they qualify all our feeling and thinking, all our doing and being. If our literature at its best, and our art at its best, has a grace which is above all the American thing in literature and art, it is because the grace of the moral world where our women rule has imparted itself to the intellectual world where men work. When it shall touch the material world to something of its own fineness, and redeem the gross business world from the low ideals which govern it, then indeed we shall have the millennium in plain sight.

The common man, with his rights and needs, is here forever; humanity has come to stay; the republic is the sense of humanity. We may, some of us, not quite like the common man, and his rights and needs may bore us, but we cannot escape their presence, and I believe the most of us do not wish to escape them. It is in our willingness to own them that we soberly confront the new century, after a cycle of the supposition that they had been fully provided for by the Declaration of Independence and the Constitution of the United States. If Europe has anything to tell us of ways and means for doing this better, we are willing to listen: we do not expect to find any help through kings and classes; they have been thoroughly tried, and they have thoroughly failed: but if Europe, under the old forms, has any secret of democracy, we are willing to consider that, and willing, upon due consideration, to give it a trial. Still, we rather look to ourselves, to our history, and to the peculiar type of human nature which we have evolved here, for suggestion; and I think we do this with a feeling of our responsibility no less devout than inarticulate. It has troubled some anxious souls hitherto that we have nowhere named God in our organic law; but with God in our hearts this is not perhaps so necessary as it has seemed. He has inclined them to such recognition of the human brotherhood as there never was before in the world; and inspired us with so great faith in one another that it does not wholly fail us in the most obstreperous moments of political difference, but revives and begins to effect itself as soon as the noise of the party tomtoms has died away.

Our patriotism is not of the earlier passion and tenderness which the day of small things inspired. These would be out of keeping with our enormous prosperity, our irresistible power. But the modern Americanism is essentially patient and tolerant. It no longer affirms that we have found the only way or the best way, but that the way to life, liberty, and the pursuit of happiness is for us the way that our fathers set out upon a hundred years ago. We have really more faith in the republic than they had, for we have found that it works, and they could merely believe that it would work. We do not preach it so much as we once did, and the terms of our rhetoric are somewhat decayed; but at least we have not now the humiliation of having slaves to keep the flies off us while we frame the praise and argument of freedom. What is most generous in our aspiration and intention is the most modern, and we can trust the future to be as true as the present to the ideals of the past.

★

OCTAVE THANET The Provincials
Scribner's 15 (May 1894): 565–572

[Octave Thanet—the pen name of Alice French—wrote prolifically for periodicals during the 1890s, first gaining recognition as a local colorist in rural Arkansas where she vacationed. "The Provincials" was originally a part of a series, "Sketches of American Types," about the 1893 World's Columbian Exposition. Here, as in the rest of her work, Thanet upheld the rural American type and the moral effects of simple living.]

A WISE OLD ENGLISHMAN once asked a clever young Englishman who was not wise, whether he had seen much of the Americans during a recent visit.

"Well, yes," answered the clever young Englishman who was not wise, "I have seen the States pretty thoroughly; I have been to all their principal cities."

"But have you visited the smaller cities and the villages?"

The young Englishman had not judged them to be of enough importance to visit.

"Then," said the wise old Englishman, brusquely, "say as little as you can about the Americans, for you haven't seen them!"

FIGURE 5 This illustration from Octave Thanet's "The Provincials" treats rural Americans as serious and astute cultural critics; the sketch echoes Thanet's career-long portrayal of rural Americans as the modern culmination of a proud, continuous American heritage. (*Scribner's*, 1894)

Sifting out the truth from the extravagance of an epigram, there remains enough to recognize. Great cities, among us, are typical of the Republic as a whole, but the citizens of our great cities have their nationality brushed off at their elbows. In the country there are still purely American communities, whose fathers and grandfathers were American before them. Moreover, in the country the foreigner becomes more quickly Americanized. In New York he hardly pays us the compliment of learning our language.

And it is not strange that the few foreigners who have either the wit or the good fortune to penetrate into what they call the "provinces," are our kindest judges; for they have seen the American at his best. They have touched both the picturesque and the gentle side of our national character. It is not in the great cities, but in the little cities and the villages, that one sees the class that Emerson loved, the plain livers and high thinkers; or another class, not so plain in its living, not so high in its thinking in one way, but practical followers of righteousness and exceedingly pleasant people to meet. Many of them have what counted for wealth in a simpler generation; all of them have education and a generous habit of mind. They love their country but they are a little shy of politics; nevertheless they furnish the pith of the Republic. They are the silent Warwicks that make and unmake party kings, asking and expecting no reward, and only half-conscious of their own power. Most of the women treasure up, somewhere, an old sword or a pair of tarnished shoulder-straps, belonging, it may be to a gray, it may be to a blue uniform, but worn by equally honest and gallant fellows. The men are in touch with the present, but they keep the sturdy virtues taught them by their fathers and, God be thanked, they will transmit them to their sons. They have the education of travel as well as of books; for the provincial travels more in proportion to his income than the people of great cities. The wealthy in cities traverse each year miles of steel or water; but, often are the same miles of the years before; the provincial varies his outing; and he travels more in his own country.

All over the provinces, too, are the people who cannot travel, but study the world in books. They are the people to whom the great Exposition gave the greatest happiness. Such people come from the unlikeliest-looking places. There are book clubs and women's clubs where they read books, in desolate prairie villages with shabby wooden shops and new wooden houses of a dazzling ugliness. One of these villages hung like a mirage before my eyes — ah, how well I know them, and the wide wheat-fields and corn-fields about them, and the lines of stunted poplar-trees outside the blue-gray fences, and the black, soggy roads that cross the railway, and the mud creased by wagon! — while my friend described to me the Gentlewoman of the Woman's Dormitories. She was a little woman, not young — there were gray hairs in her soft brown hair, brushed smoothly down over her ears — not pretty either, save as dainty neatness and delicate tints, and the sweet, vague lines about the eyes and mouth that a lifetime of remembering others' welfare first will etch on a woman's face, make it pleasant to the eye. And her clothes would have attracted attention anywhere outside of an Old Folks' Concert! She wore a glossy black silk gown, very thin, very brilliant, very old. Her cloak was of a cut unknown to Fashion since the Civil War, a long black broadcloth cloak. And she had a preposterous bonnet with wilted roses in the peak.

"She was like a character out of Miss Wilkins's stories," said my friend. But when she was described to me, she resembled a real personage, a New England woman, who being left alone in the world with a tiny house, an old black broadcloth coat of her father's, and a store of obsolete wallpaper, contrived to live and decorate her house on five dollars a year, or some such incredible sum.

While my friend studied her, wondering what manner of woman it was that could wear such clothes, and pitying her presumable embarrassment in them, she began to talk. She had an exquisite voice, and was aflame in a white heat of enthusiasm and delight; awe-struck, it seemed, before the vastness of her own pleasure. She had spent the day in the Art Palace (she invariably called all the buildings of importance by their official title; they were palaces, in truth, and she would have felt it a denial of their regal rights, to give them any meaner name), and she described the pictures and statues and architecture, as a visitor to an enchanted land might describe its wonders. She talked like one who had loved Art with unquenchable ardor; but had seen little. Spontaneously the words of the great thinkers, who had been her artistic teachers slipped to her lips. The insignificant, oddly dressed woman was eloquent. "There was a crowd about her, hanging on her words, every time," said my friend; "and I don't wonder, for it was not only that she described what she saw beautifully, in that lovely voice, but she seemed to have seen so much more in them than we had—and she was so happy!"

Often have I sketched fancy pictures of that unknown visitor to the Fair. She holds a place in my affections second only to Maria's. She was poor—one could infer that, not so much from her old-fashioned garb (which might have been merely a whim of sentiment or opinion) as from her little economies, which she recounted quite frankly. Not for her the exemplary chair-boys or, the heathen sedan-men; she knew nothing of the good beefsteak and execrable bread of the White Horse Inn, nor did she ever marvel over the tiny portions and gigantic prices of the Marine Café. She probably lived on the Fair sandwich and drank hygeia-water (not too cold for the foreign taste) at a cent a glass. It is a mistake to suppose that it was necessary to spend a large sum of money to see the Columbian Exposition. As usual, broad and pleasant was the road to financial destruction, and many there were that walked therein; but there were by-paths of economy. I, myself, know a woman, a respectable cook in a family that I love, who supported life for the space of a week, at Jackson Park, for the sum of one dollar and thirty-five cents—and had strength enough left to travel home! She bought each day a loaf of bread or a dozen rolls for ten cents, and at the butcher's or the grocer's she secured a few cents' worth of chipped beef, a Bologna sausage or the like airy and ready-made meat. Her one extravagance was an occasional cup of coffee. She said that she never was *very* hungry! But I hope the gentlewoman permitted herself more generous fare than this master economist, and that her radiant spirit had the earthly comfort of a warm meal once a day! Yet the vision of her exalted enjoyment rebukes me. Little did she think of warm meals, as little as Miss Wilkins's poetess, poor Betsey Dole. But the gentlewoman was not a New Englander, she came from an Illinois village. My friend knew nothing else of her. Did her poverty cause her to be less esteemed?

Not if her village was like any other Western village in my knowledge. The West is presumed to be helplessly given over to philistinism in its rankest form, and to worship money; but in reality, as any Westerner knows, little is demanded of educated people in the way of wealth. I am thinking, now, of the Western town that I know best, and of certain families in it, socially considered with the best, although they have neither riches nor position, nor any exceptional culture, but are simply "nice people." Moreover, I hope it may be imputed to the Western provincial for righteousness, that in the small towns character counts for a great deal. Unsuspected good is done by church-working societies and women's clubs. They have an unconscious but sweeping democracy, and "good workers" are never slighted. It is quite possible that the gentlewoman was president of her woman's club. Her queer clothes were accepted, not ridiculed. The provinces, indeed, do not suppress individuality like the cities. It is not only that the individual counts in the country; he always has counted, and always will count, just as the strong will has always ruled, and always will rule, whether one live under a mitigated despotism like Turkey's, or an unmitigated despotism, such as our socialistic friends would bind on our backs; but in the country the individual has room to grow; he is cramped in the city. To be sure, one may go his own gait more entirely in a city than anywhere, except on a desert island; but he must pay toll by an outward compliance with the conventionalities; he must look and dress and talk like everyone else. It is the aim of the citizens of a great town to each resemble the other as much as possible, and be as different as possible from the rest of the world, like a Moody and Sankey hymn-tune.

In the provinces a prominent citizen is only expected to keep the Commandments, wear whole and clean clothes, and be a good fellow. Should he choose the comfort of a silk shirt the year round or wear a coat of the fashion of his youth, that is his own and no one else's affair! The provincial magnate is generally unconventional, a man of mark in more ways than one. He has the habit of command, and does not conceal his whims, but rather respects them as part of himself, a very decent and successful fellow. What is eccentricity in the town is merely the great man's, or even the little man's, "way" in the country.

However, the younger provincials, especially the provincials from the large towns, form themselves on the best city models. When my friend Colonel Ben bowed his handsome head to us in the Midway, my New York friend asked me, "Is that an Englishman?" But when she heard him speak, she added, "No, I think he is from Chicago."

"His accent?" said I.

She shook her head, saying, "No, he has no accent, English or otherwise; it is his manner. He is too deferential to that shabby woman who is asking him the way, to be from New York!"

"But why not give him to Boston?"

"He laughs too heartily to come from Boston."

Colonel Ben belongs neither to Chicago nor New York, he is a provincial manufacturer; but his people came over in the Mayflower and he belongs to a Chicago club. The young man with him, however, gave my friend not a minute's bewilderment. Colonel Ben belongs to the class of Americans as nearly analogous to the English gentry as it is to anything. Two centuries ago, in fact, Colonel Ben's ancestors were doing their duty in that station of life to which they had been called, and caring for their tenants and grumbling at Dutch William, in the prettiest English county. Colonel Ben never mentions that he has a coat of arms; but he never forgets it. I know the young fellow well and I fancy that I listen only to the New World variation on the sturdy old English tune that power means obligation, and an honest gentleman must look after those dependent on him, when I hear him discussing with his partner how to keep their factories running, and employ as many of their men as possible, in these pinching times. It is his partner that my friend classifies without hesitation; he is a man of another type. He belongs to another, social order, although he is young like Ben (whose colonelcy came from the governor of his State and means merely a splendid uniform and a prancing steed on days of state), is invited to the same houses and courted by the same people. His father was a lawyer, a self made man, eccentric in both his opinions and his manners, but with an immense fund of hard sense back of the unconventional appearance. With a larger field for his talents, his acumen and a rough-shod but (to a jury) irresistible eloquence would have made him famous. His son inherited his father's sense and some of his oddities. He was educated in the public schools and the State university; he has never been outside of his own country, he is a provincial to his finger-tips, as the French would say. When we saw him he was clad in a suit of the best material, evidently made for him, by a good tailor, but as evidently not treated by him with the proper respect. He is clean always, as a new pin; but he does not keep his trousers properly pressed, nor preserve the harmony of his coat lines by trigly buttoning it; and his soft black hat is dented as may happen. But he is a handsome fellow, with a fine, firm chin and mouth, a beautiful brow, and good, keen, kindly eyes. Colonel Ben and he joined us and we went to the streets of Cairo (where he obligingly rode a camel for our benefit and kept the crowd in a roar of delight over his translations of what he judged the proper phrases of the desert, to increase its speed), and later he insisted on giving us a little luncheon in old Vienna. He was delighted with my friend, and in half an hour my friend was delighted with him. She went all over the black and white exhibit in the gallery of the Art Building with him, the next day. "Who would think it?" said she, "that man, with the manners of a cowboy-cavalier, is one of the finest art critics I ever met; it is so refreshing, too, to hear a picture talked about in straight English! He has a beautiful collection of etchings, your friend says. He says himself, that he hasn't money enough to have good paintings, but he can have the best etchings; so he goes in for etchings, with an occasional water-color or pen-and-ink drawing. Do you know he is what I call a magazine-cultivated man?"

"And that," said I, "is what I call a fine-sounding phrase; but I don't know what it means."

"Nothing is easier than the meaning," said she. "Mr. —— has not had the time for an exhaustive education, he has had to make a fortune; he is a splendid business man, I was told, and so decent and honest, too ——"

"*Ca va sans dire,*" interrupted the listener; "with a splendid business man, it is part of the splendor!"

My friend continued calmly, "*So*, he has been obliged to get, instead of the long, tedious culture of all sorts of studies and experiences, the short-hand culture of the magazines; and really it is a very fair working substitute."

I had nothing to say, being at this time opposite the Dahomey village and pondering on the extraordinary resemblance between one of the warriors and a waiter in a hotel of my own town; my friend continued, fancifully interested in her own train of thought: "Yes, the provinces are educated by the magazines, and the cities—"

"Are educated by books and travel and—and—and all the rest of it?" queried I.

"Not at all," said she; "the cities *talk* of being educated that way, but they are really educated by the newspapers; they don't even read the magazines, they only subscribe for them in order to dip into them, once in a way, when any especial article has excited especial attention."

"I wonder," said I; but I was not wondering whether the critic was right, but whether the ferocious warrior whose mild black eyes contradicted his scowl, could be Jim Baker.

And just at this moment a gentleman leaned over the enclosure, and the warrior sank down in a heap with the others, near enough to mutter, "Don't you know me, Mr. S——, Jim, at the Kimball House?"

I saw a cigar travelling not only to Dahomey Jim (he will have to carry that name to his coffin), but to several other black braves. And at the same time I saw a note-book flash out and a black slouch hat bent over a swift pencil. Then the pencil stopped, a boyish face that held some lines too deep for youth, was lifted and brightened with a smile. "I guess not," said the writer; "it's funny; but we don't want to damage any part of this show, just for fun!"

It was a country editor, writing up the Fair. As we walked away I pondered on this vast, subtle influence of written thought which we call the press; and how much unthanked forbearance (too much, it may be!) and kindliness there is in that irresponsible power. I thought of some of the provincial editors that I know.

Before me, amid the stately pomp of architecture and the statues outlined against the burning, blue of a Western sky, I saw a dim, innumerable caravan of benefactions that I know first issued from dingy little country offices. I saw worn-out men working when they should have slept, ringing unpopular benevolence into careless or hostile ears. I saw country editors grimly flinging furious letters from their subscribers into the fire and doggedly finishing their protests against the popular folly. I saw them forced into the procession of their party, but ready to help the tide turn. I saw a provincial editor that I know, smiling on legislators, the shrewdest and most winning of lobbyists, for—what? His own paper? His own political future? Not at all, for the better education of his State, for the better management of charitable institutions. I saw another editor who has been able to conduct charitable movements of national importance, for which he has spent his time, his money, and himself lavishly; and yet he is so shrewd, so modest, and such a good fellow, that no one accuses him of being a fanatic. I saw, too, a multitude of trivial acts of mercy and help which to the doers were nothing, done pitifully or good-naturedly, and presently forgotten, but which sometimes changed the world for frightened men and women, and sometimes have lifted up people slipping in muddy places, and always have given the sunshine a better chance. Then my thoughts went back to Colonel Ben and his class, and the fight that they and honest fellows like them are waging against anarchy on one hand, and greed on the other. And I felt a mist in my eyes. But I only said: "Yes, the provincials are not half bad!"

★

ROBERT GRANT *The Conduct of Life*
Scribner's (November 1895): 581–592

[Generally remembered for his role in the Sacco-Vanzetti case (1927) as one of the state-appointed "Hangmen in Frock Coats" who upheld the death verdicts of the Italian anarchists, Grant posits the necessity of "unadulterated Americanism," a combination of naturalness, self-respect, desire for self-improvement or success, energy, and self-reliance. Grant, who recapitulated an old stereotype in arguing that the ideal American is of Anglo-Saxon stock, here looks to a new type—the professional man.]

Now THAT MORE than a century has elapsed since our independence as a nation was accomplished, and we are sixty million strong, what do we stand for in the world? What is meant by the word American, and what are our salient qualities as a people? What is the contribution which we have made or are making to the progress of society and the advancement of civilization?

There certainly used to be, and probably there is, no such egregiously patriotic individual in the world as an indiscriminately patriotic American, and there is no more familiar bit of rhetoric extant than that this is the greatest nation on earth. The type of citizen who gave obtrusive vent to this sentiment, both at home and abroad, is less common than formerly; nevertheless his clarion tones are still invariably to be heard in legislative assemblies when any opportunity is afforded to draw a comparison between ourselves and other nations. His extravagant and highfalutin boastings have undoubtedly been the occasion of a certain amount of seemingly luke-warm patriotism on the part of the educated and more intelligent portion of the American public, an attitude which has given foreigners the opportunity to declare that the best Americans are ashamed of their own institutions. But that apparent disposition to apologize already belongs to a past time. No American, unless a fool, denies to-day the force of the national character, whatever he or she may think of the behavior of individuals; and on the other hand, is it not true that every State in the Union has a rising population of young and middle-aged people who have discovered, Congress and the public schools to the contrary notwithstanding, that we do not know everything, and that the pathway of national progress is more full of perplexities than our forests were of trees when Daniel Boone built his log cabin in the wilds of Kentucky? In short, the period of unintelligent jubilation on one side, and carping cynicism on the other, have given place to a soberer self-satisfaction. We cannot—why should we?—forget that our territory is enormous, and that we soon shall be, if we are not already, the richest nation on earth; that the United States is the professed asylum and Mecca of hope for the despondent and oppressed of other countries; and that we are the cynosure of the universe, as being the most important exemplification of popular government which the world has ever seen. At the same time, the claims put forth by our progenitors that American society is vastly superior to any other, and that the effete world of Europe is put to the blush by the civic virtues of the land of the free and the home of the brave, are no longer urged except for the purposes of rodomontade. The average American of fifty years ago—especially the frontiersman and pioneer, who swung his axe to clear a homestead, and squirted tobacco-juice while he tilled the prairie—really believed that our customs, opinions, and manner of living, whether viewed from the moral, artistic, or intellectual standpoint, were a vast improvement on those of any other nation.

But though most of us to-day recognize the absurdity of such a view, we are most of us at the same time conscious of the belief that there is a difference between us and the European which is not imaginary, and which is the secret of our national force and originality. International intercourse has served to open our eyes until they have become as wide as saucers, with the consequence that, in hundreds of branches of industry and art, we are studying Old World methods; moreover, the pioneer strain of blood has been diluted by hordes of immigrants of the scum of the earth. In spite of both these circumstances, our faith in our originality and in the value of it remains unshaken, and we are no less sure at heart that our salient traits are noble ones, than the American of fifty years ago was sure that we had the monopoly of all the virtues and all the arts. He really meant only what we mean, but he had an unfortunate way of expressing himself. We have learned better taste, and we do not hesitate nowadays to devote our native humor to hitting hard the head of bunkum, which used to be as sacred as a Hindoo god, and as rife as apple blossoms in this our beloved country.

What is the recipe for Americanism—that condition of the system and blood, as it were, which even the immigrant without an ideal to his own soul, seems often to acquire to some extent as soon as he breathes the air of Castle Garden? It is difficult to define it in set speech, for it seems almost an illusive and intangible quality of being when fingered and held up to the light. It seems to me to be, first of all, a consciousness of unfettered individuality coupled with a determination to make the most of self. One great force of the American character is its naturalness, which proceeds from a total lack of traditional or inherited disposition to crook the knee to anyone. It never occurs to a good American to be obsequious. In vulgar or ignorant personalities this point of view has sometimes manifested itself, and continues to manifest itself, in swagger or insolence, but in the finer form of nature appears as simplicity of an unassertive yet dignified type. Gracious politeness, without condescension on the one hand, or fawning on the other, is noticeably a trait of the best element of American society, both among men and women. Indeed, so valuable to character and ennobling is this native freedom from servility, that it has in cases in the past made odd and unconventional manner and behavior seem attractive rather than a blemish. Unconventionality is getting to be a thing of the past in this country, and the representative American is at a disadvantage now, both at home and abroad, if he lacks the ways of the best social world; he can no longer afford to ignore cosmopolitan usages, and to rely solely on a forceful or imposing personality; the world of London and Paris, of New York and Washington and Chicago, has ceased to thrill, and is scarcely amused, if he shows himself merely in the guise of a splendid intellectual buffalo. But the best Americanism of to-day reveals itself no less distinctly and unequivocally in simplicity bred of a lack of self-consciousness and a lack of servility of mind. It seems to carry with it a birthright of self-respect, which, if fitly worn, ennobles the humblest citizen.

This national quality of self-respect is apt to be associated with the desire for self-improvement or success. Indeed, it must engender it, for it provides hope, and hope is the touchstone of energy. The great energy of Americans is ascribed by some to the climate, and it is probably true that the nervous temperaments of our people are stimulated by the atmospheric conditions which surround us; but is it not much more true that, just as it never occurs to the good American to be servile, so he feels that his outlook upon the possibilities of life is not limited or qualified, and that the world is really his oyster? To be sure, this faith has been fostered by the almost Aladdin-like opportunities which this great and rich new country of ours has afforded. But whatever the reason for our native energy and self-reliance, it indisputably exists, and is signally typical of the American character. We are distinctly an ambitious, earnest people, eager to make the most of ourselves individually, and we have attracted the attention of the world by force of our independent activity of thought and action. The extraordinary personality of Abraham Lincoln is undoubtedly the best apotheosis yet presented of unadulterated Americanism. In him the native stock was free from the foreign influences and suggestions which affected, more or less, the people of the East. His origin was of the humblest sort, and yet he presented most saliently in his character the naturalness, nobility, and aspiring energy of the nation. He made the most of himself by virtue of unusual abilities, yet the key-note of their influence and force was a noble simplicity and farsighted independence. In him the quintessence of the Americanism of thirty years ago was summed up and expressed. In many ways he was a riddle at first to the people of the cities of the East in that, though their soul was his soul, his ways had almost ceased to be their ways; but he stands before the world to-day as the foremost interpreter of American ideas and American temper of thought as they then existed.

In the thirty years since the death of Abraham Lincoln the country has been inundated with foreign blood. Irish, Germans, English, Poles, and Scandinavians, mainly of the pauper or peasant class, have landed in large numbers, settled in one State or another, and become a part of the population. The West, at the time of the Civil War, was chiefly occupied by settlers of New England or Eastern stock—pioneers from the older cities, and towns who had sought fortune and a freer life in the new territory of prairies and unappropriated domain. The population of the whole country to-day bears many different strains of blood in its veins. The original settlers have chiefly prospered. The sons of those who split rails or followed kindred occupations in the fifties, and listened to the debates between Lincoln and Douglas, are the proprietors of Chicago, Denver, Cincinnati, Minneapolis, and Topeka. Johann Heintz now follows the plough and in turn squirts tobacco-juice while he tills the prairie; and Louis Levinsky, Paul Petrinoff, and Michael O'Neil forge the plough-shares, dig in the mine, or work in the factory side by side with John Smith and any descendant of Paul Revere who has failed to prosper in life's battle. But this is not all. Not merely are the plain people in the dilemma of being unable to pronounce the names of their neighbors, but the same is getting to be true of the well-to-do merchants and trades-people of many of our cities. The argus-eyed commercial foreigner has marked us for his own, and his kith and kin are to-day coming into possession of our dry-goods establishments, our restaurants, our cigar stores, our hotels, our old furniture haunts, our theatres, our jewelry shops, and what not. One has merely to open a directory in order to find the names in any leading branch of trade plentifully larded with Adolph Stein, Simon Levi, Gustave Cohen, or something ending in berger. They sell our wool; they float our loan, they manufacture our sugar, our whiskey, and our beer; they influence Congress. They are here for what they can make, and they do not waste their time in sentiment. They did not come in time to reap the original harvest, but they have blown across the ocean to help the free-born American spend his money in the process of trying to out-civilize Paris and London. As a consequence, the leading wholesale and retail ornamental industries of New York and of some of our Western cities are in the grip of individuals whose surnames have a foreign twang. Of course, they have a right to be here; it is a free country, and no one can say them nay. But we must take them and their wives and daughters, their customs and their opinions, into consideration in making an estimate of who are the Americans of the present. They have not come here for their health, as the phrase is, but they have come to stay. We at present, in our social hunger and thirst, supply the grandest and dearest market of the mind for the disposal of everything beautiful and costly and artistic which the Old World possesses, and all the shopkeepers of Europe, with the knowledge of generations on the tips of their tongues and in the corners of their brains, have come over to coin dowries for their daughters in the land of the free and the home of the brave. Many of them have already made large fortunes in the process and are beginning to con the pages of the late Ward McAllister's book on etiquette with a view to social aggressiveness.

Despite this infusion of foreign blood, the native stock and the Anglo-Saxon nomenclature are still, of course, predominant in numbers. There are some portions of the country where the late immigrant is scarcely to be found. True also is it that these late-comers, like the immigrants of fifty years ago, have generally been prompt in appropriating the independent and energetic spirit typical of our people. But there is a significant distinction to be borne in mind in this connection: The independent energy of the Americans of fifty years ago, whether in the East or among the pioneers of the Western frontier, was not, however crude its manifestations, mere bombastic assertiveness, but the expression of a faith and the expression of strong character. They were often ignorant, conceited, narrow, hard, and signally inartistic; but they stood for principle and right as they saw and believed it; they cherished ideals; they were firm as adamant in their convictions; and God talked with them whether in the store or workshop, or at the plough. This was essentially true of the rank and file of the people, no less true and perhaps more true of the humblest citizens than of the well-to-do and prominent.

There can be little doubt that the foreign element which is now a part of the American people represents neither a faith nor the expression of ideals or convictions. The one, and the largest portion of it, is the overflow and

FIGURE 6   Featuring the Empress Josephine, this soap advertisement invokes a majestic, elitist Eurocentric sense of "type." The ad appeared in *McClure's Magazine* in conjunction with the monthly's widely publicized, lavishly illustrated inaugural "Life of Napoleon" series, authored by Ida B. Tarbell. (*McClure's*, 1895)

riff-raff of the so-called proletariat of Europe; the other is the evidence of a hyena-like excursion for the purposes of plunder. In order to be a good American it is not enough to become independent and energetic. The desire to make the most of oneself is a relative term; it must proceed from principle and be nourished by worthy, ethical aims; otherwise it satisfies itself with paltry conditions, or with easy-going florid materialism. The thieving and venality in municipal political affairs of the Irish-American, the dull squalor and brutish contentment of the Russian-Pole, and the commercial obliquity of vision and earthy ambitions of the German Jew, are factors in our national life which are totally foreign to the Americanism for which Abraham Lincoln stood. We have opened our gates to a horde of economic ruffians and malcontents, ethical bankrupts and social thugs, and we must needs be on our guard lest their aims and point of view be so engrafted on the public conscience as to sap the vital principles which are the foundation of our strength as a people. The danger from this source is all the greater from the fact that the point of view of the American people has been changed so radically during the last thirty years as a secondary result of our material prosperity. We have ceased to be the austere nation we once were, we have sensibly let down the bars in the manner of our living; we have recognized the value of, and we enjoy, many things which our fathers put from them as inimical to republican virtue and demoralizing to society. Contact with older civilizations has made us wiser and more appreciative, and with this growth of perspective and the acquirement of an eye for color has come a liberality of sentiment which threatens to debauch us unless we are careful. There are many, especially among the wealthy and fashionable, who in their ecstasy over our emancipation are disposed to throw overboard everything which suggests the old *régime,* and to introduce any custom which will tend to make life more easy-going and spectacular. And in this they are supported by the immigrant foreigner, who would be only too glad to see the land of his adoption made to conform in all its usages to the land of his birth.

The conduct of life here has necessarily and beneficially been affected by the almost general recognition that we have not a monopoly of all the virtues, and by the adoption of many customs and points of view recommended by cosmopolitan experience. The American people still believe however, that our civilization is not merely a repetition of the older ones, and a duplication on new soil of the old social treadmill. That it must be so in a measure everyone will admit, but we still insist, and most of us believe, that we are to point the way to a new dispensation. We believe, but at the same time when we stop to think we find some difficulty in specifying exactly what we are doing to justify the faith. It is easy enough to get tangled up in the stars and stripes and cry "hurrah!" and to thrust the American eagle down the throats of a weary universe, but it is quite another to command the admiration of the world by behavior commensurate with our ambition and self-confidence. Our forefathers could point to their own nakedness as a proof of their greatness, but there seems to be some danger that we, now that we have clothed ourselves—and clothed ourselves as expensively as possible and not always in the best taste—will forget the ideas and ideals for which those fathers stood, and let ourselves be seduced by the specious doctrine that human nature is always human nature, and that all civilizations are alike. To be sure, an American now is apt to look and act like any other rational mortal, and there is no denying that the Atlantic cable and ocean greyhound have brought the nations of the world much closer together than they ever were before; but this merely proves that we can become just like the others, only worse, in case we choose to. But we intend to improve upon them.

To those who believe that we are going to improve upon them it must be rather an edifying spectacle to observe the doings and sayings of that body of people in the city of New York who figure in the newspapers of the day as "the four hundred," "the smart set," or "the fashionable world." After taking into full account the claims of the sensitive city of Chicago, it may be truthfully stated that the city of New York is the Paris of America. There are other municipalities which are doing their best in their several ways to rival her, but it is toward New York that all the eyes in the country are turned, and from which they take suggestion as a cat laps milk. The rest of us are in a measure provincial. Many of us profess not to approve of New York, but, though we cross ourselves piously, we take or read a New York daily paper. New York gives the cue alike to the Secretary of the Treasury and (by way of London) to the social swell. The ablest men in the country seek New York as a market for their brains, and the wealthiest people of the country move to New York to spend the patrimony which their rail-splitting fathers or grandfathers accumulated. Therefore it is perfectly just to refer to the social life of New York as representative of that element of the American people which has been most blessed with brains or fortune, and as representative of our most highly evolved civilization. It ought to be our best. The men and women who contribute to its movement and influence ought to be the pick of the country. But what do we find? We find as the ostensible leaders of New York society a set of shallow worldlings whose whole existence is given up to emulating one another in elaborate and splendid inane social fripperies. They dine and wine and dance and entertain from January to December. Their houses, whether in town or at the fashionable watering-places to which they move in summer, are as sumptuous, if not more so, than those of the French nobility in its palmiest days, and their energies are devoted to the discovery of new expensive luxuries and fresh titillating creature comforts. That such a body of people should exist in this country after little more than a century of democratic institutions is extraordinary, but much more extraordinary is the absorbing interest which a large portion of the American public takes in the doings and sayings of this fashionable rump. There is the disturbing feature of the case. Whatever these worldlings do is flashed over the entire country, and is copied into a thousand newspapers as being of vital concern to the health and home of the nation. The editors print it because it is demanded; because they have found that the free-born American citizen is keenly solicitous to know "what is going on in society" and that he or she follows with almost feverish interest and with open-mouthed absorption the spangled and jeweled annual social circus parade which goes on in the Paris of America. The public is indifferently conscious that underneath this frothy upper-crust in New York there is a large number of the ablest men and women of the country by whose activities the great, educational, philanthropic, and artistic enterprises of the day have been fostered, promoted, and made successful; but, this consciousness pales into secondary importance in the democratic mind as compared with realistic details concerning this ball and that dinner party where thousands of dollars are poured out in vulgar extravagance, or concerning the cost of the wedding presents, the names and toilettes of the guests and the number of bottles of champagne opened at the marriage of some millionaire's daughter.

No wonder that this aristocracy of ours plumes itself on its importance and takes itself seriously when it finds its slightest doings telegraphed from the Atlantic to the Pacific. It feels itself called to new efforts, for it understands with native shrewdness that the American people requires novelty and fresh entertainment, or it looks elsewhere. Accordingly it is beginning to be unfaithful to its marriage vows. Until within a recent period the husbands and wives of this vapid society have, much to the bewilderment of warm-blooded students of manners and morals, been satisfied to flirt and produce the appearance of infidelity, and only pretend. Now the divorce court and the whispered or public scandal bear frequent testimony to the fact that it is not so fashionable or "smart" as it used to be merely to make believe.

Was there ever a foreign court, when foreign courts were in their glory where men and women were content merely to whisper and giggle behind a rubber-tree in order to appear vicious? It may be said at least that some of our fashionables have learned to be men and women instead of mere marionettes. Still there was originality in being simpering marionettes: Marital infidelity has been the favorite excitement of every rotten aristocracy the world has ever seen.

II. A manner of life of this description can scarcely be the ideal of the American people. Certainly neither George Washington, when he delivered his farewell address, nor Abraham Lincoln, on the occasion of his second inaugural, looked forward to the evolution of any such aristocracy as the fulfillment of the nation's hopes. And yet this coterie of people has its representatives in all the large cities of the country, and there is no reason to doubt that in a short time the example set will be imitated to some extent, at least, and that one portion of the country will vie with another in extravagant social vanities and prodigal display on the part of a pleasure-seeking leisure class.

Most of these people go to church, and, indeed, some of them are ostensibly regardful of church functions and ceremonies, and, as they do not openly violate any laws so as to subject themselves to terms of imprisonment, the patriotic American citizen finds himself able merely to frown by way of showing his dissatisfaction at this form of high treason against the morals and aims of democracy. To frown and to be grateful that one is not like certain pleasure-seeking millionaires is not much of a comfort, especially when it is obvious that the ignorant and semi-ignorant mass is fascinated by the extravagances and worldly manifestations of the individuals in question, and has made them its heroes on account of their unadulterated millions. Indeed, the self-respecting, patriotic American citizen finds himself today veritably between Scylla and Charybdis in the matter of the conduct of life. We are no longer the almost homogeneous nation we were fifty years ago. There are far greater extremes of wealth and poverty. Our economic conditions, or at least the conditions which exist in our principal cities, are closely approximating those which exist in the cities of the Old World. Outside of our cities the people for the most part live in respectable comfort by the practice of what passes in America for economy, which may be defined as a high but ignorant moral purpose negatived by waste and domestic incompetence. It has always been true of our beloved country that, though the ship of state has seemed on the point of floundering from time to time, disaster has invariably been averted at critical junctures by the saving grace of the common-sense and right-mindedness of the American people. This is not so complimentary as it sounds. It really means that the average sense and intelligence of the public is apt to be in the wrong at the outset, and to be converted to the right only after many days and much tribulation. In other words, our safety and our progress have been the result of a slow and often reluctant yielding of opinion by the mass to the superior judgment of a minority. This is merely another way of stating that, where everyone has a right to individual opinion, and there are no arbitrary standards of conduct or of anything else outside the statute law, the mean is likely to fall far short of what is best. Our salvation in every instance of national perplexity has been the effectual working on the public conscience of the leaven of the best Americanism. A comparatively small proportion of the population have been the pioneers in thought and suggestion of subsequent ardent espousals by the entire public. This leaven, in the days when we were more homogeneous, was made up from all the elements of society or, in other words, the best Americanism drew its representatives from every condition of life; the farmer of the Western prairie was just as likely to tower above his fellows and become a torchbearer as the merchant or mechanic of the city.

If we as a nation have needed a leaven in the past, we certainly have no less need of one to-day, now that we are in the flush of material prosperity and consciousness of power. Fortunately we have one. The public-spirited, nobly independent, earnest, conscientious, ambitious American exists to-day as indisputable, and unmistakably as ever, and he is a finer specimen of humanity than he used to be, for he knows more and he poses much less. It is safe to assert, too, that he is still to be found in every walk of our national life. The existence of an aggravating and frivolous aristocracy on the surface, and an ignorant, unaesthetic mass underneath should not blind us to the fact that there is a sound core to our social system. The hope of the United States to-day lies in that large minority of the people who are really trying to solve the problems of life from more than a merely selfish standpoint. One has merely to think a moment in order to realize what a really numerous and significant body among us is endeavoring to promote the cause of American civilization by aspiring or decent behavior. Our clergymen, our lawyers, our doctors, our architects, our merchants, our teachers, some of our editors, our bankers, our scientists, our scholars and our philanthropists, at once stand out as a generally sane and earnest force of citizens. The great educational, charitable, artistic, and other undertakings which have been begun and splendidly completed by individual energy and liberality since the death of Abraham Lincoln bespeak eloquently the temper of a certain portion of the community. If it be true that the so-called aristocracy of New York City threatens the repute and sincerity of democracy by its heartlessness and unworthy attempts to ape the vices of a fifteenth century European nobility, New York can fairly retort that it offers in its working force of well-to-do people the most vital, interesting, sympathetic, and effective force of men and women in the nation. If the Paris of America contains the most dangerous element of society, it also contains an element which is equal to the best elsewhere, and is more attractive than any. The New York man or woman who is in earnest is sure to accomplish something, for he or she is not likely to be handicapped by ignorant provincialism of ethics or art which plays havoc with many of the good intentions of the rest of the country.

This versatile and interesting leaven of American society finds its counterpart, to a greater or less extent, in every section of the United States, but it is nowhere quite so attractive as in the Paris of America, for the reason that nowhere does the pulse of life move so keenly as there, and nowhere is the science of living absorbingly so well understood. The art of living has there reached a more interesting phase than in any part of America, if zest in life and the facilities to make the most of it are regarded as the test.

This may sound worldly. The people of the United States used to consider it worldly to admire pictures or to listen to beautiful music. Some think so still. Many a citizen of what was lately the prairie sits down to his dinner in his shirt-sleeves to-day and pretends to be thankful that he is neither an aristocrat nor a gold-bug. The next week, perhaps, this same citizen will vote against a national bankrupt law because he does not wish to pay his debts, or vote for a bill which will enable him to pay them in depreciated currency. Many a clergyman who knows better gives his flock consolingly to understand that to be absorbed in the best human interests of life is unworthy of the Christian, and that to be ordinary and unattractive is a legitimate condition of mind and body. Surely the best Americanism is the Americanism of the man or woman who makes the most of what this life affords, and throws himself or herself keenly into the thick of it. The art of living is the science of living nobly and well, and how can one live either nobly or well by regarding life on the earth as a mere log-cabin existence? If we in this country who seek to live wisely are in danger from the extravagant vanities of the very rich, we are scarcely less menaced by that narrow spirit of ethical teaching which tries to inculcate that it does not much matter what our material surroundings are, and that any progress made by society, except in the direction of sheer morality, is a delusion and a snare. Character is the basis and the indispensable requisite of the finest humanity; without it refinement, appreciation, manners, fancy, and power of expression are like so many boughs on a tree which is dead. But, on the other hand, what is more uninspiring than an unadorned soul? That kind of virtue and morality which finds no interest in the affairs of this life is but a fresh contribution to the sum of human incompetence, and but serves to retard the progress of civilization. The true and the chief reason why there is less misery in the world than formerly is that men understand better how to live. That straight-laced type of American, who is content to be moral in his own narrow way and to exclude from his scheme of life all those interests which serve to refine and to inspire, bears the same relation to the ideal man or woman that a chromo bears to a masterpiece of painting.

We have no standards in this country. The individual is free to express himself here within the law any way he sees fit, and the conduct of life comes always at last to an equation of the individual. Each one of us when we awake in the morning finds the problem of existence staring him anew in the face, and cannot always spare the time to remember that he is an American. And yet Americanism is the sum total of what all of us are. It will be very easy for us simply to imitate the civilizations of the past, but if our civilization is to stand for anything vital, and to be a step forward in the progress of humanity, we must do more than use the old combinations and devices of society in a new kaleidoscopic form. Our heritage as Americans is independence, originality, self-reliance, and sympathetic energy animated by a strong ethical instinct, and these are forces which can produce a higher and a broader civilization than the world has yet seen if we choose to have it so. But it is no longer a matter of cutting down forests and opening mines, of boasting beside the plough and building cities in a single year, of fabulous fortunes won in a trice, and of favorite sons in black broadcloth all the year round. It is a matter of a vast, populous country and a powerful, seething civilization where the same problems confront us which have taxed the minds and souls of the Old World for generations of men. It is for our originality to throw new light upon them, and it is for our independence to face them in the spirit of a deeper sympathy with humanity, and free from the canker of that utter selfishness which has made the prosperity and glory of other great nations culminate so often in a decadence of degrading luxury and fruitless culture.

No civilization which regards the blessings and comforts of refined living as unworthy to be striven for and appropriated can hope to promote the cause of humanity. On the other hand, we Americans must remember that purely selfish appropriation and appreciation of these blessings and comforts has worked the ruin of the most famous civilizations of the past. Marie Antoinette was more elegant than the most fashionable woman in New York, and yet that did not save her from the tumbrel and the axe. The best Americanism of to-day and for the future is that which shall seek to use the fruits of the earth and the fulness thereof, and to develop all the manifestations of art and gentle living in the interest of humanity as a whole. But even heartless elegance is preferable to that righteous commonness of spirit which sits at home in its shirt-sleeves and is graceless, ascetic, and unimaginative in the name of God.

★

PAULINE E. HOPKINS *Talma Gordon*

Colored American Magazine 1 (October 1900): 271–290

[Pauline E. Hopkins began writing for *Colored American Magazine* in 1900 and quickly became a major contributor and, later, the editor. *Colored American Magazine*, founded in Boston in 1900 and continuing until 1909, reached out from a Northern black elite to the rest of the nation to bring a "monthly magazine of merit into every Negro family." Hopkins published three novels, seven short stories, and numerous other selections in the periodical. In "Talma Gordon," she challenges the more usual portrait of the "tragic mulatto" (seen in the work of Charles Chesnutt, Frances Harper, and Alice Dunbar Nelson), narrating, but not exploring, the acceptance of a woman of mixed race into white society.]

THE CANTERBURY CLUB of Boston was holding its regular monthly meeting at the palatial Beacon-street residence of Dr. William Thornton, expert medical practitioner and specialist. All the members were present, because some rare opinions were to be aired by men of profound thought on a question of vital importance to the life of the Republic, and because the club celebrated its anniversary in a home usually closed to society. The Doctor's winters, since his marriage, were passed at his summer home near his celebrated sanitorium. This winter found him in town with his wife and two boys. We had heard much of the beauty of the former, who was entirely unknown to social life, and about whose life and marriage we felt sure a romantic interest attached. The Doctor himself was too bright a luminary of the professional world to remain long hidden without creating comment. We had accepted the invitation to dine with alacrity, knowing that we should be welcomed to a banquet that would feast both eye and palate; but we had not been favored by even a glimpse of the hostess. The subject for discussion was: "Expansion; Its Effect upon the Future Development of the Anglo-Saxon throughout the World."

Dinner was over, but we still sat about the social board discussing the question of the hour. The Hon. Herbert Clapp, eminent jurist and politician, had painted in glowing colors the advantages to be gained by the increase of wealth and the exalted position which expansion would give the United States in the councils of the great governments of the world. In smoothly flowing sentences marshalled in rhetorical order, with compact ideas, and incisive argument, he drew an effective picture with all the persuasive eloquence of the trained orator.

Joseph Whitman, the theologian of world-wide fame, accepted the arguments of Mr. Clapp, but subordinated all to the great opportunity which expansion would give to the religious enthusiast. None could doubt the sincerity of this man, who looked once into the idealized face on which heaven had set the seal of consecration.

Various opinions were advanced by the twenty-five men present, but the host said nothing; he glanced from one to another with a look of amusement in his shrewd gray-blue eyes. "Wonderful eyes," said his patients who came under their magic spell. "A wonderful man and a wonderful mind," agreed his contemporaries, as they heard in amazement of some great cure of chronic or malignant disease which approached the supernatural.

"What do you think of this question, Doctor?" finally asked the president, turning to the silent host.

"Your arguments are good; they would convince almost anyone."

"But not Doctor Thornton," laughed the theologian.

"I acquiesce which ever way the result turns. Still, I like to view both sides of a question. We have considered but one tonight. Did you ever think that in spite of our prejudices against amalgamation, some of our descendants, indeed many of them, will inevitably intermarry among those far-off tribes of dark-skinned peoples, if they become a part of this great Union?"

"Among the lower classes that may occur, but not to any great extent," remarked a college president.

"My experience teaches me that it will occur among all classes, and to an appalling extent," replied the Doctor.

"You don't believe in intermarriage with other races?"

"Yes, most emphatically, when they possess decent moral development and physical perfection, for then we develop a superior being in the progeny born of intermarriage. But if we are not ready to receive and assimilate the new material which will be brought to mingle with our pure Anglo-Saxon stream, we should call a halt in our expansion policy."

"I must confess, Doctor, that in the idea of amalgamation you present a new thought to my mind. Will you not favor us with a few of your main points?" asked the president of the club, breaking the silence which followed the Doctor's remarks.

"Yes, Doctor, give us your theories on the subject. We may not agree with you, but we are all open to conviction."

The Doctor removed the half-consumed cigar from his lips, drank what remained in his glass of the choice Burgundy, and leaning back in his chair contemplated the earnest faces before him.

We may make laws, but laws are but straws in the hands of Omnipotence.

"There's a divinity that shapes our ends,
Rough-hew them how we will."

And no man may combat fate. Given a man, propinquity, opportunity fascinating femininity, and there you are. Black, white, green, yellow—nothing will prevent intermarriage. Position, wealth, family, friends—all sink into insignificance before the God-implanted instinct that made Adam, awakening from a deep sleep and finding the woman beside him, accept Eve as bone of his bone; he cared not nor questioned whence she came. So it is with the sons of Adam even since, through the law of heredity which makes us all one common family. And so it will be with us in our re-formation of this old Republic. Perhaps I can make my meaning clearer by illustration, and with your permission I will tell you a story which came under my observation as a practitioner.

Doubtless all of you heard of the terrible tragedy which occurred at Gordonville, Mass., some years ago, when Capt. Jonathan Gordon, his wife and little son were murdered. I suppose that I am the only man on this side the Atlantic, outside of the police, who can tell you the true story of that crime.

I knew Captain Gordon well; it was through his persuasions that I bought a place in Gordonville and settled down to spending my summers in that charming rural neighborhood. I had rendered the Captain what he was pleased to call valuable medical help, and I became his family physician. Captain Gordon was a retired sea captain, formerly engaged in the East India trade. All his ancestors had been such; but when the bottom fell out of that business he established the Gordonville Mills with his first wife's money, and settled down as a money-making manufacturer of cotton cloth. The Gordons were old New England Puritans who had come over in the "Mayflower"; they had owned Gordon Hall for more than a hundred years. It was a baronial-like pile of granite with towers, standing on a hill which commanded a superb view of Massachusetts Bay and the surrounding country. I imagine the Gordon star was under a cloud about the time Captain Jonathan married his first wife, Miss Isabel Franklin of Boston, who brought to him the money which mended the broken fortunes of the Gordon house, and restored this old Puritan stock to its rightful position. In the person of Captain Gordon the austerity of manner and indomitable will-power that he had inherited were combined with a temper that brooked no contradiction.

The first wife died at the birth of her third child, leaving him two daughters, Jeannette and Talma. Very soon after her death the Captain married again. I have heard it rumored that the Gordon girls did not get on very well with their stepmother. She was a woman with no fortune of her own, and envied the large portion left by the first Mrs. Gordon to her daughters.

Jeanette was tall, dark, and stern like her father; Talma was like her dead mother, and possessed of great talent, so great that her father sent her to the American Academy at Rome, to develop the gift. It was the hottest of July days when her friends were bidden to an afternoon party on the lawn and a dance in the evening, to welcome Talma Gordon among them again. I watched her as she moved about among her guests, a fairylike blonde in floating white draperies, her face a study in delicate changing tints, like the heart of a flower, sparkling in smiles about the mouth to end in merry laughter in the clear blue eyes. There were all the subtle allurements of birth, wealth and culture about the exquisite creature:

> "Smiling, frowning evermore,
> Thou art perfect in love-lore,
> Ever varying Madeline,"

quoted a celebrated writer as he stood apart with me, gazing upon the scene before us. He sighed as he looked at the girl.

"Doctor, there is genius and passion in her face. Sometime our little friend will do wonderful things. But is it desirable to be singled out for special blessings by the gods? Genius always carries with it intense capacity for suffering: 'Whom the gods love die young.'"

"Ah," I replied, "do not name death and Talma Gordon together. Cease your dismal croakings; such talk is rank heresy."

The dazzling daylight dropped slowly into summer twilight. The merriment continued; more guests arrived; the great dancing pagoda built for the occasion was lighted by myriads of Japanese lanterns. The strains from the band grew sweeter and sweeter, and "all went merry as a marriage bell." It was a rare treat to have this party at Gordon Hall, for Captain Jonathan was not given to hospitality. We broke up shortly before midnight, with expressions of delight from all the guests.

I was a bachelor then, without ties. Captain Gordon insisted upon my having a bed at the Hall. I did not fall asleep readily; there seemed to be something in the air that forbade it. I was still awake when a distant clock struck the second hour of the morning. Suddenly the heavens were lighted by a sheet of ghastly light; a terrific midsummer thunderstorm was breaking over the sleeping town. A lurid flash lit up all the landscape, painting the trees in grotesque shapes against the murky sky, and defining clearly the sullen blackness of the waters of the bay breaking in grandeur against the rocky coast. I had arisen and put back the draperies from the windows, to have an unobstructed view of the grand scene. A low muttering coming nearer and nearer, a terrific roar, and then a tremendous downpour. The storm had burst.

Now the uncanny howling of a dog mingled with the rattling volleys of thunder. I heard the opening and closing of doors; the servants were about looking after things. It was impossible to sleep. The lightning was more vivid. There was a blinding flash of a greenish-white tinge mingled with the crash of falling timbers. Then before my startled gaze arose columns of red flames reflected against the sky. "Heaven help us!" I cried; "it is the left tower; it has been struck and is on fire!"

I hurried on my clothes and stepped into the corridor; the girls were there before me. Jeanette came up to me instantly with anxious face. "Oh, Doctor Thornton, what shall we do? Papa and mama and little Johnny are in the old left tower. It is on fire. I have knocked and knocked, but get no answer."

"Don't be alarmed," said I soothingly. "Jenkins, ring the alarm bell," I continued, turning to the butler who was standing near; "the rest follow me. We will force the entrance to the Captain's room."

Instantly, it seemed to me, the bell boomed out upon the now silent air, for the storm had died down as quickly as it arose; and as our little procession paused before the entrance to the old left tower, we could distinguish the sound of the fire engines already on their way from the village.

The door resisted all our efforts; there seemed to be a barrier against it which nothing could move. The flames were gaining headway. Still the same deathly silence within the rooms.

"Oh, will they never get here?" cried Talma, ringing her hands in terror. Jeannette said nothing, but her face was ashen. The servants were huddled together in a panic-stricken group. I can never tell you what a relief it was when we heard the first sound of the firemen's voices, saw their quick movements, and heard the ringing of the axes with which they cut away every obstacle to our entrance to the rooms. The neighbors who had just enjoyed the hospitality of the house were now gathered around offering all the assistance in their power. In less than fifteen minutes the fire was out, and the men began to bear the unconscious inmates from the ruins. They carried them to the pagoda so lately the scene of mirth and pleasure, and I took up my station there, ready to assume my professional duties. The Captain was nearest me; and as I stooped to make the necessary examination I reeled away from the ghastly sight which confronted me — *gentlemen, across the Captain's throat was a deep gash that severed the jugular vein!*

The Doctor paused, and the hand with which he refilled his glass trembled violently.

"What is it, Doctor?" cried the men, gathering about me.

"Take the women away; this is murder!"

"Murder!" cried Jeannette, as she fell against the side of the pagoda.

"Murder!" screamed Talma, staring at me as if unable to grasp my meaning.

I continued my examination of the bodies, and found that the same thing had happened to Mrs. Gordon and to little Johnny.

The police were notified; and when the sun rose over the dripping town he found them in charge of Gordon Hall, the servants standing in excited knots talking over the crime, the friends of the family confounded, and the two girls trying to comfort each other and realize the terrible misfortune that had overtaken them.

Nothing in the rooms of the left tower seemed to have been disturbed. The door of communication between the rooms of the husband and wife was open, as they had arranged it for the night. Little Johnny's crib was placed beside his mother's bed. In it he was found as though never awakened by the storm. It was quite evident that the assassin was no common ruffian. The chief gave strict orders for a watch to be kept on all strangers or suspicious characters who were seen in the neighborhood. He made inquiries among the servants, seeing each one separately, but there was nothing gained from them. No one had heard anything suspicious; all had been awakened by the storm. The chief was puzzled. Here was a triple crime for which no motive could be assigned.

"What do you think of it?" I asked him, as we stood together on the lawn.

"It is my opinion that the deed was committed by one of the higher classes, which makes the mystery more difficult to solve. I tell you, Doctor, there are mysteries that never come to light, and this, I think, is one of them."

While we were talking Jenkins, the butler, an old and trusted servant came up to the chief and saluted respectfully. "Want to speak with me, Jenkins?" he asked. The man nodded, and they walked away together.

The story of the inquest was short, but appalling. It was shown that Talma had been allowed to go abroad to study because she and Mrs. Gordon did not get on well together. From the testimony of Jenkins it seemed that Talma and her father had quarrelled bitterly about her lover, a young artist whom she had met at Rome, who was unknown to fame, and very poor. There had been terrible things said by each, and threats even had passed, all of which now rose up in judgment against the unhappy girl. The examination of the family solicitor revealed the fact that Captain Gordon intended to leave his daughters only a small annuity, the bulk of the fortune going to his son Jonathan, junior. This was a monstrous injustice, as everyone felt. In vain Talma protested her innocence. Someone must have done it. No one would be benefitted so much by these deaths as she and her sister. Moreover, the will, together with other papers, was nowhere to be found. Not the slightest clue bearing upon the disturbing elements in this family, if any there were, was to be found. As the only surviving relatives, Jeannette and Talma became joint heirs to an immense fortune, which only for the bloody tragedy just enacted would, in all probability, have passed them by. Here was the motive. The case was very black against Talma. The foreman stood up. The silence was intense: We "find that Capt. Jonathan Gordon, Mary E. Gordon and Jonathan Gordon, junior, all deceased, came to their deaths by means of a knife or other sharp instrument in the hands of Talma Gordon." The girl was like one stricken with death. The flower-like mouth was drawn and pinched; the great sapphire-blue eyes were black with passionate anguish, terror and despair. She was placed in jail to await her trial at the fall session of the criminal court. The excitement in the hitherto quiet town rose to fever heat. Many points in the evidence seemed incomplete to thinking men. The weapon could not be found, nor could it be divined what had become of it. No reason could be given for the murder except the quarrel between Talma and her father and the ill will which existed between the girl and her step-mother.

When the trial was called Jeannette sat beside Talma in the prisoner's dock; both were arrayed in deepest mourning. Talma was pale and careworn, but seemed uplifted, spiritualized, as it were. Upon Jeannette the full realiza-tion of her sister's peril seemed to weigh heavily. She had changed much too: hollow cheeks, tottering steps, eyes blazing with fever, all suggestive of rapid and premature decay. From far-off Italy Edward Turner, growing famous in the art world, came to stand beside his girl-love in this hour of anguish.

The trial was a memorable one. No additional evidence had been collected to strengthen the prosecution; when the attorney-general rose to open the case against Talma he knew, as everyone else did, that he could not convict solely on the evidence adduced. What was given did not always bear upon the case, and brought out strange stories of Captain Jonathan's methods. Tales were told of sailors who had sworn to take his life, in revenge for injuries inflicted upon them by his hand. One or two clues were followed, but with-out avail. The judge summed up the evidence impartially, giving the pris-oner the benefit of the doubt. The points in hand furnished valuable collat-eral evidence, but were not direct proof. Although the moral presumption was against the prisoner, legal evidence was lacking to actually convict. The jury found the prisoner "Not Guilty," owing to the fact that the evidence was entirely circumstantial. The verdict was received in painful silence; then a murmur of discontent ran through the great crowd.

"She must have done it," said one; "who else has been benefitted by the horrible deed?"

"A poor woman would not have fared so well at the hands of the jury, nor a homely one either, for that matter," said another.

The great Gordon trial was ended; innocent or guilty, Talma Gordon could not be tried again. She was free; but her liberty, with blasted prospects and fair fame gone forever, was valueless to her. She seemed to have but one object in her mind: to find the murderer or murderers of her parents and half-brother. By her direction the shrewdest of detectives were employed and money flowed like water, but to no purpose; the Gordon tragedy remained a mystery. I had consented to act as one of the trustees of the immense Gordon estates and business interests, and by my advice the Misses Gordon went abroad. A year later I received a letter from Edward Turner, saying that Jeannette Gordon had died suddenly at Rome, and that Talma, after refusing all his entreaties for an early marriage, had disappeared, leaving no clue as to her whereabouts. I could give the poor fellow no comfort, although I had been duly notified of the death of Jeannette by Talma, in a letter telling me where to forward her remittances, and at the same time requesting me to keep her present residence a secret, especially from Edward.

I had established a sanitarium for the cure of chronic diseases at Gordon-ville, and absorbed in the cares of my profession I gave little thought to the Gordons. I seemed fated to be involved in mysteries.

A man claiming to be an Englishman, and fresh from the California gold fields, engaged board and professional service at my retreat. I found him suf-fering in the grasp of the tubercle-fiend—the last stages. He called himself Simon Cameron.

Seldom have I seen so fascinating and wicked a face. The lines of the mouth were cruel, the eyes cold and sharp, the smile mocking and evil. He had money in plenty but seemed to have no friends, for he had received no letters and had had no visitors in the time he had been with us. He was an enigma to me; and his nationality puzzled me, for of course I did not believe his story of being English. The peaceful influence of the house seemed to sooth him in a measure, and make his last steps to the mysterious valley as easy as possible. For a time he improved, and would sit or walk about the grounds and sing sweet songs for the pleasure of the other inmates. Strange to say, his malady only affected his voice at times. He sang quaint songs in a silvery tenor of great purity and sweetness that was delicious to the listening ear:

> "A wet sheet and a flowing sea,
> A wind that follows fast,
> And fills the white and rustling sail
> And bends the gallant mast;
> And bends the gallant mast, my boys;
> While like the eagle free,
> Away the good ship flies, and leaves
> Old England on the lea."

There are few singers on the lyric stage who could surpass Simon Cameron.

One night, a few weeks after Cameron's arrival, I sat in my office making up my accounts when the door opened and closed; I glanced up, expecting to see a servant. A lady advanced toward me. She threw back her veil, and then I saw that Talma Gordon, or her ghost, stood before me. After the first excitement of our meeting was over, she told me she had come direct from Paris, to place herself in my care. I had studied her attentively during the first moments of our meeting, and I felt that she was right; unless something unforeseen happened to arouse her from the stupor into which she seemed to have fallen, the last Gordon was doomed to an early death. The next day I told her I had cabled Edward Turner to come to her.

"It will do no good; I cannot marry him," was her only comment.

"Have you no feeling of pity for that faithful fellow?" I asked her sternly, provoked by her seeming indifference. I shall never forget the varied emotions depicted on her speaking face. Fully revealed to my gaze was the sight of a human soul tortured beyond the point of endurance; suffering all things, enduring all things, in the silent agony of despair.

In a few days Edward arrived, and Talma consented to see him and explain her refusal to keep her promise to him. You must be present, Doctor; it is due your long, tried friendship to know that I have not been fickle, but have acted from the best and strongest motives.

I shall never forget that day. It was directly after lunch that we met in the library. I was greatly excited, expecting I knew not what. Edward was agitated, too. Talma was the only calm one. She handed me what seemed to be a letter, with the request that I would read it. Even now I think I can repeat every word of the document, so indelibly are the words engraved upon my mind:

MY DARLING SISTER TALMA: When you read these lines I shall be no more, for I shall not live to see your life blasted by the same knowledge that has blighted mine. One evening, about a year before your expected return from Rome, I climbed into a hammock in one corner of the veranda outside the breakfast-room windows, intending to spend the twilight hours in lazy comfort, for it was very hot, enervating August weather. I fell asleep. I was awakened by voices. Because of the heat the rooms had been left in semi-darkness. As I lay there, lazily enjoying the beauty of the perfect summer night, my wandering thoughts were arrested by the words spoken by our father to Mrs. Gordon, for they were the occupants of the breakfast-room.

"Never fear, Mary; Johnny shall have it all—money, houses, land and business."

"But if you do go first, Jonathan, what will happen if the girls contest the will? People will think that they ought to have the money as it appears to be theirs by law. I never could survive the terrible disgrace of the story."

"Don't borrow trouble; all you would need to do would be to show them papers I have drawn up, and they would be glad to take their annuity and say nothing. After all, I do not think it is so bad. Jeanette can teach; Talma can paint; six hundred dollars a year is quite enough for them."

I had been somewhat mystified by the conversation until now. This last remark solved the riddle. What could he mean? teach, paint, six hundred a year! With my usual impetuosity I sprang from my resting-place, and in a moment stood in the room confronting my father, and asking what he meant. I could see plainly that both were disconcerted by my unexpected appearance.

"Ah, wretched girl! you have been listening. But what could I expect of your mother's daughter?"

At these words I felt the indignant blood rush to my head in a torrent. So it had been all my life. Before you could remember, Talma, I had felt my little heart swell with anger at the disparaging hints and slurs concerning our mother. Now was my time. I determined that tonight I would know why she was looked upon as an outcast, and her children subjected to every humiliation. So I replied to my father in bitter anger:

"I was not listening; I fell asleep in the hammock. What do you mean by a paltry six hundred a year each to Talma and to me? 'My mother's daughter' demands an explanation from you, sir, of the meaning of the monstrous injustice that you have always practised toward my sister and me."

"Speak more respectfully to your father, Jeannette," broke in Mrs. Gordon.

"How is it, madam, that you look for respect from one whom you have delighted to torment ever since you came into this most unhappy family?"

"Hush, both of you," said Captain Gordon, who seemed to have recovered from the dismay into which my sudden appearance and passionate words had plunged him. "I think I may as well tell you as to wait. Since you know so much, you may as well know the whole miserable story." He motioned me to a seat. I could see that he was deeply agitated. I seated myself in a chair he pointed out, in wonder and expectation,—expectation of I knew not what. I trembled. This was a supreme moment in my life; I felt it. The air was heavy with the intense stillness that had settled over us as the common sounds of day gave place to the early quiet of the rural evening. I could see Mrs. Gordon's face as she sat within the radius of the lighted hallway. There was a smile of triumph upon it. I clinched my hands and bit my lips until the blood came, in the effort to keep from screaming. What was I about to hear? At last he spoke:

"I was disappointed at your birth, and also at the birth of Talma. I wanted a male heir. When I knew that I should again be a father I was torn by hope and fear, but I comforted myself with the thought that luck would be with me in the birth of the third child. When the doctor brought me word that a son was born to the house of Gordon, I was wild with delight, and did not notice his disturbed countenance. In the midst of my joy he said to me:

"Captain Gordon, there is something strange about this birth. I want you to see this child."

Quelling my exultation I followed him to the nursery, and there, lying in the cradle, I saw a child dark as a mulatto, with the characteristic features of the Negro! I was stunned. Gradually it dawned upon me that there was something radically wrong. I turned to the doctor for an explanation.

"There is but one explanation, Captain Gordon; there is Negro blood in this child."

"There is no Negro blood in my veins," I said proudly. Then I paused—*the mother!*—I glanced at the doctor. He was watching me intently. The same thought was in his mind. I must have lived a thousand years in that cursed five seconds that I stood there confronting the physician and trying to think. "Come," said I to him, "let us end this suspense." Without thinking of the consequences, I hurried away to your mother and accused her of infidelity to her marriage vows. I raved like a madman. Your mother fell into convulsions; her life was despaired of. I sent for Mr. and Mrs. Franklin, and then I learned the truth. They were childless. One year while on a Southern tour, they befriended an octoroon girl who had been abandoned by her white lover. Her child was a beautiful baby girl. They, being Northern born, thought little of caste distinction because the child showed no trace of Negro blood. They determined to adopt it. They went abroad, secretly sending back word to their friends at a proper time, of the birth of a little daughter. No one doubted the truth of the statement. They made Isabel their heiress, and all went well until the birth of your brother. Your mother and the unfortunate babe died. This is the story which, if known, would bring dire disgrace upon the Gordon family.

To appease my righteous wrath, Mr. Franklin left a codicil to his will by which all the property is left at my disposal save a small annuity to you and your sister.

I sat there after he had finished his story, stunned by what I had heard. I understood, now, Mrs. Gordon's half contemptuous toleration and lack of consideration for us both. As I rose from my seat to leave the room I said to Captain Gordon:

"Still, in spite of all, sir, I am a Gordon, legally born. I will not tamely give up my birthright."

I left that room a broken-hearted girl, filled with a desire for revenge upon this man, my father, who by his manner disowned us without a regret. Not once in that remarkable interview did he speak of our mother as his wife; he quietly repudiated her and us with all the cold cruelty of relentless caste prejudice. I heard the treatment of your lover's proposal; I knew why Captain Gordon's consent to your marriage was withheld.

The night of the reception and dance was the chance for which I had waited, planned and watched. I crept from my window into the ivy-vines, and so down, down, until I stood upon the window-sill of Captain Gordon's room in the old left tower. How did I do it, you ask? I do not know. The house was silent after the revel; the darkness of the gathering storm favored me, too. The lawyer was there that day. The will was signed and put safely away among my father's papers. I was determined to have the will and the other documents bearing upon the case, and I would have revenge, too, for the cruelties we had suffered. With the old East Indian dagger firmly grasped I entered the room and found—that my revenge had been forestalled! The horror of the discovery I made that night restored me to reason and a realization of the crime I meditated. Scarce knowing what I did, I sought and found the papers, and crept back to my room as I had come. Do you wonder that my disease is past medical aid?"

I looked at Edward as I finished. He sat, his face covered with his hands. Finally he looked up with a glance of haggard despair: "God! Doctor, but this is too much. I could stand the stigma of murder, but add to that the pollution of Negro blood! No man is brave enough to face such a situation."

"It is as I thought it would be," said Talma sadly, while the tears poured over her white face. "I do not blame you, Edward."

He rose from his chair, rung my hand in a convulsive clasp, turned to Talma and bowed profoundly, with his eyes fixed upon the floor, hesitated, turned, paused, bowed again and abruptly left the room. So those two who had been lovers, parted. I turned to Talma, expecting her to give way. She smiled a pitiful smile, and said: "You see, Doctor, I knew best."

From that on she failed rapidly. I was restless. If only I could rouse her to an interest in life, she might live to old age. So rich, so young, so beautiful, so talented, so pure; I grew savage thinking of the injustice of the world. I had not reckoned on the power that never sleeps. Something was about to happen.

On visiting Cameron next morning I found him approaching the end. He had been sinking for a week very rapidly. As I sat by the bedside holding his emaciated hand, he fixed his bright, wicked eyes on me, and asked: "How long have I got to live?"

"Candidly, but a few hours."

"Thank you; well, I want death; I am not afraid to die. Doctor, Cameron is not my name."

"I never supposed it was."

"No? You are sharper than I thought. I heard all your talk yesterday with Talma Gordon. Curse the whole race!"

He clasped his bony fingers around my arm and gasped: *"I murdered the Gordons!"*

Had I the pen of a Dumas I could not paint Cameron as he told his story. It is a question with me whether this wheeling planet, home of the suffering, doubting, dying, may not hold worse agonies on its smiling surface than those of the conventional hell. I sent for Talma and a lawyer. We gave him stimulants, and then with broken intervals of coughing and prostration we got the story of the Gordon murder. I give it to you in a few words:

"I am an East Indian, but my name does not matter, Cameron is as good as any. There is many a soul crying in heaven and hell for vengeance on

Jonathan Gordon. Gold was his idol; and many a good man walked the plank, and many a gallant ship was stripped of her treasure, to satisfy his lust for gold. His blackest crime was the murder of my father, who was his friend, and has sailed with him for many a year as mate. One night these two went ashore together to bury their treasure. My father never returned from that expedition. His body was afterward found with a bullet through the heart on the shore where the vessel stopped that night. It was the custom then among pirates for the captain to kill the men who helped bury their treasure. Captain Gordon was no better than a pirate. An East Indian never forgets, and I swore by my mother's deathbed to hunt Captain Gordon down until I had avenged my father's murder. I had the plans of the Gordon estate, and fixed on the night of the reception in honor of Talma as the time for my vengeance. There is a secret entrance from the shore to the chambers where Captain Gordon slept; no one knew of it save the Captain and trusted members of his crew. My mother gave me the plans, and entrance and escape were easy."

"So the great mystery was solved. In a few hours Cameron was no more. We placed the confession in the hands of the police, and there the matter ended."

"But what became of Talma Gordon?" questioned the president. "Did she die?"

"Gentlemen," said the Doctor, rising to his feet and sweeping the faces of the company with his eagle gaze, "gentlemen, if you will follow me to the drawing-room, I shall have much pleasure in introducing you to my wife— *nee* Talma Gordon."

★

THEODORE ROOSEVELT *The College Graduate and Public Life*
Atlantic Monthly 74 (August 1894): 255–260

[By the time that Theodore Roosevelt became the twenty-sixth president in 1901 after the assassination of William McKinley, many Americans saw him as the embodiment of turn-of-the-century robust masculinity and aggressive Americanism. A ubiquitous presence in the monthly periodicals at century's end, Roosevelt was the author of sixty essays and the subject of sixteen. This essay anticipates *The Rough Riders*, his glorification of the invasion of Cuba during the Spanish-American War, which was serialized in *Scribner's* throughout 1899.]

THERE ARE ALWAYS, in our national life, certain tendencies that give us ground for alarm, and certain others that give us ground for hope. Among the latter we must put the fact that there has undoubtedly been a growing feeling among educated men that they are in honor bound to do their full share of the work of American public life.

We have in this country an equality of rights. It is the plain duty of every man to see that his rights are respected. That weak good nature which acquiesces in wrongdoing, whether from laziness, timidity, or indifference, is a very unwholesome quality. It should be second nature with every man to insist that he be given full justice. But if there is an equality of rights, there is an inequality of duties. It is proper to demand more from the man with exceptional advantages than from the man without them. A heavy moral obligation rests upon the man of means and upon the man of education to do their full duty by their country. On no class does this obligation rest more heavily than upon the men with a collegiate education, the men who are graduates of our universities. Their education gives them no right to feel the least superiority over any of their fellow citizens; but it certainly ought to make them feel that they should stand foremost in the honorable effort to serve the whole public by doing their duty as Americans in the body politic. This obligation very possibly rests even more heavily upon the men of means; but of this it is not necessary now to speak. The men of mere wealth never can have and never should have the capacity for doing good work that is possessed by the men of exceptional mental training; but that they may become both a laughing-stock and a menace to the community is made unpleasantly apparent by that portion of the New York business and social world which is most in evidence in the newspapers.

To the great body of men who have had exceptional advantages in the way of educational facilities we have a right, then, to look for good service to the State. The service may be rendered in many different ways. In a reasonable number of cases, the man may himself rise to high political position. That men actually do so rise is shown by the number of graduates of Harvard, Yale, and our other universities who are now taking a prominent part in public life. These cases must necessarily, however, form but a small part of the whole. The enormous majority of our educated men have to make their own living, and are obliged to take up careers in which they must work heart and soul to succeed. Nevertheless, the man of business and the man of science, the doctor of divinity and the doctor of law, the architect, the engineer, and the writer, all alike owe a positive duty to the community, the neglect of which they cannot excuse on any plea of their private affairs. They are bound to follow understandingly the course of public events; they are bound to try to estimate and form judgment upon public men; and they are bound to act intelligently and effectively in support of the principles which they deem to be right and for the best interests of the country.

The most important thing for this class of educated men to realize is that

"Yes, Sah,

Armour's Pork and Beans are just as good as Home Made. Beans to be wholesome must be cooked right; these are."

Convenient too, these are the only Beans sold in KEY OPENING 1, 2 and 3 pound cans.

Delicious Hot or Cold.   Ready for Use.

Armour & Company, Chicago.

FIGURE 7   This advertisement features a nostalgic scene and invokes several visible "types," among them the genteel adventurers who are returning to nature, a portrait linked to the ethos of sport. Also visible is a nostalgic reference to the black servant, who is reminiscent of a Southern slave. (*Scribner's*, 1895)

they do not really form a class at all. I have used the word in default of another, but I have merely used it roughly to group together people who have had unusual opportunities of a certain kind. A large number of the people to whom these opportunities are offered fail to take advantage of them, and a very much larger number of those to whom they have not been offered succeed none the less in making them for themselves. An educated man must not go into politics as such; he must go in simply as an American; and when he is once in, he will speedily realize that he must work very hard indeed, or he will be upset by some other American, with no education at all, but with much natural capacity. His education ought to make him feel particularly ashamed of himself if he acts meanly or dishonorably, or in any way falls short of the ideal of good citizenship, and it ought to make him feel that he must show that he has profited by it; but it should certainly give him no feeling of superiority until by actual work he has shown that superiority. In other words, the educated man must realize that he is living in a democracy and under democratic conditions, and that he is entitled to no more respect and consideration than he can win by actual performance.

This must be steadily kept in mind not only by educated men themselves, but particularly by the men who give the tone to our great educational institutions. These educational institutions, if they are to do their best work, must strain every effort to keep their life in touch with the life of the nation at the present day. This is necessary for the country, but it is very much more necessary for the educated men themselves. It is a misfortune for any land if its people of cultivation take little part in shaping its destiny; but the misfortune is far greater for the people of cultivation. The country has a right to demand the honest and efficient service of every man in it, but especially of every man who has had the advantage of rigid mental and moral training; the country is so much the poorer when any class of honest men fail to do their duty by it, but the loss to the class itself is immeasurable. If our educated men as a whole become incapable of playing their full part in our life, if they cease doing their share of the rough, hard work which must be done, and grow to take a position of mere dilettantism in our public affairs, they will speedily sink in relation to their fellows who really do the work of governing, until they stand toward them as a cultivated, ineffective man with a taste for bric-a-brac stands toward a great artist. When once a body of citizens becomes thoroughly out of touch and out of temper with the national life, its usefulness is gone, and its power of leaving its mark on the times is gone also.

The first great lesson which the college graduate should learn is the lesson of work rather than of criticism. Criticism is necessary and useful; it is often indispensable; but it can never take the place of action, or be even a poor substitute for it. The function of the mere critic is of very subordinate usefulness. It is the doer of deeds who actually counts in the battle for life, and not the man who looks on and says how the fight ought to be fought, without himself sharing the stress and the danger.

There is, however, a need for proper critical work. Wrongs should be strenuously and fearlessly denounced; evil principles and evil men should be condemned. The politician who cheats or swindles, or the newspaper man who lies in any form, should be made to feel that he is an object of scorn for all honest men. We need fearless criticism; but we need that it should also be intelligent. At present, the man who is most apt to regard himself as an intelligent critic of our political affairs is often the man who knows nothing whatever about them. Criticism which is ignorant or prejudiced is a source of great harm to the nation; and where ignorant or prejudiced critics are themselves educated men, their attitude does real harm also to the class to which they belong.

The tone of a portion of the press of the country toward public men, and especially toward political opponents, is degrading, all forms of coarse and noisy slander being apparently considered legitimate weapons to employ against men of the opposite party or faction. Unfortunately, not a few of the journals that pride themselves upon being independent in politics, and the organs of cultivated men, betray the same characteristics in a less coarse but quite as noxious form. All these journals do great harm by accustoming good citizens to see their public men, good and bad, assailed indiscriminately as scoundrels. The effect is twofold: the citizen learning, on the one hand, to disbelieve any statement he sees in any newspaper, so that the attacks on evil lose their edge; and on the other, gradually acquiring a deep-rooted belief that all public men are more or less bad. In consequence, his political instinct becomes hopelessly blurred, and he grows unable to tell the good representative from the bad. The worst offense that can be committed against the Republic is the offense of the public man who betrays his trust; but second only to it comes the offense of the man who tries to persuade others that an honest and efficient public man is dishonest or unworthy. This is a wrong that can be committed in a great many ways. Downright foul abuse may be, after all, less dangerous than incessant misstatements, sneers, and those half truths that are the meanest lies.

For educated men of weak fibre, there lies a real danger in that species of literary work which appeals to their cultivated senses because of its scholarly and pleasant tone, but which enjoins as the proper attitude to assume in public life one of mere criticism and negation; which teaches the adoption toward public men and public nadirs of that sneering tone which so surely denotes a mean and small mind. If a man does not have belief and enthusiasm, the chances are small indeed that he will ever do a man's work in the world; and the paper or the college which, by its general course tends to eradicate this power of belief and enthusiasm, this desire for work, has rendered to the young men under its influence the worst service it could possibly render. Good can often be done by criticizing sharply and severely the wrong; but excessive indulgence in criticism is never anything but bad, and no amount of criticism can in any way take the place of active and zealous warfare for the right.

Again, there is a certain tendency in college life, a tendency encouraged by some of the very papers referred to, to make educated men shrink from contact with the rough people who do the world's work, and associate only with one another and with those who think as they do. This is a most dangerous tendency. It is very agreeable to deceive oneself into the belief that one is performing the whole duty of man by sitting at home in ease, doing nothing wrong, and confining one's participation in politics to conversations and meetings with men who have had the same training and look at things in the same way. It is always a temptation to do this, because those who do nothing else often speak as if in some way they deserved credit for their attitude, and as if they stood above their brethren who plough the rough fields.

Moreover, many people whose political work is done more or less after this fashion are very noble and very sincere in their aims and aspirations, and are striving for what is best and most decent in public life.

Nevertheless, this is a snare round which it behooves every young man to walk carefully. Let him beware of associating only with the people of his own caste and of his own little ways of political thought. Let him learn that he must deal with the mass of men; that he must go out and stand shoulder to shoulder with his friends of every rank, and must bear himself well in the hurly-burly. He must not be frightened by the many unpleasant features of the contact, and he must not expect to have it all his own way, or to accomplish too much. He will meet with checks and will make many mistakes; but if he perseveres, he will achieve a measure of success and will do a measure of good such as is never possible to the refined, cultivated, intellectual men who shrink aside from the actual fray.

Yet again, college men must learn to be as practical in politics as they would be in business or in law. It is surely to say that by "practical" I do not mean anything that savors in the least of dishonesty. On the contrary, a college man is peculiarly bound to keep a high ideal and to be true to it: but he must work in practical ways to try to realize this ideal, and must not refuse to do anything because he cannot get everything. One especially necessary thing is to know the facts by actual experience, and not to take refuge in mere theorizing. There are always a number of excellent and well-meaning men whom we grow to regard with amused impatience because they waste all their energies on some visionary scheme which, even if it were not visionary, would be useless. When they come to deal with political questions, these men are apt to err from sheer lack of familiarity with the workings of our government. No man ever really learned from books how to manage a governmental system. Books are admirable adjuncts, and the statesman who has carefully studied them is far more apt to do good work than if he had not; but if he has never done anything but study books he will not be a statesman at all. Thus, every young politician should of course read "The Federalist." It is the greatest book of the kind that has ever been written. Hamilton, Madison, and Jay would have been poorly equipped for writing it if they had not possessed an extensive acquaintance with literature, and in particular if they had not been careful students of political literature; but the great cause of the value of their writings lay in the fact that they knew by actual work and association what practical politics meant. They had helped to shape the political thought of the country, and to do its legislative and executive work, and so they were in a condition to speak understandingly about it. For similar reasons, Mr. Bryce's "American Commonwealth" has a value possessed by no other book of the kind, largely because Mr. Bryce is himself an active member of Parliament, a man of good standing and some leadership in his own party, and a practical politician. In the same way, a life of Washington by Cabot Lodge, a sketch of Lincoln by Carl Schurz, a biography of Pitt by Lord Rosebery, have an added value because of the writers' own work in politics.

It is always a pity to see men fritter away their energies on any pointless scheme; and unfortunately, a good many of our educated people when they come to deal with politics, do just such frittering. Take, for instance, the queer freak of arguing in favor of establishing what its advocates are pleased to call "responsible government" in our institutions, or in other words of grafting certain features of the English parliamentary system upon our own presidential and congressional system. This agitation was too largely deficient in body to enable it to last, and it has now, I think, died away: but at one time quite a number of our men who spoke of themselves as students of political history were engaged in treating this scheme as something serious. Few men who had ever taken an active part in politics, or who had studied politics in the way that a doctor is expected to study surgery and medicine, so much as gave it a thought; but very intelligent men did, just because they were misdirecting their energies, and were wholly ignorant that they ought to know practically about a problem before they attempted its solution. The English, or so-called "responsible," theory of parliamentary government is one entirely incompatible with our own governmental institutions. It could not be put into operation here save by absolutely sweeping away the United States Constitution. Incidentally, I may say it would be to the last degree undesirable, if it were practicable. But this is not the point upon which I wish to dwell; the point is that it was wholly impracticable to put it into operation, and that an agitation favoring this kind of government was from its nature unintelligent. The people who wrote about it wasted their time, whereas they could have spent it to great advantage had they seriously studied our institutions and sought to devise practicable and desirable methods of increasing and centring genuine responsibility—for all thinking men agree that there is an undoubted need for a change in this direction.

But of course much of the best work that has been done in the field of political study has been done by men who were not active politicians, though they were careful and painstaking students of the phenomena of politics. The back numbers of our leading magazines afford proof of this. Certain of the governmental essays by such writers as Mr. Lawrence Lowell and Professor A.B. Hart, and especially such books as that on the "Speakers' Powers and Duties," by Miss Follet, have been genuine and valuable contributions to our political thought. These essays have been studied carefully not only by scholars, but by men engaged in practical politics, because they were written with good judgment and keen insight after careful investigation of the facts, and so deserved respectful attention.

It is a misfortune for any people when the paths of the practical and the theoretical politicians diverge so widely that they have no common standing-ground. When the Greek thinkers began to devote their attention to purely visionary politics of the kind found in Plato's Republic, while the Greek practical politicians simply exploited the quarrelsome little commonwealths in their own interests, then the end of Greek liberty was at hand. No government that cannot command the respectful support of the best thinkers is in an entirely sound condition; but it is well to keep in mind the remark of Frederick the Great, that if he wished to punish a province, he would allow it to be governed by the philosophers. It is a great misfortune for the country when the practical politician and the doctrinaire have no point in common, but the misfortune is, if anything, greatest for the doctrinaire. The ideal to be set before the student of politics and the practical politician alike is the ideal of "The Federalist." Each man should realize that he cannot do his best, either in the study of politics or in applied politics unless he has a working knowledge of both branches. A limited number of people can do good work by the careful study of governmental institutions, but they can do it only if they have themselves a practical knowledge of the workings of these institutions. A very large number of people, on the other hand, may do excellent work in politics without much theoretic knowledge of the subject; but without this knowledge they cannot rise to the highest rank, while in any rank their capacity to do good work will be immensely increased if they have such knowledge.

There are certain other qualities, about which it is hardly necessary to speak. If an educated man is not heartily American in instinct and feeling and taste and sympathy, he will amount to nothing in our public life. Patriotism, love of country, and pride in the flag which symbolizes country may be feelings which the race will at some period outgrow, but at present they are very real and strong, and the man who lacks them is a useless creature, a mere incumbrance to the land.

A man of sound political instincts can no more subscribe to the doctrine of absolute independence of party on the one hand than to that of unquestioning party allegiance on the other. No man can accomplish much unless he works in an organization with others, and this organization, no matter how temporary, is a party for the time being. But that man is a dangerous citizen who so far mistakes means for ends as to become servile in his devotion to his party, and afraid to leave it when the party goes wrong. To deify either independence or party allegiance merely as such is a little absurd. It depends entirely upon the motive, the purpose, the result. For the last two years, the senator who, beyond all his colleagues in the United States Senate, has shown himself independent of party ties is the very man to whom the leading champions of independence in politics most strenuously object. The truth is, simply, that there are times when it may be the duty of a man to break with his liberty, and there are other times when it may be his duty to stand by his party, even though, on some points, he thinks that party wrong; he must be prepared to leave it when necessary, and he must not sacrifice his influence by leaving it unless it is necessary. If we had no party allegiance, our politics would become mere windy anarchy, and, under present conditions, our government could hardly continue at all. If we had no independence, we should always be running the risk of the most degraded kind of despotism—the despotism of the party boss and the party machine.

It is just the same way about compromises. Occasionally one hears some well-meaning person say of another, apparently in praise, that he is "never willing to compromise." It is a mere truism to say that, in politics, there has to be one continual compromise. Of course now and then questions arise upon which a compromise is inadmissible. There could be no compromise with secession, and there was none. There should be no avoidable compromise about any great moral question. But only a very few great reforms or great measures of any kind can be carried through without concession. No student of American history needs to be reminded that the Constitution itself is a bundle of compromises and was adopted only because of this fact, and that the same thing is true of the Emancipation Proclamation.

In conclusion, then, the man with a university education is in honor bound to take an active part in our political life, and to do his full duty as a citizen by helping his fellow citizens to the extent of his power in the exercise of the rights of self-government. He is bound to rank action far above criticism, and to understand that the man deserving of credit is the man who actually does the things, even though imperfectly, and not the man who confines himself to talking about how they ought to be done. He is bound to have a high ideal and to strive to realize it, and yet he must make up his mind that he will never be able to get the highest good, and that he must devote himself with all his energy to getting the best that he can. Finally, his work must be disinterested and honest, and it must be given without regard to his own success or failure, and without regard to the effect it has upon his own fortunes; and while he must show the virtues of uprightness and tolerance and gentleness, he must also show the sterner virtues of courage, resolution, and hardihood, and the desire to war with merciless effectiveness against the existence of wrong.

★

BOOKER T. WASHINGTON *The Awakening of the Negro*
Atlantic Monthly 78 (September 1896): 322–328

[The founder of Tuskegee Institute and the author of *Up from Slavery* (1901), which was originally serialized in the *Outlook* (November 1900–February 1901), Washington was known as the "Moses of his race." The years from 1895 through 1915 are often called the "Era of Booker T. Washington" because he emerged as a figure of national importance after the controversial "Atlanta Exposition Address" of 1895 in which he proposed a new and what many considered conciliatory relationship between black and white Americans.]

WHEN A MERE BOY, I saw a young colored man, who had spent several years in school, sitting in a common cabin in the South, studying a French grammar. I noted the poverty, the untidiness, the want of system and thrift, that existed about the cabin, notwithstanding his knowledge of French and other academic subjects. Another time, when riding on the outer edges of a town in the South, I heard the sound of a piano coming from a cabin of the same kind. Contriving some excuse, I entered, and began a conversation with the young colored woman who was playing, and who had recently returned from a boarding-school, where she had been studying instrumental music among other things. Despite the fact that her parents were living in a rented cabin, eating poorly cooked food, surrounded with poverty, and having almost none of the conveniences of life, she had persuaded them to rent a piano for four or five dollars per month. Many such instances as these, in connection with my own struggles, impressed upon me the importance of making a study of our needs as a race, and applying the remedy accordingly.

Some one may be tempted to ask, Has not the negro boy or girl as good a right to study a French grammar and instrumental music as the white youth? I answer, Yes, but in the present condition of the negro race in this country there is need of something more. Perhaps I may be forgiven for the seeming egotism if I mention the expansion of my own life partly as an example of what I mean. My earliest recollection is of a small one-room log hut on a large slave plantation in Virginia. After the close of the war, while working in the coalmines of West Virginia for the support of my mother, I heard in some accidental way of the Hampton Institute. When I learned that it was an institution where a black boy could study, could have a chance to work for his board, and at the same time be taught how to work and to realize the dignity of labor, I resolved to go there. Bidding my mother good-by, I started out one morning to find my way to Hampton, though I was almost penniless and had no definite idea where Hampton was. By walking, begging rides, and paying for a portion of the journey on the steam-cars, I finally succeeded in reaching the city of Richmond, Virginia. I was without money or friends. I slept under a sidewalk, and by working on a vessel next day I earned money to continue my way to the institute, where I arrived with a surplus of fifty cents. At Hampton I found the opportunity—in the way of buildings, teachers, and industries provided by the generous—to get training in the classroom and by practical touch with industrial life, to learn thrift, economy, and push. I was surrounded by an atmosphere of business, Christian influence, and a spirit of self-help that seemed to have awakened every faculty in me, and caused me for the first time to realize what it meant to be a man instead of a piece of property.

While there I resolved that when I had finished the course of training I would go into the far South, into the Black Belt of the South, and give my life to providing the same kind of opportunity for self-reliance and self-awakening that I had found provided for me at Hampton. My work began at Tuskegee, Alabama, in 1881, in a small shanty and church, with one teacher and thirty students, without a dollar's worth of property. The spirit of work and of industrial thrift, with aid from the State and generosity from the North, has enabled us to develop an institution of eight hundred students gathered from nineteen States, with seventy-nine instructors, fourteen hundred acres of land, and thirty buildings, including large and small; in all, property valued at $280,000. Twenty-five industries have been organized, and the whole work is carried on at an annual cost of about $80,000 in cash; two fifths of the annual expense so far has gone into permanent plant.

What is the object of all this outlay? First, it must be borne in mind that we have in the South a peculiar and unprecedented state of things. It is of the utmost importance that our energy be given to meeting conditions that exist right about us rather than conditions that existed centuries ago or that exist in countries a thousand miles away. What are the cardinal needs among the seven millions of colored people in the South, most of whom are to be found on the plantations? Roughly, these needs may be stated as food, clothing, shelter, education, proper habits, and a settlement of race relations. The seven millions of colored people of the South cannot be reached directly by any missionary agency, but they can be reached by sending out among them strong selected young men and women, with the proper training of head, hand, and heart, who will live among these masses and show them how to lift themselves up.

The problem that the Tuskegee Institute keeps before itself constantly is how to prepare these leaders. From the outset, in connection with religious and academic training, it has emphasized industrial or hand training as a means of finding the way out of present conditions. First, we have found the industrial teaching useful in giving the student a chance to work out a portion of his expenses while in school. Second, the school furnishes labor that has an economic value, and at the same time gives the student a chance to acquire knowledge and skill while performing the labor. Most of all, we find the industrial system valuable in teaching economy, thrift, and the dignity of labor, and in giving moral backbone to students. The fact that a student goes out into the world conscious of his power to build a house or a wagon, or to make a harness, gives him a certain confidence and moral independence that he would not possess without such training.

A more detailed example of our methods at Tuskegee may be of interest. For example, we cultivate by student labor six hundred and fifty acres of land. The object is not only to cultivate the land in a way to make it pay our boarding department, but at the same time to teach the students, in addition to the practical work, something of the chemistry of the soil, the best methods of drainage, dairying, the cultivation of fruit, the care of livestock and tools, and scores of other lessons needed by a people whose main dependence is on agriculture. Notwithstanding that eighty-five per cent of the colored people in the South live by agriculture in some form, aside from what has been done by Hampton, Tuskegee, and one or two other institutions practically nothing has been attempted in the direction of teaching them about the very industry from which the masses of our people must get their subsistence. Friends have recently provided means for the erection of a large new chapel at Tuskegee. Our students have made the bricks for this chapel. A large part of the timber is sawed by students at our own sawmill, the plans are drawn by our teacher of architecture and mechanical drawing, and students do the brick-masonry, plastering, painting, carpentry work, tinning, slating, and make most of the furniture. Practically, the whole chapel will be built and furnished by student labor; in the end the school will have the building for permanent use, and the students will have a knowledge of the trades employed in its construction. In this way all but three of the thirty buildings on the grounds have been erected. While the young men do the kinds of work I have mentioned, the young women to a large extent make, mend, and launder the clothing of the young men, and thus are taught important industries.

One of the objections sometimes urged against industrial education for the negro is that it aims merely to teach him to work on the same plan that he was made to follow when in slavery. This is far from being the object at Tuskegee. At the head of each of the twenty-five industrial departments we have an intelligent and competent instructor, just as we have in our history classes, so that the student is taught not only practical brick-masonry, for example, but also the underlying principles of that industry, the mathematics and the mechanical and architectural drawing. Or he is taught how to become master of the forces of nature so that, instead of cultivating corn in the old way, he can use a corn cultivator, that lays off the furrows, drops the corn into them, and covers it, and in this way he can do more work than three men by the old process of corn-planting; at the same time much of the toil is eliminated and labor is dignified. In a word, the constant aim is to show the student how to put brains into every process of labor; how to bring his knowledge of mathematics and the sciences into farming, carpentry, forging, foundry work; how to dispense as soon as possible with the old form of ante-bellum labor. In the erection of the chapel just referred to, instead of letting the money which was given us go into outside hands, we make it accomplish three objects: first, it provides the chapel; second, it gives the students a chance to get a practical knowledge of the trades connected with building; and third, it enables them to earn something toward the payment of board while receiving academic and industrial training.

Having been fortified at Tuskegee by education of mind, skill of hand, Christian character, ideas of thrift, economy, and push, and a spirit of independence, the student is sent out to become a centre of influence and light in showing the masses of our people in the Black Belt of the South how to lift themselves up. How can this be done? I give but one or two examples. Ten years ago a young colored man came to the institute from one of the large plantation districts; he studied in the class-room a portion of the time, and received practical and theoretical training on the farm the remainder of the time. Having finished his course at Tuskegee, he returned to his plantation home, which was in a county where the colored people outnumber the whites six to one, as is true of many of the counties in the Black Belt of the South. He found the negroes in debt. Ever since the war they had been mortgaging their crops for the food on which to live while the crops were growing. The majority of them were living from hand to mouth on rented land, in small, one-room log cabins, and attempting to pay a rate of interest on their advances that ranged from fifteen to forty per cent per annum. The school had been taught in a wreck of a log cabin, with no apparatus, and had never been in session longer than three months out of twelve. With as many as eight or ten persons of all ages and conditions and of both sexes huddled together in one cabin year after year, and with a minister whose only aim was to work upon the emotions of the people, one can imagine something of the moral and religious state of the community.

But the remedy. In spite of the evil, the negro got the habit of work from slavery. The rank and file of the race, especially those on the Southern plantations, work hard, but the trouble is, what they earn gets away from them in high rents, crop mortgages, whiskey, snuff, cheap jewelry, and the like. The young man just referred to had been trained at Tuskegee, as most of our graduates are, to meet just this condition of things. He took the three months' public school as a nucleus for his work. Then he organized the older people into a club, or conference, that held meetings every week. In these meetings he taught the people in a plain, simple manner how to save their money, how to farm in a better way, how to sacrifice,—to live on bread and potatoes, if need be, till they could get out of debt, and begin the buying of lands.

Soon a large proportion of the people were in condition to make contracts for the buying of homes (land is very cheap in the South), and to live without mortgaging their crops. Not only this: under the guidance and leadership of this teacher, the first year that he was among them they learned how, by contributions in money and labor, to build a neat, comfortable schoolhouse that replaced the wreck of a log cabin formerly used. The following year the weekly meetings were continued, and two months were added to the original three months of school. The next year two more months were added. The improvement has gone on, until now these people have every year an eight months' school.

I wish my readers could have the chance that I have had of going into this community. I wish they could look into the faces of the people and see them beaming with hope and delight. I wish they could see the two or three room cottages that have taken the place of the usual one-room cabin, the well-cultivated farms, and the religious life of the people that now means something more than the name. The teacher has a good cottage and a well-kept farm that serve as models. In a word, a complete revolution has been wrought in the industrial, educational, and religious life of this whole community by reason of the fact that they have had this leader, this guide and object-lesson, to show them how to take the money and effort that had hitherto been scattered to the wind in mortgages and high rents, in whiskey and gewgaws, and concentrate them in the direction of their own uplifting. One community on its feet presents an object-lesson for the adjoining communities, and soon improvements show themselves in other places.

Another student who received academic and industrial training at Tuskegee established himself, three years ago, as a blacksmith and wheelwright in a community, and, in addition to the influence of his successful business enterprise, he is fast making the same kind of changes in the life of the people about him that I have just recounted. It would be easy for me to fill many pages describing the influence of the Tuskegee graduates in every part of the South. We keep it constantly in the minds of our students and graduates that the industrial or material condition of the masses of our people must be improved, as well as the intellectual, before there can be any permanent change in their moral and religious life. We find it a pretty hard thing to make a good Christian of a hungry man. No matter how much our people "get happy" and "shout" in church, if they go home at night from church hungry, they are tempted to find something before morning. This is a principle of human nature, and is not confined to the negro.

The negro has within him immense power for self-uplifting, but for years it will be necessary to guide and stimulate him. The recognition of this power led us to organize, five years ago, what is now known as the Tuskegee Negro Conference,—a gathering that meets every February, and is composed of about eight hundred representative colored men and women from all sections of the Black Belt. They come in oxcarts, mule-carts, buggies, on mule-back and horseback, on foot, by railroad; some traveling all night in order to be present. The matters considered at the conferences are those that the colored people have it within their own power to control: such as the evils of the mortgage system, the one-room cabin, buying on credit, the importance of owning a home and of putting money in the bank, how to build school-houses and prolong the school term, and how to improve their moral and religious condition.

As a single example of the results, one delegate reported that since the conferences were started five years ago eleven people in his neighborhood had bought homes, fourteen had got out of debt, and a number had stopped mortgaging their crops. Moreover, a school-house had been built by the people themselves, and the school term had been extended from three to six months; and with a look of triumph he exclaimed, "We is done stopped libin' in de ashes!"

Besides this Negro Conference for the masses of the people, we now have a gathering at the same time known as the Workers' Conference, composed of the officers and instructors in the leading colored schools of the South. After listening to the story of the conditions and needs from the people themselves, the Workers' Conference finds much food for thought and discussion.

Nothing else so soon brings about right relations between the two races in the South as the industrial progress of the negro. Friction between the races will pass away in proportion as the black man, by reason of his skill, intelligence, and character, can produce something that the white man wants or respects in the commercial world. This is another reason why at Tuskegee we push the industrial training. We find that as every year we put into a Southern community colored men who can start a brick-yard, a sawmill, a tin-shop, or a printing-office,—men who produce something that makes the white man partly dependent upon the negro, instead of all the dependence being on the other side,—a change takes place in the relations of the races.

Let us go on for a few more years knitting our business and industrial relations into those of the white man, till a black man gets a mortgage on a white man's house that he can foreclose at will. The white man on whose house the mortgage rests will not try to prevent that negro from voting when he goes to the polls. It is through the dairy farm, the truck garden, the trades, and commercial life, largely, that the negro is to find his way to the enjoyment of all his rights. Whether he will or not, a white man respects a negro who owns a two-story brick house.

What is the permanent value of the Tuskegee system of training to the South in a broader sense? In connection with this, it is well to bear in mind that slavery taught the white man that labor with the hands was something fit for the negro only, and something for the white man to come into contact with just as little as possible. It is true that there was a large class of poor white people who labored with the hands, but they did it because they were not able to secure negroes to work for them; and these poor whites were constantly trying to imitate the slave-holding class in escaping labor, and they too regarded it as anything but elevating. The negro in turn looked down upon the poor whites with a certain contempt because they had to work. The negro, it is to be borne in mind, worked under constant protest, because he felt that his labor was being unjustly required, and he spent almost as much effort in planning how to escape work as in learning how to work. Labor with him was a badge of degradation. The white man was held up before him as the highest type of civilization, but the negro noted that this highest type of civilization himself did no labor; hence he argued that the less work he did, the more nearly he would be like a white man. Then, in addition to these influences, the slave system discouraged labor-saving machinery. To use labor-saving machinery intelligence was required, and intelligence and slavery were not on friendly terms; hence the negro always associated labor with toil, drudgery, something to be escaped. When the negro first became free, his idea of education was that it was something that would soon put him in the same position as regards work that his recent master had occupied. Out of these conditions grew the Southern habit of putting off till to-morrow and the day after the duty that should be done promptly to-day. The leaky house was not repaired while the sun shone, for then the rain did not come through. While the rain was falling, no one cared to expose himself to stop the leak. The plough, on the same principle, was left where the last furrow was run, to rot and rust in the field during the winter. There was no need to repair the wooden chimney that was exposed to the fire, because water could be thrown on it when it was on fire. There was no need to trouble about the payment of a debt to-day, for it could just as well be paid next week or next year. Besides these conditions, the whole South, at the close of the war, was without proper food, clothing, and shelter,—was in need of habits of thrift and economy and of something laid up for a rainy day.

To me it seemed perfectly plain that here was a condition of things that could not be met by the ordinary process of education. At Tuskegee we became convinced that the thing to do was to make a careful systematic study of the condition and needs of the South, especially the Black Belt, and to bend our efforts in the direction of meeting these needs, whether we were following a well-beaten track, or were hewing out a new path to meet conditions probably without a parallel in the world. After fourteen years of experience and observation, what is the result? Gradually but surely, we find that all through the South the disposition to look upon labor as a disgrace is on the wane, and the parents who themselves sought to escape work are so anxious to give their children training in intelligent labor that every institution which gives training in the handicrafts is crowded, and many (among them Tuskegee) have to refuse admission to hundreds of applicants. The influence of the Tuskegee system is shown again by the fact that almost every little school at the remotest cross-roads is anxious to be known as an industrial school, or, as some of the colored people call it, an "industrus" school.

The social lines that were once sharply drawn between those who labored with the hand and those who did not are disappearing. Those who formerly sought to escape labor, now when they see that brains and skill rob labor of the toil and drudgery once associated with it, instead of trying to avoid it are willing to pay to be taught how to engage in it. The South is beginning to see labor raised up, dignified and beautified, and in this sees its salvation. In proportion as the love of labor grows, the large idle class which has long been one of the curses of the South disappears. As its members become absorbed in occupations, they have less time to attend to everybody else's business, and more time for their own.

The South is still an undeveloped and unsettled country, and for the next half century and more the greater part of the energy of the masses will be needed to develop its material opportunities. Any force that brings the rank and file of the people to a greater love of industry is therefore especially valuable. This result industrial education is surely bringing about. It stimulates production and increases trade,—trade between the races,—and in this new and engrossing relation both forget the past. The white man respects the vote of the colored man who does $10,000 worth of business, and the more business the colored man has, the more careful he is how he votes.

Immediately after the war, there was a large class of Southern people who feared that the opening of the free schools to the freedmen and the poor whites—the education of the head alone—would result merely in increasing the class who sought to escape labor, and that the South would soon be overrun by the idle and vicious. But as the results of industrial combined with academic training begin to show themselves in hundreds of communities that have been lifted up through the medium of the Tuskegee system, these former prejudices against education are being removed. Many of those who a few years ago opposed general education are now among its warmest advocates.

This industrial training, emphasizing as it does the idea of economic production, is gradually bringing the South to the point where it is feeding itself. Before the war, and long after it, the South made what little profit was received from the cotton crop, and sent its earnings out of the South to purchase food supplies,—meat, bread, canned vegetables, and the like; but the improved methods of agriculture are fast changing this habit. With the newer methods of labor, which teach promptness and system, and emphasize the worth of the beautiful,—the moral value of the well-painted house, and the fence with every paling and nail in its place,—we are bringing to bear upon the South an influence that is making it a new country in industry, education, and religion.

★

SUSAN B. ANTHONY *The Status of Woman,*
Past, Present, and Future
Arena 17 (May 1897): 903–908

[Committed to a full range of political, social, and ethical debates, the *Arena*, known for its reformist bent, promoted discussions of factory conditions, child labor, and suffrage. Here, Susan B. Anthony, the preeminent organizer and strategist for women's enfranchisement, traces the effects of the Seneca Falls women's convention in 1848, contrasts "helpless, dependent, fettered" women of the past to those of the present, and predicts female suffrage and the holding of public office by women.]

A REQUEST FROM *The Arena* to state what really has come of our half century of agitation, and what is sure to come in the near future, will be used as the basis of this article.

Fifty years ago woman in the United States was without a recognized individuality in any department of life. No provision was made in public or private schools for her education in anything beyond the rudimentary branches. An educated woman was a rarity, and was gazed upon with something akin to awe. The women who were known in the world of letters, in the entire country, could be easily counted upon the ten fingers. Margaret Fuller, educated by her father, a Harvard graduate and distinguished lawyer, stood preeminently at the head, and challenged the admiration of such men as Emerson, Channing, and Greeley.

In those days the women of the family were kept closely at home, carding, spinning, and weaving, making the butter and cheese, knitting and sewing, working by day and night, planning and economizing, to educate the boys of the family. Thus the girls toiled so long as they remained under the home roof, their services belonging to father by law and by custom. Any kind of a career for a woman was a thing undreamed of. Among the poorer families the girls might go about among the neighbors and earn a miserable pittance at house work or sewing. When the boy was twenty-one, the father agreed to pay him a fixed sum per annum, thenceforth, for his services, or, in default of this, he was free to carry his labor where it would receive a financial reward. No such agreement ever was made with the girls of the family. They continued to work without wages after they were twenty-one, exactly as they did before. When they married, their services were transferred to the husband,

and were considered to be bountifully rewarded by food, shelter, and usually a very scanty supply of clothes. Any wages the wife might earn outside of the home belonged by law to the husband. No matter how drunken and improvident he might be; no matter how great her necessities and those of the children, if the employer paid the money to her he could be prosecuted by the husband and compelled to pay it again to him.

Cases were frequent where fathers willed all of their property to the sons, entirely cutting the daughters out. Where, however, the daughters received property, it passed directly into the sole possession of the husband, and all the rents and profits belonged to him to use as he pleased. At his death he could dispose of it by will, depriving the wife of all but what was called the "widow's dower," a life interest in one-third of that which was by right her own property. She lost not only the right to her earnings and her property, but also the right to the custody of her person and her children. The husband could apprentice the children at an early age, in spite of the mother's protest and at his death could dispose of the children by will, even an unborn child. The wife could neither sue nor be sued, nor testify in the courts. The phrase in constant use in legal decisions was, "The wife is dead in law," or, "Husband and wife are one, and that one the husband." According to the English common law, which then prevailed in every State in the Union except Louisiana, a man might beat his wife up to the point of endangering her life, without being liable to prosecution.

Fifty years ago no occupations were open to women except cooking, teaching, and factory work. Very few women were sufficiently educated to teach, but those who could do so received from $4 to $8 a month and "boarded round," while men, for exactly the same service, received $30 a month and board. Every woman must marry, either with or without love, for the sake of support, or be doomed to a life of utter dependence, living, after the death of parents, in the home of a married brother or sister, the druge and burden-bearer of the family, without any financial recompense, and usually looked upon with disrespect by the children. Women might work like galley slaves for their own relatives, receiving only their board and clothes and hold their social position in the community; but the moment they stepped outside of the home and became wage-earners, thus securing pecuniary independence, they lost caste and were rigidly dropped from the quilting bees, the apple-parings, and all the society functions of the neighborhood. Is it any wonder that a sour and crabbed disposition was universally ascribed to spinster-hood, or that those women should be regarded as most unfortunate, doomed to a loveless, aimless, and dependent existence,—universally considered as having made a failure of life?

Scarcely less under the ban was the woman who dared venture into the field of literature. No pen can depict the scorn and derision that expressed themselves in that word "bluestocking." The literary woman placed herself forever beyond the pale of marriage, for no man would be brave enough to take for a wife a creature who had thus unsexed herself. If she could write, it followed without question that she could not cook, sew, manage a house, or bring up children, and in such connection suggested at once an appalling scene of disorder and discomfort. This belief prevailed, to a great extent, in regard to a woman who attempted any vocation outside of domestic service, that by so doing she became at once and forever unfitted for the duties of wife and mother. Of all the old prejudices that cling to the hem of the woman's garment and persistently impede her progress, none holds faster than this. The idea that she owes service to a man instead of to herself, and that it is her highest duty to aid his development rather than her own, will be the last to die.

In that day not even woman herself had so much as a dream of entering the professions of law, medicine, and theology. When the genius of Harriet Hosmer impelled her to take up sculpture, she travelled from one end of the country to the other begging for an opportunity to make the necessary study of anatomy. When Elizabeth Blackwell determined to consecrate her life to medicine, not one of the standard medical colleges would admit her as a student, and society ostracized her. After Antoinette Brown had graduated with high honors from Oberlin College, even that institution placed every possible obstacle in the way of her entrance into the Theological Department, and one of the faculty said: "If there were any by-law, Miss Brown, by which you could be shut out, you would not be admitted."

As for the profession of law, nobody lived in those times who had even a vision of a day when woman would enter that domain which seemed so sacredly the exclusive possession of man. Politics seemed a great deal farther away than paradise, and the most radical reformer had not the prophetic eye which could discern the woman politician.

Such was the helpless, dependent, fettered condition of woman when the first Woman's Rights Convention was called just forty years ago, at Seneca Falls, N.Y., by Elizabeth Cady Stanton and Lucretia Mott. Half a century before this, Mary Wollstonecraft had written her "Vindication of the Rights of Woman," that matchless plea for the equality of the sexes. A quarter of a century before, Frances Wright, in connection with addresses on other subjects, demanded equal rights for women. In 1835, Ernestine L. Rose and Paulina Wright Davis circulated the first petition for property rights for women, and during the next ten years Mrs. Rose addressed the New York Legislature a number of times asking political equality. Mrs. Stanton also had circulated petitions and addressed the Legislature during this period. In 1847, Lucy Stone, on her return from Oberlin College, made her first woman's rights address in her brother's church in Gardner, Mass.

While there had been individual demands, from time to time, the first organized body to formulate a declaration of the rights of women was the one which met at Seneca Falls, July 19–20, 1848, and adjourned to meet at Rochester two weeks later. In the Declaration of Sentiments and the Resolutions there framed, every point was covered that, down to the present day, has been contended for by the advocates of equal rights for women. Even inequality of the existing laws and customs was carefully considered and a thorough and complete readjustment demanded. The only resolution that was not unanimously adopted was the one urging the elective franchise for women. Those who opposed it did so only because they feared it would make the movement ridiculous. But Mrs. Stanton and Frederick Douglass, seeing that the power to make laws and choose rulers was the right by which all others could be secured, persistently advocated the resolution and at last carried it by a good majority.

The proceedings of this convention were ridiculed by the press and denounced by the pulpit from one end of the country to the other. Its demands were considered the most absurd and preposterous that could be made, and so severe was the storm which raged that many who had signed the Declaration made haste to withdraw their names. Now, at the end of half a century, we find that with few exceptions, all of the demands formulated at this convention have been granted. The great exception is the yielding of political rights, and toward this one point are directed now all the batteries of scorn, of ridicule, of denunciation that formerly poured their fire all along the line. Although not one of the predicted calamities occurred upon the granting of the other demands, the world is asked to believe that all of this will happen if this last stronghold is surrendered.

There is not space to follow the history of the last fifty years and study the methods by which these victories have been gained, but there is not one foot of advanced ground upon which women stand to-day that has not been obtained through the hard-fought battles of other women. The close of this nineteenth century finds every trade, vocation, and profession open to women, and every opportunity at their command for preparing themselves to follow these occupations. The girls as well as the boys of a family now fit themselves for such careers as their tastes and abilities permit. A vast amount of the household drudgery that once monopolized the whole time and strength of the mother and daughters, has been taken outside and turned over to machinery in vast establishments. A money value is placed upon the labor of women. The ban of social ostracism has been largely removed from the woman wage-earner. She who can make for herself a place of distinction in any line of work receives commendation instead of condemnation. Woman is no longer compelled to marry for support, but may herself make her own home and earn her own financial independence.

With but few exceptions, the highest institutions of learning in the land are as freely opened to girls as to boys, and they may receive their degrees at legal, medical and theological colleges, and practice their professions without hindrance. In the world of literature and art women divide the honors with men; and our civil-service rules have secured for them many thousands of remunerative positions under the Government.

It is especially worthy of note that along this general advancement of women has come a marked improvement in household methods. Woman's increased intelligence manifests itself in this department as conspicuously as in any other. Education, culture, mental discipline, business training develop far more capable mothers and housewives than were possible under the old regime. Men of the present generation give especial thought to comradeship in the selection of a wife, and she is no less desirable in their eyes because she is a college graduate or has learned the value and the management of money through having earned it.

There has been a radical revolution in the legal status of woman. In most States the old common law has been annulled by legislative enactment, through which partial justice, at least, has been done to married women. In nearly every State they may retain and control property owned at marriage and all they may receive by gift or inheritance thereafter, and also their earnings outside the home. They may sue and be sued, testify in the courts, and carry on business in their own name, but in no State have wives any ownership in the joint earnings. In six or seven States mothers have equal guardianship of the children. While in most States the divorce laws are the same for men and women, they never can bear equally upon both while all the property earned during marriage belongs wholly to the husband. There has been such a modification in public sentiment, however, that, in most cases, courts and juries show a marked leniency toward women.

The department of politics has been slowest to give admission to women. Suffrage is the pivotal right, and if it could be secured at the beginning, women would not have been half a century in gaining the privileges enumerated above, for privileges they must be called so long as others may either give or take them away. If women could make the laws or elect those who make them, they would be in the position of sovereigns instead of subjects. Were they the political peers of man they could command instead of having to beg, petition, and pray. Can it be possible it is for this reason that men have been so determined in their opposition to grant to women power?

But even this stronghold is beginning to yield to the long and steady pressure. In twenty-five States women possess suffrage in school matters; in four States they have a limited suffrage in local affairs; in one State they have municipal suffrage; in four States they have full suffrage, local, State, and national. Women are becoming more and more interested in political questions and public affairs. Every campaign sees greater numbers in attendance at the meetings, and able woman speakers are now found upon the platforms of all parties. Especial efforts are made by politicians to obtain the support of women, and during the last campaign one of the Presidential candidates held special meetings for women in the large cities throughout the country. Some of the finest political writing in the great newspapers of the day is done by women, and the papers are extensively read by women of all classes. In many of the large cities women have formed civic clubs and are exercising a distinctive influence in municipal matters. In most of the States of the Union women are eligible for many offices, State and County Superintendents, Registers of Deeds, etc. They are Deputies to State, County, and City officials, notaries public, State Librarians, and enrolling and engrossing clerks in the Legislatures.

It follows, as a natural result, that in the States where women vote they are eligible to all offices. They have been sent as delegates to National Conventions, made Presidential electors, and are sitting to-day as members in both the Upper and Lower Houses of the Legislatures. In some towns all the offices are filled by women. These radical changes have been effected without any social upheaval or domestic earthquakes, family relations have suffered no disastrous changes, and the men of the States where women vote furnish the strongest testimony in favor of woman suffrage.

There is no more striking illustration of the progress that has been made by woman than that afforded by her changed position in the Church. Under the old regime the Quakers were the only sect who recognized the equality of women. Other denominations enforced the command of St. Paul, that women should keep silence in the churches. A few allowed the women to lift up their voices in class and prayer meetings, but they had no vote in matters of church government. Even the missionary and charity work was in the hands of men.

Now the Unitarians, Universalists, Congregationalists, Wesleyan and Protestant Methodists, Christians, Free-Will Baptists, and possibly a few others ordain women as ministers, and many parishes, in all parts of the country, are presided over by women preachers. The charity and missionary work of the churches is practically turned over to women, who raise and disburse immense sums of money. While many of the great denominations still refuse to ordain women, to allow them a seat in their councils or a vote in matters of church government, yet women themselves are, in a large measure, responsible for this state of affairs. Forming, as they do, from two-thirds to three-fourths of the membership, raising the greater part of the funds and carrying on the active work of the church, when they unite their forces and assert their right, the small minority of men, who have usurped the authority, will be obliged to yield to their just demands. The creeds of the churches will recognize woman's equality before God, as the codes of the States have acknowledged it before man and the law.

By far the larger part of the progressive movements just enumerated have taken place during the last twenty-five years, and the progress has been most rapid during the last half of this quarter of a century. With the advantages already obtained, with the great liberalizing of public sentiment, and with the actual proof that the result of enlarged opportunities for women have been for the betterment of society, the next decade ought to see the completion of the struggle for the equality of the sexes. The hardest of the battles have been fought, and, while there is still need for both generals and soldiers, the greatest necessity is for the body of women to take possession and hold the ground that has been gained. It is not sufficient that women should fill positions as well as men, they must give vastly better satisfaction in order to prove their claims. There is an urgent demand for women of the highest character and intelligence, because the whole sex will be judged by the few who come forward to assume these new duties.

While by the momentum already gained the reforms demanded would eventually come, women have learned the value of organization and united, systematic work in securing the best and speediest results. It is no longer necessary to make an effort for further educational facilities. The few universities which still close their doors to women will ultimately be compelled to open them by the exigencies of the situation. There are no longer any fences around the industrial field, although men will continue to have the best pickings in the pasture so long as women are disfranchised. There will be a gradual yielding of the laws in recognition of woman's improved position in all departments, but here also there never will be complete equality until women themselves help to make laws and elect law-makers. In view of this indisputable fact, the advanced thinkers are agreed that the strongest efforts should be concentrated upon this point.

From that little convention at Seneca Falls, with a following of a handful of women scattered through half-a-dozen different States, we have now the great National Association, with headquarters in New York City, and auxiliaries in almost every State in the Union. These State bodies are effecting a thorough system of county and local organizations for the purpose of securing legislation favorable to women, and especially to obtain amendments to their State Constitutions. As evidence of the progress of public opinion, more than half of the Legislatures in session, during the past winter, have discussed and voted upon bills for the enfranchisement of women, and in most of them they were adopted by one branch and lost by a very small majority in the other. The Legislatures of Washington and South Dakota have submitted woman-suffrage amendments to their electors for 1898, and vigorous campaigns will be made in those States during the next two years. For a quarter of a century Wyoming has stood as a conspicuous object-lesson in woman suffrage, and is now reinforced by the three neighboring States of Colorado, Utah, and Idaho. With this central group, standing on the very crest of the Rocky Mountains, the spirit of justice and freedom for women cannot fail to descend upon all the Western and Northwestern States. No one who makes a careful study of this question can help but believe that, in a very few years, all the States just west of the Mississippi river will have enfranchised their women.

While the efforts of each State are concentrated upon its own Legislature, all of the States combined in the national organization are directing their energies toward securing a Sixteenth Amendment to the Constitution of the United States. The demands of this body have been received with respectful and encouraging attention from Congress. Hearings have been granted by the Committees of both Houses, resulting, in a number of instances, in favorable reports. Upon one occasion the question was brought to a discussion in the Senate, and received the affirmative vote of one-third of the members.

Until woman has obtained "that right protective of all other rights—the ballot," this agitation must still go on, absorbing the time and energy of our best and strongest women. Who can measure advantages that would result if the magnificent abilities of these women could be devoted to the needs of government, society, home, instead of being consumed in the struggle to obtain their birthright of individual freedom? Until this be gained we can never know, we cannot even prophesy, the capacity and power of woman for the uplift of humanity. It may be delayed longer than we think, it may be here sooner than we expect, but the day will come when man will recognize woman as his peer, not only at the fireside, but in the councils of the nation. Then, and not until then, will there be the perfect comradeship, the ideal union between the sexes, that shall result in the highest development of the race. What this shall be we may not attempt to define, but this we know, that only good can come to the individual or to the nation through the rendering of exact justice.

3 ★ LABOR

D<small>URING THE</small> 1890s the sympathies of middle-class Americans, though frequently not in concert with those of the upper class, often took the side of capital when major strikes occurred for three basic reasons: they feared "foreign" agitators advocating "un-American" violence; they were inconvenienced by interrupted services; and they held to the inherited morality of the Puritan work ethic. For middle-class Americans of leisure, removed from but dependent on the work done by laborers, the essays and stories in periodicals served as a bridge to a world they knew little about; perhaps such pieces generated some sympathetic understanding in readers, if not a sense of responsibility or culpability. In fact, although descriptions of working conditions in the periodicals stress harsh reality, their emphasis is on the endurance, individualism, and heroism of workers facing adversity. For the most part, calls for reform are implicit rather than explicit; a realistic description of labor practices is emphasized rather than an analysis and reevaluation of those practices and their consequences.

The essays and stories in this section are nuanced by fears about national labor issues, in particular the consolidation of capital in the form of trusts and monopolies and the organization of labor, carried on mainly to attack owners of capital in strikes. After the Civil War, the United States experienced increased civil violence in the form of labor unrest, specifically strikes. The 1890s were particularly tumultuous; the Homestead strike, a general strike of 20,000 workers in New Orleans, and a miners' strike at Coeur d'Alene, Idaho, all in 1892, and a national miners' strike and the Pullman railroad strike of 1894 were the most significant conflicts.

Drawing their readers into scenes of hardship and arduous labor, the authors here portray workers as sympathetic individuals, but each author has a

FIGURE 8   This illustration is from a *McClure's* article on Pittsburgh's Homestead Steel Mill, originally from a series of articles on the mills. In light of the Homestead strike of 1892, working conditions were carefully scrutinized. (*McClure's*, 1894)

different purpose in doing so. In 1891, Walter A. Wyckoff, an assistant professor of political economy at Princeton University, left his "frictionless" life as a person whose physical needs were tended to by others to "learn by experience" and share in the "humblest form of labor upon which that superstructure rests." For two years Wyckoff traveled across the United States, earning his living as an unskilled laborer and working as a member of the "manual proletariat." Wyckoff's "experiment in reality," which took his readers on a detailed journey, was serialized in *Scribner's* from July 1897 to November 1898 and later published in two volumes as *The Workers—The East* and *The Workers—The West* (1899).

Wyckoff's conclusion to *The Workers*, evoking the national memory of the Civil War, is marked by a tension between his awareness of labor problems and his desire to project a nativist optimism. On the one hand, he cites "local conditions, the presence of large numbers of yet unassimilated foreign elements, [and] rapid changes in economic relations" as being responsible for "the awful sores on the body politic"; on the other, he locates salvation in "strong patriotic feeling" for a "nation whose unity has been purchased and made sure by such a cost of blood and treasure" and in a mutual commitment to labor that will bring "a fuller consciousness of national life and of the glorious mission of high destiny." Wyckoff portrays a tension between the realities of labor unrest and harsh working conditions, on the one hand, and, on the other, a desire to validate manual labor. At a time when, for some people, capitalist enterprises seemed to function as the healing glue for the nation, Wyckoff describes but does not directly question prevailing conditions of labor.

Like Wyckoff, Stephen Crane stakes a claim to authenticity by virtue of his participation and by his use of detailed realistic description; in his graphic depiction of his descent into a coal mine he accurately describes a specific kind of labor and workplace as well as the miners' inhumane working conditions. Gertrude Roscoe's tragic story of two weavers emphasizes the isolated and, indeed, "ruinous" work and living conditions of young women in the lowest-paying of jobs. Elmore Elliott Peake's railway adventure celebrates the heroism of a young wife who forces a train to meet a corporate deadline, thereby gaining her father's approval of her marriage to a laboring man. While Roscoe clearly deplores the heartless dehumanization of modern labor, Peake glorifies individual effort to accommodate corporate demands.

In an era when increasing numbers of women, particularly young women, worked, and when the preferred woman's work was in department stores and factories, essays and stories on the varieties of conditions for women's work outside the home pointed to the difficulties they would have to face as well as their opportunities for cultural growth. Florence Kelley's essay exposing the harsh conditions of sweatshops and indicting the indifferent consumers who only want cheap garments should be read in concert with Clara Davidge's more optimistic essay suggesting ways in which a few working girls could briefly mimic the lives of club women.

★

WALTER A. WYCKOFF *The Workers—The West:*
Among the Revolutionaries
Scribner's 24 (July 1898): 99–105

[Wyckoff describes his activities on a Sunday in Chicago in 1892 in three different parts of the city: downtown in a fashionable church; on the South Side, populated by southern and eastern Europeans, at a socialists' meeting; and on the West Side at the sweatshop home of a unionist. This excerpt recapitulates a debate between a Christian socialist and a communist anarchist at the socialists' meeting.]

By this time I had attended several of the Socialists' meetings, and had come to know personally a number of the members of the order, and I was not surprised, upon taking a seat in the restaurant, to catch sight of three Socialists who were nodding pleasantly to me from a neighboring table. One was the broad-minded Pedler, whose good impression made in the first speech of his which I had heard was heightened by all my later knowledge of him. Another I had learned to know as a near approach to my original preconception of a revolutionary. He was a Communistic Anarchist, and just what peculiar variation of individual belief it was which led him to ally himself with the Socialists I could never make clearly out.

It puzzled me not a little; for, by this time I had thoroughly in mind the fundamental fact that Socialism and Anarchy, as two schools of social doctrine, are at the very poles of hostile opposition to each other. And, if I may judge from the little that I have seen and heard between them, the vituperative heat of their controversies is equalled only by the warmth and malignancy which has marked the history of theological debate.

I soon learned that Socialist and Anarchist are not interchangeable terms, to be used with light indifference in describing the general advocate of revolution against established order. Indeed, to my great surprise, I found that a policy of active, aggressive revolution among these men had almost no adherents. Certainly none among the Socialists, for they repudiated the bare suggestion of violence as being wholly inadequate and absurd, and pinned their faith instead to what they called the "natural processes of evolution." These, to their belief, would, in any case, work out the appointed ends with men, but their operation could be stimulated by education, they said, and

FIGURE 9   From Walter A. Wyckoff's essay on the "revolutionaries" of the West, this illustration focuses on a passionate speaker at a meeting of socialists, treated by Wyckoff as potentially dangerous agitators, but also as domesticated family men. (*Scribner's*, 1894)

helped on by organized effort toward the achievement of manifest destiny in the highly centralized and perfected order which is to result from the common ownership and administration by all the people of all land and capital used in production and distribution, for the common good of all.

And even among the Anarchists the upholders of a policy of bloody revolt against social order were rare. Most of those whom I came to know were distinctly of a metaphysical turn of mind. It was easy to trace their intellectual kinship with the Physiocrats of the last century, in their implicit confidence in the universal efficacy of *laissez faire*. Their views, reduced to simplest terms, seemed to take the form of the epigram—that "the cure for the evils of freedom is more freedom." The removal of all artificial restraint in the form of man-made laws would result eventually, to their thinking, in a society as natural and as wholesome as is all physical order, which is the exact resultant of the free play of natural law.

It was the Socialist's conception of a highly centralized administration which drove the Anarchist into a frenzy of vehement antagonism. And it was the Anarchist's *laissez faire* ideal which roused the latent fighting-spirit of the Socialist. The Anarchist would maintain with stout conviction that centralized administration is already the core of the malady of the world, and that our need is for freedom in the absence of artificial limitations wherein natural forces can work their rightful ends. And the Socialist would retort, with rising anger, that it is from anarchy—the absence of wisely regulated system—that the world even now suffers most, and that the hope of men lies in the orderly management of their own affairs in the interests of all, and in the light of the revelations of science. They were heartily at one in their dislike for what they were fond of calling the present "*bourgeois* society," and for the existing rights of private property, which they regarded as its chiefest bulwark, but they parted company at once, and with sharp recriminations, on the grounds of their dislike, and of their purposes and hopes for a regenerated state of things.

Such Anarchists were of the "Individualistic" type. Not all of those I met were so philosophical, however. The Communistic one, who was nodding at me in a friendly manner from a near table, notably was not. Very much the reverse. He was for open revolution to the death and he made no secret of it. He had little patience for the slow pace of evolution believed in by the Socialists, but he had less, apparently, for the *laissez faire* conception of his brother Anarchists. At all events, I found him most commonly in the meetings of the former sect, where his revolutionary views were frowned down, but his invectives against society were tolerated in a spirit of free speech, and as being warranted by the evils of the existing state.

He was a German, of tall, muscular frame, erect, square-shouldered, well-poised, as a result of long service, most bitterly against his will, in the Prussian Army, and he hated kings and potentates and all governmental authority, with a burning hatred. His was the broad-featured likeness of his race, and his stiff, fair hair was brushed back in straight lines from a well-shaped forehead, while his beard, brown and streaked with white, bristled from his lower face like the bayonets of a square in full formation. He was a mechanic by trade, and a good one, as I had happened to learn.

The last of the three, like the Pedler, was a Socialist, but was very unlike his two companions as a man. My acquaintance among the Socialists had not gone far before I began to observe that I was meeting men who, whatever their mental vagaries, were craftsmen of no mean order. They were machinists and skilled workmen mostly, and some were workers in sweat-shops. All of them had known the full stress of the struggle for bread, but they were decidedly not the inefficients of their class, having fought their way to positions of some advantage in the general fight.

Here, however, was an exception in this third "comrade," and I marvelled at the rarity of his type. Incompetence was stamped on every feature. His long, lank, flabby figure, with its disjointed movements, suggested no virility. The hair grew thin and blonde from his head and from his colorless face, and his large, pale-blue eyes flitted in their movements, as though there were behind them not intelligence enough to hold them in fixed attention. The man's emotions were boundless. He had, moreover, a gift of utterance, and, when he spoke in meeting, it was sheer feeling that expressed itself in words which were marvellously void of any sane concatenation. It was a psychological phenomenon; this public speech of his. We had premonitory warnings of it, for we could see him writhing in his seat when his emotions were aroused, and starting nervously until he had gained the floor, when a half-suppressed, general groan would greet the torrent of his sentences, which flowed directly from chaotic feeling which had never reached his mind.

We four left the restaurant together, and walked on to Waverley Hall. I fell in with the Pedler, and from him I was glad to learn that the Poet was to read that afternoon his long-deferred paper on the "Opening of the Exposition Grounds on Sunday."

It was a little before the appointed hour when we reached the hall, but already there was promise of an uncommon meeting. The audience was larger than usual, the benches on both sides of the central aisle being well filled nearly to the door. The Pedler and I had some difficulty in finding seats near the front. More than ever marked was the atmosphere of keen alertness, which, from the first, had so attracted me in the gatherings of the Socialists. They might be futile, but their meetings were never dull. And, while they could not have been more orderly, they might easily have proved far less engaging than they were, had a saving sense of humor been more conspicuously a characteristic of the members.

There was a sense of pleasurable excitement in sinking back into my seat, whence, by turning a little to the right, I could command the hall. The afternoon sun was streaming through the two large windows in the south end. The heavy draperies, looped up to admit the light, were in perfect keeping with the carpet on the dais and the pulpit chairs upholstered with plush, on one of which sat the Leader, behind a reading-desk. There were other paraphernalia of the Masonic lodge which habitually held its meetings there, and among the life-sized portraits on the walls was one of Washington in the full regalia of a Mason. At small wooden tables, resting on the floor at the Leader's right, sat a few young reporters, sharpening their pencils in preparation for any points which could be turned to good account as "copy."

To the pleasure of excited interest was added the ease of some familiarity, for, besides the heads of meeting, I recognized among the gathering company the faces of *habitués*. In a seat across the aisle the Poet sat in earnest conversation with the Citizeness, holding fast a roll of manuscript in both hands. And at the end of the bench behind them was a young man who interested me far more than any of the Socialists whom I had met. A long black overcoat of cheap material concealed his work-worn garments to the knees, and his hands, dark with the dye of clothing, lay folded in his lap. His face showed faintly the marks of Jewish origin, and, although he was full three-and-twenty, he bore a strange resemblance to the Christ-child in Hoffmann's picture of Jesus Among the Doctors in the Temple.

Quite oblivious to what was passing about him, he sat in his usual mood, with an expression of much serenity on his pale face, and his great, dark, luminous eyes glowing with the ardor of his thought.

I have never lost the first impression which he made upon me; it was in one of these meetings, when an idle slur had been cast upon his race and the Leader had given him an opportunity to reply. He rose modestly to his feet, and from the first my attention was riveted by the convincing quality in his rich, deep voice. Without a word of cheap rejoinder, he simply restated the issues of debate in clear, incisive sentences, which seemed to gather force from their broken English, until he had shown the entire irrelevance of the insulting charge, even had it been true.

I had waited for him on that afternoon at the meeting's end, and we began an acquaintance which to me has been of great value. It is easy to predict for such a man an eventual escape from the bondage of a sweat-shop, but, inasmuch as he has been held in slavery to that work from his earliest infant memories of a crowded den in Poland, where he was born, I feel some measure of justice in naming him "The Victim."

Promptly on the hour the Leader called the meeting to order, and introduced the Poet, whose paper presented the topic of the day's debate. In a few moments we were all following in close attention the ready flow of the poet's voice as it passed with clear articulation over the well-chosen words of his introductory sentences. There was admirable precision in the statement of the case at issue, and we were bracing ourselves with pleasure for the logical sequences of detailed discussion, when, to our surprise, the Poet broke abruptly from all judicial treatment of his theme. At a single leap, he took the ground that certainly the Exposition should be accessible every day—that its opening on Sundays was not a subject for debate.

Then there followed a storm of hot invective. Christianity was assailed as the giant superstition of historic civilization, still daring, to the shame of high intelligence, to hold its fetich head aloft in the light of modern science. Its ministers were attacked as sycophantic parasites, whose only motive, in urging the closing of the Fair on Sundays, was the fear of the spread among working people of their enlightenment which will achieve the overthrow of capitalistic society and with it the tottering structure of the Church. Most of all, his bitterness spent itself upon these "blind leaders of the blind," as he called them, who will not themselves enter into a knowledge of a better state nor suffer others to enter in, and who grievously break the law of rest on Sundays in befooling their fellow-men, and then live through the remaining days in luxurious unproductiveness upon the labor of their dupes.

What was coming next we could not guess, and it seemed a long cry to any shout of exultation from all this, but he accomplished it with facility, for his paper closed with a peroration, wherein he rose to fervid panegyric upon the increasing intellectual emancipation of workingmen. The Romish Church, he said, keeps many of them in bondage yet, but the Protestant organizations have all but lost their hold upon them; and the widening gulf between the two great classes in society has left these churches in the nakedness of their true character, as mere centres of the social life of the very rich and of the upper *bourgeoisie*, and as a prop to the social order from which these idle classes so richly profit, at the merciless cost of the wage-earners.

Instantly this was accepted as the dominant note of the meeting. The applause which greeted it was genuine and prolonged. With light-hearted disregard of the subject appointed for debate, men began ardently to speak to this new theme: Modern Christianity a vast hypocrisy—a cloak made use of by vested interest to conceal from the common people the real nature of the grounds on which it stands.

But for the masterly qualities of the Leader, who held the meeting to strict parliamentary order, it might have degenerated into a mob. Men were crowding one another in their desire to gain the floor, but not for a moment was the peaceful conduct of the gathering disturbed. With accurate knowledge of the shades of social belief there represented and of the personalities of the men, the Leader chose for recognition with discriminating justice.

At one moment an American workman was speaking, a Socialist of the general school of Social Democracy. There was self-respecting dignity about him and a calm reserve as he began.

The Christian Church served as well as any institution of the capitalistic order, he said, to measure the growing cleavage between the classes in society. But, to his mind, the paper of the afternoon had emphasized unnecessarily the existence of the *bourgeoisie*, for, economically considered, there is no longer a middle-class to be reckoned with in vital questions. There remain simply the capitalists and the proletarians. The old middle-class which had made its living by individual enterprise, was fast being forced (by the play of natural laws, which showed themselves in the increasing centralization of capital) out of the possibility of successful competition with aggregated wealth, and down, for the most part, to the level of those who can bring to production, not land nor capital, but merely their native qualities of physical strength, or manual skill, or mental ability—proletarians, all of them, whether manual or intellectual, and coming surely, in the slow development of evolution, to a conscious knowledge of their community of interest as against the vested "rights" of monopoly in the material instruments of production. But athwart this path of progress rose the hardened structure of the Christian Church, bringing to bear against it all her temporal power and the full force of her accumulated superstitions.

But now the speaker's calm deserted him, and, with fist uplifted in threatening gesture, and his strong, bronzed face working with the fervor of his hate, he cried out against the ministers of Christ, who preach to the wronged and down-trodden poor the duty of patience with their "divinely appointed lot," and who try to soothe them to blind submission with promises of an endless future of ecstatic blessedness, when the rich of this world shall burn in the unquenchable fires of hell.

"Oh! the fiendishness of these men," he shouted, "who hide from ignorant minds the truth, which they themselves know full well, that for no mortal man is there any heaven or hell which he does not realize in the span of his earthly history, and if he misses here the happiness to which he was rightly born, he misses it forever! And the miserable paltriness of their motive in working this cruel wrong—merely that they may exempt themselves from toil and live in comfort upon the labor of others, instead of being, where most of them belong, out in the open fields hoeing corn!"

In another moment a man of widely different cult was speaking. For some time he had been trying to gain the floor, and now the Leader recognized him. He was a Christian Socialist, chief spokesman of the little band of his persuasion, who were very regular in their attendance upon these meetings. An insignificant Englishman he was, whose h's transposed themselves with consistent perversity, and whose general qualities of physique, and tone, and manner reminded one strongly of the type of parson with weak lungs and a large family who is incumbent in out-of-the-way English churches on the Continent. He was not wanting in pluck nor in a certain strength of conviction, but the gentleness of the dove was his without the wisdom of the serpent, and the words he spoke, in weak voice and apologetic manner, while they would have met with sympathy in a company of believers whose emotions were already stirred, served here only to inflame the antagonisms of men whose views were stoutly materialistic.

The Communistic Anarchist was the first to rise when the Christian Socialist sat down, and the Leader gave to him the privilege of the floor. There was the power of primal force in the suppressed passion of the man, and joined to this the exciting struggle of a human will in keeping rage in bounds. His heavy frame heaved with paroxysms of volcanic wrath, and the sibilants of English speech, augmented by the z's in Teutonic struggle to bring forth sounds, came hissing and sputtering through his teeth from a tongue which could not frame words fast enough for his impatience.

I have no power to reproduce his actual sentences, and at best I can but suggest the purport of his talk, which was in full sympathy with most of what had gone before:

"God a decaying myth, and the Bible a silly legend, and Jesus a good man seeing some human truth, but gone mad in the credulous ignorance of his age, and dead these two thousand years, and Christianity a hoary superstition, made use of in its last days by *bourgeois* civilization to stay off a little longer its own fateful day of reckoning! And here is a man, who calls himself a Socialist, who dares to bring before us this enfeebled monster of worn-out faith, which has been the tyrant of the poor from the moment of gaining temporal power, trying to hide its oppressions under a guise of so-called charity!

It has been, too, from the beginning the stubbornest foe of scientific knowledge, and even now, in the last hour of its heart-less cruelties, employs its utmost craft to put off the manifest dawn of freedom to the workers."

Breaking through the forced restraint of the beginning, his feelings bore him in resistless course until, in the full sweep of his long arms, his fingers were clutching wildly at the empty air, and his blood-shot eyes were rolling in a frenzy, and his hair stood straight on end, while his voice rose to its highest pitch in fierce scorn and denunciation.

The hall was still echoing to the roar, when a scattered number of us were on our feet, straining forward in our efforts to catch the Leader's eye. The Victim was recognized, and almost immediately the meeting began to feel the calming effect of a cool, conciliatory mind. Clearness was highly characteristic of the Victim's mental processes, and, as his ideas slowly framed themselves, in translation to English from the native language in which he thought, they took on a charming piquancy and precision, in the oddest mixtures of strange idioms and bookish phrases and the current coin of common slang.

"The assigned subject for debate this afternoon," he was saying (in a paraphrase which wholly lacks his strongly individual character), "is one which opens up questions of great economic value and importance. It is a pity, it seems to me, that the time has been consumed in a discussion of side issues, rather than of the fundamental question of the observance of Sunday as an economic institution, and the relation borne to that great issue by the present agitation over the opening of the Exposition grounds on Sundays. It is well to remember that this is a meeting of Socialists. Freedom of speech is one of our cardinal beliefs. But a freedom of speech which ignores the subject appointed for debate would make better use of its liberty by asking for a particular afternoon to be devoted to the theme which it wishes to discuss.

"Not only has the talk of to-day been wide of the mark, but it has been out of harmony with the genius of Socialism. I am proud to own myself a Scientific Socialist, and a disciple of Karl Marx. To my way of thinking, there can be no verified truth which the mind of man can accept as such aside from the established results of naturalistic science. I, therefore, attach no more value to Christianity, as an authoritative source of truth, than I do to the sacred writings of my race. Both are merely historical facts, to be dealt with precisely as are all the facts of history. This afternoon, however, they have been dealt with in a spirit of intolerance, as malignant and uncompromising as the spirit which is charged against historic Christianity. It will be well for us who profess Socialism to be on our guard, lest there grow up among us an intolerance bred of dogmatic science, which may prove in the future as destructive of free thought and of true progress as has proved in the past the bigotry of dogmatic theology."

It was now well past the ordinary time for adjourning. The Leader announced the fact, and I feared that he meant to call for a motion to adjourn without making his usual closing speech. It was his habit to sum up the discussion, and we always looked forward to that address, for the Leader had the gift of speech and a liking for it, and a knowledge, moreover, of the minds of Socialists which was by no means common. There was little of the declamatory in his habitual speaking, and he lacked the analytical skill of some of the other members, but he had a shrewd perception of the dramatic, and he could make use of it to striking purpose. He had been born and bred a workingman, and was an artisan of much ability, and he knew thoroughly the workmen's point of view. I have watched him play upon their feelings with the skill of a native orator.

He spoke now in high commendation of what The Victim had said, and deplored the fact that the afternoon had passed without discussion of the appointed theme. As a Socialist, he regretted, he said, that the talk had taken the form of an attack upon Christianity. Such a spirit was directly counter to the tolerance of Socialism. For his own part, although he had been brought up under the influence of the Protestant religion, he found himself very little in sympathy with modern Christianity. Super-naturalism he was willing to regard as a question apart, and as being entitled to fair, dispassionate discussion, but the Christian Church, as a practical embodiment of the teachings of its founder, he felt justified in judging in the light of every-day facts, and in their light he was free to say that Christianity was a failure.

"Let us take an illustration," he went on. "A very urgent problem in our city just now is that of 'the unemployed.' Certain of the newspapers have made a careful investigation in the last few weeks, and the result of their inquiry shows that, within the city limits to-day, there are at least 30,000 men out of work. There may be 50,000 but the first estimate is well within the truth.

"It is a matter primarily of supply and demand. Among these idle men there may be many inefficients and many chronic loafers, and many who, from one cause and another, are incapable of effective work. But the nature of the present status is unaffected by these considerations. It means, in its last analysis, that the local labor market is overstocked to the extent of 30,000 men. However willing to work, and however efficient as workmen they might be, these men, or their equivalent in number, under existing conditions, would invariably find themselves unemployed.

"And how does the Christian church among us hold itself in relation to this problem? Its members profess themselves the disciples of 'the meek and lowly Jesus,' whom they call 'divine.' He said of Himself that 'He had not where to lay His head,' and He was the first Socialist in His teaching of universal brotherhood.

"His followers build gorgeous temples to His worship in our city, and out of the fear, apparently, that some of the shelterless waifs, whom He taught them to know as brothers and who are in the very plight their Master was, should lay their weary heads upon the cushioned seats, they keep the churches tight locked through six days of the week, and then open them on one day for the exclusive purpose of praising that Master's name!

"Nor is this condition truer of Chicago than it is of any large industrial centre in this country, or even in all Christendom," he went on, warming to his theme as the intently listening company hailed vociferously the name of the Redeemer as the first teacher of Socialism. "Only last week news came from London that the unemployed there had grown to an army of 100,000 men. Picturing the horror of it, and the suffering, and the awful degradation, not in these men alone, but among the women and children whom they represent! Cold, and hunger, and the ravages of disease were bad enough, in the ferocity of this inclement winter; but imagine, if you can, the pitiless despair which is eating the hearts out of these our brothers, and then tell me whether we have not here a fairly good imitation of the hell where 'the worm dieth not, and the fire is not quenched.'

"Suppose, for a moment, that the Christ were to appear in the heart of that 'Christian' city. Most certainly He would be found among the poor, ministering to their needs, and comforting them in their sorrows, and bringing life and hope among them. I can imagine His perplexity at sight of the man-inflicted suffering and degradation, and the Godless tyranny of men over their brother men, in the very stronghold of Christianity and 2000 years after He had taught that, under the Fatherhood of God, to love our neighbor as ourselves is the fulfilling of the law to all who have need of our sympathy and help.

"I hear Him ask in His amazement for some authoritative head of the brotherhood which He established upon earth. I hear men tell Him that He must see the Archbishop of Canterbury. I watch Him as He picks His way to the palace of the Archbishop, along narrow streets which thunder to the din of mammon-worship and are blackened with the smoke from off its countless altars, seeing everywhere the hideous contrasts between rich and poor, and the lives of His toiling ones worn out in ceaseless labor.

"Weighed down with the heartless misery of the world, I see Him stand patiently at the palace-gate. A footman in rich livery answers to His knock.

" 'I would see the Archbishop,' says the Christ.

" 'And who shall I say wishes to see his Lordship?' asks the flunky.

" 'Tell him that his Master is at the gate.'

" 'Oh,' replies the servant, 'but his Lordship has no 'master'; he is the primate of all England!' "

Here the speaker abruptly ceased, but for that gathered company the picture was complete, and the cheers with which the hall had rung at the mention of Christ, the social teacher, were changed to hisses against the church which calls itself by His name.

★

STEPHEN CRANE *In the Depths of a Coal Mine*
McClure's (August 1894): 195–209

[After working in New York as a newspaper journalist, Stephen Crane became famous at twenty-four with his Civil War novel, *The Red Badge of Courage* (1895). Crane's realistic depiction of mining calls for a reform of harsh conditions in the mine, the "imperturbably cruel and insatiate, black emblem of greed." *McClure's Magazine* was a particularly appropriate place for Crane's essay. Founded in 1893 as a cheap alternative to the more expensive magazines, *McClure's* became notable not only for articles on science, wild animals and exploration, and notable figures such as Napoleon and Lincoln, but also for what would become known as "muckraking" journalism, that is, articles which exposed corruption in big business.]

THE "BREAKERS" SQUATTED upon the hillsides and in the valley like enormous preying monsters eating of the sunshine, the grass, the green leaves. The smoke from their nostrils had ravaged the air of coolness and fragrance. All that remained of the vegetation looked dark, miserable, half-strangled. Along the summit-line of the mountain, a few unhappy trees were etched upon the clouds. Overhead stretched a sky of imperial blue, incredibly far away from the sombre land.

We approached the colliery over paths of coal-dust that wound among the switches. The "breaker" loomed above us, a huge and towering frame of blackened wood. It ended in a little curious peak and upon its sides there was a profusion of windows appearing at strange and unexpected points. Through occasional doors one could see the flash of whirring machinery. Men with wondrously blackened faces and garments came forth from it. The sole glitter upon their persons was at their hats where the little tin lamps were carried. They went stolidly along, some swinging lunch-pails carelessly, but the marks upon them of their forbidding and mystic calling fascinated our new eyes until they passed from sight. They were symbols of a grim, strange war that was being waged in the sunless depths of the earth.

Around the huge central building clustered other and lower ones, sheds, engine-houses, machine-shops, offices. Railroad tracks extended in web-like ways. Upon them stood files of begrimed coal-cars. Other huge structures similar to the one near us up-reared their uncouth heads upon the hills of the surrounding country. From each, a mighty hill of culm extended. Upon these tremendous heaps of waste from the mines, mules and cars appeared like toys. Down in the valley, upon the railroads, long trains crawled painfully southward where a low-hanging grey cloud with a few projecting spires and chimneys indicated a town.

Car after car came from a shed beneath which lay hidden the mouth of the shaft. They were dragged creaking up an inclined cable-road to the top of the breaker.

At the top of the "breaker," laborers were dumping the coal into chutes. The huge lumps slid slowly on their journey down through the building from which they were to emerge in classified fragments. Great teeth on revolving cylinders caught them and chewed them. At places, there were grates that bid each size go into its proper chute. The dust lay inches deep on every motionless thing and clouds of it made the air dark as from a violent tempest. A mighty gnashing sound filled the ears. With terrible appetite this huge and hideous monster sat imperturbably munching coal, grinding its mammoth jaws with unearthly and monotonous uproar.

In a large room sat the little slate-pickers. The floor slanted at an angle of forty-five degrees, and the coal having been masticated by the great teeth was streaming sluggishly in long iron troughs. The boys sat straddling these troughs and as the mass moved slowly, they grabbed deftly at the pieces of slate therein. There were five or six of them, one above another, over each trough. The coal is expected to be fairly pure after it passes the final boy. The howling machinery was above them. High up, dim figures moved about in the dust clouds.

These little men were a terrifically dirty band. They resembled the New York gamins in some ways but they laughed more and when they laughed their faces were a wonder and a terror. They had an air of supreme independence and seemed proud of their kind of villainy. They swore long oaths with skill.

Through their ragged shirts we could get occasional glimpses of shoulders black as stoves. They looked precisely like imps as they scrambled to get a view of us. Work ceased while they tried to ascertain if we were willing to give away any tobacco. The man who perhaps believes that he controls them came and harangued the crowd. He talked to the air.

The slate-pickers, all through this region, are yet at the spanking period. One continually wonders about their mothers and if there are any schoolhouses. But as for them, they are not concerned. When they get time off, they go out on the culm-heap and play base-ball, or fight with boys from other breakers, or among themselves, according to the opportunities. And before them always is the hope of one day getting to be door-boys down in the mines and, later, mule-boys. And yet later laborers and helpers. Finally when they have grown to be great big men they may become miners, real miners, and go down and get "squeezed," or perhaps escape to a shattered old man's estate with a mere "miner's asthma." They are very ambitious.

Meanwhile, they live in a place of infernal dins. The crash and thunder of the machinery is like the roar of an immense cataract. The room shrieks and blares and bellows. Clouds of dust blur the air until the windows shine pallidly, afar off. All the structure is a-tremble from the heavy sweep and circle of the ponderous mechanism. Down in the midst of it, sit these tiny urchins, where they earn fifty-five cents a day each. They breathe this atmosphere until their lungs grow heavy and sick with it. They have this clamor in their ears until it is wonderful that they have any hoodlum valor remaining. But they are uncowed; they continue to swagger. And at the top of the breaker laborers can always be seen dumping the roaring coal down the wide, voracious maw of the creature.

Over in front of a little tool house, a man, smoking a pipe, sat on a bench. "Yes," he said, "I'll take yeh down, if yeh like." He led us by little cinder paths to the shed over the shaft of the mine. A gigantic fan-wheel, near by, was twirling swiftly. It created cool air for the miners, who on the lowest vein of this mine were some eleven hundred and fifty feet below the surface. As we stood silently waiting for the elevator, we had opportunity to gaze at the mouth of the shaft. The walls were of granite blocks, slimy, mossgrown, dripping with water. Below was a curtain of ink-like blackness. It was like the opening of an old well, sinister from tales of crime.

The black greasy cables began to run swiftly. We stood staring at them and wondering. Then of a sudden, the elevator appeared and stopped with a crash. It was a plain wooden platform. Upon two sides iron bars ran up to support a stout metal roof. The men upon it, as it came into view, were like apparitions from the centre of the earth.

A moment later, we marched aboard, armed with little lights, feeble and gasping in the daylight. There was an instant's creak of machinery and then the landscape that had been framed for us by the door-posts of the shed, disappeared in a flash. We were dropping with extraordinary swiftness straight into the earth. It was a plunge, a fall. The flames of the little lamps fluttered and flew and struggled like tied birds to release themselves from the wicks. "Hang on," bawled our guide above the tumult.

The dead black walls slid swiftly by. They were a swirling dark chaos on which the mind tried vainly to locate some coherent thing, some intelligible spot. One could only hold fast to the iron bars and listen to the roar of this implacable descent. When the faculty of balance is lost, the mind becomes a confusion. The will fought a great battle to comprehend something during this fall, but one might as well have been tumbling among the stars. The only thing was to await revelation.

It was a journey that held a threat of endlessness.

Then suddenly the dropping platform slackened its speed. It began to descend slowly and with caution. At last, with a crash and a jar, it stopped. Before us stretched an inscrutable darkness, a soundless place of tangible loneliness. Into the nostrils came a subtly strong odor of powder-smoke, oil, wet earth. The alarmed lungs began to lengthen their respirations.

Our guide strode abruptly into the gloom. His lamp flared shades of yellow and orange upon the walls of a tunnel that led away from the foot of the shaft. Little points of coal caught the light and shone like diamonds. Before us, there was always the curtain of an impenetrable night. We walked on with no sound save the crunch of our feet upon the coal dust of the floor. The sense of an abiding danger in the roof was always upon our foreheads. It expressed to us all the unmeasured, deadly tons above us. It was a superlative might that regarded with the supreme calmness of almighty power the little men at its mercy. Sometimes we were obliged to bend low to avoid it. Always our hands rebelled vaguely from touching it, refusing to affront this gigantic mass.

All at once, far ahead, shone a little flame, blurred and difficult of location. It was a tiny indefinite thing, like a wisp-light. We seemed to be looking at it through a great fog. Presently, there were two of them. They began to move to and fro and dance before us.

After a time we came upon two men crouching where the roof of the passage came near to meeting the floor. If the picture could have been brought to where it would have had the opposition and the contrast of the glorious summer-time earth, it would have been a grim and ghastly thing. The garments of the men were no more sable than their faces and when they turned their heads to regard our tramping party, their eye-balls and teeth shone white as bleached bones. It was like the grinning of two skulls there in the shadows. The tiny lamps on their hats made a trembling light that left weirdly shrouded the movements of their limbs and bodies. We might have been confronting terrible spectres.

But they said "Hello, Jim" to our conductor. Their mouths expanded in smiles—wide and startling smiles.

In a moment they turned again to their work. When the lights of our party reinforced their two lamps, we could see that one was busily drilling into the coal with a long thin bar. The low roof ominously pressed his shoulders as he bended at his toil. The other knelt behind him on the loose lumps of coal.

He who worked at the drill engaged in conversation with our guide. He looked back over his shoulder, continuing to poke away. "When are yeh goin't' measure this up, Jim?" he demanded. "Do yeh wanta git me killed?"

"Well, I'd measure it up t'-day, on'y I ain't got me tape," replied the other.

"Well, when will yeh? Yeh wanta hurry up," said the miner. "I don't wanta git killed."

"Oh, I'll be down on Monday."

"Humph!"

They engaged in a sort of an altercation in which they made jests.

"You'll be carried out o' there feet first before long."

"Will I?"

Yet one had to look closely to understand that they were not about to spring at each other's throats. The vague illumination created all the effect of the snarling of two wolves.

We came upon other little low-roofed chambers each containing two men, a "miner" who makes the blasts and his "laborer" who loads the coal upon the cars and assists the miner generally. And at each place there was this same effect of strangely satanic smiles and eyeballs wild and glittering in the pale glow of the lamps.

Sometimes, the scenes in their weird strength were absolutely infernal. Once when we were traversing a silent tunnel in another mine, we came suddenly upon a wide place where some miners were lying down in a group. As they up-reared to gaze at us, it resembled a resurrection. They slowly uprose with ghoul-like movements, mysterious figures robed in enormous shadows. The swift flashes of the steel-gleaming eyes were upon our faces.

At another time, when my companion, struggling against difficulties, was trying to get a sketch of the mule "Molly Maguire," a large group of miners gathered about us, intent upon the pencil of the artist. "Molly," indifferent to the demands of art, changed her position after a moment and calmly settled into a new one. The men all laughed and this laugh created the most astonishing and supernatural effect. In an instant, the gloom was filled with luminous smiles. Shining forth all about us were eyes, glittering as with cold blue flame. "Whoa, Molly," the men began to shout. Five or six of them clutched "Molly" by her tail, her head, her legs. They were going to hold her motionless until the portrait was finished. "He's a good feller," they had said of the artist, and it would be a small thing to hold a mule for him. Upon the roof were vague dancing reflections of red and yellow.

From this tunnel of our first mine we went with our guide to the foot of the main shaft. Here we were in the most important passage of a mine, the main gangway. The wonder of these avenues is the noise—the crash and clatter of machinery as the elevator speeds upward with the loaded cars and drops thunderingly with the empty ones. The place resounds with the shouts of mule-boys and there can always be heard the noise of approaching coal-cars, beginning in mild rumbles and then swelling down upon one in a tempest of sound. In the air is the slow painful throb of the pumps working at the water which collects in the depths. There is booming and banging and crashing until one wonders why the tremendous walls are not wrenched by the force of this uproar. And up and down the tunnel, there is a riot of lights, little orange points flickering and flashing. Miners stride in swift and sombre procession. But the meaning of it all is in the deep bass rattle of a blast in some hidden part of the mine. It is war. It is the most savage part of all in the endless battle between man and nature. These miners are grimly in the van. They have carried the war into places where nature has the strength of a million giants. Sometimes their enemy becomes exasperated and snuffs out ten, twenty, thirty lives. Usually she remains calm, and takes one at a time with method and precision. She need not hurry. She possesses eternity. After a blast, the smoke, faintly luminous, silvery, floats silently through the adjacent tunnels.

In our first mine we speedily lost all ideas of time, direction, distance. The whole thing was an extraordinary, black puzzle. We were impelled to admire the guide because he knew all the tangled passages. He led us through little tunnels three and four feet wide and with roofs that sometimes made us crawl. At other times we were in avenues twenty feet wide, where double rows of tracks extended. There were stretches of great darkness, majestic silences. The three hundred miners were distributed into all sorts of crevices and corners of the labyrinth, toiling in this city of endless night. At different points one could hear the roar of traffic about the foot of the main shaft, to which flowed all the commerce of the place.

We were made aware of distances later by our guide, who would occasionally stop to tell us our position by naming a point of the familiar geography of the surface. "Do yeh remember that rolling-mill yeh passed coming up? Well, you're right under it." "You're under th' depot now." The length of these distances struck us with amazement when we reached the surface. Near Scranton one can really proceed for miles, in the black streets of the mines.

Over in a wide and lightless room we found the mule-stables. There we discovered a number of these animals standing with an air of calmness and self-possession that was somehow amazing to find in a mine. A little dark urchin came and belabored his mule "China" until he stood broadside to us that we might admire his innumerable fine qualities. The stable was like a dungeon. The mules were arranged in solemn rows. They turned their heads toward our lamps. The glare made their eyes shine wondrously, like lenses. They resembled enormous rats.

About the room stood bales of hay and straw. The commonplace air worn by the long-eared slaves made it all infinitely usual. One had to wait to see the tragedy of it. It was not until we had grown familiar with the life and the traditions of the mines that we were capable of understanding the story told by these beasts standing in calm array, with spread legs.

It is a common affair for mules to be imprisoned for years in the limitless night of the mines. Our acquaintance, "China," had been four years buried.

Upon the surface there had been the march of the seasons; the white splendor of snows had changed again and again to the glories of green springs. Four times had the earth been ablaze with the decorations of brilliant autumns. But "China" and his friends had remained in these dungeons from which daylight, if one could get a view up a shaft, would appear a tiny circle, a silver star aglow in a sable sky.

Usually when brought to the surface, these animals tremble at the earth, radiant in the sunshine. Later, they go almost mad with fantastic joy. The full splendor of the heavens, the grass, the trees, the breezes, breaks upon them suddenly. They caper and career with extravagant mulish glee. Once a miner told me of a mule that had spent some delirious months upon the surface after years of labor in the mines. Finally the time came when he was to be taken back into the depths. They attempted to take him through a tunnel in the hillside. But the memory of a black existence was upon him; he knew that gaping mouth that threatened to swallow him. He had all the strength of mind for which his race is famous. No cudgellings could induce him. The men held conventions and discussed plans to budge that mule. The celebrated quality of obstinacy in him won him liberty to gambol clumsily about on the surface.

After being long in the mines, the mules are apt to duck and dodge at the close glare of lamps, but some of them have been known to have piteous fears of being left in the dead darkness. They seem then, somehow, like little children. We met a boy once who said that sometimes the only way he could get his resolute team to move was to run ahead of them with the light. Afraid of the darkness, they would trot hurriedly after him and so take the train of heavy cars to a desired place.

To those who have known the sun-light there may come the fragrant dream. Perhaps this is what they brood over when they stand solemnly in rows with slowly flapping ears. A recollection may appear to them, a recollection of pastures of a lost paradise. Perhaps they despair and thirst for this bloom that lies in an unknown direction and at impossible distances.

We were appalled occasionally at the quantity of mud we encountered in our wanderings through some of the tunnels. The feet of men and mules had churned it usually into a dull-brown clinging mass. In very wet mines all sorts of gruesome fungi grow upon the wooden props that support the uncertain-looking ceiling. The walls are dripping and dank. Upon them too there frequently grows a moss-like fungus, white as a druid's beard, that thrives in these deep dens but shrivels and dies at contact with the sun-light.

Great and mystically dreadful is the earth from a mine's depth. Man is in the implacable grasp of nature. It has only to tighten slightly and he is crushed like a bug. His loudest shriek of agony would be as impotent as his final moan to bring help from that fair land that lies, like Heaven, over his head. There is an insidious silent enemy in the gas. If the huge fan-wheel on the top of the earth should stop for a brief period, there is certain death and a panic more terrible than any occurring where the sun has shone ensues down under the tons of rock. If a man may escape the gas, the floods, the "squeezes" of falling rock, the cars shooting through little tunnels, the precarious elevators, the hundred perils, there usually comes to him an attack of "miner's asthma" that slowly racks and shakes him into the grave. Meanwhile he gets three dollars per day, and his laborer one dollar and a quarter.

In the chamber at the foot of the shaft, as we were departing, a group of the men were resting. They lay about in careless poses. When we climbed aboard the elevator, we had a moment in which to turn and regard them. Then suddenly the study in black faces and crimson and orange lights vanished. We were on our swift way to the surface. Far above us in the engine-room, the engineer sat with his hand on a lever and his eye on the little model of the shaft wherein a miniature elevator was making the ascent even as our elevator was making it. In fact, the same mighty engines give power to both, and their positions are relatively the same always. I had forgotten about the new world that I was to behold in a moment. My mind was occupied with a mental picture of this faraway engineer, who sat in his high chair by his levers, a statue of responsibility and fidelity, cool-brained, clear-eyed, steady of hand. His arms guided the flight of this platform in its mad and unseen ascent. It was always out of his sight, yet the huge thing obeyed him as a horse its master. When one gets upon the elevator down one of those tremendous holes, one thinks naturally of the engineer.

Of a sudden the fleeting walls became flecked with light. It increased to a downpour of sunbeams. The high sun was afloat in a splendor of spotless blue. The distant hills were arrayed in purple and stood like monarchs. A glory of gold was upon the near-by earth. The cool fresh air was wine.

Of that sinister struggle far below there came no sound, no suggestion save the loaded cars that emerged one after another in eternal procession and were sent creaking up the incline that their contents might by fed into the mouth of the "breaker," imperturbably cruel and insatiate, black emblem of greed, and of the gods of this labor.

★

GERTRUDE ROSCOE *A Paying Concern: A True*
Story of American Factory Life
McClure's (December 1899): 189–196

[As urban industries became more common, women increasingly left domestic work for factories where they had no support and few resources outside the workplace. Roscoe's grim portrait of women weavers' suffering in a textile mill dramatizes not only the greedy mill owner's indifference to his employees but also the particular vulnerability of women laborers.]

THIRTY-FIVE CUTS ahead of the room. How's that for No. 2 section? I tell you my weavers are hustlers. If it hadn't been for those two snails there in the corner, I would have booked an even forty more than any other fixer in the mill. Confound their lazy bones! I'll see their finish in a week or two, or my name isn't Miles Dent."

"Have you got any new method of making them tired, or is it the same old racket?" asked Delaney of No. 10 section, with a shade of sarcasm that was wasted on Dent.

"No, the regular system will do for a while, I guess. Fan was sniveling all yesterday because she couldn't get the last round of cuts off in time to have them checked on this week's pay-sheet, and all the weavers, except Nell, miles ahead of her. You ought to have seen the smart ones pretending to cry and wringing out their handkerchiefs. They were making it hot for her, I tell you."

"Has it gone so far as that?"

"Yes; and it will go further. There's no premium on lazy weavers here. Fan is about ready to give up. I've noticed that they don't hang on long after they begin to weep. But Nell is tougher. She's capable of making me a pile of trouble; but she'll go just the same."

"Where?" questioned Delaney, quietly.

"Anywhere for all I care. You might take them both over on No. 10. The slow weavers seem to gravitate toward your end of the room naturally. You are always behind the whole procession, and eight or ten cuts a week off your account wouldn't make much difference. I've got a couple of dandy weavers all ready to jump in as soon as there's a vacancy on No. 2."

Delaney looked across the room to the two weavers under discussion, but said nothing, and Miles lapsed into silence. He knew about how far it was safe to go with the fixer of No. 10.

The two men stood by Dent's workbench, in the great weaving shed of Blanton's mill, as they held the conversation partly reported above, and seeing Miles apparently at leisure, one of the girls who had incurred his displeasure approached with a shuttle in her hand. It was greatly worn, and had been irregularly whittled and sand-papered out of all true proportions. It had evidently been splintering for a long time, and when a splintered shuttle is driven through a warp by a power loom, it makes trouble of a serious kind for the weaver.

"This shuttle turns in the warp, and I can't make it run at all. I've had half a dozen bad smashes with it. The other one is nearly as bad, and I ought to have a pair of new shuttles. I haven't woven ten yards on that loom in two days. Will you come over and see how they work?"

The weaver manifested neither anger nor impatience, but she spoke with a certain effort, as though she would get through with a very disagreeable piece of work that must be done. The fixer took the shuttle, but made no reply whatever, and after a minute or two, Delaney spoke kindly, to relieve the awkward pause.

"I'm away behind all of 'em again this week, Nellie; but we will carry a lot of cloth over on the looms to begin next week with, and we'll do better than some of these extra smart fellows. Miles, here, has peeled every loom bare to make a big show."

Miles turned suddenly toward the bench, and brought the useless old shuttle down across the vise, breaking it in two. Then he turned his back to the weaver with ostentatious rudeness; and making no attempt to reply to Delaney's talk, she went wearily back to her looms.

Blanton's mill had been running behind for several years. There had been long periods of idleness for the help, longer periods of short hours, and frequent reductions of pay. Nobody quite believed those stories of running at a loss and working half-time, just to give the operatives a chance to live through the hard times, that were industriously circulated. The general impression seemed to be that the owners and managers found that these tactics best served their purpose of grinding the help down to the lowest notch of a living wage. It was better policy than to provoke strikes by sudden cut-downs when everything was running smoothly. After the mill had been closed for a few weeks, or for three or four months, the people would be glad to go to work at greatly reduced wages, and the general condition from the manager's point of view was much better than it would have been after a strike and lockout and a bitter labor contest covering the same period. There was no other large employing industry in the place, the business of which consisted largely in supplying the population gathered about the mill. Many of the traders closed their shops after disposing of the perishable goods on hand, and the whole town fell into business lethargy whenever work failed at Blanton's. All but the saloons: these seemed to flourish perennially, whether the people had employment or not.

In the fall and early winter of the year before the time of which I write, the mill had been closed for four months. New machinery had been put in, and extensive repairs made, and then it was rumored that a new agent had come from Connecticut, who announced his intention of making Blanton's a paying concern.

"There will be no more idleness and want in Blantonville," he had said to the rector of St. John's, who called on him a few days after his arrival. And the good man gave the news to his flock, and rejoiced with them that the long affliction of their enforced idleness would be ended soon.

There was a ten per cent reduction of wages when the mill started. Everybody expected that, and was prepared for it. But none was prepared for the readjustment of prices on all piece-work as soon as the new patterns were set up. Nominally, the pay was the same by the yard, or thousand, or whatever the unit of value might be for the work; but as the new work was finer, more complicated, and much slower in production, it paid proportionately less to the operative, the difference on some grades amounting to twenty-five and even thirty per cent. The people were helpless, and had to make the best of it. They had been out of work so long that nearly every family was heavily in debt, and there was no other work to be had.

The hand of the new agent was soon felt heavily in every department of the mill.

"Tighten up the gears! Tighten up the gears!" was his watchword. "Bring the teeth of the cogs together sharp; you are wasting power. You are putting a premium on laziness and incapacity." And to some of those who felt the inexorable pressure he seemed to have the fiend's own invention and insight in the selection and equipment of his human tools.

One of his first innovations had been the paying of the loom-fixers by the piece. The great weaving-shed was divided crosswise into a dozen or more sections, and a loom-fixer had charge of each of these divisions. His work was to keep the looms in repair, supply the weavers with new warps as they were needed, and look after all the petty details of their work. These men had formerly been paid fixed weekly wages; but it was argued that if they received a certain definite amount for each cut of fifty yards woven on their sections, they would look after their work more sharply, and the looms would not be allowed to stand idle waiting for repairs so frequently or so long. It is with the practical working of this rule that this true story has to do.

The fixers grumbled a good deal at first, and then set resolutely to work to use the power placed in their hands to better their condition. A sharp rivalry soon developed among them, each trying to get the largest amount of cloth to his credit. As some weavers are naturally stronger and more efficient than others, there was soon a considerable shifting about among them. Many of the slower ones got discouraged, and left voluntarily, or were discharged on some frivolous or trumped-up complaint. The fixers carried on this work covertly at first; but after a while, seeing that their superiors took no notice of it, they proceeded with arrogance to weed out the objectionable weavers.

This process had been going on for nearly a year, and Dent of No. 2 section had only two weavers left who were not able to drive through the whole week without once stopping to take breath. These two, Fanny Mace and Eleanor Barnes, were good weavers, doing their work well and performing as much as average weavers ever accomplish under normal conditions. But they could not keep the pace set by Miles Dent's picked crew of men and strong young women, who were foolishly using up five years of their lives in one to "keep solid" with the ambitious fixer. They had no homes, they had not yet gotten clear of the debts contracted during the stopping of the mill, and they steeled themselves resolutely to endure as best they could the petty tyranny to which they were subjected.

"Is your head any better to-day, Fanny?" Eleanor stopped to inquire on her way back from her fruitless attempt to get a new shuttle from Miles.

"O, Nell, you don't know how awfully it aches, and the noise seems different—farther off somehow. Isn't it strange that I don't get hungry? I haven't been near the table since Sunday."

"You ought to eat, whether you have an appetite or not. You'll be sick soon, if you don't. Neither of us can afford to be sick, you know."

"I'm sick now, and my work goes so badly that I never have a minute to rest. If Miles would only fix my looms, I know I could do as much as half of those he brags about. There's something the matter with every one of them, and he just won't do a thing that he can help. Have you got your new shuttles yet?"

"No, and he has broken one of the old ones. Miles is down on both of us, Fanny, and I wish I could find something else to do."

"If he would only let me earn my usual pay for a few weeks, I wouldn't care so much. It seems as though I never should get that back board bill paid. I can't even save a dollar from my last week's pay; and I could have had another cut off of each loom, if he hadn't been so hateful. I can't understand it. I never did anything to injure Miles in my life, but I believe he hates the sight of me."

Fanny had bound her aching head in a folded strip of wet cloth, and from under it her blue eyes with the dark circles beneath them looked out with such hopeless appeal, that Eleanor could find no words to reply. She hurried to her own looms, hardly less out of repair and quite as difficult to manage as those of her alley-mate; but she was stronger than Fanny, and knew better how to husband her strength. She found plenty to do, and could not leave her work for an instant for the rest of the day. But a little later, she saw that Fanny was crying again, and the girls all around her were hooting and screaming and pretending to cry, evidently following the lead of Dent's wife, whose looms were in the same row. Fanny went that night to the crowded, noisy boarding-house that served her for a home, feeling that her work in the mill was done. She had made a brave struggle for weeks and weeks, but the limit of her endurance was reached at last. As she carried her pitcher of water up the three long flights of stairs, she found it so heavy that she was obliged to set it down on every third stair and wait for strength to lift it and go on up to her room. She bathed in the same way, with frequent and long stops, drinking eagerly of the cold water from time to time, which seemed to revive her failing strength. Robing herself for the night in clean, white things from her trunk, she crept into bed, and almost immediately sank into unconsciousness. That night the boarders were kept awake by her raving in the delirium of brain fever, and in the morning the woman who kept the house entered her room in a fury of indignation, and ordered her to get up and pick up her things and find another boarding-place at once, for it had been reported to her that the sick girl was intoxicated. Fanny only muttered incoherently and picked busily at the sheets with aimless hands.

"Let the hussy be till she sleeps it off. I can't beat any sense into her in that condition, but she'll have to pack as soon as she can stagger out of the house," was the final word of the landlady to the chamber girl, who was peering in at the door.

When Eleanor saw that Fanny was absent from her work, she was glad that her friend had concluded to take a much-needed rest. But in a little while the report that she was howling drunk, and had kept the whole boarding-house awake all night, was circulated through the room, to the uproarious amusement of those who had actively persecuted her. This story alarmed Eleanor, and she applied at once for leave to go out and see herself how it was with Fanny. The report itself was sufficient that she must be suffering at the boarding-house for need of attention and care.

The overseer curtly refused her request, on the plea that her work would have to be stopped, as there was no spare hand; and in the afternoon it was the same. Just before the speed went down at night, a heavy casting fell on her foot, bruising it so badly that she had to be carried home in one of the mill wagons, and it was two days before she could hobble about. At noon of the third day, disregarding the pain of her injured foot, she returned to her work, going around by Fanny's house, intending to see her before entering the mill. She had worried incessantly about Fanny, knowing what it was to be sick in a factory boarding-house. But when she reached the corner of the block, she saw that it was forever too late. The undertaker's wagon stood before the door, and his men were bringing out the cheap pine coffin that the town provided for its friendless and penniless dead.

When Eleanor went down the alley to her looms, she had to pick her way around and over a perfect clutter of parts and pieces of the looms that had been Fanny's. Miles was at work on them, and was evidently bent on doing a thorough job. He took them one by one, pulled them to pieces, and seemed fairly to make them over again; and a large, cheerful girl, with many frizzes around her face, and very clean new waist and apron, took charge of those that he repaired as fast as they were in running order, leaving the rest of the set idle till they were fixed. This girl was very friendly with those who had abused Fanny, and Eleanor learned after a while that Dent's wife was her sister.

This very thing had been repeated on the section at least a dozen times within the year, and what was the use of wearing out the remnant of her health and strength in the useless contest? Better leave at once, while she was able to work. So reasoned Eleanor, watching the repairing of the purposely neglected looms. But there was one thing more to be tried. Perhaps she could get transferred to No. 10 section. Delaney was the only fixer in the room who had gone on in his usual way and absolutely refrained from using the power in his hands to favor one or injure another of the weavers whose looms were in his care.

Eleanor found the agent in the overseer's office, and a large, thickset Englishman, with square jaws and cruel little gray eyes, carrying an apron rolled in a towel under his arm. The three were talking affably together. Seeing her employer thus occupied, Eleanor would have retreated, but he called sharply to know what she wanted.

"Think you can run the self-feeders, do you?" he said, when she had preferred her request. "Well, I've got a little bone to pick with Delaney, and you may as well wait a few minutes. Perhaps you will change your mind about wanting to go to work on No. 10."

The overseer seemed in great good spirits, and there was nothing to do but stand aside and wait as he bade her, though she knew there was something dreadful going to be done when the morose man was in this mood of politeness and pleasantry. Through the glass door she saw Delaney coming, with his head a little more erect than usual. He bowed to the agent, and stood silently before the desk, looking quietly from the overseer to the Englishman, who shifted the towel and apron to his other arm, as if to attract attention to these symbols of instant preparation for work.

"How is it, Delaney, that you are so much behind the others with your work?" began the agent, taking the overseer's work out of his hands, to his no small chagrin. Everyone knew that he had reduced the heads of departments to mere automatons, but there was usually some show before the help of allowing them to do their own work.

"This business is all cut and dried," said Delaney, with a glance at the man with the apron. "You might as well give me my time at once. I can fix looms, but I've never yet done some of the work that seems to be expected of the fixers here, and I don't intend to do it. Where's the use of spinning it out?"

"Very well; take this man down to No. 10, and put him in charge of the work. Your bill will be ready as soon as you want it," said the overseer, speaking with great dignity, and the two fixers went out into the shed together. "Now, Barnes," said the overseer, with a disagreeable grin, "what can I do for you?"

"Nothing," said Eleanor quietly, "but write me a bill of my time. Miles told me yesterday that a competent weaver was all ready to take my looms if I was dissatisfied with his work, and she is welcome to the job. I shall be permanently lame if I try to work any more with my foot in its present condition.

Delaney would have been a little easy with me for a week or two, and I could have worried along with it till it gets well. But I should have no chance with the man you have hired in his place."

The overseer turned purple in the face at this plain speaking, and fairly shouted a rough command for silence. "If you think this mill is a hospital or charitable institution, you are greatly mistaken. Get out as soon as you can walk. I've no use for cripples. I want able-bodied help, and there's plenty of it waiting three deep around the door any morning."

This speech was embroidered with oaths, and more followed Eleanor out of the office, till they were drowned by the noise of the looms, as she went back into the shed for her hat and shawl. Seeing her gather up her things, the set that had tortured Fanny began hooting and shrieking, and kept it up till the door closed behind her.

When Eleanor entered the dining-room at her boarding-house that night, the landlady followed her closely. Waiting till she had laid her hand on her chair to draw it back from the table, the woman spoke in a loud, distinct voice: "You can have no supper here to-night, Miss Barnes, and I must ask you to vacate your room at once. I have stopped your pay at the office, and it will do you no good to present your bill for payment to-morrow. There's not half enough due you to pay my bill, and I shall keep your trunk till you pay the balance. I will allow you one change of clothing and your working aprons. We might as well attend to it now."

Without a word Eleanor followed her out of the room, where the people re-maining, stricken dumb and silent at the first word of the official voice of the landlady, now burst into indiscriminate gabble and laughter, mingled with the clatter of knife and dish.

This landlady had dramatic tastes, and invariably worked up a little scene whenever any opportunity offered, and her audience was always apprecia-tive. She preceded Eleanor to her room, and watched the packing of the trunk, and also of the hand-satchel that Eleanor was to be permitted to take with her. Then she locked the trunk herself, and put the key in her pocket. Holding the lamp in her hand, she stood aside for the girl to pass out, intend-ing to lock the door of the room before she went away. Then for the first time Eleanor spoke.

"I think I will dress my foot, if you have no objection, Mrs. Haines. The bandage is too tight, and I can walk better if it is loosened."

"Oh, very well, put out the light when you are ready to go. I will come up later, and close the room."

Left alone, Eleanor undressed the injured foot, bathed it in arnica, and re-placed the bandage more comfortably. The afternoon's work had made the swelling much worse, and the flesh was purple and ridged into the folds of the bandage; but the pain abated under the treatment, and she found herself able to walk down the stairs and out of the house quite steadily. Pausing on the doorstep, she turned the collar of her jacket up about her neck and drew on her mittens, for a fine snow was sifting down, and the wind drew in from the river in cold gusts. The people from the boarding-houses along the street were coming out from supper, and hurrying by in a jostling crowd. Waiting till the space in front of the house was temporarily clear, Eleanor took up her satchel, stepped carefully down to the icy sidewalk, and walked slowly away.

Two men paused on the steps of a business block to watch the crowd from the mill going by and exchange a few words at parting.

"That's about the last of the hands. There are only a few stragglers now, and we can dodge them," said one. "Look at that face passing under the lamp. Did you ever see such a peculiar color?"

"Often, at the operating-table," replied the other, who was a doctor; "but it's rather unusual on the street. That woman is suffering intense pain. It's lucky for us that we can't see and hear all that is carried behind these masks of faces."

"They've had a hard time for the last few years, but things promise to be better for the hands now employed, as well as for the rest of us. The mill has been running nearly ten months, and they tell me there are advance orders for a year to come. The new agent seems to have kept his word, and made Blanton's a paying concern."

★

ELMORE ELLIOTT PEAKE *The Night Run of the 'Overland':
A Story of Domestic Life Among the Railroad People*
McClure's (June 1900) 143–149

[Peake presents a heroine of the workers who, in the name of duty and family honor, guides the midnight train on its perilous run. Strikingly, though, the heroine in this tale of adventure and family reconciliation is also a woman of a higher class whose marriage to an honorable workingman allows her to claim both workingwoman's skills and innate courage.]

I⊤ SNOWED. The switch-lamps at Valley Junction twinkled faintly through the swirling flakes. A broad band of light from the night-operator's room shot out into the gloom, and it, too, was thickly powdered. Aside from this, the scattered houses of the little hamlet slept in darkness—all save one.

Through the drawn curtains of a cottage which squatted in the right angle formed by the intersecting tracks, a hundred yards or more from the station, a light shone dully. Inside, a young woman with a book in her lap sat beside a sick-bed. On the bed lay a young man of perhaps thirty.

They were not an ordinary couple, nor of the type which prevailed in Valley Junction. The rugged strength of the man, which shone through even the pallor of sickness, was touched and softened by an unmistakable gentleness of birth; and the dark eyes, which rested motionless upon the further wall, were thoughtful and liquid with intelligence. The young woman was yet more striking. Her loose gown, girdled at the waist with a tasseled cord, only half concealed the sturdy sweeping lines of the form beneath. Her placid, womanly face was crowned with a glorious mass of burnished auburn hair. Her blue eyes, now fixed solicitously upon her husband's face, were dark with what seemed an habitual earnestness of purpose, and her sweet mouth drooped seriously. After a moment, though, she shook off her pensive mood. "What are you thinking of, dear?" she asked, with a brightening face.

"Of you," answered her husband gravely, tightening his grasp upon the hand she had slipped into his. "Comparing your life in this wretched place, Sylvia, with what it was before I married you; and thinking of that wonderful thing called 'love,' which can make you content with the change."

The young woman bent forward with a little spasmodic movement, and laid her beautiful hair upon the pillow beside her husband's dark strands. For a little she held herself in a kind of breathless tension, her hand upon his further temple, her full passionate lips pressed tight against his cheek.

"Not content, my heart's husband, but happy!" she whispered ecstatically. After a moment she lifted herself and quietly smoothed her ruffled hair. "I mustn't do that again," she said, demurely. "The doctor said you were not to be excited. I guess I won't allow you to think any more on that subject, either," she added, with pretty tyranny. "Only this, Ben—papa will forgive us someday. He's good. Just give him time. Some day you'll put away your dear, foolish pride, and let me write to him, and tell him where we are—no matter if he did forbid it. And he'll write back, take my word for it, and say, 'Come home, children, and be forgiven.' But whether he does or not, I tell you, sweetheart, I would sooner flutter about this little dovecote of ours, and ride on the engine with you on bright days, than be mistress of the finest palace papa's money can build."

For a moment the pair looked the love they could not speak. Then the spell was broken by the distant scream of a locomotive, half-drowned in the howling wind. Sylvia glanced at the clock.

"There's the 'Overland,'" she murmured. "She's three minutes late. The wind is dead against her. Some day, dear," she added, fondly, "you will hold the throttle of that engine if you want to, and I shall be the proudest girl in the land."

With a fine unconscious loyalty to the corporation, which gave them bread and butter, they listened in silence to the dull roar of the on-coming train. But instead, a moment later, of the usual thunderous burst as the train swept by, and the trembling of earth, they heard the grinding of brake-shoes, the whistle of the air, and then, in the lull which followed, the thumping of the pump, like some great, excited heart. At this unexampled occurrence, the sick man threw his wife a startled glance, and she sprang to the front window and drew back the curtain. She was just turning away again, still unsatisfied, when there came a quick, imperative rap with the delayed train, Sylvia flung the door wide open, revealing three men, the foremost of whom she recognized as the night-operator at the Junction.

"Mrs. Fox," he began with nervous haste, "this is the general superintendent, Mr.———"

"My name is Howard, madam," said the official for himself, unceremoniously pushing forward. "We are in trouble. Our engineer had a stroke of apoplexy fifteen miles back, and I want your husband to take this train. I know he's sick but—"

"But he's too sick, sir, to hold his head up!" Sylvia exclaimed, aghast.

"What's the trouble?" called Fox sharply, from his bed.

An instant's hush fell over the little group at the door, and then they all, as if moved by one impulse, filed quickly back to the sick-room.

"Mr. Fox, I hate to ask a sick man to get out of bed and pull a train," began the general superintendent hurriedly, before Sylvia could speak. "But we're tied up here hard and fast, with not another engineer in sight; and every minute that train stands there the company loses a thousand dollars. If you can pull her through to Stockton, and will, it will be the best two hours' work that you ever did. I will give you five hundred dollars."

Fox had at first risen to his elbow, but he now sank back, dizzy and trembling from weakness. In a moment, though, he was up again. "I can't do it Mr. Howard! I'm too sick!" he exclaimed bitterly. "If it weren't a physical impossibility—if I weren't too dizzy to hold my head up—"

He broke off abruptly, and pressed his hand in a dazed way to his brow. Then he fixed his excited eyes upon his wife. The other men followed his gaze, plainly regarding him as out of his head. But Sylvia turned pale, and leaned against the wall for support. She had caught her husband's full meaning.

"She'll take the train, sir!" exclaimed Fox eagerly; "and she'll take it through safe. She knows an engine as well as I, and every inch of the road. Sylvia, you must go. It is your duty."

The superintendent staggered at this proposition, gasped, and stared at the young woman. She stood with her dilated eyes fastened upon her husband, her chest rising and falling, and blood-red tongues of returning color shooting through her cheeks. Yet even in that crucial moment, when her

little heart was fluttering like a wounded bird, something in Sylvia's eye—
something hard and stubborn—fixed the skeptical superintendent's attention, and he drew a step nearer. Sylvia, with twitching nostrils and swelling
throat, turned upon him almost desperately.

"I will go," she said, in a low, resigned voice. "But some one must stay here
with him."

"This young man will attend to all that, never fret," cried Howard gaily,
in his relief, turning to the night-operator. Whatever doubts the superintendent may have harbored yet of the fair engineer's nerve and skill were plainly
removed when Sylvia returned from the inner room, after an absence of
scarcely sixty seconds. An indomitable courage was stamped upon her handsome features, and she bore herself with the firm, subdued mien of one who
knows the gravity of her task, yet has faith in herself for its performance.
One of her husband's caps was drawn down tightly over her thick hair. She
had slipped into a short walking skirt, and as she advanced she calmly but
swiftly buttoned her jacket. Without hesitation, she stepped to the bedside
and kissed her husband good-by.

"Be brave girl!" he said encouragingly, though his own voice shook. "You
have to make seventy-five miles an hour, or better; but you've got the machine to do it with. Give her her head on all the grades except Four Mile
Creek—don't be afraid!—and give her a little sand on Beechtree Hill. Good-
by—and God keep you!"

As Sylvia stood beneath the great black hulk of iron and steel which drew
the "Overland" compared with which her husband's little local engine was
but a toy—and glanced down the long line of mail, express, and sleeping-
cars, laden with human freight, her heart almost failed her again. The mighty
boiler towered high above her in the darkness like the body of some horrible antediluvian monster, and the steam rushed angrily from the dome, as
though the great animal were fretting under unaccountable delay, and longed
again to be off on the wings of the wind, reading the tempest with its iron
snout, and awakening the sleeping hills and hollows with its hoarse shriek.

"You are a brave little woman," she heard the superintendent saying at
the cab-step. "Don't lose your nerve—but make time whatever else you do.
Every minute you make up is money in the company's pocket and they won't
forget it. Beside," he added, familiarly, "we've got a big gun aboard, and I want
to show him that a little thing like this don't frustrate us any. If you draw
into Stockton on time, I'll add five hundred dollars to that check! Remember
that." And he lifted her up to the cab.

The fireman, a young Irishman, stared at Sylvia as she stepped into the
cab as though she were a banshee; but she made no explanations, and, after
a glance at the steam and the water gages climbed up to the engineer's high

seat. The hand she laid upon the throttle-lever trembled slightly—as well it might; the huge iron horse quivered and stiffened as if bracing itself for its task; noiselessly and imperceptibly it moved ahead, expelled one mighty breath, then another and another, quicker and quicker, shorter and shorter, until its respirations were lost in one continuous flow of steam. The "Overland" was once more under way.

The locomotive responded to Sylvia's touch with an alacrity which seemed almost human, and which, familiar though she was with the work, thrilled her through and through. She glanced at the timetable. They were twelve minutes behind time. The twenty miles between Junction and Grafton lay in a straight, level line. Sylvia determined to use it to good purpose, and to harden herself at once—as, indeed, she must—to the dizzy speed required by the inexorable schedule. She threw the throttle wide open, and pushed the reverse-lever into the last notch. The great machine seemed suddenly animated with a demoniac energy, and soon they were shooting through the black, storm-beaten night like an avenging bolt from the hand of a colossal god. The headlight—so dazzling from in front, so insufficient from behind—danced feebly ahead upon the driving cloud of snow. But that was all. The track was illuminated for scarcely fifty feet, and the night yawned beyond like some engulfing abyss. Sylvia momentarily closed her eyes and prayed that no unfortunate creature—human or brute—might wander that night between the rails.

The fireman danced attendance on the fire, watching his heat and water as jealously as a doctor might watch the pulse of a fevered patient. Now the furnace-door was closed again, and now, when the ravenous maw within cried for more coal, it was flung wide open, lighting the driving cloud of steam and smoke above with a spectral glare.

Sylvia worked with the fireman with a fine intelligence which only the initiated could understand; for an engine is a steed whose speed depends upon its driver. She opened or closed the injector, to economize the heat and water, and eased the steam when it could be spared. Thus together they coaxed, cajoled, threatened, and goaded the wheeled monster until, like a veritable thing of life, it seemed to strain every nerve to do their bidding and whirled them faster and faster. Yet, as they flashed through Grafton—scarcely distinguishable in the darkness and the storm—they were still ten minutes behind time. Sylvia shut her lips tightly. If it was necessary to defy death she would.

The sticky snow on her glass now cut off Sylvia's vision ahead. It mattered little, for her life and the lives of the sleeping passengers behind were in higher hands than hers, and only the All-seeing Eye could see that night. Another train ahead, an open switch, a fallen rock or tree—one awful crash, and the engine would become a gridiron for her tender flesh, while the palatial cars behind now so full of warmth and light and comfort, would suddenly be turned into mere shapeless heaps of death. Yet Sylvia cautiously opened her door a little, and held it firmly against the hurricane while she brushed off the snow. At the same time she noticed that the headlight was burning dim.

"The headlight is covered with snow!" she called to the fireman.

The young fellow instantly drew his cap tighter, braced himself, and swung open his door. At the first cruel blast, the speed of which was that of the gale added to that of the train, he closed his eyes and held his breath; then, taking his life in his hands, he slipped out upon the wet, treacherous running-board of the pitching locomotive, made his way forward, and cleared the glass. Sylvia waited with bated breath until his head appeared in the door again.

"Fire up, please!" she exclaimed, nervously, for the steam had fallen off a pound.

As the twinkling street-lamps of Nancyville came into view, Sylvia blew a long blast. But there was no tuneful reverberation among the hills that night, for the wind, like some ferocious beast of prey, pounced upon the sound and throttled it in the teeth of the whistle. The Foxes shopped in Nancyville—they could shop fifty miles from home as easily as fifty rods—and the town, by comparison with Valley Junction, was beginning to seem like a little city to Sylvia. But tonight, sitting at the helm of that transcontinental train, which burst upon the town like a cyclone, with a shriek and a roar, and then was gone again all in a breath, she scarcely recognized the place; and it seemed little and rural and mean to her, a mere eddy in the world's big current.

One-third of the one hundred and forty-nine miles was now gone and still the "Overland" was ten minutes behind, and it seemed as if no human power could make up the time. They were winding through the Tallahula Hills, where the road was as crooked as a serpent's trail. The engine jerked viciously from side to side as if angrily resenting the pitiless goading from behind, and twice Sylvia was nearly thrown from her seat. The wheels savagely ground the rails at every curve, and made them shriek in agony. One side of the engine first mounted upward, like a ship upon a wave, then suddenly sank, as if engulfed. One instant Sylvia was lifted high above her fireman, the next dropped far below him.

Yet she dared not slacken speed. The cry of "Time! Time! Time!" was drummed into her ears with every stroke of the piston. Her train was but one wheel—nay, but one cog on one wheel in the vast and complicated machine of transportation. Yet one slip of that cog would rudely jar the whole delicate mechanism from coast to coast. Indeed, in Sylvia's excited fancy, the spirit of world-wide commercialism seemed riding on the gale above her, like Odin of old in the Wildhunt, urging her on and on.

Something of all this was in the mind of the fireman too, in a simpler way; and when he glanced at his gentle superior from time to time, as she clung desperately to the armrest with one hand and clutched the reverse-lever with the other, with white, set face but firm mouth and fearless eye, his blue eyes flashed with a chivalric fire.

The train dashed into Carbondale, and Sylvia made out ahead the glowing headlight of the east-bound train, side-tracked and waiting for the belated "Overland," her engineer and conductor doubtless fuming and fretting. For the first time during the run Sylvia allowed a morbid, nervous fear to take hold of her. Suppose the switch were open! She knew that it must be closed, but the sickening possibility presented itself over and over again, with its train of horrors, in brief space of a few seconds. She held her breath and half closed her eyes as they thundered down upon the other train, and when the engine lurched a little as it struck the switch her heart leaped into her mouth. The suspense was mercifully short, though, for in an instant, as it were, they were past the danger, past the town and once more scouring the open country.

In spite of the half-pipe of sand which she let run as they climbed Beech-tree Hill—the last of the Tallahulas—it seemed to Sylvia as if they would never reach the summit and as if the locomotive had lost all its vim. Yet the speed was slow only by contrast, and in reality was terrific; and the tireless steed upon whose high haunch Sylvia was perched was doing the noblest work of the night. At last, though, the high level of the Barren Plains was gained, and forty miles—which were reeled off in less than thirty minutes—they swept along like an albatross on the crest of a gale, smoothly and almost noiselessly in the deadening snow.

Sylvia suspected that the engine was doing no better right here than it did every night of the year, and that when on time. Yet when she glanced from the time-table to the clock, as they clicked over the switch-points of Melrose with a force which seemed sufficient to snap them off like icicles, she was chagrined to discover that they were still eight minutes behind. They were now approaching the long twelve-mile descent of Four Mile Creek, with a beautiful level stretch at the bottom through the Spirit River Valley. Sylvia came to a grim determination. Half a dozen times previously she had wondered, in her unfamiliarity with heavy trains and their magnificent speed, if she were falling short of or exceeding the safety limit; and half a dozen times she had been on the point of appealing to the fireman. But her pride, even in that momentous crisis, had restrained her; and, moreover, the time-table, mutely urging her faster and faster, seemed answer enough. But just before they struck the grade, the responsibility of her determination—contrary, too, to her husband's advice—seemed too much to bear alone.

"I am going to let her have her head!" she cried out, in her distress.

The fireman did not answer—perhaps he did not hear and, setting her teeth, Sylvia assumed the grim burden alone. The ponderous locomotive fell over the brow of the hill with her throttle agape, and the fire seething in her vitals with volcanic fury. Then she lowered her head like a maddened bull in its charge. The long, heavy train sweeping down the sharp descent, might fitly have been likened to some winged dragon flying low to earth, so appallingly flightlike was the motion. It seemed to Sylvia as though they dropped down the grade as an aerolite drops from heaven—silent, irresistible, awful, touched only by the circumambient air.

All Sylvia's familiar methods of gaging speed were now at fault, but she believed that for the moment they were running two miles to every minute. The thought that a puny human hand—a woman's hand, moreover, contrived for the soft offices of love—could stay that grand momentum, seemed wildly absurd; and as Sylvia, under the strange lassitude born of her deadly peril, relaxed her tense muscles, and drowsily closed her eyes, she smiled, with a ghastly humor, at the trust of the sleeping passengers in *her!*

She was rudely shaken out of her lethargy as the train struck a slight curve half way down the grade. The locomotive shied like a frightened steed, and shook in every iron muscle. The flanges shrieked against the rails, the cab swayed and cracked, and the very earth seemed to tremble. For a moment the startled girl was sure they were upon the ties, or at least had lost a wheel. But it was only the terrible momentum lifting them momentarily from the track, and in a few seconds—though every second meant 150 feet—the fire-eating behemoth righted itself. Yet its beautiful equilibrium was gone; and, as if abandoning itself to its driver's mad mood, the engine rolled and pitched and rose and fell, like a water-logged vessel in a storm. The bell, catching the motion, began to toll; and the dolorous sound, twisted into weird discord by the gale, fell upon the ears of the pallid engineer and fireman like the notes of a storm-tossed bell-buoy sounding the knell of the doomed.

The young fireman, who up to this time had maintained a stoical calm suddenly, sprang to the floor of the cab, with a face torn by superstitious fear.

"What if she leaves the rails!" he cried.

But instantly recovering himself, he sprung back to his seat, with the blood of shame on his cheeks.

"Am I running too fast?" shouted Sylvia.

"Not when we're behind time!" he doggedly shouted back.

As the track became smoother, the engine grew calmer; but its barred tongue licked up the flying space for many a mile before the momentum of that perilous descent was lost. As the roar of their passage over the long bridge spanning the Mattetunk, twenty miles from Stockton, died away, the fireman called out cheerily: "On time, madam!"

His voice reached Sylvia's swimming ears faint and distant as she nodded dizzily on her seat, bracing herself against the reverse-lever.

Meanwhile, in the general superintendent's private car, at the extreme rear of the train, a party of men still sat up, smoking their Havanas and sipping their wine. One member of this party was the "big gun" mentioned to Sylvia by the general superintendent—the president of the Mississippi Valley, Omaha, and Western Railway. He was a large man, with luxuriant, snow-white hair; and, though his face was benevolent, even paternal, every line of it betrayed the inflexible will which had lifted its owner from the roof of a freight car to the presidential chair of a great road.

Mr. Howard, the general superintendent, was regaling the party with an account of his experience in securing a substitute engineer at Valley Junction. For reasons afterward divulged, he suppressed, though, the most dramatic account of the heroism of the sick man, whom he unblushingly represented as having risen from his bed and taken charge of the engine.

Mr. Staniford, the distinguished guest, listened quietly until Howard was done.

"Charlie, you are a heartless wretch," he observed, smiling; and when Howard protested, with a twinkle in his eye, that there was no other way, the president added: "If it had been on my road, I should have held the train all night rather than drag a sick man from his bed."

"We all know how many trains are held all night on your road, Staniford," answered Howard, laughing. "Do you happen to remember the story of an ambitious young engineer who picked himself up out of a wreck with a broken arm, and, stepped into a new engine, and pulled his train through to the end of the run?" he asked significantly.

"I was young then and working for glory, and no superintendent ordered me to do it, or I should probably have refused," said Staniford, good-naturedly. He added soberly: "These engineers are a heroic set, and Charlie, sometimes I think we don't always do them justice."

"I'll do this one justice," answered Howard, warmly.

The party dropped off to bed, one by one. The general superintendent himself finally rose and looked at his watch. As he turned and made his way forward, his careless expression gave way to one of concern. His mind was evidently on the gentle engine-runner. Possibly he had recurring doubts of her skill and courage; but perhaps the fact that he had daughters of his own gave his thoughts, as much as anything else, a graver turn. Three cars ahead he met the conductor, who also seemed a little nervous, and they talked together for some moments. The train, at the time, was snapping around the choppy curves in the Tallahula Hills like the lash of a whip, and the two men had difficulty in keeping their feet.

"Fast, but not too fast, Dackins," observed the superintendent, half inquiringly.

"What I call a high safety," answered the conductor.

"But fearful in the cab, eh?"

"Nothing equal to it, sir," rejoined Dackins, dryly.

Howard started back toward the private car about the time the train struck Beechtree Hill. He paused in a vestibule, opened the door, and laid his practiced ear to the din outside. Then he gently closed the door, as if to slam it might break the spell, and complacently smiled. When the train reached the level of Barren Plains, and the sleepers ceased their swaying and settled down to a smooth, straightaway motion—that sure annunciator of high speed—the superintendent rubbed his palms together very much like a man shaking hands with himself. When he got back to his car, he found Mr. Staniford still up, smoking, and leaning back in the luxurious seat with half-closed eyes. Staniford motioned Howard to sit down beside him, and laid his hand familiarly on the latter's knee.

"Confound you, Charlie, you've got that sick engineer on my heart, with your inflammatory descriptions, for which you probably drew largely on your imagination. I have been sitting here thinking about him. Confess, now, that you exaggerated matters a little."

The superintendent chuckled like a man who knows a thing or two, if he only chose to tell. "Well, I did, in one respect; but in another I fell short." He paused for effect, and then continued exultingly: "Staniford, I've got the best railroad story to give the papers that has been brought out in years, and if I don't get several thousand dollars worth of free advertising out of it, my name isn't C. W. Howard. The best of it is, it's the gospel truth."

"Let's have it," said Staniford, smiling. "Well, between you and me, that man Fox was a mighty sick man—too sick to hold his head up, in fact." Howard paused inquiringly as Staniford turned sharply, and gave him a glance.

"Fox, did you say?" asked Staniford. "What's his first name?"

"I don't know. He's a tall, smooth-faced man, with dark hair and eyes. Rather intelligent-looking. What do you know about him? He's a comparatively new man with us."

The old man's fingers trembled slightly as he flicked the ashes from his cigar. "I don't know that I know him," he answered, in a constrained tone. "If he's the man I have in mind, he's all right. Go on."

"Ever run on your road?" inquired Howard, deliberately.

"Yes, yes. But that has nothing to do with it," returned Staniford, with strange impatience. "Go on."

"Well," continued the superintendent, with a mildly curious glance at his companion, "he was altogether too sick to pull a plug, but it seems that his wife has been in the habit of riding with him, and knows the road and an engine as well as he does. To come to the point—and this is my story, which I didn't tell the boys for the sake of their nerves," he added, with sparkling eyes—"the 'Overland' at this moment is in the hands of a girl, sir—Fox's wife!"

It seemed a long time before either man spoke again. Howard stared in blank amazement at the pallid face of the president, unable to understand the old railroader's agitation, and unwilling to attribute it to fear from being in the hands of an engineer who might lose her head. Then Staniford took the other's hand, and held it in an iron grip.

"Charlie, it's my own little baby girl!" he said, huskily.

Howard was familiar with the story of the elopement of Staniford's daughter with one of the M.V., O., and W. engineers, and the situation flashed over him in an instant. After a moment—during which, as he afterward confessed, he could not keep his mind off the added sensation this new fact would give his advertising story—he said enthusiastically: "She's a heroine, Staniford, and worthy of her father!"

During the perilous descent of Four Mile Creek, the private car rocked like a cradle, and cracked and snapped in every joint. Staniford clung helplessly to Howard's hand, with the tears trickling down his cheeks. When the bottom was at last reached and the danger was over—the danger at the front—the president drew his handkerchief and wiped the great drops of sweat from his brow. The ex-engineer knew the agony through which his child had passed.

The operator at Valley Junction had flashed the news along the wire, and when the "Overland" steamed up to the union depot in Stockton, at 1:07, twenty seconds ahead of time, a curious and enthusiastic throng of lay-over passengers and railroad men pressed around the engine. When Sylvia appeared in the gangway, her glorious sun-kissed hair glistening with melted snow, and her pale face streaked with soot, the generous crowd burst into yells of applause. The husky old veteran runner who was to take the girl's place stepped forward, by virtue of his office, as it were, and lifted Sylvia down. For a moment she reeled, partly from faintness, partly from the sickness caused by the pitching of the locomotive. Then she saw pushing unceremoniously through the throng the general superintendent and—she started and looked again—her father!

When President Staniford, struggling to control his emotion, clasped his daughter to his bosom, her overstrained nerves gave way under the double excitement; and laying her head wearily upon his shoulder, and with her hands upon his neck, she began to cry in a choked, pitiful little way. "Oh, papa, call me your dear little red-head once more!" she sobbed.

★

FLORENCE KELLEY *Women and Girls in Sweat-Shops*
Chautauquan (September 1897): 655–657

[Building on the *Chautauquan*'s associations with moral and religious life, Kelley, the chief inspector of factories and workshops for the state of Illinois, suggests to her solidly middle-class readers the ways in which misinformation about the garment industry allows for poor working conditions to be viewed as an asset to consumers.]

In the sweat-shops of Chicago there were found, in 1896, about seven thousand women, and rather more than one thousand girls under the age of sixteen years. This does not include the children who sew on buttons or fell seams in tenement rooms with the other members of their families; it includes merely such as the factory inspectors, while making their rounds, found in shops which the law places under inspection. While the average in all manufacturing industries in Illinois is forty-five children to one thousand male employees over sixteen years of age, in these shops the number rises to one hundred and eighty-six children to one thousand, or almost the ratio of a child to every five men. Moreover, a large part of the women in these shops are girls between sixteen and twenty years of age.

Technically, a sweat-shop is a tenement-house kitchen or bedroom in which the head of the family employs outsiders, persons not members of his immediate family, in the manufacture of garments or cigars for some wholesaler or some merchant tailor. In Illinois, since 1893, it has been a misdemeanor to maintain this form of shop. The factory inspectors, therefore, prosecute every tailor or cigar-maker whom they find working in this way. Hence the tailor now usually hires a room adjoining the flat in which his family lives, nails or screws the connecting door firmly shut, and defies the inspectors to interfere with him. If he draws the nails or unscrews and opens the door on Sundays and in the dull season there is no ground of prosecution, for the inspector calling at such a time does not find manufacture actually carried on during the visit. It is rare now to find a sweat-shop, in the proper sense of the word, in active operation; but shops of the kind just described have increased in the past four years and are still rapidly increasing. The name sweat-shop now attaches indiscriminately to any shop for the manufacture of garments or cigars in any tenement-house; and it would probably contribute to the intelligent discussion of the subject if we could substitute for this ugly word of ill-defined meaning the more general term tenement-house shop.

The women and girls found at work in these shops in Chicago are of eight nationalities: Bohemians, Poles, Russian Jews, Italians, Germans, Swedes, Norwegians, and Danes. Very few of them speak English, and fewer still read or write it. In prosecuting sweaters who have employed girls under fourteen years of age in their shops we have sometimes been obliged, when placing a child upon the witness stand, to employ an interpreter in order to obtain replies to such simple questions as, "What is your name?" "How old are you?" "Where do you live?" "Have you worked for this man?" In numerous instances the child who thus required the services of an interpreter for a conversation in words of one syllable had been living several years in Chicago, in the densely foreign colonies which form a large part of the city.

This isolation of the different groups, by reason of their having no common language, forms one of the most serious obstacles to united effort on the part of the sweaters' victims for any improvement of the conditions under which they work.

Nor does there seem to be any reasonable hope of change in this respect, since it is in the districts in which sweat-shops abound and foreign colonies are densest that the Chicago Board of Education leaves the largest numbers of children unsupplied with public school accommodations.

In the Polish sixteenth ward there are some eight thousand children in excess of the seating capacity of the public schools; and in this ward we find a large proportion of our illiterate children in the sweat-shops. In the nineteenth ward, where the children between eight and fourteen years are some three thousand in excess of the public school sittings, one of the commonest street sights is a group of women and girls in the short skirts of the south Italian peasants, carrying on their heads enormous bundles of trousers, knee-breeches, or cloaks, as they walk from the sweat-shop to their tenement dwelling. When the bundle reaches home, all the children in the tenement-house who are able to hold a needle gather about the brindle and do their share of the sewing, quite irrespective of school hours, and chattering all the while in their native patois.

There is a wide-spread belief that the prevailing cheapness of ready-made clothing is due to the utilization of the ill-paid labor of women and children in these tenement homes and shops; that the wage-earner in the non-sweated trades profits by the sufferings of these sweaters' victims, and wears better garments by reason of their poverty and the degradation of this great trade. This is, however, the exact reverse of the truth. The cheapness of our garments is attained in spite of the sweating system, not because of it. Indeed, it is doubtful whether the fall in prices of garments is commensurate with the fall in the prices of the cloth of which they are made. Certain it is that cloth is vastly cheaper than it was thirty years ago. The methods of placing goods of all kinds upon the market (garments and cloth for making garments included) have been revolutionized in the direction of cheapness within the memory of all of us. That part of the work of making garments which lies outside of sweat-shops has also been cheapened by the general application of steam machinery to garment-cutting. These three great modern improvements have enabled the corporations which control the garment trade to prolong the life of the foot-power sewing-machine and the tenement-house sweat-shop.

The purchasing public, made gullible, perhaps, by its own greed for bargains, has willingly believed that in this one set of trades alone primitive machines and petty shops maintaining a multitude of middlemen were really cheaper in the end (because they employ the worst paid women and girls to be found in the field of manufacture) than well-equipped plants, with power furnished by steam or electricity and conducted by managers of higher intelligence.

It has become an axiom in political economy that high-priced labor stimulates the application of machinery. On the other hand, the presence in the sweat-shops of girls who sew on buttons and run errands for wages ranging from thirty cents to seventy cents a week, and of women who sew at foot-power machines for $3.00 to $5.00 a week from ten to twenty hours a day during the five to seven months which form the busy season, and receive relief from public and private charities during the remainder of the year, distinctly tends to prolong the present primitive and belated equipment of this part of the garment trades. It is, perhaps, not too much to say that the seven thousand women and the thousand girls in the sweat-shops of Chicago present a serious obstacle to the process of lifting the garment trades from their present degradation to the level of the factory trades.

Under the sweating system, the wholesaler shifts the burden of rent from himself to the tailor who sews in a tenement-house kitchen or bedroom. The wholesaler farther avoids the risk attendant upon maintaining a plant equipped with steam or electricity throughout the dull season. He offsets, as far as he can, the added expense of a horde of middlemen, by subdividing the work of the women and girls in the shops and simplifying it to the utmost extreme, so that skill in the worker is reduced to the last degree, and wages follow skill in the direction of zero. Hence we find in the sweat-shops "hand girls" whose backs grow crooked over the simplest of hemming, felling, and sewing on buttons, and machine girls whose exertion of foot-power entails tuberculosis and pelvic disorders ruinous to themselves at present and to their children in the future. The foul, ill-ventilated, often damp shops, the excessive speed and intensity of the work, the ceaseless exertion of the limbs throughout interminable days, and the grinding poverty of these workers combine to render consumption the characteristic disease of these trades. The very youth of the workers increases their susceptibility to injury and disease. Young backs grow crooked over the machines, young eyes and membranes are irritated by the fluff and dust disengaged from cheaply dyed woolen goods by flying needles. The eagerness of young workers is stimulated to the highest pitch by ill-paid piece-work and the uncertainty of its continuance.

All this wretchedness, attending this belated survival of primitive organization in a great industry, surely cannot permanently survive in the face of the advantages which mechanical power possesses over foot-power. It is only a question of time when the garment trades shall be placed upon the factory level.

This change, however, cannot reasonably be expected of the corporations which control the garment trades, or of the growing intelligence of the sweaters' victims. It will be brought about, if at all, by an enlightened public's refusing to wear tenement-made garments, and embodying its will in prohibitory legislation carried much farther than the tentative measures of regulation now in force in New York, Pennsylvania, Massachusetts, Illinois, and Ohio.

A necessary preliminary to this revolt against sweater-made goods is a clear perception of the truth that no one (except possibly the wholesaler) profits by the semi-pauperism and suffering of the women and girls who work in sweat-shops.

★

CLARA SIDNEY DAVIDGE *Working-Girl's Clubs*
Scribner's 15 (May 1894): 619–628

[Describing both the necessity and the "natural selection" that bring working girls in trades and business and other "life" groups together, Davidge addresses the camaraderie of women workers, presenting their serious efforts of self-uplift through lectures on hygiene and science and participation in physical culture and musical drill. While noting the mirth and relaxation to be had at working girls' clubs, Davidge is also careful to present her subjects as workers who pursue higher culture diligently and systematically and who have few pretensions regarding their own abilities and resources.]

THE ORGANIZATIONS KNOWN as clubs or societies for working girls, in New York and other cities, represent an especial and distinctive portion of the whole body of working-women. Although the members of these societies are largely drawn from those employed in trades and business, the groups so aggregated are gathered, not by any extraneous force or influence, but by a system of natural selection such as exists in the formation of any other group, set, or clique of people with social or business aims. That "like seeks like" is a fact which simplifies the first steps toward inaugurating such societies. From the inexhaustible field of the working world come clusters of young women with kindred tastes, aims, ambitions, banding themselves by a common plan, and by means common to all, for the attainment of certain advantages.

The working-girls of large cities form a most striking, interesting, and picturesque part of the people. Driven by natural causes into semi-public

Music Drill at the University Place Hall, New York.

cause most natural, way. Even under existing conditions they seldom know a dull moment, but much more might be gained in health and enjoyment if, through some scheme of endowment or volunteer direction from women of leisure, guidance and instruction in country sports and life and interests could be supplied. Then Holiday House might be, as a girl visitor longingly remarked, "truly a nature school."

There are country-houses in connection with the other associations as well as that of New York. The Vacation Society, an independent organization, is of great value to many members of the New York clubs, as through its ar-

ing was fixed for the night on which occurred the great blizzard of 1888, and only one brave girl won her way to the doors of the hall. After that experience it was thought advisable to choose

FIGURE 10 This illustration, from Clara Davidge's article on working girls' clubs, stresses the degree to which uniformly dressed, anonymous working girls are "drilled" in culture, emphasizing the labor necessary for their acquisition of genteel behaviors. (*Scribner's*, 1894)

places, they hold the points thus gained with all simplicity. There is no pose, no glorification of their position. Necessity has sent them out into the paths they follow; by their own wits and through their own efforts they hold the right of way. In a sense, every man's hand is against them. They alone must guard their own interests, defend their individual rights. How far these rights and interests might be furthered by the perfection or full use of such organizations as benefit societies, penny provident systems, by vigilant factory inspection, honest employment bureaus, and the like, only those familiar with the abuses existing in the working world can say.

Yet, even were such protective measures fully established, and thoroughly regulated and understood, there would still be room for the working-girls' club. Formed, ten years ago, of thirteen members (like the original States of the Union), the first club chose for itself a non-sectarian, self-governing, independent platform, which has been the model and pattern for all later societies. Only a decade has passed, yet through this first club, five associations of clubs have been organized, and many scattered societies exist as well. In New York, Brooklyn, Philadelphia, and in Massachusetts and Connecticut there are associations of individual clubs, that in New York alone numbering twenty-one clubs as regular members, with six clubs as associate members.

The New York Association is governed by nine directors, in connection with a council composed of the nine directors and of the officers of all clubs belonging to the Association. Each club has its own system of government, but questions or affairs common to the whole Association are discussed and settled at council meetings, or at the meetings of the directors. A constitution and by-laws define the rights and purposes of this governing body; and many of the clubs under its jurisdiction have provided themselves with individual constitutions, framed for the special requirements of each club by its own members and officers. The officers of all clubs are elected by ballot. A monthly business meeting is held, and matters of business are decided by a majority vote.

The desire to be self-supporting and independent of outside aid renders the careful administration of club finances of first importance. The monthly dues paid by the members are fixed at twenty or twenty-five cents, with an initiation fee usually of the latter amount. A paying membership of two hundred girls will enable almost any club to carry its expenses, which, even in a large city, for rent of rooms, light, heat, and care, should average not more than $40 to $50 per month. For initial expenses of outfit or special necessaries, funds are raised by entertainments provided by the members, at which a small admission fee is asked, and from fairs and sales of articles made or contributed by members.

The women of leisure who combine with each body of working-girls to form a club, alone of all the members have time to find proper quarters, and to get them into order, to make the necessary contracts and secure skilled teachers for special classes. But these are only the most prominent among the opportunities of leisure members. There is hardly a limit to be set to the amount of work that can be developed by anyone with time and ability to give; yet a society thrives best where duties and responsibilities are divided with the girls, so that each unit feels there is a share to be borne.

An immense amount of thought and labor has been spent in the formation and conduct of these societies, and with what object? That girls may make for themselves, by co-operation, opportunities for social intercourse, self-improvement, and advancement. Primarily intended as a common meeting-ground, where differences in circumstance or degree are sunk for the time, the club is, first of all, a place where a girl may expect to enjoy herself after work-hours. There cannot be too much opportunity for recreation in such a club, yet girls seeking amusement, or excitement only rarely join clubs, or if they join are sure to drop off. Class work is soon demanded by the members themselves and the courses mapped out are suggested and discussed by the girls at business meetings, and at the "Practical Talks" which occur in most clubs at regular intervals.

If skilled and paid teachers are employed for classes, an extra fee is often charged, and only those able to pay the fee join such classes. In this way, or by the free instruction of volunteer teachers, millinery, dressmaking, cooking, first aid to the injured, and other branches are taught. By means of these classes the attendance at the club-rooms is distributed through the week, the crowded nights, when a majority of members is present, being limited to strictly social occasions, business meetings, and the "Practical Talk" nights.

At the "Practical Talks," subjects for discussion are often proposed and voted on by those present, such subjects, for example, as the following:

"What is wealth?"

"Should women be allowed to vote?"

"Why do so few girls marry nowadays, comparatively speaking?"

"Life and its struggles."

"How to tell a real lady."

"When women take men's places and cut down wages, what is the effect upon the home?"

Very often a course of subjects is chosen, such as "Famous Women," "Talks on Hygiene," "Elementary Facts of Science," and the like. The success of a series of such "Talks" naturally depends largely upon the leader and on her ability to impart information clearly and in an interesting manner. It is also important to draw as many girls as possible into the discussion that follows the "Talk," to evoke the opinion of "modest members," and to hold the attention of all.

The monthly business meetings afford training in system and order, and lead to familiarity with parliamentary rules. At these meetings the officers report as to financial condition and general affairs; heads of committees give an account of departments under their control; opinions are requested as to proposed new movements, discussion follows, and the club learns to know itself individually and as a whole. The usual outgrowths of a club, besides the class work, are clubs or meetings for junior members, the Lend-a-Hand or Relief Work undertaken by those who wish to aid others and also special organizations connected only with certain clubs, such as the "Domestic Circle" for young married women, a branch of the Thirty-eighth Street Society, and the "Literary Union" of the Endeavor Club, to which members bring their young men friends.

Each society, after successful establishment, usually develops individual characteristics, accounted for by locality, the character of members, and the nature and endowments of the officers elected by them to carry on affairs. Some societies are known for good business management and for the flourishing condition of all departments; others for zeal in Lend-a-Hand work; another is famous for its library and the intelligence and diligence of its members. One club excels in the giving of entertainments, another is known for the high spirits of its members, and yet for their extraordinary interest in the classes held in their club-rooms.

That these societies are useful, are enjoyed, and have "come to stay," is proved by their very large membership—over two thousand in New York

City alone—and by the hearty support they receive, $5,156.25 having been received as members' dues from the pockets of working-girls, in 1893. Physical culture and singing have been found the most popular of all classes, yet the most expensive and difficult to carry on in cramped club-rooms, where want of space limits the number of pupils and makes it impossible to employ and pay the best teachers.

In consequence of this difficulty several clubs combined and hired the hall of No. 9 University Place, where a capital course of physical culture and musical drill—a delightful combination of dancing and marching has been repeated for several winters. Girls whose attention cannot be held by more quiet pursuits find the drill work "the greatest thing the clubs have ever done." Gymnasium suits are worn for these exercises, as the sketch [in figure 10] shows. Classes of this kind often develop latent abilities. One pupil of such a course perfected her training at Chautauqua during two successive summers, and is now a teacher having engagements for each afternoon and evening, and with even wider openings in prospect.

The Choral Union, with a membership of one hundred and fifty, in 1892–93, has for its object a thorough and systematic course of instruction in reading music from notation. The rehearsals are held weekly during the winter months, and three concerts were given in the winter of 1892–93.

Still larger enterprises have been the outcome of the first small and modest clubs, among them the formation of the Association of Working-girls' Societies, the publication of the club paper, *Far and Near*, the organization of The Mutual Benefit Fund, and also of the Alliance Employment Bureau. For the purpose of legally holding property deeded to the societies, an incorporated body was required; hence the Auxiliary Society of the Association of Working-girls' Societies took out a charter; and in its corporate capacity, it is able to handle funds for special purposes, such as the expenses of the yearly public meetings, and the publication of the club paper and of various pamphlets descriptive of club work. The societies are taxed per capita for such expenses as are incurred by the Association for the Societies as a body.

The club paper, *Far and Near*, was for three years published under the auspices of the Association, but it is now carried on under independent management. It is edited and conducted by Maria Bowen Chapin, and has a very wide circulation, due not only to the interest of its pages, but to its practical value as a guide to those engaged in forming clubs. The paper in a sense carries on a correspondence between all such societies; in its columns difficulties common to all are canvassed and ways to meet such difficulties are suggested, fresh ideas are shared and the paths of knowledge-by-experience are smoothed and shortened.

The Mutual Benefit Fund is of the greatest importance to club members. Except through the Penny Provident Savings system, which has been introduced to some degree in the clubs, provision for emergencies is rarely made. Benefit societies, so called, although often dishonestly managed and demanding extortionate rates, are well known in factories. Their promoters prey upon employees in all branches of business, and the victims pay away a large share of their earnings that a meagre death benefit may eventually be secured by their family. In this Mutual Benefit Fund there are two classes of members. First, those paying fifty cents initiation fee and twenty-five cents monthly dues. Second, those paying fifty cents initiation fee and fifteen cents monthly dues.

The benefits are:

For members of the first class, $5.00 a week for six weeks ($30.00) during illness, not more than once a year, and $30.00 at death.

For members of the second class $3.00 a week for six weeks ($18.00) during illness, not more than once a year; and $20.00 at death.

For members joining both classes, $8.00 a week for six weeks ($48.00) during illness, not more than once a year; and $50.00 at death.

There are now two hundred and fifty members enrolled in the fund.

The Alliance Employment Bureau was opened in connection with the clubs to supply a systematic method for securing work for those without it. Certain lines of work are more popular than others, certain trades require less skill and training in those who follow them; and these avenues are crowded in proportion as population is centred. Prejudice or unfitness prevents workers from entering other fields where a living can be made, workers underbid each other in the fierce competition to secure the kind of work most desired, wages are lowered, and distress must follow. Employment offices, such as that connected with the clubs, counteract these tendencies, and can be made serviceable in canvassing the character and opportunities of shops and factories, and in filling vacancies with competent hands. Above all, such a bureau can ascertain where in the business world there is most room for workers, and try to find or fit individuals for desirable positions.

The New York Association holds in trust for the clubs a property at Miller's Place, Long Island, known as Holiday House, which is the summer resort of the members of the societies. A smaller country home at Mountainville, N.Y., is lent by its owners for club girls who need dry inland air. The Holiday House property is exceptional as to situation, neighborhood, and local conditions. The place itself has been highly improved, the two large houses—Holiday House and Holiday Harbor—having a perfect water-supply and good drainage. There are eighteen acres of land in the property, with a frontage on the North Shore of the Sound, giving the best opportunities for bathing and also for boating in a landlocked bay near by. The management of the houses has been simply the carrying out of club principles, co-operative as far as possible, the three dollars paid as weekly board by club visitors providing for current expenses, and the girls undertaking a small share in the care of the houses, although to no onerous degree. During the summer of 1893 $2,978.25 was paid by boarders. Connected with the houses, however, are expenses which the sums received for board cannot cover. Such expenses are met by the directors of the Association through their individual efforts and arrangements. Life at Holiday House in summer is a very free and happy condition. What have we of life without some familiarity with the country and its pleasures, some knowledge of nature itself! Though the new and strange features of country life—the woods, the cliffs, the beach—may have inspired something very much like fear in the first visitors at Holiday House, each successive sojourn only adds to the deep enjoyment of that first experience. Parties of girls, often in groups from the game clubs, go down to Holiday House on successive Saturdays. Usually workers in large cities are able to secure a two weeks vacation, but some, and they are often the juniors, who greatly require country air, can only be released from their work for a week. Two weeks out of fifty-two is a short tale of days, yet the experiences crowded into them by the summer visitors are lived over and over in retrospect during the rest of the year.

The facilities of Holiday House afford all that can be wished for in the way of wholesome conditions, and the ordinary country occupations and amusements. Ninety girls can be accommodated at a time in the two houses and in one or two neighboring cottages; and, had they time at their command, these hard-worked toilers could in their fortnight's holiday become familiar with the country in the most delightful, because most natural, way. Even under existing conditions they seldom know a dull moment, but much more might be gained in health and enjoyment if, through some scheme of endowment or volunteer direction from women of leisure, guidance and instruction in country sports and life and interests could be supplied. Then Holiday House might be, as a girl visitor longingly remarked, "truly a nature school."

There are country-houses in connection with the other associations as well as that of New York. The Vacation Society, an independent organization, is of great value to many members of the New York clubs, as through its arrangements summer board can be secured at mountain and other resorts.

The blending of the members of the different clubs at the country-houses has a valuable effect upon the whole. It widens the knowledge and sympathies of the societies in their mutual relations, and helps the clubs in many ways. The societies unite as a body only once a year at the annual meeting, held formerly in the month of March. On one memorable occasion the meeting was fixed for the night on which occurred the great blizzard of 1888 and only one brave girl won her way to the doors of the hall. After that experience it was thought advisable to choose a pleasanter season for the time of celebration, and the month of April was determined on for the great gathering, which is held in the hall of the Cooper Union, and though only members attend, there is seldom a vacant seat. On this occasion the societies report as to the work, achievements, and experiences of the year, and the meeting is addressed by many of the officers of the clubs and by prominent speakers as well.

In April, 1890, a Convention of Clubs was held in New York. For three successive days two sessions daily took place in the assembly-rooms of the Metropolitan Opera House. Over three hundred out-of-town delegates visited the Convention, many of whom were entertained by the New York Association at the Park Avenue Hotel. Numbers of working-girls obtained leave of absence to attend the Convention, which was conducted with the greatest enthusiasm, and also in a brisk business-like and most systematic manner. Papers on all subjects relating to clubs were read by New York women, by visiting delegates, and by working-girls themselves. The proceedings of the Convention were exhaustively reported in the papers at the time, and it was termed by one of the dailies "an event of sociologic importance." Both visitors and the press seemed much struck by the stress laid on the independent character of the clubs, as compared for instance with the English club methods, since, to quote *The Evening Post* of April 15, 1890, "half the energies of the women promoting the American clubs seem directed to disseminating the declaration that they are not a charity. Their democratic character and management are unceasingly reiterated, and the habit of the newspapers in speaking of them as a philanthropic and charitable work is lamented as a hindrance."

In addition to the longer papers read at the Convention on such subjects as "What do Working-Girls Owe One Another," "Co-operation and Organization," "Provident and Benevolent Schemes," "How to Make a Club Self-supporting" and so on, shorter papers were received and read, some of them amounting to little more than messages in length, yet striking in substance, as the following:

"We believe that the woman who is placed beyond the need of laboring for her daily bread has really received her wages in advance, and so is under greater obligation to work for the good of others than the rest of us."

"It took the world a long time to learn that work is honorable, and every human being, man or woman, should be a worker. Let us not be ashamed of the work we are doing. What we *can* do depends on natural fitness, education, and opportunities."

"A working-girl is doing other working-girls an injury when she consents to work for less than living wages."

The ideas suggested in the papers read at the Convention supplied the groundwork for many of the movements now in operation among the clubs, and the impetus since given to the societies has been a proof of the value of these inspiriting gatherings.

With the effort that has often been made to define in words exactly what a girls' club is, suggestions have come from members that are themselves apt and descriptive. By one a club is called "A meeting of girls working for each other's interests." Another says it is "A place to know yourself and others too." Perhaps the best description, to those familiar with club methods, is the negative one given by a girl president, who, when appealed to for her opinion, said, "Well, just imagine for a moment the feelings of girls who have been club members for, say a year, were their clubs to be taken from them!"

A Bostonian greatly interested in the subject of girls' clubs has said of them—and it may well stand for a final statement—"I think the most striking thing about this new form of life among us is its inexpensiveness in money, and its immense and unending cost in time, in work, in thought, in responsibility—in short, in life."

True child of the daughter of labor, it lives not by money, but by work.

4 ★ SOCIAL, ETHNIC, AND RACIAL STRIFE

THE CULTURAL IDENTITY of white "Anglo Saxon" America was in crisis by 1890. The prevailing myth of a Puritan origin sustained by largely Protestant Northern European and Western European immigration could hardly stand up to the reality of massive demographic change and terrible social inequities. Nonetheless, many Americans attempted to preserve "racial purity" by assigning very limited roles and possibilities to people seen as threats to the dominant national identity. As the last of the continent's indigenous peoples, the American Indians, were being consigned to reservations, and African Americans were struggling for legal and social equality, millions of new immigrants were arriving, straining the processes of assimilation and acceptance. The essays in this section express suspicions and fears about a changing America as well as voicing resistance to the status quo; at the very least, all of the authors argue for substantive reform, if not for full acceptance and recognition of minorities and new arrivals.

An example of the virulence with which societal changes and challenges to the status quo were attacked appears in Josiah Flynt's "Club Life Among Outcasts." A popular author, Flynt wrote more than twenty articles during the decade, almost all of them on tramps and the indigent poor who were portrayed as lazy deceivers driven by wanderlust. In this selection, a study of an American underclass, Flynt takes the reader on a dangerous adventure, exploring gangs in cities, or groups of "vagabonds, rowdies, and criminals." Presenting gangs as "a natural consequence of slum life," Flynt discusses the difficulty of reforming gang members, attacking well-meaning philanthropists for establishing organized outreach programs. Some criminals, according to Flynt, are essentially unredeemable and "must be quarantined." Fostering a fear of outsiders, of the poor, he argues for a segregated society based

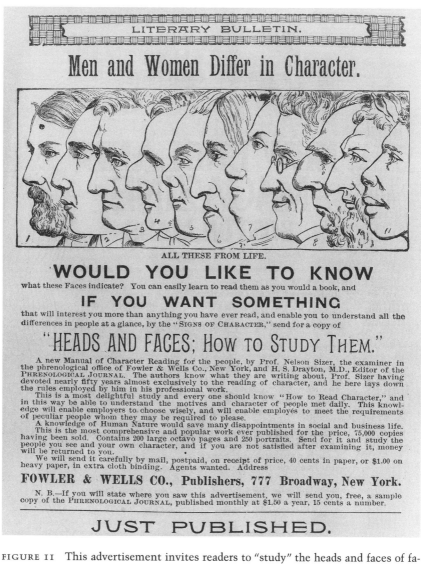

FIGURE 11 This advertisement invites readers to "study" the heads and faces of famous persons and recognizable "types," relying on ideas of ethnic and racial difference in order to reinforce implied relations among physical appearance and character, ability, and intelligence backed by the "science" of phrenology. (*Arena*, 1891)

on its members' unchangeable identities, a particularly effective strategy for addressing an audience who feared instability through change.

How to challenge or question America's status quo was also a question facing many of the authors collected here. Because they did not speak from the interests of mainstream America, dissenting voices in mainstream periodicals recognized that resistance to a dominant culture was both politically and socially dangerous for minorities. As a consequence, though dissenters often addressed the concerns of a larger group, nonetheless they were individuals who had overcome countless odds to achieve their current prominent position.

Simon Pokagon, a Potawatomi chief, for example, addressed the fate of the American Indian in response to increasing pressure to assimilate. After the massacre at Wounded Knee in 1890, which resulted in the deaths of 300 Sioux men, women, and children, military resistance to the U.S. Calvary was seen as futile, and there seemed little hope that an authentic Native American culture could survive. At the World's Columbian Exposition in 1893, Pokagon declared that the remnants of the Indian population had to accommodate themselves to the power of the United States. In contrast to his apparent acceptance of his people's fate, Pokagon had, the day before, handed out copies of "The Red Man's Rebuke" on birch bark, where he denounced the usurpation of native lands by the "pale-faced race" and predicted that the Great Spirit ultimately would cast them out of Paradise because of their abuse of the land. Pokagon's essay, "The Future of the Red Man," displays a similar tactic; his attitude appears to be one of resignation, but he also forces the reader to accept his language and his translations, and at the essay's conclusion he celebrates the fact that Indian blood has tinctured and strengthened white men.

The subtlety of Pokagon's resistance to the dominant culture proved him to be an articulate, well-educated individual who discredited the condescendingly romanticized portraits of Native Americans as stoical, primitive, and childlike. Such stereotyping was also used to justify arguments about the essential inferiority of all minority groups. When Frederick Douglass spoke out in the 1890s, he argued against the restrictions of black Americans' rights at a time when the Supreme Court debated the legal rights of the black race based on its current inferior social position. Ultimately, their decision, *Plessy v. Ferguson* (1896), legally sanctioned discrimination against African Americans by creating "separate but equal"—or segregated—public spaces; in practice, until the *Brown v. Board of Education* decision in 1954, such Jim Crow laws, as they were called, rescinded any hopes for the social equality of the race. In "Lynch Law of the South," Douglass outspokenly addresses mob executions of black men, which usually were based on fictional accounts of the rape of white women. Joining the resistance to Southern lynchings launched by Ida B. Wells-Barnett, a newspaper editor and antilynching pioneer, Douglass carried his protest to the periodical press in 1892 and to the World's Columbian Exposition in 1893. Returning to the urgency of his abolitionist writings and speeches, Douglass denounced Southern racial violence, indicting complacent lawmakers for failing to create an antilynching law and calling instead on public opinion (and therefore the dominant voices in society) to assert its intolerance of a violent, racist South.

Other authors here, among them Jacob Riis and Abraham Cahan, were themselves immigrants and had high stakes in the debate between isolationist nativism predicated on eugenics and assimilationist Angloconformism predicated on social engineering. Widespread fears surrounded the wave of immigration beginning around 1890 and extending through the first two decades of the twentieth century, during which approximately 15 million immigrants came to the United States. Considered vastly inferior to earlier waves of immigrants, these Eastern Europeans, Asians, Italians, and practicing Jews were reviled as being unskilled, lower-class, predisposed toward criminality, and unwilling to part with their national or religious heritages— unwilling, that is, to assimilate. Because such immigrants tended to settle in large urban areas, arguments about the cleansing of cities, about the dangerous "sub-cultures" of cities, and about criminality and poverty pointed to this wave of immigration. In particular, those holding a dominant hegemonic perspective asserted that America needed to be protected from new immigrants because they threatened national resources and were the root of poverty, urban sectionalism, and problems in labor relations.

Seeking to counter such widely held assumptions, Abraham Cahan, a Yiddish journalist and immigrant from Russia, tells the story of a young couple's marriage. Although the story first seems to address the false valuation of material goods held by a young couple (indicated through Goldy's anxiety about a "respectable" wedding), it shifts readers' sympathies to the couple's attack from anti-Semites and gives an ironic twist to its "happy ending" by pointing out that the impoverished and threatened pair can retreat only to an illusory state of isolation. As the story makes clear, they will never experience full cultural participation and private comfort. Similarly, Jacob Riis, born in Denmark, urges his readers to confront the problems of poverty and urban despair. Here, as in his essay on slum conditions, "How the Other Half Lives" (*Scribner's*, December 1889), Riis anatomizes the morally damaging environment of the tenement in which a "street boy" can have no other destination than the gang, a second-generation phenomenon that revealed a national social disease. While Riis presents the gang as dangerous in its gratification of "inordinate vanity," he makes it clear that the gang is the slum's "counterfeit" of social self-esteem and positions gangs as the unsavory alternative to his audience's idea of a national desideratum, military service.

In the selections grouped here, an obvious tension exists between sympathy for the dispossessed poor and an impatient and moralizing attitude that upholds a dominant hegemony. In Louise Betts Edwards's story, "Step-Brothers to Dives," these tensions arise over charitable giving. The economic depression that began in 1893 and the burgeoning wealth and philanthropic activities of industrial capitalists gave rise to debates about charity by authors such as Jane Addams, founder of the social settlement, Hull House. "Settlement" meant that educated social workers literally settled into poor areas, living in community dormitories, preaching health care and hygiene to the poor, and publicizing the plight of the poor to the nation's elite. Edwards locates the argument about charity in two characters, a fiscally responsible young man and an idealistic young woman and member of the genteel poor. Along with concerns about how much to give and how to ensure that charity is used "properly," "Step-Brothers" also alludes to the self-interested motivations of philanthropists. Edwards interjects a love story, a more human motive for philanthropy. Her story's twist, however, also indicts the two main characters, who see themselves as step-brothers to "Lazarus," or to the poor, but as the story's title suggests, they are instead actually more akin to the complacent rich, the "dives," who, as the biblical parable of Lazarus predicts, will suffer eternally for their inhumanity on earth.

★

JOSIAH FLYNT *Club Life Among Outcasts*
Harper's 90 (April 1895): 712–722

[An advocate of reform institutions, insane asylums, and prisons, Flynt has little sympathy for philanthropic organizations, arguing that would-be reformers can do little good in the slums, which they understand so poorly. Flynt does suggest that individuals who choose to live in the slums may effect change, but he remains skeptical about organized "settlements" and other attempts to reform people whom he treats as predisposed toward criminality or idleness.]

I. For several years it has been my privilege to come in contact with men and women, boys and girls, who have been turned out of respectable society, or born out of it, and who are known to the world as vagabonds, rowdies, and criminals. I have made the acquaintance of these people in a variety of ways, sometimes accidentally and sometimes purposely, but almost always voluntarily. I wanted to know what their life amounted to and what pleasures it contained. It appeals to me as a field for exploration just as Africa or Siberia appeals to so many other people, and in what follows I can say that there is no fact or opinion which is not founded on personal experience or personal inquiry.

One of the first notable features of low life is its gregariousness. To be alone, except in a few cases where a certain morbidity and peculiar fondness for isolation prevail, is almost the worst punishment that can befall the

FIGURE 12   This illustration from Josiah Flynt's article, "Club Life Among Outcasts," depicts the "court system" enforced by jail inmates, who live according to their own laws and sense of justice, according to Flynt. (*Harper's*, 1895)

ne'er-do-well. There is a variety of causes for this, but I think the main one is the wish to feel that although he is forbidden the privileges and rights of a polite society, he can nevertheless identify himself with just as definite and exclusive a community as the one he has been turned out of.

His specialty in crime and rowdyism determines the particular form and direction of his social life. If he is a tramp he wants to know his partners, and the same instinct prevails in all other fields of outlawry. In time and as he comes to see that his world is a large one—so large, in fact, that he can never understand it all—he chooses as he can those particular "pals" with whom he can get on the easiest. Out of this choice there develops what I call the outcasts' club. He himself calls it a gang, and his club-house a hang-out. It is of such clubs that I want to write in this paper. I do not pretend to know all of them. Far from it! And some of those that I know are too vile for description, but out of the various kinds that I can describe, I have picked out those which are the most representative.

II. Low life as I know it in America is composed of three distinct classes, and they are called, in outcasts' slang, the "Kids," the "Natives," and the "Old Bucks." The Kids, as their name suggests, are boys and girls, the Natives are the middle-aged outcasts, and the Old Bucks are the superannuated. Each of these classes has clubs corresponding in character and purpose to the age of the members.

The clubs of the Kids are mainly composed of mischievous children and instinctively criminal children. As a rule they are organized by boys alone, but in a few instances I have known girls to also take part in them. The lads are usually between ten and fifteen years old. Sometimes they live at home with their parents, if they have any, and sometimes in lodging-houses. They get their living, such as it is, in numerous ways—by rag-picking, selling newspapers, blacking shoes, and doing odd errands fitted to their strength. None of them, not even the criminally inclined, are able to steal enough to take care of themselves.

To illustrate, I shall take two clubs which I knew, one in Chicago and one in Cincinnati. The Chicago club belonged exclusively to a set of lads on the North Side who called themselves the "Wildcats." The most of them were homeless little fellows who lived in that district as newsboys and boot blacks. They numbered about twenty, and although they had no officially elected leader, a little fellow called Fraxy was nevertheless a recognized 'pres'dent,' and was supposed to know more about the city and certain tricks than the rest, and I think it was he who started the club. He was an attractive lad, capable of exercising considerable influence over his companions, and I can easily understand how he persuaded them to form the club. For personality counts for just as much in low life as it does in "high life," and little Fraxy had a remarkably magnetic one. He drew boys to him wherever he went, and before going to Chicago had organized a similar club in Toledo, Ohio.

The club-house of the Wildcats was a little cave which they had dug in a cabbage-field on the outskirts of the city. Here they gathered nearly every night in the week, to smoke cigarettes, read dime novels or hear them read, tell tales, crack jokes, and plan their mischievous raids on the neighboring districts. The cave contained a brick-work stove, some benches, some old pots and pans, one or two obscene pictures, and an old shoe-box, in which were stored from time to time various things to eat.

The youngest boy was ten and the oldest fourteen, and as I remember them they were not especially bad boys. I have often sat with them and listened to their stories and jokes, and although they could swear, and a few could drink like drunkards, the most of them had hearts still kind. But they were intensely mischievous. The more nuisances they could commit the happier they were; and the odd part of it all was that their misdemeanors never brought them the slightest profit, and were remarkable for nothing but their wantonness. I remember particularly one night when they stoned an old church simply because Fraxy had suggested it as sport. They left their cave about nine o'clock and went to a stone pile near at hand where they filled their pockets full of rocks. Then they started off pell-mell for the church, the windows of which they "peppered 'n' salted" till they looked like "skeeter nettin's," as Fraxy said. The moment they had finished they scampered into town and brought up at various lodging houses.

They never thieved or begged while I knew them, and not one of them had what could be called a criminal habit. They were simply full of boyishness, and having no homes, no parents, no wise friends, no refined instincts, it is no wonder that they worked off their animal spirits in pranks of this sort. Sometimes they used to take their girl friends out to the cave, too, and enlist them for a while in the same mischievousness that I have described, but they always treated them kindly, and spoke of them as their "dear little kidsy-widsies." The girls helped to make the cave more homelike, and the lads appreciated every decoration and knickknack given them.

Every city has clubs like this. They are a natural consequence of slum life, and to better them it is first necessary to better the slums themselves. Sunday-school lessons will not accomplish this; reading-rooms will not accomplish it; gymnasiums will not accomplish it; and nothing that I know of will accomplish it except personal contact with some man or boy who is willing to live among them and show them, as he alone can, a better life. There are many young men in the world who have remarkable ability, I believe, for just such work, if they would only go into it. By this I do not necessarily mean joining some organization or "settlement"—I mean that the would-be helper shall live his own individual life among these people, learn to understand their whims and passions, and try to be of use to them as a personal friend. If he is especially adapted to dealing with boys, he has only to take up his residence in any "slum" in any city and he will find plenty to do. But whatever he does, he must not let them think that he is among them as a reformer.

III. The club in Cincinnati was of a different kind. It is true that it consisted of young boys, and that some of them were boot blacks and newsboys, but in other respects they were different. Their club name was the "Sneakers," and their hang-out was an old deserted house-boat, which lay stranded on the river-bank about a mile or so out of town. Some of them had homes, but the majority lived in lodging-houses or on the boat. When I first knew them, which is over six years ago, they had been organized about three months, and a few of their number had already been caught and sent to the reform school. Their business was stealing, pure and simple. Old metals were the things they looked for chiefly, because they were the handiest to get at. They had had no training in picking pockets or "sly work" of any particular sort, but they did know some untenanted houses, and these they entered and cut away the lead pipes to sell to dealers in such wares. Sometimes they also broke into engine-houses, and, if possible, unscrewed the brass-work on the engines, and I have even known them to take the wheels off wagons to get the tires. Their boat was their storehouse until the excitement over the theft had subsided, and then they persuaded some tramp or town "tough" to dispose of their goods. They never made very much profit, but enough to keep up interest in further crimes.

I became acquainted with them through an old vagabond in Cincinnati who helped them now and then. He took me out to see them one night, and I had a good opportunity to learn what their club was made of. Most of the lads were over fourteen years of age, and two had already been twice in reform schools in different States. These two were the leaders, and mainly, I think, on account of certain tough airs which they "put on." They talked criminal slang, and had an all-wise tone that was greatly liked by the other boys. They all were saturated with criminal ideas, and their faces gave evidence of crooked characteristics. How they came to club together is probably best explained by the older vagabond. I asked him how he accounted for such an organization, and he replied:

"Got it in 'em, I guess. It's the only reason I know. Some kids always is that way. The divil's born in 'em."

I think that is true, and I still consider it the best explanation of the Sneakers. They were criminals by instinct, and such boys, just as mischievous boys, drift together and combine plots and schemes. I know of other boys of the same type who, instead of stealing, burn barns and out houses. Young as they are, their moral obliquity is so definitely developed that they do such things passionately. They like to see the blaze, and yet when asked wherein the fun lies, they cannot tell.

How to reform such boys is a question which, I think, has never been settled satisfactorily. For one, I do not believe that they can ever be helped by any clubs organized for their improvement. They have no interest in such things, and none can be awakened strong enough to kill their interest in criminal practices. They are mentally maimed, and practically belong in an insane asylum. In saying this I do not wish to be understood as paying tribute to the "fad" of some philanthropic circles, which regard the criminal as either diseased or delinquent—as born lacking in mental and moral aptitudes, or perverted through no fault of his own. Without any attempt to tone down the reproach of criminality, or to account for the facts by heredity or environment, it still remains true that in thousands of cases there is as direct evidence of insanity in a boy's crimes and misdemeanors as in a man's, and I firmly believe that a more scientific century will institute medical treatment of juvenile crime, and found reform schools where the cure of insanity will be as much an object as moral instruction and character-building.

IV. Club life among the "Natives"—the older outcasts—although in many respects quite different from that of the Kids, is in some ways strikingly similar. There are, for instance, young rowdies and roughs, whose main pleasures are mischief and petty misdemeanors, just as among the young boys I referred to in Chicago. But in place of breaking church windows and turning over horse-blocks, they join what are called "scrappin' gangs," and spend most of their time in fighting hostile clubs of the same order. They are not clever enough as yet to become successful criminals, they are too brutal and impolite to do profitable begging, and as rowdyism is about the only thing they can take part in, their associations become pugilistic clubs.

How these originated is an open question even among the rowdies themselves. My own explanation of their origin is this: Every community, if it is at all complex and varied, has different sets of outcasts and ne'er-do-wells, just as it has a variety of respectable people. In time these different sets appropriate, often quite accidentally, territories of their own. One set for example, will live mainly on the east side of a city, and another set on the west side. After some residence in their distinct quarters, local prejudices and habits are formed and, what is more to the point, a local patriotism grows. The east-sider thinks his hang-outs and dives are the best, and the west-sider thinks the same of his. Out of this conceit there comes invariably a class hatred, which grows, and finally develops into the "scrappin' gangs," the purpose of which is to defend the pride of each separate district. In New York I know of over half a dozen of these pugnacious organizations, and they fight for as many different territories. I have seen in one club young and old of both sexes joined together to defend their "kentry," as they called the street or series of streets in which they lived. The majority of the real fighters, however, are strapping fellows between the ages of eighteen and twenty-two. Sometimes they live at home, and a few pretend to do some work, but most of them are loafers, who spend their time in drinking, gambling, and petty thieving. They usually sleep in old "tenements" and cheap lodging-houses, and in the daytime they are either in the streets or at some dive, supported mainly by their patronage.

I knew such a place in the city of New York, on the east side, and not far from the Brooklyn Bridge. It was kept by an Irishman, and he had no customers other than those belonging to a "scrappin' gang" called the Rappers. There were two rooms—one fronting on the street, and used as a bar-room; the other, in the rear, was the gambling and "practisin'" room. Here they came every night, played cards, drank stale beer, and exercised themselves in fisticuffing and "scrappin'." I visited them one night, and saw some of their movements, as they called the various triangles and circles which they formed as strategic guards when attacking the hostile gangs of the west side. One of them they nicknamed "the V gang," and prided themselves on its efficiency. It was simply a triangle which they formed to charge the better into the ranks of their enemies, and it reminded me strongly of football tactics.

That same night they were to scuffle with a west side gang called the Ducks, as one of their members had been insulted by one of the Duck gang. Battle was to be joined in a certain alley not far from Eighth Avenue, and they started out, their pockets full of stones, in companies of two and three, to meet later in the alley. I accompanied the leader, a fellow called the slugger, and reached the alley about eleven o'clock. He wanted me to give my assistance, but I told him that I could play war-correspondent much better, and so was excused from action. And it was action indeed. They had hardly reached the battle-ground before the Ducks were onto them, and rocks flew and fists punched in a most terrific manner. Noses bled, coats were torn, hats were lost, and black eyes became the fashion. This went on for about fifteen minutes, and the battle was over. The Rappers were defeated fairly and squarely, but, as the slugger said, when we were all at the hang-out again, "we mought 'a' licked 'em ef we'd a-had 'em over'eer."

Such is the "scrappin' gang." Every large city supports one or two, and London has a score of them. They make some of its districts uninhabitable for respectable persons, and woe to the man who tries to interfere with them. As their members die or grow old, younger fellows come forward, often enough out of the very boys' clubs I have described, and take the place of the departed heroes. This is what rowdies call life.

Like the famous *Studenten Corps* in Germany, they need some sort of rough excitement, and the bloodier it is the happier they are. They have so much heart in them that no ordinary exercise relieves it, and they institute their foolish fighting clubs. It is possible that some sweet-natured philanthropist might go among them and accomplish wonders. In London the Salvation Army has done some splendid work with these same rowdies, and I know personally several who are to-day respectable working-men. But as for organizing polite clubs among them on any large scale I think it useless.

V. Among the other "Natives," club life, as a rule, centres around the saloon, where they gather to exchange news bulletins and meet their cronies. There are varieties of these saloons, corresponding to the varieties of outcasts, and in Chicago I know of over twenty, each one of which is supported by a different clique and species; but these are not exactly clubs. The saloons are meeting-places more than anything else, or a sort of post-office. In the main they are very much like any other saloon, except that their *clientèle* comes principally from the outcasts' world. And about all the life they afford is a boisterous joviality, which seldom takes definite shape. It is proper to say right here that criminal outcasts, as a rule, never form clubs so marked in individuality as the "scrappin' gang." The thief, the burglar, the pick-pocket, and other "professionals," although gregarious and friendly enough, do not organize simply for the sake of sociability. When they combine it is more for the sake of business than anything else, and whatever social life they seem to need is furnished them at the saloon or some private hang-out. This is also true to a great extent of all the "Natives" who have passed their thirtieth year. At that age they are usually so sobered, and have seen so much of the world, that they cannot get much pleasure out of such clubs as the younger men enjoy. The "scrappin' gang" no more appeals to them as a pastime or a source of happiness than it does to an old rounder. They feel happier in simply sitting on a bench in a saloon and talking over old times or planning new ones. Whatever excitement remains for them in life is found mainly in carousels. Of these I have seen a goodly number but I must confess that after all they are only too similar to carousels in "high life," the only noticeable difference being their greater frequency. They come just about four times as often as anywhere else, because the outcast, and especially the criminal, is intensely emotional; he can never be very long without some kind of excitement, and the older he grows the more alluring become his drinking bouts. When his opportunities in this direction are shut off by jail walls, he improvises something else, which often takes organized form; but it must be remembered that such organizations are purely make-shift, and that the members would rather sit in some low concert-hall or saloon and have an old-time carousel, if circumstances were only favorable.

VI. The most interesting of these impromptu clubs is the one called in the vernacular "The Kangaroo Court." It is found almost entirely in County jails in which petty offenders and persons awaiting trial are confined. During the day the prisoners are allowed the freedom of a large hall and at night they lodge in cells, the locks of which are sometimes fastened and sometimes not. The hall contains tables, benches, daily papers, and, in some instances, stoves and kitchen utensils. The prisoners can and do walk, jump, and play various games. After a while these games become tiresome, and "The Kangaroo Court" is formed. It consists of all the prisoners, and the officers are elected by them. The positions they fill are the "judgeship," the "searchership," the "spankership," and general "juryship." To illustrate the duties of these various officials, I shall give a personal experience in a county jail in New York State. It was my first encounter with "The Kangaroo Court."

I had been arrested for sleeping in an empty "box-car." The watchman found me and lodged me in the station-house, where I spent a most gloomy night wondering what my punishment would be. Early in the morning I was brought before "the squire." He asked me what my name might be, and I replied that "it might be Billy Rice."

"What are you doing around here, Billy?" he queried further.

"Looking for work, your Honor."

"Thirty days," he thundered at me, and I was led away to the jail proper. I had three companions at the time, and after we had passed the sheriff and his clerk, who had noted down all the facts, imaginary and otherwise, that we had cared to give him about our family histories, we were ushered pell-mell into the large hall. Surrounded in a twinkling by the other prisoners, we were asked to explain our general principles and misdemeanors. This over, and a few salutations exchanged, a tall and lanky rogue cried out in a loud voice, "The Kangru will now klect."

There were about twenty present, and they soon planted themselves about us in a most solemn manner. Some rested on their haunches, others lounged against the walls, and still others sat quietly on the flagstones. As soon as entire quiet had been reached, the tall fellow, who, by the way, was the judge, instructed a half-grown companion, whom he nick-named "the searcher," to bring his charges against the new-comers. He approached us solemnly and in a most conventional manner, and said:

"Prizners—you is charged with havin' boodle in yer pockets. Wha' does ye plead—guilty or not guilty?"

I was the first in line, and pleaded not guilty.

"Are ye willin' to be searched?" asked the judge.

"I am, your Honor," I replied.

Then the searcher inspected all my pockets, the lining of my coat, the leather band inside my hat, my shoes and socks, and finding nothing in the shape of money, declared that I was guiltless.

"You are discharged," exclaimed the judge, and the jurymen ratified the decision with a grunt.

A young fellow, a vagrant by profession, was the next case. He pleaded not guilty, and allowed himself to be searched. But unfortunately he had forgotten a solitary cent which was in his vest pocket. It was quickly confiscated, and he was remanded for trial on the charge of contempt of the "Kangru." The next victim pleaded guilty to the possession of thirty-six cents and was relieved of half. The last man, the guiltiest of all, although he pleaded innocence, was found out, and his three dollars were taken away from him instanter; he, too, was charged with contempt of court. His case came up soon after the preliminaries were over, and he was sentenced by the judge to walk the length of the corridor one hundred and three times each day of his confinement, besides washing all the dishes used at dinner for a week.

After all the trials were over, the confiscated money was handed to the genuine turnkey, with instructions that it be invested in tobacco. Later in the day the tobacco was brought into the jail and equally divided among all the prisoners.

The next day I, with the other late arrivals, was initiated as a member of the Kangaroo Court. It was a very simple proceeding. I had to promise that I would always do my share of the necessary cleaning and washing, and also be honest and fair in judging the cases which might come up for trial.

Since then I have had opportunities of studying other Kangaroo Courts, but they have all been very much like the one I have just described. They are both socialistic and autocratic, and at times they are very funny. But wherever they are they command the respect of jail-birds, and if a prisoner insults the court he is punished very severely. Moreover, it avails him nothing to complain to the authorities. He has too many against him, and the best thing he can do is to become one of them as soon as possible.

Other clubs of this same impromptu character are simple makeshifts, which last sometimes a week, and sometimes but a day, if a more substantial amusement can be found to take their place. One of which I was a member existed for six hours only. It was organized to pass the time until a train came along to carry the men into a neighboring city. They selected a king and some princes and called the club "The Royal Flush." Every half-hour a new king was chosen, in order to give as many members as possible the privileges which these offices carried with them. They were not especially valuable, but nevertheless novel enough to be entertaining. The king, for instance, had the right to order any one to fill his pipe or bring him a drink of water, while the princes were permitted to call the commoners all sorts of names as long as their official dignity lasted. So far as I know they have never met since that afternoon camp on the prairies of Nebraska. And if they are comfortably seated in some favorite saloon, I can safely say that not one of them would care to exchange places with any half-hour king.

A little experience I had some time ago in New York will show how well posted the "Natives" are about these favorite saloons. I was calling on an old friend at a saloon in Third Avenue at the time. After I had told him of my plan to visit certain Western cities, and had mentioned some of them, he said:

"Well, ye wan' ter drop in at the Half in State Street when ye strike Chi [Chicago]; 'n'doan' forget Red's place in Denver, 'n' Dutch Mary's in Omaha. They'll treat ye square. Jes left Mary's place 'bout a week ago, 'n' never had a better time. Happy all the while, 'n' one day nearly tasted meself, felt so good. There's nothin' like knowin' such places, ye know. 'F ye get into a strange town, takes ye a ter'ble while to find yer fun 'less yer posted. But you'll be all right at Red's 'n' Mary's, dead sure."

So the stranger is helped along in low life, and the "Natives" take just as much pride in passing him on to other friends and other clubs as does the high-life club-man. It gives them a feeling of importance, which is one of the main gratifications they have.

VII. Of the "Old Bucks," the superannuated outcasts, and their club life there is very little to say. Walk into any low dive in any city where they congregate and you can see the whole affair. They sit there on the benches in tattered clothes, and rest their chins on crooked sticks or in their hands, and glare at each other with bloodshot eyes. Between drinks they discuss old times, old "pals," old winnings, and then wonder what the new times amount to. And now and then, when in the mood, they throw a little crude thought on politics into the air. I have heard them discuss home-rule, free trade, the Eastern question, and at the same time crack a joke on a hungry mosquito. A bit of wit, nasty or otherwise, will double them up in an instant, and then they cough and scramble to get their equilibrium again.

Late at night, when they can sit no longer on the whittled benches, and the bartender orders them home, they crawl away to musty lodging-houses and lie down in miserable bunks. The next morning they are on hand again at the same saloon, with the same old jokes and the same old laughs. They keep track of their younger pals if they can, and do their best to hold together their close relationships, and as one of their number tumbles down and dies, they remember his good points, and call for another beer. The "Natives" help them along now and then, and even the boys give them a dime on special occasions. But as they never need very much, and as low life is often the only one they know, they find it not very difficult to pick their way on to the end. If you pity them they are likely to laugh at you, and I have even known them to ask a city missionary if he wouldn't take a drink with them.

To think of enticing such men into decent clubs is absurd; the only respectable place they ever enter is a reading-room — and then not to read. No, indeed! Watch them in Cooper Union. Half the time their newspapers are upside down and they are dozing. One eye is always on the alert, and the minute they think you are watching they grip the newspaper afresh, fairly pawing the print with their greasy fingers in their eagerness to carry out the role they have assumed. One day, in such a place, I scraped acquaintance with one of them, and, as if to show that it was the literary attraction which brought him there, he suddenly asked me in a most confidential tone what I thought of Tennyson. Of course I thought a good deal of him, and said so, but I had hardly finished before the old fellow querulously remarked,

"Don'cher think the best thing he ever did was that air charge of the seventeen hundred?"

VIII. I have already said that, so far as the older outcasts are concerned, there is but little chance of helping them with respectable clubs; they are too fixed in their ways, and the best method of handling them is to destroy their own clubs and punish the members. The "scrappin' gang," for example, should be treated whenever and wherever it shows its bloody hand with severe law, and if such a course were adopted and followed it would accomplish more good than any other method I know of. The same treatment must be applied to the associations of other "Natives," for the more widely they are separated and prevented from concourse the better will it be. It is their gregariousness which makes it so difficult to treat with them successfully, and until they can be dealt with separately, man for man, and in a prison cell if necessary, not much can be accomplished. The evils in low life are contagious, and to be treated scientifically they must be quarantined and prevented from spreading. Break up its "gangs." Begin at their beginnings. For let two outcasts have even but a little influence over a weak human being, and there are three outcasts; give them a few more similar chances, and there will be a "gang."

I would not have any word of mine lessen the growing interest in man's fellow-man, nor discourage by so much as a pen-stroke the brotherly influences on the "fallen brother" which are embodied in Neighborhood Guilds and College Settlements of the present, but I am deeply convinced that there is a work these organizations cannot, must not, do. That work must be done by law and government. Vice must be punished, and the vicious sequestrated. Public spirit and citizenship duly appreciated and exercised must precede philanthropy in the slums. Government, municipal and State, must be a John the Baptist, preparing the way and making the paths straight, ere love of man and love of God can walk safely and effectively therein.

★

SIMON POKAGON *The Future of the Red Man*
Forum 23 (August 1897): 698–708

[Simon Pokagon had been introduced to American periodical readers by B. O. Flower in "An Interesting Representative of a Vanishing Race," in *Arena* in 1896, as "simple-hearted." Here, a clearly complicated Pogakon offers a revisionist history of America that places the Indian at the center as innocent, as betrayed, and as scapegoat. Though Pogakon is partially conciliatory about assimilation through education, he imagines that America's salvation lies in a merging of the races and that the white race will be strengthened by Indian blood. The *Forum* is a suitably serious location for Pogakon's piece because it published neither fiction nor poetry and its primary concern was politics.]

OFTEN IN THE stillness of the night, when all nature seems asleep about me, there comes a gentle rapping at the door of my heart. I open it; and a voice inquires, "Pokagon, what of your people? What will their future be?" My answer is: "Mortal man has not the power to draw aside the veil of un-

FIGURE 13 This photograph accompanied an article about Native American Simon Pokagon and addressed what was commonly termed "the Indian situation." The article was titled "An Interesting Representative of a Vanishing Race." (*Arena*, 1896)

born time to tell the future of his race. That gift belongs to the Divine alone. But it is given to him to closely judge the future by the present and the past." Hence, in order to approximate the future of our race, we must consider our natural capabilities and our environments, as connected with the dominant race which outnumbers us—three hundred to one—in this land of our fathers.

First, then, let us carefully consider if Mis-ko-au-ne-ne-og' (the red man) possesses, or is devoid of, loyalty, sympathy, benevolence, and gratitude,— those heaven-born virtues requisite for Christian character and civilization. But, in doing so, let us constantly bear in mind that the character of our people has always been published to the world by the dominant race, and that human nature is now the same as when Solomon declared that "He that is first in his own cause seemeth just; but his neighbor cometh and searcheth him." In our case we have ever stood as dumb to the charges brought against us as did the Divine Master before His false accusers; hence all charges alleged against us in history should be cautiously considered, with Christian charity. There have been, and still are, too many writers who, although they have never seen an Indian in their lives, have published tragical stories of their treachery and cruelty. Mothers, for generations past, have frightened their children into obedience with that dreaded scarecrow, "Look out, or the Injuns will get you!"; creating in the infant mind a false prejudice against our race, which has given birth to that base slander, "There is no good Injun but a dead one." It is therefore no wonder that we are hated by some worse than Satan hates the salvation of human souls.

Let us glance backward to the year 1492. Columbus and his officers and crew are spending their first Christmas on the border-islands of the New World. It is not a merry, but a sad, Christmas to them. They stand crowded on the deck of the tiny ship "Nina." Four weeks since, Pinson, with the "Pinta" and her crew, deserted the squadron; and last night the flagship, "Santa Maria," that had safely borne the Admiral across an unknown sea to a strange land, was driven before the gale and stranded near the shore of Hispaniola. Deserted by her crew and left to the mercy of the breakers, she lies prostrate on the perilous sands, shivering and screaming in the wind like a wounded creature of life responsive to every wave that smites her.

It is early morning. Columbus sends Diego de Arna and Pedro Guthene to the great Chief of the Island, telling him of their sad disaster, and requesting that he come and help to save their goods from being swept into the sea. The Chief listens with all attention to the sad news; his heart is touched; he answers with his tears; and orders his people to go at once, with their canoes well manned, and help to save the stranger's goods. He also sends one of his servants to the Admiral with a message of sincere regrets for his misfortunes, offering all the aid in his power. Columbus receives the servant on shipboard; and, while he listens with gratitude to the cheering message delivered in signs and broken words, he rejoices to see coming to his relief along the shore a hundred boats, manned by a thousand men, mostly naked, bearing down upon the wrecked "Santa Maria," and swarming about her like bees around their hive. The goods disappear from the ship as by magic, are rowed ashore, and safely secured. Not one native takes advantage of the disaster for his own profit. Spanish history declares that in no part of the civilized world could Columbus have received warmer or more cordial hospitality.

Touched by such tender treatment, Columbus, writing to the King and Queen of Spain, pays this beautiful tribute to the native Carib race:—

> "They are a loving, uncovetous people, so docile in all things that I swear to your Majesties there is not in all the world a better race, or more delightful country. They love their neighbors as themselves; their talk is ever sweet and gentle, accompanied with smiles; and though they be naked, yet their manners are decorous and praiseworthy."

Peter Martyr, a reliable historian, has left on record the following:—

> "It is certain the land among these people is as common as sun and water, and that 'mine and thine,' the seed of all misery, have no place with them. They are content with so little that in so large a country they have rather a superfluity than a scarceness, so that they seem to live in the golden world, without toil, living in open gardens not intrenched or defended with walls. They deal justly one with another without books, without laws, without judges. They take him for an evil and mischievous man who taketh pleasure in doing hurt to another; and although

they delight not in superfluities, yet they make provision for the increase of such roots whereof they make bread, content with such simple diet wherewith health is preserved and disease avoided."—(Peter Martyr, Decade 1, Book 3.)

Does not this quotation most emphatically show that the red men of the New World did originally possess every virtue necessary for Christian civilization and enlightenment?

The question is often asked, What became of the numerous Caribs of those islands? They seemed to have vanished like leaves in autumn; for within a few years we find them supplanted by foreign slaves. The noble Bishop Las Casas tells us, in pity, "With mine own eyes, I saw kingdoms as full of people as hives are of bees; and now, where are they?" Almost all, he says, have perished by the sword and under the lash of cruel Spanish taskmasters, in the greedy thirst for gold.

Certain it is that in those days, which tried the souls of the Carib race, some fled from the lust and lash of their oppressors by sea to the coast of Florida, and reported to the natives there that Wau-be-au'-ne-neog' (white men), who fought with Awsh-kon-tay' Au-ne-me-kee' (thunder and lightning), who were cruel, vindictive, and without love, except a thirsty greed for gold, had come from the other side of Kons-ke-tchi-saw-me' (the ocean) and made slaves of Mis-ko-au-ne-ne-og' (the red man) of the islands, which was reported from tribe to tribe across the continent.

Scarcely a quarter-century passes since the enslavement of the Carib race, and Ponce de Leon, a Spanish adventurer, is landing from his squadron a large number of persons to colonize the coast of Florida. A few years previously, while in pursuit of the fountain of youth, he had been here for the first time, on the day of the "Feast of Flowers." Then, he was kindly received and welcomed by the sons of the forest. Now, as then, the air is perfumed with the odor of fruits and flowers; and all on shore appears pleasing and inviting. The Spaniards land, and slowly climb the terrace that bounds the sea. Here they pause, planting side by side the Spanish standard and the cross. But hark! War-whoops are heard close by. And there they come,—long lines of savages from the surrounding woods, who, with slings and darts, with clubs and stones, fall upon the dreaded Spaniards. The onslaught is terrible. Many are killed; and Ponce de Leon is mortally wounded. He now begins to realize that among the savage hosts are Caribs who have escaped from slavery and death. He well knows the bitter story of their wrong, and that this bloody chastisement is but the returning boomerang of Spanish cruelty. They fled from the avengers of blood to the ships. The report they give of the savage attack, on their return to Spain, is so terrible that years pass before another attempt is made to colonize the land of fruits and flowers.

I deem it unnecessary to explain why these peaceful natives so soon became so warlike and vindictive. Suffice it to say: "Enslave a good man and, like the wasp which stings the hand that holds it fast, he will make use of all the means which nature has placed in his power to regain his liberty." During the first century of American history, many adventurers from different European countries sailed along the eastern coast of North America,— all reporting the natives peaceable and kind when not misused.

There was a tradition among our fathers that, before the colonization of North America, an armed band of Wau-be-au'-ne-ne-og' (white men), gorgeously clad, came on the war-path from the East, reaching the Dakotas, which then extended south as far as the mouth of the Arkansas River; that they were vindictive and cruel, destroying the natives wherever they went with Awsh-kon-tay' Au-ne-me-kee' (thunder and lightning). They were looking for gold, their Man-i-to (god), and, not finding him, went down Mi-che-se-pe (the great river) and were seen no more. Those cruel adventurers, who came among us by sea and land, must have awakened hatred and revenge in the hearts of our fathers, which may have been transmitted to their children.

It should be borne in mind that several European Powers colonized this continent about the same period, among whom the English and French took the lead. Settlements were mostly made along the Atlantic coast, which was then occupied by the Algonquin family,[1] to which my tribe—the Pottawattamies—belong: they seem to have had a common origin and common language. For a time the two races lived in peace. The French in Canada seemed naturally to assimilate with our people, many of whom received the Catholic faith. In course of time there were many marriages between the two races; and we began to look upon the great king of France as our invincible sovereign: for we were taught that he was king of all kings except the King of Wau-kwing' (heaven). Their priests were devoted to their work; visiting all the tribes of the south and west, followed by French traders, planting the cross, the lilies, and the shield side by side. The tribes firmly believed that the land belonged to their great king who loved them and would, if necessary, fight their battles for them. With the exception of William Penn,[2] who settled Pennsylvania, the English who colonized the United States did not seem to have the tact of the French in their dealings with us. They were less liberal with presents and apparently less united in their religious belief. They were not so successful as the French in obtaining native converts; although some good ministers, like Roger Williams, did much to unite the races in brotherhood, and thereby delayed the final struggle.

Inroads were being continually made into Taw-naw-ke-win' (our native land); and in seeking new homes we found ourselves invading the hunting-grounds of other tribes. The warlike Iroquois of New York would not even allow the eastern tribes to pass through their country,—as a result, our forefathers seemed compelled to make a stand against the advance of the incoming race. In doing so, our villages were laid waste with fire, our people slaughtered and burned by white warriors who seemed without number for multitude. Our fathers finally gave up the contest. Some, to avoid the Iroquois, went West through Canada. Others went West through Pennsylvania, meeting in Indiana, Michigan, and Wisconsin, then known as Indian Territory, where we found French priests and traders, who gave us a hearty welcome, assuring us that we should remain safe with them. In course of time the English, finding the French traders posted along the western frontier, gave them to understand that the land they occupied belonged to the English, as well as the right to buy fur from the natives. Hence the so-called French and Indian War was inaugurated, in the course of which many outrages were committed on the frontiers, *all of them being charged to the Indians.* During this war a manifold tin box of curious make was found in a large village called Wa-gaw-nawkee-zee', which lay along Lake Michigan, between Little Traverse Bay and the Straits of Mackinaw. The unsuspecting Indians opened it, and in the innermost box found a mouldy substance. Soon after, the smallpox—a disease unknown to our fathers—broke out among them; and Odaw-yo-e-waw' Da dodse-ses' (their medicine men) all died. In fact every one taking the disease died. Lodge after lodge was filled with unburied dead. The great village was entirely depopulated. Our fathers thought the disease was sent among them by the English because the Indians had helped the French during that war. I have passed over the ancient site of this village. Its bounds are clearly marked by second-growth forests, which now cover it. It is fifteen miles long and from one to two miles wide.

Almost on the heels of this war, after France had ceded her rights to the English, came the Revolutionary war. Our people had just begun to learn that they owed allegiance to the British, who had conquered our invincible French King. They had seen the Bourbon flag taken down from the western forts, and replaced by the red cross of St. George; and they were compelled to shout, "Long live the King,—King George who rules from the Arctic Ocean to the Gulf of Mexico."

We now began selling furs to our new masters; receiving in exchange drygoods and Awsh-kon-tay' Ne-besh (fire-water), when we were called upon again to take the war-path, to aid our new king in subduing his rebellious colonies. We could not serve two masters at the same time; hence remained loyal to our new king, while the Iroquois of New York and Canada were divided. And so it was that all the dirty, cruel work of war between the revolutionists and the mother country was laid at the door of our people, whose mouths were dumb to defend or justify themselves in respect of the outrages charged against them. These outrages were generally planned, and frequently executed, by white men, as was, in after years, the Mountain

Meadow Massacre, of Mormon notoriety, for which also we were persecuted and suffered untold disgrace.

I always think of my people in those days as the dog kept by the schoolmaster to be whipped whenever a child disobeyed. During the war of 1812 we were again incited through English influence to take the war-path. Proctor, the English general of the Northwest, said to our heroic Tecumseh, "Assemble all your warriors together, join forces with us, and we will drive the Americans beyond the Ohio River, and Michigan shall be yours forever." Such a promise, from so high an authority, awakened all the native energies of our being to regain our liberty and homes, for which we had been contending against over-powering forces.

The Ottawas and Chippeways of the north, the Pottawattamies and Miamies of the south, and other tribes gathered themselves together to make the last desperate effort to regain the promised land. In this war our cause was far more sacred to us than was the Americans' to them. They had drawn the sword in defense of *one* of their rights; we, for *all of ours*; for our very existence, for our native land, and for the graves of our fathers, most sacred to our race.

The last engagement in which the confederated Algonquin tribes fought the Americans was at the battle of the Thames in Canada, on October 5, 1813, where we and the English were defeated by General Harrison, and General Tecumseh,[3] our brave leader, was killed.

After this battle our fathers became fully convinced that the small remnant of their tribes must either accept extermination, or such terms as their enemy saw fit to give. So they sued for peace; and the American warriors, uplifted by victory, and our Algonquin fathers, bowed down by defeat, stood around the grave of the hatchet—buried forever—and smoked the pipe of peace together.

At one time I felt that our race was doomed to extermination. There was an awful unrest among the western tribes who had been pushed by the cruel march of civilization into desert places, where subsistence was impossible. Starvation drove many to steal cattle from adjacent ranches; and when some of our people were killed by the cowboys, their friends were determined to take the war-path. I never failed on such occasions to declare most emphatically, "You might as well march your warriors into the jaws of an active volcano, expecting to shut off its fire and smoke, as to attempt to beat back the westward trend of civilization. You must teach your sons everywhere that the war-path will lead them but to the grave."

Having briefly reviewed some of our past history, the fact must be admitted that, when the white men first visited our shores, we were kind and confiding; standing before them like a block of marble before the sculptor, ready to be shaped into noble manhood. Instead of this, we were oftener hacked to pieces and destroyed. We further find in our brief review that the contending Powers of the Old World, striving for the mastery in the New, took advantage of our trustful, confiding natures, placing savage weapons of warfare in our hands to aid us in butchering one another.

It is useless to deny the charge, that at times we have been goaded to vindictive and cruel acts. Some of my own tribe, however, were soldiers in the Northern army during the civil war. Some of them were taken, and held prisoners in the rebel prisons, and the cruelty which, according to the tales they tell, was witnessed there was never outdone in border warfare with the scalping-knife and tomahawk. And yet I believe that, had the Northern people been placed in the South under like circumstances, their prisoners of war would have been treated with similar cruelty. It was the result of a *desperate* effort to save an expiring cause. I believe there is no reasonable person, well grounded in United States history, who will not admit that there were ten times as many who perished miserably in Southern prisons as have been killed by our people since the discovery of America. I recall these facts not to censure, but to show that *cruelty and revenge are the offspring of war, not of race*, and that nature has placed no impassable gulf between us and civilization.

It is claimed that the United States have paid out five hundred million dollars in trying to subdue the red man by military force. But now—thank Heaven!—through the influence of good men and women who have thrown the search-light of the golden rule into the great heart of the nation, her policy is changed. Where hundreds of thousands of dollars were paid out annually to fight him, like sums are now being paid yearly to educate him in citizenship and self-support; that his children may not grow up a race of savages to be again fought and again cared for at the expense of the nation. I rejoice in the policy now being pursued. If not perfect, it is certainly on the right trail to success.

While a guest at Chicago, during the World's Fair, I spent much time at the United States Indian School. There I met many delegations from different governmental schools. I was particularly interested in the delegation from Albuquerque, New Mexico, composed of Navajos, Pinas-Mojaves, Pueblos, and others. With pride I examined the articles which they had made, their clean, well-kept writing-books, and listened to their sweet vocal and instrumental music. I then and there said, in my heart: "Thanks to the Great Spirit, I do believe the remnant of our race will yet live and learn to compete with the dominant race; proving themselves worthy of the highest offices in the gift of a free people."

The Indian school at Carlisle, Pennsylvania, has done wonders in showing what can be effected for the education of our children. The test there made is a reliable one, inasmuch as that school is made up of pupils from more than sixty different tribes, from all parts of the United States. I was highly gratified a few months ago to learn that the football team from that school was able to defeat the champion Wisconsin team at Chicago, receiving many compliments from the immense crowd for their tact and self-control as well as for their physical development,—showing conclusively that our race is not, as some claim, becoming enfeebled and running out.

While I most heartily indorse the present policy of the Government in dealing with our people, I must admit—to be true to my own convictions—that I am worried over the ration system, under which so many of our people are being fed on the reservations. I greatly fear it may eventually vagabondize many of them beyond redemption. It permits the gathering of lazy, immoral white men of the worst stamp, who spend their time in idleness and in corrupting Indian morality. I do hope the Government will provide something for them to do for their own good, although it should pay her little or nothing. Again: I fear for the outcome of the Indian nations. Our people in their native state were not avaricious. They were on a common level; and, like the osprey that divides her last fish with her young, so they acted toward each other. But I find, to my sorrow, that, when you associate them with squaw men, and place them in power, they develop the wolfish greed of civilization, disregarding the rights of their less fortunate brothers. I must admit that it staggers my native brain to understand what reason, equity, or justice there is in allowing independent powers to exist within the bounds of this Republic. If the "Monroe doctrine," which has been so much petted of late years, should be enforced anywhere, it would certainly be in the line of good statesmanship to carry it out, at least in principle, at home.

Lastly, Pokagon must admit that he feels very deeply the ravages made among his people by the "intoxicating cup." Were it an open enemy outside our lines, we might meet it with success. But alas! it is a traitor within our camp, cunning as Wa-goosh (the fox). It embraces and kisses but to poison like the snake—without the warning rattle. Before I associated with white men, I had supposed that they were not such slaves to that soulless tyrant as the red man. But I have learned that the cruel curse enslaves alike the white man in his palace and the red man in his hut; alike the chieftain and the king; the savage and the sage. I am indeed puzzled to understand how it is that the white race, whose works seem almost divine, should not be able to destroy this great devil-fish, which their own hands have fashioned and launched upon the sea of human life; whose tentacles reach out into the halls of legislature and courts of law, into colleges and churches,—doing everywhere its wicked work.

As to the future of our race, it seems to me almost certain that in time it will lose its identity by amalgamation with the dominant race. No matter how distasteful it may seem to us, we are compelled to consider it as a probable result. Sensitive white people can console themselves, however, with the fact, that there are to-day in the United States thousands of men and women of high social standing whose forefathers on one side were full-blooded so-called savages; and yet the society in which they move, and in many cases they themselves, are ignorant of the fact. All white people are not ashamed of Indian blood; in fact, a few are proud of it.

At the World's Fair on Chicago Day, after ringing the new Liberty Bell, and speaking in behalf of my people, I presented Mayor Harrison, according to the programme of the day, with a duplicate of the treaty by which my father, a Pottawattamie chief, in 1833, conveyed Chicago—embracing the fair-grounds and surrounding country—to the United States for about three cents per acre. In accepting the treaty, the venerable Mayor said: "Grateful to the spirit of the past, I am happy to receive this gift from the hand of one who is able to bestow it. Chicago is proving that it recognizes the benefits conferred through this treaty. I receive this from an Indian all the more gratefully because in my own veins courses the blood of an Indian. Before the days of Pokagon, I had my origin in the blood that ran through Pocahontas. I stand to-day as a living witness that the Indian is worth something in this world."[4]

I have made diligent inquiries of the headmen of different tribes as to what estimate they place on the half-breeds among them. Their general reply has been, "They are certainly an improvement on the pale face, but not on the red man." Which no doubt is the case; for it is a lamentable fact that criminals, outlaws, and vagabonds are generally the first who seek homes among us, bringing with them nearly all the vices and diseases, and but few of the virtues, of civilization. Yet, notwithstanding such an unfortunate mixture, we find some grand characters who have been able to rise high above the sins of parentage. I have further found, by close observation, that those tinctured with our blood are far less subject to nervous diseases; but whether at the expense of intellectual force or otherwise, I am not so certain. Be that as it may, we cannot safely ignore the fact, that it is the physical development of the people of a nation that gives it strength and stability; that physical decay brings loss of executive ability, and has proved the overthrow of ancient kingdoms. I do not wish it to be understood that I advocate or desire the amalgamation of our people with the white race. But I speak of it as an event that is almost certain; and we had much better rock with the boat that oars us on than fight against the inevitable. I am frequently asked, "Pokagon, do you believe that the white man and the red man were originally of one blood?" My reply has been: "I do not know. But from the present outlook, they surely will be."

The index-finger of the past and present is pointing to the future, showing most conclusively that by the middle of the next century all Indian reservations and tribal relations will have passed away. Then our people will begin

to scatter; and the result will be a general mixing up of the races. Through intermarriage the blood of our people, like the waters that flow into the great ocean, will be forever lost in the dominant race; and generations yet unborn will read in history of the red men of the forest, and inquire, "Where are they?"
Simon Pokagon

NOTE 1. It is estimated that at the beginning of the seventeenth century the Algonquins numbered at least 250,000. Their survivors number probably not more than 30,000. Originally they occupied nearly all that portion of Canada and the United States lying west of the Mississippi River. They suffered more from advancing civilization than all the other tribes.

NOTE 2. It is said that the treaty made by William Penn with the Indians was the only treaty never sworn to and never broken, and that during seventy years not a war-whoop was sounded in Pennsylvania.

NOTE 3. At the time of this battle, Tecumseh was a brigadier-general in the English army, with Proctor. I have seen in United States histories pictures of Tecumseh, tomahawk in hand about to strike a soldier named Johnson, who claimed that he shot the dreaded chief with his pistol. But I have repeatedly heard old Indian warriors say: "After the British infantry gave way, they came to an open or clear spot in the woods, and here Tecumseh ordered his men to halt and fight the Americans once more. Just then the open space was swept by American musketry; and Tecumseh fell, saying, 'Me-daw-yo-em' o-kawd (My leg is shot off). Hand me two loaded guns. I will have the last shot. Maw-tchawn' we-wib' (Be quick and go).' These were the last words of Tecumseh." Our fathers believed that neither the Americans nor the Indians knew who fired the fatal shot.

My father, Leopold Pokagon, had been a Pottawattamie chief thirteen years before this battle, and so remained until his death, twenty-seven years after. Most of his band were sent West in 1837. He and some five hundred of his people, having embraced Christianity, were permitted to remain in Michigan. In 1866, they numbered three hundred and fifty: nearly all were of pure Indian blood. At the present time, they number two hundred and seventy-one: nearly one-half are of mixed blood.

NOTE 4. Certain it is that the families of Harrison, Rolings, Rogers, and many others tinctured with the Indian blood of Pocahontas are superior in health to, and fully as strong intellectually and morally as, those families from the same branch of pure white blood. John Randolph of Roanoke, a near descendant of this Indian woman, and strongly marked with our race lines, was several times Congressman from Virginia, once United States Senator, and minister to Russia. In his time his speeches were more read than any others. His masterly arguments were the pride of his party and the terror of his opponents.

★

FREDERICK DOUGLASS *Lynch Law in the South*
North American Review 155 (July 1892): 2–24

[Born a slave on a Maryland plantation, Douglass was one of the most forceful and eloquent orators of nineteenth-century America. Douglass gained recognition as an antislavery orator in the 1840s and as the author of *The Life of Frederick Douglass, an American Slave* in 1845. In "Lynch Law," Douglass's last published essay, he turns his attention to racial violence in the

South and to the ways in which public opinion may act as an agent for restraint and humanity.]

THE FREQUENT AND increasing resort to lynch law in our Southern States, in dealing with alleged offences by negroes, marked as it is by features of cruelty which might well shock the sensibility of the most benighted savage, will not fail to attract the attention and animadversion of visitors to the World's Columbian Exposition.

Think of an American woman, in this year of grace 1892, mingling with a howling mob, and with her own hand applying the torch to the fagots around the body of a negro condemned to death without a trial, and without judge or jury, as was done only a few weeks ago in the so-called civilized State of Arkansas.

When all lawful remedies for the prevention of crime have been employed and have failed; when criminals administer the law in the interest of crime; when the government has become a foul and damning conspiracy against the welfare of society; when men guilty of the most infamous crimes are permitted to escape with impunity; when there is no longer any reasonable ground upon which to base a hope of reformation, there is at least an apology for the application of lynch law; but, even in this extremity, it must be regarded as an effort to neutralize one poison by the employment of another. Certain it is that in no tolerable condition of society can lynch law be excused or defended. Its presence is either an evidence of governmental depravity, or of a demoralized state of society. It is generally in the hands of the worst class of men in the community, and is enacted under the most degrading and blinding influences. To break down the doors of jails, wrench off the iron bars of the cells, and in the dark hours of midnight drag out alleged criminals, and to shoot, hang, or burn them to death, requires preparation imparted by copious draughts of whiskey, which leave the actors without inclination or ability to judge of the guilt or innocence of the victims of their wrath.

The consensus of opinion in the early days of California permitted a vigilance committee, composed of respectable men, to hang a lot of thieves, thugs, gamblers and cut-throats; but it may now be fairly doubted whether even this example has not been an injury rather than a benefit to society, since it has been made the excuse for other uprisings of the people where there was no such justification as existed in California. But, granting that there may be instances where a sudden and spontaneous uprising of the populace may properly set aside the ordinary processes of the law for the punishment of crime and the preservation of society, it must still be admitted that there is, in the nature of the act itself, the essence of a crime more far-reaching, dangerous, and deadly than the crime it is intended to punish.

Lynch law violates all of those merciful maxims of law and order which experience has shown to be wise and necessary for the protection of liberty, the security of the citizen, and the maintenance of justice for the whole people. It violates the principle which requires, for the conviction of crime, that a man shall be confronted in open court by his accusers. It violates the principle that it is better that ten guilty men shall escape than that one innocent man shall be punished. It violates the rule that presumes innocence until guilt is proven. It compels the accused to prove his innocence and denies him a reasonable doubt in his favor. It simply constitutes itself not a court of trial, but a court of execution. It comes to its work in a storm of passion and thirsting for human blood, ready to shoot, stab, or burn its victim, who is denied a word of entreaty or explanation. Like the gods of the heathen these mobs have eyes, but see not, ears, but hear not, and they rush to their work of death as pitilessly as the tiger rushes upon his prey.

Some of us are old enough to remember the storm of displeasure that came up from all the regions of slavery against William H. Seward for the utterance of an idea of a higher law than the law of slavery. Then the South stood up stoutly for the authority and binding force of the regularly-enacted laws, including even the infamous Fugitive Slave Law. It took to itself credit for being the conservative element in our government, but to-day it is the bold defender of the usurpations of the mob, and its territory, in many parts, has become the theatre of lawless violence against a defenceless people. In the arguments in its defence, however, there is quite observable a slight degree of respect for the opinion of mankind and a disposition to conciliate that opinion. The crime which these usurpers of courts, laws, and juries, profess to punish is the most revolting and shocking of any this side of murder. This they know is their best excuse, and it appeals at once and promptly to a prejudice which prevails at the North as well as the South. Hence we have for any act of lawless violence the same excuse, an outrage by a negro upon some white woman. It is a notable fact, also, that it is not with them the immorality or the enormity of the crime itself that arouses popular wrath, but the emphasis is put upon the race and color of the parties to it. Here, and not there, is the ground of indignation and abhorrence. The appeal is not to the moral sense, but to the well-known hatred of one class towards another. It is an appeal that not only stops the ears and darkens the minds of Southern men, but it palliates the crime of lawless violence in the eyes of Northern men. The device is used with skill and effect, and the question of guilt or innocence becomes unimportant in the fierce tumult of popular passion.

For two hundred years or more, white men have in the South committed this offence against black women, and the fact has excited little attention, even at the North, except among abolitionists; which circumstance demonstrates that the horror now excited is not for the crime itself, but that it is based upon the reversal of colors in the participants. Yet this apology, rightly considered, utterly fails to palliate the crime of lynch law. For if the charge against the negro is true, with the evidence of his guilt overwhelming, as is usually asserted, there could be no rational doubt of his certain punishment by the ordinary processes of the law. Thus the very argument in defence of the mob proves the criminality of the mob. If in any case there could be shown an element of doubt of the certain lawful conviction and punishment of the accused, there might be admitted some excuse for this lawless method of administering justice. But for no such doubt is there any contention. No decent white man in the South will pretend that in that region there could be impannelled a jury, black, white, or mixed, which would in case of proof of the deed allow a guilty negro to escape condign punishment.

Whatever may be said of their weakness when required to hold a white man or a rich man, the meshes of the law are certainly always strong enough to hold and punish a poor man or a negro. In this case there is neither color to blind, money to corrupt, nor powerful friends to influence court or jury against the claims of justice. All the presumptions of law and society are against the negro. In the days of slavery he was presumed to be a slave, even if free, and his word was never taken against that of a white man. To be accused was to be condemned, and the same spirit prevails to-day. This state of opinion at the South not only assures by law the punishment of black men, but enables white men to escape punishment by assuming the color of the negro in order to commit crime. It is often asserted that all negroes look alike, and it is only necessary to bring one of the class into the presence of an accuser to have him at once identified as the criminal.

In apologizing for lynch law, Bishop Fitzgerald, of the Methodist Church South, says that the crime alleged against the negro makes him an outlaw, and he goes on to complain of the North that it does not more fully sympathize with the South in its efforts to protect the purity of Southern women. The answer to the first proposition of the learned and pious Bishop is that no man is an outlaw unless declared to be such by some competent authority. It is not left to a lawless mob to determine whether a man is inside or outside the protection of the law. It is not for a dozen men or for a hundred men, constituting themselves a mob, to say whether or not Bishop Fitzgerald is an outlaw. We have courts, juries and governors to determine that question, and it is a shame to the South that it holds in its bosom a Bishop of the Church of Christ who could thus apologize for the subversion of all law. As to the sympathy of the North, there never was a time when it was more fully with the Southern people than now.

The distressing circumstances in this revival of lynch law in different parts of the South is, that it shows that prejudice and hatred have increased in bitterness with the increasing interval between the time of slavery and now. I have been frequently asked to explain this phase of our national problem. I explain it on the same principle by which resistance to the course of a ship is created and increased in proportion to her speed. The resistance met by the negro is to me evidence that he is making progress. The Jew is hated in Russia, because he is thrifty. The Chinaman is hated in California because he is industrious and successful. The negro meets no resistance when on a downward course. It is only when he rises in wealth, intelligence, and manly character that he brings upon himself the heavy hand of persecution. The men lynched at Memphis were murdered because they were prosperous. They were doing a business which a white firm desired to do,—hence the mob and hence the murder. When the negro is degraded and ignorant he conforms to a popular standard of what a negro should be. When he shakes off his rags and wretchedness and presumes to be a man, and a man among men, he contradicts this popular standard and becomes an offence to his surroundings. He can, at the South, ride in a first-class car as a servant, as an appendage to a white man, but is not allowed to ride in his quality of manhood alone. So extreme is the bitterness of this prejudice that several States have passed laws making it a crime for a conductor to allow a colored man, however respectable, to ride in the same car with white men unless in the manner above stated.

To the question, What is to be the solution of this race hatred and persecution? I have two answers, one of hope and one of fear. There may come at the South satiety even in the appetite for blood. When a wall is raised to a height inconsistent with the law of gravitation, it will fall. The South is not all a wilderness. There are good men and good women there who will sooner or later make themselves heard and felt. No people can long endure the shame and disgrace of lynch law. The South, which has been compelled to keep step with the music of the Union, will also be compelled to keep step with the music of the nineteenth century, which is preeminently a century of enlightenment and progress. The grand moral forces of this century no barbarism can withstand. They met serfdom in Russia, and it fell before them. They will meet our barbarism against color, and it will fall before them. I am the more encouraged in this belief because, in various parts of the North, and especially in the State of Massachusetts, where fifty years ago there existed the same proscription which at the present time prevails in the South, all men are now treated as equals before the law and are accorded the same civil rights.

I, however, freely confess that the present prospect has for me a gloomy side. When men sow the wind it is rational to expect that they will reap the whirlwind. It is evident to my mind that the negro will not always rest a passive subject to the violence and bloodshed by which he is now pursued. If neither law nor public sentiment shall come to his relief, he will devise methods of his own. It should be remembered that the negro is a man, and that in point of intelligence he is not what he was a hundred years ago. Whatever may be said of his failure to acquire wealth, it cannot be denied that he has made decided progress in the acquisition of knowledge; and he is a poor student of the natural history of civilization who does not see that the mental energies of this race, newly awakened and set in motion, must continue to advance. Character, with its moral influence; knowledge, with its power; and wealth, with its respectability, are possible to it as well as to other races of men. In arguing upon what will be the action of the negro in case he continues to be the victim of lynch law I accept the statement often made in his disparagement, that he is an imitative being; that he will do what he sees other men do. He has already shown this facility, and he illustrates it all the way from the prize ring to the pulpit, from the plow to the professor's chair. The voice of nature, not less than the Book of books, teaches us that oppression can make even a wise man mad, and in such case the responsibility for madness will not rest upon the man but upon the oppression to which he is subjected.

How can the South hope to teach the negro the sacredness of human life while it cheapens it and profanes it by the atrocities of mob law? The stream cannot rise higher than its source. The morality of the negro will reach no higher point than the morality and religion that surround him. He reads of what is being done in the world in resentment of oppression and needs no teacher to make him understand what he reads. In warning the South that it may place too much reliance upon the cowardice of the negro, I am not advocating violence by the negro, but pointing out the dangerous tendency of his constant persecution. The negro was not a coward at Bunker Hill; he was not a coward in Haiti; he was not a coward in the late war for the Union; he was not a coward at Harper's Ferry, with John Brown; and care should be taken against goading him to acts of desperation by continuing to punish him for heinous crimes of which he is not legally convicted.

I do not deny that the negro may, in some instances, be guilty of the peculiar crime so often imputed to him. There are bad men among them, as there are bad men among all other varieties of the human family, but I contend that there is a good reason to question these lynch-law reports on this point. The crime imputed to the negro is one most easily imputed and most difficult to disprove, and yet it is one that the negro is least likely to commit. It is a crime for the commission of which opportunity is required, and no more convenient one was ever offered to any class of persons than was possessed by the negroes of the South during the War of the Rebellion.

There were then left in their custody and in their power the wives and the daughters, the mothers and the sisters of the rebels, and during all that period no instance can be cited of an outrage committed by a negro upon the person of any white woman. The crime is a new one for the negro, so new that a doubt may be reasonably entertained that he has learned it to any such extent as his accusers would have us believe. A nation is not born in a day. It is said that the leopard cannot change his spots nor the Ethiopian his skin, and it may be as truly said that the character of a people, established by long years of consistent life and testimony, cannot be very suddenly reversed. It is improbable that this peaceful and inoffensive class has suddenly and all at once become changed into a class of the most daring and repulsive criminals.

Now, where rests the responsibility for the lynch law prevalent in the South? It is evident that it is not entirely with the ignorant mob. The men who break open jails and with bloody hands destroy human life are not alone responsible. These are not the men who make public sentiment. They are simply the hangmen, not the court, judge, or jury. They simply obey the public sentiment of the South, the sentiment created by wealth and respectability, by the press and the pulpit. A change in public sentiment can be easily effected by these forces whenever they shall elect to make the effort. Let the press and the pulpit of the South unite their power against the cruelty, disgrace and shame that is settling like a mantle of fire upon these lynch-law States, and lynch law itself will soon cease to exist.

Nor is the South alone responsible for this burning shame and menace to our free institutions. Wherever contempt of race prevails, whether against African, Indian or Mongolian, countenance and support are given to the present peculiar treatment of the negro in the South. The finger of scorn at the North is correlated to the dagger of the assassin at the South. The sin against the negro is both sectional and national, and until the voice of the North shall be heard in emphatic condemnation and withering reproach against these continued ruthless mob-law murders, it will remain equally involved with the South in this common crime.

★

ABRAHAM CAHAN *A Ghetto Wedding*
Atlantic Monthly 81 (February 1898): 265–273

[Having fled Russia after involvement with antitsarist radicalism, Cahan joined the Socialist Labor Party in 1887. Cahan's written work in *Cosmopolitan*, *Century*, and *Scribner's* during the 1890s, *Yekl: A Tale of the New York Ghetto* (1896), and "Autobiography of an American Jew" (1913), were instrumental in facilitating the expansion of socialism as well as educating middle-class readers about the beliefs and customs of Eastern European Jews. "A Ghetto Wedding," which explores the hopes and gritty realities of slum life for a young Jewish couple, was published in *The Imported Bridegroom and Other Stories of the New York Ghetto* (1898).]

Had you chanced to be in Grand Street on that starry February night, it would scarcely have occurred to you that the Ghetto was groaning under the culmination of a long season of enforced idleness and distress. The air was exhilaratingly crisp, and the glare of the cafés and millinery shops flooded it with contentment and kindly good will. The sidewalks were alive with shoppers and promenaders, and lined with peddlers.

Yet the dazzling, deafening chaos had many a tale of woe to tell. The greater part of the surging crowd was out on an errand of self-torture. Straying forlornly by inexorable window displays, men and women would pause here and there to indulge in a hypothetical selection, to feast a hungry eye upon the object of an imaginary purchase, only forthwith to pay for the momentary joy with all the pangs of awakening to an empty purse.

Many of the peddlers, too, bore piteous testimony to the calamity which was then preying upon the quarter. Some of them performed their task of yelling and gesticulating with the desperation of imminent ruin; others implored the passers-by for custom with the abject effect of begging alms; while in still others this feverish urgency was disguised by an air of martyrdom or of shamefaced unwontedness, as if peddling were beneath the dignity of their habitual occupations, and they had been driven to it by sheer famine, — by the hopeless dearth of employment at their own trades.

One of these was a thick-set fellow of twenty-five or twenty-six, with honest, clever blue eyes. It might be due to the genial, inviting quality of his face that the Passover dishes whose praises he was sounding had greater attraction for some of the women with an "effectual demand" than those of his competitors. Still, his comparative success had not as yet reconciled him to his new calling. He was constantly gazing about for a possible passer-by of his acquaintance, and when one came in sight he would seek refuge from identification in closer communion with the crockery on his pushcart.

"Buy nice dishes for the holidays! Cheap and strong! Buy dishes for Passover!" When business was brisk, he sang with a bashful relish; when the interval between a customer and her successor was growing too long, his sing-song would acquire a mournful ring that was suggestive of the psalm-chanting at an orthodox Jewish funeral.

He was a cap-blocker, and in the busy season his earnings ranged from ten to fifteen dollars a week. But he had not worked full time for over two years, and during the last three months he had not been able to procure a single day's employment.

Goldy, his sweetheart, too, had scarcely work enough at her kneebreeches to pay her humble board and rent. Nathan, after much hesitation, was ulti-

mately compelled to take to peddling; and the longed-for day of their wedding was put off from month to month.

They had become engaged nearly two years before; the wedding ceremony having been originally fixed for a date some three months later. Their
joint savings then amounted to one hundred and twenty dollars,—a sum
quite adequate, in Nathan's judgment, for a modest, quiet celebration and
the humble beginnings of a household establishment. Goldy, however, summarily and indignantly overruled him.

"One does not marry every day," she argued, "and when I have at last lived
to stand under the bridal Canopy with my predestined one, I will not do so
like a beggar-maid. Give me a respectable wedding, or none at all, Nathan,
do you hear?"

It is to be noted that a "respectable wedding" was not merely a casual expression with Goldy. Like its antithesis, a "slipshod wedding," it played in
her vocabulary the part of something like a well-established scientific term,
with a meaning as clearly defined as that of "centrifugal force" or "geomet-
rical progression." Now, a slipshod wedding was anything short of a gown
of white satin and slippers to match; two carriages to bring the bride and
the bridegroom to the ceremony, and one to take them to their bridal apartments; a wedding bard and a band of at least five musicians; a spacious ball-
room crowded with dancers, and a feast of a hundred and fifty covers. As to
furniture, she refused to consider any which did not include a pier-glass and
a Brussels carpet.

Nathan contended that the items upon which she insisted would cost a
sum far beyond their joint accumulations. This she met by the declaration
that he had all along been bent upon making her the target of universal ridicule, and that she would rather descend into an untimely grave than be married in a slipshod manner. Here she burst out crying; and whether her tears
referred to the untimely grave or to the slipshod wedding, they certainly
seemed to strengthen the cogency of her argument; for Nathan at once proceeded to signify his surrender by a kiss, and when ignominiously repulsed
he protested his determination to earn the necessary money to bring things
to the standard which she held up so uncompromisingly.

Hard times set in. Nathan and Goldy pinched and scrimped; but all their
heroic economies were powerless to keep their capital from dribbling down
to less than one hundred dollars. The wedding was postponed again and
again. Finally the curse of utter idleness fell upon Nathan's careworn head.
Their savings dwindled apace. In dismay they beheld the foundation of their
happiness melt gradually away. Both were tired of boarding. Both longed for
the bliss and economy of married life. They grew more impatient and restless
every day, and Goldy made concession after concession. First the wedding
supper was sacrificed; then the pier-mirror and the bard were stricken from

the programme; and these were eventually succeeded by the hired hall and the Brussels carpet.

After Nathan went into peddling a few days before we first find him hawking chinaware on Grand Street, matters began to look brighter, and the spirits of our betrothed couple rose. Their capital, which had sunk to forty dollars, was increasing again, and Goldy advised waiting long enough for it to reach the sum necessary for a slipshod wedding and establishment.

It was nearly ten o'clock. Nathan was absently drawling his "Buy nice dishes for the holidays!" His mind was engrossed with the question of making peddling his permanent occupation.

Presently he was startled by a merry soprano mocking him: "Buy nice di-i-shes! Mind that you don't fall asleep murmuring like this. A big lot you can make!"

Nathan turned a smile of affectionate surprise upon a compact little figure, small to drollness, but sweet in the amusing grace of its diminutive outlines,—an epitome of exquisite femininity. Her tiny face was as comically lovely as her form: her apple-like cheeks were firm as marble, and her inadequate nose protruded between them like the result of a hasty tweak; a pair of large, round black eyes and a thick-lipped little mouth inundating it all with passion and restless, good-natured shrewdness.

"Goldy! What brings *you* here?" Nathan demanded, with a fond look which instantly gave way to an air of discomfort. "You know I hate you to see me peddling."

"Are you really angry? Bite the feather-bed, then. Where is the disgrace? As if you were the only peddler in America! I wish you were. Wouldn't you make heaps of money then! But you had better hear what *does* bring me here. Nathan, darling, dearest little heart, dearest little crown that you are, guess what a plan I have hit upon!" she exploded all at once. "Well, if you hear me out, and you don't say that Goldy has the head of a cabinet minister, then— well, you will be a big hog, and nothing else."

And without giving him time to put in as much as an interjection she rattled on, puffing for breath and smacking her lips for ecstasy. Was it not stupid of them to be racking their brains about the wedding while there was such a plain way of having both a "respectable" celebration and fine furniture—Brussels carpet, pier-glass, and all—with the money they now had on hand?

"Come, out with it, then," he said morosely.

But his disguised curiosity only whetted her appetite for tormenting him, and she declared her determination not to disclose her great scheme before they reached her lodgings.

"You have been yelling long enough to-day, anyhow," she said, with abrupt sympathy. "Do you suppose it does not go to my very heart to think of the way you stand out in the cold screaming yourself hoarse?"

Half an hour later, when they were alone in Mrs. Volpiansky's parlor, which was also Goldy's bedroom, she set about emptying his pockets of the gross results of the day's business, and counting the money. This she did with a preoccupied, matter-of-fact air, Nathan submitting to the operation with fond and amused willingness; and the sum being satisfactory, she went on to unfold her plan.

"You see," she began, almost in a whisper, and with the mien of a careworn, experience-laden old matron, "in a week or two we shall have about seventy-five dollars, shan't we? Well, what is seventy-five dollars? Nothing! We could just have the plainest furniture, and no wedding worth speaking of. Now, if we have no wedding, we shall get no presents, shall we?"

Nathan shook his head thoughtfully.

"Well, why should n't we be up to snuff and do this way? Let us spend all our money on a grand, respectable wedding, and send out a big lot of invitations, and then—well, won't uncle Leiser send us a carpet or a parlor set? And aunt Beile, and cousin Shapiro, and Charley, and Meyerké, and Wolfké, and Bennie, and Soré-Gitké,—won't each present something or other, as is the custom among respectable people? May God give us a lump of good luck as big as the wedding present each of them is sure to send us! Why, did not Beilké get a fine carpet from uncle when she got married? And am I not a nearer relative than she?"

She paused to search his face for a sign of approval, and, fondly smoothing a tuft of his dark hair into place, she went on to enumerate the friends to be invited and the gifts to be expected from them.

"So you see," she pursued, "we will have both a respectable wedding that we shan't have to be ashamed of in after years and the nicest things we could get if we spent two hundred dollars. What do you say?"

"What *shall* I say?" he returned dubiously.

The project appeared reasonable enough, but the investment struck him as rather hazardous. He pleaded for caution, for delay; but as he had no tangible argument to produce, while she stood her ground with the firmness of conviction, her victory was an easy one.

"It will all come right, depend upon it," she said coaxingly. "You just leave everything to me. Don't be uneasy, Nathan," she added. "You and I are orphans, and you know the Uppermost does not forsake a bride and bridegroom who have nobody to take care of them. If my father were alive, it would be different," she concluded, with a disconsolate gesture.

There was a pathetic pause. Tears glistened in Goldy's eyes.

"May your father rest in a bright paradise," Nathan said feelingly. "But what is the use of crying? Can you bring him back to life? I will be a father to you."

"If God be pleased," she assented. "Would that mamma, at least,—may she be healthy a hundred and twenty years,—would that she, at least, were here to attend our wedding! Poor mother! it will break her heart to think that she has not been foreordained by the Uppermost to lead me under the canopy."

There was another desolate pause, but it was presently broken by Goldy, who exclaimed with unexpected buoyancy, "By the way, Nathan, guess what I did! I am afraid you will call me braggart and make fun of me, but I don't care," she pursued, with a playful pout, as she produced a strip of carpet from her pocketbook. "I went into a furniture store, and they gave me a sample three times as big as this. I explained in my letter to mother that this is the kind of stuff that will cover my floor when I am married. Then I inclosed the sample in the letter, and sent it all to Russia.

Nathan clapped his hands and burst out laughing. "But how do you know that is just the kind of carpet you will get for your wedding present?" he demanded, amazed as much as amused.

"How do I know? As if it mattered what sort of carpet! I can just see mamma going the rounds of the neighbors, and showing off the 'costly table-cloth' her daughter will trample upon. Won't she be happy!"

Over a hundred invitations, printed in as luxurious a black-and-gold as ever came out of an Essex Street hand-press, were sent out for an early date in April. Goldy and Nathan paid a month's rent in advance for three rooms on the second floor of a Cherry Street tenement-house. Goldy regarded the rent as unusually low, and the apartments as the finest on the East Side.

"Oh, have n't I got lovely rooms!" she would ejaculate, beaming with the consciousness of the pronoun. Or, "You ought to see *my* rooms! How much do you pay for yours?" Or again, "I have made up my mind to have my parlor in the rear room. It is as light as the front one, anyhow, and I want that for a kitchen, you know. What do you say?" For hours together she would go on talking nothing but rooms, rent, and furniture; every married couple who had recently moved into new quarters, or were about to do so, seemed bound to her by the ties of a common cause; in her imagination, humanity was divided into those who were interested in the question of rooms, rent, and furniture and those who were not,—the former, of whom she was one, constituting the superior category and whenever her eye fell upon a bill announcing rooms to let, she would experience something akin to the feeling with which an artist, in passing, views some accessory of his art.

It is customary to send the bulkier wedding presents to a young couple's apartments a few days before they become man and wife, the closer relatives and friends of the betrothed usually settling among themselves what piece of furniture each is to contribute. Accordingly, Goldy gave up her work a week in advance of the day set for the great event, in order that she might be on hand to receive the things when they arrived.

She went to the empty little rooms, with her lunch, early in the morning, and kept anxious watch till after nightfall, when Nathan came to take her home.

A day passed, another, and a third, but no expressman called out her name. She sat waiting and listening for the rough voice, but in vain.

"Oh, it is too early, anyhow. I am a fool to be expecting anything so soon at all," she tried to console herself. And she waited another hour, and still another; but no wedding gift made its appearance.

"Well, there is plenty of time, after all; wedding presents do come a day or two before the ceremony," she argued; and again she waited, and again strained her ears, and again her heart rose in her throat.

The vacuity of the rooms, freshly cleaned, scrubbed, and smelling of white-wash, began to frighten her. Her overwrought mind was filled with sounds which her overstrained ears did not hear. Yet there she sat on the window-sill, listening and listening for an expressman's voice.

"Hush, hush-sh, hush-sh-sh!" whispered the walls; the corners muttered awful threats; her heart was ever and anon contracted with fear; she often thought herself on the brink of insanity; yet she stayed on, waiting, waiting, waiting.

At the slightest noise in the hall she would spring to her feet, her heart beating wildly, only presently to sink in her bosom at finding it to be some neighbor or a peddler; and so frequent were these violent throbbings that Goldy grew to imagine herself a prey to heart disease. Nevertheless the fifth day came, and she was again at her post, waiting, waiting, waiting for her wedding gifts. And what is more, when Nathan came from business, and his countenance fell as he surveyed the undisturbed emptiness of the rooms, she set a merry face against his rueful inquiries, and took to bantering him as a woman quick to lose heart, and to painting their prospects in roseate hues, until she argued herself, if not him, into a more cheerful view of the situation.

On the sixth day an espressman did pull up in front of the Cherry Street tenement-house, but he had only a cheap huge rocking-chair for Goldy and Nathan; and as it proved to be the gift of a family who had been set down for nothing less than a carpet or a parlor set, the joy and hope which its advent had called forth turned to dire disappointment and despair. For nearly an hour Goldy sat mournfully rocking and striving to picture how delightful it would have been if all her anticipations had come true.

Presently there arrived a flimsy plush-covered little corner table. It could not have cost more than a dollar. Yet it was the gift of a near friend, who had been relied upon for a pier-glass or a bedroom set. A little later a cheap alarm clock and an ice-box were brought in. That was all.

Occasionally Goldy went to the door to take in the entire effect; but the more she tried to view the parlor as half furnished, the more cruelly did the few lonely and mismated things emphasize the remaining emptiness of the apartments: whereupon she would sink into her rocker and sit motionless, with a drooping head, and then desperately fall to swaying to and fro, as though bent upon swinging herself out of her woebegone, wretched self.

Still, when Nathan came, there was a triumphant twinkle in her eye, as she said, pointing to the gifts, "Well, mister, who was right? It is not very bad for a start, is it? You know most people do send their wedding presents after the ceremony,—why, of course!" she added in a sort of confidential way. "Well, we have invited a big crowd, and all people of no mean sort, thank God; and who ever heard of a lady or a gentleman attending a respectable wedding and having a grand wedding supper, and then cheating the bride and the bridegroom out of their present?"

The evening was well advanced; yet there were only a score of people in a hall that was used to hundreds.

Everybody felt ill at ease, and ever and anon looked about for the possible arrival of more guests. At ten o'clock the dancing preliminary to the ceremony had not yet ceased, although the few waltzers looked as if they were scared by the ringing echoes of their own footsteps amid the austere solemnity of the surrounding void and the depressing sheen of the dim expanse of floor.

The two fiddles, the cornet, and the clarinet were shrieking as though for pain, and the malicious superabundance of gaslight was fiendishly sneering at their tortures. Weddings and entertainments being scarce in the Ghetto, its musicians caught the contagion of misery: hence the greedy, desperate gusto with which the band plied their instruments.

At last it became evident that the assemblage was not destined to be larger than it was, and that it was no use delaying the ceremony. It was, in fact, an open secret among those present that by far the greater number of the invited friends were kept away by lack of employment: some having their presentable clothes in the pawnshop; others avoiding the expense of a wedding present, or simply being too cruelly borne down by their cares to have a mind for the excitement of a wedding; indeed, some even thought it wrong of Nathan to have the celebration during such a period of hard times, when everybody was out of work.

It was a little after ten when the bard—a tall, gaunt man, with a grizzly beard and a melancholy face—donned his skull-cap, and, advancing toward the dancers, called out in a synagogue intonation, "Come, ladies, let us veil the bride!"

An odd dozen of daughters of Israel followed him and the musicians into a little side-room where Goldy was seated between her two brideswomen (the wives of two men who were to attend upon the groom). According to the orthodox custom she had fasted the whole day, and as a result of this and of her gnawing grief, added to the awe-inspiring scene she had been awaiting, she was pale as death; the effect being heightened by the wreath and white gown she wore. As the procession came filing in, she sat blinking her round dark eyes in dismay, as if the band were an executioner come to lead her to the scaffold.

The song or address to the bride usually partakes of the qualities of prayer and harangue, and includes a melancholy meditation upon life and death; lamenting the deceased members of the young woman's family, bemoaning her own woes, and exhorting her to discharge her sacred duties as a wife, mother, and servant of God. Composed in verse and declaimed in a solemn, plaintive recitative, often broken by the band's mournful refrain, it is sure to fulfill its mission of eliciting tears even when hearts are brimful of glee. Imagine, then, the funereal effect which it produced at Goldy's wedding ceremony.

The bard, half starved himself, sang the anguish of his own heart; the violins wept, the clarinet moaned, the cornet and the double-bass groaned, each reciting the sad tale of its poverty-stricken master. He began:—

> "Silence, good women, give heed to my verses!
> To-night, bride, thou dost stand before the Uppermost.
> Pray to him to bless thy union,
> To let thee and thy mate live a hundred and twenty peaceful years,
> To give you your daily bread,
> To keep hunger from your door."

Several women, including Goldy, burst into tears, the others sadly lowering their gaze. The band sounded a wailing chord, and the whole audience broke into loud, heartrending weeping.

The bard went on sternly:—

> "Wail, bride, wail!
> This is a time of tears.
> Think of thy past days:
> Alas! they are gone to return nevermore."

Heedless of the convulsive sobbing with which the room resounded, he continued to declaim, and at last, his eye flashing fire and his voice tremulous with emotion, he sang out in a dismal, uncanny high key:—

> "And thy good mother beyond the seas,
> And thy father in his grave,
> Near where thy cradle was rocked,
> Weep, bride, weep!

Though his soul is better off
Than we are here underneath
In dearth and cares and ceaseless pangs,
Weep, sweet bride, weep!"

Then, in the general outburst that followed the extemporaneous verse, there was a cry,—"The bride is fainting! Water! quick!"

"Murderer that you are!" flamed out an elderly matron, with an air of admiration for the bard's talent as much as wrath for the far-fetched results it achieved.

Goldy was brought to, and the rest of the ceremony passed without accident. She submitted to everything as in a dream. When the bridegroom, escorted by two attendants, each carrying a candelabrum holding lighted candles, came to place the veil over her face, she stared about as though she failed to realize the situation or to recognize Nathan. When, keeping time to the plaintive strains of a time-honored tune, she was led, blindfolded, into the large hall and stationed beside the bridegroom under the red canopy, and then marched around him seven times, she obeyed instructions and moved about with the passivity of a hypnotic. After the Seven Blessings had been recited, when the cantor, gently lifting the end of her veil, presented the wineglass to her lips, she tasted its contents with the air of an invalid taking medicine. Then she felt the ring slip down her finger, and heard Nathan say, "Be thou dedicated to me by this ring, according to the laws of Moses and Israel."

Whereupon she said to herself, "Now I am a married woman!" But somehow, at this moment the words were meaningless sounds to her. She knew she was married, but could not realize what it implied. As Nathan crushed the wineglass underfoot, and the band struck up a cheerful melody, and the gathering shouted, "Good luck! Good luck!" and clapped their hands, while the older women broke into a wild hop, Goldy felt the relief of having gone through a great ordeal. But still she was not distinctly aware of any change in her position.

Not until fifteen minutes later, when she found herself in the basement, at the head of one of three long tables, did the realization of her new self strike her consciousness full in the face, as it were.

The dining-room was nearly as large as the dancing-hall on the floor above. It was as brightly illuminated, and the three tables, which ran almost its entire length, were set for a hundred and fifty guests. Yet there were barely twenty to occupy them. The effect was still more depressing than in the dancing-room. The vacant benches and the untouched covers still more agonizingly exaggerated the emptiness of the room in which the sorry handful of a company lost themselves.

Goldy looked at the rows of plates, spoons, forks, knives, and they weighed her down with the cold dazzle of their solemn, pompous array.

"I am not the Goldy I used to be," she said to herself. "I am a married woman, like mamma, or auntie, or Mrs. Volpiansky. And we have spent every cent we had on this grand wedding, and now we are left without money for furniture, and there are no guests to send us any, and the supper will be thrown out, and everything is lost, and I am to blame for it all!"

The glittering plates seemed to hold whispered converse and to exchange winks and grins at her expense. She transferred her glance to the company, and it appeared as if they were vainly forcing themselves to partake of the food,—as though they, too, were looked out of countenance by that ruthless sparkle of the unused plates.

Nervous silence hung over the room, and the reluctant jingle of the score of knives and forks made it more awkward, more enervating, every second. Even the bard had not the heart to break the stillness by the merry rhymes he had composed for the occasion.

Goldy was overpowered. She thought she was on the verge of another fainting spell, and, shutting her eyes and setting her teeth, she tried to imagine herself dead. Nathan, who was by her side, noticed it. He took her hand under the table, and, pressing it gently, whispered, "Don't take it to heart. There is a God in heaven."

She could not make out his words, but she felt their meaning. As she was about to utter some phrase of endearment, her heart swelled in her throat, and a piteous, dovelike, tearful look was all the response she could make.

By and by, however, when the foaming lager was served, tongues were loosened, and the bard, although distressed by the meagre collection in store for him, but stirred by an ardent desire to relieve the insupportable wretchedness of the evening, outdid himself in offhand acrostics and witticisms. Needless to say that his efforts were thankfully rewarded with unstinted laughter; and as the room rang with merriment, the gleaming rows of undisturbed plates also seemed to join in the general hubbub of mirth, and to be laughing a hearty, kindly laugh.

Presently, amid a fresh outbreak of deafening hilarity, Goldy bent close to Nathan's ear and exclaimed with sobbing vehemence, "My husband! My husband! My husband!"

"My wife!" he returned in her ear.

"Do you know what you are to me now?" she resumed. "A husband! And I am your wife! Do you know what it means,—do you, do you, Nathan?" she insisted, with frantic emphasis.

"I do, my little sparrow; only don't worry over the wedding presents."

It was after midnight, and even the Ghetto was immersed in repose. Goldy and Nathan were silently wending their way to the three empty little rooms where they were destined to have their first joint home. They wore the wedding attire which they had rented for the evening: he a swallowtail coat and high hat, and she a white satin gown and slippers, her head uncovered,—the wreath and veil done up in a newspaper, in Nathan's hand.

They had gone to the wedding in carriages, which had attracted large crowds both at the point of departure and in front of the hall; and of course they had expected to make their way to their new home in a similar "respectable" manner. Toward the close of the last dance, after supper, they found, however, that some small change was all they possessed in the world.

The last strains of music were dying away. The guests, in their hats and bonnets, were taking leave. Everybody seemed in a hurry to get away to his own world, and to abandon the young couple to their fate.

Nathan would have borrowed a dollar or two of some friend. "Let us go home as behooves a bride and bridegroom," he said. "There is a God in heaven: he will not forsake us."

But Goldy would not hear of betraying the full measure of their poverty to their friends. "No! no!" she retorted testily. "I am not going to let you pay a dollar and a half for a few blocks' drive, like a Fifth Avenue nobleman. We can walk," she pursued, with the grim determination of one bent upon self-chastisement. "A poor woman who dares spend every cent on a wedding must be ready to walk after the wedding."

When they found themselves alone in the deserted street, they were so overcome by a sense of loneliness, of a kind of portentous, haunting emptiness, that they could not speak. So on they trudged in dismal silence; she leaning upon his arm, and he tenderly pressing her to his side.

Their way lay through the gloomiest and roughest part of the Seventh Ward. The neighborhood frightened her, and she clung closer to her escort. At one corner they passed some men in front of a liquor saloon.

"Look at dem! Look at dem! A sheeny feller an' his bride, I'll betch ye!" shouted a husky voice. "Jes' comin' from de weddin'."

"She ain't no bigger 'n a peanut, is she?" The simile was greeted with a horse-laugh.

"Look a here, young feller, what's de madder wid carryin' her in your vest-pocket?"

When Nathan and Goldy were a block away, something like a potato or a carrot struck her in the back. At the same time the gang of loafers on the corner broke into boisterous merriment. Nathan tried to face about, but she restrained him.

"Don't! They might kill you!" she whispered, and relapsed into silence.

He made another attempt to disengage himself, as if for a desperate attack upon her assailants, but she nestled close to his side and held him fast, her every fibre tingling with the consciousness of the shelter she had in him.

"Don't mind them, Nathan," she said.

And as they proceeded on their dreary way through a sombre, impoverished street, with here and there a rustling tree,—a melancholy witness of its better days,—they felt a stream of happiness uniting them, as it coursed through the veins of both, and they were filled with a blissful sense of oneness the like of which they had never tasted before. So happy were they that the gang behind them, and the bare rooms toward which they were directing their steps, and the miserable failure of the wedding, all suddenly appeared too insignificant to engage their attention,—paltry matters alien to their new life, remote from the enchanted world in which they now dwelt.

The very notion of a relentless void abruptly turned to a beatific sense of their own seclusion, of there being only themselves in the universe, to live and to delight in each other.

"Don't mind them, Nathan darling," she repeated mechanically, conscious of nothing but the tremor of happiness in her voice.

"I should give it to them!" he responded, gathering her still closer to him. "I should show them how to touch my Goldy, my pearl, my birdie!"

They dived into the denser gloom of a side-street.

A gentle breeze ran past and ahead of them, proclaiming the bride and the bridegroom. An old tree whispered overhead its tender felicitations.

★

JACOB A. RIIS *The Genesis of the Gang*
Atlantic Monthly 84 (September 1899): 302–311

[A central debate about immigrants was divided between social Darwinists and immigrant restrictionists, who argued that heredity determined character, and social reformers and proponents of assimilation, who believed that environment was destiny and that social engineering was the solution. A precursor of muckraking journalism, Riis's documentary realism reveals conflicted attitudes toward the poor; Riis employs crude stereotypes while he points to environment as the key to destiny and calls for Christian reform.]

JACOB BERESHEIM was fifteen when he was charged with murder. It is now more than three years ago, but the touch of his hand is cold upon mine, with mortal fear, as I write. Every few minutes, during our long talk on the night of his arrest and confession, he would spring to his feet, and, clutching my arm as a drowning man catches at a rope, demand with shaking voice, "Will they give me the chair?" The assurance that boys were not executed quieted him only for the moment. Then the dread and the horror were upon him again.

Of his crime the less said the better. It was the climax of a career of depravity that differed from other such chiefly in the opportunities afforded by an environment which led up to and helped shape it. My business is with that environment. The man is dead, the boy in jail. But unless I am to be my brother's jail keeper, merely, the iron bars do not square the account of Jacob with society. Society exists for the purpose of securing justice to its members, appearances to the contrary notwithstanding. When it fails in this, the item is carried on the ledger with interest and compound interest toward a day of reckoning that comes surely with the paymaster. We have heard the chink of his coin on the counter, these days, in the unblushing revelations before the Mazet Committee of degraded citizenship, of the murder of the civic conscience, and in the applause that hailed them. And we have begun to understand that these are the interest on Jacob's account, older, much older than himself. He is just an item carried on the ledger. But with that knowledge the account is at last in a way of getting squared. Let us see how it stands.

We shall take Jacob as a type of the street boy on the East Side, where he belonged. What does not apply to him in the review applies to his class. But there was very little of it indeed that he missed or that missed him.

He was born in a tenement in that section where the Tenement House Committee found 321,000 persons living out of sight and reach of a green spot of any kind, and where sometimes the buildings, front, middle, and rear, took up ninety three per cent of all the space on the block. Such a home as he had was there, and of the things that belonged to it he was the heir. The sunlight was not among them. It "never entered" there. Darkness and discouragement did, and dirt. Later on, when he took to the dirt as his natural weapon in his battles with society, it was said of him that it was the only friend that stuck to him, and it was true. Very early the tenement gave him up to the street. The thing he took with him as the one legacy of home was the instinct for the crowd, which meant that the tenement had wrought its worst mischief upon him: it had smothered that in him around which character is built. The more readily did he fall in with the street and its ways. Character implies depth, a soil, and growth. The street is all surface: nothing grows there; it hides only a sewer.

It taught him gambling as its first lesson, and stealing as the next. The two are never far apart. From shooting craps behind the "cop's" back to filching from the grocer's stock or plundering a defenseless peddler is only a step. There is in both the spice of law-breaking that appeals to the shallow ambition of the street as heroic. Occasionally the raids have a comic tinge. A German grocer wandered into police headquarters the other day, with an appeal for protection against the boys.

"Vat means dot 'cheese it'?" he asked, rubbing his bald head in helpless bewilderment. "Efery dime dey says 'cheese it' somedings vas gone."

To the lawlessness of the street the home opposes no obstacle, as we have seen. Until very recently the school did not. It might have more to offer even now. There are, at least, schools where there were none then, and so much is gained; also, they are getting better, but too many of them, in my unprofessional judgment, need yet to be made over, until they are fit to turn out whole, sound boys, instead of queer manikins stuffed with information for which they have no use, and which is none of their business anyhow. It seemed to me sometimes, when watching the process of cramming the school course with the sum of human knowledge and conceit, as if it all meant that we distrusted nature's way of growing a man from a boy, and had set out to show her a shorter cut. A common result was the kind of mental befogment that had Abraham Lincoln murdered by Ballington Booth, and a superficiality, a hopeless slurring of tasks, that hitched perfectly with the spirit of the street, and left nothing to be explained in the verdict of the reformatory, "No moral sense." There was no moral sense to be got out of the thing, for there was little sense of any kind in it. The boy was not given a chance to be honest with himself by thinking a thing through; he came naturally to accept as his mental horizon the headlines in his penny paper and the literature of the Dare-Devil-Dan-the-Death Dealing-Monster of-Dakota order, which comprise the ordinary esthetic equipment of the slum. The mystery of his further development into the tough need not perplex anybody.

But Jacob Beresheim had not even the benefit of such schooling as there was to be had. He did not go to school, and nobody cared. There was indeed a law directing that every child should go, and a corps of truant officers to catch him if he did not; but the law had been a dead letter for a quarter of a century. There was no census to tell what children ought to be in school, and no place but a jail to put those in who shirked. Jacob was allowed to drift. From the time he was twelve till he was fifteen, he told me, he might have gone to school three weeks,—no more.

Church and Sunday school missed him. I was going to say that they passed by on the other side, remembering the migration of the churches uptown, as the wealthy moved out of, and the poor into, the region south of Fourteenth Street. But that would hardly be fair. They moved after their congregations; but they left nothing behind. In the twenty years that followed the war, while enough to people a large city moved in downtown, the number of churches there was reduced from 141 to 127. Fourteen Protestant churches moved out. Only two Roman Catholic churches and a synagogue moved in. I am not aware that there has been any large increase of churches in the district since, but we have seen that the crowding has not slackened pace. Jacob had no trouble in escaping the Sunday school as he had escaped the public school. His tribe will share none until the responsibility incurred in the severance of church and state sits less lightly on a Christian community, and the church, from a mob, shall have become an army, with von Moltke's plan of campaign, "March apart, fight together." The Christian church is not alone in its failure. The Jew's boy is breaking away from safe moorings rather faster than his brother of the new dispensation. The church looks on, but it has no cause for congratulation. He is getting nothing in place of that which he lost, and the result is bad. There is no occasion for profound theories about it. The facts are plain enough. The new freedom has something to do with it, but neglect to look after the young has quite as much. Apart from its religious aspect, seen from the angle of the community's interest wholly, the matter is of the gravest import.

What the boy's play has to do with building character in him Froebel has told us. Through it, he showed us, the child "first perceives moral relations," and he made that the basis of the kindergarten and all common-sense education. That prop was knocked out. New York never had a children's playground till within the last year. Truly it seemed, as Abram S. Hewitt said, as if in the early plan of our city the children had not been thought of at all. Such moral relations as Jacob was able to make out ran parallel with the gutter always, and counter to law and order as represented by the policeman and the landlord. The landlord had his windows to mind, and the policeman his lamps and the city ordinances which prohibit even kite flying below Fourteenth Street where the crowds are. The ball had no chance at all. It is not two years since a boy was shot down by a policeman for the heinous offense of playing football in the street on Thanksgiving Day. But a boy who cannot kick a ball around has no chance of growing up a decent and orderly citizen. He must have his childhood, so that he may be fitted to give to the community his manhood. The average boy is just like a little steam engine with steam always up. The play is his safety valve. With the landlord in the yard and the policeman on the street sitting on his safety valve and holding it down, he is bound to explode. When he does, when he throws mud and stones and shows us the side of him which the gutter developed, we are shocked and marvel much what our boys are coming to, as if we had any right to expect better treatment of them. I doubt if Jacob, in the whole course of his wizened little life, had ever a hand in an honest game that was not haunted by the dread of the avenging policeman. That he was not "doing anything" was no defense. The mere claim was proof that he was up to mischief of some sort. Besides, the policeman was usually right. Play in such a setting becomes a direct incentive to mischief in a healthy boy. Jacob was a healthy enough little animal.

Such fun as he had he got out of lawbreaking in a small way. In this he was merely following the ruling fashion. Laws were apparently made for no other purpose that he could see. Such a view as he enjoyed of their makers and executors at election seasons inspired him with seasonable enthusiasm, — but hardly with awe. A slogan, now, like that raised by Tammany's last candidate for district attorney,—"To hell with reform!"—was something he could grasp. Of what reform meant he had only the vaguest notion, but the thing had the right ring to it. Roosevelt preaching enforcement of law was from the first a "lobster" to him, not to be taken seriously. It is not among the least of the merits of the man that by his sturdy personality, as well as by his unyielding persistence, he won the boy over to the passive admission that there might be something in it. It had not been his experience.

There was the law which sternly commanded him to go to school, and which he laughed at every day. Then there was the law to prevent child labor. It cost twenty-five cents for a false age certificate to break that, and Jacob, if he thought of it at all, probably thought of perjury as rather an expensive thing. A quarter was a good deal to pay for the right to lock a child up in a factory, when he ought to have been at play. The excise law was everybody's game. The sign that hung in every saloon, saying that nothing was sold there to minors, never yet barred out his "growler" when he had the price. There was another such sign in the tobacco shop, forbidding the sale of cigarettes to boys of his age. Jacob calculated that when he had the money he smoked as many as fifteen in a day, and he laughed when he told me. He laughed, too, when he remembered how the boys of the East Side took to carrying balls of cord in their pockets, on the wave of the Lexow reform, on purpose to measure the distance from the school door to the nearest saloon. They had been told that it should be two hundred feet, according to law. There were schools that had as many as a dozen within the tabooed limits. It was in the papers how, when the highest courts said that the law was good, the saloon keepers attacked the schools as a nuisance and detrimental to property. In a general way Jacob sided with the saloon keeper; not because he had any opinion about it, but because it seemed natural. Such opinions as he ordinarily had he got from that quarter.

When, later on, he came to be tried, his counsel said to me, "He is an amazing liar." No, hardly amazing. It would have been amazing if he had been anything else. Lying and mockery were all around him, and he adjusted himself to the things that were. He lied in self-defense.

Jacob's story ends here, as far as he is personally concerned. The story of the gang begins. So trained for the responsibility of citizenship, robbed of home and of childhood, with every prop knocked from under him, all the elements that make for strength and character trodden out in the making of the boy, all the high ambition of youth caricatured by the slum and become base passions,—so equipped he comes to the business of life. As a "kid" he hunted with the pack in the street. As a young man he trains with the gang, because it furnishes the means of gratifying his inordinate vanity, that is the slum's counterfeit of self-esteem. Upon the Jacobs of other days there was a last hold,—the father's authority. Changed conditions have loosened that also. There is a time in every young man's life when he knows more than his father. It is like the measles or the mumps, and he gets over it, with a little judicious firmness in the hand that guides. It is the misfortune of the slum boy of to-day that it is really so, and that he knows it. His father is an Italian or a Jew, and cannot even speak the language to which the boy is born. He has to depend on him in much, in the new order of things. The old man is "slow," he is "Dutch." He may be an Irishman with some advantages; he is still a "foreigner." He loses his grip on the boy. Ethical standards of which he has no conception clash. Watch the meeting of two currents in river or bay, and see the line of drift that tells of the struggle. So in the city's life strive the currents of the old and the new, and in the churning the boy goes adrift. The last hold upon him is gone. That is why the gang appears in the second generation, the first born upon the soil,—a fighting gang if the Irishman is there with his ready fist, a thievish gang if it is the East Side Jew,—and disappears in the third. The second boy's father is not "slow." He has had experience. He was clubbed into decency in his own day, and the night stick wore off the glamour of the thing. His grip on the boy is good, and it holds.

It depends now upon chance what is to become of the lad. But the slum has stacked the cards against him. There arises in the lawless crowd a leader, who rules with his stronger fists or his readier wit. Around him the gang crystallizes, and what he is it becomes. He may be a thief, like David Meyer, a report of whose doings I have before me. He was just a bully, and, being the biggest in his gang, made the others steal for him and surrender the "swag," or take a licking. But that was unusual. Ordinarily the risk and the "swag" are distributed on more democratic principles. Or he may be of the temper of Mike of Poverty Gap, who was hanged for murder at nineteen. While he sat in his cell at police headquarters, he told with grim humor of the raids of his gang on Saturday nights when they stocked up at "the club." They used to "hook" a butcher's cart or other light wagon, wherever found, and drive like mad up and down the avenue, stopping at saloon or grocery to throw in what they wanted. His job was to sit at the tail of the cart with a six-shooter and pop at any chance pursuer. He chuckled at the recollection of how men fell over one another to get out of his way. "It was great to see them run," he said. Mike was a tough, but with a better chance he might have been a hero. The thought came to him, too, when it was all over and the end in sight. He put it all in one sober, retrospective sigh, that had in it no craven shirking of the responsibility that was properly his: "I never had no bringing up."

There was a meeting some time after his death to boom a scheme for "getting the boys off the street," and I happened to speak of Mike's case. In the audience was a gentleman of means and position, and his daughter, who manifested great interest and joined heartily in the proposed movement. A week later, I was thunderstruck at reading of the arrest of my sympathetic friend's son for train-wrecking up the state. The fellow was of the same age as Mike. It appeared that he was supposed to be attending school, but had been reading dime novels instead, until he arrived at the point where he "had to kill some one before the end of the month." To that end he organized a gang of admiring but less resourceful comrades. After all, the plane of fellowship of Poverty Gap and Madison Avenue lies nearer than we often suppose. I set the incident down in justice to the memory of my friend Mike. If this one went astray with so much to pull him the right way, and but the single strand broken, what then of the other?

Mike's was the day of Irish heroics. Since their scene was shifted from the East Side there has come over there an epidemic of child crime of meaner sort, but following the same principle of gang organization. It is difficult to ascertain the exact extent of it, because of the well-meant but, I am inclined to think, mistaken effort on the part of the children's societies to suppress the record of it for the sake of the boy. Enough testimony comes from the police and the courts, however, to make it clear that thieving is largely on the increase among the East Side boys. And it is amazing at what an early age it begins. When, in the fight for a truant school, I had occasion to gather statistics upon this subject, to meet the sneer of the educational authorities that the "crimes" of street boys compassed at worst the theft of a top or a marble, I found among 278 prisoners, of whom I had kept the run for ten months, two boys, of four and eight years respectively, arrested for breaking into a grocery, not to get candy or prunes, but to rob the till. The little one was useful to "crawl through a small hole." There were "burglars" of six and seven years, and five in a bunch, the whole gang apparently, at the age of eight. "Wild" boys began to appear in court at that age. At eleven, I had seven thieves, two of whom had a record on the police blotter, and an "habitual liar;" at twelve, I had four burglars, three ordinary thieves, two arrested for drunkenness, three for assault, and three incendiaries; at thirteen, five burglars, one with a "record," as many thieves, one "drunk," five charged with assault and one with forgery; at fourteen, eleven thieves and housebreakers, six highway robbers,—the gang on its unlucky day, perhaps,—and ten arrested for fighting, not counting one who had assaulted a policeman, in a state of drunken frenzy. One of the gangs made a specialty of stealing baby carriages, when left unattended in front of stores. They "drapped the kids in the hallway" and "sneaked" the carriages. And so on. The recital was not a pleasant one, but it was effective. We got our truant school, and one way that led to the jail was blocked.

It may be that the leader is neither thief nor thug, but ambitious. In that case the gang is headed for politics by the shortest route. Likewise, sometimes, when he is both. In either case it carries the situation by assault.

When the gang wants a thing, the easiest way seems to it always to take it. There was an explosion in a Fifth Street tenement one night last January, that threw twenty families into a wild panic, and injured two of the tenants badly. There was much mystery about it, until it came out that the housekeeper had had a "run in" with the gang in the block. It wanted club-room in the house, and she would not let it in. Beaten, it avenged itself in characteristic fashion by leaving a package of gunpowder on the stairs, where she would be sure to find it when she went the rounds with her candle to close up. That was a gang of that kind, headed straight for Albany. And what is more, it will get there, unless things change greatly. The gunpowder was just a "bluff" to frighten the housekeeper, an installment of the kind of politics it meant to play when it got its chance. There was "nothing against this gang" except a probable row with the saloon keeper, since it applied elsewhere for house-room. Not every gang has a police record of theft and "slugging" beyond the early encounters of the street. "Our honored leader" is not always the captain of a band of cutthroats. IIe is the honorary president of the "social club" that bears his name, and he counts for something in the ward. But the ethical standards do not differ. "Do others, or they will do you," felicitously adapted from Holy Writ for the use of the slum, and the classic war cry, "To the victors the spoils," made over locally to read, "I am not in politics for my health," still interpret the creed of the political as of the "slugging" gang. They drew their inspiration from the same source. Of what gang politics means every large city in our country has had its experience. New York is no exception. History on the subject is being made yet, in the sight of us all.

Our business with the gang, however, is in the making of it. Take now the showing of the reformatory [see note], to which I have before made reference, and see what light it throws upon the matter: 71 per cent of prisoners with no moral sense, or next to none, yet more than that proportion possessed of "natural mental capacity," which is to say that they had the means of absorbing it from their environment, if there had been any to absorb. Bad homes sent half of all prisoners there; bad company 92 per cent. The reformatory repeats the prison chaplain's verdict, "weakness, not wickedness," in its own way: "Malevolence does not characterize the criminal, but aversion to continuous labor." If "the street" had been written across it in capital letters, it could not have been made plainer. Twelve per cent only of the prisoners came from good homes, and one in a hundred had kept good company; evidently he was not of the mentally capable. They will tell you at the prison that, under its discipline, 83 per cent are set upon their feet and make a fresh start. With due allowance for a friendly critic, there is still room for the three fourths labeled normal. The Children's Aid Society will give you even better news of the boys rescued from the slum before it had branded them for its own. Scarce five per cent are lost, though they leave such a black mark that they make trouble for all the good boys that are sent out from New York. Better than these was the kindergarten record in San Francisco. New York has no monopoly of the slum. Of nine thousand children from the slummiest quarters of that city who had gone through the Golden Gate Association's kindergartens, just one was said to have got into jail. The merchants who looked coldly on the experiment before brought their gold to pay for keeping it up. They were hard-headed men of business, and the demonstration that schools were better than jails any day appealed to them as eminently sane and practical.

And well it might. The gang is a distemper of the slum that writes upon the generation it plagues the recipe for its own corrective. It is not the night stick, though in the acute stage that is not to be dispensed with. Neither is it the jail. To put the gang behind iron bars affords passing relief, but it is like treating a symptom without getting at the root of the disease. Prophylactic treatment is clearly indicated. The boy who flings mud and stones is entering his protest in his own way against the purblind policy that gave him jails for schools and the gutter for a playground, that gave him dummies for laws and the tenement for a home. He is demanding his rights, of which he has been cheated,—the right to his childhood, the right to know the true dignity of labor that makes a self-respecting manhood. The gang, rightly understood, is our ally, not our enemy. Like any ailment of the body, it is a friend come to tell us of something that has gone amiss. The thing for us to do is to find out what it is, and set it right.

That is the story of the gang. That we have read and grasped its lesson at last, an item in my morning paper, which I read at the breakfast table today, bears witness. It tells that the League for Political Education has set about providing a playground for the children up on the West Side, near the model tenements which I described. Just so! With a decent home and a chance for the boy to grow into a healthy man, his political education can proceed without much further hindrance. Now let the League for Political Education trade off the policeman's club for a boys' club, and it may consider its course fairly organized.

I spoke of the instinct for the crowd in the tenement house boy as evidence that the slum had got its grip on him. And it is true of him. The experience that the helpless poor will not leave their slum when a chance of better things is offered is wearily familiar to most of us. I recall the indignant amazement of my good friend, the president of the Baron de Hirsch Fund, when, of a hundred of the neediest families chosen to be the pioneers in the experiment of transplanting the crowds of the Ghetto to the country, where homes and work were waiting for them, only seven wanted to go. They preferred the excitement of the street. One has to have resources to face the loneliness of the woods and the fields. We have seen what resources the slum has at its command. In the boy it laid hold of the instinct for organization, the desire to fall in and march in line that belongs to all boys, and is not here, as abroad, cloyed with military service in the young years,—and anyhow is stronger in the American boy than in his European brother,—and perverted it to its own use. That is the simple secret of the success of the club, the brigade, in winning back the boy. It is fighting the street with its own weapon. The gang is the club run wild.

How readily it owns the kinship was never better shown than by the experience of the College Settlement girls, when they first went to make friends in the East Side tenements. I have told it before, but it will bear telling again, for it holds the key to the whole business. They gathered in the drift, all the little embryo gangs that were tuning up in the district, and made them into clubs,—Young Heroes, Knights of the Round Table, and such like; all except one, the oldest, that had begun to make a name for itself with the police. That one held aloof, observing coldly what went on, to make sure it was "straight." They let it be, keeping the while an anxious eye upon it; until one day there came a delegation with the proposition, "If you will let us in, we will change and have your kind of a gang." Needless to say it was let in. And within a year, when, through a false rumor that the concern was moving away, there was a run on the Settlement's penny provident bank, the converted gang proved itself its stanchest friend by doing actually what John Halifax did, in Miss Mulock's story: it brought all the pennies it could raise in the neighborhood by hook or by crook and deposited them as fast as the regular patrons—the gang had not yet risen to the dignity of a bank account—drew them out, until the run ceased.

The cry "Get the boys off the street" that has been raised in our cities, as the real gravity of the situation has been made clear, has led to the adoption of curfew ordinances in many places. Any attempt to fit such a scheme to metropolitan life would probably result simply in adding one more dead-letter law, more dangerous than all the rest, to those we have. Besides, the curfew rings at nine o'clock. The dangerous hours, when the gang is made, are from seven to nine, between supper and bedtime. This is the gap the club fills out. The boys take to the street because the home has nothing to keep them there. To lock them up in the house would only make them hate it more. The club follows the line of least resistance. It has only to keep also on the line of common sense. It must be a real club, not a reformatory. Its proper function is to head off the jail. The gang must not run it. But rather that than have it help train up a band of wretched young cads. The signs are not hard to make out. When a boy has had his head swelled by his importance as a member of the Junior Street-Cleaning Band to the point of reproving his mother for throwing a banana peel in the street, the thing to be done is to take him out and spank him, if it *is* reverting to "the savagery" of the street. Better a savage than a cad. The boys have the making of both in them. Their vanity furnishes abundant material for the cad, but only when unduly pampered. Left to itself, the gang can be trusted not to develop that kink.

It comes down in the end to the personal influence that is always most potent in dealing with these problems. We had a gang start up once when my boys were of that age, out in the village on Long Island where we lived. It had its headquarters in our barn, where it planned diverse raids that aimed at killing the cat and other like outrages; the central fact being that the boys had an air rifle, with which it was necessary to murder something. My wife discovered the conspiracy, and, with woman's wit, defeated it by joining the gang. She "gave in wood" to the election bonfires, and pulled the safety valve upon all the other plots by entering into the true spirit of them,—which was adventure rather than mischief,—and so keeping them within safe lines. She was elected an honorary member, and became the counselor of the gang in all their little scrapes. I can yet see her dear brow wrinkled in the study of some knotty gang problem, which we discussed when the boys had been long asleep. They did not dream of it, and the village never knew what small tragedies it escaped, nor who it was that so skillfully averted them.

It is always the women who do those things. They are the law and the gospel to the boy, both in one. It is the mother heart, I suppose, and there is nothing better in all the world. I am reminded of the conversion of "the Kid" by one who was in a very real sense the mother of a social settlement uptown, in the latitude of Battle Row. The Kid was driftwood. He had been cast off by a drunken father and mother, and was living on what he could scrape out of ash barrels, and an occasional dime for kindling-wood which he sold from a wheelbarrow, when the gang found and adopted him. My friend adopted the gang in her turn, and civilized it by slow stages. Easter Sunday came, when she was to redeem her promise to take the boys to witness the services in a neighboring church, where the liturgy was especially impressive. It found the bigger part of the gang at her door,—a minority, it was announced, were out stealing potatoes, hence were excusable,—in a state of high indignation.

"The Kid's been cussin' awful," explained the leader. The Kid showed in the turbulent distance, red-eyed and raging.

"But why?" asked my friend, in amazement.

" 'Cause he can't go to church!"

It appeared that the gang had shut him out, with a sense of what was due to the occasion, because of his rags. Restored to grace, and choking down reminiscent sobs, the Kid sat through the Easter service, surrounded by the twenty-seven "proper" members of the gang. Civilization had achieved a victory, and no doubt my friend remembered it in her prayers with thanksgiving. The manner was of less account. Battle Row has its own ways, even in its acceptance of means of grace.

I walked home from the office tonight. The street wore its normal aspect of mingled dullness and the kind of expectancy that is always waiting to turn any excitement, from a fallen horse to a fire, to instant account. The early June heat had driven the multitudes from the tenements into the street for a breath of air. The boys of the block were holding a meeting at the hydrant. In some way they had turned the water on, and were splashing in it with bare feet, reveling in the sense that they were doing something that "went against" their enemy, the policeman. Upon the quiet of the evening broke a bugle note and the tramp of many feet keeping time. A military band came around the corner, stepping briskly to the tune of The Stars and Stripes Forever. Their white duck trousers glimmered in the twilight, as the hundred legs moved as one. Stoops and hydrant were deserted with a rush. The gang fell in with joyous shouts. The young fellow linked arms with his sweetheart and fell in too. The tired mother hurried with the baby carriage to catch up. The butcher came, hot and wiping his hands on his apron, to the door to see them pass.

"Yes," said my companion, guessing my thoughts,—we had been speaking of the boys,—"but look at the other side. There is the military spirit. Do you not fear danger from it in this country? No, my anxious friend, I do not. Let them march, and if with a gun, better still. Often enough it is the choice of the gun on the shoulder, or, by and by, the stripes on the back in the lockstep gang.

Note: Year-Book of Elmira State Reformatory, 1897. The statistics deal with 8319 prisoners received there in twenty-three years. The social stratum whence they came is sufficiently indicated by the statement that 18.3 per cent were illiterates, and 43.3 per cent were able to read and write with difficulty; 35.2 per cent had an ordinary common school education; 3.2 per cent came out of high schools or colleges.

★

LOUISE BETTS EDWARDS *Step-Brothers to Dives:*
A Moral Without a Story
Harper's 89 (August 1894): 436–440

[This story of one problematic incident of charitable giving turns on the term, "dives," or Latin for "rich man," and refers to the parable of the rich man (Luke 16: 19–31), who goes to hell while the poor beggar, Lazarus, is accepted into heaven. Engaging a debate that widely appeared in periodicals in the 1890s, Edwards, while portraying the poor as both ignorant and impractical, explores the "rights" of charity recipients as well as the motives of charitable givers.]

I. "There must be a limit to charity." Henry Benedict's long white fingers smoothed his little pointed beard reflectively as he said it. "And the limit, in this case, is set by the collection-box."

Self-satisfaction is God's best gift to man, and Henry Benedict's plentiful endowment in this direction showed itself perhaps too plainly in his face. A lawyer of thirty-two, with a select though slender clientage, backed by an agreeable certainty in the shape of an inherited income, ten years more would place him in the list of "representative citizens." Also, he was a bachelor, which is God's best gift to women. To insure him still more of divine and human favor, he was a man both religious and charitable, a warden of St. Emily's Church, with an interest in his poorer brethren only curbed by a judicious determination that his poorer brethren should not impose on him. This unusual combination of the qualities of a kind heart and a hard head had made him the unanimous choice when St. Emily's wanted a treasurer for its newly formed Indigent Relief Society. To-day an unfulfilled threat of rain had kept from the weekly meeting all but the reverend president, the secretary, the treasurer, and one other member, to whom he emphatically repeated, "There is a limit to charity."

"But this is such a needy case," said Pattie Lejeune, pleadingly.

Reflectiveness left Mr. Benedict's fingers for his face as he narrowed his gaze to hers. "Did you say a deserving case?" he asked.

"No," said Miss Lejeune, crisply, "I didn't. I said needy, which is our chief concern."

There was really only one thing to be said for Pattie Lejeune, Henry Benedict had long ago decided, and that was that she was pretty. For her name, it was some such atrocity as Patricia or Cleopatra, on which even the namby-pamby "Pattie" was an improvement; for her estate, she was poor, and had a cheerfully frank way of alluding to the subject, which seemed almost indelicate, and certainly painful, to a person who could do nothing to help it; for her character, he had heard it whispered in the Society—had even seen it proved in her own actions—that she was "injudicious" and indiscriminate in giving. Not all the dimples and devotion in the world could palliate this one sin, not all the inexperience and enthusiasm could excuse it, in Henry Benedict's eyes; and, the prejudice extending even to her protegees, he tried hard not to feel a sneaking sense of satisfaction at the rector's regretful words:

"We can't do anything this week, Miss Lejeune, I'm afraid. You just heard Mr. Benedict say that the past week's coal and provision bills have swallowed up all the ready cash, and we've cases ahead to swallow up all we are likely to get for a month to come."

"But a special appeal?" Miss Lejeune insinuated. "You remember that case last month—the church raised fifty dollars, and the family was not nearly so badly off as mine, and the husband drank, whereas mine"—she stopped in some confusion, while the effort to hide a smile went round, then continued, courageously—"hasn't touched a drop in ten years."

Undoubtedly Pattie Lejeune was very young. After it had been explained to her that two purses of fifty dollars each are not wrung out of the same church within a month's space, and Mrs. Montgomery, the secretary, had turned the empty treasury-box upside down in expressive answer to her hesitating "But haven't we actually—" the meeting broke up.

We may know a thing for a lifetime and not realize it till some sudden luminous moment. This is pre-eminently true of a man's realization of a woman's beauty. Henry Benedict, returning through the dusk for a forgotten account-book, had been aware for a year or more that Pattie Lejeune carried about with her a tumbled mass of shining hair, a pair of dark gray eyes like mountain lakes, and a complexion in which a faint suggestion of rose deepened or departed entirely in captivating dependency upon what was said to her. But his first distinct realization of it, together with his first sincere regret that she should not be more discriminating in her charity, came when he saw her standing in discouraged irresolution on the steps of the parish building.

"What did you say was the name of your case?" he asked, unwillingly.

"Nawson—No. 119 Penn Street, back garret. They've no food, no fire, and everything in pawn except the children. If you could see for yourself, Mr. Benedict—" She broke off rather lamely: "I never saw a needier case."

"Don't you think, though, that they could get along with less than fifty dollars?" He was struggling valiantly with his prejudice against the insatiable Nawsons.

"They're doing that now"—with a gleam of humor. "Of course it wouldn't take fifty dollars to help them out of their present troubles; it *would* take that much to *keep* them out, as we did with that other poor family—to give them a little freedom from the racking incertainty as to where to-morrow's bread will come from—have any of us ever felt that, Mr. Benedict?—and the unaccustomed luxury of having enough. That's the difference between living somehow and living. But we seldom see it so; less than enough is as good as a feast—for our step-brother Lazarus."

Then it was that Henry Benedict and Pattie Lejeune were both surprised at some words which seemed to utter themselves, choosing the treasure of the Indigent Relief Society as their mouth-piece: "While Dives fares sumptuously every day—true enough. Maybe I'll look up your Nawsons; then we shall see what we shall see."

With which dark prophecy he turned with some words of good-night greeting, for which he was wholly responsible this time, and purposely waited in the darkness to take the car which did *not* swallow up the shabby, stylish little hat and mackintosh which enveloped all that was earthly and heavenly of Miss Pattie Lejeune.

II. "Our step-brother Lazarus!"

Patty Lejeune's witty words (he was beginning to think her witty, which is the first position for— But that has nothing to do with the subject) haunted Benedict with unpleasant pertinacity as he toiled down three flights of sunken, splintered stairs which the wavering streaks of light from a forlorn candle end on the window-sill showed fairly polished with the accumulated grease and grime of years. The ménage Nawson, at the top of flight three, had given him a sense of mental and moral nausea as unaccustomed as unwelcome. He was wont to permit himself no profitless sentimentalities in his charitable visits; either the case was undeserving and to be ignored, or it was deserving, and then something could be done about it. To-day his soul sickened in him at a new and horrifying realization that nothing, in the wider sense, *could* be done; that the undeservingness of the case, so far from dismissing the problem, but pressed it harder; that when he had given the coal-ticket or basket of provisions or settled the month's rent for even the deserving one, the next month brought the same need of the same charity to the same person; and that if he bestowed all his goods on the poor and gave his body to be burned, it was nothing, for there would still be unhelped, unreached, unknown thousands to carry out this same ghastly mockery of existence.

Mrs. Nawson, consumptive, sad-eyed, but cleaner than might have been expected, with the latest baby (there always was a latest) sucking, with a face of wan contentment, at the empty bottle given him "to quiet his worriting"; Mary Nawson, sharp-eyed, sharp-tongued, dingily pretty, whom her mother bemoaned as having "no chance to come to any good"; the children, six of them, squalid, scrawny, hungry-faced; and Tim Nawson himself, "the indirect cause of all this misery," thought Benedict, grimly—really he was getting as caustic as Miss Lejeune—bowed and stolid, doomed at forty-two, by a slow gray film creeping over his eyes, which meant that his seeing and working days were numbered—were none more pitiful "cases" (a sudden loathing for the word arose in him) than dozens of others that he had encountered. This very fact, however, only made matters worse. It was monstrous, it was infamous, that human beings should live in this repellent destitution and dreariness and vice; in the moment's poignant distress it did not comfort him to think that he was not one of the human beings. Suppose it were his blood-brother, or Pattie Lejeune—or, of course, any other girl—would he suffer it? He a church-warden—warden of what, if not these sheep which "fainted, and were scattered abroad, as having no shepherd"?

In the same breath with these thoughts it was no surprise to meet Miss Lejeune in the doorway. Scarce giving her time for a bewildered explanation of her presence—"I brought some things for them from home"—and vouchsafing none for his, he blurted out, taking great gulps of the cold air as it blew fresh across the threshold: "See here, Miss Lejeune. I'll give you that fifty dollars—check or cash, whichever you say."

The gladness which he guessed at but could not see in her face crept into her voice in a delighted little quiver: "Oh, Mr. Benedict, I felt you would!"

"More than I felt," thought Benedict to himself, with a smile, as he waited in the vestibule for her descent, having found fresh proof of her injudiciousness in the fact that she had not only come there alone in the dark, but expected to return unattended also. Speculations—idle, of course, perfectly idle—came up in his mind as to whether such injudiciousness did not require some man, of unformulated identity, to look after it. "Certainly he would see her home;" and would most inconsistently have forgiven her lack of judgment in inviting him inside, which she did not do. All the way thither they talked Nawson, Benedict characteristically insisting that Miss Lejeune dispense only half the money to her protégés, reserving the other twenty-five until after that was gone.

"So large a sum might dazzle them, you know."

"I know it would dazzle *me*," interpolated Pattie; whereat Benedict winced, and continued:

"There would be every temptation to thriftlessness."

Just why Miss Lejeune smiled to herself so suddenly in answer to this was so interesting a problem to Benedict that when, with head down-bent, he stumbled into a crowd of gazers before a newspaper bulletin-board, he would not have looked up but for the casual remark of one man:

"Great, that about the Traders' National, isn't it?"

A cold fear, of a kind he had never felt before, palsied Benedict's tongue. In the widely known and trusted Traders' National Bank of the neighboring country town wherein he had been born and bred lay the snug little income that he owed to a father's thrift. Fear pricked his imagination to outrun his eyes, and in the second before the staring letters on the board formed themselves into intelligible words, he had seen himself plucked bare by fortune of all but the paltry stipend his incidental clients brought him; pinched, debt-ridden, worn threadbare in soul and body in the effort to keep them together. "A step-brother to Dives indeed," he thought, with a dull sickness at his heart, as a swift startled glance upward confirmed his fears.

The Traders' National had failed.

III. "DEAR MISS LEJEUNE,—I am sure you will understand my position and my regret when I tell you that I am obliged to recall the promise which I made you of a check—"

This and a number of interesting variations on it lay strewn on Henry Benedict's office table the next morning. As with all the others, a frown and a disdainful flick of the finger cut it short at this stage of completion.

"Mustn't use up paper at this rate, now I'm a pauper," muttered Benedict, who did not look as if he and Morpheus were on very good terms. "Here goes positively the last attempt:

"MY DEAR MISS LEJEUNE,—A sudden change in my financial affairs, necessitating ready money—

"Pshaw! I can't do it, and have her think me mean. Besides, they need fifty dollars more than I do. You needn't call yourself a pauper, Henry Benedict, or anything near so foolish; you've enough to live on, by strict economy and giving up nearly everything you care for (wonder if that's how Pattie Lejeune does?) and your step-brothers haven't. 'For with such sacrifices God is well pleased;' yes, that fifty will do them too much good and me too little for me to back out now."

The result was that two ten-dollar bills and a five were sent that morning in a registered letter to Miss Lejeune's address, and the church-warden of St. Emily's then set himself to the forlorn and unaccustomed task of retrenchment. For two or three days he kept unwontedly strict hours at his snug little office, and realized as never before how few and far between were the profitable visitors therein; for two or three days he realized as never before the difficulty of drawing a hard and fast line between luxuries and necessities. It would be a dismal joke, he reflected, if Miss Le—— if the members of the Indigent Relief Society could know the reluctance with which car rides, restaurant dinners, boutonnières, magazines, theatres, and so forth, were relegated to the former class by the prudent and judicious Henry Benedict. After half a week spent in industrious study of the sweet uses of adversity, an idea struck him. He would treat himself to a luxury which cost nothing—go down to the Nawsons of Penn Street, and see how they were getting along, now that their miseries had been alleviated by the gift which he had never regretted after it once had left his hand. And possibly Pattie Lejeune— But nonsense; she didn't live there.

The same crooked, evil-smelling halls, the same treacherous staircases, the same dispirited thumb's end of candle to light them; but the thought of one "good deed in a naughty world," of which he was the author, put buoyancy into Benedict's step. By the enforced self-denial of the past few days he could dimly guess at the slow consuming bitterness of an existence thus leaden-weighted by poverty.

"Fifty dollars well spent," he murmured—then stopped, surprised, before the door of the Nawson domicile. Through the crack came jerky sounds from some sort of instrument of torture which drowned his polite rap. He pushed open the door and walked in unheard. The room's only occupant was a small sharp-faced Nawson, who, seated in front of a dilapidated harmonium, clawed out of the dingy keys something sufficiently approximating music to make her throw back her head in an open-mouthed ecstasy which completed an already pronounced resemblance to a young bird.

"St. Cecilia," thought Benedict, with a twist of the mouth. Travelling round the room, his quick eye noted no improvement on the dirt and squalor and disorder save a few gaudy fans tricked out in tinsel and ribbons, which brightened the smeary walls. But—

"What are these?"

He asked it out loud in his astonishment. From the shelf of the one broken-down bureau the whole Nawson family grinned impudently at his discomfiture from a row of imperial-sized photographs—Nawson in a glory of apparel which he was some moments in discovering to be shed by gorgeous hats of lace and velvet which nodded over the heads of the feminine representation of the family, who smirked in self-satisfaction which apparently took no cognizance of the sharp contrast between this sleazy finery and the forlorn habiliments of the rest of their persons.

The spiderlike figure darted off the piano-stool to his side. "Phuttergraphs," she explained, happily. "Ain't they grand? We all got 'em the day we got our new hats and—"

The glib tongue stopped as a vision of pink and white and blue grace appeared in the doorway—Pattie Lejeune in a gown of fur-trimmed blue. A swift forward motion of surprise when she saw him, a backward step as swift and surprised when she caught sight of the gallery of grinning faces, and she gasped out his own question—

"Why, what are these?"

"These are phuttergraphs," said he, grimly. He hated himself for the mean little feeling of triumph which flared up, to die forever, as Pattie Lejeune, her quick woman's eye taking in the situation, did a thing which he had always dimly felt she did on critical occasions—put her hands up to her face and burst into tears.

Benedict called himself a fool, prefacing it with a most unchurchwardenly adjective, and then proceeded to prove it by kneeling on the dirty floor—yes, actually kneeling, and to Miss Lejeune—and completing his self-analysis by telling her that he was a brute and she mustn't cry. Her distressed sobs did not cease, however, until the sound of steps at the door made him hastily resume the normal attitude of the human biped. The rest of the Nawsons trooped jubilantly in, Nawson *père* at their head, a pitcher in his hand, whose contents, all too evident to the experienced nostrils of the two members of the Indigent Relief Society, suggested that his ten years' abstinence had been broken.

"Where's your wife?" asked Pattie Lejeune, sharply. She seemed suddenly to have become mistress of ceremonies.

"Here, Miss Lejeune," said a guilty voice under a befeathered bonnet.

"What does this mean—the harmonium, and—and everything? Is your rent paid? How much have you spent?"

She poured out the questions in an indignant volley, her great gray eyes compelling something like shame into her protégée's tones as she answered, deprecatingly:

" 'Twas such a bargain, Miss Lejeune, dear, and Katie crazy to learn to play. Only two dollars and a half. Then after we'd paid an instalment on the rent—three-fifty we give Mr. Casey, and he was very obliging, and said it would do for a week or two—you could see for yourself, Miss Lejeune, we needed some clothes."

"But not such clothes," said Pattie.

"Seems to me you've got fur on yourself, miss," said Tim Nawson, roughly.

This was too much. Ingratitude and thriftlessness were always to be expected of the poor, but when it came to impudence it was time to assert one's self, and Henry Benedict asserted himself in a brief speech whose clemency surprised even himself. He reminded them that some one had worked, and saved, and perhaps denied himself for the money they were throwing away with criminal thoughtlessness, and asked them what they expected to do for food and coal and clothing during the coming month or two when the exercise of thrift would have left them well provided. And all through his speech he himself was listening to a counter-sermon which spoke eloquently from the beady eyes of Mary Nawson, the sullen, resentful ones of her half-tipsy father, and from the limpid eyes of Pattie Lejeune alike.

"By what right," asked the tormenting voice, choosing its phrases out of the current cant of socialism, whose logic was abhorrent to him as a lawyer and whose ethics as a pietist—"do you reserve for yourself the human longing for purple and fine linen and sumptuous fare, and find fault with your brothers, cast in the same mould, for gratifying the same longing when the lifetime's chance comes for them to do it? 'Thrift?' where should they learn it, and why? Other people's money is all they get, and when this is gone they will either get more, or else will be no worse off in hunger and wretchedness than before, and the better for this brief snatch at the good things of life, which Lazarus never learns to leave sacred to Dives."

"They mighter all died, like my little Janey did, and me have no picture to remember 'em by," said Mrs. Nawson, in self-palliation at this juncture. "And you see for yourself, sir, what an air the melodgeon gives the room."

Pattie Lejeune looked penitence for a sudden irrepressible smile, and Benedict saw himself more clearly than ever a callous, unsympathetic wretch without imagination—"By Jove! not so much as these poor creatures have"—and Miss Lejeune—yes, positively she was an angel.

The pathos of the whole thing, and the hopelessness of the problem involved, smote him, together with a dim sense of some humor lurking in the situation, and when on the way home that unhappy young philanthropist informed him with tragic emphasis that the Nawsons had held a party the night before, and enjoyed for once the pleasures of having hospitality to dispense, he actually smiled before quietly remarking,

"They will never forget this week, I suppose."

"I sha'n't, I'm sure," said the angel, with downcast eyes, which sought the ground still more diligently when Benedict observed, with something like fervor, that he didn't want to forget it, and then left her, to go home to a lonely meal in a cheap eating-house.

The next day Pattie Lejeune, sitting in subdued and red-eyed meditation on her extreme injudiciousness, received a twenty-five-dollar check enclosed in a note signed "H. B.," which informed her with businesslike brevity that here was the balance of the fund held in trust for the Nawsons, and added, with a mildness which brought a twinkle into the still tearful eyes, "I think, however, it would be best for you to buy the supplies and attend to the other expenditure of the amount." Whereupon Miss Lejeune's remarks, if reported, would indicate that she was not the only angel in the world.

Then, after the Traders' National had, with a delightfully unexpected promptness, recommenced making payments, and the members of the Indigent Relief Society had become accustomed to the shock of seeing their treasurer hurry through his notes and accounts that he might walk home with Miss Lejeune, Henry Benedict conducted her to her door on one of these occasions, and instead of ringing the bell said, "Miss Lejeune!" and finding no objection raised to that remark, went on, with unwonted nervousness:

"I want you to become a step-sister—"

"To Dives? That's just what I am."

"No, to Lazarus—by marriage."

5 ★ MENTAL HEALTH & PHYSICAL TRAINING

PHYSICAL CULTURE IN THE 1890s was promoted through new ideals and models, directing attention to figures as diverse as Teddy Roosevelt and the Gibson Girl as examples of vigor and vitality. This culture stressed stature, muscularity, and dynamism in contrast to the genteel models of the past. While the Gibson Girl married lovely femininity with healthful, towering strength, Roosevelt offered the nation a strident, forceful model for masculinity rooted in what he termed "the strenuous life." Roosevelt's particular brand of muscularity was associated with robust frontierism and with his participation in the Rough Riders during the Spanish-American war, giving rise to a continued emphasis on the "health" of a nation engaged in an imperialist political agenda. This ideological position circulated fears of "race suicide" and encouraged "Anglo Saxon" Americans to become physically fit and to produce children to compete with immigrants. The concept of "fitness" therefore legitimated emerging social and cultural practices that sought to preserve the hegemonic traditions of a white, affluent, politically dominant class.

It is important to recognize that these selections point to historically specific ways of interpreting and experiencing the body. For instance, arguments about physical strength, particularly those directed to an audience of American women, highlighted personal benefits and social and familial improvement. William James in "The Gospel of Relaxation" addresses the anxieties associated with neurasthenia, or "nervousness," widely publicized as a phenomenon to which "brain workers" and women were deemed especially vulnerable. Originally delivered as an address at women's educational institutions, such as the Boston Normal School of Gymnastics, Wellesley, Bryn Mawr, and Vassar in 1895 and 1896, the essay charts the "path to cheerfulness" as a route away from paralyzing depression. James suggests self-control as an antidote to desperation and anxiety, setting forth an "ideal of a well-trained and vigorous body" for women as well as men. By advocating a strenuous ideal of womanhood and by pointing to exercise and physical strength as a source of "mental hygiene," James's approach to nervousness was markedly unusual in its day because it challenged a therapeutic ideal of sedentary femininity.

Another aspect of women's health was the argument for dress reform, which B. O. Flower advocates in "Fashion's Slaves." Emphasizing the restrictions on health and comfort stemming from fashionable dress, Flower, a social reformer, presents women as handicapped, weakened, indeed enslaved by their ridiculous costumes, an argument that other authors touch upon briefly. Here, Flower echoes the dress reform movement's attacks on the excesses of women's fashion, including the weight of clothing, its binding restrictions, and the resulting redistribution of the internal organs. Notably, Flower's attempt at a practical solution appears in the form of a "Greek" costume, a style of dress widely displayed in athletic advertisements of the period. Linked to the revival of the modern-day Olympic Games in 1896 and to classical ideals and aesthetics, Greek-styled clothing brought together the aims of dress reform and justifications for exercise, endowing both with a high-culture nuance.

One of the most popular ways to exercise, for both women and men, was on a bicycle. The development of the modern "safety" bicycle in 1884, the addition of pneumatic tires and a coaster brake in 1889 and rapidly falling costs made riding practicable. Bicycles also were controversial for a number of reasons, some relating to health (of both men and women), including fears of injury to sexual organs. Women made up one-quarter to one-third of bicycle customers, so they often were featured in bicycle narratives and illustrations of the 1890s. Critics frequently objected that the bicycle was unseemly or unfeminine because of the special clothing that biking required and because of the difficulty in chaperoning young women athletes. Edna C. Jackson's "A Fin de Cycle Incident" depicts the dilemma of a young woman who cycles in her fiancé's absence, although fearing that he would find her recreation unwomanly. The story emphasizes her capabilities as an athlete and her independent thinking.

While "physical culture" pressured women's social roles, it also challenged an emergent professionalism that entailed office work and little outdoor life for men. Recreation thus filled the void, allowing businessmen to demonstrate some connection with the "manly" ideals of the West and with American frontierism. The professional's fears of dislocation from a national ideal, however, were exacerbated by Max Nordau's *Degeneration* (1895), an assault on modern civilization that pictured the end of the century as diseased by an urban development that fostered the poor, the slum hooligan, and the immigrant. Echoing such attacks on "civilized" society, articles such as H. W. Foster's "Physical Education vs. Degeneracy" and Henry Child Merwin's "On Being Civilized Too Much," by asserting a pastoral and sometimes untamed vision of America in order to reiterate the national values of a frontier past, uphold the outdoor worker as an ideal type in the face of the extreme complications of American life. Upholding the "dignity of labor" as well as the image of American "self-reliance," Foster contends that the "countrybred boy," is exemplary because "necessity, difficulties, effort, struggle, are essential factors in maintaining a vigorous stock." Merwin, too, directs his readers to "leave the close air of the office, or the club" and "consult the teamster, the farmer, the wood-chopper, and shepherd, or the drover." Contending that the worker is "free from fads, as strong in natural impulses, as he was in Shakespeare's time," he also predicts that "from his loins, and not from those of the dilettante, will spring the man of the future." As a cure for perceived effeminacy, national corruption, and urbanization, strenuous outdoor exercise promised to mend the enervating and neurasthenic realities of modern life.

★

WILLIAM JAMES *The Gospel of Relaxation*
Scribner's 25 (April 1899): 499–507

[The preeminent pragmatist philosopher of his time, William James helped to found the academic study of psychology in America. "The Gospel of Relaxation," delivered first as a lecture, was part of a series in the *Atlantic Monthly* and was later collected in *Talks to Teachers on Psychology and to Students on Some of Life's Ideals* (1899). James argues for the restorative value of physical exercise, and he associates good moral and spiritual well-being, as well as good "mental hygiene," with physical health.]

I PROPOSE in the following informal pages to take certain psychological doctrines and show their practical applications to mental hygiene—to the hygiene of our American life more particularly. Our people, especially our teachers, are turning toward psychology nowadays with hopes of guidance, and if psychology is to justify the hopes, it must be by showing fruits in the pedagogic and therapeutic lines.

The reader may possibly have heard of a peculiar theory of the emotions, commonly referred to in psychological literature as the Lange-James theory. According to this theory our emotions are mainly due to those organic stirrings that are aroused in us in a reflex way by the stimulus of the exciting object or situation. An emotion of fear, for example, or surprise, is not a direct effect of the object's presence on the mind, but an effect of that still earlier effect, the bodily commotion which the object suddenly excites; so that, were this bodily commotion suppressed, we should not so much *feel* fear as call the situation fearful; we should not feel surprise, but coldly recognize that the object was indeed astonishing. One enthusiast has even gone so far as to say that when we feel sorry it is because we weep, when we feel afraid it is because we run away, and not conversely. The reader may possibly be acquainted with the paradoxical formula. Now, whatever exaggeration may possibly lurk in this account of our emotions (and I doubt myself whether the exaggeration be very great), it is certain that the main core of it is true, and that the mere giving way to tears, for example, or to the outward expression of an anger-fit, will result for the moment in making the inner grief or anger more acutely felt. There is, accordingly, no better known or more generally useful precept in the moral training of youth, or in one's personal self-discipline, than that which bids us pay primary attention to what we do and express, and not to care too much for what we feel. If we only check a cowardly impulse in time, for example; or if we only *don't* strike the blow or rip out with the complaining or insulting word that we shall regret as long as we live, our feelings themselves will presently be the calmer and better, with no particular guidance from us on their own account. Action seems to follow feeling, but really action and feeling go together; and by regulating the action, which is under the more direct control of the will, we can indirectly regulate the feeling, which is not.

Thus the sovereign voluntary path to cheerfulness, if our spontaneous cheerfulness be lost, is to sit up cheerfully, to look round cheerfully, and to act and speak as if cheerfulness were already there. If such conduct doesn't make you soon feel cheerful, nothing else on that occasion can. So to feel brave, act as if we *were* brave, use all our will to that end, and a courage-fit will very likely replace the fit of fear. Again, in order to feel kindly toward a person to whom we have been inimical, the only way is more or less deliberately to smile, to make sympathetic inquiries, and to force ourselves to say genial things. One hearty laugh together will bring enemies into a closer communion of heart than hours spent on both sides in inward wrestling with the mental demon of uncharitable feeling. To wrestle with a bad feeling only pins our attention on it, and keeps it still fastened in the mind, whereas if we act as if from some better feeling, the old bad feeling soon folds its tent like an Arab and silently steals away.

The best manuals of religious devotion accordingly reiterate the maxim that we must let our feelings go and pay no regard to them whatever. In an admirable and widely successful little book called "The Christian's Secret of a Happy Life," by Mrs. Hannah Whitall Smith, I find this lesson on almost every page. *Act* faithfully, and you really have faith, no matter how cold and even how dubious you may feel. "It is your purpose God looks at," writes

Mrs. Smith, "not your feelings about that purpose, and your purpose or will, is therefore the only thing you need attend to. . . . Let your emotions come or let them go, just as God pleases, and make no account of them either way. . . . They really have nothing to do with the matter. They are not the indicators of your spiritual state, but are merely the indicators of your temperament, or of your present physical condition."

But the reader knows these facts already so I need no longer press them on his attention. From our acts and from our attitudes ceaseless inpouring currents of sensation come, which help to determine from moment to moment what our inner states shall be—that is a fundamental law of psychology which I will therefore proceed to assume.

A Viennese neurologist of considerable reputation has recently written about the *Binnenleben*, as he terms it, or buried life of human beings. No doctor, this writer says, can get into really profitable relations with a nervous patient until he gets some sense of what the patient's *Binnenleben* is, of the sort of unuttered inner atmosphere in which his consciousness dwells alone with the secrets of its prison-house. This inner personal tone is what we can't communicate or describe articulately to others, but the wraith and ghost of it, so to speak, is often what our friends and intimates feel as our most characteristic quality. In the unhealthy minded, apart from all sorts of old regrets, ambitions checked by shames and aspirations obstructed by timidities, it consists mainly of bodily discomforts not distinctly localized by the sufferer, but breeding a general self-mistrust and sense that things are not as they should be with him. Half the thirst for alcohol that exists in the world, exists simply because alcohol acts as a temporary anaesthetic and effacer to all these morbid feelings that never ought to be in a human being at all. In the healthy-minded, on the contrary, there are no fears or shames to discover, and the sensations that pour in from the organism only help to swell the general vital sense of security and readiness for anything that may turn up. Consider, for example, the effects of a well-toned *motor-apparatus*, nervous and muscular, on our general personal self-consciousness, the sense of elasticity and efficiency that results. They tell us that in Norway the life of the women has lately been entirely revolutionized by the new order of muscular feelings with which the use of the *ski*, or long snow-shoes, as a sport for both sexes has made the women acquainted. Fifteen years ago the Norwegian women were even more than the women of other lands votaries of the old-fashioned ideal of femininity, the "domestic *angel*," the "gentle and refining influence," sort of thing. Now these sedentary fireside tabby-cats of Norway have been trained, they say by the snow-shoes, into lithe and audacious creatures for whom no night is too dark or height too giddy; and who are not only saying good-by to the traditional feminine pallor and delicacy of constitution, but actually taking the lead in every educational and social reform. I cannot but think that the tennis and tramping and skating habits and the "bicycle-craze" which are so rapidly extending among our dear sisters and daughters in this country are going also to lead to a sounder and heartier moral tone, which will send its tonic breath through all our American life.

I hope that here in America more and more the ideal of the well-trained and vigorous body will be maintained neck by neck with that of the well-trained and vigorous mind, as the two coequal halves of the higher education, for men and women alike. The strength of the British Empire lies in the strength of character of the individual Englishman, taken all alone by himself; and that strength, I am persuaded, is perennially nourished and kept up by nothing so much as by the national worship, in which all classes meet, of athletic out-door life and sport.

I remember, years ago, reading a certain work by an American doctor on hygiene and the laws of life and the type of future humanity. I have forgotten its author's name and its title, but I remember well an awful prophecy that it contained about the future of our muscular system. Human perfection, the writer said, means ability to cope with the environment; but the environment will more and more require mental power from us, and less and less will ask for bare brute strength. Wars will cease, machines will do all our heavy work, man will become more and more a mere director of nature's energies, and less and less an exerter of energy on his own account. So that if the *homo sapiens* of the future can only digest his food and think, what need will he have of well-developed muscles at all? And why, pursued this writer, should we not even now be satisfied with a more delicate and intellectual type of beauty than that which pleased our ancestors? Nay, I have heard a fanciful friend make a still further advance in this "new-man" direction. With our future food, he says, itself prepared in liquid form from the chemical elements of the atmosphere, pepsinated or half-digested in advance, and sucked up through a glass tube from a tin can, what need shall we have of teeth, or stomachs even? They may go, along with our muscles and our physical courage, whilst, challenging ever more and more our proper admiration, will grow the gigantic domes of our crania arching over our spectacled eyes and animating our flexible little lips to those floods of learned and ingenious talks which will constitute our most congenial occupation.

I am sure that your flesh creeps at this apocalyptic vision. Mine certainly did so; and I cannot believe that our muscular vigor will ever be a superfluity. Even if the day ever dawns in which it will not be needed for fighting the old heavy battles against Nature, it will still always be needed to furnish the background of sanity, serenity, and cheerfulness to life, to give moral elasticity to our disposition, to round off the wiry edge of our fretfulness, and make us good-humored and easy of approach. Weakness is too apt to be what the doctors call irritable weakness. And that blessed internal peace and confidence, that *acquiescentia in seipso*, as Spinoza used to call it, that wells up from every part of the body of a muscularly well-trained human being, and soaks the in-dwelling soul of him with satisfaction, is, quite apart from every consideration of its mechanical utility, an element of spiritual hygiene of supreme significance.

And now let me go a step deeper into mental hygiene and try to enlist the reader's insight and sympathy in a cause which I believe is one of paramount patriotic importance to us Yankees. Many years ago a Scottish medical man, Dr. Clouston, a mad-doctor, as they called him there, or what we would call an asylum physician (the most eminent one in Scotland), visited this country and said something that has remained in my memory ever since. "You Americans," he said, "wear too much expression on your faces. You are living like an army with all its reserves engaged in action. The duller countenances of the British population betoken a better scheme of life. They suggest stores of reserved nervous force to fall back upon, if any occasion should arise that requires it. This inexcitability, this presence at all times of power not used, I regard," continued Dr. Clouston, "as the great safe-guard of our English people. The other thing in you gives me a sense of insecurity, and you ought somehow to tone yourselves down. You really do carry too much expression, you take too intensely the trivial moments of life."

Now, Dr. Clouston is a trained reader of the secrets of the soul as expressed upon the countenance, and the observation of his which I quote seems to me to mean a great deal. And all Americans who stay in Europe long enough to get accustomed to the spirit that reigns and expresses itself there, so unexcitable as compared with ours, make a similar observation when they return to their native shores. They find a wild-eyed look upon their compatriot's faces, either of too desperate eagerness and anxiety, or of too intense responsiveness and good-will. It is hard to say whether the men or the women show it most. It is true that we do not all feel about it as Dr. Clouston felt. Many of us, far from deploring it, admire it. We say, "What intelligence it shows! How different from the stolid cheeks, the cod-fish eyes, the slow, inanimate demeanor we have been seeing in the British Isles." Intensity, rapidity, vivacity of appearance are indeed with us something of a nationally accepted ideal, and the medical notion of "irritable weakness" is not the first thing suggested by them to our mind, as it was to Dr. Clouston's. In a weekly paper not very long ago I remember reading a story in which, after describing the beauty and interest of the heroine's personality, the author summed up her charms by saying that to all who looked upon her an impression as of "bottled lightning" was irresistibly conveyed.

Bottled lightning in truth is one of our American ideals, even of a young girl's character! Now it is most ungracious, and it may seem to some persons unpatriotic, to criticise in public the physical peculiarities of one's own people, of one's own family, so to speak. Besides, it may be said, and said with justice, that there are plenty of bottled-lightning temperaments in other countries, and plenty of phlegmatic temperaments here; and that when all is said and done the more or less of tension I am making a fuss about is a very small item in the sum-total of a nation's life, and not worth solemn treatment in a magazine in which agreeable rather than disagreeable things should be made prominent. Well, in one sense the more or less of tension in our faces and our unused muscles *is* a small thing. Not much mechanical work is done by these contractions. But it is not always the material size of a thing that measures its importance, often it is its place and function. One of the most philosophical remarks I ever heard made was by an unlettered workman who was doing some repairs at my house many years ago. "There is very little difference between one man and another," he said, "when you go to the bottom of it. But what little there is is very important." And the remark certainly applies to this case. The general over-contraction may be small when estimated in foot-pounds, but its importance is immense on account of its *effects on the over-contracted person's spiritual life.* This follows as a necessary consequence from the theory of our emotions to which I made reference at the beginning of this article. For by the sensations that so incessantly pour in from the over-tense excited body, the over-tense and excited habit of mind is kept up, and the sultry, threatening, exhausting, thunderous inner atmosphere never quite clears away. If you never wholly give yourself up to the chair you sit in, but always keep your leg- and body-muscles half contracted for a rise; if you breathe eighteen or nineteen instead of sixteen times a minute, and never quite breathe out at that; what mental mood can you be in but one of inner panting and expectancy, and how can the future and its worries possibly forsake your mind? On the other hand, how can they gain admission to your mind if your brow be unruffled, your respiration calm and complete, and your muscles all relaxed?

Now, what is the cause of this absence of repose, this bottled-lightning quality, in us Americans? The explanation of it that is usually given is that it comes from the extreme dryness of our climate and the acrobatic performances of our thermometer coupled with the extraordinary progressiveness of our life, the hard work, the railroad speed, the rapid success, and all the other things we know so well by heart. Well, our climate is certainly exciting, but hardly more so than that of many parts of Europe, where, nevertheless, no bottled-lightning girls are found. And the work done and the pace of life are as extreme in every great capital of Europe as they are here. To me both of these pretended causes are utterly insufficient to explain the facts.

To explain them we must go, not to physical geography, but to psychology and sociology. The latest chapter both in sociology and in psychology to be developed in a manner that approaches adequacy is the chapter on the imitative impulse. First Tarde in France, and later Royce and Baldwin here, have shown that invention and imitation, taken together, form, one may say, the entire warp and woof of human life in so far as it is social. The American over-tension and jerkiness and breathlessness and intensity and agony of expression, are primarily social, and only secondarily physiological phenomena. They are bad habits, nothing more or less, bred of custom and example, born of the imitation of bad models and the cultivation of false personal ideals. How are idioms acquired, how do local peculiarities of phrase and accent come about? Through an accidental example set by someone, which struck the ears of others, and was quoted and copied till at last everyone in the locality chimed in. Just so it is with national tricks of vocalization or intonation, with national manners, fashions of movement and gesture, and habitual expressions of face. We, here in America through following a succession of pattern-setters whom it is now impossible to trace, and through influencing each other in a bad direction, have at last settled down collectively into what, for better or worse, is our own characteristic national type—a type with the production of which, so far as these habits go, the climate and conditions have had practically nothing at all to do.

This type, which we have thus reached by our imitativeness, we now have fixed upon us for better or worse. Now no type can be *wholly* disadvantageous; but so far as our type follows the bottled-lightning fashion, it cannot be wholly good. Dr. Clouston was certainly right in thinking that eagerness, breathlessness, and anxiety are not signs of strength; they are signs of weakness and of bad co-ordination. The even forehead, the slab-like cheek, the codfish eye, may be less interesting for the moment, but they are more promising signs than intense expression is of what we may expect of their possessor in the long run. Your dull, unhurried worker gets over a great deal of ground, because he never goes backward or breaks down. Your intense, convulsive worker breaks down and has bad moods so often that you never know where he may be when you most need his help—he may be having one of his "bad days." We say that so many of our fellow-countrymen collapse, and have to be sent abroad to rest their nerves, because they work so hard. I suspect that this is an immense mistake. I suspect that neither the nature nor the amount of our work are accountable for the frequency and severity of our breakdowns, but that their cause lies rather in those absurd feelings of hurry and having no time, in that breathlessness and tension, that anxiety of feature, and that solicitude for results, that lack of inner harmony and ease, in short, by which with us the work is so apt to be accompanied, and from which a European who should do the same work would nine times out of ten be free. These perfectly wanton and unnecessary tricks of inner attitude and outer manner in us, caught from the social atmosphere, kept up by tradition, and idealized by many as the admirable way of life, are the last straws that break the American camel's back, the final overflowers of our measure of wear and tear and fatigue.

The voice, for example, in a surprisingly large number of us has a tired and plaintive sound. Some of us are really tired (for I don't mean absolutely to deny that our climate has a tiring quality), but far more of us are not tired at all, or would not be tired at all unless we had got into a wretched trick of feeling tired by following the prevalent habits of vocalization and expression. And if talking high and tired, and living excitedly and hurriedly, would only enable us to *do* more by the way, even while breaking us down in the end, it would be different. There would be some compensation, some excuse for going on so. But the exact reverse is the case: It is your relaxed and easy worker, who is in no hurry, and quite thoughtless most of the while of consequences, who is your efficient worker; and tension and anxiety, and present and future, all mixed up together in our mind at once, are the surest drags upon steady progress and hindrances to our success. My colleague, Professor Munsterberg, an excellent observer, who came here recently, has written some notes on America to German papers. He says in substance that the appearance of unusual energy in America is superficial and illusory, being really due to nothing but the habits of jerkiness and bad co-ordination for which we have to thank the defective training of our people. I think myself that it is high time for old legends and traditional opinions to be changed; and that if anyone should begin to write about Yankee inefficiency and feebleness, and inability to do anything with time except to waste it, he would have a very pretty paradoxical little thesis to sustain, with a great many facts to quote, and a great deal of experience to appeal to in its proof.

Well, if our dear American character is weakened by all this over-tension —and I think, whatever reserves you may make, gentle reader, that you will agree as to the main facts—where does the remedy lie? It lies, of course, where lay the origins of the disease. If a vicious fashion and taste are to blame for the thing, the fashion and taste must be changed. And though it is no small thing to inoculate seventy millions of people with new standards, yet, if there is to be any relief, that will have to be done. We must change ourselves from a race that admires jerk and snap for their own sakes, and looks down upon low voices and quiet ways as dull, to one that, on the contrary, has calm for its ideal, and for their own sakes loves harmony, dignity, and ease.

So we go back to the psychology of imitation again. There is only one way to improve ourselves, and that is by some of us setting an example which the others may pick up and imitate till the new fashion spreads from east to west. Some of us are in more favorable positions than others to set new fashions. Some are much more striking personally and imitable, so to speak. But no living person is sunk so low as not to be imitated by somebody. Thackeray somewhere says of the Irish nation, that there never was an Irishman so poor that he didn't have a still poorer Irishman living at his expense; and surely there is no human being whose example doesn't work contagiously in *some* particular. The very idiots at our public institutions imitate each others' peculiarities. And if you, dear reader, should individually achieve calmness and harmony in your own person, you may depend upon it that a wave of imitation will spread from you, as surely as the circles spread outward when a stone is dropped into a lake.

Fortunately, we shall not have to be absolute pioneers. Even now in New York they have formed a society for the improvement of our national vocalization, and one perceives its machinations already in the shape of various newspaper articles intended to stir up dissatisfaction with the awful thing that it is. And, better still than that, because more radical and general, is the gospel of relaxation, as one may call it, preached by Miss Annie Payson Call, of Boston, in her admirable little volume called "Power through Repose," a book that ought to be in the hands of every instructor of youth in America of either sex. You need only be followers, then, on a path already opened up by others. But of one thing be confident—others still will follow you.

And this brings me to one more application of psychology to practical life, to which I will call attention briefly, and then close. If one's example of easy and calm ways is to be effectively contagious, one feels by instinct that the less voluntarily one aims at getting imitated, the more unconscious one keeps in the matter, the more likely one is to succeed. *Become the imitable thing,* and you may then discharge your minds of all responsibility for the imitation—the laws of social nature will take care of that result. Now, the psychological principle on which this precept reposes is a law of very deep and wide-spread importance in the conduct of our lives, and at the same time a law which we Americans most grievously neglect. Stated technically, the law is this, that *strong feeling about one's self tends to arrest the free association of one's objective ideas and motor processes.* We get the extreme example of this in the mental disease called melancholia.

A melancholic patient is filled through and through with intensely painful emotion about himself. He is threatened; he is guilty; he is doomed; he is annihilated; he is lost. His mind is fixed as if in a cramp on this sense of his own situation; and in all the books on insanity you may read that the usual varied flow of his thoughts has ceased. His associative processes, to use the technical phrase, are inhibited, and his ideas stand stock still, shut up to their one monotonous function of reiterating inwardly the fact of the man's desperate estate. And this inhibitive influence is not due to the mere fact that his emotion is *painful.* Joyous emotions about the self also stop the association of our ideas. A saint in ecstasy is as motionless and irresponsive and one-idead as a melancholiac. And without going as far as ecstatic saints, we know how in everyone a great or sudden pleasure may paralyze the flow of thought. Ask young people returning from a party or a spectacle, and all excited about it, what it was. "Oh, it was *fine!* it was *fine!* it was *fine!*" is all the information you are likely to receive until the excitement has calmed down. Probably every one of my readers has been made temporarily half-idiotic by some great success or piece of good fortune. "*Good!* Good! GOOD!" is all we can at such times say to ourselves, until we smile at our own very foolishness.

Now from all this we can draw an extremely practical conclusion. If, namely, we wish our trains of ideation and volition to be copious and varied and effective, we must form the habit of freeing them from the inhibitive influence of egoistic preoccupation about their results. Such a habit, like other habits, can be formed. Prudence and duty and self-regard, emotions of ambition and emotions of anxiety, have, of course, a needful part to play in our lives. But confine them as far as possible to the occasions when you are making your general resolutions and deciding on your plans of campaign, and keep them out of the details. When once a decision is reached and execution is the order of the day, dismiss absolutely all responsibility and care about the outcome. *Unclamp,* in a word, your intellectual and practical machinery and let it run free, and the service it will do you will be twice as good. Who are the scholars who get "rattled" in the recitation-room? Those who think of the possibilities of failure and feel the great importance of the act. Who are those who do recite well? Often those who are most indifferent. *Their* ideas reel themselves out of their memory of their own accord. Why do we hear the complaint so often that social life in New England is either less rich and expressive or more fatiguing than it is in some other parts of the world? To what is the fact, if fact it be, due, unless to the over-active conscience of the people, afraid of either saying something too trivial and obvious, or something insincere, or something unworthy of one's interlocutor, or something in some way or other not adequate to the occasion? How can conversation possibly steer itself through such a sea of responsibilities and inhibitions as this? On the other hand, conversation does flourish and society is refreshing, and neither dull, on the one hand, nor exhausting from its effort on the other, wherever people forget their scruples and take the brakes off their hearts and let their tongues wag as automatically and irresponsibly as they will.

They talk much in pedagogic circles to-day about the duty of the teacher to prepare for every lesson in advance. To some extent this is useful. But we Yankees are assuredly not those to whom such a general doctrine should be preached. We are only too careful as it is. The advice I should give to most teachers would be in the words of one who is herself an admirable teacher. Prepare yourself in the *subject so well that it shall always be on tap;* then in the class-room trust your spontaneity and fling away all further care. My advice to students would be somewhat similar, especially at periods when there are many successive days of examination impending. One ounce of good nervous tone in an examination is worth many pounds of anxious study for it in advance. If you want really to do your best in an examination, fling away the book the day before, say to yourself, "I won't waste another minute on this miserable thing, and I don't care an iota whether I succeed or not." Say this sincerely, and feel it; and go out and play, or go to bed and sleep; and I am sure the results next day will encourage you to use the method permanently. I have heard this advice given to a student by Miss Call, whose book on muscular relaxation I quoted a moment ago. In her later book, entitled "As a Matter of Course," the gospel of moral relaxation, of dropping things from the mind, and not "caring," is preached with equal success. Not only our preachers, but our friends the theosophists and mind-curers of various religious sects are also harping on this string. And with the doctors, the Delsarteans, and such writers as Prentice Mulford, Mr. Dresser, and Mr. Trine to help, and the whole band of school-teachers and magazine readers chiming in, it really looks as if a good start might be made in the direction of changing our American mental habit into something more indifferent and strong.

Worry means always and invariably inhibition of associations and loss of effective power. Of course, the sovereign cure for worry is religious faith, and this, of course, you also know. The turbulent billows of the fretful surface leave the deep parts of the ocean undisturbed, and to him who has a hold on vaster and more permanent realities the hourly vicissitudes of his personal destiny seem relatively insignificant things. The really religious person is accordingly unshakable and full of equanimity, and calmly ready for any duty that the day may bring forth. This is charmingly illustrated by a little work with which I recently became acquainted: "The Practice of the Presence of God the best Rule of a Holy Life, by Brother Lawrence, being Conversations and Letters of Nicholas Herman, of Lorraine, Translated from the French." I extract a few passages, the conversations being given in indirect discourse. Brother Lawrence was a Carmelite friar, converted at Paris in 1666. "He said that he had been footman to M. Fieabert, the Treasurer and that he was a great awkward fellow, who broke everything. That he had desired to be received into a monastery, thinking that he would there be made to smart for his awkwardness and the faults he should commit, and so he should sacrifice to God his life, with its pleasures; but that God had disappointed him, he having met with nothing but satisfaction in that state. . . .

"That he had long been troubled in mind from a certain belief that he should be damned; that all the men in the world could not have persuaded him to the contrary; but that he had thus reasoned with himself about it: *I engaged in a religious life only for the love of God, and I have endeavored to act only for Him; whatever becomes of me, whether I be lost or saved, I will always continue to act purely for the love of God. I shall have this good at least, that till death I shall have done all that is in me to love Him. . . .* That since then he had passed his life in perfect liberty and continual joy.

"That when an occasion of practising some virtue offered, he addressed himself to God, saying, 'Lord, I cannot do this unless Thou enablest me;' and that then he received strength more than sufficient.

"That when he had failed in his duty, he only confessed his fault, saying to God, I shall never do otherwise, if You leave me to myself; it is You who must hinder my failing, and mend what is amiss.' That after this he gave himself no further uneasiness about it.

"That he had been lately sent into Burgundy to buy the provision of wine for the society, which was a very unwelcome task for him, because he had no turn for business, and because he was lame, and could not go about the boat but by rolling himself over the casks. That, however, he gave himself no uneasiness about it, nor about the purchase of the wine. That he said to God, 'It was His business he was about' and that he afterward found it well performed. That he had been sent into Auvergne, the year before, upon the same account; that he could not tell how the matter passed, but that it proved very well.

"So, likewise, in his business in the kitchen (to which he had naturally a great aversion), having accustomed himself to do everything there for the love of God, and with prayer, upon all occasions, for His grace to do his work well, he had found everything easy during fifteen years that he had been employed there.

"That he was very well pleased with the post he was now in; but that he was as ready to quit that as the former, since he was always pleasing himself in every condition, by doing little things for the love of God.

"That the goodness of God assured him He would not forsake him utterly, and that He would give him strength to bear whatever evil He permitted to happen to him; and therefore that he feared nothing, and had no occasion to consult with anybody about his state. That when he had attempted to do it, he had always come away more perplexed."

The simple-heartedness of the good Brother Lawrence, and the relaxation of all unnecessary solicitudes and anxieties in him, is a refreshing spectacle.

The need of feeling responsible all the livelong day has been preached long enough in our New England. Long enough exclusively, at any rate— and long enough to the female sex. (I might as well now confess that this article was originally written for the students of a woman's college, and afterward repeated to more than one similar audience.) What our girl-students and woman-teachers most need nowadays is not the exacerbation, but rather the toning-down of their moral tensions. Even now I fear that some one of my fair readers may be making an undying resolve to become strenuously relaxed, cost what it will, for the remainder of her life. It is needless to say that that is not the way to do it. The way to do it, paradoxical as it may seem, is genuinely not to care whether you are doing it or not. Then, possibly, by the grace of God, you may all at once find that you are doing it; and, having learned what the trick feels like, may (again by the grace of God) be enabled to go on.

And that something like this may be your happy experience, dear reader, after reading this article, is my most earnest wish.

★

B.O. FLOWER from *Fashion's Slaves*
Arena (September 1891): 401–430

[B. O. Flower authored this essay, part of the *Arena*'s concentrated attack on fashionable dress, to complement another set of essays written in 1891 that advocated dress reform. The *Arena*, founded by Flower in 1889, was noted for its advocacy of the social reform of many ills, from sweatshops to slum clearance to child labor to dress reform. This article is notable for rereading the past follies of women's fashion and for presenting new and alternative fashions drawn from classical forms of dress.]

THE LAST SESSION of the International Council of Women discussed no question of greater importance to civilization than that of dress reform. The fact that this world's congress, representing the most thoughtful, conscientious, and broad-minded women of our age, has taken up this subject with a firm determination to accomplish a revolution which shall mean health and happiness to the oncoming generation, is itself a prophecy pregnant with promise of a substantial and enduring reform. It will not be surprising if in the near future it is found that this earnest though somewhat timid discussion marked a distinct step in the world's progress; certainly it was the most significant and authoritative utterance from united womanhood that has yet been made touching a problem which most vitally affects civilization.

To the student of sociology nothing is more perplexing or discouraging than society's persistency in blindly clinging to old standards and outgrown ideals which can no longer be defended by reason; and this is nowhere more marked than in the social world where fashion has successfully defied all true standards of art, principles of common sense, rules of hygiene and what is still more important, the laws of ethics which underlie all stable or enduring civilizations.

At the very threshold of this discussion, I ask the reader to, as far as pos-

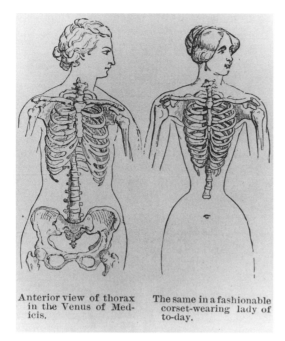

Anterior view of thorax in the Venus of Medicis.

The same in a fashionable corset-wearing lady of to-day.

FIGURE 14 From B. O. Flower's dress reform article advocating a return to classical ideals of feminine beauty, this illustration depicts the female bone structure, comparing an ancient figure with a modern, fashionable, corseted figure. (*Arena*, 1891)

sible, divest his mind of all prejudice arising from preconceived opinions, and view in a perfectly candid and judicial manner this problem upon which the last word will not be spoken until woman is emancipated. As long as free discussion is tabooed and conservatism finds it possible to dismiss the question with a flippant jest, a ribald joke, or a basely unjust imputation, the old order will stand; partly because woman feels her helplessness and largely because so few people stop to trace cause and effect or patiently reason upon results of the most serious character. Conservatism is strongly entrenched in the minds of the millions, and to a certain degree mental lethargy broods over the world. It is true that in woman's sphere to-day mental activity is more marked than in any other age, and the best brains and most thoughtful women of our time are boldly denouncing the bondage of fashion and bravely pleading for such radical reforms in dress as will secure to womanhood health and comfort, while being genuinely artistic and graceful, breathing true refinement and conforming to aesthetic principles rather than the caprice of fashion. To me there is something infinitely pathetic in the brave protests that have from time to time flashed from the outraged sensibilities of those who represent the very flower of American womanhood, when discussing this subject, for running through their almost every utterance is the plaintive note of helplessness, mingled with the consciousness of the justice of the cause for which they plead. The talented and universally respected Mrs. Abba Woolson Gould some years ago thus gave expression to her feelings when writing of the long, heavy, disease-producing skirts of women:

> Do what we will with them, they still add enormously to the weight of clothing, prevent cleanliness of attire about the ankles, overheat by their tops the lower portion of the body, impede locomotion, and invite accidents. In short, they are uncomfortable, unhealthy, unsafe, and unmanageable. Convinced of this fact by patient and almost fruitless attempts to remove their objectionable qualities, the earnest dress-reformer is loath to believe that skirts hanging below the knee are not transitory features in woman's attire, as similar features have been in the dress of men, and surely destined to disappear with the tight hourglass waists and other monstrosities of the present costume. . . . Any changes the wisest of us can to-day propose are only a mitigation of an evil which can never be done away till women emerge from this vast swaying, undefined, and indefinable mass of drapery into the shape God gave to His human beings.

Mary A. Livermore voices a sad and terrible truth when she observes:

> The invalidism of young girls is usually attributed to every cause but the right one; to hard study—co-education—which, it is said, compels overwork that the girl student may keep up with the young men of her class; too much exercise, or lack of rest and quiet at certain periods when nature demands it. All the while the physician is silent concerning the glove-fitting, steel-clasped corset, the heavy, dragging skirts, the bands engirding the body, the pinching, deforming boot, and the ruinous social dissipation of fashionable society. These will account for much of the feebleness of young women and girls. For they exhaust nervous force, make freedom of movement a painful impossibility, and frequently shipwreck the young girl before she is out of port.

> We have a theory, generally accepted in civilized society, which we never formulate in speech but to which we are very loyal in practical life. This theory, put in plain language, is as follows: God knows how to make boys; and, when He sends a boy into the world, it is safe to allow him to grow to manhood as God made him. He may be too tall or too short, for our notions, too stout or too thin, too light or too dark. Nevertheless, it is right, for God knows how to make boys. But when God sends a girl into the world, it is not safe to allow her to grow to womanhood as He has made her. Some one must take her and improve her figure, and give her the shape in which it is proper for her to grow.

> Accordingly, the young girl comes some day from the dressmaker with this demand: "Mme. —— (the dressmaker) says that I am getting

into horrid shape, and must have a pair of corsets immediately." The corsets are bought and worn, and the physical deterioration begins.

Miss Frances E. Willard thus touchingly refers to the bondage of fashion:

"But there came a day—alas! the day of my youth—on which I was as literally caught out of the fields and pastures as was ever a young colt; confronted by a long dress that had been made for me, corsets and high-heeled shoes that had been bought, hair-pins and ribbons for my stray-ing locks, and I was told that it simply 'wouldn't answer' to 'run wild' another day. Company from the city was expected; I must be made pre-sentable; 'I had got to look like other folks.'

"That was a long time ago, but I have never known a single physically reasonable day since that sweet May morning when I cried in vain for longer lease of liberty."

Mrs. Frances E. Russell, whose significant paper read at the Woman's Council elicited universal approbation, in the following extract from her able essay in *The Arena* sounds a more hopeful note than her illustrious pre-decessors, for she is nearer the dawn, and the horizon of woman's freedom is broadening:

The fiction that women have no legs is now fully discredited, for in the show windows of the largest dry goods stores stand dummies of the female figure dressed only in the combination undersuit made of wool or silk "tights," covering the whole body, except the head, hands, and feet. By this time everyone must know that woman, like man, is a biped. Can anyone give a good reason why she must lift an unnecessary weight of clothing with every step she takes,—pushing forward folds of restricting drapery and using almost constantly, not only her hands, but her men-tal power and nervous energy to keep her skirts neat and out of the way of harm to herself and others?

Much discussion has been wasted over the question whether a woman should carry the burden of her voluminous drapery from the shoulders or the hips. Why must she carry this unnecessary weight at all?

Now let us join hands, all lovers of liberty, in earnest co-operation to free American women from the dominion of foreign fashion. Let us, as intelligent women, with the aid and encouragement of all good men, take this important matter into our own hands and provide ourselves with convenient garments; a costume that shall say to all beholders that we are equipped for reasonable service to humanity.

Conservative critics have so frequently misrepresented those who have honestly pleaded for dress reform, that it is no longer safe to be frank, and this fact alone has constrained numbers of earnest writers from expressing

FIGURE 15 This illustration, one of B. O. Flower's "Liberty" dress designs, promotes the kind of garb that Flower and other dress reform enthusiasts advocated as a classical, comfortable alternative to constricting, damaging modern clothing. (*Arena,* 1891)

their sentiments who have felt it their duty to speak in behalf of health, beauty, and common sense; indeed so certain is one to be misrepresented who handles this subject in anything like a reasonable and unconventional manner, and so surely will his views be assailed as improper, owing to the age-long cast of conventional thought, that were it not that this question so intimately affects fundamental, ethical, and hygienic laws, and bears such a vitally important relation to true progress, I frankly admit that I doubt whether I should have the courage to discuss it. But I find it impossible to remain silent, believing as I do most profoundly that the baleful artificial standards so long tolerated must be abolished, that the fetish of the nineteenth century civilization must be overthrown, and that it is all-important that people be thoroughly acquainted with the far-reaching and basic significance of this problem, through courageous and persistent agitation and education, in order that manhood and womanhood be brought up to the ethical plane which marks an enduring civilization. In the examination of this subject I desire to very briefly note it from aesthetic, hygienic, and ethical points of view. It is a singular fact that every effort made toward healthful and common reform in woman's apparel has been as assailed as inartistic or immoral while fashions once disgusting, indecent, destructive to life and health, and degrading to womanhood have been readily sanctioned by conventionalism. This antagonistic attitude toward any movement for an improvement in woman's attire founded on the laws of health, art, comfort, and common sense was characteristically expressed in a recent editorial in a leading Boston daily, wherein the writer solemnly observed:

> The simple truth is, the great majority of the women *appreciate the fact that it is their mission to be beautiful,* and the dress reformers have never yet devised any garment to assist the women in fulfilling this mission.

The author of the above fairly represents the attitude of conventional thought,—its servility to fashion, its antagonism to reformative moves. The implied falsehood that fashion represents beauty and art, or is the servant of aestheticism has been reiterated so often that thousands have accepted it as truth.

In order to expose its falsity, I have reproduced in this paper plates taken from leading American and English fashion monthlies during the past three decades, in each of which it is noticeable that extremes have been reached. In 1860–65, the hoop-skirt held sway, and the wasp waist was typical of beauty. Then no lady was correctly attired according to the prevailing idea who did not present a spectacle curiously suggestive of a moving circus tent. During this era four or five fashionably dressed women completely filled an ordinary drawing-room; while the sidewalk was often practically monopolized by moving monstrosities, save when in front or behind the formidable swinging cages moved escorts, who with no less servility than American womanhood bowed to the frivolous and criminal caprice of the modern Babylon. But fashion is nothing if not changeable; fancy not art guides her mind. What to-day types beauty, is by her own voice to-morrow voted indecent and absurd. Thus we find in the period extending from 1870 to 1875 an entirely new but none the less ridiculous or injurious extreme prevails. The wonderful swinging cage, the diameter of which at the base often equaled the height of the encased figure, has disappeared, being no longer considered desirable or aesthetic, and in its place we have prodigious bustles and immense trains, by which an astonishing quantity of material is thrown behind the body, suggesting in some instances a toboggan slide, in others the unseemly hump on the back of a camel. This is the era of the enormous bustle and the train of sweeping dimensions.

When we examine the prevailing styles which marked this period, we are struck with amazement at the power exerted by fashion over the intellect and judgment of society. Imagine the shame and humiliation of a woman of fashion, endowed by nature or afflicted by disease with such an unsightly hump on the back as characterized the fashionable toilet of this period!

Toward the end of the seventies, we find another extreme reached, which if possible was more absurd and injurious than those which marked the early days of this decade. This was the period of the tie-back, or narrow skirts and enormous trains. As in 1860 fashion's slaves vied with one another in their effort to cover the largest possible circular space, now their ambitions lay in the direction of the opposite extremes: the skirts must be as narrow as possible even though it greatly impeded walking, for as will be readily observed all free use of the lower limbs was out of the question during the reign of the "tie back."

The reaction in favor of a more sensible dress which followed was of brief duration. During this time, however, the long trains were seldom seen, and thoughtful women began to hope that the arbitrary rule of fashion was over. It was not long, however, before the panier period arrived, and what was popularly known as the pull-back was accepted as the correct style in fashion's world. Of this latter conceit little need to be said, for it has so recently passed from view that all remember its peculiarity, which to the ordinary observer seemed to be a settled determination on the part of its originators to render walking as difficult and fatiguing as possible, while fully exposing the outline of the wearer's body below the waist at every step. What in '60 or '70 would have been accounted the height of indecency, is in the eighties perfectly proper in the fashionable world. During this time it was not enough to have the skirts very narrow, they must at every step give the outline of the limbs [or as our Minnesota solon would put it, *nether* limbs], hence we find the pull-backs in which "two shy knees appeared clad in a single trouser."

Such have been the inconsistencies, incongruities, and absurdities of fashion as illustrated in the past three decades, in view of which one may well ask whether in fashion's eyes women are such paragons of ugliness that these ever-varying styles (introduced, we are seriously informed, to conserve to her beauty,) are absolutely essential, and by what rule of art can we explain the fact that the ponderous hoopskirt was the essential requirement of beauty in the sixties and the enormous bustles demanded in the seventies. The truth is, fashion is supremely indifferent alike to all laws of art and beauty, health and life, decency and propriety—a fact that must be patent to any thoughtful person who examines the prevailing styles of a generation. I submit that the wildest extremes to which well-meaning but injudicious dress reformers have gone in the past have been marked by nothing more inartistic than the costume of the reigning belle in 1860. Each successive decade has been marked by an extreme which, surveyed from the vantage ground of the present, is as ridiculously absurd as it has been wanting in beauty or common sense. Nowhere have the laws of true art been so severely ignored as in the realm of fashion. Yet this view of the problem palls into insignificance when we come to examine the question from the standpoint of health and life.

One would think that after thousands of years of sickness and death, with all the advantages of increased education and a broadening intellectual horizon, we would have arrived at such an appreciation of the value of health and the solemn duty we owe to posterity, as to compel this consideration to enter into our thoughts when we adopted styles of dress; yet nowhere is the weakness of our present civilization more marked or its hollowness so visible, even to the superficial thinker, as in the realm of fashion, *where every consideration of health and even life, and all sense of responsibility to future generations are brushed aside as trivialities not to be seriously considered.* In vain have physicians and physiologists written, lectured, and demonstrated the fatal results of yielding to fashion. The learned Doctor Trall in writing on this subject wisely observes:

The evil effects of tight lacing, or of lacing at all, and of binding the clothing around the hips, instead of suspending it from the shoulders, can never be fully realized without a thorough education in anatomy and physiology. And if the illustrations here presented should effect the needed reform in fashionable dress, the resulting health and happiness to the human race would be incalculable; for the health of the mothers of each generation determines, in a very large measure, the vital stamina of the next. It is obvious that, if the diameter of the chest, at its lower and broader part, is diminished by lacing, or any other cause, to the extent of one fourth or one half, the lungs B, B are pressed in towards the heart, A, the lower ribs are drawn together and press on the liver, C, and spleen, E, while the abdominal organs are pressed downward on the pelvic viscera. The stomach, D, is compressed in its tranverse diameter; both the stomach, upper intestines, and liver are pressed downward on the kidneys, M, M, and on the lower portions of the bowels [the intestinal tube is denoted by the letters f, j, and k,] while the bowels are crowded down on the uterus, i, and bladder, g. *Thus every vital organ is either functionally obstructed or mechanically disordered,* and diseases more or less aggravated, the condition of all. In post-mortem examinations the liver has been found deeply indented by the constant and prolonged pressure of the ribs, in consequence of tight-lacing. The brain-organ, protected by a bony inclosure, has not yet been distorted externally by the contrivances of milliners and mantua-makers; but, lacing the chest, by interrupting the circulation of the blood, prevents its free return from the vessel of the brain, and so permanent congestion of that organ, with constant liability to headache, vertigo, or worse affections, becomes a "second nature." The vital resources of every person, and all available powers of mind and body, are measurable by the respiration. Precisely as the breathing is lessened, the length of life is shortened; not only this, but life is rendered correspondingly useless and miserable while it does exist. It is impossible for any child, whose mother has diminished her breathing capacity by lacing, to have a sound and vigorous organization. If girls will persist in ruining their vital organs as they grow up to womanhood, and if women will continue this destructive habit, the race must inevitably deteriorate. It may be asserted, therefore, without exaggeration that not only the welfare of the future generations, but the salvation of the race depends on the correction of this evil habit. The pathological consequences of continued and prolonged pressure on any vital structure are innutrition, congestion, inflammation, and ulceration, resulting in weakness, waste of substance, and destruction of tissue. The normal sensibility of the part is also destroyed. No woman can ever forget the pain she endured when she first applied the corsets; but in time the compressed organs become torpid; the muscles lose their contractile power, and she feels dependent on the mechanical support of the corset. But the mischief is not limited to local weakness and insensibility. The general strength and general sensibility correspond with the breathing capacity. If she has diminished her "breath of life," she has just to that extent destroyed all normal sensibility. She can neither feel nor think normally. But in place of pleasurable sensations and ennobling thoughts, are an indescribable array of aches, pains, weaknesses, irritations, and nameless distresses of body, with dreamy vagaries, fitful impulses, and morbid sentimentalities of mind. And yet another evil is to be mentioned to render the catalogue complete. Every particle of food must be aerated in the lungs before it can be assimilated. It follows, therefore, that no one can be well nourished who has not a full, free, and unimpeded action of the lungs. In the contracted chest, the external measurement is reduced one half; but as the upper portion of the lungs cannot be fully inflated until the lower portions of the lungs are fully expanded, it follows that the breathing capacity is diminished more than one half. It is wonderful how anyone can endure existence, or long survive, in this devitalized condition; yet, thousands do, and with careful nursing, manage to bring into the world several sickly children. The spinal distortion is one of the ordinary consequences of lacing. No one who laces habitually can have a straight or strong back. The muscles being unbalanced become flabby or contracted, unable to support the trunk of the body erect, and a curvature, usually a double curvature, of the spine is the consequence. And if anything were needed to aggravate the spinal curvature, intensify the compression of the internal viscera, and add to the general deformity, it is found in the modern contrivance of stilted gaiters. These are made with heels so high and narrow that locomotion is awkward and painful, the centre of gravity is shifted "to parts unknown," and the head is thrown forward and the hips projected backwards to maintain perpendicularity.

In speaking of the destructiveness to health caused by woman's dress, Prof. Oscar B. Moss, M. D., declares:

Although the corset is the chief source of constraint to the kidneys, liver, stomach, pancreas, and spleen, forcing them upward to encroach upon the diaphragm and compressing the lungs and heart, its evils are rivalled by those resulting from suspending the skirts from the waist and hips, by which means the pelvic organs are forced downward and often permanently displaced. Now, add to these errors a belt drawn snugly around the waist, and we have before us a combination of the most malignant elements of dress which it would be possible to invent.

The waist belt enforces the evils which the corset and skirts inaugurate. Every proposition of anatomy and physiology bearing upon this subject appeals to reason. Did the abdominal organs require for their well-being less room than we find in the economy of nature, less room would have been provided. Nature bestows not grudgingly, neither does she lavish beyond the requirements of perfect health.

The same laws which govern the nutrition of muscles, apply also to the vital organs. Pressure that impedes circulation of blood through them must suppress their functions proportionally. With the lungs, heart, and digestive organs impaired by external devices, which forced them into abnormal relations, health is impossible. Every other part of the body—nay, life itself— depends upon the perfection of these organs. The ancients fittingly called them the tripod of life.

Consumption, heart disease, dyspepsia, and the multiform phases of uterine and ovarian diseases are among the natural and frequent consequences of compressing the internal organs. Men could not endure such physical indignities as women inflict upon themselves. Should they attempt to do so, they would not long hold the proud position of "bread winners," which is now theirs by virtue of their more robust qualities.

It is difficult to imagine a slavery more senseless, cruel, or far-reaching in its injurious consequences than that imposed by fashion on civilized womanhood during the past generation. Her health has been sacrificed, and in countless instances her life has paid the penalty; while posterity has been dwarfed, maimed, and enervated, and in body, mind, and soul deformed at its behests. In turn every part of her body has been tortured. On her head at fashion's caprice the hair of the dead has been piled. Hats and bonnets, wraps and gowns laden with heavy beads and jet have as seriously impaired her health as they have rendered her miserable; the tight lacing required by the wasp waists has produced generations of invalids and bequeathed to posterity suffering that will not vanish for many decades. By it, as has been pointed out by the authorities cited, every vital organ in the body has been seriously affected. The heart and lungs, by nature protected by a cage of bone, have been abnormally crushed in a space so contracted as to absolutely prohibit the free action upon which health depended; while the downward pressure was necessarily equally injurious to her delicate organism. The tightly drawn corset has proved an unmitigated curse to the living and a legacy of misery and disease to posterity. And this cruel deforming of the most beautiful of God's creations was said to be beautiful simply because fashion willed it. Nor was this all; enormous bustles and skirts of prodigious dimension have borne their weight largely upon that part of her body which above all else should be absolutely free from pressure. By this means the most sensitive organs have been ruthlessly subjected to down pressing weights which for exquisite torture and for the absolute certainty of the long train of agony that must result, rival the heartless ingenuity of the Inquisition of the Middle Ages. Beyond this generation of debilitated and invalided mothers, rises a countless posterity robbed of its birthright of health while yet unborn. A possible genius deformed and dwarfed by the weight of a fashionable dress; a brain which might have been brilliant rendered idiotic by the constant pressure of a corset, and the wearisome weight of a "stylish" dress pressing about the hips; a child whose natural capacity might have carried him to the seat of a Webster or into the laboratory of an Edison, condemned to drag a weakly, diseased, or deformed body through life, with mind ever chained to the flesh, through the heartless imposition which fashion imposed on his mother! What thought can be more appalling to a conscientious woman? Yet until a revolution is accomplished and a reign of reason and common sense inaugurated, this crime against the unborn will continue. But some argue the days of these extremes are past.

I answer not past, but they are assuming other forms. Since 1890 dawned, the evils in some respects have been aggravated; for it must not be forgotten that the daughters of the present decade have, in order to be fashionable, compressed beyond all healthful bounds the flesh of their arms, retarding circulation and inviting pneumonia and other ills. And in order to look stylish, thousands of women wear dress waists so tight that no free movement of the upper body is possible; indeed in numbers of instances ladies are compelled to put their bonnets on before attempting the painful ordeal of getting into their glove-fitting dress waists. Many young women to-day, yielding to the spell of fashion, place the corset next to their flesh, while a still greater number have merely the thinnest possible undershirt between the flesh and the corset, after which they tightly draw the dress waist until it meets. This seems incredible, but it is vouched for by several ladies of my acquaintance, among whom are physicians whose large practice among their sisters gives them peculiar facilities for knowing the absolute facts. Health, posterity, and all the instincts of the higher self are ruthlessly sacrificed to the fickle folly of fashion's criminal caprice. And we must not forget that even now the sweeping train is coming in vogue and correctly attired ladies must consent to carry the germs of death with quantities of filth from the streets of our metropolitan cities into their homes of wealth and refinement.

The corset and high-heeled shoes, the two most deadly foes to maternity and posterity, are also seen at the present time, on every hand.

If outraged nature could show the procession of mothers sacrificed on fashion's altar during the past generation, or unveil the suffering and deformity being borne by posterity at the present time, through this slavery, the world would be thrilled with an indescribable horror. Health, comfort, and human life have paid the penalty of a criminal servitude to the modern juggernaut, before whose car millions of our women are bowing in abject servility, knowing full well that at each turn of its wheel new pains or fresh diseases will be inflicted. And what power controls and gives life to this mistress of modern civilization? At whose behest is this crime against reason, life, and posterity perpetrated? *The cupidity of the shrewd and unscrupulous and the caprice of the shallow and frivolous.*

The moral aspect of this subject is even more grave than the hygienic. Anything which injures the physical body, whether it be licentiousness, intemperance, gluttony, or vicious modes of dress, is necessarily evil from an ethical point of view. Not simply because the law of our being decrees that whatever drains or destroys the physical vitality must sooner or later sap the vital forces of the brain; but also because anything is ethically destructive which chains the mind to the realm of animality, when, unfettered, it should be unfolding in spiritual strength and glory. Thus it will be readily seen that any article of clothing which presses upon the vitals of the body so as to cause displacement of the delicate organism, or so cumbersome as to cause general fatigue, anything, as is the case with high heels, which throws the body out of its equilibrium, or any article of dress which makes the mind ever conscious of the body by virtue of its uncomfortableness, is injurious from an ethical point of view. This fact which has been so generally overlooked will become more apparent, if for the sake of illustration we suppose for a moment that a plant is endowed with reason and sensation, and obeying the general law of its being, and persuasive and inspiring influence of the sun and rain, is struggling to rise heavenward, and give to the radiant world above its impearled wealth—its gorgeous bloom, its marvelous fragrance and fruit; but by virtue of the bonds of a prison-house below,—a small pot or a rocky encasement, its lifework is thwarted, its bloom, perfume, and fruit, if they come at all, are stunted, limited, and imperfect. For generations woman's condition has been like that of the plant, the wealth of her nature has been dwarfed, the marvelous richness of her life has been marred by the imprisoned conditions of her body, and infinitely more sad and far-reaching have been the baleful consequences upon millions of her offspring, dwarfed, weakly, sickly, enfeebled in body and soul. *A mother whose thoughts have voluntarily or involuntarily been held in the atmosphere of the physical nature, necessarily imparts to her child a legacy of animality which, like the corpse of a dead being, clings to the soul throughout its pilgrimage.* Terrible as have been fashion's ravages on woman's physical health, the curse which she has exerted when the ethical aspect of the case is entertained, far transcends it.

It is a curious fact that almost all the opposition from women to proposed reforms in woman's dress comes from two extremes in society. Those who do no independent thinking, taking all their thoughts and opinions from the expressed views of the men with whom they associate, and the profoundly earnest and thoughtful, but conservative women of society. The opposition of the former class is merely the echo of husbands, brothers, fathers, and lovers; but the others are moved by conviction, and for this reason their views are worthy of consideration. They fear that any radical change will exert an immoral influence. Their minds are swayed by ancient thought which throughout all ages has cast its baleful shadow over the brain of the world. They are held under the spell of a conservatism which unquestioningly tolerates established institutions and existing orders; but has no confidence in aught that proposes to break with these, even though the new has reason and common sense clearly on its side. Thus time and again fashions have been tolerated, although known to be morally enervating and singularly repulsive to all refined sensibilities; while proposals from without for reforms based on the laws of health and beauty have called forth the most determined opposition from this conscientious class, merely because the proposed innovations have not conformed to ideas entertained by virtue of prevailing fashions, and have been therefore regarded immoral. And herein lies an important point to be considered. Anything which is radically unlike prevailing standards or styles to which we have become accustomed will impress most persons as being immodest or indecent. *The unusual in dress is usually denounced as immoral* because we are all prone to allow our prejudice to obscure our reason and o'ersway our judgment. This point must be recognized before any real reform can be accomplished. When humanity has grown sufficiently wise to reason broadly and view problems on their own merits, aside from preconceived opinion or inherited prejudice, real instead of false standards of morality will prevail, and we shall cease to condemn anything as pernicious simply because it is unusual, radically unlike that to which we have been accustomed or revolutionary in its tendency. Let me make this if possible more apparent by an illustration, because it bears such an important relation to the main issue. If men had for ages worn long flowing robes, completely enveloping their bodies, but on a certain day with one accord exchanged them for a costume similar to that now seen throughout the civilized world, society would experience a distinct shock; immoral, indecent, pernicious, and vulgar would mildly express the sentiment of conventional thought, until the same society had become accustomed to the change. To us at the present time it is difficult to conceive how women of sense and refinement submitted to the swinging-cage paraphernalia of the sixties, or the Grecian bend of a later date. Yet in those days the severely plain skirts of the present would have seemed positively indecent. It has been necessary to dwell on this thought in order to sufficiently remove existing prejudice to enable a fair consideration of the question in its broader aspects. . . . It is for woman and woman alone to decide what she will wear, and in this paper I am merely seeking to second the splendid work that has by her been inaugurated, and by speaking as one of the younger men of this decade, to voice what I believe American womanhood will find to be the sentiment of the rising generation, whenever she makes a concerted effort to emancipate herself from the slavery of Parisian fashions. There are many evidences that the hour is ripe for a sensible revolt, and that if the movement is guided by wise and judicious minds it will be a success. Two things seem to me to be of paramount importance.

(1.) The commission of women acting for the Council should decide definitely upon the nature and extent of changes desired. The ideal costume should be clearly defined and ever present in their mind. But it would be exceedingly unwise to attempt any radical change at once. This has been more than anything the secret of the partial or total failures of the movements of this character in the past. The changes should be gradually made. Every spring and autumn let an advance step be taken, and in order to do this an American fashion commission or bureau should be established, under the auspices of the dress reform committee of the Women's Council, which at stated intervals should issue bulletins and illustrated fashion plates. If the ideal is kept constantly in view, and every season slight changes are made toward the desired garment, the victory will, I believe, be a comparatively easy one, for the splendid common sense of the American women and men will cordially second the movement. *Concerted action, a clearly defined ideal toward which to move, and gradual changes*—these are points which it seems to me are vitally important. One reason why the most ridiculous and inartistic extremes in fashion have been generally adopted is found in this policy of gradual introduction, a fact which must impress anyone who carefully examines the fashions of the past. First there has been a slight alteration, shortly becoming more pronounced, and with each season it has grown more marked, although perhaps not for four or six years has the extreme been reached. At every step there have been complaints from various quarters, but steadily and persistently has the fashion been pushed until it reached its climax, after which we have had its gradual decline. This was the history of the hoop skirt and the Grecian bend, and has been that of most of the extremes which have marked the past, and we can readily believe that in no other way could womanhood have been insnared by such supreme and criminal folly as has characterized fashion's caprices in unnumbered instances.

(2.) Another very essential point is the proper education of the girls of to-day, for to them will fall, in its richest fruition, the blessings of this splendid reform if it be properly carried on, and if they be everywhere instructed to set health above fashion, and seek the beauty of Venus de Medici rather than the pseudo beauty of the wretched, deformed invalid, who at the dictates of the modern Babylon has trampled reason and common sense, health and comfort, the happiness of self and the enjoyment of her posterity under foot. Teach the girls to be American; to be independent; to scorn to copy fashion, manners, or habits that come from decaying civilizations, and which outrage all sentiment of refinement, laws of life, or principles of common sense. The American girl is naturally independent and well endowed with reason and common sense. Once shown the wisdom and importance of this *American* movement, and she will not be slow to cordially embrace it. In many respects the hour is most propitious, owing to a combination of causes never before present, among which may be mentioned the growing independence of American womanhood; the enlarged vision that has come to her through the wonderfully diverse occupations and professions which she has recently embraced; the growing consciousness of her ability to succeed in almost every vocation of life. The latitude enjoyed by her in matters of dress in the mountains and seashore resorts; the growth of women's gymnasiums; the emphasis given to hygienic instruction in schools, and the recent quiet introduction of a perfectly comfortable apparel for morning wear, which, strange to say, has originated where one would least expect, among the most fashionable belles of the Empire city. This significant innovation which is reported by the daily press, as becoming quite popular among the young ladies of the wealthy districts of New York, consists of a comfortable blouse worn over knickerbocker trousers. Clad in this comfortable attire, the belles come to breakfast, nor do they subsequently change their dress during the morning if they intend remaining indoors. If a sedate or fastidious caller is announced, a beautiful tea-gown, which is at hand, is slipped into, and the young lady is appropriately clad to suit even conventional requirements. The bicycle and lawn tennis costumes now becoming so popular also exercise a subtile but marked influence in favor of rational dress reform, not only giving young ladies the wonderful comfort and health-giving freedom which for ages have been denied her sex, but also by accustoming them to these radically unconventional costumes.

Another encouraging sign of the times is the increasing demand on the great and fashionable house of Liberty & Co., of London, for the Greek and other simple costumes by fashionable ladies, who are using them largely for home wear. I have reproduced two recent styles of dresses made by Liberty.

All fabrics used are rich, soft, and elegant, and the effect is said to be gratifying to lovers of art, as well as far more healthful and comfortable than the conventional dress. The most important fact, however, is the effect or influence which is sure to follow this breaking away from the ruling fashions in wealthy circles. When conventionalism in dress is fully discredited, practical reform is certain to follow. The knell of the one means the triumph of the other.

Believing as I do that the cycle of woman has dawned, and that through her humanity will reach a higher and nobler civilization than the world has yet known, I feel the most profound interest in all that affects her health, comfort, and happiness; for as I have before observed, her exaltation means the elevation of the race. A broader liberty and more liberal meed of justice for her mean a higher civilization, and the solution of weighty and fundamental problems which will never be equitably adjusted until we have brought into political and social life more of the splendid spirit of altruism, which is one of her most conspicuous characteristics. I believe that morality, education, practical reform, and enduring progress wait upon her complete emancipation from the bondage of fashion, prejudice, superstition, and conservatism.

★

MARGUERITE MERINGTON *Woman and the Bicycle*
Scribner's 17 (June 1895): 702–704

[In 1894 the U.S. Census estimated that 250,000 bicycles were in use throughout the country, a number that would rise to 1.25 million in just six years. The debate here is one part of a four-part essay that examined the bicycle as proof of the technological advances at century's end, as a means to health, and as a social equalizer.]

THE COLLOCATION OF woman and the bicycle has not wholly outgrown controversy, but if the woman's taste be for the royal pleasure of glowing exercise in sunlit air, she will do well quietly but firmly to override argument with the best model of a wheel to which she may lay hand.

Never did an athletic pleasure from which the other half is not debarred come into popularity at a more fitting time than cycling has to-day, when a heavy burden of work is laid on all the sisterhood, whether to do good, earn bread, or squander leisure; no outdoor pastime can be more independently pursued, and few are as practicable as many days in a year. The one who fain would ride, and to whom a horse is a wistful dream, at least may hope to realize a wheel. Once purchased, it needs only to be stabled in a passageway, and fed on oil and air.

FIGURE 16   This side view of the modern bicyclist accompanied a *Scribner's* series of articles on contemporary bicycling, including Marguerite Merington's. Here the bicycle is featured as a healthful means of manly exercise, whereas the more usual depiction of the bicycle stressed women's physical as well as social freedom. (*Scribner's,* 1895)

The first women cyclists of New York City seemed to rise in a heroic handful from the earth near Grant's Tomb, on Riverside Drive. That was years ago. To-day, on the broad western highway of the city a dotted line of riders, men and women, forms a fourth parallel to the dark band which the Palisades stretch across the sky, the Hudson's silver width, and the white thread of flying smoke from the trains beside the river. They ride from the first day of spring to the last privileged days of frosty winter. They ride from morning to high noon, and their lanterned wheels purr by with the gleam of a cat's eye through the dark. A moon sends hordes of their queer cobwebby shadows scurrying over the ground. In the revolving years, to the eyes of those whose windows overlook the wheelways, the woman cylist has ceased to be a white blackbird. The clear-eyed, vivified faces that speed by give no clue to the circumstances of the riders, but inquiry shows that many callings and conditions love the wheel. The woman of affairs has learned that an hour, or even half an hour, may be stolen from the working day, with profit to both woman and affairs. Now and again a complaint arises of the narrowness of woman's sphere. For such disorder of the soul the sufferer can do no better than to flatten her sphere to a circle, mount it, and take to the road. An hour of the wheel means sixty minutes of fresh air and wholesome exercise, and at least eight miles of change of scene; it may well be put down to the credit side of the day's reckoning with flesh and spirit.

The eye of the spectator has long since become accustomed to costumes once conspicuous. Bloomer and tailor-made alike ride on unchallenged; tunicked and gaitered Rosalinds excite no more remark than every-day people in every-day clothes. No one costume may yet claim to represent the pastime, for experiment is still busy with the problem, but the results are in the direction of simplicity and first principles. Short rides on level roads can be accomplished with but slight modification of ordinary attire, and the sailor hat, shirt waist, serge skirt uniform is as much at home on the bicycle as it is anywhere else the world over. The armies of women clerks in Chicago and Washington who go by wheel to business, show that the exercise within bounds need not impair the spick-and-spandy neatness that marks the bread-winning American girl. On the excursion a special adaptation of dress is absolutely necessary, for skirts, while they have not hindered women from climbing to the topmost branches of the higher education, may prove fatal in down-hill coasting; and skirts, unless frankly shortened or discarded, must be fashioned so as to minimize the danger of entanglement with the flying wheel. Knickerbockers, bloomers, and the skirt made of twin philabegs, all have their advocates; Pinero's youngest Amazon has set a pretty fashion for the cyclist, and many of the best riders make their records in a conventional cloth walking-dress with cone-shaped skirt worn over the silk trousers of an odalisque, or the satin breeks of an operatic page. This sounds costly, but it need not be. Here and there a costume strikes the spectator as an experiment, but the sincerity of all is unquestioned, for absence of self-consciousness has characterized the woman cyclist from the outset. The pastime does not lend itself to personal display, and in criticism the costume must be referred, not to the standards of the domestic hearth-rug, but to the exigencies of the wheel, the rider's positions to the mechanical demands of the motion; accordingly, the cyclist is to be thought of only as mounted and in flight, belonging not to a picture, but to a moving panorama. If she ride well, the chances are she looks well, for she will have reconciled grace, comfort, and the temporary fitness of things.

Regarding bicycling purely as exercise, there is an advantage in the symmetry of development it brings about, and a danger in riding too fast and far. The occasional denunciation of the pastime as unwomanly, is fortunately lost in the general approval that a new and wholesome recreation has been found, whose pursuit adds joy and vigor to the dowry of the race.

Having reached these conclusions, the onlooker is drawn by the irresistible force of the stream. She borrows, hires, or buys a wheel and follows tentatively. Her point of view is forever after changed; long before practice has made her an expert she is an enthusiast, ever ready to proselyte, defend—or ride!

There is full opportunity in and about New York City for the daily hour with the wheel. From Christmas to Christmas Central Park is a favorite haunt of the cyclist when the weather is kind, and indeed a fine frenzy once set rolling the eye of a poet, who told of a wintry flight among snow-laden pine-trees over sheets of frozen snow. It sounded like a Norse Saga, but the scene was Central Park, the steed a wheel, and the story true. Riverside Drive and the Boulevard offer fair roads and a breeze coming fresh from the sources of the Hudson, untainted as it sweeps by Albany; the historic ground of Washington Heights is practicable as well as picturesque, for the Father of his country outlined a clear march for the city's gigantic stride; Washington Bridge is a fine objective point where the rider will surely dismount to rest in the embrasure of the parapets, and admire the view up and down stream where the little Harlem wriggles along between its high green banks. For the longer ride, by crossing Madison Avenue Bridge a wheel-worthy road leads to Westchester and Mount Vernon. There is a ferry at Fort Lee, and a good road even in New Jersey, skirting the trap-rock battlements at whose base the Hudson lies like a broad moat. People who return from Tarrytown speak rather boastfully of the hills.

Far-reaching dreams of summer may bear the traveller of the wheel through clean stretches in the Berkshires, on sunny lanes of Normandy, among Welsh mountains, or down Roman roads between English hedgerows but all the workaday year there are highways radiating from the heart of the city to the borderland of the country, where one may breathe new inspiration for the world—the world that we persist in having too much with us in the getting and spending efforts that lay waste the powers.

★

EDNA C. JACKSON *A Fin de Cycle Incident*
Outing (June 1896): 192–198

[Centering on a vigorous young woman about to be married, Jackson's story plays out the character's anxieties about the consequences of riding a bicycle. Although exemplifying "practical" and "modern" values, the bicycle is a source of tension because bicycling seems to threaten her femininity. Against a backdrop of labor unrest, the heroine proves herself an athlete to her conservative fiancé, thereby bringing the couple to a modern sense of gender relations.]

FIGURE 17   This George Du Maurier cartoon satirizes the usefulness of the bicycle for American women. This unlikely vehicle combines the split impulses of women's lives, blending an ideal of personal exercise with the realities of caretaking. (*Harper's*, 1890)

They had been engaged just eleven minutes by the clock, and were in the stage of trying to explain how it happened. People often try the same thing ten years after but the first debate upon the question is usually most satisfactory.

"'Why do I love you,' darling?" the Professor was saying in limpid tones. "Because you are my ideal woman: so pure, so modest, so flower-like! Because, looking into your beautiful eyes, I can see the sweet soul reflected there!"

Taken literally, this was egotistical in the Professor; considering that all he saw was his own image—scholarly, rather stern-faced, with spectacles. If he had looked deeper into those blue mirrors he would have seen a flicker of guilt sneaking behind this sweetness.

"Dear Horace!" Renie exclaimed, as she put one small hand timidly against his cheek, but quickly drew it away as she saw by a slight cloudiness above the glasses that even this expression of tenderness conflicted with his rather fossilized notions of maidenly reserve.

"Whoo!" sniffed the "sweet soul," *sotto voce.* "If I didn't know what a heart of gold he really has, his notions of propriety would make me tired!"

"Your very words are flower-like, my little saint!" cooed the infatuated lover. "You have none of the bold ways and language of the so-called *fin de siècle* girl; no mannish posing as an athlete!"

Renie moaned mentally. "Saint! Must I spend my life on a pedestal? I can't—it's too condensed! I must get those antiquated ideas of his remodeled to the present century! I wish I were not so afraid of him!"

But she was—there was no denying it. Perhaps it was her love that made her dread his stern disapproval. She felt herself a pocket edition of Jekyll and Hyde; she meant to confess to the Hyde later, or else try to live up to the Jekyll. But—

> "What a tangled web we weave,
> When first we practise to deceive!"

Meanwhile, she neglected this golden opportunity to confess herself a *fin de siècle* sinner who loved yachting, rowed a shell like a mermaid, jumped gates on her trusty steed, and went in for athletics, as she often remarked, "for all she was worth." Thus she drifted deeper and deeper into this good man's confidence and away from her own.

"Do you know?" said the little saint with a swift, upward smile, "I thought you—you cared for Rill Richmond."

"Miss Richmond! I must confess that on a slight acquaintance, I was inclined to admire her; but—heavens!—she poses as an athlete, dresses in gymnastic costume, swings Indian clubs! How could one admire such a woman?"

"But," faltered the small coward, "are there not occasions when these accomplishments might be of use to a woman?"

"Not to a womanly woman," replied her lover with scathing contempt. "I cannot imagine such a woman—you, for instance, my darling—putting herself in a position to need such questionable accomplishments. But I must go." He arose with much the same kind of cheerful alacrity that Adam might have exhibited when evicted from Paradise. "I promised to meet Manager Stevens; the strikers are acting outrageously."

"Do you think they are altogether to blame?" asked Renie, putting in this weak way a question on which she had very decided ideas.

"Certainly!" he replied, in haughty surprise; "to what is the world coming when the working classes presume to dictate to their employers? But, there, little one! What are you supposed to know about the great problems of capital and labor?" He took her in his arms and held her close.

"Good night, Renie; my pearl, my angel, my own!"

"'Pearl! Angel!'" Renie drew a long breath as the door closed upon her ardent lover. She clasped her hands in mute protest as she continued: "This pedestal is growing narrower and narrower! I shall certainly tumble, and what a smash there'll be! I am not ready to be an angel; wings would be horribly in the way. Or a pearl! Shut up in a shell with an oyster—ugh!" A shiver of rebellion went over her. She dashed up the stairs and flung a door wide open.

"Jim! Oh, Jimmy, Jimmy!"

"Here!" quietly remarked a boyish voice at her elbow, "save the roof; never mind the remnants of your lungs. What's the row?"

"Hush!" cried Renie, dramatically, "I'm dying for exercise! I'm perishing for gymnastics! I'm yearning for Indian clubs!"

Suiting the action to the words, she seized a pair from the wall. Her eyes sparkled; a soft flush came into her cheeks; the lace sleeves fell back from the rounded arms, and the supple form swayed to and fro as she swung the clubs with lightning speed, round and round, above her rumpled, curly head, tossing and catching them deftly. Altogether it was a pretty picture and told of long and patient practice.

"All very well, Missie," commented her young brother, glancing critically up from his task of pumping air into the pneumatic tire of his bicycle, as Renie ended by swinging the clubs dangerously near his head, giving a blood-curdling whoop and tossing them into the farthest corner of the room, "but what would Attorney Horace P. Waldon, *alias* the 'Professor,' he of the straight-laced ideas and irreproachable walk and conversation, say if he saw you doing the Comanche act in this giddy and reprehensible style?"

Renie's face flamed scarlet as she remarked with studied indifference: "I do not know that Mr. Waldon is the ruler of my actions."

"I'm glad of it; but if I did not know that you are a girl that never fibs, Renie," returned Jim, guilelessly, "I would doubt that statement. I really thought he meant 'biz' by the token of all these flowers and visits. I'm glad he don't; for, though he is no end of a good fellow, he'd be a mighty uncomfortable sort of a brother-in-law. Do you believe in the transmigration of souls, Renie?"

"I don't know," she answered absently, as she sat curled up on the rug beside him, watching the process of adjusting the saddle with intense interest. "What's that to do with the subject under discussion, anyway?"

"Just this; you've read of those toads that wrap a solid rock around themselves and indulge in little catnaps of five thousand years or so? I imagine that sometime, way back in history, the Professor might have been one of those toads and since he has arisen to the glorious estate of man he still clings to his antique toad ideas—why, what's up?"

The mischievous eyes, so like her own, watching her furtively, saw my lady's white brow contract in a wrathful frown.

"James Raine! How dare you talk so of the best, noblest, kindest, manliest—"

"Whew! anything more? All those adjectives for a mere passing acquaintance! Then you did fib awhile ago, young woman!"

Two pairs of merry eyes met and two pairs of fresh lips laughed mischievously.

"Renie, he is a good, old chap, after all; so are you! Come along, now, and I'll teach you to ride the bike; I have borrowed a ladies' wheel purposely."

"Oh, Jim, will you?" she cried, rapturously, springing to her feet, then, with a sudden thought, sinking back again. "But–but–I guess I'd better not."

What would the Professor say if he saw his ideal floweret riding a wild, dizzy bike? In his eyes it was the cap sheaf of all unwomanly offending.

"Renie Raine! You had already promised me to ride!" exclaimed the boyish, indignant voice.

Renie looked up delighted.

"I believe I did, Jim! It wouldn't do to break a promise, would it?"

"I should think not! Come along; it's late, and nobody will be passing on Park street. Hustle!"

A minute later two young forms were hovering in excited, but solemn discussion over the wheel on the quiet, asphalt-paved street at the back of the house.

"Here! Try that saddle! Is it low enough? Now, first learn to mount. Left treadle up; foot on that; give yourself a push with the other foot; push down on left treadle and catch t'other as it comes around, see?"

"Of course I see; that's easy; g'way!" and Renie confidently placed one foot on the raised treadle and came down in an ignominious tangle with the wheel, where she lay, laughing in the most reprehensibly tomboyish manner until extricated.

"That's just like a girl!" Jim exclaimed in lofty contempt. "Goose! Don't take your other foot off the curbstone until you get ready to start! I'll hold you until you learn to steer; now," after a few minutes' drill, "try it alone."

"It's all the fault of these miserable skirts!" stormed Renie, giving the poor bike a small kick with her slippered foot. "I don't see what skirts were made for, anyhow! They are always in the way!"

"I don't know what you are going to do about it," remarked Jim, with cheerful encouragement, "unless I lend you a suit of my clothes."

"I wish you might!" sighed Renie, surveying him with mournful envy; then a reckless idea took possession of her. Once on the downward path, the wretched girl descended with lightning speed.

"Jim," she lowered her voice as she whispered the awful resolution, "I'll get bloomers!"

Jim flung himself across the wheel in an agony of suppressed hilarity.

"Oh, if my lord professor should see you in that rig — and riding the bike — you abandoned creature!—oh, me, oh, my!" his voice tapered off to a squeal of rapture as he mentally pictured the effect.

"Jim!" (there were tears on the long lashes and a suspicious quiver around the red lips) "I feel like a villain! Do you really think he would care if–if"— she added weakly, "if I wear a skirt over them?"

Jim manfully choked down the hilarity that threatened to burst forth in yells and declared with all the emphasis of truth:

"Care! Certainly not! All the girls are wearing 'em. Of course, we won't break on his enraptured sight all at once!" His voice gave a tell-tale tremble, but he recovered; "but we'll sort o' let the two facts of bloomers and bike ooze through his inner consciousness so gradually that he will get used to them before he knows it. Oh, he'll be proud of you, Renie, when he sees you flying along like an expert; indeed he will! Like as not—"

Oh, James, what a load of whoppers are you piling on your overburdened conscience!

"Like as not he will get a wheel himself and go with you."

"Do you think so, Jim, really?" cried the culprit, happily. "I wouldn't deceive him for the world, but I do want to ride the bicycle!"

The next night found the two again struggling over the problem of how to keep the center of gravity on a flying machine that seems built for the especial purpose of setting all rules of the scientist at defiance. But alas for Renie! What saintly pedestal was ever graced by a rig like this! Full Turkish pants of blue, blouse, and saucy cap crushed over boyish curls!

"That's something like!" commented Jim, approvingly, while his pupil mounted the steel steed with all the jaunty confidence of the skirt-emancipated woman.

"You must keep your feet going," explained the teacher; "you can't tip over if you keep treading. If it tips, don't try to brace up the other way, but go with it. Try again; that's right! Steady! Tread water! Go with it! Go with it! Why didn't you go with the bike?"

"Didn't I go with it?" moaned Renie, from her position prone on her left ear on the hard pavement. "Ain't I with it now? Leave me alone, James Raine! I have no breath to talk. I want to think!"

" 'There are thoughts of which we may not speak,' " quoted Jim, dancing around his pupil in unfeeling glee; then, with a sudden rush, he grasped her arm. "Run, Renie, run! Here comes His Nibs, the Professor, around the corner!"

"Jim!" whispered the culprit hoarsely, "what shall I do? I can't get past him! I'm discovered! I'm lost!"

"My mackintosh! There on the fence! Bless the Fates, he's near-sighted and this street's dark! Good evening, Mr. Waldon."

"Good evening. I–I thought I heard Miss Renie," remarked the Professor, peering around near-sightedly.

"She was here a minute ago—oh, Renie!"

"Good evening," said a soft, innocent voice near by, and a small figure hovered just in the shadow of a sheltering tree. Jim jumped on the wheel and basely deserted, much to the Professor's satisfaction.

"My darling!" he murmured fondly, "I came this way from the directors' meeting only to pass your house. I did not dream of this luck. Little violet! how like you is that dark, graceful, nun-like robe!"

Renie laughed a low, half-hysterical little peal.

"A boy's mackintosh, a mile too big, over bloomers!" she was saying inwardly. "Oh, me! Oh, my! A nun in this!"

Aloud, she said, not very enthusiastically, with her hand on the gate:
"Will you come in?"

"I cannot, darling! I have many hours of work yet to-night. Until these labor troubles are over I will have but little time even for you, my pet."

"I wish," she said, timidly, "you would not take such an active part, Horace. There is so much bitterness, and—and there is right on both sides, is there not?"

"Yes," he replied, slowly and judicially, "right and wrong. But," he smiled down on her much as if she was a tiny, white kitten, "do not trouble your pretty head about such deep subjects, pet. I am in no danger." He kissed her brow with deep reverence and tenderness. "Heaven make me worthy of you, my pearl!"

"Pearl," muttered Renie, surveying her dreadful combination rig of trousers and mackintosh with deep self-contempt. "It is an outrage to deceive him so!" she said to herself as he walked away.

"Don't you laugh, James Raine!" she continued, coming upon that young person sitting on the edge of the porch, in the moonlight; "I am going to be a good, quiet, womanly woman. You hear me? I am pure Jekyll henceforth."

"Um-m!" drawled Jim, reflectively, falling gently backward and studying the dancing vine-shadows through his half-closed lids. "What a nice pair of antiques you will be! Mr. and Mrs. Professor. Oh, say, Renie," in a brisker tone, "in that case you will not want the new bike father and I selected for you to-day?"

Renie, who had passed into the hall, was back in a flash. "Jim, you don't mean it!" she exclaimed, rapturously. "What is it like? Tell me quick!"

"It is one of those earthly vanities which you have forever renounced, young woman!" replied James, grimly. "It's a pity, too," he sighed. "Such a beauty as it is; all nickel-plated, light-running, geared up to 2:40 and the cutest little plate with your name on it. We meant it as a surprise, but, of course, since you don't want it—"

"James Jefferson Raine! who said I didn't want it! I wish it was here now. I want to try it! Will you go with me to-morrow? Oh, you dear boy!" His neck was clasped in a smothering embrace and in her bloomers she executed a wild can-can in the moonlight that would have caused Professor Horace P. Waldon to drop down dead could he have seen her.

The result of the matter was that with the downward celerity of the backslider, Renie plunged into a course of bicycle riding and became an expert in that giddy amusement in a wonderfully brief space of time. But if the sweetness of stolen fruits was hers, so was the bitter core. She even shed tears in sleepless nights of remorse over her reprehensible double life. Several times she bravely resolved, since she could not decide between her lover and her wheel, that she would boldly ride, bloomers and blouse, around by his office or his club and reveal to him her offending in all its enormity; but the next day she would weaken, seek the streets least frequented by him or fly miles into the country and try to deaden the stings of conscience with the excitements of exploration.

It was a cool morning in late July when Horace stopped at Renie's door to bid her a long farewell, after the manner of lovers who are to be severed by cruel fate for a possible space of thirty-six hours, or worse still, maybe forty-eight.

"I must go to Bulkley on horseback," he explained, "as the railroad is in danger of being blocked before I get back. But a twenty-mile ride is not much. I will come back late to-morrow, long after your blue eyes are closed, violet." He thought how fair and sweet she looked in her white, lace-trimmed wrapper.

"You should have a bicycle," suggested Renie with an Eugene-Aram-like longing to touch on the secret of her remorse. "See there."

Rill Richmond flashed past on her wheel, jaunty and charming in bloomers and cap.

"If we both rode like—like that," she faltered, "I might go with you—part way."

My lord Professor put on his haughtiest frown.

"Even for that great pleasure, Renie," he said, freezingly, "I would think I had paid a great price for your company in the loss of my ideal! But there!" taking her in his arms as the quick tears sprang to her eyes; "don't cry over such an absurdly impossible thing, my pet. It angered me even to think of your name being used in reference to such an unwomanly exhibition."

"That settles it!" declared Renie after the door closed upon him. "This must end right now! I cannot give him up—my darling!" A tragic sob gave emphasis to this last: "I will give up my bike! James! To-day ends my career as a bicyclist. This afternoon I will take a farewell ride; to-morrow you must take the wheel away—anywhere—only out of my sight!"

"Whew!" whistled Jim, bringing the front legs of his tipped-back chair to the floor with a thud, "I believe you mean it, this time, Topsey."

"I do," she said, firmly; "then I will tell him all—and—if he cannot forgive me ——"

"You'll still have your bike, Topsey!" called Jim after her with cheerful consolation, but she had gone to her room, where she succeeded in making her eyes so red and swollen that she concluded to put off her farewell appearance until the next afternoon.

Renie felt like an ingrate while she patted her willing steed caressingly. It seemed like a thing of life skimming lightly over graveled-pike and grassy paths.

"Poor old wheel! I almost wish we could meet him coming home and take our chances; but, ugh!"—a thought of his contemptuous glance at Rill Richmond came to her. "I don't dare! I must give you up, Old Faithful." As she spoke she was speeding right on over the road which she knew he must come. The long summer twilight began to deepen, and a silvery crescent hung in the sky before she realized that her last appearance as a rider must positively be drawn to a close.

"Almost night and I am miles from home," she said, slightly dismayed. "I can make it quicker by taking the wagon track through the woods. It is rather dusky." She eyed the deep shadows doubtfully. "But I can make the mile in five minutes at most."

It was shadowy under the trees, and the carpet of moist leaves made a soft and noiseless track for the wheel. That is why from the other side of a thick growth of bushes, the voices of two men who lay there lazily smoking vile-smelling pipes, reached Renic's car. Ill-favored customers they were, with hobo written all over their unkempt persons, but with a certain cold-blooded smartness in their talk that chilled the listener.

"And wot if we do have to chug him one so his skull won't hold water? It'll be laid to the strikers; everyt'ing's laid to them nowadays. Mighty good thing fer chaps like wese. Wot's that old saw: 'W'en honest men fall out rogues git their innings?' That's near enough anyhow."

"It's a gaudy streak of luck dat we found out he's carryin' dat swag ter his folks ter-night; lots er thousan's, count it later—don't savvy jest how much, but 'nuf ter save er couple er pore heathin frum perishin' er thirst fer many er day," put in the other with pensive self-gratulation.

"He needs killin' on gen'ral princ'ples," added number one, philanthropically. "He's a high an' mighty chap, Mr. H. P. Waldon! That's his name. Wot's any feller want with a job lot o'tails ter his kite like that? The last name I had wuz No. 763, an' it wuz 'neat an' serviceable,' as the cloding dealers say. But he'll likely git the killin' fast enough. Jake an' Bill's watchin' de Mill road, an' dere ain't no udder he kin come."

"Den fer er divvy an' er skip!" grinned the other, "an' all laid ter de strikers; oh, dis is pie, pard! Wot's dat?"

A soft rustle of leaves, a rush as noiseless and swift as a swallow's flight, and straight past the two startled hoboes flew a small form on a wheel. Before the tramps could start to their feet she was out of sight.

They looked at one another, and the rougher of the two laughed.

"Jest er gal on er bike; but she give me er bad turn!"

"Ye don't s'pose she heerd?" queried the other, doubtfully.

"Heerd? Nothin'! She wuz cuttin' 'cross frum the road like the wind, an' them dam' leaves deadened the sound; she never drempt we wuz on earth. But we'd best shut our traps er some one might catch on an' then—" He drew imaginary stripes around his body, and the two resumed their reclining posture and talked low.

In an incredibly short time Renie had passed through the woods and alighted on a smooth country road which, a few rods farther on, crossed the railroad. It was a very white, resolute face that she turned toward the path over which she had just come. "You are planning to murder my Horace! But you never shall do it! I don't know exactly what to do; but I'll spoil your plans, somehow." The consciousness that upon her alone rested her lover's life steadied her thoughts, and a plan outlined itself distinctly as she spoke. "It is twelve miles to the forks of this and the Mill road where those others are waiting. If I go by the road, I may not be in time, even if I get past those men; five miles this side of Bulkley this railroad crosses the Bulkley highway; I must catch him *there*; I can do it by following the railroad; it is the only way!"

"He told me he would meet the eight o'clock train there; get some valuable papers—it was that dreadful money he meant—and start immediately home." With trembling fingers she took out her watch, and calculated that she had just time enough to accomplish her purpose. "If I can only reach him in time! Oh, if that train will only be late!" With a quick motion she loosened the encumbering skirt and tossed it away; then rapidly glancing over her wheel to see that every part was in order, she sprang upon it, and in an instant had gained the track and turned to race against time. It was not exactly the ideal bicycle track. Stones and ties bumped her up and down unmercifully; but she only bent lower, and with set lips passed over rough and smooth with indifference. A mixture of moonlight and starlight faintly showed her the way; sometimes a long stretch of smooth path by the track gave her a gain in time, though the instant consumed in lifting the wheel over the rail and remounting made her frantic; then as the path disappeared, back again to the well-filled center of the track. Sometimes steep embankments towered over her, making the way dark and uncertain; then would come a strip of moonlight; again a dive into the shadow of overhanging trees, from which the cry of night-birds sounded lonesomely.

"If I can only get there in time, only in time!" she whispered to herself with white lips.

Just then with a crash and a bump she fell, striking squarely on her poor back across a sharp tie, and the bike upon her. She had run into a cattle-guard. Stunned and breathless she lay there a moment, then weakly staggered to her feet, found to her joy that the wheel was all right and mounted with the painful consciousness that her back protested against every move. The fall had hurt her badly, poor child, and struggle as she would, a deathly sickness stole over her.

"I won't faint," she muttered, as she sped on unfalteringly and half hysterically. "What is it the new school of thought teaches? All things are imaginary? I have no back! I have no back! No pain, no back, no pain no—what's that? Great Scott! a long trestle!"

Like a flash she was off her wheel and without thought of the danger if a train should come, warily she pushed the wheel before her. She thinks only of the delay. It seems an hour, though only two or three minutes that she is crawling over the giddy height. She gains the other side at last. Thank heaven! the rest of the way now is comparatively smooth and well lighted. She knows where she is now—three miles from where the Bulkley highway crosses the railroad. Can she make it, or has he already passed on to his death? She sets her teeth and bends to her work. How the wheel flies! Over rough and smooth, but she has forgotten the pain. Only for a little time! a little, little time! One mile—it must be—two! It is growing late, so late! Can he have passed by? Fly, good wheel, fly!

Suddenly before her yawned, densely black, the tunnel. She had forgotten that. And what is that far-away humming and rumbling of the rails behind her? Half a mile straight through the tunnel is the goal she seeks. She can take the road to her right; the dirt road; it leads around the hill a mile and a half. It is safe for her, but every minute may mean her lover's life. The alternative is the tunnel. She knows the meaning of that rumbling of the rails. A stone in the darkness a broken tie—a break in the wheel—in that means no escape. Will she risk it?

Not once does the brave wheel slacken; not once does its rider waver! Into the black cavern she speeds and is swallowed up in darkness. She bends lower over the machine, of which she seems to have become a part. Perhaps the angels are clearing the way—they have been credited with such things in an emergency like this one—perhaps she calls on them softly. If there be obstructions she cannot see them. The track is straight as a die, and if she keep to the smooth center there is a chance for her. She is hardly conscious; all life seems to be merged in feet and close-set lips. She begins to see a dim opening before her; how faint it is! Nearer, nearer! A scream that reverberates deafeningly against the rocky walls makes her heart leap and stand still. *The train has entered the tunnel!* It is now or never a race for life. The earth trembles. Nearer the opening comes, nearer the rushing monster. One last effort of strength!

Professor Horace P. Waldon, riding serenely along toward the crossing, thinking with hushed reverence of his fair lady love asleep in her lily bower, hears the screech of a locomotive, reins in his horse, then beholds issue from the blackness a vision that makes him spring to the ground with the impression that he has gone suddenly stark, staring mad.

That same lily maid, with bare head and flying hair that looked as if it had never heard of hairpin or comb; face showing white against smoke, headlight and starlight; in bloomers on a bike that turns off just ahead of the engine, but not so far but that, as she staggers toward him with outstretched arms, the poor wheel is caught up by the slackening train, tossed high, and falls beside the track a finished cycle.

How indignantly the workmen heard the plot which was to cover them with infamy, and how they captured the hoboes and turned them over to the authorities, does not belong to this story.

But the fact that Jim's prophecy came true is the moral thereof. Mr. and Mrs. H. P. Waldon (the title "Professor" seems to have dropped from him of late) spend most delightful hours together, perambulating the country, per cycle. The wrecked one stands as a precious relic in Mr. Waldon's library. And Renie wears bloomers. Her husband says she converted him to a belief in their utility by the first words she gasped as she staggered into his arms that night:

"I–I never could have made it with a skirt on!"

★

H. W. FOSTER *Physical Education vs. Degeneracy*
Independent 52 (August 2, 1900): 1835–1837

[Amid concerns about the loss of a fundamental, authochthonic strength and fears of encroaching debilitation in an urbanized and educated America, Foster invokes European history to warn his readers against reliance on academic education. Manufacturing a nostalgia for a simpler, rural past, Foster argues that physical training is needed to assure America's industrial and military supremacy.]

It WAS NATURAL THAT Holmes, poet, essayist, novelist, physician, believer in heredity, should be quick to observe the tendency of city breeding. He says, "I am satisfied that such a set of black-coated, stiff-jointed, soft-muscled, paste-complexioned youth as we can boast in our Atlantic cities never before sprang from loins of Anglo-Saxon lineage." "Boxing is rough play," says he, "but not too rough for a hearty young fellow. Anything is better than this white-blooded degeneration to which we all tend."

It is generally conceded that the county-bred boy has made for himself a strong record. Necessity, difficulties, effort, struggle, are essential factors in maintaining a vigorous stock. City life can be shown to lack certain essential elements in the training of a vigorous manhood. This fact becomes extremely important in view of the present drift toward the city, and the marvelous increase of the means to make life easy.

The old, ungraded, district school is often given credit for the success of the country-born. The country boy's success in the world has been attained, not because of the ungraded country school, but in spite of it. The real cause lies in the home life on the farm, and not in the district school. Through that life these elements of character are directly cultivated: fearlessness, pluck, self-reliance, activity, responsibility, patience, endurance, judgment. The boy becomes conscious of the necessity and dignity of labor, aggressive in the pursuit of his purposes; he gains skill to contrive various ways to meet difficulties, and a ready use of his physical powers. Here are the foundations of a vigorous character. Without these how shall success be attained? The boy may not, indeed, react against his environment. He will surmount his difficulties and grow thereby in manliness, or, failing to react against them, he will live unresponsive and dead to progress.

Upon the farm, labor is dignified; to rich and poor alike it is honorable. It calls for the application of intelligence. It is no mere tending of machines, to be assumed at the strident, imperious call of the whistle, to be dropped without interest the instant the whistle blows again. The child sees it not only honorable, but a necessity. Seed must be sown for the harvest, but before the sowing the plough must break the ground. Live stock must be fed, and the living animals appeal to his loving care. Fires must be supplied with fuel, that the household may enjoy the comforts of the fireside. However unwillingly he may sometimes appear to go about his toil, he never doubts the justice nor the honor of labor.

Your farm boy has responsibilities placed upon him, and his judgment is cultivated. He must rise early enough to get his chores done before school; he must get back and attend to them after school. There is wood for him to split and get in; there are cows to be milked, stables to be cleaned, live stock to be fed. He must push ahead with his work to get it done in time. He must feed judiciously, he must milk clean, so that the cows shall not go dry. He feels that he shares some of the responsibility for the sustenance of the family.

He becomes self-reliant, because he finds in himself power to do. Ox and horse are obedient to his will. The tough knot will yield at last to his vigorous axe. Where he sows, the green crops spring up and grow to maturity. He endures cold, heat and fatigue with fortitude. For his labor he is rewarded with strength of body. He must learn to manage and repair the farm implements and machines. He is compelled to be a "handy" man. The farm has furnished a training of the vigorous mind and body in that "just familiarity betwixt mind and things," which Bacon so aptly stated to be the object of education.

What has the ordinary city boy to compare with all this in his training? The upper classes of the ancient cities were compelled by the necessities of war to be trained in a vigorous fashion. The continental nations still pass their men through the physical training incident to their standing armies.

In America with years of peace there is little impulse toward physical training from this source. If future generations are to be vigorous, their training must consciously aim to secure the same results as were formerly compelled by necessity. We cannot depend upon the same training, conditions of life have changed so vastly. The boy of the village or small city a generation ago had much more in common with the country boy than the boy of to-day. He milked the family cow and drove it to pasture. He fed the horse, cleaned the stable, sawed and split wood, weeded the garden, rose in a cold room in winter; he learned to endure, and work patiently, and stick until the job was done. But now it is hard to find for the city boy endurances and tasks and responsibilities. There is no more sawing and splitting of wood; the family garden is not so much in evidence; the cow with her bare-foot driver is little seen in the outer streets; the furnace provides a few ashes to be removed daily, but it warms the house throughout, and there is no more endurance of the old, stinging cold. Comfortable school houses are provided, and it is aimed to have the boy sit quietly for five or six hours a day. What an education may be here in laziness and irresponsibility! As the conditions of life have changed so marvelously, it is all important that the education of the child of to-day shall prepare him to live without loss of vigor in the new conditions before him.

What can be supplied in place of those elements in the old life of the people which gave an all around training? The new training must be both industrial and physical. It must be industrial, not alone on account of the elements of character which such an education gives, but because of the new struggle impending between the nations, the commercial conflict. In 1866 Austria learned that a better education of the common people was needed to maintain her military prestige; in 1870 France learned the lesson. To-day England is learning that her industrial supremacy depends upon the same thing. "Made in Germany"—stamped both on the manufactured article sold over the counter in London and on the face of the youth in the counting house—here is an object lesson too plain to be overlooked. Such has been the progress in Germany in industrial education that to educate our people as well would require in this country 1,000 university professors and instructors, and 10,000 students of the highest branches of technical work; 1,000 college professors and 15,000 students in technical schools studying for superior positions in the arts, and 20,000 teachers in trade and manual training schools instructing 400,000 pupils, preparing to become skilled workmen. Only the extraordinary natural advantages of our country and the more extraordinary general intelligence and enterprise of its citizens can possibly prevent all this from telling fatally against us in the course of time, when the inevitable competition of the world shall affect us. From the time of Luther Germany has laid hold mightily upon the development of her people through her schools. All of progressive Europe has been affected by her example.

Here is something which aims to supply some of the training given by the farm. Manual education has been said to be the great triumph of the new education. Labor is dignified, the body is set to work, eye and hand and brain together. Acquaintance is made with physical difficulties to be overcome. Judgment is cultivated. It develops men who are "handy" and who have the power to grasp any manual occupation. Most people will have to labor with the body. An education which is wholly mental leaves out a most important part. When the life of the people does not provide that part, it must be made an aim of the school. In this country the importance of the matter is beginning to be appreciated, and manual education is fast securing a firm hold.

Much more, however, is demanded than can be found in industrial education to fully develop the qualities of courage, pluck, grit, endurance and activity. There should be something to directly counteract that tendency to laziness which arises through the enforced bodily inactivity of the school hours. It is a mistake to educate children into the disposition to avoid any sweat-producing activity. The value of the ordinary mental studies in the development of character is not at all to be depreciated; but they will not satisfy this demand nor will industrial education supply all the need.

In physical education are to be found forces which will meet the demand. The Greeks rise at once to mind as a nation where physical training made a vigorous race, whose mental power enabled them to place their largest impress on the world's history. Physical training, to meet the need, must take sufficient time daily throughout the whole course of a child's school life; and while, for a large part, taking advantage of the play spirit, be not afraid of downright work. It should be under the control in every city of an expert physical director. He should, indeed, where possible, be a physician especially trained for this purpose. To him should be intrusted the physical over sight of the children, including the testing for defects of sight and hearing, and examination for spinal curvature, or any deformity as well as for contagious diseases; but not, of course, the treatment, which belongs to the family physician. He should prepare the course of exercises to properly develop children, and should adapt work to abnormal cases.

The old, open-air recess, now to a very large extent discarded, appeals to us still because of its free exercise in the open air. One could not wish its return, as it was with its opportunities for evil associations, its over-exercise of the too-exuberant, or further opportunity for physical resting of the lazy, as well as its danger to health by exposure of the child half-protected in inclement weather. But there should be open air exercise in connection with the school. The school hours may be profitably lengthened to include the time necessary for physical training. There should be a gymnasium, properly fitted, connected with every school, and all necessary apparatus, selected for the work suited to the age of the children. No child should be excused from taking part, because of mere aversion to physical activity. Children not fitted for some exercises should be excused. Aside from the exercises specifically designed, there should be games which bring out manliness, as well as the bodily powers.

Football, on account of its violence and rough character, has been a subject of much complaint; but in the English public school, where it must be played by every able bodied boy, it has been the means of developing the man of energy and pluck. It is not impossible that the game might be so regulated as to exclude its dangers. The worst feature of either baseball or football is not the violence, but the fact that in America they have become so much the sole possession of experts and champions. Scarcely anything can be so demoralizing to youth as the giving over of sports to a few and placing upon them the responsibility of securing the success demanded by their backers. A careful, scientific training of every child could be made to discountenance this sort of thing. Football, baseball, the tug of war, and other vigorous sports, which have in them the element of contest, should be made a part of the physical training of every boy at the proper age.

Such an education will cost more than the old merely mental training of the schools. But the people will not object to the additional expense when they come to realize that the results are more than worth the money; that the mind responds more vigorously while the physical powers and health increase. Those who have charge of masses of children, as they come from all sorts of homes, are impressed by the bad physical condition of an extremely large part of them. They come ill-fed, even from homes of the well-to-do. They come with narrow, sunken chests, and projecting shoulder blades. Very little well directed and sufficient effort is yet made to develop them into vigorous condition. Their need cries continually for help.

★

HENRY CHARLES MERWIN *On Being Civilized Too Much*
Atlantic Monthly 79 (June 1897): 838–846

[Offering advice to readers in an overly complicated modern world, Merwin discusses the dangers of an advanced civilization and the possibility of an impending disaster stemming from a loss of visceral reactions to the world. Encouraging readers to leave their offices and return to manual labor, Merwin locates the future in the rural worker.]

THERE ARE CERTAIN phrases which people use, feeling that they express something fundamental and radical, although exactly what that something is they seldom take pains to inquire. Such is the phrase "close to nature." In the most obvious sense, a man is close to nature who prefers the country to the city, sunshine to steam heat, out of doors to indoors; who loves to buffet wind and weather, and to wander alone in the woods. So, also, a man may be described as close to nature if he deals with natural forces and objects at first-hand, as when he builds his own house, raises his own crops, milks his own cow, breaks his own colts, and constructs and sails his own boat. All these things and many similar things city people hire others to do for them, but country people know how to shift for themselves. A man who can tell the time of day by the sun is to that degree both more instructed and closer to nature than one who has recourse to a watch made by somebody else; and so of him who by natural signs, such as moss on the tree-trunks, can tell the points of the compass without the assistance of a gilded weathercock surmounting a church steeple.

Closeness to nature, in this sense, is wholesome and important to mankind; nay, it is so important that without it the human race could not long exist. The city, as we are often told, must continually be recruited from the country; and it has been remarked by President Eliot that the survival of particular families in the United States—families so strong in character as to give them in some measure a natural leadership in the community—depends upon the maintenance of a home in the country. An ideal arrangement would perhaps be one in which every family should retain its country home; one generation tilling the soil, the next leading a professional or mercantile or artisan's life in town or city, the third returning to the farm, and so on until the line was exhausted. For a generation or two, possibly for several generations, if the circumstances are favorable, a city family may keep its standing; but commonly, even in the second generation, there is a diminution of force, and in the third generation, if there be one, something as a rule gives out,—the digestion, or the heart, or the liver, or the moral character. The most successful and the ablest professional man whom I know is the son of a New Bedford whaling-captain. There is a continual stream of college-bred country boys pouring into cities like New York and Boston, and ultimately they take chief positions there at the bar, in politics, in medicine, and among the clergy. In short, man can retain his strength only by perpetually renewing his contact with Mother Earth.

But there is another and a more important sense in which a man may be described as close to nature. There are in all of us certain natural impulses, or instincts, which furnish in large measure the springs of human conduct; and these impulses, or instincts, as they may be called with some exaggeration, are apt to be dulled and weakened by civilization. While they are still strong in a man, he may be said to be close to nature, in the essential meaning of that expression. He has a certain spontaneous promptitude of action and of feeling, akin to that which is displayed by all dumb animals. Man is a compound of feeling and intellect. In the savage, feeling predominates, and the intellect plays a very subordinate part. But now take your savage in hand, cut his hair, put trousers on his legs, give him a common school education, an air-tight stove, and a daily newspaper, and presently his intellect will develop, and will exercise more and more control over his feelings. Pursue the process a little further, and soon you will have a creature who is what we call over-sophisticated and effete,—a being in whom the springs of action are, in greater or less degree, paralyzed or perverted by the undue predominance of the intellect. In every age and in every country, in the most civilized nations, and also, I suppose, in the most savage tribes, men will be found who illustrate all stages of this process. In fact, the difference is one between individuals more than between ages or races. Still, every age as well as every nation has a type of its own, which may be close to nature or far from nature. Man is at his best, does the greatest deeds and produces the greatest literature, when there is in him a perfect balance between the feelings and the intellect; when he is neither an emotional nor an intellectual being, but a happy compound of both. Such was the character of the age which produced Shakespeare and Sir Philip Sidney. If it were otherwise, if mere intellect could take the place of feeling, if knowledge could have the dynamic force of natural impulse, then indeed we might believe in that most absurd of all dreams, the perfectibility of human nature. For there is no limit to the progress of science and of education. In fact, however, every step in civilization is made at the expense of some savage strength or virtue. It is only now and then, in the history of the world, that a fortunate race strikes the right balance between the barbarism behind it and the sophistication into which it is soon to fall. "Society never advances. It recedes as fast on one side as it gains on the other. It undergoes continual changes; it is barbarous, it is civilized, it is Christianized, it is rich, it is scientific; but this change is not amelioration. For everything that is given, something is taken. Society acquires new arts, and loses old instincts." [Emerson, in the essay on Self-Reliance.]

To be close to nature is, then, to preserve certain primeval impulses, or instincts, of which the most impotent are the following: the instinct of pugnacity, the instinct of pity, and the instinct of pride. Nature herself has decided against the man who has lost these primeval impulses. He does not survive, he does not conquer and overspread the earth: and this appears most plainly when the instinct of pugnacity is considered. This instinct we share with the beasts of the field. If a dog has a bone, and a strange dog comes up and tries to take it from him, the result is a fight, which ends in the killing or disabling, or perhaps simply in the intimidation of one animal, so that the other is left to enjoy the bone of contention. In that humble contest we find the principle of most great wars. When the instinct is weakened, when people get too far from nature, they hire others to fight for them, as the

Romans did in their decadence; and when that stage is reached the end is not far off. Nature will not tolerate the suppression of the instinct of pugnacity.

But this instinct is far more beautifully shown in questions of honor than it is in questions of mere property; and here too we find ourselves at one with the inferior animals. Dogs can insult one another as well as men can; and they have the same instinct to resent an insult. You will sometimes see two dogs walking around each other on their toes and growling, until presently one flies at the other's throat, and they fight it out. The bravest man who ever died on the field of honor was actuated by the same impulse; and though dueling may be a bad and foolish manifestation or exercise of the instinct, still the instinct itself is a good one, and upon its existence depend, in the last analysis, the prosperity and permanence of nations. Before the time of the Civil War in this country, and even after the war had begun, the South thought that they would have an easy victory over the North, because, as the South supposed, the North had lost the instinct of pugnacity. They thought that we were so given over to trading and dickering, to buying and selling, that we could not fight. They thought that we were too far from nature to fight. The event proved that they were greatly in error. But nations have lost the instinct of pugnacity, they have become incapable of fighting; and when they have reached that stage, they have perished.

It is easy to see how the instinct of pugnacity is or may be weakened in the process of civilization; but it is not quite so easy to recognize the subtle way in which the instinct of pity, also, is weakened or perverted by the same process. We have all felt the instinct of pity. If we hear the cry of a drowning man, we have an impulse to jump in after him, or at least to throw him a rope. If our neighbor is ill or bereaved, our hearts go out toward him, as we say. Nature speaks in us. Upon this primeval instinct is based all pity, all charity, all benevolence, all self-sacrifice; and this instinct, too, we share not only with the savage, but also with the very beasts of the field. "The moral sense," Darwin remarks, "is fundamentally identical with the social instincts." And then he goes on to say: "The social instincts, which no doubt were acquired by man, as by the lower animals, for the good of the community, will from the first have given to him some wish to aid his fellows and some feeling of sympathy. Such impulses have served him at a very early period as a rude rule of right and wrong." In other words, Darwin bases not only benevolence, but the moral sense itself, upon the instinct of pity.

Of course, one does not mean that the instinct of pity is precisely the same in the brute or in the savage that it is in civilized man. There is far more pity among civilized than among savage people. The instinct gains as well as loses from civilization. It must remain a capricious, uncertain thing until, in the process of civilization, it acquires the strength of a principle, of a rule of life, of a conscious duty. This is the first effect of civilization. But the second effect—the effect, that is, which results when the intellect overbalances the feelings—is to dwarf and stifle the healthy instinct of pity; to make man a cold, calculating, and therefore an inefficient though it may be a conscientious person. The point is this: when it is a question of duty toward one's neighbor, the first impulse, the natural impulse, is a good one,—nature tells us to befriend him. But then reason wakes up, selfish considerations present themselves to the mind, and perhaps the natural impulse is over-borne.

Let us suppose that there is an accident in the street, and a child is about to be run over. A man is standing by, who might be described as close to nature. Without a moment's reflection, he dashes into the street to save the child's life at the risk of his own. There is no time for reflection; he cannot stop to think that it is his duty to save the child, or that the Humane Society may award him a medal for it; he has not even time to consider that he may be ashamed of himself afterward if he does not do it. He springs to the child's aid because he cannot help it; because he has an impulse to do so, just as he would have an impulse to save his own life. But let us suppose that the man who stands by is of a different character,—not so close to nature, although he may be a better man, more conscientious, a more valuable member of society. He too feels the impulse of pity, the instinct to save the child; but in him this impulse is not so strong; the selfish considerations that arise in his mind combat with it, and while he is struggling to perform his duty the moment flashes by, the child is run over; all that can now be done is to take the victim to a hospital, and that he will do, even at much personal inconvenience.

I do not intend to assert that the one is exclusively a savage, and the other exclusively a civilized type. Both kinds of men undoubtedly exist in barbarous tribes, both kinds exist in civilization; but the tendency of civilization, or of what we call civilization, is to produce the man who stands still in the moment of peril to another,—the man who is far from nature, who has lost something of primeval instinct. An illustration might be found in the case of General Gordon, whom the English government left to perish in the city of Khartoum. This, indeed, is an apt illustration, because the dangerous situation of Gordon appealed to all three of those main primeval instincts which I have mentioned, namely, the instincts of pity or benevolence, of pugnacity, and of pride. England was moved to go to Gordon's assistance, first, out of pity for him; secondly, out of anger against his enemies; and thirdly, out of wounded pride, because it was a British citizen whose life was threatened. The members of the Liberal government felt these impulses, of course, as other Englishmen felt them, but they were precisely in the situation of Rousseau's philosopher, whose impulse to do a generous act was stifled by the selfish motives which occurred to his mind; and in this case, also, the selfish dictates of reason got the upper hand of the primeval instinct. Gladstone and his cabinet found many reasons for leaving Gordon to his fate. He had got himself into the scrape, they said, and they were not responsible for the result: if a rescue were attempted, it might not be in time; an expedition would cost a large sum of money, and might involve England in a war, and so on. In short, the government did nothing, until they were compelled at last by popular clamor to do something, and then the expedition under Lord Wolseley was dispatched—but too late.

If now the question of going to Gordon's rescue or of leaving him in the hands of his enemies had been submitted, not to the Liberal government, but to the hedgers and ditchers of England, to the farmers or sailors,—to any body of men close to nature in the sense that I have indicated,—can it be doubted what the result would have been? But such men, it might be objected, would be thoughtless; they would not count the cost. That is precisely their merit,—they would not count the cost even if they had to pay it themselves, in money or in blood. England has become what she is partly by not counting the cost, by venturing upon forlorn hopes, by carving out her own path with what seemed at the time to be a reckless disregard of other nations. It was a different spirit which left Gordon to his fate, and which, later, held in check the army and navy of Great Britain while the Turks butchered the Armenians and ravished their women.

Mr. Watson's sonnet eloquently describes the degeneracy in this respect of the English government:—

> "I had not thought to hear it voiced so plain,
> Uttered so forthright, on their lips who steer
> This nation's course! I had not thought to hear
> That word re-echoed by an English thane,
> Guilt's maiden-speech when first a man lay slain,
> 'Am I my brother's keeper?' Yet full near
> It sounded, and the syllables rung clear
> As the immortal rhetoric of Cain,
> 'Wherefore should we, sirs, more than they—or they—
> Unto these helpless reach a hand to save?'
> An English thane, in this our English air,
> Speaking for England? Then indeed her day
> Slopes to its twilight, and, for Honour, there
> Is needed but a requiem, and a grave."

There always has been, and probably there always will be, this strange anomaly, as it seems at first sight; that is, a moral obtuseness in the very class which is supposed to be the most moral, which is perhaps the most conscientious, and which certainly is the best educated. The reason is plain. It is because, in this highly educated, sophisticated class, the intellect has passed beyond its legitimate borders; it has taken the place, in large measure, of those primeval instincts which exist in uneducated men and in children. The oft-quoted saying, "There is nothing so cruel as an idea," means, I suppose, that there is nothing so cruel as a man possessed by an idea. Such a man has cast off the restraints of nature. The natural impulses in him are stifled, and the misleading conclusions of the intellect have taken their place. The sensitive people, the well-educated, respectable people of the day are almost sure to be on the wrong side of every great moral question when it first arises. They mean to do right, but they trust to their logical faculties instead of to their instincts; and the consequence is that they are eager to stone those very reformers of whom, in later years, they become the most ardent admirers. These men are for unrestricted vivisection to-day, just as they were for slavery forty years ago.

In what we call the uneducated part of the community there is a striking unanimity of judgment, which is conspicuously lacking among the clever and educated people. This was strangely shown when the Civil War broke out. At that time, among the leaders of the people, there was an extreme discordance of opinion. Most of them thought that it would be impossible to preserve the Union; to many it seemed that the Union was not a thing of very great value,—certainly not so valuable as to warrant a civil war for its preservation; not a few considered that the Southern States had a right to secede, and should be permitted to exercise that right; hardly anybody thought that the North could be united in a single, direct policy; and there was only one point upon which all the public men were agreed, namely, that patriotism had died out of the country, and that only low and selfish views prevailed. This comes out very strongly in the correspondence of the time. The leading men of that day, with perhaps some exceptions, wrote to one another in a despairing mood. They had no conception of the mighty force which was soon to be aroused. But it was for the people, not for their leaders, to decide what should be done when the South seceded; and the decision was made with a wonderful approach to unanimity. The people did not sit down to reason the matter out; still less did they go to war for a theory or as a matter of duty. They went to war from impulse, from the natural, inherited instinct to defend that intangible entity which we call our country,—not the soil, for the soil of the South belonged to the people of the South. But there was an instinctive feeling at the North that a dismembered United States would lose its dignity and its pride, and the idea of consenting to such a dismemberment was not to be tolerated. Men who had never suspected that they were patriots, who had never dreamed of being such, found themselves driven to war by an impulse which they could not resist.

No doubt it will be the same in the future. When any great moral emergency arises, the people will act upon it with substantial unanimity, because they decide such matters, not by balancing arguments, but by trusting to their instincts. On the other hand, popular government would probably be impossible in a nation of clever, well-educated people. If everybody were sophisticated and artificial, if everybody reasoned about everything and took care not to act from natural impulses, harmonious political action would become impossible. We should have at first factions instead of parties, then individuals instead of factions, and then chaos. There is an approach to this condition of things in France to-day.

In Mr. Lecky's latest book there is a remarkable passage tending to uphold the theory which I maintain; and it is the more remarkable because the fact which Mr. Lecky states was forced upon his observation, and it does not readily find a place in his political philosophy. He says: "It has been the opinion of some of the ablest and most successful politicians of our time that, by adopting a very low suffrage, it would be possible to penetrate below the region where crotchets and experiments and crude Utopias and habitual restlessness prevail, and to reach the strong settled habits, the enduring tendencies, the deep conservative instincts, of the nation. Such an idea was evidently present in the minds both of Louis Napoleon and of Lord Beaconsfield, and it probably largely influenced the great statesman who based the German Constitution on universal suffrage." Bismarck himself has said: "True public opinion is that which is the outcome of certain political, religious, and social convictions, of a very simple kind, deep down in the national life, and to recognize and give effect to this is the task of the true statesman. I might call it the undercurrent of public opinion. Hence it is that I have never reckoned with our parliamentary screamers."

There is one political party or group in the United States from which, I think, a lesson can be drawn in this matter, namely, the Mugwumps. I have a great respect for them,—the sort of respect that a man naturally has for the party to which he himself belongs, or almost belongs. The Mugwumps, man for man, are about the most conscientious, the most moral, the best educated persons of our day. And yet there has always been a deep distrust of them among the people at large. I do not mean among the politicians; the politicians hate them because they are irregulars in politics. The people dislike them, in a measure because they resent what they believe (perhaps erroneously) to be an assumption of superiority on the part of the Mugwumps, but in the main, it seems to me, because they have an instinctive feeling that the Mugwumps are governed by principles entirely different from those which govern them, and are deficient in certain respects in which the mass of the people are not deficient. This is exactly the case. The Mugwumps, almost without exception, are the kind of men whom I have endeavored to describe,—the oversophisticated; they are persons who are far from nature, who distrust their natural impulses, who have substituted the feeble and erratic conclusions of the intellect for the natural promptings of the heart.

We have had recently a striking illustration of this. In the Venezuelan affair the President and his Secretary of State acted not without thought, and yet with an instinctive perception of what the honor and the ultimate welfare of the country demanded. They trusted to that instinctive perception, and the nation responded with remarkable unanimity. Even the bitterest enemies of Mr. Cleveland, in the Senate and in the House of Representatives, supported him, and the people at large, whatever their political opinions, supported their representatives. Mr. Cleveland, every one would admit, is a man close to nature, both in his virtues and in his failings, and it was almost inevitable that in such a matter as this the great bulk of his unsophisticated fellow countrymen should be at one with him. Those who objected to his policy were but a small minority. In the whole country, so far as I know, only five papers of any importance failed to support the President's position. These were the Boston Herald, the Providence Journal, the Springfield Republican, the New York Evening Post, and the New York World. Setting aside the World, which acted from well-known motives of private hatred, these are all Mugwump papers, or papers leaning in that direction. Here, then, was a remarkable coincidence. The Venezuelan affair did not in the least touch upon peculiar Mugwump principles; it was not a matter of civil service reform or of any other reform. Moreover, the position taken by the Mugwump papers was not the result of concerted action on their part; it was a position for which each paper had an obvious predilection from the start, although undoubtedly they bolstered up one another afterward. I assume that these journals were wrong. Some of my readers may refuse to grant the assumption, but at all events this much is clear, that the Mugwumps are not in sympathy with the rest of their countrymen. In some respects, at least, they stand apart from the main current of national life. The difference between them and the great mass of the people is the difference between those who are far from nature and those who are close to nature. The Mugwumps belong to the former class, and in fact they are extreme representatives of it. Their conduct in the Venezuelan affair justified that popular distrust of them which I, for one, had always regarded as a mistake, but which I now perceive was founded upon the vague perception of a real truth.

In literature, even more than in politics, one sees the evil effects of getting far from nature. In a peculiar sense literature is the business and the amusement of persons who are over-sophisticated. In fact, to take literature seriously is in itself almost a sign of decadence. It is remarkable that the times in which the greatest works have been produced were precisely those in which the least fuss was made over literature or over those who produced it. Shakespeare cut but a small figure in his day, and there were but few critics, essayists, or poetasters in his time. The greatest writers, almost without exception, being themselves close to nature and strong in natural impulses, have had a healthy contempt for their own occupation. Sir Walter Scott and Carlyle are familiar examples of this truth. But when literature is at a low ebb, the talk made about it, and the number of persons who are busy with it in one way and another, are always vastly increased.

There is a primeval or basic taste for literature. That is, it is natural for man even in a savage state, still more in childhood, to like stories in prose or in rhyme. It would be difficult to overestimate the amount of pleasure which childish readers have derived from Robinson Crusoe, for example. Who can forget the exquisite thrill of mingled horror and curiosity which he felt when Crusoe discovered the print of a human foot upon the sands of his uninhabited island! To develop and refine this natural taste is the object of a literary education, and to lay down rules for gratifying it is the chief function of literary criticism. But there comes a time when readers and critics are so sophisticated, so far from nature, that to all intents and purposes they have lost their taste for literature, and occupy themselves with the rules and principles of literary art, or with the search for some novelty to stimulate their jaded palates.

Pleasure and pain, it should always be remembered, are the only safe grades of criticism. The first, the all-important question which the critic has to ask himself is, Does this work give me pleasure or does it give me pain, or am I indifferent to it? Criticism is of no value unless the critic has this lively, instinctive taste. Charles Lamb was a superlatively good critic because his tastes were so wholesome and so strong,—strong because they were wholesome. A good thing in literature gave him the most deep and lively pleasure, and to talk about the good thing prolonged the pleasure; so that Lamb's criticism was delightful for him to write, and it is delightful for us to read. Now, Lamb was one whom it is impossible not to recognize as being close to nature. He had almost the confidence of Sterne in his own impulses and intuitions.

On the other hand, in a sophisticated age and among sophisticated people, works of literature or of the other arts almost cease to give pleasure; and a new criterion is adopted, which is, Does this thing conform to the rules? *Ought* I to like it and approve of it? I once heard a dramatic critic maintain with vehemence that a certain actress was deserving of the highest praise, and that the public were to blame for not caring much to see her act. "But," he was asked, "does her acting give you any pleasure? You are going to see her play to-night, for instance: do you look forward to the evening as something delightful to anticipate?" "No," he was candid enough to answer, "I can't say that I do." "Why, then," was the next inquiry, "do you call her a great actress?" "Oh," was his reply, "she is a great *artist*." That expressed perfectly the academic or sophisticated attitude of those who have got so far from nature that they cease to apply the test of pleasure or of pain. In other words, they endeavor to estimate chiefly by the intellect what nature intended them to estimate chiefly by their feelings.

I remember another occasion—if the reader will pardon me for recalling it—when, in a gathering of literary men, a dispute arose as to who was the greatest living poet in the United States. Some declared for this and some for that contemporary bard, but he who was most positive in his opinion fixed upon —— as the man. For this preference he gave many well-sounding reasons; but finally one of his opponents put the following question to him: "Can you repeat a single stanza, or a single line, or even a single phrase from ——'s poems?" And he was forced to acknowledge that he could not. He had derived no pleasure from ——'s poems, but nevertheless he thought that he must be a great poet because his poetry seemed to fulfill certain conditions that had been established by literary criticism. Such a man is hardly more competent to be a judge of literature than a tea-taster who had lost the sense of taste would be to fix the grade of teas.

Savages and children have a natural love for good bright colors, such as scarlet and blue; and their taste in this respect could be justified, if any justification were necessary, on physiological grounds. Everybody knows that these colors tend to raise the spirits, and therefore to improve the health; so much so, in fact, that they have been found efficacious in madhouses, in cases of melancholia. This natural, healthy sense of color may of course be cultivated and trained, so that those who possess it can learn to appreciate the beauty of more delicate shades; and in such persons there will be a happy union of natural taste with cultivation. But among the "Esthetes" of twenty years ago there was a marked absence of natural taste for color, which they supplied by a conventional and affected partiality for unlovely and depressing shades.

Nordau, in his famous work on Degeneracy, ascribes the perverted literary tastes of the present day to physical reasons, to weakness or disease either of the brain or of the nervous system. His notion, as I understand it, is that civilization and science will supply all that man can need to make him sane and successful, and that ignorance and disease are the only sources of danger. But history and experience show that there are other sources of danger, and that humanity may become ineffective without being ignorant or diseased: the project of converting man into an intellectual machine, governed solely by science and religion, will not work; it has been tried by almost every race which ever emerged from barbarism, and it has always failed. The true problem is, not to eradicate the savage in man, but so to train and control him that his strength of feeling, his spontaneousness and promptitude, shall be at the service of man's higher powers. It is for this reason that religion, which acts upon the feelings, has been, as a factor in civilization, a thousandfold more important than science, which can move only the intellect.

Nordau ascribes all those manifestations of degeneracy with which his book is concerned to a common spirit of lawlessness, an unwillingness to be hampered by morals or precedent or principle, or to submit to any kind of discipline. But all this is true rather of the degenerate authors of whom he treats than of the people who admire or affect to admire them. If we look about us, we do not see much lawlessness or much hysteria among the followers of Christian science or of Ibsen. These people are not immoral, nor ignorant, nor hysterical. On the contrary, they are usually well-to-do, well-informed, well-behaved persons, and—especially among the female portion of them—decidedly clever. Their trouble is that they are far from nature,—they have no strong root of opinion in themselves, no absolute standards, no instinctive way of separating the false from the true; and consequently they are at the mercy of every new fad as it arises. Moreover, being vaguely conscious of their own deficiencies, they have a natural readiness to take hold of any new idea or system which wears to them an aspect of strength. They cannot distinguish between strength and an hysterical appearance of strength, or between what is original and what is merely bizarre. The peculiar literary manifestations of the present day indicate an atrophy, from over-sophistication, of all genuine, natural taste for literature. Such are the chap-books, the yellow-books, and those other similar publications, composed largely by effeminate poets, who derive their inspiration sometimes from their vices and sometimes from their illnesses. "You asked me," writes one of these in a dedication, "what my aim was in those 'dramatic interludes,' which, collectively, I called 'vistas.' I could not well explain, nor can I do so now. . . . The most intimate, in the spiritual sense, [was written] when, during recovery from a long and nearly fatal illness, Lilith came to me in a vision, and was withheld in words, as soon as I could put pen to paper." Let any one compare the preface to the Endymion with this kind of thing, and he will see the difference between a man and a manikin.

And yet how little do these degenerate authors matter! How small is the section of society which even knows of their existence! Nordau himself mistakes his clinical room for the world. Leave the close air of the office, the library, or the club, and go out into the streets and the highway. Consult the teamster, the farmer, the wood-chopper, the shepherd, or the drover. You will find him as healthy in mind, as free from fads, as strong in natural impulses, as he was in Shakespeare's time and is in Shakespeare's plays. From his loins, and not from those of the dilettante, will spring the man of the future.

6 ★ THE PROMISES OF FORMAL EDUCATION

A MONG THE MOST CONSPICU-
OUSLY well-educated individuals of the period, the writers here represent the increasing diversity of formal study at the end of the century, particularly in regard to the education of minorities and women. In the 1890s, college life became increasingly attractive to American young people, with college enrollments growing fivefold during the last three decades of the nineteenth century. Women's colleges, many opening in the 1870s, were coming of age twenty years later, among them Wellesley, Smith, and Vassar. Additionally, the land-grant colleges and state institutions of the 1860s and 1870s continued to attract students from families of modest incomes. It is estimated that by the end of the century, three quarters of all colleges were coeducational in some form. And although there was no national racial integration in institutions of higher learning, the second Morril Act of 1890 helped fund the creation of state-affiliated black colleges in many Southern states. Finally, between 1877 and 1900 Congress created its own educational system for more than 20,000 Indians who were forced to learn English and menial trades. A prominent Indian institution, the Carlisle School in Pennsylvania, and the predominantly black Hampton Institute in Virginia took part in the "civilizing" process that severed children from their families, their native tongue, and all aspects of their "Indian" identity.

At century's end, educational opportunities began to have a profound impact on greater numbers of Americans seeking empowerment, respect, status, and economic freedom through institutionalized higher learning. For instance, W. E. B. Du Bois, the first African American to receive a Ph.D. from Harvard University, argued for the intellectual rights of black Americans, stating, "I sit with Shakespeare and he winces not." From Abbe Carter Goodloe's portraits of college women to Charles W. Chesnutt's fictional account of a successful African American college graduate, stories and essays in the periodicals explore the ways in which formal education authorizes an individual's claims on cultural advancement. As these authors emphasize, an individual's successes become located in peer groups and communities, which are forced to recognize educational advantages as a key component of personal worth.

In his "A Negro Schoolmaster in the New South," Du Bois tests the promises of formal education against the reality of social inequities, and he measures "progress" through the experiences of one family that fails to succeed. Du Bois demonstrates that formal education alone is not a sufficient guarantee of success for people who are also poor, culturally isolated, and black. Of the young man who fails because of the lack of social equity, Du Bois laments that "with a cultured parentage and a social caste to uphold him, he might have made a venturesome merchant or a West Point cadet," emphasizing the ways in which education's successes depend upon a network of extensive resources.

While Du Bois insists upon the ways in which communities must support educational opportunities, John Brisben Walker criticizes higher educational practices of the day as mere barbarian decoration; he deplores the commodification of education for social display. Arguing against an elite, scholarly curriculum based on the study of Greek and Latin, Walker insists on the practical needs of college students at the end of the century. He counters the traditional, conservative curriculum with a modern curriculum informed by the theories of the British social Darwinist philosopher of evolution, Herbert Spencer. For Walker, the aim of formal education should be "happiness"—by which he means satisfaction in a profession and in a marriage—which can be attained by being instructed in "reasoning."

Many authors here highlight the strains of pursuing formal education, including psychological, familial, physical, and cultural demands. Annie Payson Call focuses on the problem of stress on "college girls," as she does in her popular book *Power Through Repose* (1891), a discussion of the "disease of civilization" caused by the "mad rush" of modern life. Call, like William James, voices the widespread belief that the "excitable" nature and supposed "self-consciousness" of young women, combined with the stress of study and the "hurry" of modern life, cause them physical, mental, and emotional distress. Zitkala Sä, narrating the psychological strain of her extreme cultural and ethical dislocation, tells of her formal schooling at a Quaker school far removed from her Indian reservation home. She suffers from a sharp separation between her tribal education and her reformation as a product of white, Christian schooling, dramatizing throughout her essay the pressures of being compelled to adopt an alien and threatening culture.

A distinct break between old traditions and newer, challenging possibilities appears in moments of self-conscious change. Chesnutt's "The March of Progress" questions the decisions involved in a commitment to the "progress" of an individual as well as to a community of African Americans. The story prefigures aspects of the current debate over affirmative action as it portrays a community's choice between rewarding either a loyal, elderly white schoolteacher or a young black contender from the school's community who is a recent graduate of "Riddle University." Although Chesnutt's plantation stories, many published during the 1890s, and Paul Laurence Dunbar's poetry reveal nuances of nostalgia for older forms of prewar race relations, the selections here show situations that challenge older sets of values and that rethink attitudes which are complicit with the processes of hegemony. In "The Ingrate," Dunbar portrays the real power of formal education when the student protagonist breaks from the limited expectations placed upon him by an exploitative master and realizes the full potential of his education by exercising total citizenship.

In a story exploring the disjunctions between education's anticipated outcome and the expectations facing a central character, Abbe Carter Goodloe's "genius" is torn between two evaluative arenas, home and college, whose standards she must confront. At a time when the seriousness of women's colleges was still being questioned, Goodloe illustrates that collegiate intellectual and ethical standards were enforced through peer relations. Goodloe herself, whose stories and essays on college life appeared in *Scribner's* and in a collection titled *College Girls* (1895), exemplified one kind of success available to a female college graduate. Reviews of the book positioned Goodloe as a testament to the value of women's education. The *Boston Transcript*'s review, for example, stated: "If college is to help a woman to produce such work as this, instead of a novel thick with morbid sentiment, we say amen to each diploma."

★

W. E. BURGHARDT DU BOIS *A Negro Schoolmaster*
in the New South
Atlantic Monthly 83 (January 1899): 99–104

[W. E. B. Du Bois led the opposition to Booker T. Washington's conciliatory position on the cultural assimilation of African Americans and refused to compromise on any claim to full rights as a citizen, especially the right to higher education. "A Negro Schoolmaster in the New South," which became "Of the Meaning of Progress" in *The Souls of Black Folk* (1903), is a powerful indictment of the "Veil," the racial divide poisoning post-Reconstruction, Jim Crow America and isolating African Americans from opportunity.]

O<small>NCE UPON A TIME</small> I taught school in the hills of Tennessee, where the broad dark vale of the Mississippi begins to roll and crumple to greet the Alleghanies. I was a Fisk student then, and all Fisk men thought that Tennessee—beyond the Veil—was theirs alone, and in vacation time they sallied forth in lusty bands to meet the county school-commissioners. Young and happy, I too went, and I shall not soon forget that summer, seventeen years ago.

First, there was a teachers' Institute at the county-seat; and there distinguished guests of the superintendent taught the teachers fractions and spelling and other mysteries,—white teachers in the morning, Negroes at night. A picnic now and then, and a supper, and the rough world was softened by laughter and song. I remember how—But I wander.

There came a day when all the teachers left the Institute and began the hunt for schools. I learn from hearsay (for my mother was mortally afraid of fire-arms) that the hunting of ducks and bears and men is wonderfully interesting, but I am sure that the man who has never hunted a country school has something to learn of the pleasures of the chase. I see now the white, hot roads lazily rise and fall and wind before me under the burning July sun; I feel the deep weariness of heart and limb as ten, eight, six miles stretch relentlessly ahead; I feel my heart sink heavily as I hear again and again, "Got a teacher? Yes." So I walked on and on—horses were too expensive—until I had wandered beyond railways, beyond stage lines, to a land of "varmints" and rattlesnakes, where the coming of a stranger was an event, and men lived and died in the shadow of one blue hill.

Sprinkled over hill and dale lay cabins and farmhouses, shut out from the world by the forests and the rolling hills toward the east. There I found at last a little school. Josie told me of it; she was a thin, homely girl of twenty, with a dark-brown face and thick, hard hair. I had crossed the stream at Watertown, and rested under the great willows; then I had gone to the little cabin in the lot where Josie was resting on her way to town. The gaunt farmer made me welcome, and Josie, hearing my errand, told me anxiously that they wanted a school over the hill; that but once since the war had a teacher been there; that she herself longed to learn,—and thus she ran on, talking fast and loud, with much earnestness and energy.

Next morning I crossed the tall round hill, lingered to look at the blue and yellow mountains stretching toward the Carolinas, then plunged into the wood, and came out at Josie's home. It was a dull frame cottage with four rooms, perched just below the brow of the hill, amid peachtrees. The father was a quiet, simple soul, calmly ignorant, with no touch of vulgarity. The mother was different,—strong, bustling, and energetic, with a quick, restless tongue, and an ambition to live "like folks." There was a crowd of children. Two boys had gone away. There remained two growing girls; a shy midget of eight; John, tall, awkward, and eighteen; Jim, younger, quicker, and better looking; and two babies of indefinite age. Then there was Josie herself. She seemed to be the centre of the family: always busy at service, or at home, or berry-picking; a little nervous and inclined to scold, like her mother, yet faithful, too, like her father. She had about her a certain fineness, the shadow of an unconscious moral heroism that would willingly give all of life to make life broader, deeper, and fuller for her and hers. I saw much of this family afterwards, and grew to love them for their honest efforts to be decent and comfortable, and for their knowledge of their own ignorance. There was with them no affectation. The mother would scold the father for being so "easy"; Josie would roundly berate the boys for carelessness; and all knew that it was a hard thing to dig a living out of a rocky side hill.

I secured the school. I remember the day I rode horseback out to the commissioner's house with a pleasant young white fellow who wanted the white school. The road ran down the bed of a stream; the sun laughed and the water jingled, and we rode on. "Come in," said the commissioner,—"come in. Have a seat. Yes, that certificate will do. Stay to dinner. What do you want a month?" Oh, thought I, this is lucky; but even then fell the awful shadow of the Veil, for they ate first, then I—alone.

The schoolhouse was a log hut, where Colonel Wheeler used to shelter his corn. It sat in a lot behind a rail fence and thorn bushes, near the sweetest of springs. There was an entrance where a door once was, and within, a massive rickety fireplace; great chinks between the logs served as windows. Furniture was scarce. A pale blackboard crouched in the corner. My desk was made of three boards, reinforced at critical points, and my chair, borrowed from the landlady, had to be returned every night. Seats for the children,—these puzzled me much. I was haunted by a New England vision of neat little desks and chairs, but, alas, the reality was rough plank benches without backs, and at times without legs. They had the one virtue of making naps dangerous,— possibly fatal, for the floor was not to be trusted.

It was a hot morning late in July when the school opened. I trembled when I heard the patter of little feet down the dusty road, and saw the growing row of dark solemn faces and bright eager eyes facing me. First came Josie and her brothers and sisters. The longing to know, to be a student in the great school at Nashville, hovered like a star above this child woman amid her work and worry, and she studied doggedly. There were the Dowells from their farm over toward Alexandria: Fanny, with her smooth black face and wondering eyes; Martha, brown and dull; the pretty girl wife of a brother, and the younger brood. There were the Burkes, two brown and yellow lads, and a tiny haughty-eyed girl. Fat Reuben's little chubby girl came, with golden face and old gold hair, faithful and solemn. 'Thenie was on hand early,— a jolly, ugly, good-hearted girl, who slyly dipped snuff and looked after her little bow-legged brother. When her mother could spare her, 'Tildy came,—a midnight beauty, with starry eyes and tapering limbs; and her brother, correspondingly homely. And then the big boys: the hulking Lawrences; the lazy Neills, unfathered sons of mother and daughter Hickman, with a stoop in his shoulders; and the rest.

There they sat, nearly thirty of them, on the rough benches, their faces shading from a pale cream to a deep brown, the little feet bare and swinging, the eyes full of expectation, with here and there a twinkle of mischief, and the hands grasping Webster's blue-back spelling-book. I loved my school, and the fine faith the children had in the wisdom of their teacher was truly marvelous. We read and spelled together, wrote a little, picked flowers, sang, and listened to stories of the world beyond the hill. At times the school would dwindle away, and I would start out. I would visit Mun Eddings, who lived in two very dirty rooms, and ask why little Lugene, whose flaming face seemed ever ablaze with the dark-red hair uncombed, was absent all last week, or why I missed so often the inimitable rags of Mack and Ed. Then the father, who worked Colonel Wheeler's farm on shares, would tell me how the crops needed the boys; and the thin, slovenly mother, whose face was pretty when washed, assured me that Lugene must mind the baby. "But we'll start them again next week." When the Lawrences stopped, I knew that the doubts of the old folks about book-learning had conquered again, and so, toiling up the hill, and getting as far into the cabin as possible, I put Cicero pro Archia Poeta into the simplest English with local applications, and usually convinced them—for a week or so.

On Friday nights I often went home with some of the children; sometimes to Doc Burke's farm. He was a great, loud, thin Black, ever working, and trying to buy the seventy-five acres of hill and dale where he lived; but people said that he would surely fail, and the "white folks would get it all." His wife was a magnificent Amazon, with saffron face and shining hair, uncorseted and barefooted, and the children were strong and beautiful. They lived in a one-and-a-half-room cabin in the hollow of the farm, near the spring. The front room was full of great fat white beds, scrupulously neat; and there were bad chromos on the walls, and a tired centre-table. In the tiny back kitchen I was often invited to "take out and help" myself to fried chicken and wheat biscuit, "meat" and corn pone, string-beans and berries. At first I used to be a little alarmed at the approach of bedtime in the one lone bedroom, but embarrassment was very deftly avoided. First, all the children nodded and slept, and were stowed away in one great pile of goose feathers; next, the mother and the father discreetly slipped away to the kitchen while I went to bed; then, blowing out the dim light, they retired in the dark. In the morning all were up and away before I thought of awaking. Across the road, where fat Reuben lived, they all went outdoors while the teacher retired, because they did not boast the luxury of a kitchen.

I liked to stay with the Dowells, for they had four rooms and plenty of good country fare. Uncle Bird had a small, rough farm, all woods and hills, miles from the big road; but he was full of tales,—he preached now and then,—and with his children, berries, horses, and wheat he was happy and prosperous. Often, to keep the peace, I must go where life was less lovely; for instance, Tildy's mother was incorrigibly dirty, Reuben's larder was limited seriously, and herds of untamed bedbugs wandered over the Eddingses' beds. Best of all I loved to go to Josie's and sit on the porch, eating peaches, while the mother bustled and talked: how Josie had bought the sewing-machine; how Josie worked at service in winter, but that four dollars a month was "mighty little" wages; how Josie longed to go away to school, but that it "looked like" they never could get far enough ahead to let her; how the crops failed and the well was yct unfinishcd; and, finally, how "mcan" somc of thc whitc folks wcrc.

For two summers I lived in this little world; it was dull and humdrum. The girls looked at the hill in wistful longing, and the boys fretted, and haunted Alexandria. Alexandria was "town,"—a straggling, lazy village of houses, churches, and shops, and an aristocracy of Toms, Dicks, and Captains. Cuddled on the hill to the north was the village of the colored folks, who lived in three or four room unpainted cottages, some neat and home-like, and some dirty. The dwellings were scattered rather aimlessly but they centred about the twin temples of the hamlet, the Methodist and the Hard-Shell Baptist churches. These, in turn, leaned gingerly on a sad-colored schoolhouse. Hither my little world wended its crooked way on Sunday to meet other worlds, and gossip, and wonder, and make the weekly sacrifice with frenzied priest at the altar of the "old-time religion." Then the soft melody and mighty cadences of Negro song fluttered and thundered.

I have called my tiny community a world, and so its isolation made it; and yet there was among us but a half-awakened common consciousness, sprung from common joy and grief, at burial, birth, or wedding; from a common hardship in poverty, poor land, and low wages; and, above all, from the sight of the Veil that hung between us and Opportunity. All this caused us to think some thoughts together; but these, when ripe for speech, were spoken in various languages. Those whose eyes thirty and more years before had seen "the glory of the coming of the Lord" saw in every present hindrance or help a dark fatalism bound to bring all things right in His own good time. The mass of those to whom slavery was a dim recollection of childhood found the world a puzzling thing: it asked little of them, and they answered with little, and yet it ridiculed their offering. Such a paradox they could not understand, and therefore sank into listless indifference, or shiftlessness, or reckless bravado. There were, however, some such as Josie, Jim, and Ben,—they to whom War, Hell, and Slavery were but childhood tales, whose young appetites had been whetted to an edge by school and story and half-awakened thought. Ill could they be content, born without and beyond the World. And their weak wings beat against their barriers,—barriers of caste, of youth, of life; at last, in dangerous moments, against everything that opposed even a whim.

The ten years that follow youth, the years when first the realization comes that life is leading somewhere,—these were the years that passed after I left my little school. When they were past, I came by chance once more to the walls of Fisk University, to the halls of the chapel of melody. As I lingered there in the joy and pain of meeting old school friends, there swept over me a sudden longing to pass again beyond the blue hill, and to see the homes and the school of other days, and to learn how life had gone with my school-children; and I went.

Josie was dead, and the gray-haired mother said simply, "We've had a heap of trouble since you've been away." I had feared for Jim. With a cultured parentage and a social caste to uphold him, he might have made a venture-some merchant or a West Point cadet. But here he was, angry with life and reckless; and when Farmer Durham charged him with stealing wheat, the old man had to ride fast to escape the stones which the furious fool hurled after him. They told Jim to run away; but he would not run, and the constable came that afternoon. It grieved Josie, and great awkward John walked nine miles every day to see his little brother through the bars of Lebanon jail. At last the two came back together in the dark night. The mother cooked sup-per, and Josie emptied her purse, and the boys stole away. Josie grew thin and silent, yet worked the more. The hill became steep for the quiet old father, and with the boys away there was little to do in the valley. Josie helped them to sell the old farm, and they moved nearer town. Brother Dennis, the car-penter, built a new house with six rooms; Josie toiled a year in Nashville, and brought back ninety dollars to furnish the house and change it to a home.

When the spring came, and the birds twittered, and the stream ran proud and full, little sister Lizzie, bold and thoughtless, flushed with the passion of youth, bestowed herself on the tempter, and brought home a nameless child. Josie shivered and worked on, with the vision of schooldays all fled, with a face wan and tired,—worked until, on a summer's day, some one mar-ried another; then Josie crept to her mother like a hurt child, and slept—and sleeps.

I paused to scent the breeze as I entered the valley. The Lawrences have gone; father and son forever, and the other son lazily digs in the earth to live. A new young widow rents out their cabin to fat Reuben. Reuben is a Baptist preacher now, but I fear as lazy as ever, though his cabin has three rooms; and little Ella has grown into a bouncing woman, and is ploughing corn on the hot hillside. There are babies a plenty, and one half-witted girl. Across the valley is a house I did not know before, and there I found, rocking one baby and expecting another, one of my schoolgirls, a daughter of Uncle Bird Dowell. She looked somewhat worried with her new duties, but soon bristled into pride over her neat cabin, and the tale of her thrifty husband, the horse and cow, and the farm they were planning to buy.

My log schoolhouse was gone. In its place stood Progress, and Progress, I understand, is necessarily ugly. The crazy foundation stones still marked the former site of my poor little cabin, and not far away, on six weary boulders, perched a jaunty board house, perhaps twenty by thirty feet, with three windows and a door that locked. Some of the window glass was broken, and part of an old iron stove lay mournfully under the house. I peeped through the window half reverently, and found things that were more familiar. The blackboard had grown by about two feet, and the seats were still without backs. The county owns the lot now, I hear, and every year there is a session of school. As I sat by the spring and looked on the Old and the New I felt glad, very glad, and yet—

After two long drinks I started on. There was the great double log house on the corner. I remembered the broken, blighted family that used to live there. The strong, hard face of the mother, with its wilderness of hair, rose before me. She had driven her husband away, and while I taught school a strange man lived there, big and jovial, and people talked. I felt sure that Ben and 'Tildy would come to naught from such a home. But this is an odd world; for Ben is a busy farmer in Smith County, "doing well, too," they say, and he had cared for little 'Tildy until last spring, when a lover married her. A hard life the lad had led, toiling for meat, and laughed at because he was homely and crooked. There was Sam Carlon, an impudent old skinflint, who had definite notions about niggers, and hired Ben a summer and would not pay him. Then the hungry boy gathered his sacks together, and in broad daylight went into Carlon's corn; and when the hard-fisted farmer set upon him, the angry boy flew at him like a beast. Doc Burke saved a murder and a lynching that day.

The story reminded me again of the Burkes, and an impatience seized me to know who won in the battle, Doc or the seventy-five acres. For it is a hard thing to make a farm out of nothing, even in fifteen years. So I hurried on, thinking of the Burkes. They used to have a certain magnificent barbarism about them that I liked. They were never vulgar, never immoral, but rather rough and primitive, with an unconventionality that spent itself in loud guffaws, slaps on the back, and naps in the corner. I hurried by the cottage of the misborn Neill boys. It was empty, and they were grown into fat, lazy farm hands. I saw the home of the Hickmans, but Albert, with his stooping shoulders, had passed from the world. Then I came to the Burkes' gate and peered through; the inclosure looked rough and untrimmed, and yet there were the same fences around the old farm save to the left, where lay twenty-five other acres. And lo! the cabin in the hollow had climbed the hill and swollen to a half-finished six-room cottage.

The Burkes held a hundred acres, but they were still in debt. Indeed, the gaunt father who toiled night and day would scarcely be happy out of debt, being so used to it. Some day he must stop, for his massive frame is showing decline. The mother wore shoes, but the lion-like physique of other days was broken. The children had grown up. Rob, the image of his father, was loud and rough with laughter. Birdie, my school baby of six, had grown to a picture of maiden beauty, tall and tawny. "Edgar is gone," said the mother, with head half bowed,—"gone to work in Nashville; he and his father could n't agree."

Little Doc, the boy born since the time of my school, took me horseback down the creek next morning toward Farmer Dowell's. The road and the stream were battling for mastery, and the stream had the better of it. We splashed and waded, and the merry boy, perched behind me, chattered and laughed. He showed me where Simon Thompson had bought a bit of ground and a home; but his daughter Lana, a plump, brown, slow girl, was not there. She had married a man and a farm twenty miles away. We wound on down the stream till we came to a gate that I did not recognize, but the boy insisted that it was "Uncle Bird's." The farm was fat with the growing crop. In that little valley was a strange stillness as I rode up; for death and marriage had stolen youth, and left age and childhood there. We sat and talked that night after the chores were done. Uncle Bird was grayer, and his eyes did not see so well, but he was still jovial. We talked of the acres bought,—one hundred and twenty-five,—of the new guest-chamber added, of Martha's marrying. Then we talked of death: Fanny and Fred were gone; a shadow hung over the other daughter, and when it lifted she was to go to Nashville to school. At last we spoke of the neighbors, and as night fell Uncle Bird told me how, on a night like that, 'Thenie came wandering back to her home over yonder, to escape the blows of her husband. And next morning she died in the home that her little bow-legged brother, working and saving, had bought for their widowed mother.

My journey was done, and behind me lay hill and dale, and Life and Death. How shall man measure Progress there where the dark-faced Josie lies? How many heartfuls of sorrow shall balance a bushel of wheat? How hard a thing is life to the lowly, and yet how human and real! And all this life and love and strife and failure,—is it the twilight of nightfall or the flush of some faint-dawning day?

Thus sadly musing, I rode to Nashville in the Jim Crow car.

★

JOHN BRISBEN WALKER *Modern College Education:*
Does It Educate, in the Broadest and
Most Liberal Sense of the Term?
Cosmopolitan 22 (March 1897): 681–688

[Walker's invocation of Herbert Spencer, a controversial secularist and social Darwinist, signals engagement with one of the serious debates of the decade. Spencer's deterministic philosophy placed the individual at the mercy of society and the environment, a creature not responsible for his actions, a theory strenuously resisted by William James, who posited free will and moral agency. By aligning himself with Spencer, Walker endorses Spencer's argument for a practical, professional education instead of traditional, classical training. Though today's readers might think *Cosmopolitan* to be an unlikely place for such a serious article, that magazine in the 1890s, reaching an audience of 300,000, had departments covering socioeconomic, American, and international political issues as well as education, transportation, and science.]

THE PURSUIT OF ALL mankind is happiness. There is no other basis upon which any tenable theory of education for youth may be built, except that the training received tends, in the highest degree, toward those conditions of mind and body which will best serve to bring happiness to the individual educated and to those about him. That, at least, is the ideal toward which education must move with ever-quickening strides.

It is worth while, just at the close of the nineteenth century, to step aside from beaten paths and consider what may be worth the student's attention, as calculated to best fit him for his place in the world. The decided progress made within the quarter which closes the century has been due to criticism. Every general discussion of the utility of existing method has been followed by a progressive movement. Every college course, as it differs to-day from those of the English universities of the sixteenth century, marks a contest made by some independent mind against that conservatism which takes deepest root within cloistral walls. It is with this thought in mind that the editor of the COSMOPOLITAN has undertaken to present a series of articles upon the value and defects of the education in vogue at our great universities. Certainly, discussion can do no harm and it ought to be productive of wide benefit.

With a view to arranging the proposed series upon the broadest lines, visits were made to Yale, the Johns Hopkins, Harvard and other leading institutions for mental and physical training. President Eliot, of Harvard, President Dwight, of Yale, and President Gilman, of the Johns Hopkins, and many noted professors were among the number who gave up their valuable time to a consideration of the lines upon which such a discussion might be arranged. Alert in behalf of progress, they were free to recognize the necessity of moving beyond existing excellence, while the weaknesses of the average college curriculum were discussed with as little of prejudice as might be. One distinguished gentleman, whose name stands for the most advanced thought upon educational matters, said with entire frankness, "Unquestionably our system is bad. With us, it is not the question of the ideal, but of making headway, not only against tradition, but against the men who are steeped in tradition."

Proceeding upon the hypothesis that all education is intended to bring man or woman into a condition of mind and body best calculated to produce happiness, the papers which will follow in succeeding numbers of THE COSMOPOLITAN are in reply to this question: "Does the college education of the present day do all that it might to fit men or women for every day life and the achievement of the greatest good?"

If a commission made up of men, from all classes of useful work, were to be brought together to formulate that scheme of education best calculated to meet the requirements of every-day life, as it will be at the beginning of the twentieth century, they would probably begin the work by tabulating the various branches of knowledge, putting first that which seems most essential, and next that which comes second in value.

I have tried to imagine myself a member of such a commission. It would be necessary, in the beginning, for each to submit his own ideas, however crude. The tables presented by the individual members would form a basis for discussion; and from the careful comparison of these plans would ultimately be worked out the report of the commission. I do not hesitate, therefore, to present as a nucleus the following:

SCHEME OF EDUCATION: divided into nine groups, in order of relative importance.

FIRST GROUP—WISDOM

ETHICS: General principles of the professions: A complete course of lectures by experienced men, both in favor of and against each profession, in order that there may be set forth for them all the advantages, drawbacks, temptations and opportunities, to the end that each man may select his profession knowingly.

LOVE: Practical lessons taught by: study of weak and strong characters; ambitious men; useful men; lives of wise and unwise men of modern times analyzed; study of novels conveying lessons.

Relations of the sexes: what attraction means; selecting a wife; courtship; conditions of married happiness.

Relations with fellow-men: good feeling necessary to place in society; organized bodies, as trades' unions; business relations.

BUSINESS PRINCIPLES: Difference between right and wrong trading— What constitutes legitimate business in: law, mercantile pursuits, journalism, manufacturing, transportation.

SECOND GROUP—LIFE

PHYSIOLOGY: animal; vegetable

PHENOMENA OF THE MIND: general principles of, as applied to everyday life; recognition of inherited tendencies; control over self; cultivation of temper; just estimates of own abilities.

SCIENCE OF HEALTH: prevention of disease; treatment of disease; exercise, compulsory; athletics, wise and unwise; food.

THIRD GROUP—SCIENCE

MATHEMATICS; MECHANICS; CHEMISTRY

FOURTH GROUP—LANGUAGES

1st. ENGLISH: complete course in English literature, embracing a full knowledge, not only of the classics, but of best authors of the day; style— a course beginning with letter writing and extending to thorough practice in all forms of writing likely to be useful. 2d. French: sufficiently thorough to open up the literature of the language. 3d. German: sufficiently thorough to open up the literature of the language. 4th. Dead Languages: going beyond the rudimentary only in the case of students whose abilities enable them to carry Greek and Latin in addition to thoroughly mastering the more important French and German.

FIFTH GROUP—ACCOMPLISHMENTS

1st. Voice culture; 2d. conversation; 3d. charm of manner; 4th. memory culture; 5th. how to walk.

SIXTH GROUP—BUSINESS PREPARATION

1st. study of general principles and best examples of: manufacturing, government, transportation, store-keeping, newspapers; 2d. the keeping of accounts; 3rd. the filing of papers; 4th. general ideas of legal responsibility.

SEVENTH GROUP—CITIZENSHIP

1st. duties of a citizen of a republic; 2d. practical exercises of citizenship; 3d. dependence of citizen upon good government; 4th. studies of other forms of government; 5th. history; 6th. political geography.

1st. general knowledge of mechanical arts; 2d. the fine arts: drawing and music, rudimentary, except when talent is shown.

Ninth Group—Manual Training: Useful forms of.

It is the theory of the existing system of education that the most important knowledge required for a man's life will come to him after graduation if he has had at school a sufficiently vigorous training in Greek. But it must be confessed that observation of life does not confirm this theory. A young man goes out from college well fitted to reason about many intricate problems; but, as a rule, it would have been of greater value to him to have had those problems stated to him while in college.

There are some things that a young man is liable to do shortly after graduation. One is to choose a profession, and the other is to choose a wife. Either of these things, done with imperfect knowledge, is sufficient to wreck his life.

Take for instance the selection of a profession. Upon a wise choice depends not only agreeable duty but the measure of success. It is quite true that, at the present time, there is no course in any of the leading colleges which in any adequate way provides for the young man's proper equipment in this direction. On the contrary, he, as a rule, permits his fancy to run wild regarding his proper sphere in life. He "takes a fancy" to be a lawyer. He had an uncle whom he greatly admired; he was a lawyer. He "feels it in his bones," as one young man said to me at the Johns Hopkins, that he should be a doctor. Or perhaps he thinks it an easy sort of a profession where, scientific progress after graduation is not too closely inquired into. Or perhaps the good mother has an ambition that her son should be a clergyman.

Apologists for the failure to instruct the youth in that which so vitally concerns his future happiness will say that the undergraduate has many opportunities for acquiring information regarding the professions, and that after leaving the college he may give himself up to exhaustive inquiry. But we must take the average experience as our guide. The graduate does not go systematically to work to post himself regarding the professions, and in nine cases out of ten he selects his life work as most men select a house and lot, because it is the best of which he happens to know.

As a rule, he has only the opportunities which special prejudice may afford and no more. His mind is determined by hearing one-sided pleas, so that long before graduation a decision is made which but too often is freighted with the direst consequences.

Knowing that during college term the average youth selects his career and that upon a wise choice depends the after-life of the man, it would seem that too much time could scarcely be given to this most important matter. Should he not be compelled to hear lectures by at least two fair minded men upon each of the professions and upon the various kinds of business life—one arguing in favor of and the other against—so that all sides shall be presented? It will not do to say that there is not time in a four-years' course for such work. Time must be found by throwing overboard other studies. The educational motto for the twentieth century must be

TIME FOR THE MOST IMPORTANT STUDIES:
OMIT THE LEAST IMPORTANT.

What is being done in our colleges to-day to form the young man's ideals of character? "Plutarch's Lives" is about as near as we come to a course of training along practical lines. But the glimpses we catch of human nature in these long-distance sketches are as little available for forming a modern life as may be. We have, in the history of our own times, material that is so rich in moral, that it will serve as a guide for the dullest intellect. What is failure in its truest aspect? What is the success that is failure, in spite of millions gained? This is the knowledge that can be used, as a guiding oar, when in the whirlpool of real life the frail boat on which we are embarked is roughly tossed over foaming waters.

Besides the choice of profession, which a young man makes immediately upon leaving college, there is that other choice which is but too often made with equal haste, and which exercises an even greater influence upon his future happiness. The partnership of matrimony carries with it possibilities of life-long happiness, or the opportunities of a hell upon earth. Largely, it is a question of temperament, of previous environment and of inherited tendencies. Beyond these things must be taken into consideration certain physical and psychical phenomena. I do not mean, of course, that any lectures, however wise, will enable a man to exercise dispassionate reason in choosing a wife. But I have no question that they would so far guide him that the present large percentage of unhappy marriages would be materially decreased.

A striking commentary of the methods in vogue was afforded recently by the experiences of a young man who, presumably, had the advantages of all that the existing system could accomplish. The son of a man many times a millionaire, he was sent to one of the leading universities, after a careful preparation under the best auspices. Probably a total of twelve or fourteen years was consumed in school and college education. Nothing that money could secure was omitted. The father's guardianship was careful and wise so that neither extravagance nor idleness interfered with securing the best results.

Finally the youth received his degree and was dispatched into the world to perform the duties of a station important by reason of the large fortune at his command. Thrown into general society he found himself amply supplied with knowledge of Greek and Latin tongues, which is, in its way, an equipment betokening much admirable training. But in those large problems of life which were to concern his immediate future, he was a mere child. There had been no course at college which gave even the most inadequate idea of the strange phenomena which are constantly being produced in the human heart. Courtship, the affect of inherited tendencies upon character, the qualities calculated to produce happy marital union, the simplest laws of psychology—all these things were as if written in an unknown tongue.

His education has been conducted upon the theory that all this would come in that post-graduate course which is popularly described as "having one's eye teeth cut." But very often it happens that serious steps are taken before there is time for post-graduate study of this description. And so it happened in this case. A marriage was contracted under conditions calculated to almost certainly bring about disaster in the one affair most important of all to human happiness. Yet a dozen carefully prepared lectures by a fairly wise man would have given such an insight into the affairs of the existence of men and women that a blunder of this description would have been an improbability.

The relations of father and son came into the discussion prior to the marriage. Uneducated regarding the duties which a grateful son owes to parents who have sacrificed much for his sake, there was developed a friction which brought misery to the father sufficient to destroy health and bring him to death's door.

Then came another development. The course at college which taught the science of health, enforced by physical training, had been crude and insufficient. His knowledge of methods of bodily preservation was too slight and imperfect to enable him to meet the extraordinary demands made by serious troubles of the mind. Of what avail was the mental training which had been so long pursued in order that his faculties might be developed, if those faculties were paralyzed by ignorance of the most essential data regarding the common thing, of everyday life?

In the course of time the young man would undoubtedly have acquired this knowledge. But unfortunately for the practical outcome, it was the equipment which, as it happened, was needed above all others, immediately after his departure from college. Perhaps it is too strong to say that the failure to provide such equipment is almost as if a recruit were to be sent into battle, minus sword or gun, with the idea that he could best learn the use of arms by seeing how his enemies managed them.

The reply to the criticism here made is, as I am well aware, that the imparting of such knowledge belongs to the parent and that the father and mother should see to it. But unfortunately fathers and mothers are, ordinarily, not trained teachers. They are commonly incapable of giving such instruction and even those who are capable, ordinarily neglect their duties in this respect.

My examination of the methods in vogue in educational institutions has brought me to the belief that the most lamentable gaps in existing systems arise from this false hypothesis, that somewhere in previous or in subsequent conditions, important omissions have been, or will be in due time, made good. The actual facts should be confronted fairly and squarely, and college education should be provided upon a basis of, not what ought to have been taught, but what has been taught, in the case of the average young man; and not what the graduate may with effort acquire in the world, but what he actually needs for the immediate battle of life, and yet, in the majority of instances, only obtains when too old to avail himself of.

Let me give an instance of obscure and little valued accomplishment which, nevertheless, may be one of the most important factors in a successful career. Voice culture is so little esteemed that nowhere is it mentioned on the pages of any college curriculum. Yet you and I know that the average man of our acquaintance is handicapped by his voice. It rasps and distresses you. On the contrary, a soft, well-modulated, pleasing voice is almost a fortune to any man or woman. In a woman it is a constant charm. Given to a man, it opens an easy path to the esteem of his fellow men and makes the most difficult business negotiations simple. Time and again I have witnessed the spectacle—at a meeting of a board of directors, for instance—of the man of soft and pleasing voice prevailing over his neighbor of higher intellectual parts. Who ever heard of either school or college training commensurate with the practical importance of this matter? The college course is founded upon the supposition that the student has had his voice trained in the preparatory school, and the preparatory school course is based upon the idea that the parents have attended to it; or, at most, the voice is subjected to some trivial or even ridiculous exercises. Yet half an hour a day, from earliest childhood to senior graduation, would not be incommensurate with the part which such training would have upon the happiness of after living.

In the arrangement of the table here given it will be observed that it is intended to cover both school and college work and that the groups are arranged in the order of relative importance. It does not follow that the last group may not be the first to be taken up by the youth. But the intention is that the arrangement shall cover all that is most important in a liberal education. Having distinctly in mind what constitutes such an education, it is possible to calculate the number of hours available, and the average capacity; and then assign studies solely with reference to that which may be accomplished in the allotted time, keeping the most important groups constantly in mind as the necessities of education, and giving only so much of the least important as the time at disposal will permit.

In apology for the grouping, it may be argued that life itself is of little value without wisdom; but that having wisdom, the next step is to preserve life. The college courses make rather a pretense of teaching the important facts connected with the preservation of life, than practical accomplishment. The supposition is rather on this order—that doctors are graduated in order to fight disease.

But the man who must depend upon the advice of his physician to teach him the leading facts regarding the preservation of his body, is one likely to have had his constitution seriously impaired before he reaches the doctor's care.

Physical exercise is just as much required for the senior as for the freshman; and, above all things, the weakly of body should be required to build themselves up into health. President Eliot, of Harvard, was kind enough to take me to his splendidly equipped gymnasium to prove to me the excellence of the physical training. I spent half an hour under this distinguished guidance in admiring the system and the facilities for training. But the young men present numbered but a few hundred, and nine-tenths of them were athletes of splendid physical proportions and already developed muscles. As we walked back to the President's offices we met dozens of young men hurrying back to their rooms, who were not well developed and who looked pale and sickly. These were the men who should have been in the gymnasium. But they were not athletes and took no pleasure in measuring their hollow chests and puny arms alongside their more favored brothers. Therefore I make the argument that daily physical training must be a compulsory feature of college life; otherwise those who stand most in need of its benefits will not be reached. Against the few hundred athletes at work in the Harvard gymnasium there were nearly three thousand absent ones whose physical training was of the slightest, because such training is optional.

Besides exercise of the muscles, there is much that can be taught to a young man or woman that will count for his or her happiness and the pleasure of those about them. Health may be preserved and the advances of disease repelled by following the simplest rules. The average men and women have never had such instruction as would enable them to check the first indications of approaching illness. Usually, when the doctor arrives, the symptoms which could have been easily eradicated at the earliest stages, have become serious. How to breathe seems a matter that requires no teaching: yet not one person in a thousand understands this first mechanical effort of the body. And not one man or woman in five hundred knows how to walk.

Our own prosperity and our children's children's happiness depends upon an intelligent exercise of citizenship. A republic composed of unreasoning men and women must fall. A republic guided by persons of high intelligence will not only reward its citizens, but stand out as a guide to distressed peoples. What more important, then, than that the college graduate should carry into the world a thorough understanding of his government and of the practical duties of citizenship?

Thirty-seven years ago Herbert Spencer wrote his arraignment of the educational system of the day. At the close of the century, we find that his seemingly unanswerable logic has produced but little effect upon those whom it was intended to influence. Is it not more than strange that while Spencer's psychological, sociological and biological work should have been received with such profound respect in the universities of the world, his theory of education should have been treated with such marked contempt?

Are we, after all, but little more than the Orinoco savage whom he describes as appearing in public unclothed without embarrassment, but deeply respectful of the custom which requires the body to lie gaudily decorated with paint of many hues?

Speaking of the condition of education in his chapter on "What Knowledge is of the Most Worth?" Spencer wrote: "Among mental as among bodily acquisitions, the ornamental comes before the useful. Not only in times past, but almost as much in our own era, that knowledge which conduces to personal well-being has been postponed to that which brings applause. In the Greek schools, music, poetry, rhetoric and a philosophy, which, until Socrates taught, had but little bearing upon action, were the dominant subjects; while knowledge aiding the arts of life had a very subordinate place. And in our own universities and schools at the present moment the like antithesis holds. We are guilty of something like a platitude when we say that throughout his after-career a boy, in nine cases out of ten, applies his Latin and Greek to no practical purposes. The remark is trite that in his shop, or his office, in managing his estate or his family, in playing his part as director of a bank or a railway, he is very little aided by this knowledge he took so many years to acquire—so little, that generally the greater part of it drops out of his memory; and if he occasionally vents a Latin quotation, or alludes to some Greek myth, it is less to throw light on the topic in hand than for the sake of effect. If we inquire what is the real motive for giving boys a classical education, we find it is simply in conformity to public opinion. Men dress their children's minds as they do their bodies, in the prevailing fashion. As the Orinoco Indian puts on his paint before leaving his hut, not with a view to any direct benefit, but because he would be ashamed to be seen without it; so, a boy's drilling in Latin and Greek is insisted on, not because of their intrinsic value, but that he may not be disgraced by being found ignorant of them— that he may have "the education of a gentleman"—the badge marking a certain social position, and bringing a consequent respect."

*　　*　　*

"And that it is which determines the character of our education. Not what knowledge is of the most real worth, is the consideration; but what will bring most applause, honor, respect—what will most conduce to social position and influence—what will be most imposing. As throughout life, not what we are, but what we shall be thought is the question, so in education, the question is, not the intrinsic value of knowledge, so much as intrinsic effects on others. And this being our dominant idea, direct utility is scarcely more regarded than by the barbarian when filing his teeth and staining his nails."

* * *

"Men read books on this topic, and attend lectures on that; decide that their children shall be instructed in these branches of knowledge, and shall not be instructed in those; and all under the guidance of mere custom, or liking, or prejudice; without even considering the enormous importance of determining in some rational way what things are really most worth learning. It is true that in all circles we have occasional remarks on the importance of this or the other order of information. But whether the degree of its importance justifies the expenditure of the time needed to acquire it; and whether there are not things of more importance to which the time might be better devoted; are queries which, if raised at all, are disposed of quite summarily, according to personal predilections."

* * *

"Had we time to master all subjects we need not be particular. To quote the old song:

> 'Could a man be secure
> That his days would endure
> As of old, for a thousand long years,
> What things might he know!
> What deeds might he do!
> And all without hurry or care.'

"But we who have but 'span-long lives' must ever bear in mind our limited time for acquisition. And remembering how narrowly this time is limited, not only by the shortness of life, but also still more by the business of life, we ought to be especially solicitous to employ what time we have to the greatest advantage. Before devoting years to some subject which fashion or fancy suggests, it is surely wise to weigh with great care the worth of the results, as compared with the worth of various alternative results which the same years might bring if otherwise employed."

* * *

"In education, then, this is the question of questions, which it is high time we discussed in some methodic way. The first in importance, though the last to be considered, is the problem—how to decide among the conflicting claims of various subjects on our attention. *Before there can be a rational curriculum, we must settle which things it most concerns us to know; or, to use a word of Bacon's, now unfortunately obsolete—we must determine the relative values of knowledges."*

*   *   *

"How to live?—that is the essential question for us. Not how to live in the mere material sense only, but in the widest sense. The general problem which comprehends every special problem is—the right ruling of conduct in all directions under all circumstances. In what way to treat the body; in what way to treat the mind; in what way to manage our affairs; in what way to bring up a family; in what way to behave as a citizen; in what way to utilize all those sources of happiness which nature supplies—how to use all our faculties to the greatest advantage of ourselves and others—how to live completely. And this, being the great thing needful for us to learn, is, by consequence, the great thing which education has to teach. To prepare us for complete living is the function which education has to discharge; and the only rational mode of judging of any educational course is, to judge in what degree it discharges such function."

Is Spencer as clear a thinker on the subject of education as upon other matters, wherein his philosophy carries weight? Then why for nearly forty years should his words be brushed aside as of no moment? Or is it possible that there are those who think that the educational system of to-day conforms in any degree to Spencer's philosophy?

But enough has been said in the way of criticism to introduce the more serious discussion which will follow in subsequent numbers of THE COSMO-POLITAN from the pens of men better able to view the problems involved, from the standpoint of practical experience. As was said in the beginning, the closing hours of the nineteenth century is an appropriate time to look back upon the progress of a hundred years and ask ourselves:

Is this education the best we can offer to the youth of the twentieth century?

★

ANNIE PAYSON CALL *The Greatest Need of College Girls*
Atlantic Monthly 69 (January 1892): 102–109

[Focusing on the educational discrepancies facing "boys" and "girls," or unmarried young people, Call advocates the benefits of "physical culture" for college girls, arguing for "muscular training" and asserting the therapeutic value of exercise. Physical culture is presented as a means of alleviating tension and achieving the appearance of controlled ease expected of a social woman.]

The colleges for women in America have not as a rule been developed from lower forms of boarding-schools; they have been copies of the colleges for men. The demand for the higher education of women has been in part the result of dissatisfaction with the existing finishing-schools, so called; in part the result of an attempt to diminish the inequalities of condition between men and women. The chances for men in the intellectual sphere were seen to be vastly superior to those for women, and in a country where public education of the lower grades was free and equal for girls and boys, it was inevitable that a state of affairs could not be permanent which saw the academy doors close behind both boys and girls, and the college doors open only to boys.

In the experiments which have been made to satisfy this demand for the higher education of women, there have been and still are three general forms: the college in which the two sexes meet on equal terms, the annex in which the appliances of an existing college are used for a coordinate institution, and the college exclusively for women. In studying the essential conditions of collegiate life for women it is best to take this last form, since it permits the freest development, and offers the most open field for observation and experiment.

The college for women, then, in America has naturally been modeled as closely as possible upon the lines of existing colleges for men. It is the ambition of Vassar, of Smith, of Wellesley, to give as thorough an education to young women as the colleges whose curricula they substantially adopt give to young men. They would efface all intellectual distinctions of sex. In one particular only is there an obvious discrimination. The part which athletics plays in college life for men has no answering equivalent in college life for women. No one who has watched the gymnasium and the field in the one case would contend that there is a corresponding condition in the other. It is true that in well-equipped colleges for women the gymnasium is found, and that the higher forms of outdoor athletics are practiced; but it by no means follows that the difference is one only of degree, that in the development of these colleges there will be an approximation to the physical culture which exists in the colleges which they copy. The boldest advocate of an intellectual parity which should discover no distinction between the sexes in the class room would shrink from demanding or expecting a physical parity in the gymnasium or on the field.

Now in the education of the man athletics represents, not physical development integrally, but physical development as related to intellectual, moral, and religious development. That is to say, physical culture is a means to an end, not an end in itself; and the perversion of this doctrine, apparent as it is in the case of individual men, does not impair the fundamental truth. It is the constant study of college authorities to regulate athletics just as they regulate courses of study with reference to the symmetrical and sane development of manhood, and the practical problem is in the repressing, not the encouragement, of athletic zeal.

How is it in colleges for women? The situation is almost reversed. The constant study of the authorities is, not to regulate, but to enforce physical culture; not to encourage, but to repress intellectual excitability. This broad distinction marks a radical difference between the sexes, and any consideration of the true development of colleges for women must take it into account. However closely these colleges may copy their models in matters of scholarship and discipline, they are bound to recognize the divergence of nature in this particular of physical culture. They cannot blindly follow the lead of colleges for men, and think they have gained their end when they have set up a gymnasium, made exercise compulsory, and provided for boating, tennis, and grace hoops.

The muscular training of men is a primal physical need. In the order of time, of scale, and of logic, it is first. The success with which it is accomplished determines in a very considerable degree the success to be attained in mental and moral development. This may be asserted of the college as a whole, though there are marked examples of intellectual success secured in the face of immense physical disabilities.

It does not require acute perception to find the greatest physical need among women in our schools and colleges. A collective need is most often an exaggeration of the average individual short-coming. No one who has been an inmate of a large college for women will deny the general state of rush and hurry which prevails there. "No time" is the cry from morning until night. Worry and hurry mark the average condition of the schoolgirl. If she is not hurried or worried herself, through the happy possession of a phlegmatic temperament, she cannot entirely resist the pressure about her. The spirit of the place is too strong for an individual to be in it and not of it. The strain is evident in the faces of students and teachers. It is evident in the number who annually break down from overstudy. More pitiably evident is it in those who have not wholly broken down, but are near enough the verge of disaster to have forgotten what a normal state of mind and body is. We can only think, in the presence of such an one, what a magnificent specimen of womanhood that might have been, with a constitution that holds its own through such daily strain, and does not give in completely. This greatest physical need among studious women is so evident that those who will can see it. Those who will not see it are living in so abnormal a state themselves that they do not recognize the want because of their own necessity. Men and women can breathe bad air and not know it, but one coming directly from out-of-doors will be sickened at once.

To see the strain at its height, it must be watched during examinations. The average schoolgirl—or schoolwoman—would not feel that she had taken her examination properly unless she had taken it in a condition of worry, hurry, fright, and general excitement. Mark the contrast in this respect between colleges for men and those for women. Students in the former are not without their share of nervous strain, especially in examinations, but the strain is noticeably far less than among the women. The explanation of the difference is commonly found to lie in the physical exercise taken in football, rowing, and other out-of-door sports, which give men new life for study and restore the balance of the nervous system. But if girls should try this corrective to the same extent, they would devote such intense nervous energy to play, they would have so little real abandon, that the result would be in most cases a nervous strain and excitement, from which they must in turn recover before going on with study. The balance is to be restored by some other means.

Let us look a little deeper into the temperamental reason for this strain. A woman's self-consciousness is her greatest enemy. Custom is partly to blame for this, because it is so generally felt that man is to admire, and woman to be admired. Thus a woman is born into and inherits a "to-be-admired" state of mind, and her freedom is delayed in proportion. Few realize the absolute nervous strain in self-consciousness; and if to self-consciousness we add a sensitive conscience, we have come near to a full explanation. Mr. Howells perhaps exaggerates when he tells us that a New England woman is not strong intellectually, but she has a conscience like the side of a house. He might be truthful and give her a larger allowance of brains, but he could not rightly reduce the dimensions of the conscience. Men have not so great a strain in self-consciousness, and the tyranny of a morbid conscience is less real to them. In the atmosphere of men's colleges, either among the faculty or the students, there is not a tenth part of the unnecessary excitement that we find in women's colleges. The faces of the students tell their own story. Nervous strain is far less evident.

Another contrast will help toward an understanding of the terms of the problem. English women are showing a marked superiority over American women in the college career. They are taking prizes and attaining marked intellectual distinction, not because their scholastic advantages are greater nor because of superior intellectual gifts, but because of better physique, more normal nervous systems, and consequently greater power of endurance.

These contrasts emphasize the proposition which I maintain, namely, that the first, the greatest physical need for women is a training to rest: not rest in the sense of doing nothing, not repose in the sense of inanity or inactivity, but a restful activity of mind and body, which means a vigorous, wholesome nervous system that will enable a woman to abandon herself to her study, her work, and her play with a freedom and ease which are too fast becoming, not a lost art, but lost nature. We have jumped at the conclusion that the style of training which is admirably suited to men must be equally adapted to women. However that may be in the future, there is a prior necessity with women. After their greatest physical need is supplied, they may—will, probably—reach the place where their power will be increased through vigorous exercise.

It is evident that the gymnasiums and various exercises established in schools and colleges for women have done little or nothing toward supplying this greatest need. The girls are always defeating the end of the exercise: first, by entering into every motion of the exercise itself with too much nervous strain; second, by following in their manner of study, in their general attitude of mind and habit of body, ways that must effectually tell against the physical power which might be developed by the exercise. Truly the first necessity now is to teach a girl to approach her work, physical or mental, in a normal, healthy way,—to accomplish what she has to do naturally, using only the force required to gain her point; not worrying all the time she studies for fear the lesson will not be learned; not feeling rushed from morning to night for fear her work will not be done; not going about with a burden of unnecessary anxiety, a morbid fear of her teachers, and a general attitude toward life which means strain, and constant strain. A glance forward intensifies the gravity of the case. Such habits once developed in a girl who is fitting herself to teach are strongly felt by her pupils when she takes the position of teacher. The nervous strain is reflected back and forth from teacher to pupil, and is thus forcing itself upon the notice of others, and proving day by day more clearly what is the greatest physical need.

Those who have observed this tendency are wont to say, "Give the girls plenty of exercise, plenty of fresh air, see that they sleep and eat well, and this greatest need will be supplied without thought." If the unhealthy condition we have noted were just making its appearance, the remedy would be sufficient. As it is, such a remedy suffices in a few cases, in most cases partially, but in some not at all. The habit has stood now through too many generations to be overcome without a distinct recognition of the loss of power, and a strong realization of the need of regaining this power. Indeed, so great a hold on the community has this want of quiet and easy activity in study and in play that it is not rare to find young girls who believe the abnormal to be the natural life, and the other unnatural. As one girl told me once in perfect good faith, "I keep well on excitement, but it tires me *terribly* to carry a pitcher of water upstairs." This I know is an extreme instance, and yet not so uncommon as I wish it were. To swing such a girl, or one approaching so abnormal a state, suddenly back into the normal would be most disastrous; she would not recognize the world or herself, and would really suffer intensely. She must be carried step by step. To restore her is like curing a drunkard.

Let us suppose a school started in the United States having in its scheme a distinct intention of eliminating all hurry and worry, and training girls to a normal state of active repose. Suppose that to be the main idea of the school. To get rid of the "no time" fever, the teachers would need to accept the fundamental principle that it is not the acquisition of knowledge, but the training of power to think, which is the justification of school or college. A girl can at most gain in her school life but an iota of the knowledge which is possible to her, but she can attain the power of acquiring knowledge; and if this end is kept in view on the part both of teachers and pupils, more regard will be paid to the order of studies and the method in each than to the quantity of facts gathered in any one study. With a subordination of the desire to amass knowledge, every course of study followed will help other courses taken at the same time, and others to come, and make it comparatively easy for the student to acquire more after the school years are over. A mind truly trained attracts and absorbs unconsciously, it digests and it produces, and the way is never stopped with useless facts. As the unity of intellectual work is recognized, the greatest physical need will be more readily met; for by an insistence upon that which is of first importance intellectually the cry of "no time" will subside. When a girl feels rushed she begins to lose mental power in proportion, however well she may seem to work at any one time.

This is the first change which our model school would effect, and its next most important reform would be so to arrange the daily work that there would be a marked rhythm in the alternation of studies. A body and mind, to be wholesome, must be trained to action and reaction, not action and inaction. There is often the most perfect rest in freeing one set of faculties entirely and working another. Indeed, action and reaction is the order of being, for in sleep, the most entire rest, the body is busy receiving supplies for near activity when it shall awake. There must be vigorous exercises, plenty of food carefully chosen, long sleeping times; a friendly attitude and perfect confidence between students and teachers must be cultivated, but without emotionalizing. Now, supposing so wholesome a state of things to be organized, the end is not yet. The hurry and worry will creep in and will be strongly felt, because of the girls' mothers and grandmothers and great-grandmothers, not to mention the inheritance which often comes from the paternal ancestry. There still remains for our school a distinct power to cultivate, a power to be gained through repose; not a forced, a studied, or a flabby repose, but a natural repose which is self-forgetful, and often delightfully active. "Freedom" is a better word than "repose." Freedom includes repose; and for freedom, physical and mental, women should have special training now. If special training to that end is needed in our imaginary school, established with that purpose in view and with the spirit of true freedom animating its entire faculty, it certainly is sadly needed in the schools and colleges where power through repose is often as fatally lacking in teachers as in the girls under their charge.

The work must begin with physical training, including a training of the voice. If the course be followed carefully, it will soon affect the mental work, and special exercises to help the activity of mind will follow. But let us lay the foundation first, stand the girls on their feet, and demonstrate that a perfect physical balance means a better working head. As the physical work progresses, every lesson may contain the application of true freedom to study and recitation. Thus the mental and physical will each help the other, and the whole woman will feel that she is dropping chains. A freedom from the limitations of self will lead to a freedom from self-consciousness, which is possible only to a wholesome nervous system. A woman so trained will be beyond the apparent necessity of controlling herself, for she will have learned how to let nature control her.

I cannot content myself with a general assertion of the need of this training. I must attempt an outline, at least, of what it might be. Let us follow an imaginary class in physical training, the more truly to gain an idea of the practical working of our principle. All through the class work deep breathing should be practiced, not only for its quieting and restful effect, but for the new vigor that comes with it, and the steady, even development which deep breathing so greatly assists. The deep breathing also prevents an extreme relaxation, which is as harmful as extreme tension, and prevents too quick a reactionary effect when a tense body is at once relaxed. In beginning with the deep breaths, it will be found that few members of a large class can take a deep breath at all, and not one has an idea of what it is to breathe quietly. The soothing effect of a long quiet breath is never realized until one has been trained to inhale and exhale with the least possible effort. Even before this power has been gained, regular breathing will quiet a mild case of hysteria, as it will do away with stage fright. Members of the class must, to some degree, be trained separately for the deep breaths, in order that it be made clear to each what a deep quiet breath is; what it is to feel as if the breath took her, and not as if she took the breath. It is also requisite to avoid the curious strain which one often experiences under the impression that by holding herself as if in a vise while she inhales she is taking a quiet breath.

Quiet should be the first aim, in this class for physical culture,—a natural quiet, not a forced quiet. This can be gained collectively to a delightful degree, for one mind acts upon another, and, in a large class, the weaker brains feel the influence of the stronger. Each member of the class having a general idea of a deep breath, the quiet should be gained through the breathing exercises, which cannot be given here. Suffice it to say, the teacher should have always in mind, from the first, natural quiet as an end, and lead to that through long regular breaths—rhythmic breaths from twenty-five to fifty—and other forums of exercise. The result of this training is strongly apparent in a single person and still more when a class works together. The action upon the brain of deep breathing is well known. It is not only deep breathing, but deep breathing with the least possible effort, that does the good work. The class should take slow, regular exercises for the relaxation of the muscles and further quieting of the nerves, interspersed always with deep breathing. After the special deep-breathing and the relaxing exercises, the voice training should begin and continue as a part of the regular work. A want of natural equilibrium tells more in the sound of the voice and manner of speaking than in any other one physical action; and a woman should be trained to the true freedom of her voice with the rest of her body.

The exercises for suppleness of the joints and muscles would come next; these should include the direction of force, and often be very rapid, but must increase in rapidity only as they can be taken with perfect ease. The exercises must be taken with only the part of the body meant to be used, allowing no superficial "sympathy" in any other part. Then should follow motions for finer balance and for spring; and the class work might end with the quiet breathing and voice training. This course should be taken gradually, so that a clear idea of what they are aiming at will dawn upon the girls without too much hard thinking. Although the teacher must never once lose her central aim, it is better for the girls to follow the exercises more or less automatically. If they fail to come out of such a class not only with new vigor, but with a clearer idea each day of how to let nature's laws work through them in study and in play, such failure will show a want of the true spirit in the teacher who leads them; or it may be that the air of the room has not been fit for breathing. Two elements are necessary in the teacher of such a class: that she should have the daily habit of obeying the laws she teaches; and that she should pretend in no way to stand as a perfect example of the laws, but should impress her pupils with the idea that they are all students together, and subject to the same laws. With this and a loving patience, a woman cannot fail to rouse other women to their best, unless her environment is entirely against her.

I have tried simply to follow the regular physical work in a class which trains a woman to vigor and restful activity through a process which trains her first to supply her greatest need, the power of rest. With this should come a training to meet sudden emergencies with a clear head; to drop the excitement of such emergencies when once the trouble is removed, and even before it has wholly disappeared; to have the power of ignoring nagging worries. Indeed, a great end is accomplished when a girl has acquired the ability to distinguish herself from her nervous system so far as to recognize when a worry is an effect of indigestion or some other physical derangement, and treat it as such; when she can bear it as a pain, if it must be, and will not increase it by admitting that it has any real foundation, and will drop it as soon as it can be dropped. Much useless suffering will be saved women who learn in school how to meet the various annoyances and cares that are sure to come in some form later. Many a woman is the slave of her nervous system because she does not know it; and a nervously magnified conscience will whip a woman into all sorts of absurd work which simply drains her beyond recovery, because she has not been taught how she may distinguish herself from a set of tired or disordered nerves. To all this may be added the help which will come from women to other women through realizing when they are not to be taken seriously, however it may be necessary to appear serious.

The popular mind seldom makes allowance for difference in temperament. Some time ago I watched two girls in a tennis match, one of whom was under the process of training to a better freedom; her movements were quick, graceful, and supple, but her excitable nervous system, inherited from intellectually active parents, still mastered her. Her expression was intense. Nearly all in the audience were her friends and admirers, eager to have her win. She was not only vividly alive to every personal wish for her, but acutely conscious of herself as the centre of attraction. The other player, the daughter of a country-man, was apparently stolid, with splendid muscular power. Her expression hardly changed. She did not know the audience nor realize their presence, apparently, although she must have been perfectly aware of their partiality for her opponent. She played directly, and her whole mind was upon every stroke of her racket. Of course she won the game. A bystander said to me, with a superior smile and not a little scorn, "You see this 'relaxing' does not always win." My answer was, "It certainly does. Your country girl was the more 'relaxed.'" The girl who lost had a most sensitive nervous organization, with a power far beyond the other, but one that must take longer to find its balance. The winner had her equilibrium on a much lower plane. Take Diana herself and put her in this country, surrounded with all its influences, and after five years she would lose the first tennis match against just such phlegmatic temperament. With equal scorn our critic might say, "You see, my friends, a goddess does not always win."

What then can we expect of our highly bred women who have generations of nervous strain back of them? Diana would win the second match, for she would at once see her mistake, and have her constitution to back her in correcting it. The compensation to the goddess would be great in an acute realization of what it is to allow a fine, wholesome nervous system to work according to its own laws. We need to train our girls first to the wholesomeness which must come through the power to rest, and then to the normal use of the real power as it grows upon them. They have much more to work against than Diana after her five years, and their appreciation would be keener in proportion.

In connection with the whole subject there is a fundamental principle to be carefully noted. To make the best of this training which is meant to help toward a natural way of doing whatever may be before us, the life itself must be regular and normal. It is a great mistake for a woman to train herself to do her work more easily in order to crowd more work or play into her life than she ought to carry. No woman has the natural spirit of repose who, finding she can attend to particulars with increasing facility, crowds her life in general. Much more can be accomplished, of course, by learning how to rest and how not to waste force; but that gives all the stronger reason for recognizing one's limitations and being guided by them. In the one way, the limitations decrease; in the other, they increase to a startling extent. People wonder that a training for rest should result in fatigue, without noting the fact that the training itself has been presumed upon. So must the whole spirit of our schools be changed if they are to educate women to absolutely wholesome bodies and the best possible use of their minds. A young man rising from a severe fit of illness was told by his physician that it was useless for him to try to get through college; he had not the strength for the continued work. He obtained the physician's consent to study two hours a day. By realizing the best use of those two hours, he passed through college, and graduated among the first of his class. But he rested entirely the remaining hours of the day. If, finding that he had gained such power of concentration, he had tried to use it every hour in the day without reaction, the result would have been disastrous.

This country seems now like a precocious child. Because it shows wonderful powers and intense activity, it is pushed to display itself more and more; and unless the child is quieted, and made to enjoy natural, childlike ways, there is danger that the man will fall far short of the brilliancy promised by the child. Surely the mothers of the country need the quiet most, and need it first.

In brief, in the men and women who are healthy workers and players there is a complete reaction from every action; they drop on the ground and give up to gravity when "time is called;" the others walk up and down, and worry over their past plays and wonder over those to come. These last can be led through physical training and moral suasion until they are in the same wholesome current. They can be, if they will be; if the training commences early enough, they must be. The greatest strength of a college will come when this active repose or restful activity can be so taken as a matter of course that it need never be thought of at all. Under these conditions men and women would be sensitive to the slightest disobedience of such natural laws and correct it at once, as they are now sensitive to more flagrant disobedience of other laws. Then would come a freedom of mind and body such as we see now only in the most healthy little children.

A woman's education should prepare her to hold to the best of her ability whatever position life may offer. A training to help her to a wholesome use of a normal nervous system must be the foundation upon which she stands if she would perform in the best way the work which lies before her. No womanly woman wants to be a very good man, but a very true woman, and as such she not only holds her own place firmly, but helps man to hold his. A man's life in the world is in this age full of temptation to nervous strain and worry. If he takes the overwrought state home only to find a similar state in his wife, increased by just so much as the natural intensity of the feminine nervous system exceeds that of the masculine, he does not go home to rest, but to more nervous strain; and the wearing effect upon one of the excited and tired nervous system of another who is nearly related is more fatiguing in a few hours than would be as many days of severe work.

In contrast to this place the ideal of repose that may be found in a woman, and the influence it may have upon a man, not only because of the restful atmosphere to which he returns, but the certainty throughout the day that there is the quiet strength at home, and that he will surely find it.

Because the nerves of the average woman are far more excitable than those of the average man, we could not only reach the man by means of the woman, but by training the mothers reach more surely the next generation, so that later this natural economy of our nervous force may come, in school and out as a matter of course. And where could we better begin the training than in our schools and colleges for women?

★

ZITKALA-ŠĂ *The School Days of an Indian Girl*
Atlantic Monthly 85 (February 1900): 185–194

[Zitkala-Šă, also known as Gertrude Bonnin, was born on the Pine Ridge Reservation to a Sioux mother and a white father and at eight was taken to a Quaker missionary school in Wabash, Indiana. Tormented by her estrangement from her mother and her heritage, she described the painful and permanently damaging process of cultural dislocation in three articles for the *Atlantic Monthly*, of which this is the first.]

I. THE LAND OF RED APPLES.

There were eight in our party of bronzed children who were going East with the missionaries. Among us were three young braves, two tall girls, and we three little ones, Judéwin, Thowin, and I.

We had been very impatient to start on our journey to the Red Apple Country, which, we were told, lay a little beyond the great circular horizon of the Western prairie. Under a sky of rosy apples we dreamt of roaming as freely and happily as we had chased the cloud shadows on the Dakota plains. We had anticipated much pleasure from a ride on the iron horse, but the throngs of staring palefaces disturbed and troubled us.

On the train, fair women, with tottering babies on each arm, stopped their haste and scrutinized the children of absent mothers. Large men, with heavy bundles in their hands, halted near by, and riveted their glassy blue eyes upon us.

I sank deep into the corner of my seat, for I resented being watched. Directly in front of me, children who were no larger than I hung themselves upon the backs of their seats, with their bold white faces toward me. Sometimes they took their forefingers out of their mouths and pointed at my moccasined feet. Their mothers, instead of reproving such rude curiosity, looked closely at me, and attracted their children's further notice to my blanket. This embarrassed me, and kept me constantly on the verge of tears.

I sat perfectly still, with my eyes downcast, daring only now and then to shoot long glances around me. Chancing to turn to the window at my side, I was quite breathless upon seeing one familiar object. It was the telegraph pole which strode by at short paces. Very near my mother's dwelling, along the edge of a road thickly bordered with wild sunflowers, some poles like these had been planted by white men. Often I had stopped, on my way down the road, to hold my ear against the pole, and, hearing its low moaning, I used to wonder what the paleface had done to hurt it. Now I sat watching for each pole that glided by to be the last one.

In this way I had forgotten my uncomfortable surroundings, when I heard one of my comrades call out my name. I saw the missionary standing very near, tossing candies and gums into our midst. This amused us all, and we tried to see who could catch the most of the sweetmeats. The missionary's generous distribution of candies was impressed upon my memory by a disastrous result which followed. I had caught more than my share of candies and gums, and soon after our arrival at the school I had a chance to disgrace myself, which, I am ashamed to say, I did.

Though we rode several days inside of the iron horse, I do not recall a single thing about our luncheons.

It was night when we reached the school grounds. The lights from the windows of the large buildings fell upon some of the icicled trees that stood beneath them. We were led toward an open door, where the brightness of the lights within flooded out over the heads of the excited palefaces who blocked the way. My body trembled more from fear than from the snow I trod upon.

Entering the house, I stood close against the wall. The strong glaring light in the large whitewashed room dazzled my eyes. The noisy hurrying of hard shoes upon a bare wooden floor increased the whirring in my ears. My only safety seemed to be in keeping next to the wall. As I was wondering in which direction to escape from all this confusion, two warm hands grasped me firmly, and in the same moment I was tossed high in midair. A rosy-checked paleface woman caught me in her arms. I was both frightened and insulted by such trifling. I stared into her eyes, wishing her to let me stand on my own feet, but she jumped me up and down with increasing enthusiasm. My mother had never made a plaything of her wee daughter. Remembering this I began to cry aloud.

They misunderstood the cause of my tears, and placed me at a white table loaded with food. There our party were united again. As I did not hush my crying, one of the older ones whispered to me, "Wait until you are alone in the night."

It was very little I could swallow besides my sobs, that evening.

"Oh, I want my mother and my brother Dawee! I want to go to my aunt!" I pleaded; but the ears of the palefaces could not hear me.

From the table we were taken along an upward incline of wooden boxes, which I learned afterward to call a stairway. At the top was a quiet hall, dimly lighted. Many narrow beds were in one straight line down the entire length of the wall. In them lay sleeping brown faces, which peeped just out of the coverings. I was tucked into bed with one of the tall girls, because she talked to me in my mother tongue and seemed to soothe me.

I had arrived in the wonderful land of rosy skies, but I was not happy, as I had thought I should be. My long travel and the bewildering sights had exhausted me. I fell asleep, heaving deep, tired sobs. My tears were left to dry themselves in streaks, because neither my aunt nor my mother was near to wipe them away.

II. THE CUTTING OF MY LONG HAIR.

The first day in the land of apples was a bitter-cold one; for the snow still covered the ground, and the trees were bare. A large bell rang for breakfast, its loud metallic voice crashing through the belfry overhead and into our sensitive ears. The annoying clatter of shoes on bare floors gave us no peace. The constant clash of harsh noises, with an undercurrent of many voices murmuring an unknown tongue, made a bedlam within which I was securely tied. And though my spirit tore itself in struggling for its lost freedom, all was useless.

A paleface woman, with white hair, came up after us. We were placed in a line of girls who were marching into the dining room. These were Indian girls, in stiff shoes and closely clinging dresses. The small girls wore sleeved aprons and shingled hair. As I walked noiselessly in my soft moccasins, I felt like sinking to the floor, for my blanket had been stripped from my shoulders. I looked hard at the Indian girls, who seemed not to care that they were even more immodestly dressed than I, in their tightly fitting clothes. While we marched in, the boys entered at an opposite door. I watched for the three young braves who came in our party. I spied them in the rear ranks, looking as uncomfortable as I felt.

A small bell was tapped, and each of the pupils drew a chair from under the table. Supposing this act meant they were to be seated, I pulled out mine and at once slipped into it from one side. But when I turned my head, I saw that I was the only one seated, and all the rest at our table remained standing. Just as I began to rise, looking shyly around to see how chairs were to be used, a second bell was sounded. All were seated at last, and I had to crawl back into my chair again. I heard a man's voice at one end of the hall, and I looked around to see him. But all the others hung their heads over their plates. As I glanced at the long chain of tables, I caught the eyes of a paleface woman upon me. Immediately I dropped my eyes, wondering why I was so keenly watched by the strange woman. The man ceased his mutterings, and then a third bell was tapped. Everyone picked up his knife and fork and began eating. I began crying instead, for by this time I was afraid to venture anything more.

But this eating by formula was not the hardest trial in that first day. Late in the morning, my friend Judéwin gave me a terrible warning. Judéwin knew a few words of English; and she had overheard the paleface woman talk about cutting our long, heavy hair. Our mothers had taught us that only unskilled warriors who were captured had their hair shingled by the enemy. Among our people, short hair was worn by mourners, and shingled hair by cowards!

We discussed our fate some moments, and when Judéwin said, "We have to submit, because they are strong," I rebelled.

"No, I will not submit! I will struggle first!" I answered.

I watched my chance, and when no one noticed I disappeared. I crept up the stairs as quietly as I could in my squeaking shoes,—my moccasins had been exchanged for shoes. Along the hall I passed, without knowing whither I was going. Turning aside to an open door, I found a large room with three white beds in it. The windows were covered with dark green curtains, which made the room very dim. Thankful that no one was there, I directed my steps toward the corner farthest from the door. On my hands and knees I crawled under the bed, and cuddled myself in the dark corner.

From my hiding place I peered out, shuddering with fear whenever I heard footsteps near by. Though in the hall loud voices were calling my name, and I knew that even Judéwin was searching for me, I did not open my mouth to answer. Then the steps were quickened and the voices became excited. The sounds came nearer and nearer. Women and girls entered the room. I held my breath, and watched them open closet doors and peep behind large trunks. Some one threw up the curtains, and the room was filled with sudden light. What caused them to stoop and look under the bed I do not know. I remember being dragged out, though I resisted by kicking and scratching wildly. In spite of myself, I was carried downstairs and tied fast in a chair.

I cried aloud, shaking my head all the while until I felt the cold blades of the scissors against my neck, and heard them gnaw off one of my thick braids. Then I lost my spirit. Since the day I was taken from my mother I had suffered extreme indignities. People had stared at me. I had been tossed about in the air like a wooden puppet. And now my long hair was shingled like a coward's! In my anguish I moaned for my mother, but no one came to comfort me. Not a soul reasoned quietly with me, as my own mother used to do; for now I was only one of many little animals driven by a herder.

III. THE SNOW EPISODE.

A short time after our arrival we three Dakotas were playing in the snow-drifts. We were all still deaf to the English language, excepting Judéwin, who always heard such puzzling things. One morning we learned through her ears that we were forbidden to fall length-wise in the snow, as we had been doing, to see our own impressions. However, before many hours we had forgotten the order, and were having great sport in the snow, when a shrill voice called us. Looking up, we saw an imperative hand beckoning us into the house. We shook the snow off ourselves, and started toward the woman as slowly as we dared.

Judéwin said: "Now the paleface is angry with us. She is going to punish us for falling into the snow. If she looks straight into your eyes and talks loudly, you must wait until she stops. Then, after a tiny pause, say, 'No.'" The rest of the way we practiced upon the little word "no."

As it happened, Thowin was summoned to judgment first. The door shut behind her with a click.

Judéwin and I stood silently listening at the keyhole. The paleface woman talked in very severe tones. Her words fell from her lips like crackling embers, and her inflection ran up like the small end of a switch. I understood her voice better than the things she was saying. I was certain we had made her very impatient with us. Judéwin heard enough of the words to realize all too late that she had taught us the wrong reply.

"Oh, poor Thowin!" she gasped, as she put both hands over her ears.

Just then I heard Thowin's tremulous answer, "No."

With an angry exclamation, the woman gave her a hard spanking. Then she stopped to say something. Judéwin said it was this: "Are you going to obey my word the next time?"

Thowin answered again with the only word at her command, "No."

This time the woman meant her blows to smart, for the poor frightened girl shrieked at the top of her voice. In the midst of the whipping the blows ceased abruptly, and the woman asked another question: "Are you going to fall in the snow again?"

Thowin gave her bad password another trial. We heard her say feebly, "No! No!"

With this the woman hid away her half-worn slipper, and led the child out, stroking her black shorn head. Perhaps it occurred to her that brute force is not the solution for such a problem. She did nothing to Judéwin nor to me. She only returned to us our unhappy comrade, and left us alone in the room.

During the first two or three seasons misunderstandings as ridiculous as this one of the snow episode frequently took place, bringing unjustifiable frights and punishments into our little lives.

Within a year I was able to express myself somewhat in broken English. As soon as I comprehended a part of what was said and done, a mischievous spirit of revenge possessed me. One day I was called in from my play for some misconduct. I had disregarded a rule which seemed to me very needlessly binding. I was sent into the kitchen to mash the turnips for dinner. It was noon, and steaming dishes were hastily carried into the dining room. I hated turnips, and their odor which came from the brown jar was offensive to me. With fire in my heart, I took the wooden tool that the paleface woman held out to me. I stood upon a step, and, grasping the handle with both hands, I bent in hot rage over the turnips. I worked my vengeance upon them. All were so busily occupied that no one noticed me. I saw that the turnips were in a pulp, and that further beating could not improve them; but the order was, "mash these turnips," and mash them I would! I renewed my energy; and as I sent the masher into the bottom of the jar, I felt a satisfying sensation that the weight of my body had gone into it.

Just here a paleface woman came up to my table. As she looked into the jar, she shoved my hands roughly aside. I stood fearless and angry. She placed her red hands upon the rim of the jar. Then she gave one lift and a stride away from the table. But lo! the pulpy contents fell through the crumbled bottom to the floor! She spared me no scolding phrases that I had earned. I did not heed them. I felt triumphant in my revenge, though deep within me, I was a wee bit sorry to have broken the jar.

As I sat eating my dinner, and saw that no turnips were served, I whooped in my heart for having once asserted the rebellion within me.

IV. THE DEVIL

Among the legends the old warriors used to tell me were many stories of evil spirits. But I was taught to fear them no more than those who stalked about in material guise. I never knew there was an insolent chieftain among the bad spirits, who dared to array his forces against the Great Spirit, until I heard this white man's legend from a paleface woman.

Out of a large book she showed me a picture of the white man's devil. I looked in horror upon the strong claws that grew out of his fur-covered fingers. His feet were like his hands. Trailing at his heels was a scaly tail tipped with a serpent's open jaws. His face was a patchwork: he had bearded cheeks, like some I had seen palefaces wear; his nose was an eagle's bill, and his sharp-pointed ears were pricked up like those of a sly fox. Above them a pair of cow's horns curved upward. I trembled with awe, and my heart throbbed in my throat, as I looked at the king of evil spirits. Then I heard the paleface woman say that this terrible creature roamed loose in the world, and that little girls who disobeyed school regulations were to be tortured by him.

That night I dreamt about this evil divinity. Once again I seemed to be in my mother's cottage. An Indian woman had come to visit my mother. On opposite sides of the kitchen stove, which stood in the centre of the small house, my mother and her guest were seated in straight-back chairs. I played with a train of empty spools hitched together on a string. It was night, and the wick burned feebly. Suddenly I heard some one turn our door-knob from without.

My mother and the woman hushed their talk, and both looked toward the door. It opened gradually. I waited behind the stove. The hinges squeaked as the door was slowly, very slowly pushed inward.

Then in rushed the devil! He was tall! He looked exactly like the pictures I had seen of him in the white man's papers. He did not speak to my mother, because he did not know the Indian language, but his glittering yellow eyes were fastened upon me. He took long strides around the stove, passing be-hind the woman's chair. I threw down my spools, and ran to my mother. He did not fear her, but followed closely after me. Then I ran round and round the stove, crying aloud for help. But my mother and the woman seemed not to know my danger. They sat still, looking quietly upon the devil's chase after me. At last I grew dizzy. My head revolved as on a hidden pivot. My knees became numb, and doubled under my weight like a pair of knife blades without a spring. Beside my mother's chair I fell in a heap. Just as the devil stooped over me with outstretched claws my mother awoke from her quiet indifference, and lifted me on her lap. Whereupon the devil vanished, and I was awake.

On the following morning I took my revenge upon the devil. Stealing into the room where a wall of shelves was filled with books, I drew forth The Stories of the Bible. With a broken slate pencil I carried in my apron pocket, I began scratching out his wicked eyes. A few moments later, when I was ready to leave the room, there was a ragged hole in the page where the picture of the devil had been.

V. IRON ROUTINE.

A loud-clamoring bell awakened us at half past six in the cold winter mornings. From happy dreams of Western rolling lands and unlassoed freedom we tumbled out upon chilly bare floors back again into a paleface day. We had short time to jump into our shoes and clothes, and wet our eyes with icy water, before a small hand bell was vigorously rung for roll call.

There were too many drowsy children and too numerous orders for the day to waste a moment in any apology to nature for giving her children such a shock in the early morning. We rushed down stairs, bounding over two high steps at a time, to land in the assembly room.

A paleface woman, with a yellow-covered roll book open on her arm and a gnawed pencil in her hand, appeared at the door. Her small, tired face was coldly lighted with a pair of large grey eyes.

She stood still in a halo of authority, while over the rim of her spectacles her eyes pried nervously about the room. Having glanced at her long list of names and called out the first one, she tossed up her chin and peered through the crystals of her spectacles to make sure of the answer "Here."

Relentlessly her pencil black-marked our daily records if we were not present to respond to our names, and no chum of ours had done it successfully for us. No matter if a dull headache or the painful cough of slow consumption had delayed the absentee, there was only time enough to mark the tardiness. It was next to impossible to leave the iron routine after the civilizing machine had once begun its day's buzzing; and as it was inbred in me to suffer in silence rather than to appeal to the ears of one whose open eyes could not see my pain, I have many times trudged in the day's harness heavy-footed, like a dumb sick brute.

Once I lost a dear classmate. I remember well how she used to mope along at my side, until one morning she could not raise her head from her pillow. At her deathbed I stood weeping, as the paleface woman sat near her moistening the dry lips. Among the folds of the bedclothes I saw the open pages of the white man's Bible. The dying Indian girl talked disconnectedly of Jesus the Christ and the paleface who was cooling her swollen hands and feet.

I grew bitter, and censured the woman for cruel neglect of our physical ills. I despised the pencils that moved automatically, and the one teaspoon which dealt out, from a large bottle, healing to a row of variously ailing Indian children. I blamed the hard-working, well-meaning, ignorant woman who was inculcating in our hearts her superstitious ideas. Though I was sullen in all my little troubles, as soon as I felt better I was ready again to smile upon the cruel woman. Within a week I was again actively testing the chains which tightly bound my individuality like a mummy for burial.

The melancholy of those black days has left so long a shadow that it darkens the path of years that have since gone by. These sad memories rise above those of smoothly grinding school days. Perhaps my Indian nature is the moaning wind which stirs them now for their present record. But, however tempestuous this is within me, it comes out as the low voice of a curiously colored sea-shell, which is only for those ears that are bent with compassion to hear it.

VI. FOUR STRANGE SUMMERS.

After my first three years of school, I roamed again in the Western country through four strange summers.

During this time I seemed to hang in the heart of chaos, beyond the touch or voice of human aid. My brother, being almost ten years my senior, did not quite understand my feelings. My mother had never gone inside of a schoolhouse, and so she was not capable of comforting her daughter who could read and write. Even nature seemed to have no place for me. I was neither a wee girl nor a tall one; neither a wild Indian nor a tame one. This deplorable situation was the effect of my brief course in the East, and the unsatisfactory "teenth" in a girl's years.

It was under these trying conditions that, one bright afternoon, as I sat restless and unhappy in my mother's cabin, I caught the sound of the spirited step of my brother's pony on the road which passed by our dwelling. Soon I heard the wheels of a light buckboard, and Dawee's familiar "Ho!" to his pony.

He alighted upon the bare ground in front of our house. Tying his pony to one of the projecting corner logs of the low-roofed cottage, he stepped upon the wooden doorstep.

I met him there with a hurried greeting, and, as I passed by, he looked a quiet "What?" into my eyes.

When he began talking with my mother, I slipped the rope from the pony's bridle. Seizing the reins and bracing my feet against the dashboard, I wheeled around in an instant. The pony was ever ready to try his speed. Looking backward, I saw Dawee waving his hand to me. I turned with the curve in the road and disappeared. I followed the winding road which crawled upward between the bases of little hillocks. Deep water-worn ditches ran parallel on either side. A strong wind blew against my cheeks and fluttered my sleeves. The pony reached the top of the highest hill, and began an even race on the level lands. There was nothing moving within that great circular horizon of the Dakota prairies save the tall grasses, over which the wind blew and rolled off in long, shadowy waves.

Within this vast wigwam of blue and green I rode reckless and insignificant. It satisfied my small consciousness to see the white foam fly from the pony's mouth.

Suddenly, out of the earth a coyote came forth at a swinging trot that was taking the cunning thief toward the hills and the village beyond. Upon the moment's impulse, I gave him a long chase and a wholesome fright. As I turned away to go back to the village, the wolf sank down upon his haunches for rest, for it was a hot summer day; and as I drove slowly homeward, I saw his sharp nose still pointed at me, until I vanished below the margin of the hilltops.

In a little while I came in sight of my mother's house. Dawee stood in the yard, laughing at an old warrior who was pointing his forefinger, and again waving his whole hand, toward the hills. With his blanket drawn over one shoulder, he talked and motioned excitedly. Dawee turned the old man by the shoulder and pointed me out to him.

"Oh han!" (Oh yes) the warrior muttered, and went his way. He had climbed the top of his favorite barren hill to survey the surrounding prairies, when he spied my chase after the coyote. His keen eyes recognized the pony and driver. At once uneasy for my safety, he had come running to my mother's cabin to give her warning. I did not appreciate his kindly interest, for there was an unrest gnawing at my heart.

As soon as he went away, I asked Dawee about something else.

"No, my baby sister, I cannot take you with me to the party to-night," he replied. Though I was not far from fifteen, and I felt that before long I should enjoy all the privileges of my tall cousin, Dawee persisted in calling me his baby sister.

That moonlight night, I cried in my mother's presence when I heard the jolly young people pass by our cottage. They were no more young braves in blankets and eagle plumes, nor Indian maids with prettily painted cheeks. They had gone three years to school in the East, and had become civilized. The young men wore the white man's coat and trousers, with bright neckties. The girls wore tight muslin dresses, with ribbons at neck and waist. At these gatherings they talked English. I could speak English almost as well as my brother, but I was not properly dressed to be taken along. I had no hat, no ribbons, and no close-fitting gown. Since my return from school I had thrown away my shoes, and wore again the soft moccasins.

While Dawee was busily preparing to go I controlled my tears. But when I heard him bounding away on his pony, I buried my face in my arms and cried hot tears.

My mother was troubled by my unhappiness. Coming to my side, she offered me the only printed matter we had in our home. It was an Indian Bible, given her some years ago by a missionary. She tried to console me. "Here, my child, are the white man's papers. Read a little from them," she said most piously.

I took it from her hand, for her sake; but my enraged spirit felt more like burning the book, which afforded me no help, and was a perfect delusion to my mother. I did not read it, but laid it unopened on the floor, where I sat on my feet. The dim yellow light of the braided muslin burning in a small vessel of oil flickered and sizzled in the awful silent storm which followed my rejection of the Bible.

Now my wrath against the fates consumed my tears before they reached my eyes. I sat stony, with a bowed head. My mother threw a shawl over her head and shoulders, and stepped out into the night.

After an uncertain solitude, I was suddenly aroused by a loud cry piercing the night. It was my mother's voice wailing among the barren hills which held the bones of buried warriors. She called aloud for her brothers' spirits to support her in her helpless misery. My fingers grew icy cold, as I realized that my unrestrained tears had betrayed my suffering to her, and she was grieving for me.

Before she returned, though I knew she was on her way, for she had ceased her weeping, I extinguished the light, and leaned my head on the window sill.

Many schemes of running away from my surroundings hovered about in my mind. A few more moons of such a turmoil drove me away to the Eastern school. I rode on the white man's iron steed, thinking it would bring me back to my mother in a few winters, when I should be grown tall, and there would be congenial friends awaiting me.

VII. INCURRING MY MOTHER'S DISPLEASURE.

In the second journey to the East I had not come without some precautions. I had a secret interview with one of our best medicine men, and when I left his wigwam I carried securely in my sleeve a tiny bunch of magic roots. This possession assured me of friends wherever I should go. So absolutely did I believe in its charms that I wore it through all the school routine for more than a year. Then, before I lost my faith in the dead roots, I lost the little buckskin bag containing all my good luck.

At the close of this second term of three years I was the proud owner of my first diploma. The following autumn I ventured upon a college career against my mother's will.

I had written for her approval, but in her reply I found no encouragement. She called my notice to her neighbors' children, who had completed their education in three years. They had returned to their homes, and were then talking English with the frontier settlers. Her few words hinted that I had better give up my slow attempt to learn the white man's ways, and be content to roam over the prairies and find my living upon wild roots. I silenced her by deliberate disobedience.

Thus, homeless and heavy-hearted, I began anew my life among strangers.

As I hid myself in my little room in the college dormitory, away from the scornful and yet curious eyes of the students, I pined for sympathy. Often I wept in secret, wishing I had gone West, to be nourished by my mother's love, instead of remaining among a cold race whose hearts were frozen hard with prejudice.

During the fall and winter seasons I scarcely had a real friend, though by that time several of my classmates were courteous to me at a safe distance.

My mother had not yet forgiven my rudeness to her, and I had no moment for letter-writing. By daylight and lamplight, I spun with reeds and thistles, until my hands were tired from their weaving, the magic design which promised me the white man's respect.

At length, in the spring term, I entered an oratorical contest among the various classes. As the day of competition approached, it did not seem possible that the event was so near at hand, but it came. In the chapel the classes assembled together, with their invited guests. The high platform was carpeted, and gayly festooned with college colors. A bright white light illumined the room, and outlined clearly the great polished beams that arched the domed ceiling. The assembled crowds filled the air with pulsating murmurs. When the hour for speaking arrived all were hushed. But on the wall the old clock which pointed out the trying moment ticked calmly on.

One after another I saw and heard the orators. Still, I could not realize that they longed for the favorable decision of the judges as much as I did. Each contestant received a loud burst of applause, and some were cheered heartily. Too soon my turn came, and I paused a moment behind the curtains for a deep breath. After my concluding words, I heard the same applause that the others had called out.

Upon my retreating steps, I was astounded to receive from my fellow students a large bouquet of roses tied with flowing ribbons. With the lovely flowers I fled from the stage. This friendly token was a rebuke to me for the hard feelings I had borne them.

Later, the decision of the judges awarded me the first place. Then there was a mad uproar in the hall, where my classmates sang and shouted my name at the top of their lungs; and the disappointed students howled and brayed in fearfully dissonant tin trumpets. In this excitement, happy students rushed forward to offer their congratulations. And I could not conceal a smile when they wished to escort me in a procession to the students' parlor, where all were going to calm themselves. Thanking them for the kind spirit which prompted them to make such a proposition, I walked alone with the night to my own little room.

A few weeks afterward, I appeared as the college representative in another contest. This time the competition was among orators from different colleges in our state. It was held at the state capital, in one of the largest opera houses.

Here again was a strong prejudice against my people. In the evening, as the great audience filled the house, the student bodies began warring among themselves. Fortunately, I was spared witnessing any of the noisy wrangling before the contest began. The slurs against the Indian that stained the lips of our opponents were already burning like a dry fever within my breast.

But after the orations were delivered a deeper burn awaited me. There, before that vast ocean of eyes, some college rowdies threw out a large white flag, with a drawing of a most forlorn Indian girl on it. Under this they had printed in bold black letters words that ridiculed the college which was represented by a "squaw." Such worse than barbarian rudeness embittered me. While we waited for the verdict of the judges, I gleamed fiercely upon the throngs of palefaces. My teeth were hard set, as I saw the white flag still floating insolently in the air.

Then anxiously we watched the man carry toward the stage the envelope containing the final decision.

There were two prizes given, that night, and one of them was mine!

The evil spirit laughed within me when the white flag dropped out of sight, and the hands which furled it hung limp in defeat.

Leaving the crowd as quickly as possible, I was soon in my room. The rest of the night I sat in an armchair and gazed into the crackling fire. I laughed no more in triumph when thus alone. The little taste of victory did not satisfy a hunger in my heart. In my mind I saw my mother far away on the Western plains, and she was holding a charge against me.

★

CHARLES W. CHESNUTT *The March of Progress*
Century 61 (January 1901): 422–428

[Charles W. Chesnutt, who served as the principal of a normal school before pursuing a legal career, addresses both the promises and difficulties of self-uplift among black communities, focusing on the ways in which loyalty to one's "own people" affects the selection of a schoolteacher in a North Carolina community. The story emphasizes the newfound possibility of recognizing leadership from within the black race, thus igniting complex issues of allegiance, dedication, and cultural tutelage.]

THE COLORED PEOPLE of Patesville had at length gained the object they had for a long time been seeking—the appointment of a committee of themselves to manage the colored schools of the town. They had argued, with some show of reason, that they were most interested in the education of their own children, and in a position to know, better than any committee of white men could, what was best for their children's needs. The appointments had been made by the county commissioners during the latter part of the summer, and a week later a meeting was called for the purpose of electing a teacher to take charge of the grammar school at the beginning of the fall term.

The committee consisted of Frank Gillespie, or "Glaspy," a barber, who took an active part in local politics; Bob Cotten, a blacksmith, who owned several houses and was looked upon as a substantial citizen; and Abe Johnson, commonly called "Ole Abe" or "Uncle Abe," who had a large family, and drove a dray, and did odd jobs of hauling; he was also a class-leader in the Methodist church. The committee had been chosen from among a number of candidates—Gillespie on account of his political standing, Cotten as representing the solid element of the colored population, and Old Abe, with democratic impartiality, as likely to satisfy the humbler class of a humble people. While the choice had not pleased everybody,—for instance, some of the other applicants,—it was acquiesced in with general satisfaction. The first meeting of the new committee was of great public interest, partly by reason of its novelty, but chiefly because there were two candidates for the position of teacher of the grammar school.

The former teacher, Miss Henrietta Noble, had applied for the school. She had taught the colored children of Patesville for fifteen years. When the Freedmen's Bureaus, after the military occupation of North Carolina, had called for volunteers to teach the children of the freedmen, Henrietta Noble had offered her services. Brought up in a New England household by parents who taught her to fear God and love her fellow men, she had seen her father's body brought home from a Southern battle-field and laid to rest in the village cemetery; and a short six months later she had buried her mother by his side. Henrietta had no brothers or sisters, and her nearest relatives were cousins living in the far West. The only human being in whom she felt any personal interest was a certain captain in her father's regiment, who had paid her some attention. She had loved this man deeply, in a maidenly, modest way; but he had gone away without speaking, and had not since written. He had escaped the fate of many others, and at the close of the war was alive and well, stationed in some Southern garrison.

When her mother died, Henrietta had found herself possessed only of the house where she lived and the furniture it contained, neither being of much value, and she was thrown upon her own resources for a livelihood. She had a fair education and had read many good books. It was not easy to find employment such as she desired. She wrote to her Western cousins, and they advised her to come to them, as they thought they could do something for her if she were there. She had almost decided to accept their offer, when the demand arose for teachers in the South. Whether impelled by some strain of adventurous blood from a Pilgrim ancestry, or by a sensitive pride that shrank from dependence, or by some dim and unacknowledged hope that she might sometime, somewhere, somehow meet Captain Carey—whether from one of these motives or a combination of them all, joined to something of the missionary spirit, she decided to go South, and wrote to her cousins declining their friendly offer.

She had come to Patesville when the children were mostly a mob of dirty little beggars. She had distributed among them the cast-off clothing that came from their friends in the North; she had taught them to wash their faces and to comb their hair; and patiently, year after year, she had labored to instruct them in the rudiments of learning and the first principles of religion and morality. And she had not wrought in vain. Other agencies, it is true, had in time coöperated with her efforts, but any one who had watched the current of events must have been compelled to admit that the very fair progress of the colored people of Patesville in the fifteen years following emancipation had been due chiefly to the unselfish labors of Henrietta Noble, and that her nature did not belie her name.

Fifteen years is a long time. Miss Noble had never met Captain Carey; and when she learned later that he had married a Southern girl in the neighborhood of his post, she had shed her tears in secret and banished his image from her heart. She had lived a lonely life. The white people of the town, though they learned in time to respect her and to value her work, had never recognized her existence by more than the mere external courtesy shown by any community to one who lives in the midst of it. The situation was at first, of course, so strained that she did not expect sympathy from the white people; and later, when time had smoothed over some of the asperities of war, her work had so engaged her that she had not had time to pine over her social exclusion. Once or twice nature had asserted itself, and she had longed for her own kind, and had visited her New England home. But her circle of friends was broken up, and she did not find much pleasure in boarding-house life; and on her last visit to the North but one, she had felt so lonely that she had longed for the dark faces of her pupils, and had welcomed with pleasure the hour when her task should be resumed.

But for several reasons the school at Patesville was of more importance to Miss Noble at this particular time than it ever had been before. During the last few years her health had not been good. An affection of the heart similar to that from which her mother had died, while not interfering perceptibly with her work, had grown from bad to worse, aggravated by close application to her duties, until it had caused her grave alarm. She did not have perfect confidence in the skill of the Patesville physicians, and to obtain the best medical advice had gone to New York during the summer, remaining there a month under the treatment of an eminent specialist. This, of course, had been expensive and had absorbed the savings of years from a small salary; and when the time came for her to return to Patesville, she was reduced, after paying her traveling expenses, to her last ten-dollar note.

"It is very fortunate," the great man had said at her last visit, "that circumstances permit you to live in the South, for I am afraid you could not endure a Northern winter. You are getting along very well now, and if you will take care of yourself and avoid excitement, you will be better." He said to himself as she went away: "It's only a matter of time, but that is true about us all; and a wise physician does as much good by what he withholds as by what he tells."

Miss Noble had not anticipated any trouble about the school. When she went away the same committee of white men was in charge that had controlled the school since it had become part of the public-school system of the State on the withdrawal of support from the Freedmen's Bureau. While there had been no formal engagement made for the next year, when she had last seen the chairman before she went away, he had remarked that she was looking rather fagged out, had bidden her good-by, and had hoped to see her much improved when she returned. She had left her house in the care of the colored woman who lived with her and did her housework, assuming, of course, that she would take up her work again in the autumn.

She was much surprised at first, and later alarmed, to find a rival for her position as teacher of the grammar school. Many of her friends and pupils had called on her since her return, and she had met a number of the people at the colored Methodist church, where she taught in the Sunday-school. She had many friends and supporters, but she soon found out that her opponent had considerable strength. There had been a time when she would have withdrawn and left him a clear field, but at the present moment it was almost a matter of life and death to her—certainly the matter of earning a living—to secure the appointment.

The other candidate was a young man who in former years had been one of Miss Noble's brightest pupils. When he had finished his course in the grammar school, his parents, with considerable sacrifice, had sent him to a college for colored youth. He had studied diligently, had worked industriously during his vacations, sometimes at manual labor, sometimes teaching a country school, and in due time had been graduated from his college with honors. He had come home at the end of his school life, and was very naturally seeking the employment for which he had fitted himself. He was a "bright" mulatto, with straight hair, an intelligent face, and a well-set figure. He had acquired some of the marks of culture, wore a frock-coat and a high collar, parted his hair in the middle, and showed by his manner that he thought a good deal of himself. He was the popular candidate among the progressive element of his people, and rather confidently expected the appointment.

The meeting of the committee was held in the Methodist church, where, in fact, the grammar school was taught, for want of a separate school-house. After the preliminary steps to effect an organization, Mr. Gillespie, who had been elected chairman, took the floor.

"The principal business to be brought befo' the meet'n' this evenin'," he said, "is the selection of a teacher for our grammar school for the ensuin' year. Two candidates have filed applications, which, if there is no objection, I will read to the committee. The first is from Miss Noble, who has been the teacher ever since the grammar school was started."

He then read Miss Noble's letter, in which she called attention to her long years of service, to her need of the position, and to her affection for the pupils, and made formal application for the school for the next year. She did not, from motives of self-respect, make known the extremity of her need; nor did she mention the condition of her health, as it might have been used as an argument against her retention.

Mr. Gillespie then read the application of the other candidate, Andrew J. Williams. Mr. Williams set out in detail his qualifications for the position: his degree from Riddle University; his familiarity with the dead and living languages and the higher mathematics; his views of discipline; and a peroration in which he expressed the desire to devote himself to the elevation of his race and assist the march of progress through the medium of the Patesville grammar school. The letter was well written in a bold, round hand, with many flourishes, and looked very aggressive and overbearing as it lay on the table by the side of the sheet of small note-paper in Miss Noble's faint and somewhat cramped handwriting.

"You have heard the readin' of the applications," said the chairman. "Gentlemen, what is yo' pleasure?"

There being no immediate response the chairman continued:

"As this is a matter of consid'able importance, involvin' not only the welfare of our schools, but the progress of our race, an' as our action is liable to be criticized, what ever we decide, perhaps we had better discuss the subjec' befo' we act. If nobody else has anything to obse've, I will make a few remarks."

Mr. Gillespie cleared his throat, and, assuming an oratorical attitude, proceeded:

"The time has come in the history of our people when we should stand together. In this age of organization the march of progress requires that we help ourselves, or be left forever behind. Ever since the war we have been sendin' our child'n to school an' educatin' 'em; an' now the time has come when they are leavin' the schools en' colleges, an' are ready to go to work. An' what are they goin' to do? The white people won't hire 'em as clerks in their sto's an' factories an' mills, an' we have no sto's or factories or mills of our own. They can't be lawyers or doctors yet, because we have n't got the money to send 'em to medical colleges an' law schools. We can't elect many of 'em to office, for various reasons. There's just two things they can find to do—to preach in our own pulpits, an' teach in our own schools. If it was n't for that, they'd have to go on forever waitin' on white folks, like their fo'-fathers have done, because they could n't help it. If we expect our race to progress, we must educate our young men an' women. If we want to encourage 'em to get education, we must find 'em employment when they are educated. We have now an opportunity to do this in the case of our young friend an' fellow-citizen, Mr. Williams, whose eloquent an' fine-lookin' letter ought to make us feel proud of him an' of our race.

"Of co'se there are two sides to the question. We have got to consider the claims of Miss Noble. She has been with us a long time an' has done much good for our people, an' we'll never forget her work an' frien'-ship. But, after all, she has been paid for it; she has got her salary regularly an' for a long time, an' she has probably saved somethin', for we all know she has n't lived high; an', for all we know, she may have had somethin' left her by her parents. An' then again, she's white, an' has got her own people to look after her; they've got all the money an' all the offices an' all the everythin',—all that they've made an' all that we've made for fo' hundred years,—an' they sholy would look out for her. If she don't get this school, there's probably a dozen others she can get at the North. An' another thing: she is gettin' rather feeble, an' it 'pears to me she's hardly able to stand teachin' so many child'n, an' a long rest might be the best thing in the world for her.

"Now, gentlemen, that's the situation. Shall we keep Miss Noble, or shall we stand by our own people? It seems to me there can hardly be but one answer. Self-preservation is the first law of nature. Are there any other remarks?"

Old Abe was moving restlessly in his seat. He did not say anything, however, and the chairman turned to the other member.

"Brother Cotten, what is yo' opinion of the question befo' the board?"

Mr. Cotten rose with the slowness and dignity becoming a substantial citizen, and observed:

"I think the remarks of the chairman have great weight. We all have nothin' but kind feelin's fer Miss Noble, an' I came here to-night somewhat undecided how to vote on this question. But after listenin' to the just an' forcible arguments of Brother Glaspy, it 'pears to me that, after all, the question befo' us is not a matter of feelin', but of business. As a business man, I am inclined to think Brother Glaspy is right. If we don't help ourselves when we get a chance, who is goin' to help us?"

"That bein' the case," said the chairman, "shall we proceed to a vote? All who favor the election of Brother Williams—"

At this point Old Abe, with much preliminary shuffling, stood up in his place and interrupted the speaker.

"Mr. Chuhman," he said, "I s'pose I has a right ter speak in dis meet'n'? I *s'pose* I is a member er dis committee?"

"Certainly, Brother Johnson, certainly; we shall he glad to hear from you."

"I s'pose I's got a right ter speak my min', ef I is po' an' black, an' don' weah as good clo's as some other members er de committee?"

"Most assuredly, Brother Johnson," answered the chairman, with a barber's suavity, "you have as much right to be heard as any one else. There was no intention of cuttin' you off."

"I s'pose," continued Abe, "dat a man wid fo'teen child'n kin be 'lowed ter hab somethin' ter say 'bout de schools er dis town?"

"I am sorry, Brother Johnson, that you should feel slighted, but there was no intention to igno' yo' rights. The committee will be please' to have you ventilate yo' views."

"Ef it's all been an' done reco'nized an' 'cided dat I's got de right ter be heared in dis meet'n', I'll say w'at I has ter say, an' it won't take me long ter say it. Ef I should try ter tell all de things dat Miss Noble has done fer de niggers er dis town, it'd take me till ter-morrer mawnin'. Fer fifteen long yeahs I has watched her incomin's an' her outgoin's. Her daddy was a Yankee kunnel, who died fighting fer ou' freedom. She come heah when we—yes, Mr. Chuhman, when you an' Br'er Cotten—was jes sot free, an' when none er us did n' have a rag ter ou' backs. She come heah, an' she tuk yo' child'n an' my child'n, an' she teached 'em sense an' manners an' religion an' book-l'arnin'. When she come heah we did n'hab no chu'ch. Who writ up No'th an' got a preacher sent to us, an' de fun's ter buil' dis same chu'ch-house we're settin' in ter-night? Who got de money f'm de Bureau to s'port de school? An' when dat was stop', who got de money f'm de Peabody Fun'? Talk about Miss Noble gittin' a sal'ry! Who paid dat sal'ry up ter five years ago? Not one dollah of it come outer ou' pockets!

"An' den, w'at did she git fer de yuther things she done? Who paid her for teachin' de Sunday-school? Who paid her fer de gals she kep' f'm throwin' deyse'ves away? Who paid fer de boys she kep' outer jail? I had a son dat seemed to hab made up his min' ter go straight ter hell. I made him go ter Sunday-school, en' somethin' dat woman said teched his heart, an' he behaved hisself, an' I ain' got no reason fer ter be 'shame' er 'im. An' I can 'member, Br'er Cotten, when you did n' own fo' houses an' a fahm. An' when yo' fus wife was sick, who sot by her bedside an' read de Good Book ter 'er, w'en dey wuz n' nobody else knowed how ter read it, an' comforted her on her way across de col', dahk ribbers? An' dat ain' all I kin 'member, Mr. Chuhman! When yo' gal Fanny was a baby, an' sick, an' nobody knowed what was de matter wid 'er, who sent fer a doctor, en' paid 'im fer comin', an' who he'ped nuss dat Chile, an' tol' yo' wife w'at ter do, an' save' dat chile's life, jes as sho' as de Lawd has save' my soul?

"An' now, aftuh fifteen yeahs o' slavin' fer us, who ain' got no claim on her, aftuh fifteen yeahs dat she has libbed 'mongs' us an' made herse'f one of us, an' endyoed havin' her own people look down on her, aftuh she has growed ole an' gray wukkin' fer us an' our child'n, we talk erbout turnin' 'er out like a' ole hoss ter die! It 'pears ter me some folks has po' mem'ries! Whar would we 'a' be'n ef her folks at de No'th had n' 'membered us no bettuh? An' we had n' done nothin', neither, fer dem to 'member us fer. De man dat kin fergit w'at Miss Noble has done fer dis town is unworthy de name er nigger! He oughter die an' make room fer some 'spectable dog!

"Br'er Glaspy says we got a' educated young man, en' we mus' gib him sump'n' ter do. Let him wait; ef I reads de signs right he won't hab ter wait long fer dis job. Let him teach in de primary schools, er in de country; en' ef he can't do dat, let 'im work awhile. It don't hahm a' educated man ter work a little; his fo'fathers has worked fer hund'eds of years, an' we's worked, an' we're heah yet, an' we're free, an' we 's gettin' ou' own houses en' lots an' hosses an' cows—an' ou' educated young men. But don't let de fus thing we do as a committee be somethin' we ought ter be 'shamed of as long as we lib. I votes fer Miss Noble, fus, las', an' all de time!"

When Old Abe sat down the chairman's face bore a troubled look. He remembered how his baby girl, the first of his children that he could really call his own, that no master could hold a prior claim upon, lay dying in the arms of his distracted young wife, and how the thin, homely, and short-sighted white teacher had come like an angel into his cabin, and had brought back the little one from the verge of the grave. The child was a young woman now, and Gillespie had well-founded hopes of securing the superior young Williams for a son-in-law; and he realized with something of shame that this later ambition had so dazzled his eyes for a moment as to obscure the memory of earlier days.

Mr. Cotten, too, had not been unmoved, and there were tears in his eyes as he recalled how his first wife, Nancy, who had borne with him the privations of slavery, had passed away, with the teacher's hand in hers, before she had been able to enjoy the fruits of liberty. For they had loved one another much, and her death had been to them both a hard and bitter thing. And, as Old Abe spoke, he could remember, as distinctly as though they had been spoken but an hour before, the words of comfort that the teacher had whispered to Nancy in her dying hour and to him in his bereavement.

"On consideration, Mr. Chairman," he said, with an effort to hide a suspicious tremor in his voice and to speak with the dignity consistent with his character as a substantial citizen, "I wish to record my vote fer Miss Noble."

"The chair," said Gillespie, yielding gracefully to the majority, and greatly relieved that the responsibility of his candidate's defeat lay elsewhere, "will make the vote unanimous, and will appoint Brother Cotten and Brother Johnson a committee to step round the corner to Miss Noble's and notify her of her election."

The two committeemen put on their hats and, accompanied by several people who had been waiting at the door to hear the result of the meeting, went around the corner to Miss Noble's house, a distance of a block or two away. The house was lighted, so they knew she had not gone to bed. They went in at the gate, and Cotten knocked at the door.

The colored maid opened it.

"Is Miss Noble home?" said Cotten.

"Yes; come in. She 's waitin' ter hear from the committee." The woman showed them into the parlor. Miss Noble rose from her seat by the table, where she had been reading, and came forward to meet them. They did not for a moment observe, as she took a step toward them, that her footsteps wavered. In her agitation she was scarcely aware of it herself.

"Miss Noble," announced Cotten, "we have come to let you know that you have be'n 'lected teacher of the grammar school fer the next year."

"Thank you; oh, thank you so much!" she said. "I am very glad. Mary"— she put her hand to her side suddenly and tottered—"Mary, will you–"

A spasm of pain contracted her face and cut short her speech. She would have fallen had Old Abe not caught her and, with Mary's help, laid her on a couch.

The remedies applied by Mary, and by the physician who was hastily summoned, proved unavailing. The teacher did not regain consciousness.

If it be given to those whose eyes have closed in death to linger regretfully for a while about their earthly tenement, or from some higher vantage-ground to look down upon it, then Henrietta Noble's tolerant spirit must have felt, mingling with its regret, a compensating thrill of pleasure; for not only those for whom she had labored sorrowed for her, but the people of her own race, many of whom, in the blindness of their pride, would not admit during her life that she served them also, saw so much clearer now that they took charge of her poor clay, and did it gentle reverence, and laid it tenderly away amid the dust of their own loved and honored dead.

Two weeks after Miss Noble's funeral the other candidate took charge of the grammar school, which went on without any further obstacles to the march of progress.

★

PAUL LAURENCE DUNBAR The Ingrate
New England Magazine 20 (August 1899): 676–681

[Paul Laurence Dunbar was best known for *Lyrics of Lowly Life* (1896), a collection of poems in the tradition of plantation stories of the "Old South" by Joel Chandler Harris and Charles W. Chesnutt. However, in this story of poetic justice, Dunbar contrasts the appearance of a seemingly simple slave with the reality of a fully empowered man who attains his intellectual and civic freedom.]

I. Mr. Leckler was a man of high principle. Indeed, he himself had admitted it at times to Mrs. Leckler. She was often called into counsel with him. He was one of those large soured creatures with a hunger for unlimited advice, upon which he never acted. Mrs. Leckler knew this, but, like the good, patient little wife that she was, she went on paying her poor tribute of advice and admiration. Today her husband's mind was particularly troubled— as usual, too, over a matter of principle. Mrs. Leckler came at his call.

"Mrs. Leckler," he said, "I am troubled in my mind. I—in fact, I am puzzled over a matter that involves either the maintaining or relinquishing of a principle."

"Well, Mr. Leckler?" said his wife, interrogatively.

"If I had been a scheming, calculating Yankee, I should have been rich now; but all my life I have been too generous and confiding. I have always let principle stand between me and my interests." Mr. Leckler took himself all too seriously to be conscious of his pun, and went on: "Now this is a matter in which my duty and my principles seem to conflict. It stands thus: Josh has been doing a piece of plastering for Mr. Eckley over in Lexington, and from what he says, I think that city rascal has misrepresented the amount of work to me and so cut down the pay for it. Now, of course, I should not care, the matter of a dollar or two being nothing to me; but it is a very different matter when we consider poor Josh." There was deep pathos in Mr. Leckler's tone. "You know Josh is anxious to buy his freedom, and I allow him a part of whatever he makes; so you see it's he that's affected. Every dollar that he is cheated out of cuts off just so much from his earnings, and puts further away his hope of emancipation."

If the thought occurred to Mrs. Leckler that, since Josh received only about one-tenth of what he earned, the advantage of just wages would be quite

FIGURE 18 This portrait of Paul
Laurence Dunbar was originally
published with "The Ingrate," a
portrait that delineated Dunbar
as a black author and as someone
culturally and socially positioned
to comment on the intersection
of privilege and relative educational advantages. (*New England
Magazine*, 1899)

as much her husband's as the slave's, she did not betray it, but met the
naive reasoning with the question, "But where does the conflict come in, Mr.
Leckler?"

"Just here. If Josh knew how to read and write and cipher—"

"Mr. Leckler, are you crazy?"

"Listen to me, my dear, and give me the benefit of your judgment. This is a
very momentous question. As I was about to say, if Josh knew these things,
he could protect himself from cheating when his work is at too great a distance for me to look after it for him."

"But teaching a slave—"

"Yes, that's just what is against my principles. I know how public opinion
and the law look at it. But my conscience rises up in rebellion every time I
think of that poor black man being cheated out of his earnings. Really, Mrs.
Leckler, I think I may trust to Josh's discretion, and secretly give him such
instructions as will permit him to protect himself."

"Well, of course, it's just as you think best," said his wife.

"I knew you would agree with me," he returned. "It's such a comfort to
take counsel with you, my dear!" And the generous man walked out on the
veranda, very well satisfied with himself and his wife, and prospectively
pleased with Josh. Once he murmured to himself, "I'll lay for Eckley next
time."

Josh, the subject of Mr. Leckler's charitable solicitations, was the plantation plasterer. His master had given him his trade, in order that he might do

whatever work was needed about the place; but he became so proficient in his duties, having also no competition among the poor whites, that he had grown to be in great demand in the country thereabout. So Mr. Leckler found it profitable, instead of letting him do chores and field work in his idle time, to hire him out to neighboring farms and planters. Josh was a man of more than ordinary intelligence; and when he asked to be allowed to pay for himself by working overtime, his master readily agreed—for it promised more work to be done, for which he could allow the slave just what he pleased. Of course, he knew now that when the black man began to cipher, this state of affairs would be changed; but it would mean such an increase of profit from the outside that he could afford to give up his own little peculations. Anyway, it would be many years before the slave could pay the two thousand dollars, which price he had set upon him. Should he approach that figure, Mr. Leckler felt it just possible that the market in slaves would take a sudden rise.

When Josh was told of his master's intention, his eyes gleamed with pleasure, and he went to his work with the zest of long hunger. He proved a remarkably apt pupil. He was indefatigable in doing the tasks assigned him. Even Mr. Leckler, who had great faith in his plasterer's ability, marveled at the speed with which he had acquired the three R's. He did not know that on one of his many trips a free Negro had given Josh the rudimentary tools of learning, and that since the slave had been adding to his store of learning by poring over signs and every bit of print that he could spell out. Neither was Josh so indiscreet as to intimate to his benefactor that he had been anticipated in his good intentions.

It was in this way, working and learning, that a year passed away, and Mr. Leckler thought that his object had been accomplished. He could safely trust Josh to protect his own interests, and so he thought that it was quite time that his servant's education should cease.

"You know, Josh," he said, "I have already gone against my principles and against the law for your sake, and of course a man can't stretch his conscience too far, even to help another who's being cheated; but I reckon you can take care of yourself now."

"Oh, yes, suh, I reckon I kin," said Josh.

"And it wouldn't do for you to be seen with any books about you now."

"Oh, no, suh, su't'n'y not." He didn't intend to be seen with any books about him.

It was just now that Mr. Leckler saw the good results of all he had done, and his heart was full of a great joy, for Eckley had been building some additions to his house, and sent for Josh to do the plastering for him. The owner admonished his slave, took him over a few examples to freshen his memory, and sent him forth with glee. When the job was done, there was a discrepancy of two dollars in what Mr. Eckley offered for it and the price which accrued from Josh's measurements. To the employer's surprise, the black man went over the figures with him and convinced him of the incorrectness of the payment—and the additional two dollars were turned over.

"Some o' Leckler's work," said Eckley, "teaching a nigger to cipher! Close-fisted old reprobate—I've a mind to have the law on him."

Mr. Leckler heard the story with great glee. "I laid for him that time—the old fox." But to Mrs. Leckler he said: "You see, my dear wife, my rashness in teaching Josh to figure for himself is vindicated. See what he has saved for himself."

"What did he save?" asked the little woman indiscreetly.

Her husband blushed and stammered for a moment, and then replied, "Well, of course, it was only twenty cents saved to him, but to a man buying his freedom every cent counts; and after all, it is not the amount, Mrs. Leckler; it's the principle of the thing."

"Yes," said the lady meekly.

II. Unto the body it is easy for the master to say, "Thus far shalt thou go, and no farther." Gyves, chains, and fetters will enforce that command. But what master shall say unto the mind, "Here do I set the limit of your acquisition. Pass it not"? Who shall put gyves upon the intellect, or fetter the movement of thought? Joshua Leckler, as custom denominated him, had tasted of the forbidden fruit, and his appetite had grown by what it fed on. Night after night he crouched in his lonely cabin, by the blaze of a fat pine brand, poring over the few books that he had been able to secure and smuggle in. His fellow-servants alternately laughed at him and wondered why he did not take a wife. But Joshua went on his way. He had no time for marrying or for love; other thoughts had taken possession of him. He was being swayed by ambitions other than the mere fathering of slaves for his master. To him slavery was deep night. What wonder, then, that he should dream, and that through the ivory gate should come to him the forbidden vision of freedoms? To own himself, to be master of his hands, feet, of his whole body—something would clutch at his heart as he thought of it; and the breath would come hard between his lips. But he met his master with an impassive face, always silent, always docile; and Mr. Leckler congratulated himself that so valuable and intelligent a slave should be at the same time so tractable. Usually intelligence in a slave meant discontent; but not so with Josh.

Meanwhile the white hills of the North were beckoning to the chattel, and the north winds were whispering to him to be a chattel no longer. Often the eyes that looked away to where freedom lay were filled with a wistful longing that was tragic in its intensity, for they saw the hardships and the difficulties between the slave and his goal, and, worst of all, an iniquitous law—liberty's compromise with bondage, that rose like a stone wall between him and hope—a law that degraded every free-thinking man to the level of a slave-catcher. There it loomed up before him, formidable, impregnable, insurmountable. He measured it in all its terribleness, and paused. But on the other side there was liberty; and one day when he was away at work, a voice came out of the woods and whispered to him, "Courage!"—and on that night the shadows beckoned him as the white hills had done, and the forest called to him, "Follow."

"It seems to me that Josh might have been able to get home to-night," said Mr. Lecklcr, walking up and down his veranda; "but I reckon it's just possible that he got through too late to catch a train." In the morning he said: "Well, he's not here yet; he must have had to do some extra work. If he doesn't get here by evening, I'll run up there."

In the evening he did take the train for Joshua's place of employment, where he learned that his slave had left the night before. But where could he have gone? That no one knew, and for the first time it dawned upon his master that Josh had run away. He raged; he fumed; but nothing could be done until morning, and all the time Leckler knew that the most valuable slave on his plantation was working his way toward the North and freedom. He did not go back home, but paced the floor all night long. In the early dawn he hurried out, and the hounds were put on the fugitive's track. After some nosing around they set off toward a stretch of woods. In a few minutes they came yelping back, pawing their noses and rubbing their heads against the ground. They had found the trail, but Josh had played the old slave trick of filling his tracks with cayenne pepper. The dogs were soothed, and taken deeper into the wood to find the trail. They soon took it up again, and dashed away with low bays. The scent led them directly to a little wayside station about six miles distant. Here it stopped. Burning with the chase, Mr. Leckler hastened to the station agent. Had he seen such a Negro? Yes, he had taken the northbound train two nights before.

"But why did you let him go without a pass?" almost screamed the owner.

"I didn't," replied the agent. "He had a written pass, signed James Leckler, and I let him go on it."

"Forged, forged!" yelled the master. "He wrote it himself."

"Humph!" said the agent, "how was I to know that? Our niggers round here don't know how to write."

Mr. Leckler suddenly bethought him to hold his peace. Josh was probably now in the arms of some Northern abolitionist, and there was nothing to be done now but advertise; and the disgusted master spread his notices broadcast before starting for home. As soon as he arrived at his house, he sought his wife and poured out his griefs to her.

"You see, Mrs. Leckler, this is what comes of my goodness of heart. I

taught that nigger to read and write, so that he could protect himself—
and look how he uses his knowledge. Oh, the ingrate, the ingrate! The very
weapon which I give him to defend himself against others he turns upon
me. Oh, it's awful—awful! I've always been too confiding. Here's the most
valuable nigger on my plantation gone—gone, I tell you—and through my
own kindness. It isn't his value, though, I'm thinking so much about. I could
stand his loss, if it wasn't for the principle of the thing, the base ingratitude
he has shown me. Oh! if I ever lay hands on him again!" Mr. Leckler closed
his lips and clenched his fist with an eloquence that laughed at words.

Just at this time, in one of the "underground" railway stations, six miles
north of the Ohio, an old Quaker was saying to Josh: "Lie still; thee'll be perfectly safe there. Here comes John Trader, our local slave catcher; but I will
parley with him and send him away. Thee need not fear. None of thy brethren who have come to us have ever been taken back to bondage.—Good evening, Friend Trader!" and Josh heard the old Quaker's smooth voice roll on,
while he lay back half smothering in a bag, among other bags of corn and
potatoes.

It was after ten o'clock that night when he was thrown carelessly into a
wagon and driven away to the next station, twenty-five miles to the northward. And by such stages, hiding by day and traveling by night, helped by
a few of his own people who were blessed with freedom, and always by the
good Quakers wherever found, he made his way into Canada. And on one
never-to-be-forgotten morning he stood up, straightened himself, breathed
God's blessed air, and knew himself free!

III. To Joshua Leckler this life in Canada was all new and strange. It was a
new thing for him to feel himself a man and to have his manhood recognized
by the whites with whom he came into free contact. It was new, too, this
receiving the full measure of his worth in work. He went to his labor with
a zest that he had never known before, and he took a pleasure in the very
weariness it brought him. Ever and anon there came to his ears the cries of
his brethren in the South. Frequently he met fugitives who, like himself, had
escaped from bondage; and the harrowing tales that they told him made him
burn to do something for those whom he had left behind. But these fugitives
and the papers he read told him other things. They said that the spirit of freedom was working in the United States, and already men were speaking out
boldly in behalf of the manumission of the slaves; already there was a growing army behind that noble vanguard, Sumner, Phillips, Douglass, Garrison.
He heard the names of Lucretia Mott and Harriet Beecher Stowe, and his
heart swelled, for on the dim horizon he saw the first faint streaks of dawn.

So the years passed. Then from the surcharged clouds a flash of lightning
broke, and there was the thunder of cannon and the rain of lead over the

land. From his home in the North he watched the storm as it raged and wavered, now threatening the North with its awful power, now hanging dire and dreadful over the South. Then suddenly from out the fray came a voice like the trumpet of God to him: "Thou and thy brothers are free!" Free, free, with the freedom not cherished by the few alone, but for all that had been bound. Free, with the freedom not torn from the secret night, but open to the light of heaven.

When the first call for colored soldiers came, Joshua Leckler hastened down to Boston, and enrolled himself among those who were willing to fight to maintain their freedom. On account of his ability to read and write and his general intelligence, he was soon made an orderly sergeant. His regiment had already taken part in an engagement before the public roster of this band of Uncle Sam's niggers, as they were called, fell into Mr. Leckler's hands. He ran his eye down the column of names. It stopped at that of Joshua Leckler, Sergeant, Company F. He handed the paper to Mrs. Leckler with his finger on the place.

"Mrs. Leckler," he said, "this is nothing less than a judgment on me for teaching a nigger to read and write. I disobeyed the law of my state and, as a result, not only lost my nigger, but furnished the Yankees with a smart officer to help them fight the South. Mrs. Leckler, I have sinned—and been punished. But I am content, Mrs. Leckler; it all came through my kindness of heart—and your mistaken advice. But oh, that ingrate, that ingrate!"

★

ABBE CARTER GOODLOE *The Genius of Bowlder Bluff*
Scribner's 17 (June 1895): 713–719

[Goodloe's story explores the strain of attempting to meet the lofty goals of an ambitious lower class father who fancies his daughter a young genius. While trying genuinely to fulfill her role as the caretaking daughter, the "genius" of the story's title, facing a dilemma about integrity, questions how a college education suits a woman for life after school. Here, as in her other stories, Goodloe asserts that traditional femininity is not challenged by the college experience.]

M ISS ARNOLD found him wandering aimlessly, though with a pleased, interested look, around the dimly lit College Library. She had gone there herself to escape for a few moments from the heat and lights and the crowd around the Scotch celebrity to whom the reception was being tendered, and was looking rather desultorily at an article in the latest *Revue des Deux Mondes*, when he emerged from one of the alcoves and stood hesitatingly be-

FIGURE 19   Depicting a "student parlor," this illustration from a nonfiction essay by Abbe Carter Goodloe on her alma mater, Wellesley, emphasizes the social side of college life, particularly among the more affluent students. (*Scribner's*, 1898)

fore her. She saw that he was not a guest. He was not in evening dress—it occurred to her even then how entirely out of his element he would have looked in a conventional dress-suit—but wore new clothes of some rough material which fitted him badly. He was so evidently lost and so painfully aware of it that she hastened to ask him if she could do anything for him.

"I'm lookin' fur my daughter, Ellen Oldham," he said, gratefully. "Do you know her?"

He seemed much surprised and a little hurt when Miss Arnold shook her head, smilingly.

"You see, there are so many ——" she began, noting his disappointed look.

"Then I s'pose you can't find her fur me. You see," he explained, gently, "I wrote her I wuz comin' ter-morrer, an' I came ter-night fur a surprise—a surprise," he repeated, delightedly. "But I'm mighty disappointed not ter find her. This is the first time I ever wuz so fur east. But I hed to see Ellen—couldn't stan' it no longer. You see," he continued, nervously, "I thought mebbe I could stay here three or four days, but last night I got a telegram from my pardner on the mountain sayin' there wuz trouble among the boys an' fur me ter come back. But I—I jest couldn't go back without seein' Ellen, so I came on ter-night fur a surprise, but I must start back right off, an' I'm mighty disappointed not ter be seein' her all this time. Hed no idea yer college wuz such a big place—thought I could walk right in an' spot her," he ran on meditatively. "I thought it wuz something like Miss Bellairs's an Miss Tompkins's an' Miss Rand's all rolled inter one. But Lord! it's a sight bigger'n that! Well I'm glad of it. I've thought fur years about Ellen's havin' a college eddication, an' I'm glad to see it's a real big college. Never hed no schoolin' myself, but I jest set my heart on Ellen's havin' it. Why shouldn't she? I've got ther money. Hed to work mighty hard fur it, but I've got it, an' she wanted ter come to college, an' I wanted her ter come, so of course she came. I met another young woman," he continued, smiling frankly at the girl before him; "she wasn't so fine-lookin' as you, but she was a very nice young woman, an' she promised to send Ellen ter me, but she hasn't done it!"

Miss Arnold felt a sudden interest in the old man.

"Perhaps," she began, doubtfully, "if you could tell me what her class is, or in what building she has her rooms, I might find her."

He looked at the young girl incredulously.

"Ain't you never heard of her?" he demanded. "Why, everybody knew her at Miss Bellairs's. But p'r'aps"—in a relieved sort of way—"p'rhaps you ain't been here long. This is Ellen's second year."

Miss Arnold felt slightly aggrieved.

"I am a Senior," she replied, and then added, courteously, "but I am sure the loss has been mine."

She could not make this man out, quite—he was so evidently uncultivated, so rough and even uncouth, and yet there was a look of quiet power in his honest eyes, and he was so unaffectedly simple and kindly that she instinctively recognized the innate nobility of his character. She felt interested in him, but somewhat puzzled as to how to continue the conversation, and so she turned rather helplessly to her magazine.

But he came over and stood beside her, looking down wonderingly at the unfamiliar words and accents.

"Can you read all that?" he asked, doubtfully.

Miss Arnold said "Yes."

"Jest like English?" he persisted.

She explained that she had had a French nurse when she was little, and afterward a French governess, and that she had always spoken French as she had English. He seemed to be immensely impressed by that and looked at her very intently and admiringly, and then he suddenly looked away, and said, in a changed tone:

"I never hed no French nurse fur Ellen. Lord! it wuz hard enough to get any kind in them days," he said, regretfully. "But she's been studyin' French fur two years now—p'rhaps she speaks almost as good as you do by this time— she's mighty smart."

Miss Arnold looked up quickly at the honest, kindly face above her with the hopeful expression in the eyes, and some sudden impulse made her say, quite cheerfully and assuringly, "Oh, yes—of course."

She was just going to add that she would go to the office and send someone to look for Miss Oldham, when a slender, rather pretty girl passed the library door, hesitated, peering through the half-light, and then came swiftly toward them.

With a cry of inexpressible tenderness and delight the old man ran toward her.

"Ellen!" he said, "Ellen!"

She clung to him for a few moments and then drew off rather shyly and awkwardly, with a sort of *mauvaise honte* which struck disagreeably on Miss Arnold, and looked inquiringly and almost defiantly from her father to the girl watching them.

"This young woman," he said, understanding her unspoken inquiry, "has been very kind to me, Ellen—we've been talkin'."

Miss Arnold came forward.

"I think we ought to be friends," she said, graciously. "I am Clara Arnold. Your father tells me this is your Sophomore year."

The girl met her advances coldly and stiffly. She had never met Miss Arnold before, but she had known very well who she was, and she had envied her, and had almost disliked her for her good looks and her wealth and her evident superiority. She comprehended that this girl had been born to what she had longed for in a vague, impotent way and had never known. She wished that Miss Arnold had not witnessed the meeting with her father— that Miss Arnold had not seen her father at all. And then with the shame at her unworthy thoughts came a rush of pity and love for the man standing there smiling so patiently and so tenderly at her. She put one hand on his arm and drew herself closer to him.

"Father!" she said.

Miss Arnold stood looking at them, turning her clear eyes from one to the other. It interested her tremendously—the simple, kindly old man, in his rough clothes, and with his homely talk and his fatherly pride and happiness in the pretty, irresolute-looking girl beside him. It occurred to her suddenly, with a thrill of pity for herself, that she had never seen her father look at her in that way. He would have been inordinately surprised and— she felt sure—very much annoyed, if she had ever kissed his hand or laid her head on his arm as this girl was now doing. He had been an extremely kind and considerate father to her. It struck her for the first time that she had missed some thing—that after providing the rather pretentiously grand-looking house and grounds, and the servants and carriages and conservatories, her father had forgotten to provide something far more essential. But she was so much interested in the two before her that she did not have much time to think of herself. She concluded that she did not want to go back to the Scotch celebrity, and resolutely ignored the surprised looks of some of her friends who passed the library door and made frantic gestures for her to come forth and join them. But when they had moved away it occurred to her that she ought to leave the two together, and so she half rose to go, but the man, divining her intention, said, heartily:

"Don't go—don't go! Ellen's goin' to show me about this big college, an' we want you to go, too."

He was speaking to Miss Arnold, but his eyes never left the girl's face beside him, while he gently stroked her hair as if she had been a little child.

And so they walked up and down the long library, and they showed him the Milton shield, and dragged from their recesses rare books, and pointed out the pictures and autographs of different celebrities. He seemed very much interested and very grateful to them for their trouble, and never ashamed to own how new it all was to him nor how ignorant he was, and he did not try to conceal his pride in his daughter's education and mental superiority to himself. And when Miss Arnold realized that, she quietly effaced herself and let the younger girl do all the honors, only helping her now and then with suggestions or statistics.

"You see," he explained, simply, after a lengthy and, as it seemed to Miss Arnold, a somewhat fruitless dissertation on the splendid copy of the "Rubaiyat" lying before them—"you see I don't know much about these things. Never hed no chance. But Ellen knows, so what's the use of my knowin'! She can put her knowledge to use; but, Lord! I couldn't if I hed it.

"You see it was like this," he continued, cheerfully, turning to Miss Arnold, while the girl at his side raised her head for an instant and uttered a low exclamation of protest. "We lived out West—in a minin' camp in Colorado— Bowlder Bluff wuz its name. Awfully lonesome place. No schools—nothin', jest the store—my store—an' the mines not fur off. Ellen wuz about twelve then"—he turned inquiringly to the girl, but she would not look up—"about twelve," he continued, after a slight pause and another gentle caress of the brown hair; "an' I hedn't never given a thought to wimmen's eddication, an' Ellen here wuz jest growin' up not knowin' a thing—except how I loved her an' couldn't bear her out of my sight" (with another caress), "when one day there came to ther camp a college chap. He wuz an English chap, an' he wuz hard-up. But he wuz a gentleman an' he'd been to a college—Oxford wuz the name—an' he took a heap of notice of Ellen, an' said she wuz mighty smart— yes, Ellen, even then we knew you wuz smart—an' that she ought to have schoolin' an' not run aroun' the camp any more. At first I didn't pay no attention to him. But by an' by his views did seem mighty sensible, an' he kep' naggin' at me. He used to talk to me about it continual an' at night we'd sit out under the pines an' talk—he with a fur-away sort of look in his eyes an' the smoke curl in' up from his pipe—an' he'd tell me what eddication meant to wimmen—independence an' happiness an' all that, an' he insisted fur Ellen to go to a good school. He said there wuz big colleges fur wimmen just like there wuz fur men, an' that she ought to have a chance an' go to one.

"An' then he would read us a lot of stuff of evenin's—specially poetry. Shelley in particular. And yet another chap, almost better'n Shelley. Keats wuz his name. Pr'aps you've read some of his poetry?" he inquired, turning politely to Miss Arnold. Something in her throat kept her from speaking, so she only lowered her head and looked away from the drawn, averted face of the girl before her. "He wuz great! All about gods an' goddesses an' things one don't know much about; but then, as I take it, poetry always seems a little fur off, so it wuz kind of natural. But Shelley wuz our favorite. He used to read us somethin' about the wind. Regularly fine—jest stirred us up, I can tell you. We knew what storms an' dead leaves an' 'black rain an' fire an' hail' wuz out on them lonesome mountains. An' sometimes he'd read us other things, stories from magazines, an' books, but it kind of made me feel lonesomer than ever.

"But Ellen here, she took to it all like a duck to water, an' the college chap kep' insistin' that she ought to go to a good school, an' that she showed 'great natural aptitude'—them wuz his words—an' that she might be famous some day, till at last I got regularly enthusiastic about wimmen's eddication, an' I jest determined not to waste any more time, an' so I sent her to Miss Bellairs's at Denver. She wuz all I hed, an' Lord knows I hedn't no particular reason to feel confidence in wimmen folks"—a sudden, curious, hard expression came into his face for a moment and then died swiftly away as he turned from Miss Arnold and looked at the girl beside him. "But I sent her, an' she ain't never been back to the camp, an' she's been all I ever hoped she'd be."

They had passed from the faintly lighted library into the brilliant corridors, and the man, towering in rugged strength above the two girls, cast curious glances about him as they walked slowly along. Everything seemed to interest him, and when they came to the Greek recitation-rooms he insisted, with boyish eagerness, upon going in, and the big photogravures of the Acropolis and the charts of the Ægean Sea and even a passage from the "Seven against Thebes" (copied upon the walls doubtless by some unlucky Sophomore), and which was so hopelessly unintelligible to him, seemed to fascinate him. And when they came to the physical laboratories he took a wonderful and as it seemed to Miss Arnold an almost pathetic interest in the spectroscopes and Romanoff coils, and the batteries only half-discernible in the faintly flaring lights.

And as they strolled about he still talked of Ellen and himself and their former life, and the life that was to be—when Ellen should become famous. For little by little Miss Arnold comprehended that that was his one fixed idea as he talked, slowly it came to her what this man was, and what his life had been—how he had centred every ambition on the girl beside him; separated her from him, at what cost only the mountain-pines and the stars which had witnessed his nightly struggles with himself could tell; how he had toiled and striven for her that she might have the education he had never known. She began to understand what "going to college" had meant to this girl and this man—to this man especially. It had not meant the natural ending of a preparatory course at some school and a something to be gone through with—creditably, if possible, but also, if possible, without too great exertion and with no expectation of extraordinary results. It had had a much greater significance to them than that. It had been regarded as an event of incalculable importance, an introduction into a new world, the first distinct step upon the road to fame. It had meant to them what a titled offer means to a struggling young American beauty, or a word of approbation to an under-lieutenant from his colonel or a successful maiden speech on the absorbing topic of the day, or any other great and wonderful happening, with greater and more wonderful possibilities hovering in the background.

She began to realize just how his hopes and his ambitions and his belief in this girl had grown and strengthened until the present and the future held nothing for him but her happiness and advancement and success. It was a curious idea, a strange ambition for a man of his calibre to have set his whole heart upon, and as Miss Arnold looked at the girl who was to realize his hopes, a sharp misgiving arose within her and she wondered with sudden fierce pity, why God had not given this man a son.

But Ellen seemed all he wanted. He told, in a proud, apologetic sort of way, while the girl protested with averted eyes, how she had always been "first" at "Miss Bellairs's" and that he supposed "she stood pretty well up in her classes" at college. And Miss Arnold looked at the white, drawn face of the girl and said, quite steadily, she had no doubt but that Miss Oldham was a fine student. She was an exceptionally truthful girl, but she was proud and glad to have said that when she saw the look of happiness that kindled on the face of the man. Yet she felt some compunctions when she noted how simply and unreservedly he took her into his confidence.

And what he told her was just such a story as almost all mothers and fathers tell—of the precocious and wonderful intellect of their children and the great hopes they have of them. But with this man it was different in some way. He was so deeply in earnest and so hopeful and so tender that Miss Arnold could scarcely bear it—"Ellen" was to be a poet. Had she not written verses when she was still a girl and had not the "college chap" and her teachers declared she had great talents? Wait—he would let Miss Arnold judge for herself. Only lately he had written to Ellen, asking her if she still remembered their lonely mountain-home, and she had sent him this. They had strolled down the corridor to one of the winding stairways at the end. He drew from his large leather purse a folded paper. The girl watched him open it with an inexpressible fear in her eyes, and when she saw what it was she started forward with a sort of gasp, and then turned away and steadied herself against the balustrade.

He spread out the paper with exaggerated care, and read with the monotonously painful intonations of the unpractised reader:

> Ye storm-winds of Autumn!
> Who rush by, who shake
> The window, and ruffle
> The gleam lighted lake;
> Who cross to the hill-side
> Thin sprinkled with farms,
> Where the high woods strip sadly
> Their yellowing arms—
> Ye are bound for the mountains!
> Oh! with you let me go
> Where your cold, distant barrier,
> The vast range of snow,
> Through the loose clouds lifts dimly
> Its white peaks in air—
> How deep is their stillness!
> Ah! would I were there!

As he read, Miss Arnold turned her eyes, burning with an unutterable indignation and scorn, upon the girl, but the mute misery and awful supplication in her face checked the words upon her lips. When he had finished reading, Miss Arnold murmured something, she hardly knew what, but he would not let her off so easily.

What did she think of it?—did she not think he ought to be proud of Ellen? and was the "gleam-lighted lake" the lake they could see from the piazza?

He ran on, taking it for granted that Miss Arnold was interested in his hopes and dreams, and almost without waiting for or expecting replies. And at last he told her the great secret. Ellen was writing a book. He spoke of it almost with awe—in a suppressed sort of fashion. She had not told him yet much about it, but he seemed wholly confident in its future success. He wondered which of the big publishing houses would want it most.

Miss Arnold gave a quick gasp of relief. There was more to this girl, then, than she had dared to hope. She glanced eagerly and expectantly toward her, and in that one look she read the whole pitiable lie. Ellen was looking straight ahead of her, and the hopeless misery and shame in her eyes Miss Arnold never forgot. All the pretty, weak curves about the mouth and chin had settled into hard lines, and a nameless fear distorted every feature. But the man seemed to notice nothing, and walked on with head uplifted and a proud, almost inspired look upon his rugged face.

"When will the book be finished, Ellen?" he asked, at length.

The girl looked up, and Miss Arnold noted with amazement her wonderful control.

"It will not be very long now, father," she replied. She was acting her difficult part very perfectly. It occurred to Miss Arnold that for many years this girl had been so acting, and as she looked at the strong, quiet features of the man she shuddered slightly and wondered how it would be with her when he knew.

When the carriage which was to take him to the station for the midnight train into Boston had driven from the door, the two girls looked at each other steadily for an instant.

"Come to my study for a few moments," said the younger one, imperiously. Miss Arnold acquiesced silently, and together they moved down the long corridor to Miss Oldham's rooms.

"I want to explain," she began, breathlessly, leaning against the closed door and watching with strained, wide-opened eyes Miss Arnold's face, upon which the light from the lamp fell strong and full.

"I want to explain," she repeated, defiantly this time. "You had no right to come between myself and my father! I wish with all my heart you had never seen him, but since you *have* seen him I must explain. I am not entirely the hypocrite and the coward you take me for." She stopped suddenly and gave a low cry. "Ah! what shall I say to make you understand? It began so long ago—I did not mean to deceive him. It was because I loved him and he thought me so clever. He thought because I was quick and bright, and because I was having the education I *was* having, that I was—different. In his ignorance how could he guess the great difference between a superficial aptitude and real talents? How could I tell him—how could I," with a despairing gesture, "that I was just like thousands of other girls, and that there are hundreds right here in this college who are my superiors in every way? It would have broken his heart." Her breath came in short gasps and the pallor of her face had changed to a dull red.

Miss Arnold leaned forward on the table.

"You have grossly deceived him," she said, in cold, even tones.

"Deceived him?—yes—a thousand times and in a thousand ways. But I did it to make him happy. Am I really to blame? He expected so much of me—he had such hopes and such dreams of some great career for me. I *am* a coward. I could not tell him that I was a weak, ordinary girl, that I could never realize his aspirations, that the mere knowledge that he depended and relied upon me weighed upon me and paralyzed every effort. When I loved him so could I tell him this? Could I tell him that his sacrifices were in vain, that the girl of whom he had boasted to every man in the mining camp was a complete failure, that he had been dishonored by the mother, and that he was duped by her daughter?"

She went over to the table and leaned her head upon her shaking hand.

"If my mother—if I had had a brother or sister, it might have been different, but I was alone and I was all he had. And so I struggled on, half hoping that I might become something after all. But I confessed to myself what I could not to him, that I would never become a scholar, that my intellect was wholly superficial, that the verses I wrote were the veriest trash, that I was only doing what ninety-nine out of every hundred girls did, and that ninety-eight wrote better rhymes than I. There is a whole drawer full of my 'poetry'"—she flung open a desk disdainfully—"until I could stand it no longer, and one day when he asked me to write something about the mountains, in desperation I copied those verses of Matthew Arnold's. I knew he would never see them. After that it was easy to do so again." She stopped and pressed her hands to her eyes.

"I am the most miserable girl that lives," she said.

Miss Arnold looked at her coldly.

"And the book?" she said at length.

Miss Oldham lifted her head wearily.

"It was all a falsehood. He kept asking me if I were not writing a book. He thought one had only to write a book to become famous. It seemed so easy not to oppose the idea, and little by little I fell into the habit of talking about 'the book' as if it were really being written. I did not try to explain to myself what I was doing. I simply drifted with the current of his desires and hopes. It may seem strange to you that a man like my father should have had such ambitions, and stranger still that he should have ever dreamed I could realize them. But one *has* strange fancies alone with one's self out on the mountains, and the isolation and self-concentration of the life give an intensity to any desire or expectation that you, who live in an ever-changing world, cannot understand."

Miss Arnold looked at the girl curiously. She wondered for the first time if there was any excuse for her. She had a singularly strong moral nature herself, and she could not quite understand this girl's weakness and deceit. The fact that she loved her father so deeply only added to the mystery.

She arose. "If I were you"—she began, coldly, but Miss Oldham stopped her.

"It is all finished now," she said. She, too, had arisen, and was standing against the door, looking down and speaking in the monotonous tone of someone reciting a lesson.

"I have decided, and I shall go to my father, and I shall say, 'I have deceived you; I have neither courage nor honesty. There might have been an excuse for another girl—a girl who did not understand you or who did not love you, or who did not know just how much her success meant to you. For me there is none. I, who knew how strange the idea at first seemed to you of your daughter's being an educated, accomplished girl; I, who knew how little by little the idea became a passion with you, how proud and how fond you were of her, how you worked and prayed that she might be something different and better than the rest—than her mother—I, who knew all this, have still deceived you. There is but one thing I dare ask you, Will you not let me go back to the mountain with you, and serve you and be to you the daughter I have not been as yet?'"

She stopped suddenly and looked at Miss Arnold.

"That is what I must do, is it not?" she asked, dully.

Miss Arnold went over to her.

"That is what you must do," she said, gently.

It was almost two weeks later when Miss Arnold, coming in from a long walk, found a letter lying on her table. It bore an unfamiliar postmark, and the superscription had evidently been written in great haste or agitation. She tore it open with a feeling of apprehension.

"My punishment has come upon me," it ran. "My father is dead. I got a telegram at Denver—they met me at the foot of the mountain. I cannot say anything now. As yet I have but one thought and one comfort—he never knew! Think of me as you will—I am glad he never did!   E. O."

7 ★ THE FUTURE & CULTURAL CHANGE

AT THE TURN OF THE century there was a growing recognition that the nation's future lay in its cities and in their vast potential to invite their inhabitants into the promises of cultural enrichment. Filled with institutional and economic expansion based on new technologies, cities bespoke the richness of a modern future. However, cities also were increasingly associated with disruptive political communities and immigrant settlements. For the authors grouped here, the city appears as a deeply contradictory site containing both the most energizing and corroding elements of modern life.

While the nation's cities were widely portrayed as creating and exacerbating a host of economic, social, and cultural problems, for many authors the "White City" constructed for the Chicago World's Columbian Exposition in 1893 was the paradigmatic metropolis of the future. Covered by virtually every weekly and monthly publishing at the time, the white city was termed the "city of realized dreams" and the "dream city" and was idealized by writers. In "What a Great City Might Be," John Coleman Adams posits a belief that the white city proves that modern cities can be models of civilization rather than sites of degeneration and breeding grounds for poverty, disease, indigency, and crime.

In depictions of the city, assertions about technological or cultural advantage often are countered by anxieties about the nation's rapidly changing demographic and political profile. By 1900, as the nation's population shifted to cities, the country was less dominated by agrarian or frontier regions. By century's end more than two-fifths of the population dwelt in cities as opposed to less than one-fifth in 1860. Though the number of people in the entire country grew by 26 percent during the 1890s, the urban population increased by 56 percent and the rural by only 13 percent. The growth of cities was hastened not only by a shifting and increasing population, but also by rapidly developing technologies that improved extant means of transportation and introduced new ones (among them the street railway, cable car, and electrified streetcar or trolley).

During a time of urban growth, which fostered a perception that the expansion of cities was transforming a pastoral landscape, new ideas about the West and conservation increasingly addressed concerns over the decline of rural America and the psychological consequences of a vanishing national identity based on frontierism. John Muir, author of *The Mountains of California* (1894), had addressed the conservation of national resources, and in periodical pieces published in the 1880s and 1890s he continued to write about the West. For many Americans, the West was understood not only as a geographic reality, but also as an ideological basis for an essential American identity. Declaring that the frontier—an area of "free land" so crucial to American expansion and advancement—was now "closed," Frederick Jackson Turner nonetheless reiterated the frontier's primacy in American identity in "The Significance of the Frontier in American History," delivered at the 1893 World's Columbian Exposition and World's Fair in Chicago. In "The Problem of the West," Turner returned to and elaborated on this theme by arguing that the continued expansion of the frontier was the key to national economic and social growth, thus laying the groundwork for an imperialist foreign policy. While Turner addresses the national dimension of the central relationship between Americans and the land, Anna Weeks posits an individual and spiritual connection to nature that must be preserved. In "The Divorce of Man from Nature," Weeks predicts an urbanized future in which socialist communities communicate through global technologies.

Some of the writers collected here evaluate characters according to their ability to incorporate new technologies into their lives, suggesting that many of society's existing difficulties will be faced by those individuals most invested in the promises of modern life. Edward Everett Hale's comic piece, "Susan's Escort," depicts the dilemma of a young single woman determined to explore the city's cultural riches, even as she experiences a considerable and energizing anxiety about the lurking "dangers" of the nocturnal city. While depicting the gendering of cultural enrichment available to women, who generally had more leisure time than their male counterparts, the story satirizes a male escort's scant ability to absorb cultural works. In "Twenty-Four: Four," the advances obvious in telephone communication are explored by a woman who attempts to incorporate modern technology into her everyday life. As an antidote to boredom, a "mental stimulus" to a "drowsy and dreamy life," the telephone serves as a replacement for a man. For all of its benefits and conveniences, however, the telephone also appears as a representative of an uncertain technology, as an occasional affront to female dignity, and as a mystical force that is, at one point, viewed as an ominous and uncontrollable device for communicating with the dead.

For some, technology posed a serious threat. For instance, the historian Henry Adams in *The Education of Henry Adams* expressed his fear that the future was rushing toward disasters, propelled by the ever-increasing speed of the new sciences. Likewise, Robert Barr's science fiction tale, "Within an Ace of the End of the World," depicts the kind of scientific catastrophe that Adams had predicted could come with the "pushing" of science, namely, the destruction of the world, beginning with its cities, in a virtually apocalyptic event.

★

JOHN COLEMAN ADAMS *What a Great City Might Be—*
A Lesson from the White City
New England Magazine 14 (March 1896): 3–13

[Adams takes up a popular theme in periodicals in the 1890s when he contrasts the ideal qualities of the "White City" with the problems of unregulated cities. Because of its controlled plan and proper maintenance, its cleanliness, "fitness," and "absolute safety," the "White City" corrects the "blot and failure of modern civilization."]

WHILE MANY observers during the great Chicago Exposition, made public their impressions of the artistic and industrial phases of the White City, and much was written of its dramatic side, the stream of incident flowing through the six months of its existence, the human procession marching and countermarching in its avenues, there is one whole aspect of the Exposition which received altogether too little attention. Yet it is a side which contained as much food for thought certainly as any other for the American citizen. Nothing in any of the exhibits within the walls of those great buildings, illustrating the achievements of human skill and power, was half so interesting, so suggestive, so full of hopeful intimations, as the Fair in its aspect as a city by itself. In the midst of a very real and very earthly city, full of the faults which Chicago so preeminently displays, we saw a great many features of what an ideal city might be, a great many visions which perhaps will one day become solid facts, and so remove the blot and failure of modern civilization, the great city of the end of the century. The White City has become almost a dream; but it is well to go back to it, after this interval, and study anew some of its lessons.

In the first place, when one entered the gates of the White City, he felt that he was in the presence of a system of arrangements which had been carefully

FIGURE 20 This photograph of "The White City" of the 1893 Chicago World's Columbian Exposition originally appeared with J. C. Adams's article on the fair. Both the picture and the article emphasize the magnitude of the technical and artistic accomplishments at the fair. (*New England Magazine*, 1896)

and studiously planned. The city was orderly and convenient. The plotting of the grounds, the manner of their development, the placing of the buildings, the communicating avenues and canals and bridges, all exhibited a prevision, a plan, an arrangement of things with reference to each other. The problem of the architect, the landscape gardener and the engineer had been thoroughly thought out before the gates were opened. The result was preeminently satisfying. The features of the Fair could be studied as a whole, or the details could be taken up without loss of time or distraction of attention. The mind was helped and not hindered by the planning of the various parts. They seemed to be the details of an organism, not the mere units of an aggregation. The buildings were not a heap and huddle of walls and roofs; they were a noble sketch in architecture. The streets were not a tangle of thoroughfares representing individual preference or caprice; they were a system of avenues devised for the public convenience.

Of course every dweller in a great city will recognize the fact that these particulars represent just what most of our larger cities are not. If we except some of the newer cities of the West, we have extremely few in which there are any evidences of deliberate and intelligent plan, the perception of the end to be attained, and the effort to gain that end. Life in our cities would be vastly easier if only they had been planned with some reasonable foresight as to results and some common-sense prevision in behalf of the people who were coming to live in them. The great blemish upon our cities is the fact that their natural advantages have been squandered by uses which had no forethought of future needs. The blunders and stupidity of those who have developed them have laid heavy expense upon those who shall come after and try to remodel the territory they have spoiled. That work has hardly begun. When it is undertaken there will be anathemas profound and unsparing upon the short-sightedness which permitted narrow streets and omitted frequent parks and open squares; which reared monumental buildings, and failed to dig tunnels for local transportation; which carried sewage away in drain pipes, only to bring it back by the water tap.

Of course the answer and defence made to this complaint is a general denial of the possibility of doing otherwise, and a claim that the conditions in the two cases were all so different that it is unfair to expect like results. The claim may be partly conceded. The American city is, in general, a surprise to its own inhabitants. It grows beyond all prophecy; it develops in unexpected directions; it increases in territory and population at a pace which is scarcely less than appalling. All these conditions make foresight difficult and possibly debar hindsight from criticism. But the trouble has been that the builders of our cities have been blind because they would not see. They have erred because they chose. They have neglected opportunities which offered. When London suffered from its great fire in 1666, Sir Christopher Wren was ready with admirable plans for rebuilding it with broad streets conveniently arranged, with such a quay as the Victoria Embankment, and with beautiful buildings advantageously disposed. But his plans were not adopted, and an opportunity was lost which will perhaps never recur, of making London a beautiful, well-arranged city. Boston had a like opportunity under a like calamity, and likewise refused it. She threw a tub to the whale of travel and traffic in the shape of a few parings of territory to widen streets; but the whale still chases her perplexed and weary citizens through crooked and narrow thoroughfares. For many years it has been possible to forecast the growth of our cities as certainly as it was possible to predict that the daily population of the White City would be anywhere from 100,000 to 800,000 people. Our mistakes are therefore gratuitous and wilful.

But there were other hints of the order which might exist in our great cities, conveyed in the general cleanliness and neatness of the Exposition grounds. The management had grave difficulties in its way. It had to contend with a great untaught multitude which had never learned in real cities how to be neat in this mimic one. They were as careless and untidy here as they were in their own cities and towns. They littered the ground; they covered the floors; they filled the waters with the rubbish of lunch baskets and the debris of unconsumed luncheons; they tore up their letters and tossed the tatters into the air, they threw away in one building the cards and circulars they had collected in others. But every night when they were gone the patient attendants did their best to clean up after them and to present the grounds fresh and bright for the new crowd next day. When shall we carry the same methods into our municipal affairs? Why may we not at once take a hint in our every-day towns from this city of a few weeks? There is no reason (save such as are discreditable alike to our minds and our morals) why New York and Philadelphia, Boston and Chicago, should not be swept and scrubbed every night in preparation for the uses of every new day. Sometime they will be. Perhaps that day will come all the sooner for the lesson of the White City.

It may be cited as an evidence of what the American populace might be trained to do in the care of its own city premises, that no great multitude of people ever took better care of itself nor showed more love of order in behavior than the throng which came and went every day through the gates of Jackson Park. That fact has been too often cited with praise to demand any emphasis here. It is only called up to show that the American people possesses that self control which can be made the basis of municipal neatness and order. The American citizen understands that he can have a good time without boisterousness or disorder. He knows that the good order of a crowd is only the good order of every individual in it. Once teach him that neatness in the streets can only be secured by the care of every man, woman and child who walks those streets, and we shall be as distinguished for our clean cities as we are for our well-behaved and good-natured crowds.

A word ought to be said just here in behalf of those excellent officials whose personal bearing and courteous, intelligent manner of performing their duties were almost ideal. Many witnesses have testified to their value as an object-lesson in the possibilities of a police force; though perhaps no one has spoken more forcibly than Mr. John Brisben Walker who called them "not bulky, burly punishers of the law's infractions, but public servants placed there to aid in maintaining the law by advice and assistance, ready at all times with kindly word of information, alert to the necessities of visitors and determined to make the day of each in their precincts as pleasant as possible." If one were to sketch a picture of the policeman of the future he could not do better than get a Columbian Guard to pose as a model,—a good specimen of physical manhood, not chosen for his "pull" or his political utility, or for his mere brute bulk, but selected on account of his fitness, drilled into perfect familiarity with his duties, mindful of his own responsibilities to law, and discharging them with intelligence as well as conscientiousness. It may be remarked incidentally that it would have been entirely feasible to secure such a sketch, because the White City policeman, unlike the policemen of so many cities, was a tangible reality at the points when he was needed. He was no absentee official, either in mind or body, but was always visible when on duty, and that, too, in every part of the territory he was set to guard.

But the White City presented yet another hint of a possibility of every great city, in the remarkable safety which it afforded its temporary citizens. Every provision was made to take care of the people and to guard their lives and limbs. The sense of absolute safety within those avenues was delicious. The visitor could give his whole mind to the business in hand without one thought of peril—of falling into any hole, of being hit by any missile. Coming to these grounds from the crowded thoroughfares of Chicago, where the sharp gong of the street cars and the rumble of vehicles was an interminable reminder of the constant threat to personal safety in the crowded streets, it was an unspeakable and indescribable relief to move freely in the midst of the great throngs and not feel in imminent danger. The visitor did not have to think of his personal safety at all. The slow watering-carts and the occasional ambulance on its errand of relief were all that interfered with pedestrians. The railway overhead and the lagoon at one side furnished all the rapid transit without interference of any sort with the sightseers. Suppose that the same sort of care were taken of our lives and persons in a modern great city. It would be worth one's while if he could be as safe in Brooklyn or New York as he was in the streets of the Exposition. But he never will be as long as selfish and mercenary corporations are allowed to capture our thorough-fares and disregard the rights of the people in their use of them.

A word might not be out of place just here as to the provisions made for the comfort as well as the safety of these people. It was possible to do in the Fair what you cannot do in any city that I know of. You did not need to walk five minutes if you were thirsty without finding a place where you could slake your thirst. And there were no open bars at the Fair, either. Water was there for the thirsty, free as air, if you wished it free, at a penny's cost if you felt that a drink could not be real unless you paid for it. I have sometimes thought that the cause of temperance could be promoted by a little more attention to the physical fact that men will get thirsty and that a cool fountain once in every half mile of sidewalk would discourage the trade of the saloons. In a great city you cannot get a cup of cold water even if you want it without begging for it like a tramp,—and much harm comes therefrom. In the great White City you could not get a glass of strong drink unless you went into a restaurant and sat down at a table; and there was no actual suffering, apparently, on account of the absence of the open bars. Possibly there may have been some connection between these facilities for quenching the thirst in a harmless way, and the marked absence of drunkenness in the White City. If it should ever become impossible to obtain any food in our restaurants less obnoxious to the digestion than welsh rarebits and mince-pies, the people could scarcely be blamed for the dyspepsia which would surely ensue.

Much the same things might be said of the facilities for cleanliness and comfort which in the White City were so amply provided. It was a decided novelty, anywhere in America, to be in a miniature great city, where for a nickel one could get at frequent intervals clean hands and face and a smooth head of hair. But the novelty was of a sort which commanded universal approval. Everybody liked the arrangements at the Fair, and everybody would doubtless like to see similar arrangements in his own city. Who will be first to furnish them? A good profit awaits his investment.

No doubt the people who did not go to Chicago are saying even now: "Let us hear no more of the beauty of the buildings at the Fair,"—being like those Athenians who wearied of hearing Aristides' praises continually dinned in their ears; and those who went there are never quite ready to forgive any lack of enthusiasm on that theme. Let me rather do my duty by the most wonderful revelation of the century to Americans, than ease the unwilling minds of those who still sit in the darkness of ignorance. Inquiry was made of several of the most critical observers of the World's Fair what in their judgment would be its most marked and impressive effect upon American thought and enterprise. The unanimous opinion was that it would give a great impulse to architecture, to the construction of civic buildings, to the study of artistic effects in public and private constructions. Not that anybody expects to see those great buildings reproduced anywhere else. That would be to repeat the old stupidities of our architectural bungling and botches, which have given us Greek temples for dwelling houses and an enlargement of the settler's log cabin for a church. But there will be a new spirit growing out of the discovery of what is possible in the way of beautiful public buildings. We have had very little so far in our national life; and we have had, certainly until this latest time, extremely little good private architecture. After the awful monotony of ugliness in the domestic and public architecture of cities like Brooklyn and New York and Philadelphia, the White City was not only a revelation but a benediction. But it forecast a duty, too. It is time we awoke from our nightmare of ugliness and builded better. We are on the eve of a great revival in architecture. When it comes we shall not find men building barns for city halls and court houses and churches, nor making houses by the mile, so like each other that a man could not tell his own house in the block by broad daylight except for its number or some private chalk-marks.

The American visitor to the Fair was permitted another sensation as unusual as it was agreeable, and as strange as it was unexpected. He was treated to the extraordinary experience of feeling that all this beauty, order, protection and display were for his sake, to minister to his enjoyment and to his ease. He knew that the White City was built and furnished on his account, and that everything had been done with a view to making him feel at home in the enjoyment of his inheritance. There was not another place in America where the American citizen could feel so much of the pride of popular sovereignty as he could after he had paid his half dollar and become a naturalized resident of this municipality. Once within those grounds he was monarch of all he surveyed. He could go anywhere. He could see everything. He was welcome to all that he found inside those gates. He could feel for once in his life that he was not liable to be snubbed by the police, nor bullied by car-conductors, nor brow-beaten by salesmen. His temporary citizenship entitled him to the same large privileges which are his by right in any permanent city,—with this difference, that for once his title was recognized and his rights respected. It was a great experience for the patient, submissive, long-suffering American. It gave him a hint of his own deserts. It taught him what he had a right to expect by virtue of his citizenship. It revealed to him what a mock-freedom is really his, when every petty upstart, clad with a little brief authority, feels at liberty to domineer over him. We imagine that we, the people, are the state, and we pride ourselves upon our sovereignty. But was ever a monarch so shame-faced, so put upon, so humiliated? Let this "popular sovereign" try to walk the streets of his own city with any such feeling as filled his heart in the White City, and see how mortifying a lot is his. If he meets a policeman he cannot help feeling afraid under some very innocent circumstances, that he may be arrested merely for being out of doors. If he attempts to cross a street, the swift and death-dealing trolley- or cable-car will soon teach him that the public thoroughfare does not belong to him but to some corporation. If he enters these or any other public vehicle, he realizes that they are run, not to accommodate him, but to make money for somebody else. The sidewalks are not his, but the grocer's, the furniture dealer's, the house builder's and the street contractor's. Even in his own house, the dust from ill-kept streets, the crash and racket over bad pavements, teach him that the city is cared for, not by a government of the people, by the people, and for the people, but by a government of the politicians, by the politicians, for the politicians. But, perhaps, as he understands all these things, he will long for a day to come when he can walk abroad with uplifted head, in the comfortable assurance that the city belongs to him and not to the corporations and the politicians.

Such an era of real liberty in which the city is devoted to the good of the citizen, is perfectly possible, but only under the same conditions as those which made the White City so conspicuous. The splendid administration of that six-months' city was secured by enlisting in its service the best brains and the best dispositions available. The talent and the character of at least one city government in America were level with the task which was set for them. The source and secret of the order, the safety, the beauty, the devotion to the good of the people, which were found in that one small municipality, lay in the fact that the best were called upon to produce the best. Those beautiful grounds were planned by the best minds that could be brought to the undertaking. The beautiful buildings were decorated by the best artists who could be secured. The president of the Directory was one of the foremost business men of Chicago. The executive talent in that wonderful city (which abounds in that particular commodity) was laid under contribution to administer the enterprise. It was a clear case of cause adequate to effect. When our great cities can and will observe the same law; when they realize that it takes the best to make the best; when they feel that personal comfort, safety, and enjoyment are worth having and worth working for; then indeed we may expect to see the ideals suggested in the White City realized in Boston, New York, Brooklyn and Chicago, in every great city in the land.

The great White City has disappeared. Its walls have fallen, its attractions have vanished, its glories have faded like the summer which marked its life. But in its place, heirs of its uses, its beauties, its order, we shall yet see springing into being throughout the land cities which shall embody in permanent form the splendors, the noble suggestions, the dignified municipal ideals of this dream city. In the day in which the better, the best, American city shall become a common spectacle, we shall perceive how much sooner it came by reason of the vision of the White City which we all beheld upon the shores of the great lake.

★

FREDERICK J. TURNER *The Problem of the West*
Atlantic Monthly 78 (September 1896): 289–297

[Invoking evolutionary theory, Frederick Jackson Turner conceives of the American West not as an "area" but as a "form of society" on "free land," a society in which man would undergo a transformational process, adapting and evolving into a "new political species" and a new "type" of man, the "frontiersman," who would be the antithesis of East Coast men, both the Eurocentric "civilized" man and the "degraded" urban immigrant. Turner heralds the frontiersman as a "new natural type," a "homogeneous type" caught in a middle stage of development in an organic, meliorist process of expansion, a process that, of necessity, would lead to heterogeneous unity predicated on a specifically American dynamic and dominant individualism.]

THE PROBLEM OF the West is nothing less than the problem of American development. A glance at the map of the United States reveals the truth. To write of a "Western sectionalism," bounded on the east by the Alleghanies, is, in itself, to proclaim the writer a provincial. What is the West? What has it been in American life? To have the answers to these questions, is to understand the most significant features of the United States of to-day.

The West, at bottom, is a form of society, rather than an area. It is the term applied to the region whose social conditions result from the application of older institutions and ideas to the transforming influences of free land. By this application, a new environment is suddenly entered, freedom of opportunity is opened, the cake of custom is broken, and new activities, new lines of growth, new institutions and new ideals, are brought into existence. The wilderness disappears, the "West" proper passes on to a new frontier, and, in the former area, a new society has emerged from this contact with the backwoods. Gradually this society loses its primitive conditions, and assimilates itself to the type of the older social conditions of the East; but it bears within it enduring and distinguishing survivals of its frontier experience. Decade after decade, West after West, this rebirth of American society has gone on, has left its traces behind it, and has reacted on the East. The history of our political institutions, our democracy, is not a history of imitation, of simple borrowing; it is a history of the evolution and adaptation of organs in response to changed environment, a history of the origin of new political species. In this sense, therefore, the West has been a constructive force of the highest significance in our life. To use the words of that acute and widely informed observer, Mr. Bryce, "The West is the most American part of America. . . . What Europe is to Asia, what England is to the rest of Europe, what America is to England, that the Western States and Territories are to the Atlantic States."

The West, as a phase of social organization, began with the Atlantic coast, and passed across the continent. But the colonial tide-water area was in close touch with the Old World, and soon lost its Western aspects. In the middle of the eighteenth century, the newer social conditions appeared along the upper waters of the tributaries of the Atlantic. Here it was that the West took on its distinguishing features, and transmitted frontier traits and ideals to this area in later days. On the coast were the fishermen and skippers, the merchants and planters, with eyes turned toward Europe. Beyond the falls of the rivers were the pioneer farmers, largely of nonEnglish stock, Scotch-Irish and German. They constituted a distinct people, and may be regarded as an expansion of the social and economic life of the middle region into the back country of the South. These frontiersmen were the ancestors of Boone, Andrew Jackson, Calhoun, Clay, and Lincoln. Washington and Jefferson were profoundly affected by these frontier conditions. The forest clearings have been the seed plots of American character.

In the Revolutionary days, the settlers crossed the Alleghanies and put a barrier between them and the coast. They became, to use their phrases, "the men of the Western waters," the heirs of the "Western world." In this era, the backwoodsmen, all along the western slopes of the mountains, with a keen sense of the difference between them and the dwellers on the coast, demanded organization into independent States of the Union. Self-government was their ideal. Said one of their rude, but energetic petitions for statehood: "Some of our fellow-citizens may think we are not able to conduct our affairs and consult our interests; but if our society is rude, much wisdom is not necessary to supply our wants, and a fool can sometimes put on his clothes better than a wise man can do it for him." This forest philosophy is the philosophy of American democracy. But the men of the coast were not ready to admit its implications. They apportioned the state legislatures so that the property-holding minority of the tide-water lands were able to outvote the more populous back counties. A similar system was proposed by federalists in the Constitutional Convention of 1787. Gouverneur Morris, arguing in favor of basing representation on property as well as numbers, declared that "he looked forward, also, to that range of new States which would soon be formed in the West. He thought the rule of representation ought to be so fixed, as to secure to the Atlantic States a prevalence in the national councils." "The new States," said he, "will know less of the public interest than these; will have an interest in many respects different; in particular will be little scrupulous of involving the community in wars, the burdens and operations of which would fall chiefly on the maritime States. Provision ought, therefore, to be made to prevent the maritime States from being hereafter outvoted by them." He added that the Western country "would not be able to furnish men equally enlightened to share in the administration of our common interests. The busy haunts of men, not the remote wilderness, was the proper school of political talents. If the Western people get power into their hands, they will ruin the Atlantic interest. The back members are always most averse to the best measures." Add to these utterances of Gouverneur Morris the impassioned protest of Josiah Quincy, of Massachusetts, in the debates in the House of Representatives, on the admission of Louisiana. Referring to the discussion over the slave votes and the West in the Constitutional Convention, he declared, "Suppose, then, that it had been distinctly foreseen that, in addition to the effect of this weight, the whole population of a world beyond the Mississippi was to be brought into this and the other branch of the legislature, to form our laws, control our rights, and decide our destiny. Sir, can it be pretended that the patriots of that day would for one moment have listened to it? . . . They had not taken degrees at the hospital of idiocy. . . . Why, sir, I have already heard of six States, and some say there will be, at no great distance of time, more. I have also heard that the mouth of the Ohio will be far to the east of the centre of the contemplated empire.... You have no authority to throw the rights and property of this people into 'hotch-pot' with the wild men on the Missouri, nor with the mixed, though more respectable, race of Anglo-Hispano-Gallo-Americans who bask on the sands in the mouth of the Mississippi.... Do you suppose the people of the Northern and Atlantic States will, or ought to, look on with patience and see Representatives and Senators from the Red River and Missouri, pouring themselves upon this and the other floor, managing the concerns of a seaboard fifteen hundred miles, at least, from their residence; and having a preponderancy in councils into which, constitutionally, they could never have been admitted?"

Like an echo from the fears expressed by the East at the close of the eighteenth century come the words of an eminent Eastern man of letters at the end of the nineteenth century, in warning against the West: "Materialized in their temper; with few ideals of an ennobling sort; little instructed in the lessons of history; safe from exposure to the direct calamities and physical horrors of war; with undeveloped imaginations and sympathies—they form a community unfortunate and dangerous from the possession of power without a due sense of its corresponding responsibilities; a community in which the passion for war may easily be excited as the fancied means by which its greatness may be convincingly exhibited, and its ambitions gratified.... Some chance spark may fire the prairie."

Here, then, is the problem of the West, as it looked to New England leaders of thought in the beginning and at the end of this century. From the first, it was recognized that a new type was growing up beyond the mountains, and that the time would come when the destiny of the nation would be in Western hands. The divergence of these societies became clear in the struggle over the ratification of the federal constitution. The interior agricultural region, the communities that were in debt and desired paper money, opposed the instrument; but the areas of intercourse and property carried the day.

It is important to understand, therefore, what were some of the ideals of this early Western democracy. How did the frontiersman differ from the man of the coast?

The most obvious fact regarding the man of the Western waters is that he had placed himself under influences destructive to many of the gains of civilization. Remote from the opportunity for systematic education, substituting a log hut in the forest clearing for the social comforts of the town, he suffered hardships and privations, and reverted in many ways to primitive conditions of life. Engaged in a struggle to subdue the forest, working as an individual, and with little specie or capital, his interests were with the debtor class. At each stage of its advance, the West has favored an expansion of the currency. The pioneer had boundless confidence in the future of his own community, and when seasons of financial contraction and depression occurred, he, who had staked his all on confidence in Western development, and had fought the savage for his home, was inclined to reproach the conservative sections and classes. To explain this antagonism requires more than denunciation of dishonesty, ignorance, and boorishness as fundamental Western traits. Legislation in the United States has had to deal with two distinct social conditions. In some portions of the country there was, and is, an aggregation of property, and vested rights are in the foreground: in others, capital is lacking, more primitive conditions prevail, with different economic and social ideals, and the contentment of the average individual is placed in the foreground. That in the conflict between these two ideals an even hand has always been held by the government would be difficult to show.

The separation of the Western man from the seaboard, and his environment, made him in a large degree free from European precedents and forces. He looked at things independently and with small regard or appreciation for the best Old World experience. He had no ideal of a philosophical, eclectic nation, that should advance civilization by "intercourse with foreigners and familiarity with their point of view, and readiness to adopt whatever is best and most suitable in their ideas, manners, and customs." His was rather the ideal of conserving and developing what was original and valuable in this new country. The entrance of old society upon free lands meant to him opportunity for a new type of democracy and new popular ideals. The West was not conservative: buoyant self-confidence and self-assertion were distinguishing traits in its composition. It saw in its growth nothing less than a new order of society and state. In this conception were elements of evil and elements of good.

But the fundamental fact in regard to this new society was its relation to land. Professor Boutmy has said of the United States, "Their one primary and predominant object is to cultivate and settle these prairies, forests, and vast wastelands. The striking and peculiar characteristic of American society is that it is not so much a democracy as a huge commercial company for the discovery, cultivation, and capitalization of its enormous territory. The United States are primarily a commercial society, and only secondarily a nation." Of course, this involves a serious misapprehension. By the very fact of the task here set forth, far-reaching ideals of the state and of society have been evolved in the West, accompanied by loyalty to the nation representative of these ideals. But M. Boutmy's description hits the substantial fact, that the fundamental traits of the man of the interior were due to the free lands of the West. These turned his attention to the great task of subduing them to the purposes of civilization, and to the task of advancing his economic and social status in the new democracy which he was helping to create. Art, literature, refinement, scientific administration, all had to give way to this Titanic labor. Energy, incessant activity, became the lot of this new American. Says a traveler of the time of Andrew Jackson, "America is like a vast workshop, over the door of which is printed in blazing characters, 'No admittance here, except on business.'" The West of our own day reminds Mr. Bryce "of the crowd which Vathek found in the hall of Eblis, each darting hither and thither with swift steps and unquiet mien, driven to and fro by a fire in the heart. Time seems too short for what they have to do, and the result always to come short of their desire."

But free lands and the consciousness of working out their social destiny did more than turn the Westerner to material interests and devote him to a restless existence. They promoted equality among the Western settlers, and reacted as a check on the aristocratic influences of the East. Where everybody could have a farm, almost for taking it, economic equality easily resulted, and this involved political equality. Not without a struggle would the Western man abandon this ideal, and it goes far to explain the unrest in the remote West to-day.

Western democracy included individual liberty, as well as equality. The frontiersman was impatient of restraints. He knew how to preserve order, even in the absence of legal authority. If there were cattle thieves, lynch law was sudden and effective: the regulators of the Carolinas were the predecessors of the claims associations of Iowa and the vigilance committees of California. But the individual was not ready to submit to complex regulations. Population was sparse, there was no multitude of jostling interest, as in older settlements, demanding an elaborate system of personal restraints. Society became atomic. There was a reproduction of the primitive idea of the personality of the law, a crime was more an offense against the victim than a violation of the law of the land. Substantial justice, secured in the most direct way, was the ideal of the backwoodsman. He had little patience with finely drawn distinctions or scruples of method. If the thing was one proper to be done, then the most immediate rough and ready, effective way was the best way.

It followed from the lack of organized political life, from the atomic conditions of the backwoods society, that the individual was exalted and given free play. The West was another name for opportunity. Here were mines to be seized, fertile valleys to be preempted, all the natural resources open to the shrewdest and the boldest. The United States is unique in the extent to which the individual has been given an open field, unchecked by restraints of an old social order, or of scientific administration of government. The self-made man was the Western man's ideal, was the kind of man that all men might become. Out of his wilderness experience, out of the freedom of his opportunities, he fashioned a formula for social regeneration,—the freedom of the individual to seek his own. He did not consider that his conditions were exceptional and temporary.

Under such conditions, leadership easily develops,—a leadership based on the possession of the qualities most serviceable to the young society. In the history of Western settlement, we see each forted village following its local hero. Clay, Jackson, Harrison, Lincoln, were illustrations of this tendency in periods when the Western hero rose to the dignity of national hero.

The Western man believed in the manifest destiny of his country. On his border, and checking his advance, were the Indian, the Spaniard, and the Englishman. He was indignant at Eastern indifference and lack of sympathy with his view of his relations to these peoples; at the short-sightedness of Eastern policy. The closure of the Mississippi by Spain, and the proposal to exchange our claim of freedom of navigating the river, in return for commercial advantages to New England, nearly led to the withdrawal of the West from the Union. It was the Western demands that brought about the purchase of Louisiana, and turned the scale in favor of declaring the War of 1812. Militant qualities were favored by the annual expansion of the settled area in the face of hostile Indians and the stubborn wilderness. The West caught the vision of the nation's continental destiny. Henry Adams, in his History of the United States, makes the American of 1800 exclaim to the foreign visitor, "Look at my wealth! See these solid mountains of salt and iron, of lead, copper, silver, and gold. See these magnificent cities scattered broadcast to the Pacific! See my cornfields rustling and waving in the summer breeze from ocean to ocean, so far that the sun itself is not high enough to mark where the distant mountains bound my golden seas. Look at this continent of mine, fairest of created worlds, as she lies turning up to the sun's never failing caress her broad and exuberant breasts, overflowing with milk for her hundred million children." And the foreigner saw only dreary desert, tenanted by sparse, ague-stricken pioneers and savages. The cities were log huts and gambling dens. But the frontiersman's dream was prophetic. In spite of his rude, gross nature, this early Western man was an idealist withal. He dreamed dreams and beheld visions. He had faith in man, hope for democracy, belief in America's destiny, unbounded confidence in his ability to make his dreams come true. Said Harriet Martineau in 1834, "I regard the American people as a great embryo poet, now moody, now wild, but bringing out results of absolute good sense: restless and wayward in action, but with deep peace at his heart; exulting that he has caught the true aspect of things past, and the depth of futurity which lies before him, wherein to create something so magnificent as the world has scarcely begun to dream of. There is the strongest hope of a nation that is capable of being possessed with an idea."

It is important to bear this idealism of the West in mind. The very materialism that has been urged against the West was accompanied by ideals of equality, of the exaltation of the common man, of national expansion, that make it a profound mistake to write of the West as though it were engrossed in mere material ends. It has been, and is, preeminently a region of ideals, mistaken or not.

It is obvious that these economic and social conditions were so fundamental in Western life that they might well dominate whatever accessions came to the West by immigration from the coast sections or from Europe. Nevertheless, the West cannot be understood without bearing in mind the fact that it has received the great streams from the North and from the South, and that the Mississippi compelled these currents to intermingle. Here it was that sectionalism first gave way under the pressure of unification. Ultimately the conflicting ideas and institutions of the old sections struggled for dominance in this area under the influence of the forces that made for uniformity, but this is merely another phase of the truth that the West must become unified, that it could not rest in sectional groupings. For precisely this reason the struggle occurred. In the period from the Revolution to the close of the War of 1812, the democracy of the Southern and Middle States contributed the main streams of settlement and social influence to the West. Even in Ohio political power was soon lost by the New England leaders. The democratic spirit of the Middle region left an indelible impress on the West in this its formative period. After the War of 1812, New England, its supremacy in the carrying trade of the world having vanished, became a beehive from which swarms of settlers went out to western New York and the remoter regions. These settlers spread New England ideals of education and character and political institutions, and acted as a leaven of great significance in the Northwest. But it would be a mistake to believe that an unmixed New England influence took possession of the Northwest. These pioneers did not come from the class that conserved the type of New England civilization pure and undefiled. They represented a less contented, less conservative influence. Moreover, by their sojourn in the Middle region, on their westward march, they underwent modification, and when the farther West received them, they suffered a forest-change, indeed. The Westernized New England man was no longer the representative of the section that he left. He was less conservative, less provincial, more adaptable and approachable, less rigorous in his Puritan ideals, less a man of culture, more a man of action.

As might have been expected, therefore, the Western men, in the era of good feeling, had much homogeneity throughout the Mississippi valley, and began to stand as a new national type. Under the lead of Henry Clay they invoked the national government to break down the mountain barrier by internal improvements, and thus to give their crops an outlet to the coast. Under him they appealed to the national government for a protective tariff to create a home market. A group of frontier States entered the Union with democratic provisions respecting the suffrage, and with devotion to the nation that had given them their lands, built their roads and canals, regulated their territorial life, and made them equals in the sisterhood of States. At last these Western forces of aggressive nationalism and democracy took possession of the government in the person of the man who best embodied them, Andrew Jackson. This new democracy that captured the country and destroyed the older ideals of statesmanship came from no theorist's dreams of the German forest. It came, stark and strong and full of life, from the American forest. But the triumph of this Western democracy revealed also the fact that it could rally to its aid the laboring classes of the coast, then just beginning to acquire self-consciousness and organization.

The next phase of Western development revealed forces of division between the northern and southern portions of the West. With the spread of the cotton culture went the slave system and the great plantation. The small farmer in his log cabin, raising varied crops, was displaced by the planter raising cotton. In all except the mountainous areas, the industrial organization of the tidewater took possession of the Southwest, the unity of the back country was broken, and the solid South was formed. In the Northwest this was the era of railroads and canals, opening the region to the increasing stream of Middle State and New England settlement, and strengthening the opposition to slavery. A map showing the location of the men of New England ancestry in the Northwest would represent also the counties in which the Free Soil party cast its heaviest votes. The commercial connections of the Northwest likewise were reversed by the railroad. The result is stated by a writer in De Bow's Review in 1852 in these words:—

"What is New Orleans now? Where are her dreams of greatness and glory? . . . Whilst she slept, an enemy has sowed tares in her most prolific fields. Armed with energy, enterprise, and an indomitable spirit, that enemy, by a system of bold, vigorous, and sustained efforts, has succeeded in reversing the very laws of nature and of nature's God,—rolled back the mighty tide of the Mississippi and its thousand tributary streams, until their mouth, practically and commercially, is more at New York or Boston than at New Orleans."

The West broke asunder, and the great struggle over the social system to be given to the lands beyond the Mississippi followed. In the Civil War the Northwest furnished the national hero,—Lincoln was the very flower of frontier training and ideals,—and it took into its hands the whole power of the government. Before the war closed, the West could claim the President, Vice-President, Chief Justice, Speaker of the House, Secretary of the Treasury, Postmaster-General, Attorney-General, General of the army, and Admiral of the navy. The leading generals of the war had been furnished by the West. It was the region of action, and in the crisis it took the reins.

The triumph of the nation was followed by a new era of Western development. The national forces projected themselves across the prairies and plains. Railroads, fostered by government loans and land grants, opened the way for settlement and poured a flood of European immigrants and restless pioneers from all sections of the Union into the government lands. The army of the United States pushed back the Indian, rectangular Territories were carved into checker-board States, creations of the federal government, without a history, without physiographical unity, without particularistic ideas. The later frontiersman leaned on the strong arm of national power.

At the same time the South underwent a revolution. The plantation, based on slavery, gave place to the farm, the gentry to the democratic elements. As in the West, new industries, of mining and of manufacture, sprang up as by magic. The New South, like the New West, was an area of construction; a debtor area, an area of unrest; and it, too, had learned the uses to which federal legislation might be put.

In the mean time the old Northwest [the present States of Ohio, Indiana, Illinois, Michigan, and Wisconsin] has passed through an economic and social transformation. The whole West has furnished an area over which successive waves of economic development have passed. The Indian hunters and traders were followed by the pioneer farmers, engaged in raising unrotated crops; after this came the wave of more settled town life and varied agriculture; the wave of manufacture followed. These stages of development have passed in succession across large parts of the old Northwest. The State of Wisconsin, now much like parts of the State of New York, was at an earlier period like the State of Nebraska of to-day; the granger movement and the greenback party had for a time the ascendancy; and in the northern counties of the State, where there is a sparser population, and the country is being settled, its sympathies are still with the debtor class. Thus the old Northwest is a region where the older frontier conditions survive in parts, and where the inherited ways of looking at things are largely to be traced to its frontier days. At the same time it is a region in many ways assimilated to the East. It understands both sections. It is not entirely content with the existing structure of economic society in the sections where wealth has accumulated and corporate organizations are powerful; but neither has it seemed to feel that its interests lie in supporting the programme of the prairies and the South. In the Fifty-third Congress it voted for the income tax, but it rejected free coinage. It is still affected by the ideal of the self-made man, rather than by the ideal of industrial nationalism. It is more American, but less cosmopolitan than the seaboard.

We are now in a position to see clearly some of the factors involved in the Western problem. For nearly three centuries the dominant fact in American life has been expansion. With the settlement of the Pacific coast and the occupation of the free lands, this movement has come to a check. That these energies of expansion will no longer operate would be a rash prediction; and the demands for a vigorous foreign policy, for an interoceanic canal, for a revival of our power upon the seas, and for the extension of American influence to outlying islands and adjoining countries, are indications that the movement will continue. The stronghold of these demands lies west of the Alleghanies.

In the remoter West, the restless, rushing wave of settlement has broken with a shock against the arid plains. The free lands are gone, the continent is crossed, and all this push and energy is turning into channels of agitation. Failures in one area can no longer be made good by taking up land on a new frontier; the conditions of a settled society are being reached with suddenness and with confusion. The West has been built up with borrowed capital, and the question of the stability of gold, as a standard of deferred payments, is eagerly agitated by the debtor West, profoundly dissatisfied with the industrial conditions that confront it, and actuated by frontier directness and rigor in its remedies. For the most part, the men who built up the West beyond the Mississippi, and who are now leading the agitation, came as pioneers from the old Northwest, in the days when it was just passing from the stage of a frontier section. For example, Senator Allen of Nebraska, president of the recent national Populist Convention, and a type of the political leaders of his section, was born in Ohio in the middle of the century; went in his youth to Iowa, and not long after the Civil War made his home in Nebraska. As a boy, he saw the buffalo driven out by the settlers; he saw the Indian retreat as the pioneer advanced. His training is that of the old West, in its frontier days. And now the frontier opportunities are gone. Discontent is demanding an extension of governmental activity in its behalf. In these demands, it finds itself in touch with the depressed agricultural classes and the workingmen of the South and East. The Western problem is no longer a sectional problem; it is a social problem on a national scale. The greater West, extending from the Alleghanies to the Pacific, cannot be regarded as a unit; it requires analysis into regions and classes. But its area, its population, and its material resources would give force to its assertion that if there is a sectionalism in the country, the sectionalism is Eastern. The old West, united to the new South, would produce, not a new sectionalism, but a new Americanism. It would not mean sectional disunion, as some have speculated, but it might mean a drastic assertion of national government and imperial expansion under a popular hero.

This, then, is the real situation: a people composed of heterogeneous materials, with diverse and conflicting ideals and social interests, having passed from the task of filling up the vacant spaces of the continent, is now thrown back upon itself, and is seeking an equilibrium. The diverse elements are being fused into national unity. The forces of reorganization are turbulent and the nation seems like a witches' kettle:

"Double, double, toil and trouble,
Fire burn and cauldron bubble."

But the far West has its centres of industrial life and culture not unlike those of the East. It has state universities, rivaling in conservative and scientific economic instruction those of any other part of the Union, and its citizens more often visit the East, than do Eastern men the West. As time goes on, its industrial development will bring it more into harmony with the East.

Moreover, the old Northwest holds the balance of power, and is the battle-field on which these issues of American development are to be settled. It has more in common with all regions of the country than has any other region. It understands the East, as the East does not understand the West. The White City which recently rose on the shores of Lake Michigan fitly typified its growing culture as well as its capacity for great achievement. Its complex and representative industrial organization and business ties, its determination to hold fast to what is original and good in its Western experience, and its readiness to learn and receive the results of the experience of other sections and nations, make it an open-minded and safe arbiter of the American destiny. In the long run the centre of the Republic may be trusted to strike a wise balance between the contending ideals. But she does not deceive her self; she knows that the problem of the West means nothing less than the problem of working out original social ideals and social adjustment for the American nation.

★

ANNA R. WEEKS *The Divorce of Man from Nature*
Arena 9 (January 1894): 227–232

[This essay attempts to reconcile new scientific thought with religion and burgeoning urbanization with civic responsibility. Anna Weeks posits a spiritual, specifically Christian, relationship between man and the land, which ultimately cannot be severed by Darwinism or compromised by the demonized city, and which will evolve into an ideal socialist, globalized, technology-based future.]

"A flaming sword which turned every way to keep the way of the tree of life."

MAN'S LOVE OF nature, their divorce, and the wickedness of a social scheme which causes this, have haunted me all through a long summer and autumn. Until I speak my mind the ghost cannot rest.

If theories of evolution are true, if the new belief of life in all things be true, then is man, as to earth, "bone of her bone, flesh of her flesh." That wonderful allegory in Genesis once more flashes a response to science and the inner light when it says, "And the Lord God formed man of the dust of the ground." And it is that which is dear to man, whenever he has been allowed to come in contact with it in its pristine state.

There is no time of year in which one may get away from the city that this love of nature does not assert itself.

Go out in January and see how the heart thrills at the purity of the snow, unsoiled by city grime; how the eye feasts upon the grace and tints of the bare tree branches, and on the tasseled pines beplumed with snow; what velvet in the mosses, what peace under the stars.

Watch the leaves come out in May; call to the answering chipmunk, hide to watch the birds at their love making and nest building.

> *Each little form celestial seems,*
> *Untouched, unspoiled, a harp with wings;*
> *Each little sprite a message brings,*
> *A glimpse of heaven while he sings.*

The flashing gulls above like silver stars on wing, the snow of the rabbit's breast, the dirt of the squirrel's plume, the rain on the cottage roof, the rustle of the wren, the warm breath of the pines, the rattle of the nuts on the crisp brown leaves, the chatter of departing blackbirds;—what are all these but messages of brotherhood from the humbler of God's creation to the higher?

Go to the Great Lake beaches in midsummer and autumn; press joyful feet upon them, breathe full and free in unison with the jubilant waves; read ancient stories in the stones they toss you. But ever between all this and you comes the face of the proletariat; it dims the sunrise, it gazes from the incandescent sumach, from the soft glory of the maple. When lingering cottagers sat on the grassy bluff that September Sabbath eve, when the moon rose from the lake, when they sang soft evensongs to her, where were the toilers? *Not there.* Have they, then, no ear for these lofty tidings from nature? Alas! only those at the court may receive the envoy. Man is in the great city, struggling with his brother. What to him can all this beauty bring? Can a fighting man stop to enjoy the sunrise? To him it means only another heroic day; it is but his battle reveille.

The child who should be like the squirrel peers through the grime of the factory window to envy the sparrow. Even the field mice are happier than the poor babes in Chicago; they gather their seeds and berries, they lack not for acorns and nuts, they sip the dew from the fallen leaf. The very cows are better cared for than is the poverty-stricken mother in Babylon. While the summer was in its glow it came to her only as a fierce fiend of fire on the attic roof; it made a place of death of her miserable alley rooms when the steam of her washing stifled her. Or mayhap she sat with her babe on her lap to watch it die, while her faith in man—and so in God—went slowly out.

Some spirits are blind and some are heartless; either of these will dismiss the complaint with the *ipse dixit*, "But the poor flock incessantly to the cities." Aye, they do. Is it not better to starve with one's fellows than alone? But thoughtful and gentle hearts will continue to ask, "Whence come these wrongs?"

The competitive system is responsible. The man of the peasant class or middle class is compelled by misfortune to mortgage his little farm, and never is able to get ahead enough to redeem it; at last the mortgage is foreclosed, and his means of production gone. Or his place was paid for, and he does not mortgage, but the ground becomes a millstone round his neck; the crops fail, or he can get no market, or the usurpers of the public highway exact such freight tribute as leaves him to famish. At the same time the chicane of the "village promoter" puts a fictitious value on his land; the tax becomes excessive and yet he cannot sell. Then he "strikes for his altars and his fires" by a desperate flight to the city. Surely there is much work where there are so many to be served.

But there is another force which makes exiles of the farmer class; that is, the barrenness of their lives as regards music, literature, the drama, pictorial art, and society. All love these things more or less, in the degree that they are aware of their existence; but to pursue them in the country costs much, and is only possible to a limited degree, as country life now is. In the city the young man or woman who has these tastes can find libraries and night schools, and he supposes that he will also find choice society. He has heard of the charms of that great centre; he dreams of the parks, the boulevards, the theatres, palaces, schools, picture galleries; neighbors all about one, instead of half a mile away. He has seen but the hard side of nature and is as yet somewhat unconscious of her beauty, or, associating it with his Dead Sea life, he really hates it. The gregarious instinct masters him, and the "earth longing" is for the moment eclipsed. He, too, embarks in the municipal whirlpool.

Here, then, are the two classes of men and women who are so rapidly shifting from prairie and village to the city, and it is poverty which drives them both; in one bodily hunger, and in the other soul hunger. But they soon discover that one cannot enjoy even the public parks, the drives, the schools, unless he has at least a little money; even a car fare is frequently more than they dare to take from the rent coming due; it takes time to go to those distant fairy fields—they do not live in a quarter near them. Only the prosperous can do that. To the children of these families the schools are naught, for the child, too, must toil in Vanity Fair.

And society? One place opens its doors—aye, two; the saloon and the house of hell. These are always filled with light, music, games, and gayety.

Neighbors? He finds that in cities people seldom have neighbors, unless on those magnificent streets where wealth allows one to live a lifetime. His dearest may die, and those on the other side of the wall may not know it until they see the hearse. He seems not to understand that, while every man is at war with his brother, Ishmael cannot guard his munitions too carefully. And so in the urban maelstrom he is more pitifully alone than on the bitter barrens of the Dakotas. He sees at last that he is driven not only from agrarian life, but even from human relations. Thus does the two-edged flaming sword of industrial war bar the gate of his Eden, from whence he becomes doubly exiled.

Is man, then, to be permanently separated from the earth? Not only has he left the pasture and wood, but in the towns his shelter lifts higher and higher, nearer the stars, but surely not nearer heaven. He helplessly talks of roof gardens, he accepts for his little ones the pitiful dole of the Fresh Air Fund.

"The Fresh Air Fund"! Can the successful class imagine what that means? Had we not once a phrase, "as free as air"? It is obsolete. Few commodities now cost as much as air. The monster office buildings increase in number and in grotesque want of symmetry. They shut out the air and light of day from adjoining houses and from the street. Men work constantly by artificial light till they

> Scarce can hold it true
> That in distant lanes the lilies blossom under skies of blue.

The herding goes on. The crowds in the street congest travel until local transportation seems a Sphinx riddle. Citizens' committees are appointed to consider it; every solution but the right one is tried, and proved ineffectual or palliative only. And yet in all that throng there is scarcely a man who does not dream of a little home under the skies, with trees and vines and birds! Should the masses at last conclude that this dream is but a phantasm, then may our *quasi* civilization beware. But let us hope that ere the giant awakes he will be restored to that which he loves, the society of nature.

There is but one way to do this with absolute success, and that is, the great city of to-day must go. This is to be brought to pass by a socialistic order which shall conduct its manufactures, its schools, its society, on such a basis as will for a time convert centripetal forces into centrifugal; an order which shall set the stream of life flowing back again in its natural channel, and make it possible for men to live without this dragnet huddling. The modern metropolis is an enormity, and must be decentralized; as there should be no vast wastes untrodden by man, neither should there be any wilderness of masonry where myriads of prisoners stay out their weary years. Says August Bebel:

No one can regard the development of our large towns as a healthy product. The present economic and industrial system is constantly attracting great masses of the population hither. . . . All round the towns and immediately adjoining them, the villages are also assuming the character of towns, and an enormous mass of proletariat is collecting within them. Meanwhile the villages increase in the direction of the town and the town in the direction of the villages, until at length they fall into the town, like planets that have come too near the sun. But their mutual conditions of existence are not improved thereby. On the contrary these aggregations of masses, these centres of revolution, as one might call them, were a necessity during the present phase of development; when the new community is constituted, their object will have been fulfilled. Their gradual dissolution becomes inevitable.

To those who have never thought that the capitals of the competitive age could vanish, the suggestion of such a thing may seem as a foolish dream. Certainly none of us shall see it in the flesh, but there are conditions foreshadowed which, if considered, will lend to this conception an air of feasibility.

Cumulative modern invention and cumulative psychic light are intensely unifying the race. To be in and of the world it will not always be necessary that we shall be piled above one another in brick and mortar, or that we shall every day behold the tangible faces of the crowd. Electricity, aluminum, and the thought force promise to serve us far more in the future than as yet.

The Adam and Eve of the new Eden will have a home for life, with its plot of ground or its share in the common park about the dwellings. Factories will be, not in a few congested, barren spots, but wherever the raw material is produced. Improved roads, the bicycle, the telegraph, the telephone, the ocean cable, pneumatic tubes, air ships, electric cars, and telepathy will keep us near one another and near our needs. Immense concourses of people can in an hour unite in great auditoriums scattered here and there, but they need not gather thus for daily work. Each public building will be not a tower but a palace; its harmony will be restored, and the space about it will allow its proportions to be understood at a glance. Its inner beauty, too, will be increased by the freedom with which shall enter light, air, and odors of flowers.

The prophet of humanity still insists that there shall be a New Jerusalem, but it will have neither walls nor gates; its streets shall be not of gold but of grass; flowing through it no stream of filth, death laden, but "the river of the water of life, clear as crystal." On its banks are the trees of life and their "leaves are for the healing of the nations." The coming age shall be a perpetual feast of tabernacles without the sacrifice of helpless beasts, "and all the congregation of them that are come again out of captivity" shall "make booths and sit under the booths." Behold, the tabernacle of Good is with men, and she will dwell with them. "What therefore God hath joined together, let no man put asunder."

★

EDWARD EVERETT HALE *Susan's Escort*

Harper's 80 (1890): 908–918

[Edward Everett Hale, a prolific story writer and Boston minister, contributed to many literary periodicals over a period of thirty years. Among his most famous pieces were "The Man Without a Country" (1863) and his memoir, "A New England Boyhood," which appeared in the *Atlantic Monthly* in 1892.]

I. Susan Ellsworth is as nice a girl as I know. I wish that you and I, dear readers, knew more such. She lived just out from Boston; not at Jamaica Plain, but at one of the most convenient stations on that admirable Providence Railroad—my road, so far as a person may be said to own it who by many punch-tickets builds up the fortunes of the stockholders. Susan Ellsworth was and is a school-mistress in one of the public schools of Boston. Like most such ladies, she had a fancy for living at a great distance from her school, and went and came by rapid or slow transit as the gods and Mr. Whitney might provide. This was in the daytime, and was easy.

But Susan had more difficulty in the evenings. Her brothers lived, one in Alaska, one in Yokohama, and a third was studying medicine in Vienna. She was engaged then to a man far away, and is now, if, indeed, she be not married before this story goes to press. Still, she had what I may call a passion for evening concerts and lectures—nay, let me whisper it, for a rollicking, laughing burlesque, if the Vokeses or some other nice people came along, and, most of all, for the opera when it was really good. Now all these brothers were earning their own board bills, so that Susan Ellsworth was not fleeced by them, as most good school-mistresses known to me are by their brothers. And as her salary was good, she could indulge her passion for these evening entertainments, for she was still young.

She tried at first bold independence. Boston, she said, was a civilized city. The streets were light, and when electricity came in they were very light even at night. So she pretended to be bold when she was frightened. She went into the station at Park Square by rail. She took street car or sidewalk to the Institute, the Opera-house, to Mr. Hale's reading, to the Old South lectures, to the Museum, or wherever she went. When the entertainment was over she crowded into a car, or put herself in the wake of some large walking party going her way. And so she pretended to herself and to fellow-graduates from

FIGURE 21 From Edward Everett Hale's short story, this illustration features a progressive, cultured young woman who creates her own escort for evening cultural events held in the city. (*Harper's*, 1890)

Vassar, to whom she wrote descriptions of her independent Boston life, that she was not afraid.

All the same she was afraid, and knew she was; and she was always well pleased when, just in time for the theatre train out to Readville, she found herself safe in that hospitable station.

And one night her fears were justified. She had gone to a natural history lecture. It was really the best thing in Boston that winter, the most exciting, the newest, and the most entertaining. So dear Boston had let it wisely alone, and there were not a hundred people in the hall. No one, as fate ordered, went Susan's way, and so it happened that a drunken dog on two legs staggered up to her, and asked if he should not see her home. Susan was horribly frightened. She said nothing, but almost ran. Fortunately that friendly policeman, the old man who patrols that section, came round the corner. She gasped rather than spoke. He saw the trouble, gave the drunken dog a bit of his mind, and walked with Susan to the station. But she had learned her lesson very thoroughly. She dared not try mock courage again, nor purchase her independence so dearly. For a fortnight, almost a month, she was horribly dependent.

"Dear Sarah, if you are going to the opera to-night, may I join your party? I have a ticket, but," etc.

"Dear Mr. Primrose, are you going to hear the bishop? May I," etc., etc.

"Dear Mrs. Armitage, would it trouble you and Mr. Armitage," etc., etc., etc.

And generally it proved that Mr. Primrose was not going, or that Sarah was to stay in town, or that it would trouble Mr. and Mrs. Armitage. Sometimes poor Susan bought two tickets to the opera and treated some cub of a pupil. But this was intolerable in the long-run. She really thought she should have to abjure the world, have her beautiful hair all cut off, give up all the modest amusements and vanities of her life, and enter a convent.

II. But necessity is the mother of invention. One day when Susan was at Hollander's to be measured for a new walking dress she saw whence her safety might come. For she actually stepped back a moment for a lady to pass her, and then it proved that the lady was no flesh and blood lady, but only the frame of a lady, with her frock stretched over her neatly, and a bonnet where the head is usually. Susan recovered herself from her little blunder, passed her hand within the sack, and lifted the pretty creature from the ground. She found that she was by no means heavy.

You see, of course, what she determined on. In two days she had made for herself an escort. She bought a cheap and light gossamer overcoat, a travelling cap, a dozen toy masks, and at a second-hand clothing store a pair of badly worn check pantaloons. She also bought rattan enough, and the wire of hoop-skirts, for her purpose. She sewed to the bottom of the pantaloons two right-foot arctics, which Hugh had left when he went to Vienna, because they matched only too well. From the rattan, with an old umbrella slide, she made a backbone and two available legs to support the mackintosh and on the top of the backbone she could adjust either of the masks which she preferred with the travelling cap. The whole thing would shut together like a travelling easel. The mask would go into her leather bag, which, like others of her sex, she carried everywhere. The rest could then be slid into a long umbrella case rather large for a patent umbrella, but not so large as to challenge attention. Susan finished her little manikin early in the afternoon. The hours crawled, they stood still, till evening came, when she was first to put him to his trial. He was to go to *Lohengrin* with her, and she had bought only one ticket for both.

Fortunately it rained like fury. It did not seem curious that one should carry two umbrellas. She might be returning one, for virtuous and true people, like Susan, do return umbrellas sometimes. Arrived in Boston, Susan went out-doors to that sheltered lee where you wait for Cambridge street cars. In an instant she had opened up her new friend to his own proportions, and in a moment more, by an act not dissimilar, she opened her own umbrella. A moment more, and she slid her arm under the cape she had sewed on his mackintosh, and they crossed Park Square together.

He was a little man, he stooped in walking, and was ungraceful in movement. But most men are this and do thus, Susan said bravely and truly to herself. He was not so tall as she; neither were any of the school-boy cubs on whom she had been depending. He had nothing to say; neither had they. Better than this, he said nothing; alas, most of them were not so wise. He could be squeezed into a very small corner if they were waiting for a crowd, or at a crossing; but they stepped out and tried to perform deeds of gallantry. So that, as she walked with him, delighted to see how people turned out for them, Susan, as she balanced his advantages and his disadvantages, said that the good far surpassed the evil, as Robinson Crusoe did on a similar emergency, and as the reader will, if he will fairly compare the plus and the minus of this well-governed world. Both parties sped down Boylston Street safely, and arrived without any adventure before the Boston Theatre. There Susan walked into the alley by the side with him, as if she had been a carefully attended ballet girl a little late. In a second more his face was in her bag, and his bones in her light umbrella case, and Susan—alone as it seemed, but really never less alone—was on her way up to the family circle, where her two umbrellas took place beside her, in time for all to see daybreak in the opera.

III. Prosperous and happy girl, Susan followed her new career with success and cheerfulness such as she had never looked forward to. There was in her life none of the embarrassment which the other girls felt, who did not know whether they should or should not insist on paying their own car fares when their attendants offered to pay. Her escort never proposed that they should stop on their way to the train to eat an ice, and never terrified her by waiting so long in the ice-cream saloon that she thought they had both missed the train. Her escort never annoyed her by depreciating Wagner, or by overpraising that sweet air in *Trovatore*. On the other hand, she saw in a week that the other girls regarded her with a certain sort of respect, not to say admiration and awe, which she had never been conscious of before. To be met in the street, now with a dark Italian, now with a foolish-looking Irishman, now with a German who scowled and knew everything, now with a lighthearted Yankee who seemed a Harvard Junior or Sophomore—this affected Susan's reputation among her young friends of her own sex. They were not surprised. No; they knew she was well worthy of any amount of admiration. Not surprised,—no, only,—well,—yes, it was different from what it was the year before, when Susan had been poking about as if she were nobody and nobody cared for her.

It would be wrong to say that Susan cared for respect of admiration so cheaply bought. But if you had asked her she would have owned that she was glad that she was no longer the subject of commiseration among her young friends. In truth, she took a higher grade than a girl engaged to only one person, and hers is a grade much higher than the girl who had six brothers.

Yet I really think it was a mistake that one evening when Susan, having a pocketful of complimentary tickets for the recital, took Mr. Mackintosh into Chickering Hall with her, and let him sit by her side to listen, instead of leaving him with her umbrella in the anteroom. But the recital was really first-rate, so the audience was very small. Susan was very much interested in the success of the young lady who was giving her first concert, and she thought that every seat that was filled was an advantage to her. But you see, of course, that it made other people talk. Here was this handsome young man sitting by Susan, and for a week her fair friends were asking who he was, and how she came to know him. But she did not at first appreciate this, so she made the mistake more than once, and I think he heard more good music than was good for him.

But as for her, in "these halcyon days of his first success," she enjoyed her winter as she had never enjoyed a winter before. If you choose, in Boston, there is nothing you may not see and hear and know and understand in the heavens above, or the earth beneath, or the waters that are supposed to be under the earth. Susan found her time full, her hands full, her heart full, and her brain very much more than full. When she was not in school she was writing up her notes or reading, that she might be in a measure prepared for Mr. Barton, or Mr. Goodale, or Mr. Shaler, or Mr. Wright, or the rest of the *savants*. She knew the difference between a kame and a drumlin; she knew the difference between a moth and a behemoth, and how the trunk of one was related to the trunk of the other. She knew that she was herself an ascidian, and she was as eager as any one to work out the links which connected her with her grandfather's great-grandfather. She dipped into Buchner and Helmholz, and even went back to Helvetius and D'Holbach that she might get the doctrine at the fountain. So she understood that if a giraffe without a long neck only wants one enough, he will get it by stretching up his neck to the top of the palm-trees, and that if a seal on the beach wants a pair of legs, and tries for them hard enough, he will develop them, and that what there is left of his tail will dwindle down into insignificance. This is the doctrine of the *nisus*, or effort. Susan, who was a good girl, satisfied herself with the effort to be very wise, and hoped that it would come out all right, but little did she think all the time how the same doctrine was soaking into Mr. Mackintosh's empty head, and what a nuisance it would be to her.

This is the reason why I feel sure it would have been better to have left him in his case with the umbrellas at the door. But, as you will see, it was an annoyance, if you were walking to a lecture with a party, to have to make some ridiculous excuse for staying outside; and also it seems rather cheap to confess that you always go to the play or lecture with a man who cares nothing about Shakespeare or geology, and prefers to stay elsewhere. It was to the scientific lectures and the really first-class concerts that she took him most, for to those a school-mistress of her grade was almost sure to have free tickets sent her. As to places where she paid for tickets, she never dreamed of taking him there.

But it was really as great a misfortune to him as it was to her. Empty-headed creature as he was, of course he listened to nothing, heard nothing, and understood nothing at first. And it never occurred to Susan that things would not stay on this easy and cheerful basis. But nothing stays on the thoroughly comfortable basis. People always attempt improvements, which often result in ruin. So it is that Voltaire says that "the better is the enemy of the good."

One night there were some very bright and wonderful stereoscopes. And poor addle-pated Mr. Mackintosh could not help having the rays come through his gray glass eyes into that empty camera-obscura of his head. And of course the picture could not help showing itself all upside-down and hind side before. But it amused him and pleased him. And that night his mask had very large ears, so that he could not help listening a little. And then he listened more. For the man was gesticulating and quoting and illustrating and making it very plain, so that if Mr. Mackintosh would only "make an effort," as Mrs. Chick said, all would be well. I suppose he did "make an effort," as far as rattan and whalebone could, and so he formed that habit, which proved bad for him, of listening to the man more. As for keeping his eyes and ears open, he could not help that, for none of the masks were made with eyes or ears that opened or shut, and he had to look and listen whether he wanted to or not. The rest of us are more fortunate.

Susan, quite unconsciously, hurried on the mischief which had been begun, by talking to him herself as they walked home from the lectures and concerts. I do not think she did this for practice in talking. For she talked a good deal in the school-room, and, though she is a modest girl, I think she must know that without special practice she is as good a talker as you shall meet with in a long day. But she was sensitive and conscious about the deception which she was keeping up with Mr. Mackintosh—or with the public in the affair of Mr. Mackintosh. Dr. Primrose preached that terrible sermon of his about "Truth" just then, and made it clear that any conscious deception was a lie, whether you said a word or not. This worried her a little. For was she not consciously deceiving every loafer on Washington Street or Boylston Street? Had she not made Mr. Mackintosh on purpose that she might deceive them? But a certain under-consciousness that she meant no wrong sustained her against Dr. Primrose, and at first the stings of conscience only pricked her so deep as to make her resolve that she would not be found out— no, not if she met Dr. Primrose and Mrs. Primrose both. So she thought it more prudent—that was the word she used in discussing it with herself—to keep up an animated conversation with Mr. Mackintosh in the street when she observed that any one was near them. And indeed this proved so agreeable, as conversation is apt to when you do all the talking, that she kept it up all the time from the lecture or concert to the station. After they came to the station, she always folded him up in some recess of the ladies' waiting-room. For the Providence Railway conductors are pitiless, and would have been sure to demand a ticket for him.

"That is a magnificent harmony at the end of the third act." No audible reply,—but one so seldom hears both sides of a conversation. "I was not sure but Gloria strained a little in striking the *non;* but it was all so good that it is absurd to pick out flaws." Again Mr. Mackintosh's voice is lost as those firemen rush by. Or, "Could you quite follow him in what he said about the permanence of type? How can it be, if the type is permanent, that we should notice the transition, as Mr. Shaler pointed it out Tuesday? But then, I am not quite sure if Mr. Shaler and Mr. Barton quite agree about that. You must remind me to ask him. Or we might send a note to *Notes and Queries.*" Now if the bishop himself had heard that, or Mrs. Bishop, neither wouldn't have minded, or remembered afterward, that Mr. Mackintosh said nothing.

IV. But, alas, simple Susan carried on this rattling and interesting conversation quite too far and too long. Mr. Mackintosh had been making all the "nisus" or "effort" he could, in listening to the stereoscope man, and he had all the encouragement of the success of the giraffe and the seals. Now here was this bright, wise, merry Susan Ellsworth who bore him along, who was the result of just such efforts as he was making. And he found it much more agreeable to listen to her sweet, low-toned voice just in his ear, her breath fragrant as clover, and her hand under his arm beating a pulse in keeping with all she said—he found this much more agreeable than straining his poor little new wits to make out what the man on the platform a hundred feet away was howling about. So he was always distressed when any of her friends joined them to take advantage of his protection, and when Susan turned away from him to speak to Maud or Clara. To say the truth, this did not happen often. For Maud and Clara had the same proper pride about hitching on upon other people's escorts as had governed Susan in her independent days.

While poor Mr. Mackintosh made this nisus or effort to hear, he was all the time making wild and futile efforts to speak. For these he had wretched organs and more wretched opportunities. For one night in the family circle, where Susan had unfolded him after they had passed the ticket gate, he had seen the policeman seize two boys who were catcalling, and hale them off he knew not whither. So poor Mr. Mackintosh was frightened, and did not dare to try experiments in-doors. Then, as soon as they came to the railway station, Susan always ruthlessly shut him up, and he had no organization at all. Literally he "went to pieces," and it was not slang to say so. One night, in a high gale, Susan was dragging him beside her—or rather behind her—and he tried to speak, but nothing but a great howl came out, which was half a sneeze. She did not suspect that he had anything to do with it. And the poor creature was dreadfully mortified by his failure.

But another night, very imprudently she left him sitting in a chair, in the anteroom of the hall of the "Sons of Idleness." The hall had been hired for a "reception" which was given by the graduates of Vassar to one of the professors who was going to Germany on his sabbatical visit. Susan thought she was safe in leaving Mr. Mackintosh in a dark corner without folding him up. And so she was. He sat, with his chin on his hands, as she left him, and thus he had, for once, the chance to try his various gruntings and howlings, and to pass through the experiments of the ascidian to the more articulate language of the man.

Fortunately for him, he had some lessons just when he needed them most and expected them least.

For one of the other escorts, who had been taken into the reception hall, came running out, and helplessly rushed up and down the waiting-room, annoyed that he found no one there. But in his despair he saw Mr. Mackintosh.

"Ugh–ah–glad to see somebody–ugh–could you–can you–yes,–would you tell me, please,–ugh, you know,–don't you see?–where the water is?–Miss Maelstrom–ugh–is faint–you know!"

Mr. Mackintosh's time had come. Imitation was his cue, clearly, as in Rosenthal and Prendergast. With one sublime effort, he echoed the other, wondering, as he did so, whether perhaps he had as much brain.

"Ugh,"—tremendously prolonged,—"ah,"—shorter, but very long,—"glad to see somebody,"—this hopelessly indistinct from eagerness, like an Edison turned three times too fast; "could you–can you–can you–could you,"—this slower,—"water–Maelstrom–ugh–ah–yes, you know." But fortunately, in his agony gesticulating like a school-boy who forgets his piece, he pointed his finger to the looking-glass, where stood pitcher and tumbler in full sight of both of them.

"Ugh–oh–thanks–yes–so much—so much obliged, you know,–thanks—ugh, oh, Miss Maelstrom"—and Mr. Knowitz vanished with his tumbler.

Mr. Mackintosh had tried and had succeeded, and on these sounds he practiced all the evening.

Would she give him another chance for practice? Alas, no! or it seemed no. That night as they went home there was a great group of Vassarites, all bubbling over with fun—effervescing and sputtering as so many bottles of XX might do which had been warmed at a sociable all the evening. And he thought Susan had never been so remorseless as she was in undoing him that night. The next evening was worse. A gentleman joined her on the other side. And poor Mackintosh was afraid for his very life as they swung along.

It was not till the third night that he had a chance, or so it seemed to the poor witless creature.

V. But on the third night the chance came. Susan was in the highest spirits. The night was clear and cold, and they devoured the pavement as she rushed him along. "Well, my dear Mac," said she, mercilessly, "that was first-rate. I do not wonder women want to speak, if they could speak like that. Mac, if I could get Mr. Edison to give me one of his plates, I would attach it to you, and you should repeat the end of Mr. Bryce's lecture."

"Ugh–ah–you know–well–Miss Susan–ugh, ah–give me a chance–you know–and I will do 'em all." The end was badly run together.

"What, you—my dear Mac!" This was all Susan said, and she almost dropped him in the gutter in her surprise, and she lost her own speech for laughing. She laughed so that she shook him from his cap to his arctics, and all the poor breath he had in his limp ribs was knocked out of him. And when she came to herself, all she could say was, "Poor dear Mac! I beg your pardon, but"—then she broke down again—"but whoever dreamed of your talking?"

But then it was poor Mac's turn. She had to listen, and he told her, with many unnecessary "ughs" and "ahs," and "you knows," and "don't you sees," that he was sure he only needed more practice to speak quite well. It was true that he could not manage r, and he always called th d; but so did many gentlemen he met. He needed extra breath, but "ugh" and "oh" seemed to help in this. And when he had not an idea, he could fill in with "don't you see," and "you know."

"You poor dear thing," said Susan, compassionately, as she unscrewed his head and put it in her bag, "you are really eloquent."

VI. But the reader will see that a good girl like Susan could not shut up the face just now eager in its entreaties, and go to sleep, after she had silenced it, without serious thought. Here was a matter of conscience more formidable than that question about veracity which Dr. Primrose had started. Was it quite honorable in her, was it fair, nay, was it right, to start this poor feeble creature in his career, to let him partake of a little taste of the wonders of science, of art, and of music, and then to snuff him out, like a candle, simply because she chose to? Susan tossed in her bed a good deal before she went to sleep, with these questions troubling her. And early in the morning, when the singing birds first wakened her by their carols to the rising sun, she rose, screwed Mr. Mackintosh together, tied him to an armchair in her entry, and left him to enjoy the sunrise. As she went to sleep again she could hear him practicing an imitation of this morning hymn of the birds, who were Plymouth Rock cockerels. The poor brainless creature did not know any better; he had taken it for granted that these were the morning songs of men. Susan was pleased with herself for this act of mercy, and she did not take him to pieces till it was time for her to go to school.

As it happened, he was this time shut up—and, so to speak ceased to be as an individual—longer than had ever happened to him before. For, to her delight, as the school recess came, Susan received a card, and visit close following, from George Farmer, the fine young engineer officer to whom, as I said, she was engaged. By good luck, and by good strategy of his own, he had got himself ordered to Boston, to make a contract for some ice for the meat cars of the Cattaraugus and Opelousas Railroad. With good luck, this ice contract and certain subsidiary negotiations were made to last a fortnight, and during that whole time Susan needed no escort other than George, and, in truth, thought very little of any other. But at last the last day of George's visit came, as last days will, and then she began to think how dreadful it would be to have nobody but Mr. Mackintosh to go anywhere with her. Still, she was less disposed than ever to cut off her hair and to retire into a convent.

Wisely, therefore, the girl submitted the question to her lover. But she did it in a guarded way, which I would not recommend to other good girls in a like position; if, indeed, there ever may be such girls. As they came home from the Symphony on that wretched farewell night she said: "George, I want your advice. You are so good, and—and you are never jealous. You see, when you are away, I have no one to go with me to the concerts, you know, and the lectures."

"No; you used to boast of your independence when I first knew you."

"I know—yes, I did. But I was very foolish." And then she told him of that horrid fright she had. And he was very angry, and swore—just a little—and made her promise to run no such risk again. This made it easier for her to go on.

"No; I knew you would not let me. That is why I did not write you about it. But what I did—you must not be angry—was to hire a poor stick there was, with nothing to do, to come and go with me. You do not mind that, do you?" And here she looked up at him with her most roguish and confiding smile. But George's face clouded; she could see it did.

"I don't know," said he. "That would depend. What sort of creature is he— an old man?"

"Oh, I do not know. Don't be jealous, now. I do not suppose he is very old perhaps he is very young. You see he was deaf—and dumb—and blind—and could hardly walk. So I did not suppose you would care."

At this George grinned a somewhat ghastly smile, and said he didn't care quite so much; but asked how, if the man was deaf, he could enjoy the concerts.

You will observe also that Susan wandered from Dr. Primrose's instructions. She said Mr. Mackintosh "was" deaf and dumb—she did not dare say "he is"—and there was conscious deception again. In answer to her lover she said: "Enjoy the concerts? Who ever said he enjoyed the concerts?" She was a little reassured, as women are, because he had made an unimportant mistake. "You do not suppose I ever bought a concert ticket for him, do you? No; I take him as I would take a cab after the concert was over. Dear George, you must not be jealous of him more than you would be of a cab man."

"You do not take a cabman's arm," said George, a little irresolutely; and Susan shuddered as she recollected with how firm a grip she had to take all the arm Mr. Mackintosh had. "What is the wretch's name?" continued he.

"Name?" said Susan. "Do you ask your cabman's name? I never asked him. We call him Mr. Mackintosh, from the coat he wears, but I never asked him his name. I do not believe he has any."

This encouraged George a little; but still he said he did not think it was nice or wise, and that nobody but as innocent and sweet a girl as Susy would ever have fallen into so silly a plan. He even asked if other girls in Boston had to hire their escorts. At which Susy said that other girls had escorts who did not live in the Rocky Mountains, or in Opelousas either; and at that Mr. George had to come down from his high horse. It ended by a compromise. She agreed, when she went anywhere alone, to order a cab regularly at a stable he named, and he declared that the next time he came to Boston he should pay the bill. Whether she would let him or not was left undecided in the final ceremonies of the farewell. For he left in that horrible train which goes off at eleven at night, and there was no question but that he must go.

So all Susan had got by asking advice was that she was worse off than she was when she asked for it. This is what is apt to happen, dear Clara, when you do not tell your whole story to your adviser.

VII. And now she must deal with Mr. Mackintosh alone, by her own unassisted sense, such as it was. Really it was stronger as the reader has seen, in the inventive and mechanical lines than it was in the philosophical and ethical lines.

Of course she could have left Mr. Mackintosh where he was—his legs and arms in the glazed umbrella case, his masks in her alligator-skin bag, and his arctics on the floor of her closet. But, as has been said, she did not think this fair. She had thought of burning him up. But she was too strong a Protestant; her reminiscences of Smithfield and John Rogers were too strong, and that she would not do. She had called him into such being as he had, poor creature, and she would not destroy her own work. "That would be simply mean," she said to herself; "that would not be fair."

So she took another morning when the cocks were crowing, and screwed him together, and tied him to a chair as before. Poor Mr. Mackintosh did not know how long he had ceased to exist, any more than Mr. Hyde knew how long Dr. Jekyll had been running the machine. Nor was the poor thing as wretched as the girl chose to fancy him. For, as he had none of that essence which loves and fears, hopes, admires, and worships, he had nothing worth remembering, if he could remember, as he could not; and nothing to look forward to, if he could look forward, as he could not. But this, simple Susan did not consider. She simply screwed him together. He listened to the cock-a-doodles, as he did before; and if he had thought, as he could not and did not, he would have thought that this was thus and then was now.

Then Susan went to bed and slept till the dressing-bell rang. As she dressed, she began a little note to George, for she had promised to write to him twice a day. But after breakfast, before school-time, she came up and brought Mr. Mackintosh into her room and locked the door. He had never been in that room before.

"Mac," said she, "I shall not want you any more. What do you want to do? What do you like to do most?"

"Oh, ugh, ah–you know–don't you see–well, you know–"

And Susan was patient, for she often had such remarks addressed to her by her partners who were not skilful in extempore speech. So she waited. And at last it came, as gas comes after the puff of air in a poor gas-pipe.

"If—you know, Miss Susan—I could go to some of those parties—receptions—like that of the Sons of Idleness. Indeed, Miss Susan, I can talk as well—as the young men I see there."

"I think you can," said Susan. "I should be ashamed of my work if you could not. I had thought of that, Mac. But I cannot do it, for you have no pumps nor patent-leather shoes. And your trousers are not good. I have no money to throw away on parties. Think of something else, Mac."

It is not worth the while to load the page with poor Mac's "ohs" and "ughs" and other "spaces." In substance he then asked if he might not be a juryman. "I thought I could; you know they do not have to know anything, and, indeed, are better when they do not."

"That is good, Mac. I had not thought of that, but I will," said the girl. And so she took his head off and shut him up, and took this plan into consideration.

But of course she did not assent to it. That same day she read the Court Calendar, and was distressed to think that she had yielded even for an hour. When she went home she put Mac together, and told him that this would not do.

"Then," said he, very piteously, "might I not be an under-editor to an independent journal. You know they do not have any opinions, and are very proud that they do not. I am sure I never had any opinions. I do not know what an opinion is." But this time Susan was not deceived; this was only the jury plan under another form.

Then Mac pleaded, quite eloquently for him, that he might stay just what he was. He had seen the red-capped messenger men at the station. He envied one of them his one arm, because practically poor Mac had no arms at all.

"Now I could not go of errands, Miss Susan. But you say yourself I do my work well. You could fasten me at the door, and any one who wanted me would unfasten me."

"My dear Mac, you do not see. The secret would be discovered, and then the roughs would not mind you. Don't you see, Mac, you cannot knock a man down. You might as well be a woman, for all the good you are in your own business, unless people think you are a man. And if they do think so, it is because I 'consciously deceive' them. Oh dear! Oh dear! I wish you had never been born!" And the poor girl broke out crying. But she did not say, "I wish I had never been born," for the memory of George's last kiss came to her.

"I had thought," said Mac, "of voting. What you say of women reminds me that they cannot vote; but I can."

"No, you can't," said Susan, smartly, for she knew. "You have not registered, and you have not been assessed."

"I could register," said Mac.

"You can't register; it's a very smart person who knows how to register; and besides, you can't read the Constitution. So it would be of no use if you could register."

"No," said Mac, sadly, "I cannot read the Constitution. You don't think I could be a minister?"

"No, you couldn't. There are some kinds that know very little, but they all have to know something."

"Nor a doctor?"

"No, Mac; at least, I believe not. I think they have to know something."

"Nor a lawyer?"

"No, certainly not. You have no eye-teeth. And they have to be cut before you are a lawyer. I heard Judge Jeffries say so."

And then they waited. "I will talk to you again by-and-by," she said. And then she ran down stairs to meet the postman, and found just a little postal-card on which George had written in French that she was the dearest girl in the world and that he should always love her. Immediately on this she took Mr. Mackintosh to pieces, dressed herself for the Appalachian Club, went to Boston, and tried her pretty cab for the first time. It was really an elegant little coupé, and the stable-keeper had put the driver in livery. George had written to him from Springfield that the coupé must wait for Miss Ellsworth every evening.

But the next morning Susan brought her little drama to an end.

She screwed Mr. Mac together once more, and said, "Tell me yourself what you want to be."

"Could I not be Vice-President," he said; "till the President died, you know; or Lieutenant-Governor, or something like that?"

"Oh no, Mac; they might not know when to unscrew you."

"Could I not be a trustee? I believe trustees have to be cautious, and not do the rash things other people do."

"I had thought of that, Mac, and I inquired. But you would have to give bonds. Now no one would give bonds for you. I am sure I would not." This was cruel in Susan; but sometimes she is cruel.

"Then, Miss Susan, why cannot I be what I am?"

"Because I do not want you."

"But somebody else might want me. I could stand in front of tailors' shops with new clothes on. I should like to be that. I see a great many young men who do that and nothing else, and they seem to like it very much."

"You dear old Mac!" cried the girl; "you have more sense than any of us— at least more than I have. It is the best sense possible to be what you are, and pretend to nothing more. I knew that, though I have never tried it, for Mr. Emerson says so."

So she went with him to Cutter and Dresser's that very day. They are the great ready-made clothing men. And they took Mac at once off her hands literally. And they put on him that handsome Garrick you saw me wearing yesterday. That was the way I came to know the story.

And—will you believe it?—one day when they had dressed him in a cos-tumer's suit as Dromio of Syracuse, old Mac forgot, and began walking up and down the balcony on which he was standing. The people in the street saw it, and fancied he was a wonderful automaton. They stopped in hundreds to see him, and of the hundreds scores went in to buy.

That was the beginning of the triumphant success of Cutter and Dresser. They owed it all to Susan, and I think they will send her a pair of salt-spoons for her wedding.

★

ELIZABETH STUART PHELPS *Twenty-Four: Four*
Harper's 92 (1895): 264–277

[Essayist, story writer, novelist, and poet, Elizabeth Stuart Phelps Ward made nearly thirty appearances in the periodicals of the 1890s. Her autobiography, *Chapters in a Life*, was first published in *McClure's* in December 1895, as was *The Story of Jesus Christ* in 1897. "Twenty-four: Four" was later published in *The Empty House and Other Stories* in 1910.]

MRS. FORTITUDE FILLEBROWN had neuralgia at the base of the brain, and Melissy Pulsifer had sent for the doctor. When Melissy experienced a similar

FIGURE 22   This illustration accompanied Phelps's short story on the telephone. The varying expressions of the two women attest to their different class positions; ultimately, their relationship with the telephone exaggerates these existing hierarchies. (*Harper's*, 1896)

disorder she called it a headache behind. But Mrs. Fillebrown had neuralgia at the base of the brain.

Now it snowed—only a New England February knows *how* it snowed— and the road to the village was blocked. Melissy got badly drabbled wading over to Silas Whey's to ask Silas to send Adoniram out with old Peter Parley to bring the doctor. Melissy came home soaked.

"You'll be down yourself," sighed Mrs. Fillebrown. "We might die here for all anybody would know or care."

"I've got my bitters," said Melissy, dryly.

"Then you have to recover from the bitters," suggested Melissy's employer, with the tinge of sarcasm which a neuralgic diathesis lends to the workings of the most literal mind.

One does not say Melissy's "mistress." Melissy was a Yankee and a neighbor. She did not serve. She "accommodated." But she had accommodated Mrs. Fillebrown affectionately for nearly ten years—ever since Joe Fillebrown died, and was buried in Northwest Peony churchyard, and Mrs. Fillebrown had erected a dutiful slab of Rutland marble to his not altogether blessed memory.

There is no fidelity more attractively loyal than the fidelity of an American domestic, when one is privileged to command a good specimen of its intelligence and energy. Mrs. Fillebrown had been thus fortunate. The two women had grown fond of each other, as solitary women do (unless they hate) in silent, manless country homes, where the little that life has to offer is shared and made the most of with pathetic and democratic interest.

"It *dooz* snow," observed Melissy, looking out of the window at the white whirlwind. It swept between the two women and their nearest neighbor, a revolving wall, solid and sardonic. It seemed to shut them apart from all the world.

"It's reely r'arin' up," said Melissy. "I guess the doctor 'll hev high jinks wallerin' through them drifts along by Silas's."

Mrs. Fillebrown groaned. Melissy Pulsifer would have dug her way through the snow to the village on her hands and knees if she could have cured the base of Mrs. Fillebrown's brain. But in that finer activity which we call tact, Melissy did not excel. Mrs. Fillebrown thought that this was because Melissy was too healthy.

It grew later, and late. It grew dull, and dusk. The doctor did not come. The storm increased viciously. The drift began to block the back yard, an ominous garrison, tall and impregnable, piling against the shed; and over towards Silas Whey's the road lay even and high, winding like a white, unbroken river to the unseen town.

Adoniram and Peter Parley had not been known to return. The stanch old-fashioned house, dating from the days when carpenters built "on honor," trembled through all its oaken skeleton. Now and then plaster rattled from somewhere overhead; a blind broke loose in the kitchen, and swung slapping till it smashed the window-pane. When Melissy went to fix it, she came back covered with snow.

"Do brush it off!" complained Mrs. Fillebrown. "You look like a dead person. Isn't that doctor in sight yet?"

"I've het you up some beef tea," replied Melissy, cheerfully.

It was growing quite dark in the sitting-room. Melissy pugnaciously delayed to light the lamps, showing therein the possession of more delicacy of imagination than we gave her credit for.

"She don't know how late it is," thought Melissy. "And there ain't no call she should."

The faces of the two women stood out like satin masks, white above their dark dresses, in the gathering dusk. Their forms were scarcely visible to each other. Neither spoke. The maid stood by the window, staring out. The mistress, from the lounge, where she lay covered with the blue and red afghan that Melissy crocheted at Christmas, watched her.

Mrs. Fillebrown thought how important Melissy was to her. There was no one else—she had nobody else in the world. This seemed worse sometimes than neuralgia at the base; and Mrs. Fillebrown's imagination could no farther go.

Her face twitched with two kinds of pain—the one that the doctor prescribed for, when be could get there, and the one that no doctor could cure. She had been a handsome woman when Joe Fillebrown courted her; trouble had taken her color and contour, but had left her fineness of feature, and that carriage of the head which only a woman who is or once was beautiful ever has.

Now Melissy had never been handsome. But there was a look about her kind eyes and resolute white mouth that seemed beautiful to the other lonely woman, as Melissy stood sturdily challenging the storm for the first symptom of the doctor's approach.

" 'Tain't no use," said Melissy, suddenly, at last. "He's blocked. We've gotter make a night on't without him. I'll het you up the soapstones, and get you to bed, and set by you. I can sleep in my blanket-wrapper as comf't'ble as they make 'em. There ain't no use mincin' of it. He ain't a-comin'. Ee's wallerin' on the road someheres with Adoniram and Peter Parley."

She smoothed her white apron over her chocolate calico dress, drew the curtains decidedly, and lighted the double burner with blue crepe silk shade. The faces of the two women took on a moribund hue in the cold color of the lamp.

Melissy's prophecy, as is not at all sure to be the case with the pessimism of optimistic people, proved accurately correct. The doctor did not get through till daylight; and Mrs. Fillebrown's neuralgia, with the eccentricity characteristic of that wilful disorder, had fled before him.

She was so much better when he dug his way to her front gate that she was delightfully cross. The doctor treated the symptom gleefully, as he would the squalls of a convalescent baby.

"I won't go through another such night, not even to please Providence!" snapped Mrs. Fillebrown. "We might starve, or freeze, or be murdered in our beds here—for all Northwest Peony. It's no sort of way to live. I'm going to have a man in the house if I live till the snowplough gets out!"

"There ain't nobody but Adoniram and old Mr. Ginger. He's deaf as a seraphim on a gravestone, and drags on the left side sence he had his stroke," remarked Melissy. "An' I'd like to know how long you'd hev Adoniram perfumin' up this house—feelin' the way you do about caows."

"Have a telephone," suggested the doctor, with the cosmopolitan air that he wore when he had been to Boston, and felt that he was what he called "in touch with the world." "It is cheaper than a man, and more protection. You are quite able, Mrs. Fillebrown, to afford these modern improvements. Really, I should feel much easier about you."

These last words touched Mrs. Fillebrown; for the doctor, with the emotional economy of his kind, was not lavish of his sympathy. She said to Melissy twice that day, "The doctor says he should feel easier about me."

She told Mrs. Whey so, when that good neighbor came in after the storm to verify the startling rumor that Mrs. Fillebrown had ordered a telephone put up in her bedroom, possible burglars and actual neuralgia being offered as the chief excuses for this incredible act. Silas came himself, and Mrs. Fillebrown's lawyer, Wiley X. Toyl, the minister's wife, the grocer from Peony Centre, the dressmaker, the sweet potato man, and four of Mrs. Fillebrown's Sunday-school class. Mrs. Fillebrown had not received so many calls—who could say when? She grew quite chatty and cheerful. She was not used to being an object of public interest or attention.

"I have signed the contract," she said, "under Mr. Wiley X. Toyl's advice. The instrument is to go in next week. The doctor says he shall feel so much easier about me."

She repeated this phrase with a pathetic comfort at which it is not easy for a fine sympathy to smile. She was so starved for common human affection that she eagerly devoured the professional substitute for it—that pseudo-sympathy, that discreet dose of friendly interest, which is all that so many ailing and lonely women get from any source. Not that there was the palest tinge of sentiment in the attitude of her mind towards her doctor. She would as soon have thought of romancing about Silas Whey, or even old Mr. Ginger. She was an experienced, indeed a cynical, widow, holding all masculine admiration at a cold distance, and the doctor was the infatuated bridegroom of a brand new second wife. But he was the only person in the world (except Melissy) who knew how Mrs. Fillebrown felt, was sorry, and sometimes said so.

Most of us learn some one lesson out of life's primer better than all the rest put together. Many of us study it in the form of a reiterated or monotonous trouble by which the unseen Power seems trying to screw some particular idea into our dull heads. Fortitude Fillebrown had learned the weakness of man, and what it means to woman. We might add that she had discovered the incurability of neurotic disorders; but that is secondary. You have seen carpenters screwing "bits" into hard wood, and have watched the shrinking, shrieking fibre as the tool bores its way. Supplant the wood by the living human brain, and that is neuralgia. But the boring, physical agonies of all the years of her lonely life, in which she had so little else to think of except the bit and the bore, were transport beside that other kind of pain which a strong and loving woman endures when she first admits to herself that the man she loves does not deserve her warm and wasted trust, and that her marriage is a definite mistake.

It had come gradually to Fortitude Fillebrown, as the consciousness of most such misfortunes comes. There was the slight but growing neglect, the intermittent tenderness, the increasing absence from home, the sharp and sharper word, the cooling indifference, unrecognized by the man himself, the occasional, then the frequent, domestic "scene."

When he lost his situation (Joe was a railroad man), from that sheer carelessness of temperament which we hesitate to call shiftlessness when we find it in one we love, she did not take the incident too much to heart. She owned their pretty home, and had enough for two to live on, with the old-fashioned economy to which her father had trained her. (He was master of the Peony Centre High-School, and had written an arithmetic successful in its day.) But Joe liked other ways. He developed habits as foreign to her simple ideas as the *milieu* of Monte Carlo. It took her a long time to understand what these meant. The wife is the last person to hear the truth about the life of a dissipated man. Rumors reached her on vague wings, and she buffeted them away as if they had been bats. But one night he came home unmistakenly and savagely drunk.

From that hour she began to cast up the black items in the long sum by which a woman tries to solve the problem—given dead honor and dying love, how preserve enough happiness to keep alive on and save a home?

"Give me time, Forty," Joe said, in one of his best moments, "and I'll come out right yet. You're quick, my girl you know. Let a fellow have his rope, and don't yank him in and give him up because he tugs on it. I'm not *all* bad yet, Forty. Be patient with me, girl, as long as you *can*—won't you?"

Joe wore upon his watch-guard a little iron Greek cross that his wife had put there once to signalize some one of his repentant vows to be or do something that she had asked him, and when he said this, Joe fingered the iron cross nervously. He always did the day after a spree. The trinket grew to have a sickly association in her mind with the piteous reaching out of irreclaimable weakness after strength which it is too weak to know that it cannot command.

Patient at first she was, or she thought she was; it amounted to the same thing in her mind, if not in Joe's. But, as Joe said, Fortitude was "quick." The recorder of her history does not claim that she was a perfect wife. There are some women nearly that; one wonders at their number.

But Fortitude Fillebrown was more human than superior—a loving, impulsive, warm-hearted, quick-tongued woman. She found it hard to forgive. Things rankled. She brooded. Sometimes she nagged. Her sense of outraged womanhood was stronger in her than the warm, maternal pity for a man, which is often the sweetest thing in the wife of a better husband than Joe Fillebrown.

"You women don't understand us men," Joe said, one day, rather drearily.

In short, Fortitude's patience broke when her heart did, and this was bad.

Her courage followed her patience. Bitterly sometimes she gibed at the irony of her own brave name. When things were at their worst she was half conscious that she had not the pluck of women she had read of, or of one or two she had known. But she did not know a great many people. She lived an uneventful life. After Joe died it grew secluded. She dreamed, and remembered, and had neuralgia, and answered Melissy.

Indeed, Joe took himself off in a painful way; and one need not wonder that Fortitude was never quite the woman after that black time that she was before.

Only Melissy ever knew the facts; but Melissy was in the dining room putting away the silver, and the door was not latched.

Joe had come home very drunk the night before; had slept through the stupor which disgusts a woman with his sex in a way that no man can ever understand and was "coming to," after supper, in a ferocious mood. He had put on his hat to go out again. His wife remonstrated. He turned and clinched his fist, and without a moment's hesitation brought it down on her neck and shoulders. It was the first time he had ever struck her. She cried out, and he struck her again.

She staggered, and her face turned a terrible color. She was not hurt much —in her flesh—a mere bruise that passed away next day. But her heart received a mortal wound.

All the pride of her sex, her maiden years, her father's name, her wifehood—its outraged fidelity and tenderness—leaped up. She walked with a firm step to the front door and opened it. She stretched her hand out—she had a hand with a fine profile—and pointed into the dark.

"Go!" she articulated, distinctly.

"Very well," said Joe; "that'll suit me. The house is yours, as you say."

Now Fortitude had said nothing of the kind. She only stood still—that was all—and pointed through the open door.

Joe gave one sodden glance at her majestic figure; he scarcely raised his eyes to the face, solemn as an antique marble, that frowned above the level of his low gaze. He stood feebly fingering the iron cross upon his watch-chain.

She remembered afterwards that he took off his hat; then he went down the steps. He called back once through the dark, "Good-by, girl."

She did not answer. And she never saw Joe again.

She expected him for a few days, and Melissy set his plate at the table every night. But he did not come. And one evening Mrs. Silas Whey came in, with the minister and his wife, and the three divided between them, as best they could the news which they bore.

There had been a fire at Peony Centre; it was in a low hotel or boarding-house. Joe was staying there: he had been on a steady spree since he left home. It was a bitter night, and blew a gale. The rustic fire department used up the water-supply, and looked on while the house went down.

Seven people—some men, some women, some drunk, some sober, were smothered or burned.

Joe had got out of the building, it was quite certain. But he was seen to go back.

There was a cry that a little serving-maid, an uncouth, ignorant Swede, but a week in the country, was entrapped and perishing in the attic. It was believed that Joe went back to save the little maid.

They covered his face and brought him home to his wife. His clothes were ashes, but the iron cross on his watch-guard had not burned. Pitiful symbol of the metal that was lacking in the man! Sacred sign of the touch of dedication which transmutes feebler frailty than Joe's into character! Pathetic memory of those unrecorded scenes, those hopes and despairs, those ecstasies and agonies, known only to the dead man and to his living wife!

She broke when she saw the iron cross, and the women about her trembled before her cry.

With her own shaking fingers she removed the cross from Joe's poor body. From that hour she wore it on a ribbon, out of sight, against her heart. And from that hour she mourned and loved him.

Now Melissy marvelled much at this. A few months after Joe was buried, "I calc'late," said Melissy to herself, "she'd take another lickin' to get him back agin."

When Joe had been dead so many years that Melissy almost lost track of them, "Lordy," thought Melissy, "I calc'late she'd take a lickin' every day to set her eyes on him for a spell."

Melissy supposed it was because she had never been married that she found it so hard to understand the grief of the drunkard's widow. The old maid did not respect the wife altogether for this mystery of conjugal allegiance.

"When a man ain't wuth it," mused Melissy, "he ain't *wuth.*"

Melissy welcomed anything, even a modern improvement, that would alleviate the desolation of the house She was very much interested in the telephone.

"It's all over taown!" she cried, gleefully. "Some they call it onchristian extravagance, and some says the money'd better go to the A.B.C.F.M., or the W.C.T.U., or the Widder's Mite. But Silas Whey he's a-talkin' of puttin' one in himself; an' him a deacon!—He says, seein' the poles run right by, he didn't s'pose the company'd charge nothin'extry. And Wiley X. Toyl, I hear he's ordered already. You've sot the fashion now, I do declare."

"So it seems," said Mrs. Fillebrown, blushing importantly. "These modern improvements are very interesting."

She went to the post-office that morning herself, although the wind was northwest and neuralgic, to mail a letter subscribing to a popular scientific periodical. She felt that she called a mental stimulus quite new to her drowsy and dreamy life.

She was gone some time—so many people stopped her to say how glad they were to see her out, and when was her "instrument" going in?—and when she came home she was surprised to hear voices in the house.

She stepped into the hall softly, and closed the door without noise. Melissy's obvious ones rose with their own familiar positiveness upon her employer's astonished ear.

"You don't catch me! What? *Me!* Put my mouth into that hole? Lordy! give me the cullender and show me how to handle the darn thing. Looks like a tunnel a man had got a patent on without askin' his wife if it would let syrup through. So? I feel like a fritter fried too long. What'll I do *naow?*"

Mrs. Fillebrown walked softly through the dining-room. The door of her bedroom was open. In that sacred apartment boldly appeared Melissy and a man. The "instrument," in the visible form of the neat oaken desk of the long-distance and metallic circuit, stood already in position against the wall.

Melissy sat at the desk. The local manager, in no wise loath to expend the time of the corporation in Melissy's stimulating society, stood twitching an amused mustache behind her. Neither of the two observed Mrs. Fillebrown.

"Now talk," said the affable manager. "Say something."

Melissy put her mouth to the transmitter and the receiver to her ear. She flushed with embarrassment, and sat in abnormal silence.

"Look a-here," said Melissy, meekly. "I can't think of a dumb thing to say."

She laid the receiver down weakly. Her strong, red fingers fumbled on the desk.

"Then it's the first time, I'll warrant," suggested the manager, wickedly.

Melissy fired at the fuse. She picked up the receiver stoutly, and in a defiant tone began:

"Here-you. Hello! Hel-*lo!* Yes. I hear you. Yes, I *said* I heard you. Hel-hum-ho! This corporation's got an awful sarsy manager. I'll say that for it."

Melissy choked, and sank back.

"Ring up now," directed the manager, amiably. "Call up some one else. You've got to learn."

"I don't know who to call," pleaded Melissy, faintly.

Who had ever seen Melissy embarrassed before? It took the greatest of contemporaneous monopolies to disconcert the Yankee girl who "accommodated" for an income.

"Call up your grocer, and see if there isn't somebody in the store you know," observed the manager, with the ingenuity of his class. "Ask for 32:5."

"32:5!" demanded Melissy, in a fierce and resolute tone. "Mercy to Betsy! he says what do I want. What *do* I want?"

"Tell him you thought your young man was in the store, and you wanted a few words with him," commanded the godless manager.

Now Melissy's head was so muddled by this time, that she retained few if any intelligent ideas beyond the conviction that, the corporation must be obeyed, on forfeit of the instrument.

Mechanically she repeated the terrible language which the manager put into her mouth. There was a moment's significant silence in the telephone. Then Melissy could hear peals of profane masculine laughter reverberating through the grocery store.

"*I'll* answer the lady," broke in a sturdy voice. "Hullo, Miss Melissy! I'm proud to talk to ye!"

Melissy's face burned a dark, brick red.

"Child of sin and sorrow!" she gasped. "That's Adoniram Whettlestone! That's Silas Whey's Adoniram! Mercy to Betsy! I never can hold up my head in Northwest Peony again. I'm done for. Adoniram Whey? *Be* you Adoniram Whettlestone?"

"Yes. I hear you. I wisht I didn't."

"No, I didn't. I never did. I'd 'a' died fuss. This feller give me the order of them words. This is the sarsiest corporation I ever—No. I hadn't got nothin' to say to you over no blamed Noo York and Noo England Telephone instrumunt. No, sir. You may tell 'em so, too."

"What's that?"

"I'm a goin' to put this blame thing down offen my ear. I won't hear another word."

"What did you say? I didn't just get that. Say it again. Speak a little louder."

"Mercy to Betsy!"

At this juncture Mrs. Fillebrown made her presence manifest, and Melissy, with a burning face, flew to her for protection. "Take it!" she cried, throwing down the receiver. "Take the blame thing, an' do the foolin' for this here fambly yerself! It's fit to bring scandal on any decent house of women folks!"

With this, weeping for mortification, yet bridling through her tears, Melissy fled from the room.

It was now Mrs. Fillebrown's turn. She sat down with dignity, and picked up the receiver daintily, with her little finger crooked out the way she held a teaspoon in company.

"It is very interesting," she sighed. "Whom shall I talk to?"

"How would the doctor do?" suggested the astute manager.

"Shall I have to pay for a professional call?" asked the lady, anxiously. "I haven't got two dollars' worth of neuralgia to-day."

Being reassured on this point, she put her lips to the transmitter and faintly murmured: "Is the doctor in? Somebody says he isn't in," she added, in a disappointed tone. "I think it is his second wife."

"Are you sure it isn't his first?" asked the jocular manager.

"I'm not a spiritualist," replied the new subscriber, with dignity. The manager, who was no natural fool, perceived that he had unwittingly called out the concealed severity of an amiable woman—had stumbled on the subject of Mrs. Fillebrown's dearest aversion. He murmured a deprecating apology.

"Dear me!" said Mrs. Fillebrown, suddenly blushing. "They say there are twins at the sweet-potato man's, and they can't tell when to expect the doctor."

At this instant the call-bell rang loudly. Mrs. Fillebrown jumped and trembled. The manager explained that this was not her own call, but a chronic interruption to which she was expected to pay no attention.

"Hev we got ter hev that kerwollopin' in our ears night 'n' day?" demanded Melissy at the door. "I'd sooner *hev* twins—or the Last Trumpet."

Four musical rings now pealed prettily through the solemn house.

"You answer it!" pleaded Mrs. Fillebrown. "I feel somehow—it is very foolish, I know—a little afraid of it. Well, if you think it best—Who's that? Doctor? Why, *Doctor!*" Her pale face flushed with pleasure. "Why, I can recognize his voice—that big, bass tone he has when he's hungry and cross. Doctor? Why, this is delightful. Thank you; I am very much better. I haven't had an attack for ten days. Now, if anything *does* happen, I can call you up, can't I? Two boys, did you say? How interesting! It never occurred to me that a sweet-potato man *could* have twins. I don't think I even knew he was a married man. You see, one thinks of him as a sweet-pota—Yes. Good-by, Doctor. You are always so kind! He says he shall feel so much easier about me," sighed Mrs. Fillebrown, gently, as she hung the receiver in its place. The manager bowed gravely.

"What have you been doing in the front hall, Melissy?" asked Mrs. Fillebrown, after the representative of the corporation had left the house.

"Oh, nothin'," observed Melissy, carelessly—"only offerin' that feller a hot apple tart I had."

"Dear me, Melissy! I don't know about that. Is it quite—" Mrs. Fillebrown paused for a word. Had the telephone already begun to corrupt the manners of her irreproachable household?

"Waal," said Melissy, grimly, "I thought he needed a little more sarse. I told him so. I het it up, and put a tablespoonful cayenne pepper inside. Then I stirred in a teaspoonful of my bitters and a little lixypro 'n' some mustard. I told him I was lookin' to get a husband on my repootation for cookin'."

"Mercy on us, Melissy! Did the poor young man eat that tart?"

"A big mouthful!" cried Melissy, savagely. "He took a chaw when he got outside. I seen him."

With this spicy prelude the telephone entered Mrs. Fillebrown's household, and there it had been cherished for nearly a year at the time when these records find themselves again concerned with it.

It would be impossible to overestimate the importance of this third member of the family. As Melissy said, it was worth twenty men folks. She said it had better habits, and was more civil. Melissy averred that it was a sight more useful than a husband, and consider'ble less trouble than a family of children.

Mrs. Fillebrown did not say much; but the apparent fact was that the grave without a hope would now have had less terror for her than existence without a telephone connection. The little nickel bell of 24:4 was always tinkling merrily through the lonely house. Business occasions demanding the use of the wire crowded upon the imagination of the subscriber. Friendship, neighborhood charity, and religion in turn combined their forces to supply Mrs. Fillebrown's telephone with steady occupation. Trade and the professions re-enforced each other in keeping the lady busy at her oaken desk. Silas Whey and Wiley X. Toyl added their addresses to the year-book, and their connections to Mrs. Fillebrown's list of electric intimacies. The monthly bills at the grocer's and the butcher's increased so fast that it ceased to be a mystery how these rural tradesfolk could afford telephones. Who could count the unnecessary chops and salads, the delusive patent soaps and dyspeptic canned things, that got into the kitchen because it was so easy for them to get through the telephone? Equally impossible was it to estimate the social excitements which that "instrument" brought into Mrs. Fillebrown's solitary life. Sitting there alone on winter days, in her desolate rooms, she visited, she entertained. Across that tiny, trembling wire all her little world came to her, and thereby she ventured out to it.

One day the Northwest Peony Church (having heard it rumored in Boston that the modern improvements in religion called upon all active parishes to keen open church), in a burst of Christian good sense, put a telephone into the vestry. *Then* Mrs. Fillebrown may be said to have begun to live; for then she found her hands and heart full (or, more precisely and telephonically speaking, her ears and mouth full) of the miseries of other people; and her own, like dissolving figures thrown through a stereopticon, retreated gently. In a word, the wife with a history, the widow with a bitter memory fill in the place of a holy grief, the nervous invalid, the cynical recluse, had been added to the noble army of women whose romance has been sublimated into sacrifice. It took a year, but at the end of that year she was well on her way to become one of those neighborhood angels who glorify so many of the villages of New England with a gleam of splendid, moral life—some people name it altruism; some prefer an old-fashioned word, and call it Christianity.

24:4 had become the busiest number on the local exchange. The musical bell sang through its glass window at all hours of the day and many of the night.

It had become quite the fashion in Northwest Peony to expect Mrs. Fillebrown to "fill up"—to meet those gaps in things which nobody else did or could. Was a watcher needed? Was a girl in trouble which only another woman and an older could understand? Was a young fellow bothered about his debts or his class oration? Ring up 24:4! Who will start the subscription to keep a forgotten old lady out of the poorhouse? Who will help out at the minister's while his wife brings the new baby into the world at the precise time when the other children have the measles? Who will look after those girls whom a drunken father sold to a Russian Finn? That boy who has been all winter with no flannels, and one old jacket over his little cotton shirt? Call up 24:4!

"We'll have to charge you hotel rates, Mrs. Fillebrown, if this goes on," said the manager, soothing his mustache. But he wouldn't have done it for his situation. He was proud of 24:4. Most people in Northwest Peony were. When three calls on this busy number came in one week from the Fresh-air Fund, and one from the State Industrial School, and another from the Women's Prison, the manager felt that his most important subscriber reflected credit on the exchange and on the corporation.

One night in early January Mrs. Fillebrown was very tired. She had been answering the bell all day when she was in, and it had been calling snappily for her all the time she was out. It was late. Melissy had gone to bed with a toothache. The house was quiet. The yard and street were still with the heavy stillness of a windless, winter night when the thermometer is low, and the moon is on the snow.

The last calls of a busy day were over. She had directed Wiley X. Toyl to pay the coal bill that he disputed for those poor Portuguese who had the grippe. She had told the dressmaker not to put on that expensive trimming. She had asked Mrs. Silas Whey how Silas's throat was and wasn't there anything she could do? Oh, and how was Peter Parley's left hind ankle? She had ordered lemons from the grocer's for Rebecca at the Well. She had ordered extract of beef from the druggist's for the wife of the sweet-potato man, who had blessed the sweet-potato man and shocked the village by adding a cross-eyed, red-haired girl to her year-old twins.

Mrs. Fillebrown had told one of her Sunday-school scholars how to break an engagement, and another how to trim a bonnet. She had talked quite a while with the minister about the Junior Endeavor Convention and as long again with his wife about the baby's croup and the little girl's composition. She had asked the doctor what she should do for Melissy's wisdom-tooth, and now she had hung the receiver up and was lying on the lounge in the sitting-room under Melissy's blue and red afghan.

In one respect alone it should be said, 24:4 had proved an astonishing disappointment to its subscriber. So little occasion to summon the doctor had lately arisen that Mrs. Fillebrown sometimes felt as if the final cause of her connection with the corporation had been defeated. Beyond a word in behalf of Melissy's toothache, or a prescription for old Mr. Ginger's "left side" or a friendly suggestion what to do for those girls in the parish who were making themselves preeminent by eating slate-pencils and chewing the margins of the religious newspapers, the doctor had found limited professional occupation over the wires of 24:4.

Mrs. Fortitude Fillebrown had grown round and rosy, cheerful and calm. The electric spark which completed her circuit with the warm, human world had bought into her life as much as it carried out.

If Mrs. Fillebrown was not quite a well woman, or if she never would be, she was too busy a one to have the time to know it; and on this particular evening it was an angry surprise suddenly to find that old bit boring "at the base of the brain." She met the fact with that exasperated scorn by which the mind receives those foes of the body which it believed itself to have routed. She would not telephone for the doctor—she set her teeth and clinched her hands and lay still. She felt as ashamed as if neuralgia had been a felony.

"I am only tired out," she said.

The call-bell rang and she rose wearily to answer it. A young mother in the village who had lost her little girl that winter was going to Boston to consult a spiritualistic medium to-morrow. She telephoned to ask Mrs. Fillebrown to go with her.

"Not a step!" snapped Mrs. Fillebrown with the decision of a kindly woman whose pet antipathy is unexpectedly aroused. "I won't go an inch with you on any such fool of an errand! You stay at home Alicia and say your prayers, and take round the subscription for the Orphans' Home, and put poor little Allie's dresses in a Home Missionary barrel. That's all I've got to say to *you!*"

She came back to the lounge, and crept under the blue and red afghan rather weakly. Indeed she was tired—soul and body tired out. She had reached one of those crevices to be found on the steeps of the most noble of lives, where sacrifice itself takes on the weariness and doubtfulness of all human endeavor, and where the climb seems hardly worth the muscle. To crawl in and stop seemed just for that one hour the intelligent thing to do.

Suddenly, as she lay there in this supine mood which all strong beings know but few talk about, it seemed to her that she would give the whole— the whole brave, lonely play—for one of her husband's kisses.

This pang of womanly weakness surprised Mrs. Fillebrown the more because she really had thought so little about Joe for some time past. She was rather glad when the telephone rang again, and she had to stagger in to the bedroom to answer it. The summons came from the manager, who wished to know how she liked the looks of her name and number on the new yearbook, and regretted that he should not have the pleasure of serving so valuable a subscriber much longer. He was going to marry a Boston operator and expected to be promoted to a city exchange.

She had not left the desk before the bell struck once more and Mr. Adoniram Whettlestone presented his compliments to Miss Melissy Pulsifer, and would like to know if she received that evening.

"She's gone to bed with a toothache, Adoniram," said Mrs. Fillebrown, patiently. "And I must say I should be obliged to you if you wouldn't call us up again to-night. It is the seventh time to-day and, really I must have a little rest myself. If you want Melissy, come after her, man fashion; but I can't do second-hand courting over the telephone for a steady occupation."

It seemed hardly worth while to go back into the sitting-room after this, and Mrs. Fillebrown lay down on her bed, too tired and too ill either to undress or to sit up. It must have been half past nine o'clock when the bell rang with a loud, imperious cry.

"Well?" said Mrs. Fillebrown, wearily. (A subscriber seldom says hilloa.)

"Mrs. Fillebrown," replied the manager, in the voice of an operator moved with the unexpected importance of a country exchange, "here's a Long Distance call for you."

"Who is it?" asked Mrs. Fillebrown, with reviving interest.

"I don't know. It is a call from Chicago."

"Must be some mistake. I don't know anybody in Chicago."

"There is no mistake. The call is from Chicago—24:4—Mrs. Fortitude Fillebrown. No mistake at all. I will shut everything else off, and keep the wire clear for you. Speak distinctly, but don't holer. Line connected."

"Good-evening, Chicago," cried Mrs. Fillebrown, thickly, at the top of her lungs.

"Are you Northwest Peony, 24:4?"

"Yes."

"Is this Mrs. Fillebrown's house?"

"Yes."

"Mrs. Fortitude Fillebrown's?"

"Yes."

"Mrs. Joseph Fillebrown's?"

"This is the house."

"Are *you* Mrs. Fortitude Fillebrown?"

"I am the lady."

"*Forty!*" called the voice from space, tremulously, "don't you know me?"

The receiver shook in Mrs. Fillebrown's hand. Her face and neck went a mortal color. Women have dropped dead from far less shocks.

"No," she said, after a moment's terrible silence, "I do not know you."

"Very well," from a thousand miles away replied the voice, in disappointment so evident as to have something piteous about it—"very well, that will suit me."

"*Who* are you?" gasped Mrs. Fillebrown, now in great agitation.

"I used to be Joe," said the unseen, more quietly. He spoke with remarkable distinctness and power of tone. The conversation which followed took place without more difficulty than Mrs. Fillebrown might have experienced in calling up Boston in a snow-storm or a gale. "Now listen to me closely, Forty. It's a long pull, and you'll have to give trained attention."

"I am listening. I am attending closely."

"So you say—Joe died?"

"Joe died, and I buried him."

"Good riddance, wasn't it? Got along better without him, didn't you, girl? Wouldn't want me back if you could get me, would you?"

"Are you Joe's ghost? For God's sake, what are you?"

"Wouldn't want him round again, did you say?—Forty! Forty! *tell* a fellow! What's that? Did you say you'd be willing to take him back?"

"I'd thank God for the chance!"

"Rich or poor?"

"Rich or poor."

"Lucky or unlucky?"

"Lucky or unlucky."

"Good or bad?"

"Good or bad."

"Dead or living?"

"Dead or living," said the widow, solemnly. "I'd bless God for the chance to take my poor husband back."

"Then I'll call again," replied the voice from the winter night. "Good-by."

Silence succeeded. She strained her throat in calling, her ears in listening. No words followed. The wire roared in the frosty atmosphere.

"Finished!" cried the manager. She hung up the receiver, and for the first time in her life Mrs. Fillebrown fainted quite away.

She was a woman used to keeping her own counsel, and she told no person what had happened to her. When she came to her senses, lying stiff and uncovered there across her bed in the winter night, she found herself quaking with that terror which is not of this earth nor of its laws. For her hand touched the iron cross, cold upon her bosom beneath her loosened dress. The incredible significance of this little circumstance struck her chill and dumb.

Joe was dead. She had buried him. Her own hands had taken the trinket from his poor burned body.

Then *who* had tampered with the half-understood electric powers which men fancied themselves to have controlled? Then *what* had called to her across a thousand miles of winter night?

She thought, with a sudden flame upon her ashy cheeks, how impatient she had been with that woman whose little girl was dead. Suppose she had gone to the Boston medium with Alicia?

"Perhaps I should have found out—something," she thought, vaguely. Then, with the natural energy of a practical woman who has a morbidness in a healthy direction, she scorned herself for the thought. Towards all other human weakness trouble had taught her to be motherly and tolerant; but with the feebler side of mysticism, taken in the only form in which she knew it, that of the lower, vulgar order of séances and rappings and communications, she had never felt even a civil patience.

Now she trembled before a mystery more incredible, more unreasonable, than any tale of the dusk which she had ever read or heard.

"Such things are phenomena," she said. For she had been reading the scientific magazine to which she had subscribed.

The next night she locked herself in with her telephone, but the "phenomena" were not repeated. The night after and the day and night following passed without event. Mrs. Fillebrown dared not go out of hearing of the call-bell of 24:4. She shut herself into the house, and sent Melissy on all the errands, real and imaginary, which she found it possible to invent.

On the third night Adoniram was in the kitchen, and Melissy was thoroughly preoccupied. Mrs. Fillebrown was alone in her sleeping-room, with the bolt drawn. The lamp with the ghastly blue silk shade was burning, and in its deadly color the widow in her black dress, sat stolidly. No call had come in since supper. Mrs. Fillebrown watched the telephone with eyes in which there was more terror than longing. At half past nine she fancied that she saw the bell quiver behind its glass case. Then it struck.

She sprang to the desk. The manager was speaking.

"Mrs. Fillebrown, here's a Long Distance call for you again—New York."

"New York!"

"Connected."

With a clearness and distinctness which one might call appalling when one thought of the distance involved, the volume and articulation of voice began:

"Are you Northwest Peony, 24:4?"

"I am."

"Mrs. Fortitude Fillebrown's?"

"I am Mrs. Fillebrown."

"You are a mighty good operator for a subscriber. Hilloa, girl! Can you hear what I say?"

"I hear perfectly. But I don't know who you are."

"Try again! You've got a good Long Distance wire. You *ought* to recognize a voice no further than New York city. —Say, Forty! Come! Don't you know me?"

The woman's teeth chattered against the edge of the transmitter. Know the voice? Good God! She could not lie to Joe, just because he was a dead man. She *did* know the voice.

It was the voice that had courted her—and the voice that had cursed her. From that voice she had heard tenderness and blasphemy, manly love and unmanly recrimination, sodden song, self-pity, penitence, vows made only to be broken, and oh, what love-making! Enough to melt and hold the heart of the stoniest woman in the bitter world.

"*Joe!*" she wailed; and three hundred miles of sensitive wire vibrated to her cry.

"Well, well, Forty! Why, girl! Why, my poor girl! Why, I thought—Upon my word, the girl thinks she's talking to a ghost. Say, Forty! I know I *ought* to be dead, but the fact is—can you make out to bear it?—you see, I'm *not*."

"Joe Fillebrown!" called the widow, with an access of moral and physical strength, "just because you're a dead spirit, you needn't take advantage of a poor live woman to deceive her. . . . I took the iron cross off your burned corpse, and it's hanging around my neck."

"Whe-ew! You did, did you? I say, Forty! You always *were* almighty clever. I guess that evidence would hold in any court—and he'd be no kind of a ghost who didn't lose his case on it."

"Well, then!" cried the widow, in uncanny triumph. She felt an awful exaltation. She wondered what Alicia would say to this tremendous thing. How petty, how paltry, all those vulgar Boston "manifestations" seemed beside her own elect experience!

"Forty!" called the voice from New York, in a strange, changed tone. "Girl, I hate to disappoint you. But it isn't true."

"*What* isn't true?"

"You took the cross off the wrong fellow." . . . But now from 24:4 there came no reply.

"Forty! Has somebody cut us off?"

"No; we are not cut off."

"I say, Forty! You see, I was a little tight that night, and this chap, he won at poker and I was short of funds. . . . I *was* short, you know, occasionally, those days. So I was too tight to know any better—and I think I must have given him my watch."

"*You—gave away—my iron cross!*"

The words came with terrible distinctness. That little offence seemed worse to the woman at that moment than abuse, desertion, or death.

"Well," said the voice from New York, "haven't I been punished enough? *I* wasn't coming back to disgrace you! I meant—why, girl, don't you see?— I meant to try my hand at making a man of myself. It took a good while. I was going to make sure of it first."

Dead silence answered.

"If I haven't done that, I've done the next thing to it," urged the voice that was, but could not be, Joe's voice. "I've been manager of a big Western exchange. I telephone. That's my business. I can have any position I want. I'm doing well, Forty. And I haven't got drunk for six years and three months. I meant to serve seven steady years for you; but ten years without you (drunk or sober) is a good while, and—I couldn't stand it any longer, girl. I've got to that pass."

Then over the New York wire there broke the strangest message which that great line had ever known. It was the inarticulate pleading of a woman's sobs. They came one upon another far down from the depths which strong women never fathom in their own griefs—agonized entreaties, protests, appeals from fate to Heaven, and perhaps God knows what unuttered or unutterable forebodings.

"Oh, Forty! Why, Forty! Why, my poor girl! If you feel so badly—as *that!*— I won't bother you, my dear. I won't disgrace you. I meant to come home— when I'd made a man of myself, when I could make up to you for what happened; but I—can—give it . . . up. I'll go back. I meant to take—the first train—to you."

"Joe! *Joe!* As soon as I *can* speak—Joe! Oh, for God's sake, *don't* let anybody cut us off *now!*"

"Forty! Do you want me? Did you say you did? Don't you bother about the wire. I'd like to see 'em cut off a manager on a D. H. message! Did you say you *wanted* me? Then, I swear, all hell sha'n't keep me! I'll be with you— dead or living—by to-morrow night!"

The communication shut down. Silence put her delicate finger upon the throbbing wire. The receiver fell from Mrs. Fillebrown's hand. She sat staring about her lonely room. She got up and snatched off the blue lamp shade; she hated the color suddenly. She wondered where that rose-red one had gone to that Joe used to like.

All the next day she lived in one of those sublimated dreams which make it possible for one to understand what it may be like to be a disembodied creature. Cherishing the thrilling secret, which still she did not dare to share with any living, she trod the floors of her house as if they had been floating clouds.

Melissy watched her; the Yankee girl's jaw dropped. "What in mercy to Betsy's got ye? There ain't no comp'ny comin'. Ain't this here house clean enough for you? And I'd like to know what you're a-movin' round the furnitoor in your room for. That bureau hadn't stood there sence Mr. Fillebrown was buried. Why, that old red silk quilt's ben in the rag-bag this five year! Be you out of your senses?"

But Mrs. Fillebrown stared at Melissy solemnly. The question troubled her. Perhaps she was. She would not talk to Melissy. She spent the day in putting little things as Joe used to fancy them.

Towards night she got into a white cashmere tea gown that she sometimes wore with black ribbons. She sent Melissy to a Christian Endeavor meeting with Adoniram Whey, and herself remained alone in the house.

The evening trains came in and went out. Time to ride, to walk, to crawl from the station elapsed. The last train roared down the valley. Wheels were heard; they passed the house. It came on to be nine o'clock. Her pale lips moved stiffly.

"If there's anything *to* it, he'll call me up again." But he did not call her up again. She sat by her telephone all night long. The bell did not ring. . . . There was nothing to it.

Joe was dead; and she had been fooled, like the weakest of women, by a "manifestation."

"It is nothing but a modern improvement in spiritualism," she thought, coldly.

In the morning she put on her black dress again, and carried her insomniac face proudly to the breakfast table, where Melissy took one look at it, and rang up the doctor immediately.

But Mrs. Fillebrown said nothing to the doctor. He prescribed for neuralgia at the base of the brain. She looked at him, and said, "Thank you, doctor," and he went away.

A week passed; two; four. No more Long Distance messages came to the Peony Centre exchange for 24:4. Mrs. Fillebrown eyed her telephone with a sick horror, as she might some evil spirit that had conspired with all that was freakish and weak in Joe to work her this unutterable misery.

One night, at a late hour, it being nearly twelve of the clock, she lay in bed with the light burning. She could not sleep. Then, suddenly, while she lay watching the nickel bell through its glass protector, it rang. It rang with the wilful and commanding peal familiar to the business in the transmission of messages from officer to operator of the line.

In her night-dress as she was, she leaped to the receiver; and through it, as before, came the prudent prelude:

"Is this 24:4, Peony Centre?"

"It is."

"Is this Mrs. Joseph Fillebrown's?"

"I am Mrs. Fortitude Fillebrown."

"Forty! . . . . I'm almost home. I'm in Boston."

"I hear you"—coldly.

"Girl, I've been sick—"

"Yes. I hear what you say."

"On my honor, Forty! I wasn't well when I started. I only got so far and stopped. I've had pneumonia at the City Hospital. I've been delirious. I couldn't get to you."

"Lord have mercy upon me!" wailed Mrs. Fillebrown, piteously. . . . It had all begun all over again. Joe had been on a spree.

"*Fortitude Fillebrown!*" A thunderous cry rushed across the wires. "You think—I've been drinking again! I say, if you do, I won't come home—I'll never come home till I *am* a ghost. If you can't trust me, girl—*now*—I did my best to get to you, Forty," tremulously. "But I see you don't believe me. Good-by. Good-by, girl—good-by."

"I'll believe in you when I see you," said the widow, stoutly. "It's asking too much of me to believe in deceiving spirits. It isn't Scriptural. You come home, Joe, and give me a chance to believe in you."

"Will you *want* me, Forty?"—timidly.

"Come home and find out for yourself, Joe."

"*Sure* you want me?"

"Sure."

"Poor or rich? Lucky or unlucky?"

"Yes—God knows—yes."

"Sick or well?"

"Sick or well."

"Dead or living?"

"*Dead or living.*"

"Then I'll be there to breakfast," said the unseen.

The message shut off abruptly. But in a few moments the bell called again.

"Forty! I forgot to tell you. I've kept track of you, you know, all this while. I never meant to let you get into any scrape. I wasn't so bad as that. And, girl, I can have the exchange at Peony Centre if you'd rather stay on in the old home. It's a small job—there's a bigger in Boston for the taking—but I'd like to please you. Think it over, will you?"

"I'll think it over, Joe."

"And, Forty, girl, do you think you care enough for me"—

"I never cared for any man but you, Joe Fillebrown, in all my life."

—"When I come, if I should want to kiss you, Forty? I might, you know."

"I'll tell you when I see you," said Mrs. Fillebrown, evasively, persisting in the shelter of her phrase.

She went to bed and slept like a little girl. In the morning she woke quietly. Ghost or man, she had somehow ceased to be afraid of Joe. She felt the sacred power of the marriage bond close around her solemnly. Better, oh, best, a thousand times, forever be true wife, let shame, misery, mystery, death, come as they will!

She told Melissy, vouchsafing no explanation of this fearful domestic irregularity to wait breakfast for a little, and then she opened the front door and looked out.

The first train from the city was screaming down the valley. There would be no cab at the station. She almost wished she had sent Adoniram with old Peter Parley. But then she remembered that one cannot ask the use of a neighbor's carriage to meet a spirit.

She stood in her black dress looking down the road. A man was walking feebly up the little hill. It was slushy, and the walking was hard. He crawled along with bent head. As he came nearer she saw that his hair was gray. Her heart gave one wild leap, and fell. For, oh, Joe's curls were brown as a seal, and as soft! Poor Joe! Dead Joe! She stepped back into the house. Then, God knew why, she turned.

He had seen her, and, appalled at her abrupt retreat, had stopped there in the snow and leaned against the fence. He was breathing fast and weakly. It would have taken less than the least of the little whims which control the great decisions of life to make the man turn back.

For it was Joe. And he thought she was ashamed of him, or that she was sorry she had told him to come home.

She ran out into the slush and got to him. He held out his hand, and she put hers into it.

Now at that moment she found these dreadful words in her mind: "This was the hand that struck me."

She looked up into his face. Haggard as it was with mortal sickness, still the firm lines and the direct eye of long abstinence were there. All the witnesses of Joe's face took oath for him.

In hers a solemn jury held its verdict back. A piteous mental confusion ran riot in her. What were those old words about being born again? Her *Scien-*

tific Monthly had omitted to quote them in that strong paper treating of the physiological renewal of the cells conceded to occur once in so many years.

"The hand that did that died. This is a new Joe," she thought. And then she thought no more. But she took his wasted fingers and bent over them, and laid her lips to them and kissed them.

When she saw how sick a man he was, very naturally and quietly she said, "Breakfast is all ready, Joe," just as if nothing had happened, and he had only been out all night, and was sorry, and had come home quite himself.

★

ROBERT BARR *Within an Ace of the End of the World:*
Being some account of the fearful disaster which overtook
the inhabitants of this earth through scientific
miscalculation in the year 1904
McClure's 14 (1900): 545–554

[Barr, a reporter for the *Detroit Free Press*, was an early popularizer of the new fictional device of presenting civic criticism, ecological concerns, and global ethnic cleansing in the guise of science fiction. His story ends with the survivors, a group of Oxford "boys" and Vassar "girls," gazing on the ruins of New York City and anticipating a "pure" and "civilized" world.]

THE SCIENTIST'S SENSATION: The beginning of the end was probably the address delivered by Sir William Crookes to the British Association at Bristol, on September 7, 1898, although Herbert Bonsel, the young American experimenter, alleged afterward that his investigations were well on the way to their final success at the time Sir William spoke.

All records being lost in the series of terrible conflagrations which took place in 1904, it is now impossible to give any accurate statement regarding Sir William Crookes's remarkable paper, but it is known that his assertions attracted much attention at the time, and were the cause of editorial comment in almost every newspaper and scientific journal in the world.

The sixteen survivors out of the many millions who were alive at the beginning of 1904 were so much occupied in the preservation of their own lives, a task of almost insurmountable difficulty, that they have handed down to us, their descendants, an account of the six years beginning with 1898 which is, to say the least, extremely unsatisfactory to an exact writer.

Man, in that year, seems to have been a bread-eating animal, consuming, per head, something like six bushels of wheat per annum. Sir William appears to have pointed out to his associates that the limit of the earth's production of wheat had been reached and he predicted universal starvation, did not science step in to the aid of a famine-stricken world.

Science, however, was prepared. What was needed to increase the wheat production of the world to something like double its then amount was nitrate of soda; but nitrate of soda did not exist in the quantity required—viz., some 12,000,000 tons annually. However, a supposedly unlimited supply of nitrogen existed in the atmosphere surrounding the earth, and from this storehouse science proposed to draw, so that the multitude might be fed.

Nitrogen in its free state in the air was useless as applied to wheat-growing, but it could be brought into solid masses for practical purposes by means of electricity generated by the waterfalls which are so abundant in many mountainous lands. The cost of nitrates made from the air by water-power approached $25 a ton, as compared with $130 a ton when steam was used. Visionary people had often been accused of occupying castles in the air, but now it was calmly proposed to feed future populations from granaries in the air. Naturally, as has been said, the project excited much comment, although it can hardly be asserted that it was taken seriously.

It is impossible at this time, because of the absence of exact data, to pass judgment on the conflicting claims of Sir William Crookes and Mr. Herbert Bonsel; but it is perhaps not too much to say that the actual beginning of disaster was the dinner given by the Marquis of Surrey to a number of wealthy men belonging to the city of London, at which Mr. Bonsel was the guest of the evening.

THE DINNER AT THE HOTEL CECIL: Early in April, 1900, a young man named Herbert Bonsel sailed for England from New York. He is said to have been a native of Coldwater, Michigan, and to have served some sort of apprenticeship in the workshops of Edison at Orange, New Jersey. It seems that he did not prosper there to his satisfaction, and after trying to interest New York people in his experiments, he returned to Coldwater, where he worked for some time in a carriage-building establishment. Bonsel's expertness with all kinds of machinery drew forth the commendation of his chief, and begot a friendship between them which ultimately led to Bonsel's divulging to the other at least part of his secret. The obstacle in the way of success was chiefly scarcity of money, for the experiments were costly in their nature. Bonsel's chief, whose name is not known, seems to have got together a small syndicate, which advanced a certain amount of capital, thus enabling the young man to try his fortune once more in New York. Again his efforts to enlist capital in New York were fruitless; therefore, in April he sailed for England.

Bonsel's evil star being in the ascendant, he made the acquaintance of the wealthy Marquis of Surrey, who became much interested in the young man and his experiments. The Marquis bought out the Coldwater syndicate, returning the members tenfold the money they had invested, and took

Bonsel to his estate in the country, where, with ample means now at his disposal, the youthful scientist pushed his investigations to success with marvelous rapidity. Nothing is known of him until December of that year, when the Marquis of Surrey gave a dinner in his honor at the Hotel Cecil, to which were invited twenty of the richest men in England. This festival became known as "The Millionaires' Dinner"; and although there was some curiosity excited regarding its purport, and several paragraphs appeared in the papers alluding to it, no surmise concerning it came anywhere near the truth. The Marquis of Surrey presided, with Bonsel at his right and the Lord Mayor of London at his left. Even the magnates who sat at that table, accustomed as they were to the noted dinners in the City, agreed unanimously that they had never partaken of a better meal, when, to their amazement, the chairman asked them, at the close, how they had relished it.

A STRIKING AFTER-DINNER SPEECH: The Marquis of Surrey, before introducing the guest of the evening, said that, as they were all doubtless aware, this was not a social, but a commercial dinner. It was the intention, before the company separated, to invite subscriptions to a corporation which would have a larger capitalization than any limited liability concern that had ever before been floated. The young American at his right would explain the discoveries he had made and the inventions he had patented, which this newly formed corporation would exploit. Thus introduced, Herbert Bonsel rose to his feet and said:

"Gentlemen, I was pleased to hear you admit that you liked the dinner which was spread before us to-night. I confess that I never tasted a better meal, but most of my life I have been poor, and therefore I am not so capable of passing an opinion on a banquet as any other here, having always been accustomed to plain fare. I have, therefore, to announce to you that all the viands you have tasted and all the liquors you have consumed were prepared by me in my laboratory. You have been dining simply on various forms of nitrogen, or on articles of which nitrogen is a constituent. The free nitrogen of the air has been changed to fixed nitrogen by means of electricity, and the other components of the food placed on the board have been extracted from various soils by the same means. The champagne and the burgundy are the product of the laboratory, and not of the wine-press, the soil used in their composition having been exported from the vine-bearing regions of France. More than a year ago, Sir William Crookes announced what the nitrogen free in the air might do for the people of this world. At the time I read his remarks I was engaged in the experiments that have now been completed. I trembled, fearing I was about to be forestalled; but up to this moment, so far as I know, there has been made no effort to put his theories into practical use. Sir William seemed to think it would be sufficient to use the nitrates extracted from the atmosphere for the purpose of fertilizing the ground. But this always appeared to me a most roundabout method. Why should we wait on slow-footed nature? If science is capable of wringing one constituent of our food from the air, why should it shrink from extracting the others from earth or water? In other words, why leave a job half finished? I knew of no reason; and, luckily, I succeeded in convincing our noble host that all food products may be speedily compounded in the laboratory, without waiting the progress of the tardy seasons. It is proposed, therefore, that a company be formed with a capital so large that it can control practically all the water-power available in the world. We will extract from earth, air, and water whatever we need, compound the products in our factories, and thus feed the whole world. The moment our plant is at work, the occupations of agriculturist, horticulturist, and stock-breeder are gone. There is little need to dwell on the profit that must accrue to such a company as the one now projected. All commercial enterprises that have hitherto existed, or even any combination of them, cannot be compared in wealth-producing power to the scheme we have now in hand. There is no man so poor but he must be our customer if he is to live, and none so rich that he can do without us."

THE GREAT FOOD CORPORATION (Limited): After numerous questions and answers, the dinner party broke up, pledged to secrecy, and next day a special train took the twenty down to the Marquis of Surrey's country place, where they saw in operation the apparatus that transformed simple elements into palatable food. At the mansion of the Marquis was formed The Great Food Corporation (Limited), which was to have such an amazing effect upon the peoples of this earth. Although the company proved one of the most lucrative investments ever undertaken in England, still it did not succeed in maintaining the monopoly it had at first attempted. In many countries the patents did not hold, some governments refusing to sanction a monopoly on which life itself depended, others deciding that, although there were certain ingenious novelties in Bonsel's processes, still the general principles had been well known for years, and so the final patents were refused. Nevertheless, these decisions did not interfere as much as might have been expected with the prosperity of The Great Food Producing Corporation (Limited). It had been first in the field, and its tremendous capitalization enabled it to crush opposition somewhat ruthlessly, aided by the advantage of having secured most of the available water-power of the world. For a time there was reckless speculation in food-manufacturing companies, and much money was lost in consequence. Agriculture was indeed killed, as Bonsel had predicted, but the farmers of Western America, in spite of the decline of soil-tilling, continued to furnish much of the world's food. They erected windmills, with which electricity was generated, and, drawing on the soil and the air, they manufactured nourishment almost as cheaply as the great water-power corporation itself. This went on in every part of the world where the

Bonsel patents were held invalid. In a year or two every one became accustomed to the chemically compounded food, though a few old fogies kept writing to the newspapers proclaiming that the former manner of cultivation was better, and that they would never forsake the ancient wheaten loaf for its modern equivalent; yet nobody paid any attention to these conservatives, looking on them as harmless enthusiasts; and presently even they could not get the wheaten loaf of bygone days, as grain was no longer grown except as a curiosity in some botanist's garden.

REMARKABLE SCENE IN THE GUILDHALL: The first three years of the twentieth century were notable for the great increase of business confidence all over the world. A reign of universal prosperity seemed to have set in. Political questions appeared easier of solution. The anxieties that hitherto had oppressed the public mind, such as the ever-present poverty problem, provision for the old age of laborers, and so forth, lifted like a rising cloud, and disappeared. There were still the usual number of poor people; but, somehow, lack of wealth had lost its terror. It was true that the death-rate increased enormously; but nobody seemed to mind that. The episode at the Guildhall dinner in 1903 should have been sufficient to awaken the people, had an awakening been possible in the circumstances; but that amazing lesson, like others equally ominous, passed unheeded. When the Prime Minister who had succeeded Lord Salisbury was called upon to speak, he said:

"My Lord Mayor, Your Royal Highnesses, Your Excellencies, Your Graces, My Lords and Gentlemen: It has been the custom of Prime Ministers from time immemorial to give at this annual banquet some indication of the trend of mind of the Government. I propose, with your kind permission, to deviate in slight measure from that ancient custom (cheers). I think that hitherto we have all taken the functions of government rather more seriously than their merits demanded and a festive occasion like this should not be marred by the introduction of debatable subjects (renewed cheering). If, therefore, the band will be good enough to strike up that excellent tune, 'There will be a hot time in the old town to-night,' I shall have the pleasure of exhibiting to you a quick-step I have invented to the rhythm of that lively composition (enthusiastic acclaim)."

The Prime Minister, with the aid of some of the waiters, cleared away the dishes in front of him, stepped from the floor to his chair, and from the chair to the table, where, accompanied by the energetic playing of the band, he indulged in a break-down that would have done credit to any music-hall stage. All the applauding diners rose to their feet in the wildest excitement. His Royal Highness the Crown Prince of Alluria placed his hands on the shoulders of the Lord Mayor, the German Ambassador placed his hands on the shoulders of the Crown Prince, and so on down the table, until the distinguished guests formed a connected ring around the board on which the

Prime Minister was dancing. Then all, imitating the quick-step, and keeping time with the music, began circling round the table, one after the other, shouting and hurrahing at the top of their voices. There were loud calls for the American Ambassador, a celebrated man, universally popular; and the Prime Minister, reaching out a hand, helped him up on the table. Amidst vociferous cheering, he said that he took the selection of the tune as a special compliment to his countrymen, the American troops having recently entered a conquered city to its melodious strains. His Excellency hoped that this hilarious evening would cement still further the union of the English-speaking races, which in fact it really did, though not in the manner the honorable gentleman anticipated at the time of speaking. The company, headed by the band and the Prime Minister, then made their way to the street, marched up Cheapside, past St. Paul's, and along Fleet Street and the Strand, until they came to Westminster. Every one along the route joined the processional dance, and upward of 50,000 persons were assembled in the square next to the Abbey and in the adjoining streets. The mob was exuberant in its approval of the proceedings. The Prime Minister, waving his hands toward the Houses of Parliament, cried, "Three cheers for the good old House of Commons!" These being given with a tiger appended, a workingman roared, "Three cheers for 'is Lordship and the old duffers what sits with 'im in the 'Ouse of Lords." This was also cheered—until the echoes reached the Mansion House.

The "Times" next morning, in a jocular leading article, congratulated the people of England on the fact that at last politics were viewed in the correct light. There had been, as the Prime Minister truly said, too much solidity in the discussion of public affairs; but, linked with song and dance, it was now possible for the ordinary man in the street to take some interest in them, etc., etc. Foreign comment, as cabled from various countries, was entirely sympathetic to the view taken of the occurrence by all the English newspapers, which was that we had entered a new era of jollity and good will.

A WARNING FROM OXFORD: I have now to speak of my great-grandfather, John Rule, who, at the beginning of the twentieth century, was a science student at Balliol College, Oxford, aged twenty four. It is from the notes written by him and the newspaper clippings which he preserved that I am enabled to compile this imperfect account of the disaster of 1904 and the events leading to it. I append, without alteration or comment, his letter to the "Times," which appeared the day after that paper's flippant references to the conduct of the Prime Minister and his colleagues:

To the Editor of the "Times":

"*Sir*,—The levity of the Prime Minister's recent conduct; the levity of your own leading article thereon; the levity of foreign reference to the deplorable episode, indicate but too clearly the crisis which mankind is called upon to face, and to face, alas, under conditions which make the averting of the greatest calamity well-nigh impossible. To put it plainly, every man, woman, and child on this earth, with the exception of eight persons in the United States and eight in England, are drunk—not with wine, but with oxygen. The numerous factories all over the world which are working night and day making fixed nitrates from the air, are rapidly depleting the atmosphere of its nitrogen. When this disastrous manufacture was begun, 100 parts of air, roughly speaking, contained 76.9 parts of nitrogen and 23.1 parts of oxygen. At the beginning of this year, the atmosphere round Oxford was composed of nitrogen 53.218, oxygen 46.782. And here we have the explanation of the largely increased death-rate. Man is simply burning up. To-day the normal proportions of the two gases in the air is nearly reversed, standing nitrogen, 27.319, oxygen 72.681, a state of things simply appalling: due in a great measure to the insane folly of Russia, Germany, and France competing with each other in raising mountain ranges of food products as a reserve in case of war, just as the same fear of a conflict brought their armies to such enormous proportions a few years ago. The nitrogen factories must be destroyed instantly, if the people of this earth are to remain alive. If this is done, the atmosphere will gradually become nitrogenized once more. I invite the editor of the 'Times' to come to Oxford and live for a few days with us in our iron building, erected on Port Meadow, where a machine supplies us with nitrogen and keeps the atmosphere within the hut similar to that which once surrounded the earth. If he will direct the policy of the 'Times' from this spot, he may bring an insane people to their senses. Oxford yesterday bestowed a degree of D.C.L. on a man who walked the whole length of the High on his hands; so it will be seen that it is time something was done.

"I am, sir, yours, etc.,

"John Rule.

"Balliol College, Oxford."

The "Times" in an editorial note said that the world had always been well provided with alarmists, and that their correspondent, Mr. Rule, was a good example of the class. That newspaper, it added, had been for some time edited in Printing House Square, and it would continue to be conducted in that quarter of London, despite the attractions of the sheet-iron house near Oxford.

THE TWO NITROGEN COLONIES: The coterie in the iron house consisted of the Rev. Mr. Heburn, who was a clergyman and tutor; two divinity students, two science students, and three other undergraduates, all of whom had withdrawn from their colleges, awaiting with anxiety the catastrophe they were powerless to avert. Some years before, when the proposal to admit women to the Oxford colleges was defeated, the Rev. Mr. Hepburn and John Rule visited the United States to study the working of co-education in that country. There Mr. Rule became acquainted with Miss Sadie Armour of Vassar College on the Hudson, and the acquaintance speedily ripened into friendship, with a promise of the closer relationship that was yet to come. John and Sadie kept up a regular correspondence after his return to Oxford, and naturally he wrote to her regarding his fears for the future of mankind, should the diminution of the nitrogen in the air continue. He told her of the precautions he and his seven comrades had taken, and implored her to inaugurate a similar colony near Vassar. For a long time the English Nitrogenists, as they were called, hoped to be able to awaken the world to the danger that threatened; and by the time they recognized that their efforts were futile, it was too late to attempt the journey to America which had long been in John Rule's mind.

Parties of students were in the habit of coming to the iron house and jeering at the inmates. Apprehending violence one day, the Rev. Mr. Hepburn went outside to expostulate with them. He began seriously, then paused, a comical smile lighting up his usually sedate face, and finally broke out into roars of laughter, inviting those he had left to come out and enjoy themselves. A moment later he began to turn somersaults round the iron house, all the students outside hilariously following his example, and screaming that he was a jolly good fellow. John Rule and one of the most stalwart of the divinity students rushed outside, captured the clergyman, and dragged him into the house by main force, the whirling students being too much occupied with their evolutions to notice the abduction. One of the students proposed that the party should return to Carfax by hand-springs, and thus they all set off, progressing like jumping-jacks across the meadow, the last human beings other than themselves that those within the iron house were to see for many a day. Rule and his companions had followed the example set by continental countries, and had, while there was yet time, accumulated a small mountain of food products inside and outside of their dwelling. The last letter Rule received from America informed him that the girls of Vassar had done likewise.

THE GREAT CATASTROPHE: The first intimation that the Nitrogenists had of impending doom was from the passage of a Great Western train running northward from Oxford. As they watched it, the engine suddenly burst into a brilliant flame, which was followed shortly by an explosion, and a moment later the wrecked train lay along the line blazing fiercely. As evening drew on, they saw that Oxford was on fire, even the stonework of the colleges seeming to burn as if it had been made of wax. Communication with the outside world ceased, and an ominous silence held the earth. They did not know then that London, New York, Paris, and many other cities had been consumed by fire; but they surmised as much. Curiously enough, the carbon dioxide evolved by these numerous and widespread conflagrations made the outside air more breathable, notwithstanding the poisonous nature of this mitigant of oxygenic energy. For days they watched for any sign of human life outside their own dwelling, but no one approached. As a matter of fact, all the inhabitants of the world were dead except themselves and the little colony in America, although it was long after that those left alive became aware of the full extent of the calamity that had befallen their fellows. Day by day they tested the outside air, and were overjoyed to note that it was gradually resuming its former quality. This process, however, was so slow that the young men became impatient, and endeavored to make their house movable, so that they might journey with it, like a snail, to Liverpool, for the one desire of each was to reach America and learn the fate of the Vassar girls. The moving of the house proved impracticable, and thus they were compelled to remain where they were until it became safe to venture into the outside air, which they did some time before it had reached its normal condition.

It seems to have been fortunate that they did so, for the difficulties they had to face might have proved insurmountable had they not been exhilarated by the excess of oxygen in the atmosphere. The diary which John Rule wrote showed that within the iron house his state of depression was extreme when he remembered that all communication between countries was cut off, and that the girl to whom he was betrothed was separated from him by 3,000 miles of ocean, whitened by no sail. After the eight set out, the whole tone of his notes changed, an optimism scarcely justified by the circumstances taking the place of his former dismay. It is not my purpose here to dwell on the appalling nature of the foot journey to Liverpool over a corpse-strewn land. They found, as they feared, that Liverpool also had been destroyed by fire, only a fringe of the river front escaping the general conflagration. So enthusiastic were the young men, according to my great-grandfather's notes, that on the journey to the seaport they had resolved to walk to America by way of Behring Straits, crossing the English Channel in a row-boat, should they find that the shipping at Liverpool was destroyed. This seems to indicate a state of oxygen intoxication hardly less intense than that which had caused the Prime Minister to dance on the table.

A VOYAGE TO RUINED NEW YORK: They found the immense steamship "Teutonic" moored at the landing-stage, not apparently having had time to go to her dock when the universal catastrophe culminated. It is probable that the city was on fire when the steamer came in, and perhaps an attempt was made to board her, the ignorant people thinking to escape the fate that they felt overtaking them by putting out to sea. The landing-stage was packed with lifeless human beings, whole masses still standing up, so tightly were they wedged. Some stood transfixed with upright arms above their heads, and death seemed to have come to many in a form like suffocation. The eight at first resolved to take the "Teutonic" across the Atlantic, but her coal bunkers proved nearly empty, and they had no way of filling them. Not one of them knew anything of navigation, and Rule alone was acquainted with the rudiments of steam-engineering. They selected a small steam yacht, and loaded her with the coal that was left in the "Teutonic's" bunkers. Thus they started for the West, the Rev. Mr. Hepburn acting as captain and John Rule as engineer. It was fourteen days before they sighted the coast of Maine, having kept much too far north. They went ashore at the ruins of Portland; but embarked again, resolved to trust rather to their yacht than undertake a long land journey through an unknown and desolated country. They skirted the silent shores of America until they came to New York, and steamed down the bay. My great-grandfather describes the scene as somber in the extreme. The Statue of Liberty seemed to be all of the handiwork of man that remained intact. Brooklyn Bridge was not entirely consumed, and the collapsed remains hung from two pillars of fused stone, the ragged ends of the structure which once formed the roadway dragging in the water. The city itself presented a remarkable appearance. It was one conglomerate mass of gray-toned, semi-opaque glass, giving some indication of the intense heat that had been evolved in its destruction. The outlines of its principal thoroughfares were still faintly indicated, although the melting buildings had flowed into the streets like lava, partly obliterating them. Here and there a dome of glass showed where an abnormally high structure once stood, and thus the contour of the city bore a weird resemblance to its former self—the likeness that the grim outlines of a corpse over which a sheet has been thrown might bear to a living man. All along the shore lay the gaunt skeletons of half-fused steamships. The young men passed this dismal calcined graveyard in deep silence, keeping straight up the broad Hudson. No sign of life greeted them until they neared Poughkeepsie, when they saw, flying above a house situated on the top of a hill, that brilliant fluttering flag, the Stars and Stripes. Somehow its very motion in the wind gave promise that the vital spark had not been altogether extinguished in America. The great sadness which had oppressed the voyagers was lifted, and they burst forth into cheer after cheer. One of the young men rushed into the chartroom, and brought out the Union Jack, which was quickly hauled up to the mast-head, and the reverend captain pulled the cord that, for the first time during the voyage, let loose the roar of the steam whistle, rousing the echoes of the hills on either side of the noble stream. Instantly, on the veranda of the flag-covered house, was seen the glimmer of a white summer dress, then of another and another and another, until eight were counted.

AND FINALLY: The events that followed belong rather to the region of romance than to a staid, sober narrative of fact like the present; indeed, the theme has been a favorite one with poets and novelists, whose pens would have been more able than mine to do justice to this international idyll. America and England were indeed joined, as the American Ambassador had predicted at the Guildhall, though at the time his words were spoken he had little idea of the nature and complete accord of that union. While it cannot be denied that the unprecedented disaster which obliterated human life in 1904 seemed to be a calamity, yet it is possible to trace the design of a beneficent providence in this wholesale destruction. The race which now inhabits the earth is one that includes no savages and no war lords. Armies are unknown and unthought of. There is no battleship on the face of the waters. It is doubtful if universal peace could have been brought to the world short of the annihilation of the jealous, cantankerous, quarrelsome peoples who inhabited it previous to 1904. The Lord destroyed humanity once by flood, and again by fire; but whether the race, as it enlarges, will deteriorate after its second extinguishment, as it appears to have done after its first, must remain for the future to determine.

BIBLIOGRAPHY OF RECENTLY
PUBLISHED SECONDARY SOURCES

Allen, Robert G. *Horrible Prettiness: Burlesque and American Culture.* Chapel Hill: U of North Carolina, 1991.

Ames, Kenneth L. *Death in the Dining Room and Other Tales of Victorian Culture.* Philadelphia: Temple UP, 1992.

Ammons, Elizabeth. *Conflicting Stories: American Women Writers at the Turn into the Twentieth Century.* New York: Oxford UP, 1991.

Ardis, Ann. *New Women, New Novels: Feminism and Early Modernism.* New Brunswick, N.J.: Rutgers UP, 1990.

Banta, Martha *Imaging American Women: Idea and Ideals in Cultural History.* New York: Columbia UP, 1987.

Bederman, Gail. *Manliness and Civilization: A Cultural History of Gender and Race in the United States, 1880–1917.* Chicago: U of Chicago P, 1995.

Bijker, Wiebe E. *Of Bicycles, Bakelites, and Bulbs: Toward a Theory of Sociotechnical Change.* Cambridge, Mass.: MIT P, 1995.

Blair, Karen J. *The Torchbearers: Women and Their Amateur Arts Associations in America, 1890–1930.* Bloomington: Indiana UP, 1994.

Bledstein, Burton J. *The Culture of Professionalism: The Middle Class and the Development of Higher Education in America.* New York: Norton, 1976.

Blumin, Stuart M. *The Emergence of the Middle Class: Social Experience in the American City, 1760–1900.* New York: Cambridge UP, 1989.

Bordman, Gerald. *The American Theater: A Chronicle of Comedy and Drama: 1869–1914.* Oxford: Oxford UP, 1994.

Boyer, Paul. *Urban Masses and Moral Order in America, 1820–1920.* Cambridge, Mass.: Harvard UP, 1978.

Briggs, Asa, and Daniel Snowman, eds. *Fins de Siècle: How Centuries End: 1400–2000.* New Haven, Conn.: Yale UP, 1996.

Brodhead, Richard H. *Cultures of Letters: Scenes of Reading and Writing in Nineteenth-Century America.* Chicago: U of Chicago P, 1993.

Bronner, Simon J., ed. *Consuming Visions: Accumulation and Display of Goods in America, 1880–1920.* New York: Norton, 1989.

Burke, Martin J. *The Conundrum of Class: Public Discourse on the Social Order in America.* Chicago: U of Chicago P, 1995.

Burt, Nathaniel. *Palaces for the People: A Social History of the American Art Museum.* Boston: Little, Brown, 1977.

Bushman, Richard L. *The Refinement of America: Persons, Houses, Cities.* New York: Vintage, 1993.

Carnes, Mark C. *Secret Ritual and Manhood in Victorian America.* New Haven, Conn.: Yale UP, 1989.

Carnes, Mark C., and Clyde Griffen, eds. *Meanings for Manhood: Constructions of Masculinity in Victorian America.* Chicago: U of Chicago P, 1990.

Cashman, Sean Dennis. *America in the Gilded Age: From the Death of Lincoln to the Rise of Theodore Roosevelt.* New York: New York UP, 1993.

Chielens, Edward E., ed. *American Literary Magazines: The Eighteenth and Nineteenth Centuries.* Westport, Conn.: Greenwood P, 1986.

Cotkin, George. *Reluctant Modernism: American Thought and Culture, 1880–1900.* New York: Twayne, 1992.

Coultrap-McQuin, Susan. *Doing Literary Business: American Women Writers in the Nineteenth Century.* Chapel Hill: U of North Carolina P, 1990.

Davidson, Cathy, ed. *Reading in America: Literature and Social History.* Baltimore: Johns Hopkins UP, 1989.

Denning, Michael. *Mechanic Accents: Dime Novels and Working-Class Culture in America.* New York: Verso, 1987.

Foy, Jessica H., and Thomas J. Schlereth. *American Home Life, 1880–1930: A Social History of Spaces and Services.* Knoxville: U of Tennessee P, 1992.

Freedman, Jonathan. *Professions of Taste: Henry James, British Aestheticism, and Commodity Culture.* Stanford, Calif.: Stanford UP, 1990.

Flint, Kate. *The Woman Reader, 1837–1914.* Oxford: Oxford UP, 1993.

Fox, Richard Wightman, and T. J. Jackson Lears, eds. *The Culture of Consumption.* New York: Pantheon, 1983.

Gale, Robert L. *The Gay Nineties in America: A Cultural Dictionary of the 1890's.* Westport, Conn.: Greenwood P, 1992.

Garvey, Ellen Gruber. *The Adman in the Parlor: Magazines and the Gendering of Consumer Culture, 1880s to 1910s.* Oxford: Oxford UP, 1996.

Gere, Anne Ruggles. *Intimate Practices: Literacy and Cultural Work in U.S. Women's Clubs, 1880–1920.* Urbana: U of Illinois P, 1997.

Glazener, Nancy. *Reading for Realism.* Durham, N.C.: Duke UP, 1997.

Goetzmann, William H., and William N. Goetzmann. *The West of the Imagination.* New York: Norton, 1986.

Gordon, Ian. *Comic Strips and Consumer Culture, 1890–1945.* Washington, D.C.: Smithsonian Institution P, 1998.

Green, Harvey. *Fit for America: Health, Fitness, Sport and American Society.* New York: Pantheon, 1986.

Grier, Katherine C. *Culture and Comfort: Parlor Making and Middle-Class Identity, 1850–1930.* Washington, D.C.: Smithsonian Institution P, 1997.

Grover, Kathryn, ed. *Hard at Play: Leisure in America, 1840–1940.* Amherst: U of Massachusetts P, 1992.

Grunden, Robert M. *American Salons: Encounters with European Modernism, 1885–1917.* Oxford: Oxford UP, 1993.

Gutman, Herbert G. *Power and Culture: Essays on the American Working Class.* New York: Pantheon, 1986.

Haber, Samuel. *The Quest for Authority and Honor in the American Professions, 1750-1900.* Chicago: U of Chicago P, 1991.

Halle, David. *Inside Culture: Art and Class in the American Home.* Chicago: U of Chicago P, 1993.

Hapke, Laura. *Tales of the Working Girl: Wage-Earning Women in American Literature, 1890-1925.* New York: Twayne, 1992.

Harris, Susan. *Nineteenth-Century Women's Novels: Interpretive Strategies.* Cambridge: Cambridge UP, 1990.

Higham, John. *Send These to Me: Immigrants in Urban America.* Baltimore: Johns Hopkins UP, 1984.

———. *Strangers in the Land: Patterns of American Nativism, 1865-1925.* New Brunswick, N.J.: Rutgers UP, 1994.

Hilkey, Judy. *Character Is Capital: Success Manuals and Manhood in Gilded Age America.* Chapel Hill: U of North Carolina P, 1997.

Hyde, Anne Farrar. *An American Vision: Far Western Landscape and National Culture, 1820-1920.* New York: New York UP, 1990.

Jones, Maldwyn Allen. *American Immigration.* Chicago: U of Chicago P, 1992.

Joselit, Jenna Weisman. *The Wonders of America: Reinventing Jewish Culture, 1880-1950.* New York: Hill and Wang, 1994.

Kaestle, Carl F. *Literacy in the United States: Readers and Reading Since 1880.* New Haven, Conn.: Yale UP, 1991.

Kaplan, Amy. *The Social Construction of American Realism.* Chicago: U of Chicago P, 1988.

Kaplan, Amy, and Donald E. Pease, eds. *Cultures of United States Imperialism.* Durham, N.C.: Duke UP, 1993.

Kammen, Michael. *Mystic Chords of Memory: The Transformation of American Society in the Twentieth Century.* New York: Knopf, 1991.

Kern, Stephen. *The Culture of Time and Space, 1880-1918.* Cambridge, Mass.: Harvard UP, 1983.

Klein, Marcus. *Easterners, Westerners, and Private Eyes: American Matters, 1870-1900.* Madison: U of Wisconsin P, 1994.

Knupfer, Anne Meis. *Toward a Tenderer Humanity and a Nobler Womanhood: African American Women's Clubs in Turn-of-the-Century Chicago.* New York: New York UP, 1996.

Leach, William. *Land of Desire: Merchants, Power, and the Rise of a New American Culture.* New York: Vintage, 1994.

Lears, T. J. Jackson. *Fables of Abundance: A Cultural History of Advertising in America.* New York: Basic, 1994.

———. *No Place of Grace: Anti-Modernism and the Transformation of American Culture, 1800-1920.* Chicago: U of Chicago P, 1994.

Levine, Lawrence W. *Highbrow/Lowbrow: The Emergence of Cultural Hierarchy in America.* Cambridge, Mass.: Harvard UP, 1988.

Lynes, Russell. *The Lively Audience: A Social History of the Visual and Performing Arts in America, 1890-1950.* New York: Harper, 1985.

Marchalonis, Shirley. *College Girls: A Century in Fiction.* New Brunswick, N.J.: Rutgers UP, 1995.

Michaels, Walter Benn. *The Gold Standard and the Logic of Naturalism.* Berkeley: U of California P, 1995.

Munslow, Alan. *Discourse and Culture: The Creation of American Society, 1870-1920.* New York: Routledge, 1992.

Murolo, Priscilla. *The Common Ground of Womanhood: Class, Gender, and Working Girls' Clubs, 1884-1928.* Urbana: U of Illinois P, 1997.

Murphy, Brenda. *American Realism and American Drama, 1880-1940.* Cambridge: Cambridge UP, 1987.

Musser, Charles. *The Emergence of Cinema: The American Screen to 1907.* Berkeley: U of California P, 1994.

Nackenoff, Carol. *The Fictional Republic: Horatio Alger and American Political Discourse.* Oxford: Oxford UP, 1994.

Newton, Sarah E. *Learning to Behave: A Guide to American Conduct Books Before 1900.* Westport, Conn.: Greenwood P, 1994.

Noble, David W. *The Progressive Mind, 1890-1917.* Minneapolis: U of Minnesota P, 1981.

Odem, Mary E. *Delinquent Daughters: Protecting and Policing Adolescent Sexuality in the United States, 1885-1920.* Chapel Hill: U of North Carolina P, 1995.

Ohmann, Richard. *Selling Culture: Magazines, Markets, and Class at the Turn of the Century.* New York: Verso, 1996.

Orvell, Miles. *The Real Thing: Imitation and Authenticity in American Culture, 1880-1940.* Chapel Hill: U of North Carolina P, 1989.

Petroski, Henry. *Engineers of Dreams: Great Bridge Builders and the Spanning of America.* New York: Vintage, 1996.

Price, Kenneth M., and Susan Belasco Smith, eds. *Periodical Literature in Nineteenth-Century America.* Charlottesville: UP of Virginia, 1995.

Reed, David. *The Popular Magazine in Britain and the United States, 1880-1960.* Toronto: U of Toronto P, 1997.

Rubin, Joan Shelly. *The Making of Middlebrow Culture.* Chapel Hill: U of North Carolina P, 1992.

Rotundo, E. Anthony. *American Manhood: Transformations in Masculinity from Revolution to the Modern Era.* New York: Basic, 1993.

Rydell, Robert W. *All the World's a Fair: Visions of Empire at America's International Expositions, 1876-1916.* Chicago: U of Chicago P, 1984.

Scanlon, Jennifer. *Inarticulate Longings: The Ladies' Home Journal, Gender and the Promises of Consumer Culture.* New York: Routledge, 1995.

Schlereth, Thomas. *Victorian America: Transformations in Everyday Life: 1876-1915.* New York: Harper, 1991.

Shi, David E. *Facing Facts: Realism in American Thought and Culture, 1850-1920.* Oxford: Oxford UP, 1995.

Shore, Bradd. *Culture in Mind: Cognition, Culture, and the Problem of Meaning.* New York: Oxford UP, 1996.

Smith, Joseph. *The Spanish-American War: Conflict in the Caribbean and the Pacific, 1895-1902.* New York: Longman, 1994.

Smith, Robert A. *A Social History of the Bicycle.* New York: American Heritage P, 1972.

Sollors, Werner. *Beyond Ethnicity: Consent and Descent in American Culture.* Oxford: Oxford UP, 1986.

Sowell, Thomas. *Ethnic America: A History.* New York: Basic, 1981.

Stevenson, Louise L. *The Victorian Homefront: American Thought and Culture, 1860-1880.* New York: Twayne, 1991.

Sundquist, Eric. *To Wake the Nation: Race in the Making of American Literature.* Cambridge, Mass.: Belknap P of Harvard UP, 1993.

Susman, Walter I. *Culture as History: The Transformation of American Society in the Twentieth Century.* New York: Pantheon, 1984.

Takaki, Ronald. *A Different Mirror: A History of Multicultural America.* Boston: Little, Brown, 1993.

———. *Iron Cages: Race and Culture in Nineteenth-Century America.* Oxford: Oxford UP, 1990.

———, ed. *From Different Shores: Perspectives on Race and Ethnicity in America.* New York: Oxford UP, 1987.

Tate, Claudia. *Domestic Allegories of Political Desire: The Black Heroine's Text at the Turn of the Century.* New York: Oxford UP, 1992.

Theriot, Nancy M. *Mothers and Daughters in Nineteenth-Century America: The Biosocial Construction of Femininity.* Lexington: UP of Kentucky, 1996.

Thernstrom, Stephen, et al. *The Harvard Encyclopedia of American Ethnic Groups.* Cambridge, Mass.: Belknap P, 1980.

Thomas, Brook. *American Literary Realism and the Failed Promise of Contract.* Berkeley: U of California P, 1997.

Tichi, Cecelia. *Shifting Gears: Technology, Literature, and Culture in Modernist America.* Chapel Hill: U of North Carolina P, 1987.

Townsend, Kim. *Manhood at Harvard: William James and Others.* New York: Norton, 1996.

Trachtenberg, Alan. *The Incorporation of America: Culture and Society in the Gilded Age.* New York: Hill and Wang, 1982.

Traxel, David. *1898: The Birth of the American Century.* New York: Knopf, 1998.

Truether, William H., ed. *The West as America: Reinterpreting Images of the Frontier, 1820–1920.* Washington, D.C.: Smithsonian Institution P, 1991.

Vallone, Lynne. *Disciplines of Virtue: Girls' Culture in the Eighteenth and Nineteenth Centuries.* New Haven, Conn.: Yale UP, 1995.

Wald, Priscilla. *Constituting Americans: Cultural Anxiety and Narrative Form.* Durham, N.C.: Duke UP, 1995.

Walker, Cheryl. *Native American Literature and Nineteenth-Century Nationalisms.* Durham, N.C.: Duke UP, 1997.

Wheeler, Marjorie Spruill. *One Woman, One Vote.* Troutdale, Ore.: New Sage P, 1995.

Whorton, James C. *Crusaders for Fitness: The History of American Health Reformers.* Princeton, N.J.: Princeton UP, 1982.

INDEX